EUROPEAN HISTORY AND CULTURE	MUSIC	AND CULTURE
	1653–1713: Archangelo Corelli	
1661–1682: Versailles constructed	**1659–1695:** Henry Purcell	
	1678–1741: Antonio Vivaldi	
1684–1721: Jean Antoine Watteau	**1685–1750:** Johann Sebastian Bach	
	1685–1759: George Frideric Handel	
1688–1689: Glorious Revolution in England	**1689:** Purcell, *Dido and Aeneas*	
1703–1770: Boucher	**1710–1736:** Giovanni Battista Pergolesi	
	1712: Vivaldi, Concerto grosso, Op. 3, No. 8	
	ca. 1720: J. S. Bach, *Brandenburg Concerto* No. 5	
	1724: Handel, *Julius Caesar in Egypt*	
	1731: J. S. Bach, Cantata No. 140 (*Wachet auf*)	
	1732–1809: Joseph Haydn	
1740–1786: Reign of Frederick the Great in Prussia	**1742:** Handel, *Messiah*	
1756–1763: Seven Years' War	**1756–1791:** Wolfgang Amadeus Mozart	**1755–1763:** French and Indian War
	ca. 1759: Haydn's first symphony	
1762: Rousseau, *The Social Contract*		**1765:** Stamp Act
	1770–1827: Ludwig van Beethoven	
1774: Goethe, *Sorrows of Young Werther*	**1772:** Haydn, *Farewell* Symphony (No. 45)	**1773:** Boston Tea Party
1776: Adam Smith, *The Wealth of Nations*		**1776:** Declaration of Independence
1781: Kant, *Critique of Pure Reason*		**1783:** Treaty of Paris
	1786: Mozart, *The Marriage of Figaro;* Piano Concerto, K. 488	**1787:** *Federalist Papers;* U.S. Constitution
1789: Outbreak of French Revolution	**1791:** Mozart, *The Magic Flute; Requiem*	**1789:** Inauguration of George Washington as first president
1793–1794: Reign of Terror in France	**1794:** Haydn, *Military* Symphony (No. 100)	**1794-1796:** Thomas Paine, *The Age of Reason*
	1797: Haydn, *Emperor* Quartet, Op. 76, No. 3	**1798:** Alien and Sedition Acts
1798: Wordsworth and Coleridge, *Lyrical Ballads*	**1797–1828:** Franz Schubert	
	1801: Beethoven, *Moonlight* Sonata, Op. 27, No. 2	
	1803–1869: Hector Berlioz	**1803:** Louisiana Purchase
1804: Napoleon proclaimed emperor		
1808: Goethe, *Faust* (Part I)	**1808:** Beethoven, Symphonies No. 5 and 6 (*Pastoral*)	
	1809–1847: Felix Mendelssohn	
	1810–1849: Frédéric Chopin	
	1810–1856: Robert Schumann	
	1811–1886: Franz Liszt	
1812–1818: Byron, *Childe Harold's Pilgrimage*	**1813–1883:** Richard Wagner	**1812–1815:** War of 1812
	1813–1901: Giuseppe Verdi	
1814–1815: Congress of Vienna	**1814:** Schubert, *Gretchen am Spinnrade*	
	1821: Weber, *Der Freischütz*	**1820:** Missouri Compromise
1825: Stockton-Darlington Railway in England	**1825:** Beethoven, String Quartet, Op. 132	**1823:** Monroe Doctrine
	1826: Mendelssohn, *A Midsummer Night's Dream* Overture	
	1828: Schubert, *Winterreise*	

The Musical Art offers a musicologically rich overview of Western music. Organized historically, it leads introductory students through the evolution of Western music—beginning with the Middle Ages and continuing into the twentieth century.

An objective music historian, author R. Larry Todd presents a comprehensive treatment of all important periods including the often-neglected avant-garde music of the twentieth century. Guided by his crisp and eloquent writing style, students embark on a compelling and impressive journey filled with the wonder and richness of Western music.

The fundamentals of music—pitch, rhythm, texture, classification of the instruments, and notation—are reviewed in a concise appendix. Throughout the text, general terms and concepts are carefully introduced as they apply to the music of a specific historical period. For example, tonality is presented in conjunction with its systematic application in the music of the Baroque period, and each of the instruments is introduced as it is encountered during the historical progression.

The Musical Art also includes—

- A repertoire containing carefully selected masterworks from each period, as well as interesting, lesser known material to provide variety in the classroom

- Historical timelines—engaging historical introductions to each musical period that enable students to place composers and compositions in the broader context of European and American history and culture

- Suggestions for further listening—at the end of each chapter

- Discussions of women composers such as Hildegard of Bingen, Clara Schumann, and Ellen Taaffe Zwilich

About the author—

R. Larry Todd (Ph.D, Yale University) is Professor of Music at Duke University. He served as the Director of Graduate Studies in Music at Duke from 1981 to 1985 and as Valentine Distinguished Visiting Professor at Amherst College during the fall 1989 semester. A prolific and respected author, Todd has written *Mendelssohn's Musical Education: A Study and Edition of His Exercises in Composition* (Cambridge University Press, 1983) and has co-edited *Mendelssohn and Schumann Essays: Perspectives on Their Music and Its Context* (Duke University Press, 1984). He has contributed to *19th Century Music, The Musical Quarterly, Music and Letters,* and other scholarly journals.

The Musical Art: An Introduction to Western Music

The Musical Art

An Introduction to Western Music

R. Larry Todd
Duke University

Wadsworth Publishing Company
Belmont, California
A Division of Wadsworth, Inc.

Music Editor: Suzanna Brabant
Developmental Editor: Everett M. Sims
Editorial Assistant: Andrea Varni
Production Editor: Jerilyn Emori
Managing and Text Designer: James Chadwick
Cover Designer: Harry Voigt
Print Buyer: Randy Hurst
Art Editor: Marta Kongsle
Copy Editor: Carole Crouse
Autographer: Mansfield Music-Graphics
Cover Art: Raoul Dufy, *La Console jaune au violon
(Yellow Console with Violin),* 1949, oil on canvas.
Art Gallery of Ontario, Toronto; gift of Sam
and Ayala Zacks. Copyright © 1989 A.R.S.
NY/SPADEM.

Illustration and music credits appear on p. 575 at the
end of the book.

Printed in the United States of America   34

1 2 3 4 5 6 7 8 9 10—94 93 92 91 90

**Library of Congress
Cataloging-in-Publication Data**

Todd, R. Larry.
   The musical art : an introduction to Western
music / R. Larry Todd.
      p.   cm.
   ISBN 0-534-09840-1
   1. Music appreciation.   I. Title.   89-37860
   MT6.T62M9   1990   CIP
   781.1'7--dc20   MN

BRIEF CONTENTS

DETAILED CONTENTS

PREFACE

The Musical Art provides an overview of Western music for introductory courses in music literature and appreciation. In American universities and colleges today, wide varieties of musical backgrounds are typically represented in introductory music courses. Some students have few or no musical skills, others already have the ability to read music to some degree, and still others enroll in the course with a high level of musical achievement. A considerable challenge for the teacher—and the textbook writer—is, therefore, to strike a suitable level of instruction that meets the varying needs of the enrollment. *The Musical Art* is written for students with limited or no musical backgrounds, yet it contains material that will also enrich the more musically equipped students.

HISTORICAL METHOD

In methodology, this book follows a historical approach: Its principal aim is to offer the layperson a discussion of how Western musical style evolved from the Middle Ages to the twentieth century. Several years of teaching music appreciation and the valued advice of many colleagues who have taught similar courses have convinced the author of the legitimacy of this method. Music appreciation students are evidently best served if introduced to a chronological series of musical masterworks presented in their historical contexts. Students' appreciation of a composition is enhanced if they understand its historical roots and the cultural environment within which it was created. As exciting as it is to listen to Beethoven's Fifth Symphony, the abstract experience becomes much more meaningful if students can grasp something of the Napoleonic era and Beethoven's "heroic" period and, further, if students can compare their appreciation of the work with that of an earlier symphonic masterpiece by Mozart or Haydn.

SELECTION OF REPERTORY

Many courses in music literature and appreciation are designed to be taught during one semester of an academic year. Consequently, hard decisions must be made about the repertory of compositions to be examined. For the most part, *The Musical Art* relies upon a selection of familiar masterworks to provide systematic coverage of the acknowledged masters and the principal musical genres in which they excelled. Generally, works are discussed in their entirety, except, of course, in cases where the length of the composition precludes a full treatment. Instructors should encounter few surprises in the selection of material for the main body of the book, Chapters 3–19, which concern music from the baroque period to modern times; the music examined there is drawn from the common repertory of the concert hall. Also included are discussions of Clara Schumann's *Variations on a Theme of Robert Schumann* and Ellen Taaffe Zwilich's Symphony No. 1—in recognition of new research in music by women composers.

TREATMENT OF MUSICAL ELEMENTS

Because music is an art with an abstract language and notation of its own, a consideration of its special vocabulary and technical elements is unavoidable in music courses at the basic level. Unfortunately, there is no completely satisfactory solution for apportioning this sort of material in a textbook. Though the student should begin to acquire some familiarity with technical concepts early in the course, burdening the student from the outset with a wealth of unfamiliar technical material poses its own problems. For example, there is no particular reason why a student need grasp the principles of tonality in the first few classes, only to plunge into an examination of music of the Middle Ages and the Renaissance, to which those principles do not apply. Such an approach risks encumbering the student prematurely (and needlessly) with "technical baggage."

In *The Musical Art,* technical material is presented in two stages. In the introductory sections for the main historical periods (the first parts of Chaps. 1–3, and all of Chaps. 6, 10, and 15), technical material appropriate to each period is considered as needed. Thus, for the Middle Ages, the concept of modality and the church modes are discussed (Chap. 1, pp. 8–9); for the Renaissance, during which triadic harmony became ever more meaningful, the concept of the triad is presented (Chap. 2, pp. 38–39); and for the baroque period, the system of tonality is examined (Chap. 3, pp. 68–72). For the classical and romantic periods, and for the twentieth century, individual chapters (6, 10, and 15) introduce the relevant technical terms, forms, and concepts. In this way, students approach the language of music in much the same way as they would the study of a foreign language, learning theoretical concepts step-by-step in accumulative fashion, but not all at once. The Appendix ("The Elements of Western Music") discusses the basic rudiments of Western music, including pitch, intervals, elementary scales, rhythm and meter, notation, the concepts of counterpoint and harmony, and dynamics and timbre, and an introduction to common Western instruments. Intended here is a succinct treatment of the bare essentials.

HISTORICAL BACKGROUND SECTIONS

Each of the principal periods is introduced by a brief "Background" section and a historical timeline. These six background sections seek to provide the student with general historical and cultural contexts for the surveys of music that follow. The timelines summarize in parallel columns key events and figures in European history, arts, letters, and music. To give the chronologies a special relevance to the American undergraduate, additional timelines of key events and figures in American history and culture are offered for Parts III, IV, V, and VI. A separate timeline is included for Part V, Chapter 14, "Late Nineteenth-Century Music," in an effort to set off somewhat the latter part of the nineteenth century from the earlier impact of romanticism. Finally, students may find simplified historical timelines in the endpapers.

STUDY DIAGRAMS

In the Contents, instructors may find a list of those compositions discussed at some length in the book. Many of these compositions are supported in the text by study diagrams, which offer summaries of their essential features—typically, a few details of the thematic and formal organization, dynamics, rhythm and meter, texture, or scoring (in the case of an orchestral work)—that should help students find their way through even highly complex scores with some degree of ease. Each chapter concludes with a summary of Suggested Listening, including the principal works discussed in the chapter, but also additional suggestions for students who wish to pursue their listening further.

ACKNOWLEDGMENTS

One of the most gratifying tasks that befalls an author is the opportunity to acknowledge those who contribute in so many ways to the book's completion. Several colleagues patiently read portions of *The Musical Art* in draft and offered valuable suggestions; I have drawn heavily on their collective wisdom and classroom experiences. They include Bryan Gilliam, James Henry, Paula Higgins, Stephen Jaffe, Lorenzo Muti, Robert C.

Parkins, and Alexander Silbiger, all of Duke University; and Dolores Pesce of Washington University. To Bryan Gilliam I owe a special debt for extended discussions about the selection of repertory and general pedagogical method. Paul Bryan and Peter Williams, of Duke University, and Stephen Hefling, of Case Western Reserve University, contributed illustrative material; for considerable assistance with the selection and preparation of the art program I wish to acknowledge John Druesedow, J. Samuel Hammond, and Judy Tsou. For assistance of various kinds with the manuscript I wish to thank Donna Lynn, Anne Parks, Orest Pelech, and Ann Wharton.

I am also indebted to the following people who reviewed the manuscript at various stages during the writing process:

Thomas Bauman
University of Washington

Donald R. Boomgaarden
St. Mary's College of Maryland

Graeme M. Boone
Harvard University

Susan Hicks Brashire
University of Kansas

Martha Braswell
University of Georgia

Richard Brooks
Nassau Community College

Lester Brothers
University of North Texas

Bruce B. Campbell
Michigan State University

Gregory Carroll
University of North Carolina

Malcolm S. Cole
University of California, Los Angeles

Laurence Dreyfus
Yale University

John R. Duke
Middle Tennessee State University

Mark Ellis
Ohio State University

Peter Gano
Ohio State University

William B. George
San Jose State University

Sharon Girard
San Francisco State University

John W. Goodall
Stephen F. Austin State University

Calvin Huber
University of Tennessee

Mark Johnson
Michigan State University

Marita P. McClymonds
University of Virginia

James P. McCormick
California State University, Sacramento

Jeremiah W. McGrann
Boston College

Dale Monson
University of Michigan

Richard Norton
University of Illinois

David Oakley
University of Missouri

Dolores Pesce
Washington University

Dwayne Pigg
Middle Tennessee State University

Katherine Powers
University of California, Santa Barbara

William Prizer
University of California, Santa Barbara

Martha Rearick
University of South Florida

Katherine T. Rohrer
Princeton University

Ronald Steele
University of Massachusetts

Homer Rudolf
University of Richmond

Anne Swartz
Baruch College

John I. Schwarz, Jr.
Lock Haven University

Michael C. Tusa
University of Texas, Austin

Douglass Seaton
Florida State University

E. Chappell White
Kansas State University

Elaine R. Sisman
Columbia University

Stephen Willier
University of Illinois

R. John Specht
Queensborough Community College

Lynn Wood-Newman
Emory University

This volume has been greatly enhanced by the expertise of my editors and the production staff at Wadsworth. Thanks are owed in particular to Sheryl Fullerton, who first suggested the project to me; Suzanna Brabant, who followed the course of the manuscript with characteristic good humor and unerring critical judgment; Ev Sims, whose editorial acumen is reflected in any number of suggestions incorporated in the book; Carole Crouse, who expertly and efficiently undertook the copyediting of the manuscript; James Chadwick, who prepared an elegant design; Marty Kongsle, who conscientiously oversaw the art program; and Jerilyn Emori, who expedited the production of the volume and resolved some of its thornier problems.

Finally, to my wife, Karin A. Yoch, I owe the greatest debt of all. Her scrutiny of the manuscript and intuitive sense of the nature of music led to a wealth of constructive revisions. In watching the progress of the volume, she has come to know it intimately; it is an immeasurably enriched volume for her unflagging support, love, and encouragement.

FOR THE STUDENT

*T*he random sounds of a murmuring brook, the rumble of thunder, the cacophony of the streets, and the clanking of machines arouse unpredictable responses, or perhaps no response at all, as they strike our ears. But the sounds of music—traditionally, sounds arranged in some artful way—have been calming, delighting, and astonishing men and women in the Western world for nearly twenty centuries. Down through the ages a tradition of serious "art" music has been cultivated in the churches of the Middle Ages, in the courts of the emerging nation states of the Renaissance, and in the urban centers of the Industrial Revolution. Folk music and popular music too have had a long, colorful history and at times have vigorously influenced art music. In our own century, the accelerating technological revolutions of the electronic and computer ages have made music an intimate and constant companion that conditions our daily life. Today we hear music in concert halls, at rock festivals, in commercial establishments, and, through various mass media, in our homes. Music remains, as it has always been, an integral part of our lives.

How Western music has developed is the subject of this book. We shall endeavor to sketch the general outlines of that development and to discover ways to enhance our appreciation of it. Historically broad, our topic ranges over more than ten centuries of music. During this vast spectrum of time composers developed ever-changing means of creating, developing, and notating musical material as the very meaning and purpose of music was continually being challenged and redefined. By investigating the music of the past we shall seek to discover the roots of our own present-day music.

The Musical Art: An Introduction to Western Music

PART 1 THE MIDDLE AGES

EUROPEAN HISTORY	EUROPEAN CULTURE AND IDEAS	EUROPEAN MUSIC
4th century: Christianity established as official religion in Rome **306–337:** Reign of Constantine (Constantinople recognized as Eastern capital of the Roman Empire, 330)	**ca. 340–420:** Jerome, compiler of the *Vulgate*	
	413–426: Augustine, *The City of God*	
451–452: Huns invade Western Europe **476:** Last Roman emperor deposed; beginning of the Dark Ages **ca. 480–544:** Benedict of Nursia		
ca. 571–632: Muhammed **590–604:** Pope Gregory the Great	**524:** Boethius, *The Consolation of Philosophy*	**6th–12th centuries:** Standardization of Gregorian chant
711: Muslims invade Spain **732:** Muslims repelled by Charles Martel near Poitiers **768–814:** Reign of Charlemagne, King of the Franks and Lombards		
800: Charlemagne crowned Emperor of the Romans **871–899:** Alfred the Great		**9th–10th centuries:** Early polyphony **9th–12th centuries:** Additions to the Catholic liturgy (sequences and tropes)
9th–10th centuries: Viking, Hungarian, and Muslim invasions **1054:** Great schism between Eastern and Western Churches **1066:** Battle of Hastings; Norman conquest **1095:** Calling of First Crusade	**ca. 1000:** *Chanson de Roland* **11th–12th centuries:** Romanesque architecture **1098–1179:** Hildegard of Bingen	**ca. 991–ca. 1033:** Guido d'Arezzo
ca. 1182–1226: Francis of Assisi **1215:** *Magna Carta*	**mid 12th–early 15th centuries:** Gothic architecture **1163:** Construction begun on Cathedral of Notre Dame, Paris **1267–1273:** Thomas Aquinas, *Summa Theologica* **1267–1337:** Giotto	**ca. 1135–1201:** Leonin active at Notre Dame, Paris **ca. 1200:** Perotin active at Notre Dame, Paris **12th–13th centuries:** Troubadours and trouvères in France **ca. 1160–ca. 1320:** French *ars antiqua* **12th–14th centuries:** Minnesingers in Germany **13th century:** Estampies, motets **1291–1361:** Philippe de Vitry
1305–1378: Papacy in Avignon **1338–1453:** 100 Years' War **1348–1350:** Black Death **1378–1417:** Papal Schism **1453:** Fall of Constantinople to Turks	**1308–1320:** Dante, *Divine Comedy* **ca. 1340–1400:** Chaucer	**14th century:** French *ars nova;* Italian *trecento* **ca. 1300–1377:** Guillaume de Machaut **1316:** *Le Roman de Fauvel* **ca. 1325–1397:** Francesco Landini

BACKGROUND FOR THE MIDDLE AGES

The vast stretch of time known as the Middle Ages marks the first flowering of Western music. This unwieldy period of approximately one thousand years began with the overthrow of the last Roman emperor in A.D. 476 and extended to the fall of Constantinople, the capital of the Eastern church, in 1453. With the rise of the Renaissance in the fifteenth century, the millennium just past came to be regarded as a time of cultural stagnation and steady decline in the West. The cultured men and women of the Renaissance described it as medieval—a pejorative term referring to the "middle ages" between antiquity and their own golden age. They called the early medieval centuries—a turbulent time of political instability—the Dark Ages, and described the architecture of the later centuries as gothic,★ meaning grotesque or uncouth.

Today, historians view the period more positively and recognize the rich diversity of its contributions to Western culture. During the eighth and ninth centuries, for example, arts and letters enjoyed a vigorous revival. Charlemagne (ruled 768–814, from 800 as the Holy Roman Emperor) introduced a system of primary education throughout his empire in an effort to promote literacy and to disseminate classical and Christian culture. In the tenth and early eleventh centuries, scholarship revived, and manuscript illustration reached new levels of refinement. During the eleventh and early twelfth centuries, countless churches and cathedrals were built in the Romanesque style, with its massive rounded arches. In the subsequent Gothic style (roughly, from the mid-twelfth to the early fifteenth century), the emphasis in architecture shifted to soaring, pointed arches and great panels of stained glass. The late Middle Ages saw the chartering of universities in Oxford, Bologna, and Paris, and the rise of scholasticism, a movement in Christian logic that drew on the ancient Greeks as well as the early church fathers. And over all those centuries—centuries of cultural slumber and awakening—Western art music grew steadily more versatile and complex as efforts were made to preserve it in notation.

Throughout the Middle Ages, the Church was a guardian of Western culture. In the East, its center was Constantinople, the capital of the Byzantine Empire. In the West, its center was Rome, where its alliance with a succession of Frankish and German emperors eventually took shape as the Holy Roman Empire. Early on, there were signs that the nascent Western culture was breaking away from the heritage of antiquity. By the third century, the church father Tertullian had asked, "What has Athens to do with Jerusalem?" Tertullian was arguing against pagan values and for the supremacy of faith over the philosophical method of the Greeks. For some three hundred years, Christians had endured persecution at the hands of the Roman emperors, so it is not surprising that the early church fathers were eager to abandon their Roman heritage.

Still, Graeco-Roman culture continued to assert itself, and the Church was obliged to come to terms with certain aspects of the pagan past. Early Christian writers tried to reconcile the philosophy of Plato (ca. 427–347 B.C.) with the tenets of their new faith. Augustine (ca. A.D. 354–430) "baptized" Plato for the Church and in *The City of*

★ A reference to the Goths, a Germanic people who periodically invaded the Roman Empire from the third century.

St. Ouen, Rouen, interior from organ loft showing pointed Gothic arches.

God described an ideal Christian city that resembled the ideal city-state Plato had set forth in *The Republic*. The philosopher Boethius (ca. 480–524) described music as one of the liberal arts of classical antiquity, the cornerstone of higher learning. In the thirteenth century, Thomas Aquinas studied the logic of Aristotle (384–322 B.C.), and in the fourteenth century, Dante introduced the Roman poet Virgil (70–19 B.C.) into his *Divine Comedy*. Through much of the Middle Ages, this long process of acculturation significantly shaped the course of music as well.

1

MUSIC IN THE MIDDLE AGES

*W*e know regrettably little about ancient Greek music—its structure, its notation, how it was performed—and even less about ancient Roman music. We do know, however, that the music of the Middle Ages owed a considerable debt to the music of antiquity, especially to Greek music. For that reason, our exploration of Western music begins with classical antiquity.

GREEK AND ROMAN MUSIC

Music played a central role in Greek society and culture. Greek poetry was sung, and the tragedies of Aeschylus, Sophocles, and Euripides (fifth century B.C.) were performed in a kind of rhythmic speech, perhaps by skilled singers accompanied by instruments. Music figured in the curricula of Greek schools and was highly valued for its civilizing role. Still, apart from some fragments in a primitive alphabetic notation, little survives to indicate just how the music of the ancient Greeks sounded.

Most of what we know comes from the writings of Greek philosophers and mathematicians, who began to set down their theories about music around the fourth century B.C. Their writings reveal that Greek music was based on **modes,** scalelike arrangements of pitches with differing patterns of intervals. The names of the modes, such as *Dorian* and *Phrygian,* suggest that they were originally named after tribes in various regions of Greece.

The Greek modes differed from our major and minor scales in significant ways. Like our modern major scale (see p. 68), they comprised steplike successions of intervals that spanned the octave. However, instead of limiting themselves to half steps and whole steps—the intervals of our modern major scale—the Greeks introduced into their theoretical system intervals smaller than the half step, known as **microtones,** as well as intervals somewhat larger than the whole step. There were several modes, each with its own set of intervals and its own character; exactly how they were applied in Greek music remains unclear.

Greek music was **monophonic**—that is, it consisted of a single line of melody. There was no harmony, as we know it, to support the melodic line. Apart from the modes, the character of Greek music was determined by its rhythms, likely drawn from the patterns of Greek poetry. Apparently, improvisation figured prominently in the music of the Greeks. In performing a particular melody in a particular mode, each member of a group of instrumentalists or vocalists might execute a personal version of the basic melody. Performance of this sort is known as **heterophony** (from the Greek meaning "different voices").

To the Greeks, music possessed a special property called *ethos:* the ability to arouse the emotions of listeners and even to influence their moral behavior. Plato discussed this property at length in *The Republic,* as did Aristotle in *The Politics.* So concerned was Plato about the effect of music on listeners that he permitted only certain types of music in his ideal city-state. He rejected flute playing, which he felt had a corrupting effect. He preferred instead music performed by a singer accompanied by the *kithara,* a harplike instrument, or by the *lyre,* a tortoise shell with strings stretched across it. Plato

Greek calyx krater, ca. 450–440 B.C., with lyre player.

permitted only music in the Dorian and Phrygian modes—the Dorian because it was thought to instill courage in the defenders of the Republic, the Phrygian because it was thought to encourage temperance and restraint. He believed that other modes engendered moral lassitude and, consequently, forbade them in the Republic. Aristotle, too, remarked on the ability of music to affect the minds and the morals of the citizenry. Somewhat more moderate in his views than Plato, he preferred the Dorian mode because it represented for him the mean of the various modes. How or why the Greeks perceived the various modes in those ways remains a vexing question.

We know that the Romans, too, cultivated music, though detailed information about their musical customs is meager indeed. Music played a practical role in military campaigns, where brass instruments, including the trumpetlike *tuba* and the curved, hornlike *cornu,* sounded military signals and sometimes served to deceive the enemy. Instruments also played a role in Roman theaters, in the triumphal processions of victorious Roman legions, and in religious ceremonies, where the *tibia,* a double-pipe wind instrument, was employed.

Roman music drew on a variety of sources, including the music of the Etruscans, who had inhabited west-central Italy before the rise of the Romans, and the music of Syria and Egypt. Greek music was the most important source, however. In 146 B.C. the Romans sacked the city of Corinth and conquered Macedonia, establishing their control over Greece. They exported their system of government and jurisprudence to Greece, but in return they continued to preempt its mythology, its literature, and its musical practices.

According to the Roman historian Suetonius, the emperor Nero (ruled A.D. 54–68) was an ardent student of music. As a youth, Nero studied the lyre and singing, and made his debut in Naples. Every five years, he held a public music contest, in imitation of the Greeks, in which he himself competed. To ensure his success, he hired a claque of spectators who greeted his performances with enthusiastic applause. When he ordered that Rome be set on fire, Nero watched the burning city from a tower, dressed as a tragedian and singing an epic poem about the fall of Troy. He was reputed to have claimed that only the Greeks could appreciate his singing.

Nowhere was the power of music to influence behavior more celebrated than in the Greek myth of Orpheus, the fabled musician who was the object of adulation in Orphic cults and in the Latin poetry of Ovid and Virgil. With his music, Orpheus could tame wild beasts, move lifeless rocks, and restore to life his dead wife, Euridice. The myth of Orpheus continued to inspire Western composers (see p. 77), even to our own century.

MUSIC AND THE EARLY CHRISTIAN CHURCH

The early Christians found in the Bible a wealth of references to music and music making. The Book of Genesis identifies Jubal, a descendant of Cain, as the "ancestor of those who play the harp and pipe." (So persistent was the Greek influence, however, that throughout the Middle Ages and beyond, Pythagoras—see p. 8—was also given

The ancient Greeks were apparently among the first to study scientifically the nature of musical pitches. Pythagoras, a sixth-century B.C. philosopher-mathematician chiefly remembered for his theorem about right-angle triangles, is also credited with discovering the basic ratio that underlies the common octave. The octave may be expressed as the ratio 2:1; that is, two fixed strings, columns of air, or other sound-emitting media in a 2:1 ratio produce two pitches one octave apart. Similarly, the ratio 3:2 produces a fifth; and the ratio 4:3, a fourth. In short, basic integers may be used to represent basic musical intervals.

Pythagorean thought was highly esteemed in the West for centuries. Not only was Pythagoras often recognized as the discoverer of music, but he was also pictured as the discoverer of the ratios of basic intervals. He was shown plucking strings of different tensions regulated by variously sized weights, or playing flutes or bells of different sizes, or, in the woodcut reproduced here from a sixteenth-century music treatise, forging and weighing hammers of different sizes. When struck on an anvil, the hammers, it was thought, produced the desired intervals.

credit for discovering music.) The Book of Psalms attributes much of its lyric poetry to David (fl. 1000–975 B.C.), who, like the Greek Orpheus, was renowned for his musical prowess. According to the first book of Samuel, David's music was powerful enough to dispel the evil spirits besetting Saul.

For centuries, the singing of psalms had formed an essential part of the Jewish service, and the early Christians incorporated this practice, known as **psalmody,** into their own liturgy. In their churches and basilicas, they chanted the psalms without instrumental support, following the custom in Jewish synagogues. (Considerably earlier in Jewish history, instruments had been used in synagogues and in Solomon's temple; in fact, several psalms specify that the Lord be praised with harps, cymbals, and *psalteries,* zitherlike instruments played by plucking the strings.)

Although the Christian church derived its psalmody from the Jews, it derived its music theory from the Greeks. This complex process of assimilation occurred slowly, over several centuries, before the Church had in place a more or less standardized musical system. The Church also devised a system of modes, later known as the **church modes,** to which were later applied—incorrectly, as it turned out—the names of the ancient Greek modes.

There were four basic church modes: the *Dorian,* the *Phrygian,* the *Lydian,* and the *Mixolydian.* These modes constituted scales on the pitches D, E, F, and G, which served as their fundamental pitches:

The Church Modes

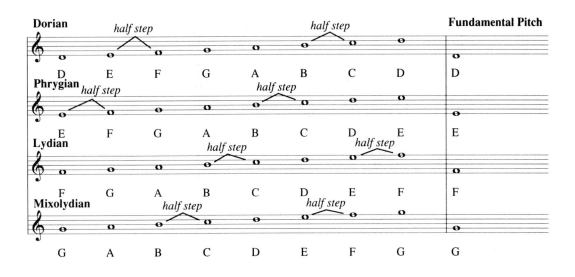

As our example indicates, each mode had its own fundamental pitch and its own con-figuration of whole steps and half steps. The placement of half steps differed from mode to mode, so that no two modes were alike. Thus, in the Dorian mode, the half steps occurred between the second and third pitches and between the sixth and seventh pitches; in the Phrygian mode, a half step occurred at the very beginning of the mode. Such differences gave the modes their individual characters. From these four basic modes, church musicians created additional variant versions.

HYMN, *AVE MARIS STELLA*

As an example of music written in a church mode, we look briefly at the **hymn** *Ave maris stella* ("Hail, Star of the Sea"), which was performed in the church liturgy during feasts honoring the Blessed Virgin Mary. Set to poems in praise of God, hymns were among the simplest forms of sacred modal music composed during the Middle Ages. Typically, their texts consisted of short phrases in a regular series of stressed and unstressed syllables. Here are the text and the music for the first stanza of this hymn. The same music is used for succeeding stanzas:

Ăvĕ márĭs stéllă,   Hail, star of the sea,
Dĕí Mátĕr álmă,   Cherished Mother of God,
Ătquĕ sémpĕr Vírgŏ,   And forever a Virgin,
Félĭx cáelĭ pórtă.   Joyous gate of heaven.

Hymn, Ave Maris Stella

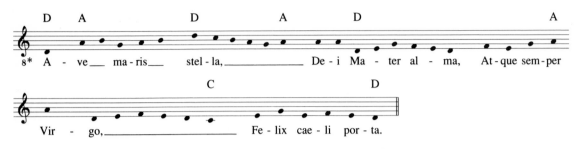

* Sounds one octave lower.

The melody for *Ave maris stella* is in the Dorian mode, the first of the four modes in our example. Its arrangement of pitches is therefore drawn from the scale on D, its fundamental pitch. The hymn begins on D, leaps a fifth above, where it encircles A, and ascends to a high D for the word "stella," or "star," before falling gently back to A and, in the second line, to the fundamental pitch, D. The music for the third line of the stanza reaches A and then drops to the lowest pitches of the mode; actually, it descends as far as one step below D to C. The music for the fourth line remains in the lower range and ends by reasserting D as the fundamental pitch of the mode. Throughout the hymn, the music moves by gentle leaps of a fifth or smaller, or by stepwise motion that seems to hover around a specific pitch. The ever-changing melodic contours of the hymn, its supple melodic flow that surges and subsides, and its ultimate descent to the fundamental pitch are all characteristic of medieval modal melodies.

The church modes provided the raw materials of **modality,** the musical system that would prevail in Western music until the seventeenth century. They were the forerunners of our modern major and minor scales. To modern ears, the ancient church modes sound somewhat exotic; they do not quite fit the patterns of the major and the minor scales to which we are accustomed. Yet, long after the church modes were superseded by our modern scales, modal music survived in the anonymous repertory of folk music, and for centuries, composers seeking an alternative to the major and minor scales have occasionally introduced modal elements into their music.

SACRED MEDIEVAL MONOPHONY: PLAINCHANT

Most medieval music that has come down to us was written for performance in church services. That music was created only over a considerable period (roughly, from the sixth to the twelfth century) and was eventually consolidated for use throughout the Christian realm. Just as generations of anonymous artisans designed and built the great medieval cathedrals, so generations of anonymous composers created a repertory of church music that was meant to endure for centuries. Like the gothic cathedrals reaching to heaven, the early church music was dedicated to the glory of God.

The music of the medieval Church is called **plainchant** (also **plainsong** or **chant**). It consists of thousands of monophonic vocal settings of liturgical texts, such as the hymn *Ave maris stella,* that were chanted by a group of celebrants during worship. Over time, the Church came to recognize certain versions of the chants as the authorized plainchant. At first, however, there was little in the way of regular notation, making it difficult to record accurate versions of the chants. Apparently, they were handed down from generation to generation by oral tradition, perhaps with hand signals used as teaching aids. Eventually, scribes devised a system in which, above the lines of text, they entered a configuration of dashes, dots, and curved figures resembling hooks. These primitive musical symbols, known as **neumes,** merely suggested the contours of the chant melody. Later, scribes improved on this crude method by raising and lowering the neumes to indicate the relative level of adjacent pitches. They also introduced horizontal lines into their manuscripts, with each line representing a certain pitch. By positioning the neumes either on those lines or between them, they achieved still greater accuracy. The first writer to describe this line system was Guido d'Arezzo, an eleventh-century monk in northern Italy, who suggested ruling manuscripts with yellow and red lines to designate specific pitches. From these modest but ingenious beginnings, Western musical notation evolved. Not for several centuries, however, did it come to resemble modern notation.

As the chants were composed, they tended to cluster in repertories indigenous to specific areas. For instance, the Ambrosian chant was centered in Milan, the old Roman chant in Rome, the Gallican chant in Gaul, and the Mozarabic chant on the Iberian peninsula. These local repertories, each with its own version of plainchant, differed considerably from one another.

In 800 an event occurred that helped to expedite the standardization of the various chant repertories. On Christmas Day in Rome, Pope Leo III proclaimed Charlemagne (reigned 768–814) Holy Roman Emperor. That act united Charlemagne's Frankish empire, which included parts of Germany, France, Switzerland, and Italy, in faith as well as in governance. Charlemagne adopted the Roman liturgy and the Roman repertory of chants and had them copied and disseminated throughout his kingdom. Some two centuries before, however, Pope Gregory I (reigned 590–604) had codified the liturgy and standardized the church calendar and had encouraged the adoption of uniform practices in the singing of chants. According to legend (possibly encouraged by Charlemagne), Gregory himself, under divine inspiration, had composed the chant melodies. So it was that the authorized plainchant of the Church came to be known as **Gregorian chant.**

Gregorian chant was used for two types of service. The **Divine Office,** also known as the canonical hours, comprised eight services conducted throughout the day and during the evening and night. In each service, psalms, hymns, and canticles★ were sung, and passages from Scripture were read.

The **Mass,** the second type of service, was, and is, the symbolic re-creation of Christ's Last Supper with the twelve apostles, in which the consecrated bread and wine are shared in Holy Communion. Early on, this daily affirmation of faith became the

---

★ Psalmlike scriptural texts that appear outside the Book of Psalms. Perhaps the best known is the *Magnificat* ("My soul doth magnify the Lord"), from Luke 1:46–55.

most solemn and the most complex service of the Church. The Mass consisted of readings from Scripture, prayers, and the singing of chants.

The chants sung during the Mass were of two sorts. The chants of the **Proper** were all sung to texts appropriate to, or "proper" to, the saint or the occasion that was being celebrated on a particular day. Many of them were elaborately structured and included passages that were sung by trained soloists. The texts of the chants of the **Ordinary** (including the *Kyrie*, *Gloria*, *Credo*, *Sanctus*, and *Agnus Dei*) did not change from day to day. They were usually sung by the congregation and were simpler in structure than the chants of the Proper.

The various texts and melodies of the chants were recorded in chant books. *Antiphonaries* contained the chants for the Office, *graduals* contained the chants for the Proper of the Mass, and *kyriales* contained the chants for the Ordinary of the Mass. Typically, the chants were arranged according to the Christian calendar, with the focal points at Christmas and Easter, preceded by the penitential seasons of Advent and Lent, respectively.

The chants were sung according to different plans. For **antiphonal** chants, the choir was divided into two groups that sang alternately. For **responsorial** chants, a soloist and the choir alternated. Finally, some chants were sung by the entire choir in **unison.**

GRADUAL, *VIDERUNT OMNES*

The responsorial chant *Viderunt omnes,* for the Mass on Christmas Day, is an example of a *Gradual,* one of the chants of the Proper. It consists of a Respond (*A*), a Verse (*B*), and a repetition of the Respond. The Respond and the Verse begin with music for a soloist, which is answered by music for the choir. The overall form takes the symmetrical shape of *ABA,* as the study diagram shows.

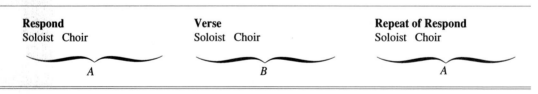

Gradual, *Viderunt omnes*

Respond	**Verse**	**Repeat of Respond**
Soloist Choir	Soloist Choir	Soloist Choir
A	*B*	*A*

The psalm text on which this Gradual is based is exuberant in tone, in keeping with the joyful character of Christmas:

Respond

Viderunt omnes fines terrae salutare Dei nostri:	All the realms of the earth have seen the salvation of our Lord:
Jubilate Deo omnis terra.	Rejoice in the Lord, all the earth.

A page from an Italian gradual, ca. 1420. The chant *Viderunt omnes* begins on the third stave.

Verse

Notum fecit Dominus salutare suum:	The Lord has proclaimed His salvation:
Ante conspectum gentium revelavit justitiam suam.	Before the sight of nations He has revealed His justice.

On first hearing this chant, the listener may be struck by its elastic rhythmic quality. There are no measure lines, no regular meter. Rather, the music gently ebbs and flows, pausing at appropriate points of articulation in the text. Sometimes, a single note is assigned to a syllable of text (**syllabic** text setting). At other times, several notes are assigned to a syllable (**neumatic** text setting). At still other times, a florid display of notes, called a **melisma,** is assigned to a syllable (**melismatic** text setting).

Gradual, Viderunt omnes

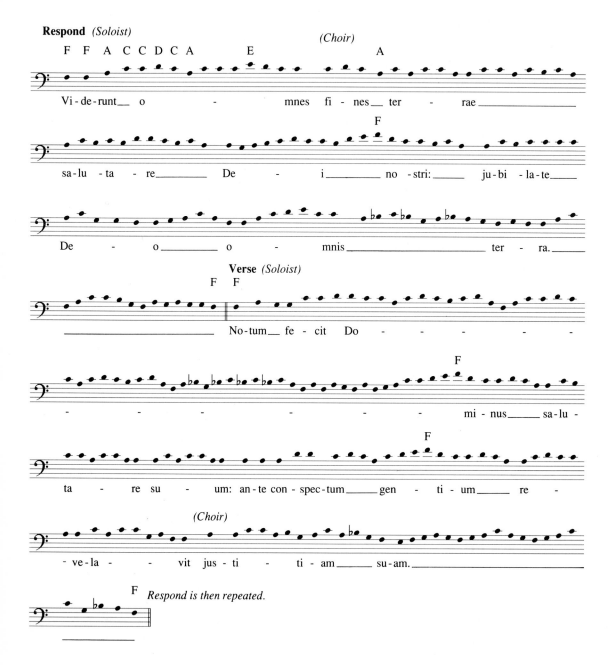

In the opening music of the Respond, several melismas enhance the meaning of the text. The first melisma expands on the first syllable of "omnes" ("all"). Others occur on "terrae" ("earth"), on "Dei" and "Deo" ("Lord"), and again on "omnis" and "terra." But these examples hardly compare with what occurs in the Verse: a rhapsodic melisma on the first syllable of "Dominus" ("Lord") that dwarfs all preceding melismas to suggest the Lord's omnipotence.

Viderunt omnes is in the Lydian mode on F (see p. 9). Rising from F, its fundamental pitch, the music floats for much of the Respond on or around the pitch C. (The third pitch of the mode, A, serves as a prominent intermediary pitch.) On the first syllable of "omnes," the music surges to the high pitch E; later, it stretches to the climactic high F on "Dei" before gradually falling to the F an octave lower. Similarly, the Verse, beginning on F, thrusts upward, twice reaching its apex an octave higher (on "Do-" and "gen-"), and then gradually recedes through a series of lesser crests to the F. The anonymous composer of *Viderunt omnes* invested its celebratory text with a melodic freshness that remains undiminished today.

Disarmingly subtle modal melodies and texts of this sort served as the building blocks for much of Western art music for centuries to come. During the twelfth century, as we shall see, composers were to build the new, multivoice art of polyphony on chants of the Proper. During the Renaissance, composers were to cite chants (and other modal melodies) in great cyclical settings of the Ordinary.

Alongside the Gregorian plainchant, other forms of monophonic music found their way into church music during the Middle Ages. By the ninth century, creative musicians were beginning to supplement the official corpus with texts and melodies of their own, called **tropes.** Some tropes were newly created texts and melodies that appeared either as a preface to a chant or as glosslike insertions between the lines of a chant. Other tropes were simply new texts fitted to existing melismas. Still others were new textless melodies fitted to established chants.

Some of the tropes grew quite lengthy and began to be performed in dramatic fashion. Eventually, they evolved into more or less self-sufficient liturgical dramas, religious plays that included monophonic music. *Quem queritis* ("Whom do you seek?"), originally a trope associated with the beginning of Easter Mass, was widely performed from the tenth century on. This liturgical drama features a dialogue before the tomb of Christ between the three Marys and the angels, who inform them that Christ has arisen. Other liturgical dramas represented the journey to Emmaus, the three Magi, and the Slaying of the Innocents. Still others are based on the Book of Daniel and the miracles of the saints. Scholars trace the origins of modern drama in part to such liturgical dramas, tropes that outgrew their original function.

Another addition to the liturgy was the **sequence.** This was an extended melody, appended to certain chants of the Proper, either with a proselike text or, later on, with rhyming verses. We have one account that may shed some light on the origins of the sequence. According to that account, a monk named Notker Balbulus (Notker "the Stammerer," ca. 840–912), at the Benedictine monastery of St. Gall in Switzerland, found that he could memorize the music more easily by setting various texts to the lengthy textless melismas of certain Proper chants known as Alleluias, with one syllable of text for each note of the melisma. What we now know as the sequence thus may have originated as a mnemonic device.

Great collections of tropes and sequences were set down in medieval manuscripts known as tropers, which were used widely for several centuries. Finally, however, the Council of Trent (1545–1563) summarily banned all tropes and all but a handful of sequences. The most famous sequence to survive is the *Dies irae,* in the **Requiem** Mass for the dead. The text, eighteen rhymed stanzas attributed to the thirteenth-century poet Thomas of Celano, describes in grim imagery the reckoning of Judgment Day. Here are its opening lines:

Dies irae, dies illa,	Day of wrath, that day,
Solvet saeclum in favilla;	Will turn the world to ashes
Teste David cum Sibylla.	As David and the Sibyl are witnesses.

The haunting melody of this anonymous chant attracted many later composers, including Hector Berlioz (see p. 311), Franz Liszt, and Camille Saint-Saëns in the nineteenth century, and Sergei Rakhmaninov in the twentieth, for all of whom it conjured up macabre associations:

Sequence, Dies irae

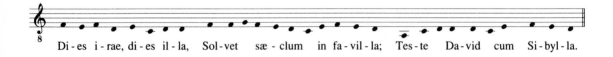

Di - es i - rae, di - es il - la, Sol-vet sæ - clum in fa - vil - la; Tes - te Da - vid cum Si - byl - la.

By and large, the composition and performance of sacred monophony during the Middle Ages was a male-dominated activity. Still, records survive of women who sang in religious services and, further, composed plainchant. The ninth-century Byzantine nun Kassia, for example, wrote sacred poems that she set to music. Hildegard of Bingen (1098–1179) produced a substantial amount of monophony. The abbess of a German convent, she won renown as the Sibyl of the Rhine for her prophecies and mystical visions. A valued adviser to popes and emperors, Hildegard wrote the earliest surviving morality play, a dramatized allegory about the struggle between the Devil and the sixteen Virtues for possession of the Soul. Titled *Ordo virtutum* (*The Order of Virtues*), the play comes down to us with more than eighty monophonic melodies by Hildegard.

SECULAR MONOPHONY

Secular as well as sacred monophonic music was written and performed during the Middle Ages, though relatively little of it has survived. The record of instrumental monophonic music is especially scanty. Surely such music existed, for medieval art abounds in images of instruments of many types. King David is usually shown playing

A sampling of medieval musical instruments. At the top is King David, who plays a psaltery; in the center is *Musica,* personification of music, who plays a portable organ, or portative. On the right, from top to bottom, are a bowed string instrument, possibly a vielle; tambourine; and bagpipe and shawm. On the left, from top to bottom, are a lute, hand-held clappers, and buisines. The figure at the bottom plays a pair of drums.

a string instrument such as a lyre, a harp, or a psaltery, surrounded by other instrumentalists. Angels are shown playing a variety of instruments, including fiddles (known as *vielles*), pear-shaped string instruments (*rebecs*), guitars (*gitterns*), small portable organs (*portatives*), double-reed woodwinds (*shawms*), and herald trumpets (*buisines*). There were also lutes, bagpipes, hurdy-gurdies, flutes, recorderlike pipes, bells, and various kinds of cymbals, triangles, and drums. Some of these instruments were of Arabic provenance; first introduced into Europe after the Moslem invasion of Spain in the eighth century, they were also brought back later by Crusaders returning from the Holy Land.

The organ became associated with church music early on. The medieval world knew organs of various types, including the *hydraulis,* operated by hydraulic pressure, and organs operated by bellows. Such instruments as the *pipe and tabor* (a three-hole flute played with one hand and a small drum played with the other) were more suitable for lively, secular dances or for accompanying monophonic songs.

Instrumental music was doubtless improvised by secular performers long before it was written down for posterity. Only with the thirteenth century do we begin to find notated examples, including largely anonymous, textless dances known as **estampies.** These were sectional dances composed primarily of a series of double phrases (*aa, bb, cc,* and so on). Estampies represent the earliest significant repertoire of notated instrumental music.

Secular monophonic music for voice also was cultivated during the twelfth and thirteenth centuries, mainly at the courts of the nobility. There, the knights observed a strict code of chivalry that dealt with honor, duty, sacrifice, and romantic love. The music of aristocratic poet-composers, who worked at courts throughout western Europe, reflects that code.

The most famous were the **troubadours** from southern France, who wrote lyrics in the Provençal language, and the **trouvères** from northern France, who wrote in a vernacular dialect known as Old French. These skillful artists composed epiclike poems about the deeds of heroes, laments over the death of noblemen, songs about the Crusades, pieces that told of encounters between knights and shepherdesses in pastoral settings, and morning songs about watchmen standing guard over lovers. The troubadours left the job of singing their compositions to itinerant musicians; other, highly skilled musicians held regular posts in the retinues of the troubadours and their patrons.

Outside France, secular monophony developed in England, Italy, and Germany. In Germany, the *Minnesingers* sang of a spiritualized version of love (*Minne*). Most active from the twelfth through the fourteenth century, the Minnesingers gave way in the fifteenth and sixteenth centuries to the Meistersingers (literally, "master singers"), who performed their music in guildlike associations.

These medieval poet-musicians produced thousands of secular melodies and poems, and came to be venerated in legend. According to one legend, King Richard the Lion-Hearted, who had been imprisoned in Austria in 1194 on his return from a crusade, was rescued by his minstrel, Blondel de Nesle, when he sang back in response to Blondel's singing. Centuries later, romantic operas were written about these secular musicians, including Giuseppe Verdi's *Il trovatore* (*The Troubadour,* 1853, set in fifteenth-century Spain) and Wagner's *Tannhäuser* (1849, based on the thirteenth-century Minnesingers Heinrich von Ofterdingen and Tannhäuser), among others.

GUILLAUME DE MACHAUT: VIRELAI, "DOUCE DAME JOLIE"

As late as the fourteenth-century, the French poet-composer Guillaume de Machaut (ca. 1300–1377) was still composing secular monophonic music. Though he is best remembered for his polyphonic music (see p. 27), Machaut wrote many monophonic songs that drew on the art of the trouvères.

Machaut's "Douce dame jolie" is an example of a **virelai,** one of the standard forms of medieval French lyric poetry. Typically, the virelai consisted of three stanzas, each beginning and ending with a refrain. The basic formal scheme of each stanza was *AbbaA,* in which *A* represents the text and melody of the refrain, *b* represents a new text and new melody, and *a* represents the melody of the refrain with new text. In the score given here, 1 and 5 stand for *A,* 2 and 3 stand for *b,* and 4 stands for *a.* **Repeat marks** (‖: :‖) are used to signal the repetition of *b.* Here is the first stanza (freely translated) of "Douce dame," with the various sections marked off:

A(1)   *Douce dame jolie,*
       Pour Dieu ne penses mie,
       Que nulle ait signourie,
       Seur moy fors vous seulement.

b(2)   *Qu'ades sans tricherie,*
       Chierie,
       Vous ay et humblement

b(3)   *Tous les jours de ma vie,*
       Servie,
       Sans vilein pensement.

a(4)   *Helas! et je mendie,*
       D'esperance et d'aie,
       Dont ma joie est fenie,
       Se pite ne vous en prent.

A(5)   Refrain (*Douce dame jolie,* etc.)

Sweet, delightful lady, for the sake of God do believe that only you sway my heart. All the days of my life, dearest, I have served you humbly and without deceit. Alas! Now I beg for hope and consolation. My joy is lost, if you do not take pity.

Sweet, delightful lady, (etc.)

Machaut sets this poem to lively syncopated rhythms and infectious melodic turns. Notice how the higher register of the *b* section (the music between the repeat marks) clearly sets it off from the refrain. (An instrumental drone★ may have been added to the music in Machaut's time.)

★ A sustained bass tone typically held for several measures.

Machaut: Virelai, "Douce dame jolie"

1.5. Dou - ce da - me jo - li - e, Pour Dieu ne pen - ses mi - e, Que
4. He - las! et je men - di - e, D'es - pe - rance et d'a - i - e, Dont

nulle ait sig - nou - ri - e, Seur moy fors vous seu - le - ment._____ 2. Qu'a - des sans
ma joie est fe - ni - e, Se pi - te ne vous en prent._____ 3. Tous les jours

|1.*

tri - che - ri - e, Chie - ri - e, Vous ay et hum - ble - ment._____ vi - lein
de ma vi - e, Ser - vi - e, Sans

|2.*

pen - se - ment._____

★ The numerals 1 and 2 refer to a first and a second ending. The first ending is used for the text of line 2; the second ending is used for the text of line 3.

THE RISE OF POLYPHONY

The plainchant and secular music we have been discussing are examples of monophonic music—that is, music designed to be performed as a single line. When two or more musical lines are performed simultaneously, the result is **polyphony.** The turn to polyphony during the Middle Ages opened up a new direction in Western music. The first composers to set musical lines against each other were practicing what came to be known as **counterpoint** (see p. 524). Over time, counterpoint evolved into a rigorous musical discipline that enabled composers to achieve an extraordinary degree of inventiveness and complexity that simply could not be achieved in a single-strand, monophonic texture. Some music scholars regard the appearance of polyphony as the most significant event in the evolution of Western music.

And yet the origins of polyphony are obscure. Some early references to it appear in music treatises from about 900. There the terms **organum** (the Latin for "organ," derived from the Greek for "instrument" or "tool"; pl., *organa*) and **diaphony** (from the Greek for "separate sounds") are used interchangeably to describe this radically new kind of music. The earliest organa were modest compositions in which a second, newly composed musical line was set against an established plainchant. From the first, these compositions were intended to adorn the plainchant, not to replace it. Nevertheless, for the medieval musician trained in counterpoint, organum offered a new outlet for artistic expression.

The parts of the early polyphony moved in an uncomplicated fashion, note against note. At first, the parts were arranged so that only certain consonant intervals were produced between them. In the following example, found in an eleventh-century treatise, the added voice mirrors the chant at a fixed interval, here the interval of a fourth. The procedure is known as **parallel organum,** because the motions of the two voices parallel one another and move in **parallel motion:**

Eleventh-Century Parallel Organum

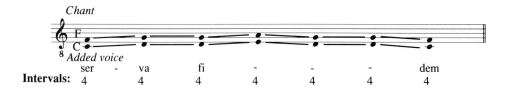

This type of polyphony was relatively straightforward and made few demands on performers. Indeed, musicians educated in the principles of parallel organum could probably improvise the added voice on their own. Inevitably, however, composers grew more adventurous. In the following example, probably from the early twelfth century, the voices move in different, contrary directions rather than in parallel directions, and they occasionally cross. This type of motion is known as **contrary motion.**

Twelfth-Century Organum

The chant is shown by downward stemmed notes. The organal voice is shown by upward stemmed notes.

Note that the ten vertical intervals in this example include no fewer than seven different types, ranging from the unison (U) to the octave (8). This greater diversity of intervals and the contrary motion of the voices give the music a dynamic quality that is all but lacking in the preceding example.

The new polyphony spread quickly. In northern Italy, the Benedictine Guido d'Arezzo set down rules for composing organa in the *Micrologus,* a widely read music treatise of the eleventh century. At the cathedral monastery of Winchester in England, organa were notated in the margins of a great musical troper. In southwest France, a florid, elaborate style of organum developed. A similar type of polyphony thrived in Compostela in Spain, a popular pilgrimage site where the relics of James the Apostle were preserved. At each center, polyphony was associated with the liturgy of the Church and was performed by church musicians trained in the new style. As polyphonic compositions became more complex, new notational techniques were devised to ensure their proper performance.

NOTRE DAME POLYPHONY—LEONIN: ORGANUM, *VIDERUNT OMNES*

The new polyphony achieved a high degree of sophistication in twelfth-century Paris. Known as the French Athens, Paris was the center of a great cultural awakening that was encouraged in part by the rise of the French monarchy and the consolidation of the French state. Intellectual life was quickened by the chartering of a university in 1200, and spiritual life was stimulated by the founding of monastic houses and by the building of the great cathedral of Notre Dame. The cornerstone of Notre Dame was laid in 1163, and construction continued into the 1220s.

Notre Dame, Paris, view showing flying buttresses of nave.

The music composed at Notre Dame has come down to us in carefully prepared manuscripts, and because of the testimony of one writer, we can attribute the music to two named composers. These are the earliest Western composers whose polyphony can be examined and evaluated in detail. The first of them, Magister Leoninus ("Master Leonin"), is described as the best maker of organum. He lived from about 1135 to at least 1201 and was likely a poet and a priest as well as a composer.

Leonin composed polyphony for Proper chants selected from the main feasts of the liturgical calendar; he gathered his work together in a sizable volume known as the *Magnus Liber,* or "Great Book." His compositions were essentially enhancements of responsorial chants like the Gradual *Viderunt omnes* we examined earlier. Leonin's contribution was to add a new part above the ornate solo sections of the chant, creating a composition with two parts. In Gradual chants, the solo sections occurred at the opening of the Respond and the Verse (see p. 12). The other sections Leonin left to be sung as monophony by the full choir, as our plan shows. As you study Leonin's polyphonic setting of *Viderunt omnes,* you may wish to refer to the transcription of the chant (p. 14) on which it is based.

Two types of polyphony are evident in *Viderunt omnes.* Leonin uses the first type for those portions of the chant that display syllabic and neumatic text setting (for example, "Viderunt"; see also p. 14), and the second type for those portions of the chant that display melismatic text setting (for example, "omnes"; see also p. 14). In the first type, the lower voice holds one note of the chant while the upper voice executes a series of freshly composed melodic flourishes. Leonin employs consonant and dissonant intervals, though consonant intervals—chiefly the octave, the fifth, and the fourth—tend to dominate. The lower voice, which is entrusted with the chant, is called the **tenor** (from the Latin for "hold"; compare "tenacious"), and the upper voice is called the *duplum* ("double"). In this type of polyphony, the chant note is held for the equivalent of many measures in modern notation, while the upper voice executes comparatively rapid groups of notes. The elongated, slowly moving tenor thus contrasts with the energetic motion of the duplum. By this simple means, Leonin transforms individual pitches of the chant into lively polyphonic musical passages.

Notre Dame Organum: Plan for Polyphonic Gradual

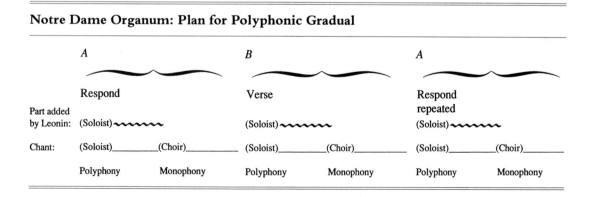

In his setting of *Viderunt omnes,* Leonin follows this florid style until he reaches the word "omnes," where the tenor sings the fifth pitch of the chant (m. 35). At this point, the chant reaches its first melisma, with a proliferation of pitches for the syllable "o" (see p. 14). Rather than continue with the first type of polyphony, Leonin here shifts to the second type, in which the tenor is speeded up so that it approaches the pace of the upper voice. Then, having exhausted the melisma of the chant, he reverts to the first type of polyphony (m. 41) and eventually brings "omnes" to a **cadence,** or close (m. 55). This much of the composition, for the solo part of the Respond, is transcribed here into modern notation.

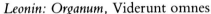

Leonin: Organum, Viderunt omnes

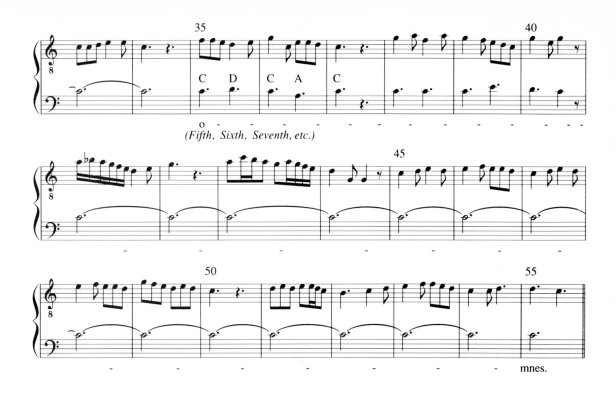

In Leonin's time, polyphony had become complex enough that some sort of systematized rhythmic notation was needed to ensure the proper coordination of the parts. To serve that need, Leonin and his contemporaries devised a system of six rhythmic patterns known as rhythmic modes. These modes had values that today are generally represented by eighth notes (♪), quarter notes (♩), and dotted-quarter notes (♩. = ♩ ♪):

Mode 1   ♩ ♪ ♩ ♪

Mode 2   ♪ ♩ ♪ ♩

Mode 3   ♩. ♪ ♩

Mode 4   ♪ ♩ ♩.

Mode 5   ♩. ♩.

Mode 6   ♫♪ ♫♪

We are not sure just how medieval composers decided on these six modes, though they may have taken them over from the poetic meters of antiquity. In Leonin's *Viderunt omnes,* mode 1 (long–short) tends to dominate.

The new polyphonic style grew even more ornate in the music of Leonin's great successor at Notre Dame, Perotin, who flourished around the turn to the thirteenth century. Perotin composed a group of "improved" snatches of polyphony designed to replace portions of Leonin's original settings. In addition, he produced several compositions for three voices and two complex works for four voices (including an elaborate version of *Viderunt omnes*). Perotin explored several of the rhythmic modes, whereas Leonin had preferred the long–short pattern of the first rhythmic mode. In short, Perotin extended the scope of Leonin's polyphony by testing further the intricate relationships between distinct musical lines—the essence of counterpoint.

THE THIRTEENTH-CENTURY MOTET

During the thirteenth century, the new polyphony made its appearance in secular music with the rise of the **motet.** At first, poets simply appropriated two-part pieces from the Notre Dame repertory and added new Latin texts to the upper parts. These Latin texts were little more than glosses on the texts of the old tenors. In a second development, French texts began to appear in the upper part, and the compositions became known as motets (from *mot*, the French for "word"). With this shift to the vernacular, the thirteenth-century motet departed from its liturgical origins.

The transition created certain problems, however. For one, it was not always easy to fit new texts to music that already existed. Moreover, the borrowed segments were relatively short sections of music, and composers needed some way of expanding the motet to make it suitable as secular entertainment. A common solution to this problem was simply to repeat the given tenor part, thereby extending its length and building a more extended foundation for the motet.

In another stage in the evolution of the motet, composers created a fresh line of music with French text above a chant tenor, or they added two new lines, with two different texts, above the old tenor. The new texts were in French, in Latin, or in a combination of French and Latin. Just as the motet acquired layers of different texts, so it acquired layers of different rhythmic character. The tenor continued to move at a slow pace, reflecting its previous role in the earlier Notre Dame repertory. The second part moved at a slightly faster pace, and the third part in still more sprightly rhythms.

Unlike the Latin texts that had been added, the French texts bore seemingly little relation to the subject of the Gregorian tenor; unabashedly secular in tone, they were concerned with matters of the heart. Thus, a tenor with the text "Domino" ("Lord") might appear beneath a second part with a text that spoke of lovesickness and a third part that celebrated the joys of love. A tenor in praise of the Blessed Virgin Mary might appear beneath other parts that described the pastoral sport of shepherds and shepherdesses.

In short, what had begun as an offshoot of Notre Dame polyphony emerged as a fully developed variety of secular polyphony. By the end of the thirteenth century, all but the most persistent ties of the motet to its origins in organum had been severed. Composers were now constructing their own tenors or borrowing secular tunes, overlaying them with new sophisticated rhythmic patterns. In the upper voices of their motets, they stretched the system of rhythmic modes to its limits. No longer were the older methods of notation suitable for the complexities of the new music. Finally, at the turn to the fourteenth century, the polyphony of Leonin and Perotin came to be referred to as *ars antiqua* ("ancient art") and was deemed antiquated. That style gave way to a powerful new impetus in music—the *ars nova* ("new art").

MUSIC IN THE FOURTEENTH CENTURY

The growing secularization of the times was evident in a remarkable fourteenth-century allegorical poem of some three thousand verses, *Le Roman de Fauvel (The Romance of Fauvel,* 1316), written by a notary of the French court. Among the manuscripts preserving this poem is an especially lavish one that contains over one hundred monophonic and polyphonic compositions to accompany a reading of the poem. In the poem, Fauvel is an asslike creature, whose name derives from the French words for the six vices of flattery, avarice, villainy, duplicity, envy, and lasciviousness. A trenchant satire, *Le Roman de Fauvel* presents a scathing indictment of the moral lassitude of fourteenth-century French society.

Contributing to the trend toward secular music was the waning influence of the Church. Between 1305 and 1378, the papacy was centered not in Rome but in Avignon, where it fell under the influence of the French court. A great schism followed as various contenders struggled to gain control of the papacy. Other worldly events, too, shook the foundations of Europe. At the middle of the century, Europe was struck by the Black Death, the bubonic plague that wiped out much of the population. And for much of the century and beyond, France and England were locked in struggle in the devastating Hundred Years' War.

During this tumultuous period, French secular music was in the ascendancy. Philippe de Vitry (1291–1361) was one of its leading composers. After studying at the Sorbonne, Vitry became a soldier, a diplomat, and a bishop, as well as a gifted composer. About 1320 he set down his thoughts on contemporary practices in composition and defended the rhythmically complex new style that had come to be known as *ars nova.* His own motets, some of which figure in *Le Roman de Fauvel,* had a decidedly intellectual bent and earned him the praise of mathematicians, astronomers, and the great Italian poet Petrarch.

The most versatile composer of the century, however, was Guillaume de Machaut (ca. 1300–1377), who was also the premier French poet of the time. Like Vitry, Machaut was also a diplomat and a cleric. His many compositions, meticulously notated, have survived in a series of opulently appointed manuscripts, the preparation of which he supervised. Although most of Machaut's music is secular, he wrote some sacred motets and, more significantly, attempted the first great polyphonic setting of the Ordinary of the Mass, a composition on a much larger scale than the refined love songs for which he was celebrated.

We have already examined Machaut's "Douce dame jolie," an example of his secular monophonic music (p. 19). Machaut also fashioned a wealth of polyphonic settings of his own poetry, patterned, like "Douce dame," on the standard forms of French medieval lyric poetry.

GUILLAUME DE MACHAUT: BALLADE, "DE TOUTES FLOURS"

Machaut's "De toutes flours" is an example of the **ballade,** a form that consists of a series of eight-line stanzas of poetry. The first four lines of each stanza have the rhyme scheme *abab*. In composing music for these four lines of text, Machaut uses the same music for the third and fourth lines as he uses for the first two (which we designate as *A*). He sets the remaining four lines of the stanza (*ccdd*) to fresh music (which we label *B*). So, the overall form of the music for the stanza is *AAB*. Here are the text and a free translation of the first stanza of "De toutes flours":

A ⎡ *De toutes flours n'avoit et de tous fruis*	*a*	
⎣ *En mon vergier fors une seule rose.*	*b*	
A ⎡ *Gastes estoit li seurplus et destruis*	*a*	
⎣ *Par Fortune qui durement s'oppose*	*b*	
B ⎡ *Contre ceste doulce flour*	*c*	
⎢ *Pour amatir sa colour et s'odour.*	*c*	
⎢ *Mais se cueillir la voy ou trebuchier,*	*d*	
⎣ *Autre après li jamais avoir ne quier.*	*d*	

A ⎡ Of all the flowers and fruits	*a*	
⎣ In my garden there is a solitary rose.	*b*	
A ⎡ All the rest has been destroyed	*a*	
⎣ By Fortune who now is intent	*b*	
B ⎡ Against this sweet flower	*c*	
⎢ To fade its color and dispel its fragrance.	*c*	
⎢ But if it is plucked or withers	*d*	
⎣ Another will not content me.	*d*	

Machaut's setting has four parts. In ascending order they are the *tenor*, the lowest sounding; the *contratenor* (literally, "against the tenor"), which occasionally crosses the tenor; the *cantus* (Latin for "song"), which carries the text; and the *triplum* ("third" part above the tenor), the uppermost part. The cantus is performed by a singer; the remaining parts are designed for instruments, though the instruments are not specified. There is evidence that Machaut intended the ballade as a three-part composition, including the cantus, the tenor, and either the triplum or the contratenor.

Machaut: Ballade, "De toutes flours"

Triplum and cantus parts sound one octave lower than written.

Machaut's harmonies typify fourteenth-century practice. Consonant intervals—especially fourths, fifths, and octaves—prevail, though occasionally the parts clash with one another, injecting a certain piquancy into the music. Relatively rare is the rounded, mellow sound of the interval of the third, characteristic of our modern triad; on a first hearing, Machaut's ballade may sound somewhat hollow or wooden.

In Italy the fourteenth century, known as the *trecento,* also saw a burgeoning of polyphony. The new Italian music was primarily secular. Its leading composer was Francesco Landini (ca. 1325–1397), who served, though blind, as cathedral organist in Florence. Landini set secular poems, possibly his own, in several musical types. The most colorful of all, the *caccia,* was a composition for three parts; its upper two parts engaged in a **canon** in which one voice pursued and imitated the other literally (the word *caccia* means "chase"; see also p. 525). The texts used for the caccia teemed with naturalistic imagery, such as birdcalls and calls of the hunt.

In England, too, polyphony had become well entrenched by the fourteenth century, in both sacred and secular music. Here the Notre Dame style of polyphony had taken hold more firmly than it had in Italy; in fact, one of the primary manuscripts of Leonin's music is of English or Scottish provenance. English polyphony acquired a character of its own, however, and evolved independently of newer French musical currents. English composers preferred mellow intervals, such as the third and the sixth, and tended to avoid the dissonant clashes found in French music. Instead of the open, hollow sonorities that were prevalent on the Continent, they preferred triads as the basic harmonic materials.

The English also delighted in the intricacies of counterpoint. One notable example is the thirteenth-century "Sumer is icumen in," a celebration of the return of summer. This charming composition is in the form of a four-part canon constructed on a foundation in which two additional voices exchange their own musical phrases. All told, then, there are six vocal parts; indeed, "Sumer is icumen in" is the first known example of six-part polyphony.

Our knowledge of early English music is sketchy at best; most of it is by anonymous composers. By the fifteenth century, however, named composers, including Lionel Power and John Dunstable, were perfecting a suave musical style rooted in triadic harmony. Sometime during the early decades of that century, this style found its way to the Continent. There, known as the *contenance angloise* ("English manner"), it was to figure prominently in the music of the Renaissance.

Suggested Listening

* Gradual, *Viderunt omnes*
* Hymn, *Ave maris stella*
* Leonin: Organum, *Viderunt omnes*
* Machaut, Guillaume de: Ballade, "De toutes flours"
* _____: Virelai, "Douce dame jolie"

Works marked with an asterisk are the principal works discussed in the text.

PART II THE RENAISSANCE

EUROPEAN HISTORY	EUROPEAN CULTURE AND IDEAS	EUROPEAN MUSIC
	1304–1374: Petrarch	
	1313–1375: Boccaccio	
1364–1477: Rise to power of dukes of Burgundy	**1377–1446:** Brunelleschi	
	ca. 1386–1466: Donatello	**ca. 1390–1453:** John Dunstable
	ca. 1400-1468: Johann Gutenberg	**ca. 1400–1474:** Guillaume Dufay
	1401–1429?: Masaccio	
1434: Beginning of Medici rise to power in Florence	**1440s:** Gutenberg's printing press	
	1444–1510: Botticelli	**ca. 1440–1521:** Josquin Desprez
1455–1485: Wars of the Roses	**1452–1519:** Leonardo da Vinci	
1461–1483: Reign of Louis XI in France	**ca. 1466–1536:** Erasmus	
	1469–1527: Machiavelli	
1473–1543: Copernicus	**1471–1528:** Dürer	
1478: Establishment of Spanish Inquisition	**1475–1564:** Michelangelo	
1483–1546: Martin Luther	**1483–1520:** Raphael	
1485–1603: Reign of Tudors in England		
1492: Granada, last stronghold of Moors, recaptured; Columbus reaches San Salvador		
1494–1498: Girolamo Savonarola seizes power in Florence	**1497–1543:** Holbein the Younger	
1509–1547: Reign of Henry VIII in England		**1501:** Petrucci, *Odhecaton A*
		ca. 1510–1586: Andrea Gabrieli
1513: Balboa crosses the Isthmus of Panama to the Pacific Ocean	**1513:** Machiavelli, *The Prince*	**ca. 1525–1594:** Giovanni Pierluigi da Palestrina
	ca. 1520–1569: Brueghel the Elder	
1517: Luther's 95 Theses		
1519–1522: Magellan circumnavigates the world	**1528:** Castiglione, *The Courtier*	**1532–1594:** Orlande de Lassus
1534: Church of England established; Ignatius Loyola founds the Jesuit Order		
1543: Copernicus, *De revolutionibus orbium coelestium*	**1541–1614:** El Greco	**1543–1623:** William Byrd
	1547–1616: Cervantes	
1545–1563: Council of Trent		
1558–1603: Reign of Elizabeth I in England	**1564–1616:** Shakespeare	**ca. 1556–1612:** Giovanni Gabrieli
	1568: Vasari, *Lives of the Artists* (2nd ed.)	**1563–1626:** John Dowland
1588: England defeats Spanish Armada		**1576–1623:** Thomas Weelkes
	1590s: Spenser, *The Faerie Queene*	**1601:** *Triumphs of Oriana*

BACKGROUND FOR THE RENAISSANCE

*T*he Renaissance was an age of cultural revival that arose in Italy in the latter part of the fourteenth century and then, in the fifteenth and sixteenth centuries, spread throughout western Europe. Nineteenth-century historians were the first to apply to this period the term *renaissance*, or "rebirth," which they saw as the beginning of "modern" history. The thinkers, writers, and artists of the Renaissance saw themselves as the agents of a cultural regeneration prompted in part by their rediscovery of the culture of classical antiquity.

The music theorist Johannes Tinctoris, in a counterpoint treatise written in Milan in 1477, praised the music of the recent past but dismissed earlier music of the Middle Ages as unworthy in comparison. The philosopher Marsilio Ficino, writing late in the fifteenth century in Florence, viewed his century as a new golden age that had rescued the traditional liberal arts, including music, from oblivion. In *Lives of the Artists* (1568), the Florentine Giorgio Vasari likened the perceived decline of the arts after the fall of Rome to the atrophying of a body, and their recent brilliant period to a miraculous rebirth. To dramatize that revival, he sketched the lives of distinguished painters, sculptors, and architects of recent centuries: Giotto, Masaccio, Brunelleschi, Donatello, Botticelli, Leonardo da Vinci, Raphael, and Michelangelo, among others.

Pervading the culture of the Renaissance was the concept of humanism, which extolled the ability of man to raise himself from ignorance to knowledge. This emphasis on human values dated back to classical antiquity. Aristotle had declared that the duty of mankind was "to know and to act," and Cicero had determined humanity (*humanitas*, from which we get the word "humanities") to be the proper pursuit of mankind. For the ancients, the innate dignity of man raised him to the stature of a mortal god.

The Renaissance humanist Pico wrote an *Oration on the Dignity of Man* (1486). The Italian diplomat Castiglione described the "universal man" in his celebrated *Courtier* (1528). For Castiglione, the Renaissance gentleman was well educated in the humanities, well read in Latin and Greek literature, proficient in arms, chivalrous in love, and skillful in athletics. Perhaps the greatest exemplar of that versatility was Leonardo da Vinci (1452–1519), scientist, artist, writer, inventor, and musician.

Although the humanists embraced the values of classical antiquity, they were devout Christians who glorified the creations of God. Rejecting the dogmatic thought of the late Middle Ages, they turned to the writings of the early church fathers, which led them inevitably back to the culture of the Greeks and the Romans. They studied ancient ruins, statues, and coins. They sought out the great works of Greek and Roman literature, translating for the first time the complete works of Plato and rediscovering the comedies of Terence and Plautus. The humanists were exacting scholars whose goal was to rescue pagan culture and to make it available to their contemporaries. To do so, they chose the language of classical Latin, modeling their style on the elegantly turned prose of Cicero's orations.

For the humanists, man was also *homo creator,* man the creator. Painters and sculptors chose as their subject the human figure, always realistically detailed and often unclothed. Art was further humanized through the use of three-dimensional perspective, a technique that was probably introduced by the Florentine architect Brunelleschi

Giovanni Bellini, *Saint Francis,* 1470s. Bellini uses perspective to draw the viewer's gaze into the painting.

in the 1420s and was brilliantly employed by his contemporaries Donatello, a sculptor, and Masaccio, a painter. Perspective enabled painters to render objects on the flat surface of their canvases so as to suggest depth.

Composers, too, came to see themselves as individual creators rather than as anonymous practitioners. Thus, Guillaume Dufay, the principal composer of the early Renaissance, inserted his own name into the text of one of his secular compositions, and in a deeply moving setting of *Ave Regina caelorum,* he presented himself as a penitent seeking forgiveness. Josquin Desprez, perhaps the greatest musical genius of the period, wrote a motet with a text in which his own name appears as an acrostic. These musical signatures demonstrated the emergence of music as more and more an independent art practiced by individual composers with highly personal styles.

Today, scholars view the Renaissance as a transition to modern times rather than as an abrupt change of course. Medieval feudalism, with its decentralized political authority supported by a land-based economy, was giving way to the nation-states of England, France, and Spain, in which authority was exercised by monarchs and wealth was amassed through commerce. In Italy, the great city-states of Florence, Milan, and Venice were rising in power. Columbus, Magellan, Vasco da Gama, Vespucci, and Balboa were venturing out onto the oceans, doubling the area of the world known to Europeans. Copernicus proposed his revolutionary theory of a heliocentric solar system, and Leonardo da Vinci created detailed drawings of the human anatomy. With the invention of printing and engraving, the means were at hand to disseminate the new knowledge—and the new music.

The Renaissance gave rise to a new human curiosity about the world and mankind's place in it. The medieval world view, in which the present life was a time of self-denial, a sobering preparation for the blissful hereafter, gave way to a burst of confidence in the faculties of mankind. With the dawning of the new age, composers rose to the new challenge: They still wrote music to glorify God, but they also wrote music to celebrate human experience, both trivial and exalted.

2

MUSIC IN THE RENAISSANCE

*M*usic and the other arts underwent a genuine revitalization during the fifteenth and sixteenth centuries. In some ways, however, music continued to follow the traditions of the past. Composers still drew on courtly love poetry (see p. 18) for their secular music. They continued to build their sacred polyphony on the foundation of authentic Gregorian plainchant, a technique that dated back to twelfth-century polyphony in Paris (p. 22), and they continued to adhere to the principles of modality based on the medieval church modes.

Nevertheless, new attitudes about music began to assert themselves. Fifteenth-century composers were ambitiously exploring their craft, creating works on a larger scale that demanded new approaches to musical structure. They began to make decisions for purely musical reasons rather than merely to accommodate the requirements of the text or its liturgical purpose. Among their innovations were the expansion of the church modes and the application of new principles of harmony and counterpoint.

The medieval system of church modes carried over to the Renaissance. Moreover, additional modes on A and C, known as the Aeolian and the Ionian, came to be used with increasing frequency:

Aeolian and Ionian Modes★

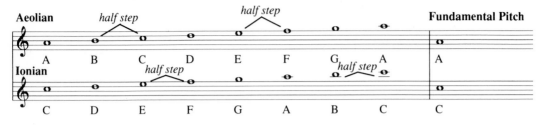

★See also p. 9.

(The full significance of the new modes, however, became apparent only later; during the seventeenth century, they emerged as the basis of our modern minor and major scales.)

Renaissance composers also developed a new approach to harmonic relationships. The **triad,** built up by superimposing thirds (for example, C-E-G), became the preferred sonority. By using triads, composers could create music that sounded sweeter, richer, and more full-bodied than the sonorities of medieval music, which, often lacking the third, sounded pointed and austere in comparison. Triads, in short, added a new dimension to music and affected the way in which composers treated harmony. By using progressions of harmonies that featured recurring triads, they achieved a new sense of harmonic direction. In the following passage from Dufay's *Ave Regina caelorum,* triads on C (with pitches C, E, and G, or C, E-flat, and G) and on G (with pitches G, B, and D, or G, B-flat, and D) tend to dominate.

Dufay: Ave Regina caelorum *(III)*

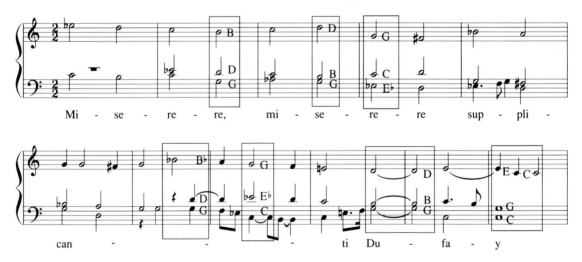

Text: Have pity on your supplicant Dufay.

The harmonic progressions of this passage resemble those of later times, making the music sound more modern, more familiar, than, say, a motet from the thirteenth or fourteenth century.

Composers were also revising their attitudes toward counterpoint. Medieval composers had typically written the parts of their music successively, one at a time, a technique that sometimes produced clashes between the parts. Renaissance composers, however, with their new enthusiasm for triadic harmonies, tended to compose all parts simultaneously, creating a euphonious complex of triadically related parts.

FIFTEENTH-CENTURY MUSIC: GUILLAUME DUFAY AND THE FRANCO-FLEMISH STYLE

We usually think of Italy as the wellspring of the Renaissance. A great succession of Italians—the poets Dante, Petrarch, Boccaccio, Ariosto, and Tasso; the statesmen Machiavelli and Castiglione; and the brilliant succession of painters, sculptors, and architects—did indeed lead the way in the visual arts and letters. In music, however, the Renaissance arose in a small area of northeastern France, Belgium, and Holland. There, during the fifteenth century, composers influenced by innovations in English music refined a Franco-Flemish art of polyphony. Many of them left their homelands to work in Italy, where their transplanted art found further nourishment. Known as the *oltremontani,* these northerners from "beyond the mountains" filled the ranks of musicians at the Papal Chapel in Rome and at Italian ducal courts and chapels well into the sixteenth century. Only then did Italy produce native composers of the first rank.

Throughout much of the fifteenth century, the Franco-Flemish style was centered in the duchy of Burgundy, southeast of Paris, and in the various territories (including much of Holland, Belgium, Luxembourg, and northeastern France) under the control of the duchy. Many of the most famous musicians of the day were associated with the Burgundian court, including Guillaume Dufay (ca. 1400–1474), Gilles Binchois (ca. 1400–1460), Antoine Busnois (ca. 1430–1492), and Josquin Desprez (ca. 1440–1521). The arts flourished in Burgundy, especially under the patronage of Philip the Good (reigned 1419–1467) and Charles the Bold (reigned 1467–1477), the last duke of Burgundy.

After serving as a choirboy at the cathedral of Cambrai, Dufay traveled as a young man to Italy. There, in the 1420s, he entered the service of the ruling Malatesta family in Pesaro and Rimini and later sang in the papal choir in Rome. At one time or another, he lived in Florence and Ferrara and at the court of Savoy in northern Italy. Finally, at the height of his fame, he returned to Cambrai, where he died in 1474.

Dufay was a prolific composer who worked in a variety of genres. Many of his compositions are relatively simple polyphonic settings of chants for use in church services. These settings generally have three voices, with the chant in the upper voice and with the lower voices providing accompaniment. Dufay gives the chant prominence by assigning it to the top voice, where it is clearly audible. Instead of merely citing the

Mary with the Child and angel musicians, Flemish, Jacob Cornelisz von Oostsanen (1493–1544). Mary and the infant Jesus are shown with a host of angel musicians. Among the instruments illustrated are the lute, hurdy-gurdy, recorder, fiddle, harp, and shawm.

chant, however, he leaves his own mark on it by taking certain liberties with it. He smooths it out by adding connecting notes between pitches and embroiders it with graceful melodic ornaments. The result is a highly personalized version of the chant. This technique of providing an existing melody with fresh melodic elaboration, known as **paraphrase,** was adopted by many Renaissance composers. Although Dufay did not invent the technique—he took it over from earlier English music—he was the first major composer to explore thoroughly its potential.

Dufay also composed several secular songs, known as **chansons.** In Dufay's chansons, a treble melody for solo singer is accompanied by two lower parts, evidently to be performed by instruments. Although the theme of chivalrous love betrays the medieval origins of these pieces, their lithe, lyrical melodic lines and rounded triadic harmonies are uniquely Dufay's.

Dufay directed his major efforts, however, to the polyphonic motet and the Mass. Some thirty of his motets survive, many of them written for such specific occasions as the coronation of a pope, the signing of a treaty, or the celebration of a state marriage. One of them, *Nuper rosarum flores,* was written for the consecration of Brunelleschi's dome for the Cathedral of Florence in 1436. In several of his motets, Dufay continued to rely on medieval techniques by using slow-moving tenor parts based on plainchant. But he also employed a wealth of forward-looking techniques. For example, he varied the texture of his motets, from finely wrought duets to dense contrapuntal thickets in as many as five parts. He wrote free polyphony in which the voices carry different strands; he wrote imitative polyphony in which the voices imitate each other's material; and occasionally he wrote canons in which the voices strictly duplicate each other. Later composers were to enrich their own polyphony by emulating Dufay's remarkable range of compositional techniques.

DUFAY: *MISSA SE LA FACE AY PALE* (KYRIE)

By Dufay's time, the polyphonic Mass had developed into a multimovement cycle consisting of settings of the five major texts of the Ordinary: the *Kyrie, Gloria, Credo, Sanctus,* and *Agnus Dei.* Often, these Masses are built around a recurring melodic line known as a **cantus firmus** ("fixed voice"). Typically a sacred plainchant, the cantus firmus appears prominently in one voice in each movement and gives unity to the whole. English composers of the early fifteenth century were the first to develop the new technique, but Dufay applied it on a large scale and established the cyclic Mass as the most imposing musical genre of the time.

One of Dufay's crowning achievements was the Mass (*Missa*) *Se la face ay pale,* a work possibly written about 1450, toward the middle of his career. Remarkably, Dufay turned for its cantus firmus not to plainchant but to a melody from one of his own secular chansons, the love song "Se la face ay pale" ("If the face is pale, the cause is love"). Dufay's choice of a secular melody for treatment in a sacred Mass is striking evidence of the rise of humanistic values in the music of the fifteenth century.

Dufay wrote this Mass for a small choral ensemble in four parts. (Whether he intended instruments to double the parts remains open to debate.) The tenor unfolds the cantus firmus in slow-moving rhythmic values while the three other voices weave a tapestry of freely composed counterpoint around it. We have seen how in earlier, medieval music the tenor had generally served as the lowest-sounding part of a composition. In Dufay's Mass, however, the tenor is supported by a lower-sounding bass voice. Working independently of the tenor, the bass reinforces the pitches of the upper three voices (soprano, alto, and tenor), thereby reinforcing the recurring triads of the music.

Although Dufay uses the chanson melody as a cantus firmus throughout the Mass, he varies his treatment of it from movement to movement. In certain sections, he omits the cantus firmus altogether and reduces the texture from four to three (or even two) voices. In other sections, he changes the rhythmic values of the cantus firmus from one statement of the melody to the next. Generally, the chanson melody appears in **augmented,** or elongated, values two or three times as long as the basic pulse of the other voices. Sometimes, Dufay presents several consecutive statements of the complete cantus firmus with increasingly faster note values. This speeding up of the cantus firmus until it matches the motion of the other parts creates a strong sense of increasing rhythmic momentum.

A brief look at the Kyrie of the Mass reveals further aspects of Dufay's style (see study diagram). Traditionally, the text of the Kyrie is in three sections: a first section on "Kyrie eleison" ("Lord have mercy"), a second section on "Christe eleison" ("Christ have mercy"), and a third section on "Kyrie eleison," with the overall plan of *ABA.* Dufay follows this plan for the Kyrie of his *Missa Se la face ay pale.* For the first and third sections, those on "Kyrie eleison," he employs the full chorus, with the slowly moving cantus firmus—the melody of the love song "Se la face ay pale"—in the tenor voice. The following example shows the opening measures of the Mass. (Here the soprano, alto, and bass are transcribed in the meter of $\frac{3}{2}$, with three half notes or their equivalent per measure. The tenor moves in a meter half as fast, $\frac{3}{1}$, with three whole notes or their equivalent per measure. The note value ⌗, called a breve, is the equivalent of two whole notes.)

Dufay: Mass, *Se la face ay pale* (Kyrie)

A "Kyrie eleison"	*B* "Christe eleison"	*A* "Kyrie eleison"
Four-part polyphony (soprano, alto, tenor, bass), with cantus firmus in long values in tenor	Two-part polyphony, duets between soprano and alto, alto and bass, and soprano and bass; no cantus firmus	Four-part polyphony (soprano, alto, tenor, bass), with cantus firmus in long values in tenor

---

Dufay: Mass, Se la face ay pale *("Kyrie eleison")*

★ Sounds one octave lower.

As the study diagram shows, in the second section, on "Christe eleison," Dufay aims for contrast: He drops the tenor voice and, with it, the cantus firmus. In contrast to the full-bodied sound of the preceding "Kyrie eleison," the "Christe eleison" offers comely duets between soprano and alto, alto and bass, and soprano and bass. The third and last section of the movement, with its text again on "Kyrie eleison," returns to the full-bodied, four-part sound of the opening, with the cantus firmus once again intoned in the tenor.

We have said that in the "Christe eleison," Dufay omits the cantus firmus and thus sets off the "Christe eleison" from the opening "Kyrie eleison." Nevertheless, he takes other steps to link the two sections: He begins the "Christe" with a short musical figure, or **motive,** that has already been heard in the opening measure of the preceding "Kyrie." This motive, which descends by steps in the soprano, is bracketed in the following example, from the "Christe eleison," and in the preceding example, from the opening "Kyrie eleison":

Dufay: Mass, Se la face ay pale *("Christe eleison")*

*Sounds one octave lower.

The recurrence of the motive provides a measure of unity between the "Kyrie" and the "Christe."

JOSQUIN DESPREZ

After Dufay's death, generations of Franco-Flemish composers continued to practice the art of sacred polyphony. The composer who brought it to a new pinnacle of achievement in the sixteenth century was Josquin Desprez, who was active in France and in Italy. Josquin invested his music with an expressiveness and a nobility that were ideally suited to the meaning of his texts. He advanced Dufay's use of triadic harmony and often introduced passages of block chords that featured recurring triads. Most important, he perfected a new style of counterpoint that was to influence music for centuries to come.

We know quite little about Josquin's early years. He was probably born about 1440 near Picardy in northern France. He may have studied with the composer Johannes Ockeghem (ca. 1410–1497), who served at the court of the French kings; Josquin composed a heartrending lament in Ockeghem's memory. In Italy by 1459, Josquin served as a singer at the cathedral in Milan. He remained there for several years and eventually entered the service of the ruling Sforza family.

During the 1480s and 1490s, Josquin sang in the Papal Chapel in Rome and later entered the service of Duke Ercole d'Este of Ferrara. He finally returned to France, where he may have established ties to the French court of Louis XII and to the Flemish court of Queen Margaret of Austria.

Josquin's fame as a composer spread throughout western Europe and survived long after his death. Martin Luther once remarked that only Josquin could bend the notes of music to his will. His reputation was undoubtedly enhanced by the appearance of music printing at the beginning of the sixteenth century. By the last quarter of the fifteenth century, liturgical chant books were being printed from woodblocks instead of having to be copied by hand. Then, in 1501, the Venetian printer Ottaviano Petrucci succeeded in printing polyphonic music from movable type. His landmark publication was *Harmonice musices Odhecaton A (One Hundred Songs of Harmonic Music),* an anthology of about one hundred secular vocal pieces, including several by Josquin. Later, Petrucci published volumes of Josquin's Masses and issued many of his motets.

JOSQUIN: *MISSA PANGE LINGUA* (KYRIE)

Josquin wrote about one hundred polyphonic motets and some two dozen polyphonic cyclic Masses. In addition, he composed numerous settings of French and Italian secular texts; the animated style and homophonic texture of these settings are evident in some of his later sacred works as well.

One of Josquin's most highly regarded works is the *Missa Pange lingua,* from his late period. Like Dufay's *Missa Se la face ay pale,* this Mass is based on a preexistent melody—not a secular song tune, as in the Dufay, but the sacred hymn *Pange lingua.* Also, Josquin does not set off the melody as a cantus firmus in long note values, as did Dufay, nor does he even state the chant melody once in its entirety. Instead, he paraphrases it and distributes segments of his paraphrase among all four voices of the chorus. Josquin often applies the technique of **imitative polyphony:** In one voice, he typically introduces a motive, drawn from his paraphrase of the chant, and then has another voice or series of voices imitate it. The statement of the motive and its subsequent reuse in imitation together create a **point of imitation.**

The chant that inspired Josquin's Mass is a hymn for the feast of Corpus Christi ("The Body of Christ"). The text, in stanzas of six lines (rhyming *ababab*), was written by Thomas Aquinas in 1263. Here are the hymn, the text, and a translation of the first stanza:

Pange lingua gloriosi	Sing, O tongue, of that
Corporis mysterium,	glorious body's mystery
Sanguinisque pretiosi,	and of that precious blood
Quem in mundi pretium	which, a reward to mankind,
Fructus ventris generosi	the fruit of the generous womb,
Rex effudit gentium.	the King of all peoples has poured out.

Hymn, Pange lingua

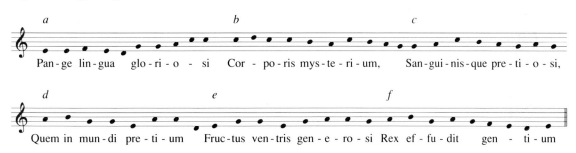

In the original hymn, each line of text has its own, distinctive melodic phrase. (The six phrases are labeled *a–f* in the musical example.) In his Mass, Josquin paraphrases, or reworks, these six melodic phrases and expands each into a point of imitation.

The Kyrie of this Mass is a masterful example of Josquin's command of paraphrase techniques and imitative polyphony. The paraphrased portions of the hymn are distributed throughout the three main parts of the Kyrie: the "Kyrie eleison," the "Christe eleison," and the second "Kyrie eleison." Josquin develops the first two phrases of the hymn (*a* and *b*) in the opening "Kyrie eleison"; the third and fourth (*c* and *d*), in the central "Christe eleison"; and the fifth and sixth (*e* and *f*), in the concluding "Kyrie eleison." By themselves, Josquin's paraphrase techniques offer exquisite examples of the composer's melodic art. They range in scope from phrase *a*, in which Josquin closely observes the contours of the original hymn, to phrase *f*, in which he systematically reworks the original in a profusion of notes that prolong the graceful descending close of the hymn.

Josquin: Paraphrase Technique in Missa Pange lingua, *Kyrie*

PARAPHRASE OF *a*

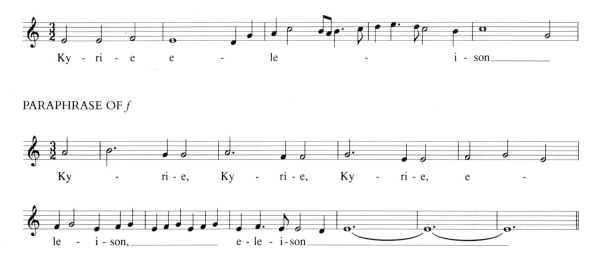

Josquin begins the Mass with the first phrase of the paraphrased hymn (*a*) in the tenor and has the bass imitate it:

Josquin: Missa Pange lingua, *Kyrie*

After a few measures, as these parts drop out, the phrase is heard in the overlapping soprano voice, imitated by the alto. Through his use of paired entries, Josquin is able to articulate clearly the paraphrased phrases of the chant. The result is a coordinated, balanced musical structure permeated with the ever-present paraphrase of the chant. In this Mass, the notes of the hymn do bend to the artistry of Josquin and to his consummate contrapuntal skill.

Josquin was the brightest point in a constellation of Franco-Flemish composers who mastered the art of imitative polyphony. Possibly his greatest contemporary was Heinrich Isaac (ca. 1450–1517), who served in the magnificent courts of Lorenzo de' Medici in Florence and Emperor Maximilian I in Vienna. Isaac's monumental collection *Choralis Constantinus,* a cycle of several hundred polyphonic settings for the Proper of the Mass (see p. 12), was published after his death, in 1550 and 1555.

After Josquin and Isaac, the Franco-Flemish style persisted well into the sixteenth century. Orlande de Lassus (1532–1594), one of the last great Franco-Flemish composers and one of the most productive and versatile of the Renaissance masters, wrote some two thousand compositions. His works encompass a variety of styles and include settings of Latin, Italian, French, and German texts.

As the dominant style, imitative polyphony continued to be developed throughout the sixteenth century. Composers began to thicken the texture of their music by writing for choruses with five or more parts. Occasionally, they borrowed and reworked substantial sections of earlier polyphonic compositions, a process known as **parody technique.** Finally, they became more responsive to the texts they set to music, sharpening the meaning of the texts by making them more explicit through strikingly expressive gestures in the music.

GIOVANNI PIERLUIGI DA PALESTRINA

During the second half of the sixteenth century, Italian composers began to rival the long line of distinguished Franco-Flemish composers. The preeminent Italian composer was Giovanni Pierluigi da Palestrina (ca. 1525–1594), who brought the Franco-Flemish style of imitative polyphony to its ultimate perfection. Born in the town of Palestrina, he spent most of his adult life in Rome. After serving for a time in the Sistine Chapel,

Matthias Grünewald, Isenheim Altarpiece, second view, ca. 1510–1515. The central panel shows the Virgin and Child. The angels play a variety of viols.

he was dismissed because his marriage broke the rule of celibacy (even though he was not a priest). Subsequently, he held posts at some of the great churches of Rome.

Palestrina's prolific output—among his works are 104 Masses and nearly 400 motets—reflects the spirit of the Counter-Reformation, the reaction of the Catholic church to the Protestant Reformation. A major event in the Counter-Reformation was the Council of Trent, which was convened in 1545 and remained in session intermittently until 1563. The purpose of the Council was to review the doctrines of the Church, to correct certain excesses of the past (some of which had prompted Martin Luther to proclaim his 95 Theses in 1517), and to reaffirm and reinvigorate the Catholic faith.

The bishops who participated in the Council turned their attention to music as well. As early as 1555, during a short, three-week reign, Pope Marcellus II had enjoined the singers of his Chapel (including Palestrina) to perform their music in a dignified style and in a manner that permitted its text to be clearly understood. By the 1560s, one of his successors, Pius IV, began to consider more severe measures, including a ban on polyphony and a return to the singing of plainchant. Apparently in response to these views, Palestrina composed one of his greatest works, the *Missa Papae Marcelli* (*Pope Marcellus* Mass), which was published in 1567. This masterpiece was conceived as a defense of church polyphony, a statement of its ideal embodiment. Not based on a preexistent cantus firmus, the Mass is freely composed. It employs an expanded, six-part chorus that engages in luxurious imitative counterpoint; yet—and this was Palestrina's great accomplishment—the polyphony is fluent and clear throughout. By emphasizing consonances and by carefully regulating dissonances, Palestrina constantly focuses attention on the text of the Mass. So successful was the *Pope Marcellus* Mass that Palestrina came to be regarded as the savior of church music. His great Mass was regarded as a standard of perfection to which other composers should aspire.

PALESTRINA: MOTET, *SICUT CERVUS*

Another example of Palestrina's sacred polyphony is the motet *Sicut cervus,* a setting of the first three verses of Psalm 42 for four-part choir:

Sicut cervus desiderat ad fontes aquarum,	As the hart panteth after the water brooks,
Ita desiderat anima mea ad te Deus.	So panteth my soul after thee, O God.
Sitivit anima mea ad Deum fortem vivum,	My soul thirsteth for God, for the living God:
Quando veniam et apparebo ante faciem Dei?	When shall I come and appear before His face?
Fuerunt mihi lacrymae meae panes die ac nocte,	My tears have been my bread day and night,
dum dicitur mihi quotidie: ubi est Deus tuus?	Saying daily unto me, Where is thy God?

Imitative polyphony prevails in much of the motet, except for the final line, where Palestrina turns to a homophonic texture and treats the chorus in block-chordal fashion.

The motet opens with a lucid point of imitation in which a gracefully rising motive is carried through all four voices, one by one. After the tenor introduces the motive, it is taken up in turn by the alto, the soprano, and the bass. Our example gives the first ten measures, which make up the point of imitation. Palestrina carefully controls his use of dissonances; relatively few occur, and when they do, they fall primarily on weak, unaccented beats. The result is a graceful contrapuntal flow of lines that, taken together, project a series of smooth, consonant harmonies:

Palestrina: Motet, Sicut cervus

POINT OF IMITATION

Palestrina's reputation as a reforming contrapuntal purist endured long after his death. The eighteenth-century Austrian composer Johann Joseph Fux devised a system of counterpoint based on Palestrina's music that was used to instruct generations of composers in the high art of counterpoint. Nineteenth-century romantic composers admired the spiritual qualities of Palestrina's music and formed a kind of Palestrina cult. In the twentieth century, Hans Pfitzner transformed the composer into a romantic genius in the opera *Palestrina* (1917), which shows him in a state of divine inspiration as he creates his *Pope Marcellus* Mass.

NEW CURRENTS: NATIONAL STYLES

Outside the churches and cathedrals of sixteenth-century Europe, lighter, secular styles of music were gaining popularity. In Germany, many collections of secular songs were being published. In Spain, the *villancico,* a composition of several stanzas separated by a recurring refrain, was disseminated. In France, the publisher Pierre Attaignant was issuing collections of a new genre, known as the Parisian chanson, which featured a lively melody, accompanied by chords, repeated for successive stanzas. The composer Clément Janequin (ca. 1485–1558) delighted in filling his chansons with such natural imagery as birdsongs, street cries, and battle cries.

Italian composers, too, were catering to the popular taste for secular music. The *frottola* was a polyphonic vocal composition that featured lighthearted, amorous poetry. The frottola had a chordal, four-part texture, with little imitative polyphony. It was usually performed by a solo voice (the top part) with instrumental accompaniment (the three lowest parts).

The most important of all the new secular genres, however, was the Italian **madrigal.** Madrigals had texts of high literary merit; the music displayed both chordal, homophonic passages and more intricate passages drawn in imitative polyphony. Although scholars disagree about the origins of the sixteenth-century madrigal, it seems to have arisen in the first half of the century as part of a movement to promote vernacular Tuscan as a worthy literary language. The most vigorous advocate in this literary movement was Cardinal Pietro Bembo (1470–1547), who brought out editions of Dante and Petrarch early in the century. The madrigalists were especially impressed by Petrarch's *Canzoniere,* a collection of Tuscan sonnets that attested the poet's love for the unknown Laura, and by the vernacular poetry of Ariosto, Tasso, and Sannazaro. Madrigalists set these and other distinguished texts in vivid musical idioms that matched the inflections, nuances, and rhythms of the poetry. Typically, madrigals had four vocal parts and were performed with one singer for each part; in the second half of the sixteenth century, madrigals for five or more parts became increasingly common.

The first collection of Italian madrigals, which appeared during the 1530s, contained works by foreign composers living in Italy—among them, Philippe Verdelot and Jacques Arcadelt—and works by the Italian composer Costanzo Festa. As the century advanced, numerous composers, both foreign and Italian, developed the madrigal into a highly charged musical expression. Among them were the Flemish composers Adrian Willaert, Cipriano de Rore (a pupil of Willaert), and Giaches Wert—all employed in Italian courts—and several Italian composers, including Marenzio, Andrea Gabrieli, Gesualdo, and Claudio Monteverdi, the master of early Italian baroque music. Carlo Gesualdo, prince of Venosa (ca. 1560–1613), carried the genre into the early years of the seventeenth century. Many of his late creations can best be described as bizarre: His mannered madrigals shock us with sharp rhythmic and textural contrasts, jolting dissonances, and extreme, convoluted harmonic turns that seem to tear asunder the musical fabric—all depicting cogently texts of unrelenting grief and sorrow.

In the later years of the sixteenth century, the madrigal became the favorite show-piece of highly trained singers performing in the academies and courts of Europe. The composer Orlande de Lassus cultivated the genre in Munich, and in Vienna Philippe de Monte turned out over eleven hundred madrigals. The madrigal was popular in France and as far afield as Denmark. In England, it enjoyed a spectacular heyday for a few decades before and after 1600.

THE ENGLISH MADRIGAL

Before the madrigal reached England, a tradition of popular song had emerged during the long reign of Elizabeth I (1558–1603). The composer who did much to raise its artistic level was William Byrd (1543–1623), easily the most renowned and versatile musician in Elizabethan England. Byrd composed many secular settings in a polyphonic style but excelled in a peculiarly English genre known as the consort song. This was a solo song accompanied by a "consort," or set of instruments, such as an ensemble of viols (bowed string instruments played upright) or an ensemble of recorders (woodwind instruments with whistle-type mouthpieces). For the most part, Byrd managed to avoid the direct influence of Italian madrigals, which became available in "Englished" texts only toward the end of the sixteenth century.

Byrd also wrote a great quantity of church polyphony. A Catholic, he composed Latin Masses but also magisterial Anglican services for the newly established Church of England. He also wrote a fair amount of keyboard music; we shall study one example later in this chapter (see pp. 56–57).

THOMAS MORLEY: MADRIGAL, "HARD BY A CRYSTAL FOUNTAIN"

Between 1590 and 1609, the English madrigalists Thomas Morley (ca. 1557–1602), Thomas Weelkes (1576–1623), and John Wilbye (1574–1638) published several collections of madrigals, and in 1601 Morley collected two dozen madrigals by various composers in a volume titled *The Triumphs of Oriana*. All the pieces in this collection honor Elizabeth I, the Virgin Queen, who appears throughout as Oriana. The queen is accompanied by Vesta (goddess of the Vestal Virgins), Diana (goddess of the hunt), and various satyrs, fauns, nymphs, demigods, and other divinities—all of whom pay homage to Oriana.

Each madrigal concludes with the lines "Then sang the shepherds and nymphs of Diana: Long live fair Oriana." Though the poetry impresses as somewhat flat and uninspired, the composers enliven it through the use of **madrigalisms,** or **word paintings.** These are musical turns of phrase that heighten the meaning of the text and reinforce its nuances and allusions. For example, the composer might use ascending and descending phrases to suggest the idea of rising or falling, fast or slow note values to suggest motion or repose, and harsh dissonances to suggest grief or other strong emotions.

One of the most celebrated madrigals in *The Triumphs of Oriana* is Morley's "Hard by a Crystal Fountain," based, as it turns out, on an Italian madrigal by Giovanni Croce (ca. 1557–1609). For his text, Morley used an "Englished" version of Croce's Italian text that had already appeared in a collection titled *Musica transalpina* (1588). Then, taking Croce's madrigal as a point of departure, Morley fashioned an English madrigal that was considerably more elaborate than its prototype.

Here is the "Englished" text:

Hard by a crystal fountain
Oriana the bright lay down a-sleeping.
The birds they finely chirped, the winds were stilled,
Sweetly, with these accenting the air was filled;
This is that fair whose head a crown deserveth
Which heaven for her reserveth.
Leave shepherds your Lambs keeping
Upon the barren mountain,
And, nymphs, attend on her and leave your bowers,
For she the shepherds' life maintains and yours.
Then sang the shepherds and Nymphs of Diana,
Long live fair Oriana!

Our music example gives some instances of how Morley used madrigalisms to suit his music to the text: "Fountain" (line 1) is set to an undulating, flowing figure; "a-sleeping" (line 2) and "stilled" (line 3) are matched by a rhythmic lull; "accenting" (line 4) is given a stress in the middle of the measure; "crown" (line 5) and "heaven" (line 6) attain the uppermost range of the ensemble. Morley sets the concluding line, "Long live fair Oriana," as an elaborate, extended passage in imitative counterpoint; in the final measures, he has the lowest voice, the bass, draw out a single pitch for several measures, a conspicuous reminder of Elizabeth's long reign.

Word Paintings in Morley, "Hard by a Crystal Fountain"

(continued)

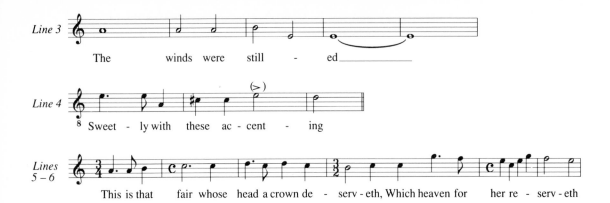

Line 3

The winds were still - ed

Line 4

Sweet - ly with these ac - cent - ing

Lines 5 – 6

This is that fair whose head a crown de - serv - eth, Which heaven for her re - serv - eth

The madrigal was not the only English import from Italy. Shakespeare's plays and sonnets are fraught with Italian references, and Sir Edmund Spenser's epic poem *The Faerie Queene* is indebted to the arcadian poetry of Ariosto. Though English composers began by imitating the Italian madrigal, however, they soon transformed the genre into a distinctly English form of entertainment.

THE RISE OF INSTRUMENTAL MUSIC

One of the most far-reaching, though often overlooked, developments during the Renaissance was the rise of instrumental music. Here we find the ultimate source of such later masterpieces as the eighteenth-century fugues of Johann Sebastian Bach and the piano concertos of Mozart. True, there was music for instruments well before the Renaissance, but not until the sixteenth century did composers produce substantial quantities of instrumental music that was carefully notated for posterity. By the end of the century, they were busily engaged in developing new instrumental genres.

Much of the new instrumental music comprised adaptations of familiar vocal compositions, including motets, portions of Mass settings, and such secular genres as the French chanson and the Italian madrigal. Composers transcribed this music for keyboard instruments, such as the organ or the harpsichord and its family of instruments, in which the keyboard activated a set of quills that plucked enclosed sets of strings; for a variety of lutes; and for consorts of a family of instruments (such as recorders or viols).

In some of this instrumental music, composers used preexistent material as a cantus firmus, or they used a bass pattern that was repeated several times to form the foundation of a composition. Against this foundation, they worked out ingenious sets of variations in which they explored diverse musical textures and counterpoints.

Another category of instrumental music, the dance movement, was especially popular during the sixteenth century. Often, slow dances and fast dances appeared in pairs. A common arrangement paired a **pavan,** a slow, ceremonial dance in duple meter, and a **galliard,** a sprightly, fast dance in triple meter.

The **ricercar** (from the Italian, "to seek out"; compare the French *recherché*) and the **fantasia** (compare "fantasy" or "fancy") were polyphonic instrumental compositions built around consecutive points of imitation, in a technique borrowed from the imitative style of Renaissance vocal polyphony. According to Thomas Morley, the composer of a fantasy was free to take "a point at his pleasure," "wresting" and "turning" it as he liked, "making either much or little of it according as shall seem best in his own conceit." Another genre, the **canzona,** which began as instrumental versions of French secular chansons, evolved into a composition that consisted of several contrasting sections, often in imitative polyphony. Still other instrumental pieces were improvisatory in character and apparently served as short preludes to compositions in a more serious and learned style.

As the sixteenth century advanced, Italian and French collections of lute music and German collections of organ and harpsichord music became more and more available throughout Europe. In England, the works of such Elizabethan keyboard composers as William Byrd and John Bull were gathered into great anthologies that have come down to us both in manuscript (the *Fitzwilliam Virginal Book,* compiled between 1609 and 1619) and in print (the *Parthenia* of about 1612, which contained the "first musicke that ever was printed for the Virginalls"★). The English lutenist John Dowland (1563–1626) popularized the solo song with lute accompaniment, known as a **lute ayre.** His most famous ayre, "Flow my tears," also known as *Lachrymae* (Latin for "tears"), was transcribed, reworked, and imitated by composers in innumerable versions for instruments alone.

DOWLAND: LUTE AYRE, "FLOW MY TEARS"
BYRD: *PAVANA LACHRYMAE* FOR HARPSICHORD

One of the most celebrated lutenists of the Elizabethan and Jacobean periods, John Dowland studied music at Oxford and perhaps at Cambridge. He traveled widely on the Continent, where four volumes of his lute ayres and various instrumental works were widely admired. The lute ayre "Flow my tears" originally appeared in Dowland's *Second Book of Songes,* published in 1600. The text, possibly by Dowland himself, is a sorrowful lament in five stanzas. Here is the first of five stanzas of poetry:

> Flow my teares, fall from your springs,
> Exilde for ever: Let mee morne
> where nights black bird hir sad infamy sings,
> there let mee live forlorne.

Dowland captures the sadness of the text with expressive leaps, with drooping, falling lines, and with dissonant harmonies. The lute provides a discreet accompaniment of chords and occasionally ventures into delicate melodic detailing. The emphasis, however, is clearly on the solo voice and its plaintive melody:

★ The virginal was the generic English term for the harpsichord (see also p. 87).

Dowland: Lute Ayre, "Flow my tears"

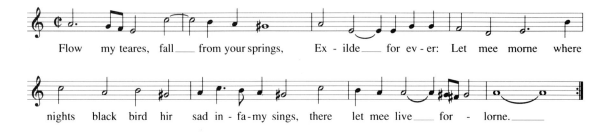

In the many instrumental elaborations based on "Flow my tears," composers were free to explore Dowland's memorable melody beyond the confines of the text. Since Dowland's original lute ayre resembles the pavan in its meter, mood, and structure, its instrumental transformations became known as *Lachrymae* pavans. In 1604 Dowland himself brought out a collection of instrumental pavans called "Seven Teares," all freely based on "Flow my tears." Each bore a Latin title, such as *Lachrymae gementes* ("Groaning Tears") and *Lachrymae amantis* ("Tears of the Lover"). Written for a consort of five viols and one lute, these pieces exhibit colorful textures of freely composed polyphony into which Dowland weaves strands of the original ayre.

Among the many other settings of Dowland's *Lachrymae* is a keyboard version by William Byrd, which appears in the *Fitzwilliam Virginal Book* along with several other keyboard works of the composer. Dowland's original lute ayre is suitable for variation, a technique especially favored by instrumental composers of the time. In his setting, Byrd varies the melody by introducing fresh ornaments and counterpoints. Here is the opening of Byrd's *Pavana lachrymae:*

Byrd: Pavana lachrymae

In the first few measures, Byrd presents the original melody intact in the upper voice. But when he subsequently repeats the first section, he subjects the melody to an ingenious contrapuntal transformation:

Notice how Byrd imitates the new, freely flowing upper line in a lower voice, and how in the second bar he extends the descent of the melody further (in Dowland's lute ayre, corresponding to the words "fall from your springs").

GIOVANNI GABRIELI: *CANZONA SEPTIMI TONI,* NO. 2 (1597)

By the end of the sixteenth century, composers were experimenting with instrumental music on a much grander scale. A major center of experimentation was Venice, the resplendent Italian maritime republic known as "La serenessima," the "most serene." There, such artists as Giorgione, Titian, and Veronese were adorning the ducal palace and the great churches of the city. Enterprising Venetian publishers were releasing volumes of the latest musical compositions. Such distinguished musicians as the northerners Adrian Willaert and Cipriano da Rore, the Italian organist Claudio Merulo, and the Italian composers Andrea and Giovanni Gabrieli were directing music on a lavish scale at St. Mark's Cathedral.

St. Mark's was the center of Venetian musical life. Dating back to the eleventh century, this great structure was lavishly adorned with Byzantine mosaics under five golden domes. Inside, raised galleries and two facing organ lofts provided ideal placement for vocalists and instrumentalists and encouraged composers to experiment with split choirs. As many as four choirs of musicians could be pitted against one another in a new style known as **polychoral music.**

The leader of this type of composition was Giovanni Gabrieli (ca. 1556–1612), nephew of the Venetian organist and composer Andrea Gabrieli (ca. 1510–1586). In his *Sacrae symphoniae* (*Sacred Symphonies*) of 1597, Gabrieli applied the polychoral style to sacred motets, using instruments to reinforce the vocal parts. He also included several polychoral works for instruments alone, usually not specified but featuring groups of brass instruments such as the *sackbut* (the ancestor of the modern trombone), wind instruments such as the *cornett* (a wooden instrument with a cuplike mouthpiece), and violins.

Gabrieli called these instrumental pieces sonatas and canzonas. **Sonata** was a general term used to distinguish instrumental compositions from vocal compositions (the Italian *suonare* means "to sound"). Gabrieli's canzonas imitated the popular rhythms and homophonic textures of the French chanson.

Gabrieli's *Canzona septimi toni* appeared in his collection of 1597. The title means "Canzona of the seventh mode"—in this case, a work using a mode based on G (see

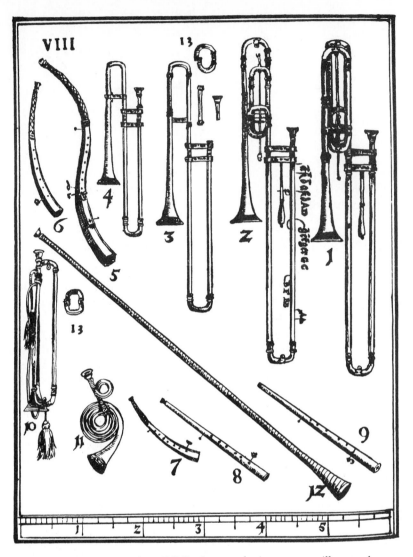

Praetorius, *Syntagma musicum* (1618). Among the instruments illustrated are a variety of trombones (1–4), a cornett (5), and examples of a related instrument, the zinck (6–9).

p. 9). The work is scored for eight parts divided into two instrumental choirs: The choirs exchange short musical gestures and occasionally overlap to form a grand, eight-part ensemble. Gabrieli achieves a question-and-answer effect by using contrasts in dynamics. (He actually titled one of his instrumental compositions *Sonata pian' e forte,* or "Sonata, soft and loud.")

This canzona begins with a crisp rhythmic motive in duple time (♩♩♩♩ | ♩), not unlike certain rhythmic motives common in French secular songs of the time:

Giovanni Gabrieli: Canzona septimi toni, *No. 2*

Instrumental Choir I

Instrumental Choir II

The motive is taken up by both instrumental choirs, which elaborate on it and exchange it back and forth, a polychoral technique frequently employed in Gabrieli's canzonas. Several distinct sections follow: a contrasting section in triple time, a more substantial section in duple time that forms the core of the piece, another section in triple time, and a final section in duple time. Toward the end, Gabrieli brings back the opening motive to round out the shape of the piece and to impose unity on its loose, sectional structure.

Several seventeenth-century composers explored further the Venetian instrumental style, notably the German composers Michael Praetorius (ca. 1571–1621) and Heinrich Schütz (1585–1672). Indeed, in the eighteenth century, Johann Sebastian Bach employed double choruses in some of his greatest church music.

Gabrieli's work brought a new stature to instrumental music. His application of block-chord formations in antiphonal choirs—now divided, now massed together—imposed a new rigor on harmonic progressions and prepared the way for the new hierarchy of tonal harmonic relationships that came to the fore in the seventeenth century. The Venetian style brought the Renaissance to a brilliant close and set in motion currents of change that found full expression in the baroque.

Suggested Listening

- ★ Byrd: *Pavana lachrymae*
- ★ Dowland: Lute ayre, "Flow my tears"
  Dufay: Chanson, "Se la face ay pale"
- ★ _____: Mass, *Se la face ay pale*
- ★ Gabrieli, Giovanni: *Canzona septimi toni,* No. 2
- ★ Josquin Desprez: Mass, *Pange lingua*
- ★ Morley: Madrigal, "Hard by a Crystal Fountain"
- ★ Palestrina: Motet, *Sicut cervus*

Works marked with an asterisk are the principal works discussed in the text.

PART III THE BAROQUE

EUROPEAN HISTORY AND CULTURE	AMERICAN HISTORY	EUROPEAN MUSIC
1561–1626: Francis Bacon		
1564–1642: Galileo Galilei		**1567–1643:** Monteverdi
1571–1630: Kepler		
1573–1610: Caravaggio		
1573–1652: Inigo Jones		
1577–1640: Rubens		**1583–1643:** *Frescobaldi*
	1584: "Lost Colony" on Roanoke founded by Sir Walter Raleigh	**1585–1672:** Heinrich Schütz
1596–1650: Descartes		
1598–1680: Bernini		
1599–1660: Velásquez		
1603–1625: Reign of James I of England		
1606–1669: Rembrandt		
1606–1684: Corneille	**1607:** Jamestown Colony founded	**1607:** Monteverdi, *Orfeo*
1608–1674: Milton		
1613: Romanov dynasty founded in Russia		**1616–1667:** Froberger
1618–1648: Thirty Years' War	**1620:** Plymouth Colony founded	
1622–1673: Molière		
1625–1649: Reign of Charles I of England		
1632: Galileo, *Essay on the Solar System*		**1632–1687:** Lully
1632–1675: Vermeer		
1632–1723: Christopher Wren	**1636:** Harvard College founded	
1639–1699: Racine		
1642–1727: Newton		
1643–1715: Reign of Louis XIV of France		
1646–1716: Leibnitz		**1653–1713:** Corelli
1649–1660: Commonwealth in England		**1656:** Froberger, Suite No. 2, in A major
		1659–1695: Purcell

BACKGROUND FOR THE BAROQUE

Few period terms have an origin as fanciful as that for baroque, the term used to designate music from roughly 1600 to 1750. A French word, *baroque* comes from the Portuguese *barroco,* meaning an irregularly shaped pearl. When the term began to be applied to the arts during the eighteenth century, it acquired various pejorative meanings—"rough," "misshapen," and "deformed"—as well as negative connotations such as "affective," "grandiose," and "extravagant." In the nineteenth century, *baroque* was used to designate a period of decline in art after the high Renaissance style of Michelangelo. In the twentieth century, *baroque* was appropriated to designate a fundamental period in music that encompassed the rise of opera in the seventeenth century and the music of Johann Sebastian Bach in the eighteenth. Only in the twentieth century did *baroque* shed its pejorative meanings, though such connotations as "affective," "gran-

EUROPEAN HISTORY AND CULTURE	AMERICAN HISTORY	EUROPEAN MUSIC
1660–1685: Reign of Charles II of England		
1661–1682: Versailles constructed		
1666: Great Fire in London		**1668–1733:** François Couperin
		1678–1741: Vivaldi
	1681: Charter of Pennsylvania granted to William Penn	**1681–1767:** Telemann
		1683–1764: Rameau
1684–1721: Watteau		
1685–1688: Reign of James II of England		**1685:** Corelli, Trio Sonata, Op. II, No. 6
1687: Newton, *Philosophiae naturalis principia mathematica*		**1685–1750:** Johann Sebastian Bach
1688–1689: Glorious Revolution in England		**1685–1757:** Domenico Scarlatti
		1685–1759: Handel
1689–1702: Reign of William of Orange in England		**1689:** Purcell, *Dido and Aeneas*
1689–1725: Reign of Peter the Great in Russia		
1702–1714: Reign of Queen Anne in England		**1710–1736:** Pergolesi
1703–1770: Boucher		**1712:** Vivaldi, Concerto grosso in A minor, Op. 3, No. 8
1713: Treaty of Utrecht		**ca. 1720:** J. S. Bach, *Brandenburg Concerto* No. 5
1714–1727: Reign of George I of England		**1724:** Handel, *Julius Caesar in Egypt*
1727–1760: Reign of George II of England	**1733:** Founding of Georgia	**1731:** J. S. Bach, Cantata No. 140, *Wachet auf*
		1742: J. S. Bach, *Well-Tempered Clavier,* Book II
		1742: Handel, *Messiah*
	1755:–1763: French and Indian War	
1763: Treaty of Paris	**1759:** Battle of Québec	

diose," and "extravagant" endured. So it was that a jeweler's term came to describe one hundred fifty years of music—including the sublime masterpieces of one of the most profound musical geniuses of all time.

The fountainhead of the baroque was Italy. There, during the latter part of the sixteenth century, an exaggerated, mannered style in the arts began to depart from the serene balance and cool discipline of Renaissance art. With the start of the seventeenth century, baroque art emerged full blown, in all its grandeur. It was a powerful art that displayed monumental, sometimes overwhelming effects. It was a forceful, dramatic art, characterized by strong contrasts and bold statements of instability and imbalance. It was a lavish art, richly ornamented and sumptuously detailed. And it was an expressive, intensely charged art that had as its principal aim to capture the tortuous passions and affections of humankind.

The painter Caravaggio (1573–1610), in *The Calling of St. Matthew* (ca. 1598), shows the tax collector Matthew in a lowly tavern. Light streaming in from the side

Caravaggio, *The Calling of St. Matthew,* ca. 1598.

over the raised hand of the Savior falls on Matthew's face and on the twisting figures beside him as they are overtaken by the divine presence. On a more monumental scale, the great colonnade of Gian Lorenzo Bernini (1598–1680) embraces the vast area before St. Peter's in Rome. Inside the lavishly decorated cathedral, Bernini's towering bronze tabernacle supported by four convoluted, spiraling pillars stands before his splendid Throne of St. Peter (begun 1656), a spectacular baroque setting in marble, stucco, and bronze of that saint's lowly wooden stool.

From Italy, the baroque style spread throughout western Europe. In the southern Netherlands, Rubens created heroic canvases on a grand scale. In Spain, the new style was prepared by El Greco (1541–1614), who filled his canvases with elongated, distorted figures. The Spanish baroque found full expression in the brilliantly colored portraiture of Velásquez (1599–1660), court painter to Philip IV. In the northern Netherlands, baroque art reached its zenith in the luminous paintings of Rembrandt.

Interior of St. Peter's, Rome, showing Bernini's Tabernacle (1624–1633).

In France, the seventeenth century was *le grand siècle,* the "grand century" of Louis XIV, the Sun King, who maintained his absolutist rule by divine right. The symbol of his long reign was the magnificent Palace of Versailles, not far from Paris. Designed to accommodate thousands, this vast structure, with its glittering Hall of Mirrors, sweeping vistas, and elegant fountains and gardens, was the envy of European monarchs well

Palace of Versailles.

into the eighteenth century. French taste in the arts was mandated by official academies created by Colbert, Louis's tireless, efficient minister. French literature entered a neoclassical phase in the works of the dramatists Corneille and Racine, who applied Aristotelian principles in their passionate tragedies engulfing figures of antiquity.

The sciences, influenced by Sir Francis Bacon's inductive method of observation, made dramatic advances during the seventeenth century, sustaining the spirit of inquiry that was the legacy of the Renaissance. New instruments were invented, including the telescope and the microscope. Powerful minds were at work in all areas of scientific exploration: Galileo in astronomy and physics, Descartes in analytical geometry, Leibnitz in the calculus, Harvey in anatomy, and Newton in the calculus and physics. Their revolutionary work dealt a death blow to the medieval cosmology that had first been challenged during the Renaissance. Descartes's pithy pronouncement *cogito, ergo sum* ("I think, therefore I am") opened the way to the eighteenth-century Age of Enlightenment.

Throughout the baroque, composers were creating strong, ardent music that mirrored the emotionalism of the age. That music ranged from the dramatic operas of Monteverdi and Purcell to the polished chamber music of Corelli, the buoyant concertos of Vivaldi, the exuberant operas and oratorios of Handel, and the cerebral fugues of Johann Sebastian Bach.

3

MUSIC IN THE BAROQUE

*R*unning like a thread through the diverse styles of the baroque is a compelling interest in human passions. In painting, Caravaggio, Rubens, and Rembrandt exhibited the new emotionalism in their exaggerated contours, emphatic lighting, and contorted human figures. In drama, Racine showed an acute, almost clinical psychological insight into human attitudes and behaviors. In music, composers of instrumental music favored rich contrasts and intensified effects, and composers of vocal music strove to capture the emotional intensity of texts dealing with powerful emotional states or with affections, such as love, rage, or sorrow.

Baroque composers were especially concerned with the relationship between text and music. Eager to depict the essence of their texts more cogently than ever before, they pushed music to new limits of expressiveness. By the early decades of the seventeenth century, a fundamental change in musical style had taken place: Composers now observed a modern, or "second," practice instead of the older, "first" practice. It was the Italian composer Claudio Monteverdi who in 1605 distinguished between the two practices when he replied to some scathing criticism of his recent madrigals. For Monteverdi, the older practice was exemplified by Renaissance imitative polyphony, which had evolved through the fifteenth and sixteenth centuries and had reached a high level of achievement in the music of Palestrina (see pp. 48–51). With his carefully controlled use of dissonance and crystalline part writing, Palestrina had treated the music as ruler of the text. The newer practice, Monteverdi pointed out, reversed that relationship by making the music more responsive to the text, freeing the composer to employ audacious musical licenses previously not contemplated.

Baroque music thus came to contrast sharply with the music of the Renaissance. New musical resources were employed to achieve the goals of the second practice. Chief among these was the development of tonality and systematic exploration of harmonic progressions based on triads, the widespread use of the *basso continuo,* and new approaches to melody, rhythm, and dynamics.

THE DEVELOPMENT OF TONALITY

For centuries, composers had respected the system of modality based on the ancient church modes. Then, during the Renaissance, composers had gradually recognized the triad as a fundamental harmonic sonority. Finally, during the seventeenth century, the modern minor and major scales emerged, and the triads built on them became the basis of the hierarchical harmonic relationships we know as **tonality.** The shift from modality to tonality was gradual. Signs of tonality are detectable in Renaissance music, and vestiges of modality were to linger for some time in baroque music. Composers continued to experiment with tonal procedures throughout the seventeenth century, and by the end of the century, the system of tonality was well established. It was to stand unchallenged until late in the nineteenth century, and in fact, alternatives to tonality were not seriously contemplated or adopted until the twentieth century.

Tonality is based on a constellation of triads that revolve around a primary triad. In turn, that primary triad represents through its lowest pitch a tonal center, or **key,** toward which the other triads gravitate. Keys are based on the major and minor scales. We look first at a simple example, the C major scale (see also p. 516). This scale consists of a succession of whole steps and half steps:

C Major Scale

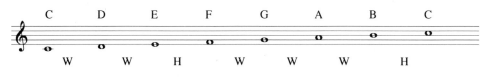

W = whole step; H = half step.

By constructing triads on the steps of this scale, we can derive the harmonic building blocks—the primary triad and its satellites, so to speak—typical of compositions in the key of C major:

Triads on the C Major Scale

Not all these triads have equal weight, however. After the triad on the first pitch, known as the **tonic** triad, the most important are the triads built on the fourth and fifth pitches of the scale, known respectively as the **subdominant** and **dominant** triads. The tonic triad—that is, the primary triad—determines the key of a tonal composition; it usually appears in some form at the opening of a composition and always at the conclusion. The tonic triad acts as a center of gravity, attracting the subdominant and dominant triads and working in association with them. The strongest association is between the tonic triad and the dominant triad. It is the tension between those triads that holds a tonal composition together. Motion away from the tonic to the dominant triad increases that tension, and motion from the dominant back to the tonic relaxes it. Next in importance is the subdominant triad, which interrelates with both the tonic and the dominant triads. Finally, all the triads on the various pitches of the scale may play a role in the **harmonic progressions**—that is, the movement from one triad to another—that a composer employs throughout a tonal composition.

The following example shows several basic harmonic progressions in the key of C major. In the example, one pitch in each triad is used twice (or doubled), so that instead of a succession of three-note triads, we in fact have a succession of four-note chords in **four-part harmony.** The roman numerals beneath the bass identify the triads embedded in the harmonies, with I for tonic (C major triad, pitches C, E, and G), IV for subdominant (F major triad, pitches F, A, and C), and V for dominant (G major triad, pitches G, B, and D):

Harmonic Progressions in the Key of C Major

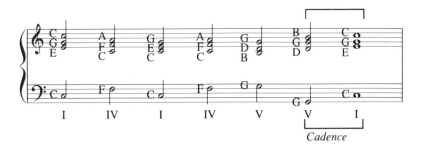

Baroque composers came to recognize the lowest-sounding line, or bass line, as the supporting line of such harmonic progressions. In particular, they used certain bass-line patterns, or cadences, to suggest a sense of arrival in a particular key. The final progression of the preceding example, from dominant to tonic (V–I), represents a common cadence—in this case, a cadence in C major.

Baroque composers employed minor and major keys based on pitches other than C—all with their own constellations of triads. Here, for example, is a major scale based on G—that is, with G as the tonic pitch, and the G major triad as the tonic triad:

G Major Scale

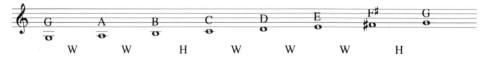

W = whole step; H = half step.

Notice that the succession of whole steps and half steps in the G major scale is the same as that used in the C major scale. The G major scale requires one modification. Because its seventh and eighth pitches—F and G—form a whole step instead of the required half step, the F is raised by a sharp sign, yielding the half step F#–G. Other keys require sharps for raising pitches or flats for lowering pitches. During the baroque, composers began to identify the keys of their compositions by using **key signatures,** or listings of the sharps or flats called for (see p. 514). Composers of tonal music still follow that convention.

To summarize, all major scales, on which the major keys are based, use the same succession of whole steps and half steps. The major scales are said to be **transpositions★** of the basic plan represented by the C major scale. What distinguishes each key from other keys is its tonic pitch: In the C major scale, C is the tonic pitch; in the G major scale, G is the tonic pitch. In the A-flat major scale, A-flat is the tonic pitch. Similarly, each key has its own group of triads. In the following example, the three triads on G, C, and D are the tonic, subdominant, and dominant triads in the key of G major:

Triads on the G Major Scale

(Recall that in comparison, triads on C, F, and G are the tonic, subdominant, and dominant triads in the key of C major.)

★ Repetitions of the same musical line or idea beginning on a different pitch.

We can also construct triads on minor scales, the other type of scale (see p. 517) that was incorporated in the system of tonality. Here, for example, is the scale of C minor:

(see p. 517)

C Minor Scale

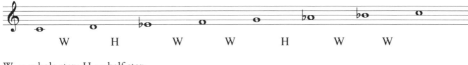

W   H   W   W   H   W   W

W = whole step; H = half step.

The most important triads for a key based on a minor scale are, after the tonic triad, the **mediant** triad (on the third pitch), the subdominant triad (on the fourth pitch), and the dominant triad (on the fifth pitch):

Triads on the C Minor Scale

I   III   IV   V   I
Tonic   *Mediant Subdominant Dominant*   *Tonic*

By transposing the C minor scale to other pitches, we can produce the various other minor scales, on which the minor keys are based, and their triads.

All the major and minor keys—twelve each, for a total of twenty-four keys—were worked out together with their triads during the baroque period. We can represent that scheme as a circle on which the keys appear in order of transposition by fifths: ascending fifths on one side and descending fifths on the other (the two series overlap midway). In the diagram (p. 72), major keys appear with uppercase letters; minor keys appear with lowercase letters. Thus, the key of G major lies a fifth above the key of C major, and the key of F major lies a fifth below the key of C major. Similarly, the key of B minor lies a fifth above the key of E minor, and the key of C minor lies a fifth below the key of G minor. This arrangement reveals how closely any two keys are related: Two adjacent keys are the most closely related, two nonadjacent keys are less closely related, and two keys opposite each other are least closely related. Thus, for example, C and G, B-flat and F, or e and b are closely related keys; C and F-sharp, or f and b, on the other hand, are least closely related.

Such, in brief, are the principles of tonality developed during the seventeenth century. Unlike the modal system, which depended on several unique modes, the tonal system relies on only two types of scales—the major scale and the minor scale—which can be transposed to begin on any of the twelve basic pitches. Triads built on these scales are arranged in a hierarchical order. The tonic is the principal triad, and the

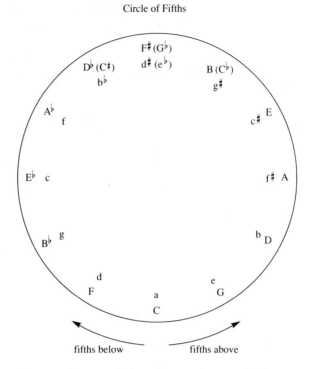

Circle of Fifths

Uppercase letters = major keys; lowercase letters = minor keys.

relationship of the tonic triad to the dominant triad creates the harmonic tension that supports the sense of key.

THE *BASSO CONTINUO*

The turn to tonality encouraged composers to extend the number and the types of harmonies in their music, using triads of various keys as building blocks. A new type of performance practice, called **basso continuo** ("continuous bass"), or simply **continuo,** exemplified the new tonal logic of baroque music. The basso continuo enabled composers to notate in abbreviated fashion the basic succession of harmonies of a composition. To accomplish that, they provided the bass line, which sounded more or less continuously throughout the composition, with a series of numbers, sharps, and flats that indicated chords that were to be played, or **realized,** above it. The chords served to fill the texture between the bass line and whatever treble instruments were called for (perhaps a violin or an ensemble of violins). The continuo was executed by an instrument capable of playing chords (usually a keyboard instrument such as a harpsichord or an organ, but also other instruments, such as members of the lute family), or by a bass instrument (for example, a cello or a viol), or by both. The bass instrument (sometimes there were more than one) played the bass line, and the keyboard instrument played both the bass line and the chords indicated by the numbers. The discipline of realizing the numbers—that is, converting them into chords—was known as **figured bass** or **thoroughbass.** A trained keyboard musician could interpret a figured bass at a glance and could readily furnish a steady harmonic background for the composition.

Most of the baroque compositions we shall examine include a figured bass performed by a group of continuo instruments. Indeed, in some types of music, this practice survived well beyond the baroque period and became obsolete only in the nineteenth century.

MELODY, RHYTHM, AND DYNAMICS IN BAROQUE MUSIC

Baroque composers made extravagant use of melody, rhythm, and dynamics to overwhelm listeners with the richness and the complexity of their music. Much of the exuberance and grandiloquence of baroque music resides in the cumulative effect of its long, ornate melodies, driving rhythmic patterns, and forceful contrasts in dynamics.

The following passage from a *partita* (a multimovement keyboard work) by Johann Sebastian Bach suggests how melody and rhythm might be combined to splendid effect:

J. S. Bach: Partita in B-flat major, Allemande

Here, Bach carries the melody along in an unwavering series of sixteenth notes (♫♫). Once he has set the pulse of the music, he refuses to abandon it; the melodic flow moves steadily forward, describing a winding, intricate contour in groups of sixteenth notes marked off into a regular meter of $\frac{4}{4}$ time (notated by the C at the beginning of the music).

Another movement of Bach's partita, the *praeludium,* exhibits a second characteristic of baroque melody: its tendency toward lavish ornamentation. Underlying Bach's melody is a simple enough ascending idea that reaches three successively higher crests. We can summarize the melody this way:

J. S. Bach: Partita in B-flat major, Praeludium

SUMMARY OF MELODY

In Bach's version, this basic idea is elaborated and liberally embellished. The result is a brilliant overlay of decorative pitches that resemble in their effect the opulent finery of baroque painting and sculpture. In the example, the figure ∿ is performed by adding adjacent pitches to the notated pitch beneath it:

J. S. Bach: Partita in B-flat major, Praeludium

BACH'S VERSION

Although Bach does not specify the dynamics (see p. 528) in these examples, contrasts between soft and loud levels of sound did play an important role in music of the baroque. The notations *piano* (soft) and *forte* (loud) now occurred with increasing frequency. In a technique that later came to be known as **terraced dynamics,** composers called for abrupt shifts from one dynamic level to another, for example from *forte* to *piano,* with no intervening gradations. Here again baroque composers were striving to intensify the impact of their music.

CLAUDIO MONTEVERDI AND THE RISE OF ITALIAN OPERA

The first great master of the baroque was Claudio Monteverdi (1567–1643), who was both heir to the Renaissance and a bold stylistic innovator. His early career centered in the court of the duke of Mantua, where he served as *maestro di cappella,* or music director. In 1613 he succeeded Giovanni Gabrieli as music director at St. Mark's in Venice. There he remained for some thirty years, modernizing the musical resources of the cathedral and enriching its already distinguished musical life.

In his early years, Monteverdi was often content not to venture beyond the sixteenth-century style of imitative polyphony. He collected these finely crafted works into four volumes of madrigals **a cappella,** that is, for voices alone (1587–1603). Then, with the fifth volume (1605), he began to use an instrumental continuo to accompany the vocal ensemble. Finally, he elevated the role of the instruments further by writing madrigals in which they no longer just provided a continuo but also enjoyed an individuality of their own. His most successful experiments with mixed scoring for voices and instruments (also known as the "concerted" manner) were the *canti guerrieri,* or "songs of war," which appeared along with *canti amorosi* ("songs of love") in his eighth volume of madrigals (1638). In the *canti guerrieri,* he gave the instruments intense, rapidly repeated musical figures, to suggest what he termed the *stile concitato* ("agitated style"), his musical representation of the passion of anger.

In addition to these secular madrigals, Monteverdi composed sacred choral music. His great collection of Vesper settings (1610) contains an abundance of different styles and genres, including the older polyphonic Mass and polychoral choruses in the style of Gabrieli. It also includes movements in the new concerted manner and intimate settings for solo voice and continuo. Such striking syntheses of old and new reveal Monteverdi as a principal figure in the transition from Renaissance to baroque. His most influential achievements, however, were in an essentially new type of music—opera.

EARLY ITALIAN OPERA

An **opera**★ is a dramatic work, set to more or less continuous music, that is acted out on a stage with singers, costumes, and scenery. Typically, an opera calls for soloists, ensembles, choruses, and an orchestra. A librettist furnishes the text of the drama, known as the **libretto** (Italian for "little book"), and a composer sets that text to music. The emergence of opera about the beginning of the seventeenth century marks a milestone in the history of music. Now the rich resources of music were joined to drama to produce a sophisticated and enduring synthesis of the arts. This alliance of music and drama arose in Italy as a form of court entertainment and then, during the seventeenth century, spread throughout western Europe.

In the closing decades of the sixteenth century, the stage was set for opera in lavish, theatrical court entertainments. At the same time, humanist noblemen were seeking to explore ancient Greek practices of singing. One group, which met in Florence during the 1570s and 1580s, attempted to emulate a practice in classical Greek drama in which the text was delivered in a kind of heightened speech that resembled singing. Vincenzo Galilei (d. 1591), a principal of the Florentine group and father of the famous astronomer

---

★ Italian word for "work," and the plural of the Latin word for "work," *opus.*

A scene from an Italian opera by Antonio Draghi (Vienna, 1674). Note the profusion of ornamental detail and the presence of musical instruments on stage, including trumpets and drums.

Galileo, set down guidelines for composers of such works to follow. The texts, he stipulated, should be carried by a single vocal line accompanied only by a continuo section. This type of composition, known as **monody,** was to be sung by highly skilled, virtuoso singers. In Galilei's view, monody was superior to the older Renaissance style of imitative polyphony. Polyphony, he argued, obscured the text by enmeshing it in a network of competing vocal lines. The advantage of monody was that listeners could concentrate on a single vocal line that could reflect the natural accents and rhythms of the individual words of the text.

Responding to these new ideas, two Italian composers—Jacopo Peri (1561–1633) and Giulio Caccini (ca. 1545–1618)—created works based on pastoral subjects taken from Greek mythology. Staged in Florence in 1598 and 1600, these works were the first operas ever to be performed. The first musically dramatic masterpiece in the new genre, however, came in 1607, when Monteverdi's opera *Orfeo* (*Orpheus*) was produced in Mantua.

The Orpheus myth was an ideal subject for the new operas. In classical mythology, Orpheus was the follower (or the son) of the god Apollo. Both poet and musician, Orpheus set his verses to music so moving that he could induce animals and even inanimate objects to do his will. Orpheus was the embodiment of the power of song, and monody was a musical style that glorified the persuasive powers of singing.

In Monteverdi's opera, Orfeo tries to win back his wife, Euridice, who has died of a serpent's sting and has crossed the river Styx to join the souls in Hades, Pluto's underworld realm. Orfeo journeys to the underworld and wins permission to lead Euridice back to the upper world on condition that he not look back at her along the way. He does glance at her, however, and loses her once again. Here the libretto departs from the myth: The god Apollo, appearing like a *deus ex machina,*★ comforts Orfeo over his loss and transports him to the heavens, where he can gaze forever upon his beloved Euridice.

For much of this pioneering score, Monteverdi employs the monodic style of solo singing with simple continuo accompaniment. But he also inserts lively choruses for the pastoral setting of Orfeo's Thracian homeland, subdued choruses for the shadowy realm of Hades, and various instrumental dances and movements, robust or reserved as the scene dictates.

Monteverdi matches the diversity of the music with an uncommonly elaborate ensemble of instruments, or **orchestra.** Earlier Florentine experiments with dramatic music had generally called for meager instrumental forces. Monteverdi's *Orfeo,* however, which was intended as a sumptuous court entertainment, was conceived on a more opulent scale. The orchestra consisted of nearly forty players, including a string section of violins and various viols, several trombones and valveless trumpets, *cornetti* (for an illustration of a cornett, see p. 58), and recorders. For his continuo section, Monteverdi called variously for harpsichords, a double harp (a harp with two sets of strings), *chitarroni* (lutelike instruments with elongated necks), and small chamber organs (two with wooden pipes and one, known as a *regal,* with reeds). Nowhere in the score, however, does Monteverdi amass the full power of his multifarious ensemble; rather, he draws selectively on its resources, associating the colors of particular instruments with various characters and settings. He specifies the harsh reed organ for the implacable Charon, guardian of the river Styx, and the somber trombones with Pluto's underworld court. He uses the brighter colors of the recorder to enliven pastoral scenes set in the upper world.

In the third act, Orfeo encounters Charon, who ferries the dead across the river Styx to the underworld. By lulling Charon to sleep with his music, Orfeo is able to cross the river and enter Pluto's realm. Monteverdi prepares this memorable scene with a short passage for instruments alone. Orfeo then appears, accompanied by Speranza (Hope), who has guided him to the bank of the river Styx. Denied entry to the infernal regions, Speranza now departs and leaves the despairing Orfeo to his own devices.

★ "A god from a machine," a figure introduced unexpectedly in a play to provide a contrived resolution to the drama.

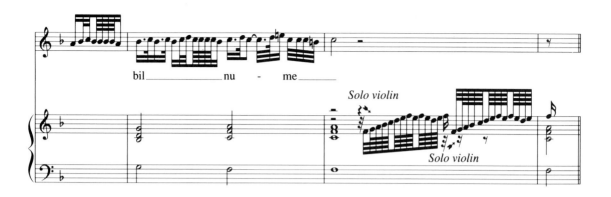

bil_____ nu - me_____

Solo violin

Solo violin

Such an emotional outpouring, enhanced by the accumulating colors of the solo instruments, represents Monteverdi's art at its most imaginative. Still, Charon is not convinced. After singing several unsuccessful stanzas of text, Orfeo abandons his florid melodic style, and the solo instruments fall silent. Now Orfeo resorts to a direct, forceful style. Only with a last, desperate plea to the spirits of murky Tartarus★ does Orfeo finally succeed in lulling Charon to sleep. He then proceeds across the river, intent on reclaiming Euridice from Pluto's court with the sheer power of his song.

After *Orfeo,* Monteverdi wrote several other dramatic works, many of which have been lost. The major surviving work of his late period is the opera *L'incoronazione di Poppea* (*The Coronation of Poppea,* 1642), which marks another milestone in the history of opera. Unlike *Orfeo,* intended as a court entertainment, *Poppea* was performed in a public opera house in Venice. For its subject, Monteverdi turned from Greek mythology to a lurid chapter in Roman history. Poppea, the mistress of the emperor Nero, intrigues to displace the empress Octavia. When the philosopher Seneca expresses his disapproval, Nero orders him to commit suicide. Monteverdi's ability to capture musically the emotions of a wealth of characters again provides impressive evidence of his musical and dramatic genius—and his success in responding to the needs of a new opera-attending public.

THE SPREAD OF OPERA

By the middle of the seventeenth century, opera had spread throughout Italy, in part through the efforts of Francesco Cavalli (1602–1676), a pupil of Monteverdi, and abroad. The opening of public opera houses—in Venice (1637), Hamburg (1678), and elsewhere—made opera accessible to new, music-loving audiences. No longer was it performed exclusively as entertainment for the nobility. In addition, two types of solo vocal music now became standard. Recitative, the hallmark of early Italian opera, was reserved for texts that set forth the essential dramatic action. A second, more melodic and more highly organized type of solo music, known as an **aria** (or air), was reserved

---

★ In mythology, the lowest region of Hades.

for texts in which the characters paused to comment on or react to the dramatic action. Often, a recitative, with its dry, rapid declamation, introduced a lyrical, tuneful aria, so that an act might consist largely of a series of alternating recitatives and arias.

In Germany, two early attempts at opera were composed by Heinrich Schütz, who studied in Italy and eventually settled in Dresden as music director to the Saxon court. There he produced a large body of sacred music, including psalm settings for voices and for combinations of voices and instruments. His German operas, based on the Daphne myth and the Orpheus myth, were mounted in 1627 and 1638. Though neither has survived, we may safely assume that they were heavily indebted to Italian models.

Opera came to France only later in the century. There were several reasons for its delayed appearance. The ballet, which was well entrenched at the royal court, was a highly attractive form of entertainment, as was French drama. Also, composers and librettists at first found it difficult to render French texts into recitative. Actually, the composer responsible for establishing French opera was an Italian, Giovanni Battista Lulli, better known by his French name, Jean-Baptiste Lully (1632–1687). An accomplished violinist in the court orchestra of Louis XIV, Lully first gained attention through his music for court ballets, to which the playwright Molière occasionally contributed. Lully then turned to writing French opera, which he termed *tragédie lyrique* ("lyrical tragedy"). A royal patent issued by the king guaranteed Lully absolute control over the composition and production of French operas; during the 1670s and 1680s, he created more than a dozen. The librettos for these operas, drawn from classical mythology, were written by the dramatists Philippe Quinault and Pierre Corneille.

Lully's music reflects the neoclassical grandeur of the French baroque. Typically, his operas begin with a stately instrumental **overture** in two sections. The first is a majestic, dignified march in an elevated style with **dotted rhythms** (in patterns of long and very short rhythms, ♪ ♪ ♪ ♪); this section traditionally marks the entry of the king. The second, with livelier rhythms, displays complex imitative counterpoint. The opening section sometimes returns at the end to round out the overture. The entire movement, known as the **French overture,** was widely emulated by later baroque composers (see pp. 83 and 138).

In a general sense, Lully intended his operas as musical celebrations of Louis XIV. The opera itself often opened with a prologue dedicated to the king. Sprinkled throughout were elaborate spectacles, filled with dancing and singing, called *divertissements* (literally, "diversions"), which, though they had little to do with the dramatic thread, provided entertainment for the Sun King.

In England, too, opera arrived only late in the seventeenth century. The English court had its own favorite form of entertainment, the **masque,** a spectacle in which poetry, music, masked dancers, and elaborate sets were all organized around some allegorical subject. Especially popular at the courts of James I (1603–1625) and Charles I (1625–1649), the masque achieved a high quality in the collaboration of playwright Ben Jonson and architect Inigo Jones. During the Restoration, the masque became popular in English theaters; both the poet John Dryden and Henry Purcell (1659–1695), one of England's most distinguished composers, contributed to the later masque repertoire.

During his short life, Purcell served as the organist of Westminster Abbey and of the Chapel Royal. He composed keyboard and other instrumental works, scores of

A page from *Orpheus Britannicus* (2nd ed., 1706), a collection of Purcell's songs with "a thorough bass [figured bass] to each song figur'd for the organ, harpsichord, or theorbo-lute." The selection shows the opening of Purcell's song "If Music be the food of love," on a text from Shakespeare's *Twelfth Night.* The figures indicate which chords are to be played above the bass line.

sacred **anthems**★ for the Anglican church, ceremonial compositions for court, and "dramatic" operas, including *King Arthur* (1691) and *The Fairy Queen* (1692, based on Shakespeare's *A Midsummer Night's Dream*). He is remembered today mainly for his *Dido and Aeneas* (1689), the first English opera of note. This work contains a French-style overture, recitatives, airs, ensembles, choruses, dances, and instrumental interludes.

★ English choral works, occasionally with instrumental accompaniment, for performance in a church service.

Dido and Aeneas was premiered at a girls' boarding school in Chelsea. Purcell took for his subject the tragic love affair of Dido and Aeneas as related in the fourth book of Virgil's epic poem, *The Aeneid*. Aeneas, forced to flee Troy as the Greeks sack the city, sets out on a long journey. Ultimately, impelled by destiny (and by the gods), he founds the city of Rome. Along the way, he lands at Carthage, where he falls in love with the queen, Dido. In Virgil's version, Mercury appears and orders Aeneas to leave Carthage. In despair, Dido immolates herself on a funeral pyre as Aeneas' fleet weighs anchor.

Purcell's opera is set to an English version of the episode newly prepared by Nahum Tate that deviates from Virgil's account. Instead of Mercury, a group of witches forces Aeneas to abandon Dido, and Tate makes a great deal of their scheming in his libretto. Moreover, there is provision for choruses sung by the witches and Aeneas' sailors, and several dances, including a rousing "Echo Dance of Furies."

In this short opera (it takes less than an hour to perform), Purcell drew on a range of musical styles. The work commences with a French overture featuring majestic dotted rhythms (♪. ♪ ♪. ♪). In the course of the opera, there is a rich selection of instrumental interludes and dances that reflect the English masque tradition. There are choruses, recitatives, and arias, some of which are based on recurring bass patterns after the Italian manner.

PURCELL: *DIDO AND AENEAS*, ACT III, "WHEN I AM LAID IN EARTH"

The most dramatic moment comes at the conclusion of the opera, when the forsaken Dido sings a lament in preparation for death. "When I am laid in earth" is a special moment in Purcell's music—and in the history of opera. A somber chorus prepares for the scene ("Great minds against themselves conspire, And shun the cure they most desire"). Then Dido enters and delivers a short recitative in which she addresses her sister, Belinda:

Purcell: Dido and Aeneas, *Act III: Recitative*

(continued)

rest

etc.

The supple line of the recitative mirrors the expressive nuances of the text as Dido, overcome by grief, welcomes death. Her steadily descending line is accompanied only by a figured bass line, realized, according to baroque practice, by a continuo section of a bass instrument and harpsichord.

THE VIOLIN FAMILY

*T*he seventeenth century marked the ascendancy of the violin family of string instruments (see p. 534). Played with a bow of horsehair, the violin is today held under the musician's chin. It has four strings (made today of gut or steel), stretched over a hollow wooden case and tuned in fifths:

G   D   A   E

The violinist produces these pitches by bowing the four "open" strings; by stopping the strings with fingers, the violinist can obtain intervening and higher pitches. At the violinist's disposal are several special effects: plucking the strings (*pizzicato*), bowing two or more strings simultaneously to produce chords, and even tapping the strings with the wood of the bow (*col legno*).

Similar in appearance to the violin is the viola, with its four strings tuned a fifth lower:

C   G   D   A

Slightly larger in size, the viola has a darker, less powerful tone than the brilliant, sweet sound of the violin. The cello (also violoncello), the third member of the violin family, is played upright. Its strings are tuned one octave below those of the viola:

C   G   D   A

Its lower range makes it an ideal instrument for playing bass lines. Finally, the large, seemingly unwieldy double bass (also bass viol,

string bass, violone, and contrabass), also played upright, has the lowest range of the string instruments, with a tuning in fourths:

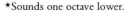
E   A   D   G
*8va** -

*Sounds one octave lower.

The double bass is descended from the viol family of instruments, which the violin family supplanted in the eighteenth century. In the modern orchestra, the double bass is used to reinforce the bass line.

Because of its great versatility and powerful tone, the violin quickly became a favored instrument of virtuosos. String sections, made up of violins, violas, cellos, and double basses, eventually became the core of the orchestras used for operas and of the modern orchestra as we know it.

For the air that follows Dido's recitative, Purcell employs a small chamber orchestra of strings. The air is built on a descending bass pattern that is reiterated several times with modifications in the accompaniment and in the vocal line. This technique, known as a **ground bass** or **basso ostinato** (compare "obstinate"), was favored by Monteverdi and other seventeenth-century Italian opera composers and by later baroque composers of instrumental music. The particular descending pattern of Purcell's air was recognized during the baroque as a symbol of grief and death. Purcell introduces the pattern by itself in the bass; then, he has Dido sing melodic phrases to the following text against the repeating bass pattern:

When I am laid in earth
May my wrongs create
No trouble in thy breast.
Remember me, but ah! forget my fate.

Purcell: Dido and Aeneas, *Act III, Dido's Lament*

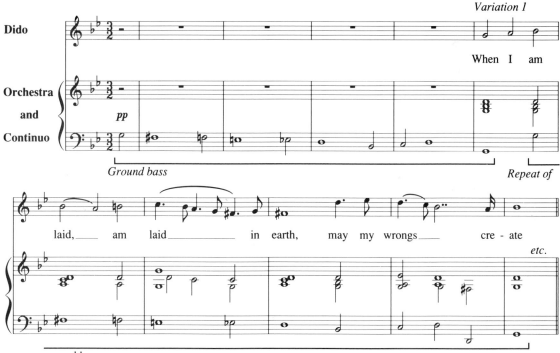

Her somber music falls into eight variations grouped into four pairs. The second and fourth pairs are repetitions of the first and third pairs (see the study diagram). With the recurring statements of the ground bass, there accumulates a powerful tension that is

Purcell: *Dido and Aeneas*, Act III, "When I am laid in earth"

Orchestra	Dido and _____	Orchestra
	Orchestra	Imitative
		counterpoint,
		sighlike gestures
Ground	Variation	
bass	1 2 3 4 5 6 7 8 9 10	

|__| |__| |__| |__|

Repeat of 1 and 2   Repeat of 5 and 6

only released with Dido's poignant farewell, "Remember me!" After her eighth phrase, Dido concludes, and the orchestra continues by itself through two more variations. At this point, the music suggests a series of drooping sighs. Pulled ever downward, the clashing string parts produce a highly dissonant, contrapuntal conclusion. This lament conveys the nobility of the queen and translates into music the emotionalism of the baroque spirit.

THE DEVELOPMENT OF INSTRUMENTAL MUSIC

The seventeenth century brought an astonishing proliferation of instrumental music. During the baroque, great national schools of instrumentalists were formed in Italy, France, England, Germany, and the Netherlands. This was an age of instrumental virtuosos—brilliant performers like the Italian violinists Arcangelo Corelli and Antonio Vivaldi, the French lutenist Denis Gaultier, and the French musicians Antoine Forqueray and Marin Marais, who favored the viol (also known as the viola da gamba). Several generations of keyboardists excelled in the harpsichord and the organ—two instruments that enjoyed special favor during the period (see pp. 87 and 115). Among the most distinguished keyboardists were the Italian Frescobaldi, the Netherlander Sweelinck, the Germans Froberger and Buxtehude, the French Chambonnières and Louis and François Couperin, and in the late baroque, the Germans Johann Sebastian Bach and George Frideric Handel.

In the seventeenth century, many instrumental compositions were simply called sonatas (from *suonare*, "to sound"), a catchall term used to distinguish them from vocal music. But some instrumental types still used techniques common in vocal music. In particular, the imitative polyphonic style of the Renaissance was adapted to new instrumental genres, especially well suited to keyboard instruments, on which performers could sustain several musical parts simultaneously in complicated contrapuntal textures.

Other instrumental types consisted of a series of sophisticated virtuoso variations on ground bass patterns, many of them drawn from popular dances of the period. Still

THE HARPSICHORD

*T*wo keyboard instruments, the harpsichord and the organ, came to prominence during the baroque (for a discussion of the organ, see p. 115). The harpsichord (in German and Italian, *cembalo*; in French, *clavecin*) has a set (or sets) of strings that were plucked to produce its characteristically crisp, cleanly articulated sound. The plucking agent, known as a *plectrum,* was a piece of stiff quill affixed to a strip of wood known as a *jack.* Beneath the jack lay the end of a key. When the harpsi-

chordist depressed a key, the jack was forced upward and the *plectrum* came into contact with and plucked a string. When the harpsichordist released the key, the jack fell back to its original position and a small piece of cloth muted the string.

Harpsichords were in use as early as the fifteenth century, though they were most widely used during the baroque period. They not only served as continuo instruments but also responded to the artistic whims of such great vir-

tuosos as Frescobaldi, Froberger, Bach, and Handel. In the second half of the eighteenth century, their popularity was gradually eclipsed by the new fortepiano (see p. 227), the forerunner of our modern piano.

Shown here is a lavishly decorated instrument with two keyboards, or manuals, by Andreas Ruckers the Elder, built in 1608. A harpsichord revival that began in the twentieth century continues today as builders seek to re-create the sound of the early instruments.

other instrumental compositions, including the **prelude,** a relatively short instrumental work often used to introduce a more substantial instrumental work, were more freely conceived, in the manner of improvisations. Among them we find some of the most innovative and brilliant creations of the baroque.

Finally, many instrumental compositions of the period were composed as dances, or as stylized dances meant to be enjoyed for their music alone. Seventeenth-century composers assembled great collections of dances, such as the *Terpsichore*★ of Michael Praetorius (1612), with over four hundred arrangements of dance tunes, and the *Banchetto musicale* (*Musical Banquet*) of Johann Schein (1617), with about one hundred groups of dances. A selection of dances arranged in some order came to be known as a **suite** (from the French for "following" or "sequence"). By the middle of the century, the older Renaissance coupling of a slow dance and a fast dance had given way to a suite consisting of four dance movements of different character. The trend toward standardization of the suite is evident in the work of the German composer Johann Jakob Froberger (1616–1667), who served for much of his career as court organist in Vienna.

FROBERGER: SUITE NO. 2, IN A MAJOR (1656)

Froberger's Suite No. 2, in A major, for harpsichord solo, includes four separate dances, labeled *allemande, gigue, courante,* and *sarabande.* As is typical of baroque suites, this work is unified tonally in that all four dances are in the same key. Each dance begins and ends in A major, which serves as the tonic. Moreover, each dance uses the same musical form—binary form—and follows similar internal tonal plans. In this suite of 1656, the principles of tonality that were to govern Western music until the twentieth century are already firmly established.

Although binary form seems a simple enough scheme in these short dances, it subsequently evolved into a much more complicated form—sonata form—which we shall take up in Part IV. As its name implies, **binary form** consists of two sections, each of which is repeated. We shall label these two sections A and A', and represent the form as ‖: A :‖: A' :‖. In binary-form dances, the two sections are characteristically cut from the same musical cloth: Similar melodic ideas and harmonic progressions appear in the two sections, as if the whole dance were spun from the same basic thread. The A and A' sections differ, however, in their internal tonal plan. The A section begins in the tonic key, but as it approaches the end of the section designated by the repeat mark, it **modulates,** or changes key, from the tonic to a second key, usually the dominant. At the end of the section, there is a strong cadence in the second key. In the second section, the process is reversed: A' begins in the second key and then, through a modulation, returns to the tonic key, which is reaffirmed at the conclusion by a strong cadence on the tonic.

The accompanying diagram shows how Froberger uses binary form in the four movements of his suite. The tonal trajectory is traced by the line at the bottom. Straight segments represent stable sections that remain within a particular key; jagged segments represent modulations that effect the changes of key.

★ In classical mythology, Terpsichore was the Muse of dance.

Binary Form in Froberger, Suite No. 2, in A major (1656)

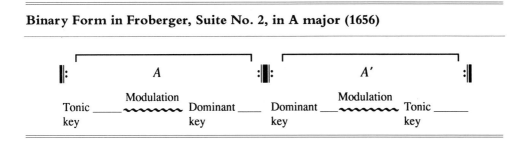

Froberger begins his suite with an **allemande,** a dance that probably originated in Germany during the sixteenth century (*allemande* is the French word for "German"). Allemandes are typically in duple meter (for example, $\frac{4}{4}$ or $\frac{2}{4}$). They begin with an upbeat and sometimes display bits of contrapuntal imitation among the various voices. At the beginning of Froberger's allemande, the rising upbeat figure in the treble is imitated (though not literally) in a lower voice:

Froberger: Suite No. 2, in A Major (1656)

ALLEMANDE

The **gigue,** the second movement of this suite, is a fast dance, usually (though not here) in compound meter (for example, $\frac{6}{8}$ or $\frac{12}{8}$) and probably of English origin (compare "jig"). Sprightly rhythmic patterns lend Froberger's gigue an irresistible verve. Like the allemande, it begins with a rising upbeat figure, which is immediately imitated in lower voices:

GIGUE

Eventually, as the suite became standardized, baroque composers placed the gigue as the fourth movement, bringing their suites to lighthearted conclusions.

The third movement of Froberger's suite is a **courante,** a fast French dance, usually in triple meter (for example, $\frac{3}{4}$, here, however, $\frac{3}{2}$; *courante* means "coursing" in French). In this movement, Froberger focuses the main interest in the upper part, accompanying it with a simple chordal support:

COURANTE

The fourth and final movement of the suite is a **sarabande,** a triple-meter dance that may have been imported from Latin America to Spain during the sixteenth century, and from there to the rest of Europe. The sarabande evolved into a slow, stately dance, though one variety kept a faster tempo. The rhythmic patterns of many sarabandes were influenced by formulas that stretched the second beat in the measure, as in

all of which occur in Froberger's sarabande (mm. 1, 3, and 4, respectively):

SARABANDE

The popularity of the suite persisted throughout the rest of the seventeenth century and into the eighteenth. In Germany, the four-movement plan was brought to perfection in the eighteenth century by Johann Sebastian Bach. In France, the suite culminated in the extended collections of François Couperin (1668–1773). In comparison with Froberger's miniatures, Couperin's suites were conceived on an ambitious scale, often with as many as twenty movements, from which the performer could select a group. Some of the dances bore the names of Couperin's contemporaries, and others carried such ambiguous titles as *La misterieuse* ("The Mysterious One").

In keeping with baroque performance practice, Couperin lavishly decorated his music by superimposing crisp surface **ornaments** on the underlying melodic line. (The composer explained his system of ornamentation in a treatise on keyboard playing, one of many such primers published during the baroque.) Often, it seems, performers took it upon themselves to supply their own ornaments, and Couperin was not alone in requesting performers not to add ornaments beyond those notated in the music. The various trills and turnlike figures gave baroque instrumental music a resplendent, overwhelming effect, much like the ornaments used in baroque ceiling paintings and on building exteriors.

THE TRIO SONATA

Baroque composers also wrote instrumental music for chamber ensembles. The most important of the ensemble genres, which came to be known as the **trio sonata,** was introduced in Italy in the seventeenth century. Trio sonatas featured two solo treble instruments (usually two violins or, later on, two wind instruments) and a bass instrument. In addition, a continuo instrument, usually a harpsichord or organ, played the bass line and filled in the harmonies indicated by the figured bass. Thus, despite its name, the trio sonata was performed by four musicians.

The outstanding composer of the new trio sonata was Arcangelo Corelli (1653–1713). Born near Bologna, Corelli spent most of his career in Rome, where, under the patronage of Cardinal Pietro Ottoboni, he was acclaimed for his violin virtuosity. Almost all his compositions were for strings. He published his works in six collections, which appeared as Opus I through Opus VI between 1681 and 1714. The first four collections contained trio sonatas, while the fifth contained sonatas for solo violin and continuo. The sixth was a collection of concertos, another baroque instrumental genre, which we shall discuss on pages 97–101.

CORELLI: TRIO SONATA, OP. II, NO. 6 (1685)

By Corelli's time, a distinction between two types of instrumental music had emerged: music to be performed in church services and music to be performed in chamber settings. (Some sought to define a third type, music for theater.) In Corelli's collections, half the trio sonatas (Opus I and Opus III) are labeled **sonata da chiesa** ("church sonata"), and the other half (Opus II and Opus IV) are labeled **sonata da camera** ("chamber sonata"). The church sonatas are generally in four movements, in the sequence slow–fast–slow–fast. Though their individual movements may derive from common dances of the time, the church sonatas tend to be in a learned, proper style of composition, with a good deal of contrapuntal writing. The chamber sonatas, on the other hand, are generally dance suites in three or four movements, in a lighter style, and with the individual dances labeled.

Corelli's Trio Sonata, Op. II, No. 6, is a sonata da camera in three short movements, each in binary form with repeats. The slow first movement, an allemande, is followed by two fast movements, a corrente and a gigue. We give the complete score of the work on pages 92–97. The top two lines are played by two violins; the third line is played by a bass instrument or a keyboard instrument (or both). The keyboard instrument (here a harpsichord) realizes the figured bass.

In the stately Allemande, the two violins frequently cross each other in range, like competing musical strands, but play in unison at the strong cadences that conclude each section. In the fast Corrente, animated by a stream of eighth notes in triple meter (♩♩♩♩♩♩), the main thematic material is assigned to the first violin; the second violin and the bass line play an accompanying role. The lively, concluding Gigue is in a compound meter, with a group of three eighth notes (♪♪♪) as the principal metrical subdivision. Throughout this vivacious dance, the first violin, which is supported by the second violin, cuts an especially jagged melodic line with many unpredictable leaps.

Corelli's music was widely imitated, both during and after his lifetime. In fact, François Couperin glorified the composer in *Le Parnasse ou L'apothéose de Corelli* (*Parnassus, or the Apotheosis of Corelli*, 1724). The German composer Georg Philipp Telemann composed "Corellisirende" ("Corelli-ized") sonatas, and Johann Sebastian Bach assimilated elements of Corelli's style into his own music.

Corelli: Trio Sonata, Op. II, No. 6

ALLEMANDE

(continued)

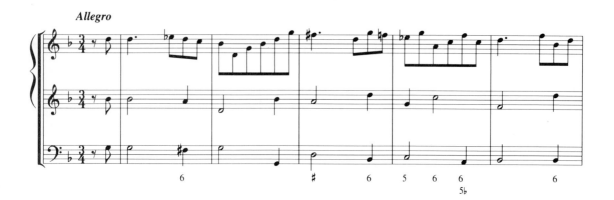

GIGUE

(continued)

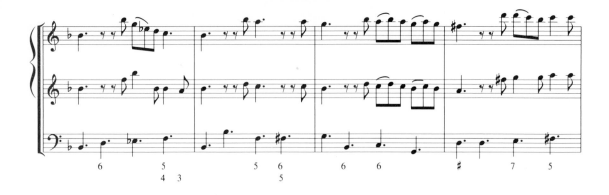

THE BAROQUE CONCERTO

Another major instrumental genre of the baroque period was the **concerto.** The word *concerto* comes either from the Italian verb *concertare,* meaning to concert or join in harmony, or from the Latin verb *concertare,* meaning to compete or dispute. The term was applied in the early seventeenth century to choral music, especially for church, that had a complement of supporting instrumental parts. In the closing decades of the seventeenth century, the concerto was taken to be a purely instrumental composition in which the instruments competed with one another while concerting in harmony.

The main type of baroque concerto was the **concerto grosso** ("large concerto"). The concerto grosso called for two groups of instruments: the **concertino,** a small group of soloists generally from two to five or six in number, accompanied by the **ripieno,** a larger group of musicians, generally string players, who made up the orchestra. From time to time, the soloists and the orchestra came together to form the **tutti**

Ritornello Form

Section:	R_X	S	R_X	S	R_X	...	R_X
Instrumental Forces:	T (C and R together)	C accompanied by R	T	C accompanied by R	T	...	T
Key Plan:	Tonic	〜〜〜	Related key	〜〜〜	Related key	...	Tonic

R_X = Ritornello; S = Solo; T = Tutti; C = Concertino; R = Ripieno

(Italian for "all"). The interaction of the concertino, the ripieno, and the tutti constituted the principal structural idea behind the concerto grosso.

Usually *concerti grossi* were written in three movements: fast–slow–fast. Although composers experimented with various forms in these movements, they often employed what is known as **ritornello form.** In a movement in ritornello form, the music begins with a **ritornello** (pl., *ritornelli*), an opening passage for the tutti that recurs, like a refrain, in whole or in part throughout the movement (see also p. 79). After the ritornello, the solo instruments of the concertino display their wares in a freer *solo* section, with a reduced accompaniment by the ripieno. The remainder of the movement alternates between ritornelli and solo sections, and concludes with a ritornello. What gives the form its vitality is the contrast between the two. The ritornelli are sturdy sections centered on particular keys. The first and last ritornelli are always in the tonic key, and the intermediate ritornelli are in keys closely related to the tonic or, occasionally, in the tonic. The ritornelli, in short, provide the movement with its basic tonal plan and give it its structural outline. The solo sections are considerably freer in nature. They provide the composer an opportunity to modulate from the key of one ritornello to the key of the next. Sometimes, the solo sections reuse ideas from the opening ritornello; at other times, they develop material that highlights the virtuoso potential of the solo instruments.

The study diagram summarizes the essential features of ritornello form. (In the diagram, *R* stands for the refrain or *ritornello; S,* for *solo; C,* for *concertino; R,* for *ripieno;* and *T,* for *tutti.*) The ritornello and the solo passages are quite different in texture: The full sound of the ritornello contrasts noticeably with the thinner sound of the solo passages.

VIVALDI: CONCERTO GROSSO IN A MINOR FOR TWO VIOLINS AND ORCHESTRA, OP. 3, NO. 8 (FROM *L'ESTRO ARMONICO*, 1712)

Several Italian composers contributed to the development of the concerto grosso. Among them were Corelli, whose twelve concertos (1714) are essentially trio sonatas reinforced with a ripieno, Giuseppe Torelli (1658–1709), and Tomaso Albinoni (1671–1751). But the most prolific and imaginative composer of concertos was the Venetian Antonio

Vivaldi (1678–1741), who wrote nearly five hundred concertos, along with some forty operas and a wealth of sacred music. A priest, Vivaldi served as the music director of a Venetian orphanage school for girls. There he performed his music with a highly trained orchestra in a famous series of concerts on Sundays and special feast days.

Distinguished as a violinist, Vivaldi thoroughly explored the technical resources of his instrument in hundreds of violin concertos, but he was equally capable of writing concertos for other string and wind instruments. He even wrote concertos for the mandolin and for instruments that became obsolete during the eighteenth century, such as the lute. Vivaldi wrote not only concerti grossi but also concertos for single solo instruments. The second type, the solo concerto, eventually became the standard type of concerto in the eighteenth century.

Vivaldi assigned fanciful titles to some of his most distinctive concertos. He was an important proponent of **program music**—that is, instrumental music that alludes to some extramusical idea or object. He wrote concertos depicting violent tempests, nocturnal settings, and dream states, and a series of concertos imitating various birds (such as the goldfinch and the cuckoo). Most famous of all is his *Four Seasons,* four concertos for solo violin and orchestra that depict spring, summer, fall, and winter. The score was published about 1725 with anonymous sonnets that give clues to its meaning. For Spring we have birdcalls, murmuring brooks, a thunderstorm, and a peasants' dance (Ludwig van Beethoven would treat similar subjects in his *Pastoral* Symphony; see p. 232). Summer depicts the ardent sun; Fall glorifies the hunt; and Winter suggests bone-chilling cold.

Among Vivaldi's most popular works is Op. 3, No. 8, from a collection of twelve concertos titled *L'estro armonico* (*The Harmonic Whim,* ca. 1712). This is a concerto grosso for two solo violins and orchestra consisting of strings and continuo. We shall look briefly at its first movement as an example of ritornello form.

The movement begins with a ritornello played by the soloists and the orchestra. Like many of Vivaldi's ritornelli, this one falls into several parts, providing the material on which Vivaldi draws for subsequent ritornelli in the movement:

Vivaldi: Concerto Grosso, Op. 3, No. 8, First Movement

FIRST RITORNELLO

(continued)

In the first part of the ritornello (*a*), vigorous descending and ascending scales impart a sense of forward thrust. The second part (*b*) plays on a simple motive of a half step that is the mirror of the first three notes of *a*. The third part (*c*) develops the step motive by systematically repeating it on lower pitches. The fourth and fifth parts (*d* and *e*), rhythmically less energetic, reinforce the home key of A minor.

After the opening ritornello, the two violins enter with their solo material. Their initial ascent recalls the second measure of *a*; subsequently, ornamental **trills★** decorate the course of their melodic detailing:

FIRST SOLO

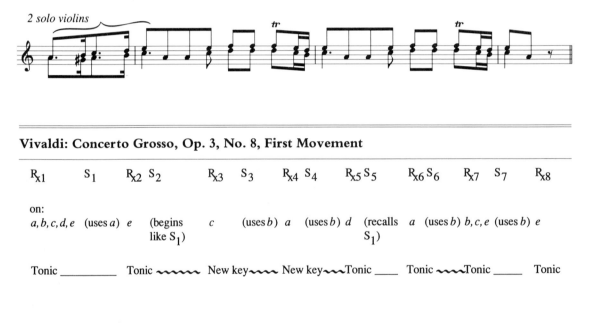

Vivaldi: Concerto Grosso, Op. 3, No. 8, First Movement

R_{x1}	S_1	R_{x2} S_2	R_{x3}	S_3	R_{x4} S_4	R_{x5} S_5	R_{x6} S_6	R_{x7}	S_7	R_{x8}

on:

a,b,c,d,e	(uses a) e	(begins like S_1)	c	(uses b) a	(uses b) d	(recalls S_1) a	(uses b) b,c,e	(uses b) e

Tonic _____	Tonic ⌇⌇⌇	New key⌇⌇	New key⌇⌇Tonic ____	Tonic ⌇⌇Tonic ____	Tonic

R_x = Ritornello; S = Solo

★ Embellishments in which two adjacent pitches alternate rapidly. The symbol **tr** is placed above the principal note on which the trill is executed.

They are soon interrupted by the second ritornello—this one a short, compact quotation of *e*. The second ritornello in turn gives way to the second solo, which begins like the first solo but then blossoms into violinistic figurations that are sustained for several measures. And so the movement proceeds, with alternating ritornello and solo sections moving through a series of keys before returning to the tonic, A minor. In all, there are fifteen sections, including eight ritornelli and seven solos. The plan for the entire movement is laid out in the study diagram.

Vivaldi enjoyed great acclaim during his lifetime, but he died in poverty in 1741, and his vast quantity of music was more or less forgotten until it was revived in the twentieth century. During his lifetime, however, reports of his facile technique and his concertos reached well beyond Italy. They had a profound influence on a German master of the late baroque, Johann Sebastian Bach.

Suggested Listening

*Corelli: Trio Sonata, Op. II, No. 6
*Froberger: Suite No. 2, in A major (1656)
*Monteverdi: *Orfeo*
*Purcell: *Dido and Aeneas*
*Vivaldi: Concerto Grosso for Two Violins and Orchestra, Op. 3, No. 8

Works marked with an asterisk are the principal works discussed in the text.

4

JOHANN SEBASTIAN BACH

"Not *Bach* ["brook"] but *Meer* ["sea"] should be his name." That was Beethoven's tribute to Johann Sebastian Bach (1685–1750). Today, as in Beethoven's time, aspiring musicians learn their craft from Bach's timeless keyboard works, especially the *Well-Tempered Clavier*, two encyclopedic keyboard cycles of paired preludes and fugues in the twenty-four major and minor keys—forty-eight preludes and fugues in all. Bach's prodigious cycles of church cantatas, his *St. Matthew Passion* and *St. John Passion*, and his colossal B minor Mass mark what may well be the summit of Western sacred music. His magisterial compositions for organ and resplendent concertos and suites are consummate examples of the illustrious tradition of baroque instrumental music. His unsurpassed last masterpieces, *The Musical Offering* and *The Art of Fugue,* are towering, ornate monuments to the florid art of baroque counterpoint.

Acclaim did not always greet Bach during his lifetime, however. He was a provincial German musician recognized in his homeland as a brilliant church organist, but he enjoyed little international standing as a composer. Though he worked throughout his life in Germany, he was able to absorb and master the best Italian and French music of the time. His productivity has been matched by few composers, though incredible as it may seem, little of his music was known or even published at the time of his death. Full recognition of his enormous achievement came only later, gathering momentum in the nineteenth century, when a heavily romanticized image of the man and his genius gained currency.

J. S. Bach.

BACH'S LIFE AND CAREER

Bach came from a long line of German musicians that reached back into the sixteenth century. His forbears were versatile church, town, and court musicians, and a few of them earned recognition as composers. Some of Bach's own children, of whom there were twenty, carried on that worthy tradition. Two of them—Carl Philipp Emanuel (the "Hamburg" Bach, 1714–1788) and Johann Christian (the "London" Bach, 1735–1782)—in fact were far better known in their day than their father had been in his. Johann Sebastian once boasted that he could assemble a musical ensemble to be reckoned with from the members of his own family. He trained his children himself and wrote special compositions for their musical education. Engrained in the family tradition was a deep appreciation of music as a craft to be mastered and handed down.

Bach was born in Eisenach, a small village in a region of central Germany known as Thuringia. He probably received his first musical instruction, in string playing, from his father, who died when the boy was 10. For five years, young Bach was raised by an elder brother, who presumably gave him his first instruction in keyboard instruments. According to one unconfirmed story, he secretly copied out a volume of keyboard music from his brother's library by moonlight, but he was found out and had to surrender his tediously produced work. Though the authenticity of the story has been challenged, the suggestion that young Bach learned by copying whatever music became available to him is probably accurate enough.

Bach received a sound elementary education and was well read in theology and Latin, though he did not attend a university. Instead, after filling several minor musical posts, he found employment in 1708 as court organist to the duke of Weimar. There he remained until 1717, having been promoted to Konzertmeister ("concertmaster") in 1714.

It was in Weimar that Bach composed the majority of his organ works, including the *Orgelbüchlein* (*Little Organ Book*), a collection of Protestant chorale settings, and possibly the imposing Passacaglia in C minor (BWV 582★) and the Toccata and Fugue in D minor (BWV 565). His services were also in demand, in Weimar and elsewhere, for inspecting and overseeing the maintenance and repair of organs. A proud man, Bach took offense when he learned that he had been passed over for the position of Kapellmeister, or director of music, in Weimar. When he secured a new position in Cöthen and asked to be released, the duke had him imprisoned for several weeks. Such was the social status of a court musician in the early eighteenth century.

As Kapellmeister in Cöthen, where he served from 1717 to 1723, Bach composed a fair amount of instrumental music for the prince, who loved music. Much of it was arranged in collections; some examples from the Cöthen period include the six cello suites, the first volume of the *Well-Tempered Clavier,* and the six *Brandenburg Concertos.* He also produced collections of keyboard pieces for the instruction of his second wife, Anna Magdalena, and of his son Wilhelm Friedemann.

In 1723 Bach moved to Leipzig, where he served as Kantor of the Thomaskirche (St. Thomas's Church) and the Thomasschule, an affiliated boarding school for boys, and as music director for the city of Leipzig. He was responsible for composing and directing music for the principal churches of the city and for important civic functions as well. As Kantor of the Thomasschule, he was also expected to instruct the students in Latin, a task he particularly disliked. Bach was not the first choice of the city authorities for the joint appointment; they approached him only after other applicants, including the distinguished composer Georg Philipp Telemann (1681–1767), had turned them down.

Since the Reformation, Leipzig had enjoyed a rich musical tradition. Bach was determined not only to preserve that tradition but also to raise the quality of the city's musical life even further. The local authorities found his musical standards exceptionally rigorous, however, and conflict was inevitable.

Still, Bach remained in Leipzig for nearly thirty years, somehow managing to cope with a demanding work schedule. For the weekly church services he wrote organ preludes, *a cappella* motets, and arrangements of chorales. His major contributions were the great cycles of **cantatas,** multimovement works for chorus, soloists, and orchestra that generally preceded the Creed. In his first two years in Leipzig, Bach wrote a new cantata every week, each based on a text appropriate to the liturgical calendar. In all, he composed nearly three hundred church cantatas, about one hundred of which have,

---

★ BWV is the abbreviation for *Bach-Werke-Verzeichnis,* the standard catalog of Bach's music.

The Thomaskirche in Leipzig.

unfortunately, been lost. For several years, he also directed the *Collegium musicum,* an ensemble of professional musicians and university students who performed weekly public concerts for the music-loving middle class of German burghers.

Toward the end of his life, in 1747, Bach was invited to visit the court of Frederick the Great in Potsdam, near Berlin. There he improvised on a subject suggested by Frederick; this "royal theme" later formed the basis of Bach's contrapuntal *tour de force, The Musical Offering.* During the 1740s, he was also at work on another monumental instrumental cycle, *The Art of Fugue.* He intended that this compendium of fugal techniques culminate in a contrapuntal treatment of the letters of his own name, which in German nomenclature correspond to the following notes:

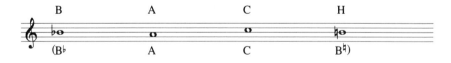

Regrettably, during his last years Bach suffered from the gradual loss of his vision, and when he died, in 1750, he left to posterity the unfinished *Art of Fugue,* and the great bulk of his music in manuscript.

Bach is generally regarded as the most accomplished contrapuntist of all time. In many ways, his music brought to a final perfection the centuries-old tradition of polyphony, the learned art of combining musical lines into an intricate web of sound. Even in Bach's own day, younger composers were beginning to adopt new musical fashions that signaled the decline of complex part writing. It remained for later generations to rediscover the peerless artistry of Bach's contrapuntal craft.

Bach's favored type of contrapuntal composition was the **fugue.** Though not the first to write fugues, he was unquestionably the most distinguished master of the fugue. The term *fugue* comes from the Latin (and Italian) word *fuga,* meaning "flight." In a fugue, separate musical lines, or voices, engage in pursuit of a musical figure known as the **subject.** The number of voices determines the complexity of the fugal texture. In the most common arrangement, the fugue has four parts, labeled by convention soprano, alto, tenor, and bass. (Those terms are used whether the fugue calls for vocal or instrumental forces.) Fugues for three parts, five parts, or more are not uncommon, however.

Historians still puzzle over the early evolution of the fugue. Renaissance masters, including Dufay, Josquin, and Palestrina, had used the term in their sacred masses for a type of imitative polyphony in which one voice is literally imitated by the others. In time, such strict imitation, the most rigorous type of counterpoint, became known as **canon.** (Bach himself wrote numerous erudite examples of this sort.) It seems likely, however, that the baroque fugue evolved from sixteenth- and seventeenth-century instrumental genres based on such vocal models as the motet and the chanson, which featured imitative passages. Though technically not a fugue, the gigue of the Froberger suite that we examined earlier (p. 89) displays a fuguelike, imitative texture; furthermore, in Corelli's trio sonatas, the two solo violin parts often engage in a similar imitative play. But whatever its precise evolution, the fugue achieved its highest form of development in the hands of Bach.

Throughout the course of a fugue, Bach brought a range of specialized contrapuntal techniques to bear on the *subject,* the theme presented at the outset that permeates the music of the fugue. He followed no prescribed form in his fugues; rather, he let his fertile imagination invent a seemingly inexhaustible variety of approaches. We may identify, however, some general principles of organization. Of fundamental significance is the **fugal exposition,** with which Bach's fugues—and other fugues—typically begin.

In a fugal exposition, the voices are introduced one at a time. The first voice states the fugal subject by itself in the tonic key. As the first voice continues, either with fresh material or material derived from the subject, the second voice presents a statement of the fugal subject on the dominant, called the **answer.** Then the other voices enter in turn in different registers, alternating between the subject (in the tonic) and the answer (in the dominant), until all the voices have appeared. Our diagram offers a typical plan of a fugal exposition in four parts, with an initial subject in the soprano, an answer in the tenor, another statement of the subject in the alto, and another answer in the bass. (Note that the voices may enter in various orders.)

Typical Exposition for Fugue in Four Parts

(New or derived material)

Soprano   Subject _____ ∿∿∿∿∿∿∿∿∿∿∿∿∿∿∿

Alto   Subject _____ ∿∿∿∿∿

Tenor   Answer _____ ∿∿∿∿∿∿∿∿∿

Bass   Answer _____

The rest of the fugue generally consists of further statements of the subject and free passages known as **episodes.** The material of the episodes may be new or may be derived from the fugal subject; in any event, in episodes, the composer avoids direct, complete statements of the fugal subject. Often, the entrances of the subject and the episodes alternate, so that the fugue takes this overall shape:

    Full exposition / episode / subject entrance(s) / episode / subject entrance(s) . . .

Bach was a master at applying certain learned techniques to his fugal subjects. For example, in what is known as **mirror inversion,** he might reverse the melodic contours of the subject without altering its rhythmic structure. Here, for example, is a fugal subject from the second volume of Bach's *Well-Tempered Clavier:*

Fugue in C minor (Well-Tempered Clavier, *Book II*)

SUBJECT

Here is the same subject in mirror inversion, with the contours reversed:

SUBJECT IN MIRROR INVERSION

In a technique known as **augmentation,** Bach might increase the rhythmic values of the subject by a factor of 2 or some other number (for example,  instead of):

SUBJECT IN AUGMENTATION

Sometimes, he combined these and other techniques in masterly fashion. In the following display of erudition from the same fugue, we find the original subject in the upper voice, the augmented subject in the middle voice, and the subject in mirror inversion in the lowest voice:

SUBJECT COMBINED WITH SUBJECT IN AUGMENTATION AND MIRROR INVERSION

Using still other techniques, he might shorten the rhythmic values of the subject by some factor (**diminution;** for example, instead of) or compress the distance between adjacent entries of the subject so that they overlapped (**stretto,** from the Italian for "narrow" or "compressed").

One technique frequently encountered in Bach's fugues is independent of the fugal subject. This is the **pedal point,** in which a single pitch is sustained for several measures while the other voices engage in contrapuntal work. This technique creates a tension between the static quality of the pedal point and the contrapuntal momentum of the other voices. In Bach's organ music, pedal points usually occur in the bass voice and are often performed by the pedals beneath the organist's feet. Although pedal points (also called organ points) may appear at various points within a fugue, they make their most dramatic impact near the end of a fugue, where they prepare for the summation of the closing measures.

FUGUE IN E MAJOR (*WELL-TEMPERED CLAVIER,* BOOK II)

We now look more closely at the ninth fugue from the second volume of the *Well-Tempered Clavier*★(1742). For this fugue, in E major, Bach appropriates a subject with

---

★ *Clavier:* German word for keyboard instrument, such as an organ or a harpsichord. Bach's *Well-Tempered Clavier* was most likely intended for the harpsichord.

a rich heritage. Compact in range, it begins on the tonic pitch, E, rises gently, and falls back to the tonic:

*Fugue in E major (*Well-Tempered Clavier, *Book II)*

Before Bach, other composers had treated this subject contrapuntally. After Bach's treatment, the subject continued to appear in fugues, most notably in the spectacular fugal finale of Mozart's *Jupiter* Symphony (1788). Although Bach was certainly more than capable of devising his own fugal subjects—and usually did so—his borrowing here of a preexistent subject shows him to be a respectful student of counterpoint.

We give the music of the E major fugue in its entirety, along with a study diagram mapping its structure. Concentrated within the forty-three measures of the composition are no fewer than twenty-six statements of the fugal subject, all labeled in the score. The first four appear at the beginning in ascending order in the fugal exposition (bass, tenor, alto, and soprano), announcing that this is a four-voice fugue. By measure 9, Bach turns to stretto, so that entries 5, 6, 7, and 8 overlap in a compressed format. Alternating stretto passages and episodes fill out most of the remainder of the fugue. A special case obtains in entries 13, 14, and 15, where Bach presents a paraphrased version of the remainder of the subject:

ENTRY 13 (PARAPHRASE OF SUBJECT)

Beginning in measure 26, Bach combines stretto with a version of the subject in diminution (♩♩♩♩♩ instead of 𝅝♩♩♩♩). The original subject is restored in measure 30 and is used again in a final stretto passage that begins in measure 35. The ultimate entrance appears in the bass voice (m. 40); this meticulously crafted composition comes to an elegant close shortly thereafter.

Bach: Fugue in E major (*Well-Tempered Clavier*, Book II)

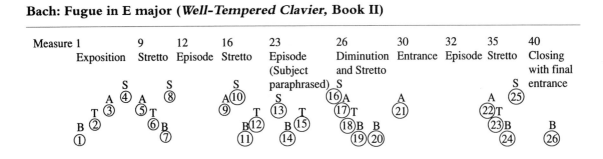

S = Soprano; A = Alto; T = Tenor; B = Bass; circled numbers designate entrances of the subject.

*Fugue in E major (*Well-Tempered Clavier, *Book II, No. 9)*

(continued)

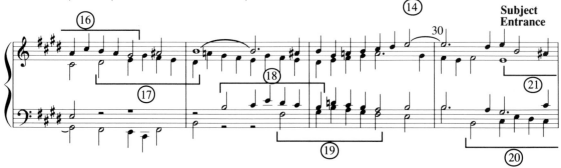

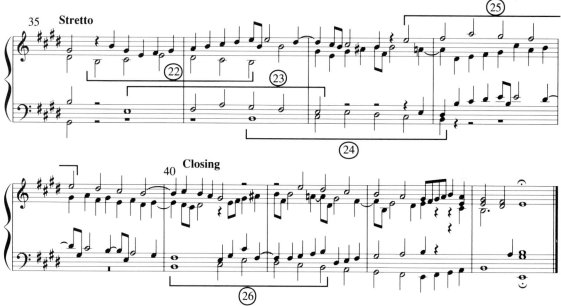

It was said that Bach could deduce straightaway the potential of a subject for fugal development on first hearing—that he could, so to speak, shake fugal intricacies out of his sleeve. Clearly, great intellectual effort went into the writing of the E major fugue; yet, for all its carefully calculated techniques, we can enjoy the fugue beyond its intellectual level. Bach's part writing is so fluent that it sounds effortless, and not a note seems wasted.

BACH'S OTHER INSTRUMENTAL MUSIC

In other works, Bach brought baroque instrumental music to new heights of complexity and refinement that rivaled the intellectual mastery of his fugues. Ever the synthesizer of earlier styles and idioms, he brought together the best of the German, Italian, French, and English instrumental traditions and invested them with an unprecedented splendor.

Bach systematically mastered each of the principal types of baroque instrumental music. The *Goldberg Variations* (ca. 1742), for example, is a stunning series of thirty variations on a recurring bass subject of thirty-two bars, just one of Bach's several contributions to the baroque **ostinato** bass repertoire (see p. 85; a cycle of canons, interpolated with every third variation, adds to the technical perfection of this masterpiece). He wrote dozens of suites, including individual series for harpsichord, violin, cello, and lute, and four magnificent suites for orchestra. He wrote sonatas for flute (with harpsichord) and for violin (with and without harpsichord), as well as trio sonatas after the Corellian model. He wrote several Italianate concertos as well.

Bach's compositions for the organ occupy a special position in his list of works. The supreme keyboard virtuoso of his age, he was the last—and most significant—in a long line of distinguished baroque keyboardist-composers. The tradition had been established during the early baroque by such Italian masters as Andrea and Giovanni Gabrieli, and the boldly imaginative Girolamo Frescobaldi, whose compositions frequently alternated between flights of rhapsodic fancy and intense, imitative counterpoint. The tradition was nourished by the Dutch composer Jan Pieterszoon Sweelinck (1562–1621), who learned much of his craft from the music of earlier English harpsichordists, and, finally, by a succession of German composers. Among them were Samuel Scheidt (1587–1654), who based much of his organ music on Protestant chorales; Johann Pachelbel (1653–1706), who wrote an abundance of fugues for organ; and Dietrich Buxtehude (ca. 1637–1707), whom young Bach, it is said, traveled several weeks on foot to hear perform.

Bach was equally fluent in all the established traditions of organ music. The Passacaglia in C minor (BWV 582), for example, is another series of variations on a bass ostinato subject; this one concludes with a grandiose fugue. He wrote numerous separate organ fugues, many of them introduced by preludes in freer styles. Much of his organ music is founded on the cherished, familiar repertory of Protestant chorales.

TOCCATA AND FUGUE IN D MINOR (BWV 565)

Not all Bach's keyboard works were based on ostinato patterns, fugal subjects, or chorales. Some of his most flamboyant music is found in the **toccatas,** which he composed for organ and for harpsichord. The toccata is a keyboard work in free style, with running scales, arpeggios,★ and other florid passagework, and thickly scored chords. Patchworklike, toccatas are often pieced together in sections alternating between free passages and stricter passages in fugal style. Occasionally, the fugal sections are developed enough to warrant mention in the title, as in Bach's Toccata and Fugue in D minor (BWV 565). As celebrated as this work is, it comes down to us not in Bach's autograph manuscript but in eighteenth-century copies by others, and there is some question about whether the version for organ is actually the original version.

The work consists of three sections, of which the first and third are in a free, improvisational style. Bach opens with a simple yet arresting flourish, a high treble note

---

★ Chordlike figures with notes executed in succession instead of simultaneously. The word derives from the Italian verb meaning "to play the harp."

THE ORGAN

Mozart called the organ the king of instruments. The design of this magisterial instrument includes a set (or sets) of tuned pipes through which air, generated by a bellows and controlled by one or more manual keyboards and usually a set of pedals, is allowed to enter, setting in motion the vibrations that create sounds.

Of all Western keyboard instruments, the organ has enjoyed the greatest longevity. The Greeks and the Romans used organs operated by bellows as well as hydraulic organs operated by a water-pumping mechanism. As early as the tenth century, an organ celebrated for the strength of its sound was in place at the monastery of Winchester in England, where it may have been used to perform some of the early polyphony recorded in manuscripts there. The most brilliant period of organ construction came during the baroque. By the seventeenth century, great organs were filling the cathedrals and churches of Europe with their rich blends of sound. Their ornate architectural design provided a visual counterpart to the music.

The most impressive baroque organs visually had several keyboards, a pedalboard, and ranks of pipes of different tone color and pitch that could be engaged by knobs known as stops. At the time, these great machines were of unequaled complexity, built on an unprecedented scale. Bach, the most celebrated master of the instrument, was not only an organist and a composer of organ music but also a connoisseur of the technical design of organs.

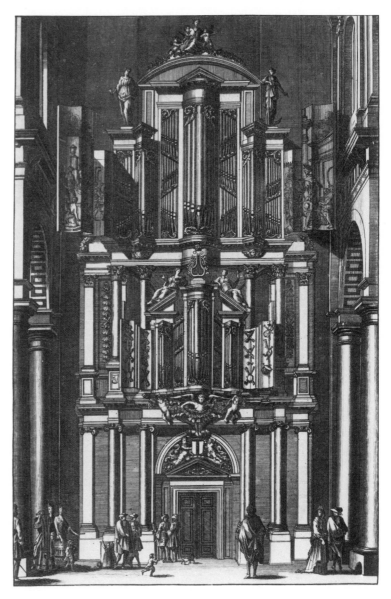

Shown here is an engraving of the organ in the Westerkerk, Amsterdam, an instrument dating from the 1680s.

decorated by a short ornament; this abruptly breaks off and yields to a lunging, descending scale figure. He repeats the flourish dramatically in lower registers, with pauses between its plummeting statements:

Toccata and Fugue in D minor (BWV 565)

Then, a low pitch on the pedalboard is sounded and a dissonant chord slowly accumulated above it, thickening and darkening the texture. After the chord resolves, Bach launches into a rapid-fire *prestissimo* ("very fast"), with both hands sharing the figuration. The music now gains momentum, though it is interrupted periodically by solemn chords and reverberant rests. Eventually, a passage for the pedals leads to a conclusive cadence in the tonic key, D minor. Bach then proceeds to the main portion of the toccata, a four-part fugue.

His fugal subject comprises a figure that fans out from a single, repeated pitch. As in a fully developed fugal exposition, the subject is answered immediately, here by a second voice above:

Before the anticipated third entrance of the subject, however, Bach abandons the exposition in favor of several free measures, and after the third entrance of the subject, he introduces additional free measures before he allows the fourth and final entrance of the exposition to sound in the pedals. Such licenses produce a rather relaxed four-part fugue, in keeping with the unrestrained, at times capricious, character of the toccata.

Instead of bringing the fugue to a proper conclusion, Bach interrupts it with yet another willful gesture: a held chord that announces the third and final section. Here again he resorts to rapid scales and precipitous figural work. In particular, he obtains a dazzling effect by dividing the material between the hands. In the following example, after the held chord (denoted by the **fermata,** ⌒), the notes stemmed upward are played by the right hand, and the notes stemmed downward are played by the left hand:

This toccata—now rhapsodic, now learnedly contrapuntal—reveals in splendid fashion the full play of the master's imagination.

BRANDENBURG CONCERTO NO. 5

In his concertos, Bach drew on the works of the Italians who had popularized the genre, composers such as Corelli and Vivaldi. Here again we find Bach adopting the fundamental features of an established type of composition. Thus, he took over the idea of contrast between ripieno and solo groups, and the idea of the ritornello (see pp. 97–98). Bach diligently transcribed for organ solo several of Vivaldi's concertos, including the Vivaldi concerto we examined in Chapter 3, so that he could study them. What is more, he transferred certain features of the concerto—the ritornello concept, for example— to some of his nonconcerto works, both instrumental and vocal. Still, though Bach began by assimilating the best foreign models of the concerto, his own concertos far surpassed those models in sophistication and sheer brilliance.

Several of Bach's concertos are for one or more harpsichords and orchestra. Two call for three harpsichords. Another, for four harpsichords, is a transcription of a Vivaldi concerto for four violins. Others are scored for violin or for violins and orchestra. His masterpiece in the genre is the series of *Brandenburg Concertos,* composed between 1711 and 1720 and dedicated to the margrave of Brandenburg, a minor German territory. A compendium of concerto writing, this impressive collection features six concertos with different combinations of instruments. For example, the second is a concerto grosso with a concertino of four solo instruments, including a recorder, an oboe, a trumpet, and a violin. In contrast, the fourth has a concertino of three solo instruments, one violin and two recorders.

THE BAROQUE ORCHESTRA

By Bach's time, the orchestra had evolved into a musical ensemble centered on a string section, an arrangement already favored at the French court of Louis XIV in the closing decades of the seventeenth century. At Leipzig, Bach preferred to have a string section of some thirteen musicians, including four to six violins (in two groups), four violas, two cellos, and one double bass.

The string section was supplemented by wind instruments, most notably the soprano-range flute and oboe and the bass-range bassoon. Of the three, the oboe, with its distinctly nasal, penetrating sound, appears to have been the first to win a secure place in the orchestra; Bach often included parts for two oboes in his cantatas. The oboe descended from the double-reed shawm, a wind instrument common during the Renaissance and used as late as the seventeenth century. Made of wood, the oboe has a tubelike body, at the top of which are inserted two reeds that are bound together. Through the reeds the player blows air that activates the vibrating column within the instrument. A system of holes bored into the instrument and carefully aligned keys enables the player to shorten or lengthen the vibrating column, thereby producing all the necessary pitches. Baroque oboes had only one or two keys; the complex keywork of the modern oboe (see p. 535) evolved during the nineteenth century.

The baroque flute included two basic types, both constructed of wood. The recorder (see p. 40) was held straight from the mouth and was thus "end-blown." The transverse flute was held sideways, like the modern flute; the player blew across an opening in the instrument. Today the flute is made of metal instead of wood; it has a complex series of holes and keys, unlike its baroque predecessor, which had only a few holes and one key. The flute has a higher range than the oboe and is able to execute rapid passages with relative ease (see p. 535).

The baroque bassoon may have descended from large, bass-pitched versions of the shawm. Like the oboe, the bassoon has a double reed. Its low range requires an extra length of tubing, which is folded double, giving the instrument its distinctive breadth (p. 535). During the baroque, the bassoon was often used as a continuo instru-

Bach's scoring of the fifth *Brandenburg Concerto* is particularly noteworthy. Its ripieno, or orchestra proper, consists of strings in four parts (violin, viola, cello, and double bass). Its concertino consists of a flute, a violin, and a harpsichord. In keeping with tradition, the harpsichord serves as a continuo instrument in this concerto; but, departing from tradition, Bach often frees the harpsichord from that role to permit it to serve as a solo instrument as well, the first such example in the history of the concerto. So, in the tutti sections, the harpsichord performs its duties as a continuo instrument, blending with the full orchestra. In the solo sections, however, it emerges to perform a virtuoso part that is carefully coordinated with the solo parts of the flute and violin. Needless to say, Bach tailored the harpsichord solos to suit his own style of virtuosity. The culmination of the harpsichord part comes toward the end of the first movement, in a lavish **cadenza** (an improvisatory, virtuoso passage for the soloist alone), the first keyboard cadenza in the concerto repertoire.

The *Brandenburg Concerto* No. 5 consists of three movements in the order fast–slow–fast. The first movement is patterned after the ritornello principle observed in many movements of Italian baroque concertos (see p. 98). Bach announces his ritornello theme in the opening measures, played by the tutti:

ment to double a bass line. The flute, the oboe, and the bassoon later became grouped in a class known as **woodwind** instruments because they were constructed of wood. (A fourth member of the woodwinds, the clarinet, came into favor later in the eighteenth century; see p. 535.)

Bach also wrote for trumpets and horns, members of the **brass** instruments, when he desired an especially rich sound from the orchestra. Brass instruments have cup-shaped mouthpieces and lengths of coiled metal tubing that flare out into a bell. Pitches are produced by varying the tension of the lips on the mouthpiece and the pressure of the airflow into the instrument. In modern brass instruments, the length of the air column can be altered by opening and closing a series of valves. In Bach's day, detachable metal strips known as crooks had to be inserted into the instruments. The trumpet, the most brilliant of the brass, had its origins in military functions; it covers the soprano range and can project a powerful, piercing tone (p. 535). The horn, known today as the French horn, seems to have had its origins as an instrument of the hunt (p. 535). It has a more mellow sound quality and a lower range than that of the trumpet. (Two bass brass instruments, the trombone and the tuba, became standard instruments in the orchestras of the nineteenth century.)

Finally, for special occasions, Bach wrote for two kettle drums, also known as timpani, the one type of **percussion** instrument that we encounter in his music. These instruments have membranes stretched over a kettle-shaped copper shell. By tightening or loosening the membrane, the player can produce definite pitches. In Bach's day, the membrane was tightened by a screwlike apparatus, a tedious procedure. Today, timpanists generally employ timpani with foot pedals to facilitate retuning (see p. 534).

The center of Bach's orchestra was the string section. A small number of woodwinds were frequently employed, and for an especially brilliant sound, one or two trumpets or horns (or both) and two timpani were added. But there was still no standard orchestra as such, with a regular order of instruments or number of musicians. That development occurred later in the eighteenth century (see p. 182).

Brandenburg Concerto *No. 5, First Movement*

TUTTI

This long, arching theme, not unlike Vivaldi's concerto openings, is the epitome of baroque melody. Steadily propelled by unrelenting sixteenth notes (♪♪♪♪), it begins with ascending triadic skips followed by a descending scale. It reaches two climaxes, in measures 3 and 6, before subsiding to its beginning pitch. From the theme, Bach extracts a descending four-note motive, nothing more than a portion of a scale (bracketed in the preceding example), for use in the ensuing solo section. We hear the motive in the flute (also in the harpsichord accompaniment; see the circled notes), then in the violin (and harpsichord accompaniment), and again in the flute. The last statement is especially ingenious: Here, the bass part of the solo harpsichord parallels the motive, while the mirror version of the motive (in ascending motion) is embedded in the treble part of the harpsichord:

SOLO

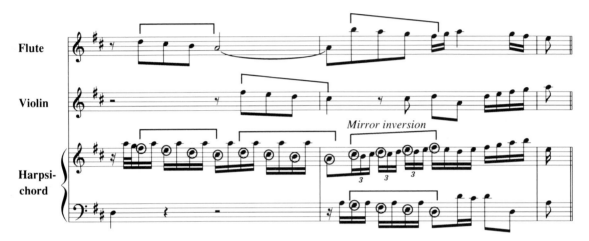

Thus, the music of the solo is saturated with a motive extracted from the opening ritornello. Such a tightly knit motivic structure is characteristic of Bach's music, as is the complex interplay of the various parts.

The main body of the movement alternates between increasingly adventurous solo sections featuring the soloists and sturdy statements of the ritornello material for the full ensemble. Eventually, in the final solo, against a torrent of scales in the harpsichord, Bach thins out the texture to prepare for the harpsichord cadenza: a sparkling—and lengthy—display of keyboard artistry before the concluding ritornello.

Bach scores the slow middle movement for the three soloists alone. More intimate in mood, this music contrasts with the pulsating energy of the first movement. Marked *Affettuoso* ("tenderly"), its tempo, too, contrasts with the brisk *Allegro* of the first movement. Finally, its minor key contrasts with the bright major key of the first movement. The texture of the Affettuoso recalls the trio sonata: Two treble instruments, in this case flute and violin, introduce an ascending theme marked by dotted rhythms in imitative counterpoint while the harpsichord plays a bass line and improvises chords above from a series of figures, according to the continuo tradition:

Brandenburg Concerto *No. 5, Second Movement*

But in the fifth measure, the role of the harpsichord changes; instead of playing chords against the bass line, it now takes up the opening melody of the violin and flute and plays the role of a soloist (one telltale sign of this change in the music is the disappearance of the figures beneath the bass line). Then, a few measures later (not shown), Bach reverts to the original arrangement and has the harpsichord function again as a continuo instrument; it continues to play a double role throughout the movement.

The third movement is a frolicking, giguelike Allegro (see p. 89). In duple meter ($\frac{2}{4}$), the beats are subdivided into triplets,

creating the effect of a fast $\frac{6}{8}$ meter,

The first section of the movement (*A*) begins with the solo instruments (in the order violin, flute, and harpsichord), which enter in turn with a lively, disjunct subject that seems to announce a fugue:

Brandenburg Concerto *No. 5, Third Movement*

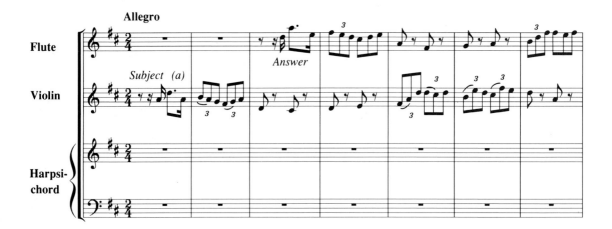

THE BAROQUE

When the orchestra enters, it, too, takes up the fugal subject (*a*). Finally, having wrung it dry, Bach concludes his fuguelike display and proceeds to a contrasting section. This second section (*B*) features a theme (*b*) in the flute. It begins with some leaps that recall the opening of the fugal subject (*a*). But the new theme is rhythmically less energetic than *a*; what is more, instead of being presented as a fugal subject, the new theme is accompanied by flowing chords in the orchestra:

The theme is subsequently taken up by the violin and the harpsichord before it is lost for a while among the swirling chords of the orchestra. To round out the movement, Bach simply repeats the first section literally. The result is thus a three-part *ABA* form, with active exchanges throughout the three sections between the soloists and the orchestra.

In the *Brandenburg Concerto* No. 5, Bach devised three formidable movements of different character and structure, though in all three, the basic principle of contrasting solo and ripieno groups is observed. The first movement is a ritornello movement along the lines of the Vivaldi concerto movement we examined in Chapter 3. The second movement is a trio-sonata movement, after the example of Corelli's chamber sonatas. The third movement is a hybrid structure that combines elements of a fugue and a dancelike gigue with an *ABA* form. Bach's virtuosity, in short, amazes us not only in the irrepressible flare of his solo writing but also in his ever-imaginative treatment of musical form.

JOHANN SEBASTIAN BACH   123

BACH'S SACRED MUSIC

Bach's cantatas claim the largest share of his sacred music. The cantata had arisen in seventeenth-century Italy as a vocal composition in several sections or movements, usually for solo voice and continuo accompaniment. The word *cantata* (from *cantare,* "to sing") was used to distinguish these compositions from the *sonata,* a term loosely applied to instrumental compositions. Most of the early Italian cantatas employed secular texts. By the turn to the eighteenth century, however, the cantata was taken over by German church composers, who employed sacred texts and **chorales,** the hymn tunes of the Lutheran church. Moreover, they expanded the cantata to include a mixture of choral movements and recitatives and arias for soloists. What is more, they expanded the modest continuo accompaniment to include a small chamber orchestra of strings that might be complemented by wind instruments and, on festive occasions, by brass and drums.

Bach discovered the texts for many of his cantatas in the great repertory of Lutheran chorales, which had continued to accumulate throughout the seventeenth century. Typically, Bach's **chorale cantatas,** as those based on chorales are called, begin with a complex polyphonic choral movement built upon a chorale melody and conclude with a simpler, homophonic setting of the same chorale melody. The intermediate movements often contain virtuoso music for solo singers and intricate solo parts for instruments. Usually, a recitative introduces a solo aria, an arrangement borrowed from opera. (Though Bach composed no operas himself, this debt of his cantatas did not pass unnoticed by his contemporaries.) The texts of these intermediate movements consist either of additional verses of the chorale or of newly composed devotional poetry that elucidates the chorale text.

CANTATA NO. 140, *WACHET AUF, RUFT UNS DIE STIMME* ("AWAKEN, THE VOICE SUMMONS US")

Bach composed Cantata No. 140 in 1731, for performance in Leipzig on the twenty-seventh Sunday after Trinity. In seven movements, the cantata is scored for solo singers, a chorus, and an orchestra that includes two oboes, an *oboe da caccia,*★ a horn, a *violino piccolo,*† a string ensemble in four parts (first violin, second violin, viola, and bass, with multiple instruments per part), and continuo. The chorale that gives the cantata its name was written by the German theologian Philipp Nicolai (1556–1608), who set his text to an earlier melody and published it in 1599. Bach uses verses from Nicolai's chorale for the first, fourth, and seventh movements; for the other movements, he uses verses by an unknown poet.

The text of the chorale refers to the parable of the wise and foolish virgins in Matthew 25. Five of the virgins brought oil for their lamps; the others did not. Only the provident could greet the bridegroom (the Savior), who arrived at midnight. The last line of the parable, "Keep awake then; for you never know the day or the hour,"

★ An eighteenth-century oboe with a lower range than the modern oboe. It was apparently associated with hunting music.

† A small violin with strings tuned higher than those of the ordinary violin.

prompts the opening line of the chorale text, "Awaken, the voice summons us," a call to vigilance.

Here are the famous melody and text:

Chorale, "Wachet auf"

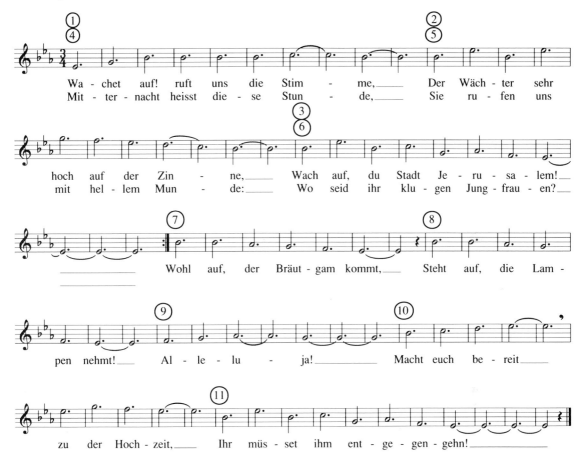

Wachet auf, ruft uns die Stimme,
Der Wächter sehr hoch auf der Zinne,
Wach auf, du Stadt Jerusalem!
Mitternacht heisst diese Stunde,
Sie rufen uns mit hellem Munde:
Wo seid ihr klugen Jungfrauen?
Wohl auf, der Bräutgam kommt,
Steht auf, die Lampen nehmt!
Alleluja!
Macht euch bereit zu der Hochzeit,
Ihr müsset ihm entgegengehn!

Awaken, the voice summons us,
High atop the tower the watchmen call,
Awaken, O town of Jerusalem!
This hour is midnight,
They summon us with cheerful voices:
Where are you, wise virgins?
Arise, the Bridegroom comes,
Arise, and take your lamps!
Alleluja!
Prepare yourselves for the wedding,
You must go out to greet him!

JOHANN SEBASTIAN BACH   125

Bach: Cantata No. 140, *Wachet auf, ruft uns die Stimme*

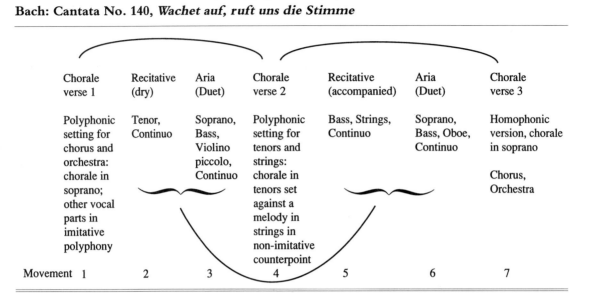

Chorale verse 1	Recitative (dry)	Aria (Duet)	Chorale verse 2	Recitative (accompanied)	Aria (Duet)	Chorale verse 3
Polyphonic setting for chorus and orchestra: chorale in soprano; other vocal parts in imitative polyphony	Tenor, Continuo	Soprano, Bass, Violino piccolo, Continuo	Polyphonic setting for tenors and strings: chorale in tenors set against a melody in strings in non-imitative counterpoint	Bass, Strings, Continuo	Soprano, Bass, Oboe, Continuo	Homophonic version, chorale in soprano

Chorus, Orchestra |
| Movement   1 | 2 | 3 | 4 | 5 | 6 | 7 |

The chorale contains a total of eleven phrases, some of which are reused. The first three, which describe a rising and falling arch, are repeated as the fourth, fifth, and sixth. The seventh and eighth comprise identical stepwise descents. The ninth phrase is a short exclamation on "Alleluia." The tenth phrase (broken by Bach into two portions) reuses material from the second phrase, and the eleventh phrase is the same as the third (sixth) phrase, giving the chorale a rounded symmetry. This soaring melody attains two highpoints in the second and tenth phrases. These highpoints coincide with references in the second line to the watchmen on high ("hoch") who await the Savior's arrival, and in the tenth line to the anticipated wedding ("Hochzeit," or, literally, "high time") of the Savior and the Soul.

The seven movements of the cantata follow a carefully worked-out sequence. The first, fourth, and seventh movements make use of the chorale melody. The remaining movements fall into two pairs of recitatives and arias, both of which are duets for soprano and bass. The study diagram summarizes the plan of the whole.

First Movement: Chorale (Chorus and Orchestra) The cantata opens with an energetic orchestral statement. In part, that energy emanates from the steady pacing of the bass line, which persists unabated for nearly the entire movement. Such a bass line, known as a walking bass, is common in baroque music:

Cantata No. 140, First Movement

Walking bass line

Its purpose here is to suggest the approach of the Savior. In addition, Bach works with two ideas in this initial orchestral section. The first idea (*a*) is a dotted figure (♩.♪), associated during the baroque with themes of majesty or (as in the French overture) of royalty. The second idea (*b*) is a faster-moving, upward-surging figure that is exchanged between the violin and oboe parts. At first, this second idea is checked by tied notes (see p. 519) that interrupt its progress. But then it breaks into an extravagant flourish of ascending scales, suggesting breathless expectation:

First Movement

Now the chorus enters. The soprano intones the first strain of the chorale in long, held notes, as the other choral voices envelop it with thick, rich polyphony:

First Movement

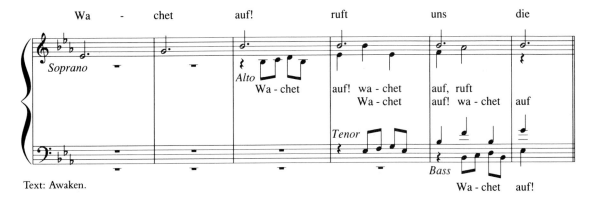

Text: Awaken.

The orchestra supports this animated discourse with a background of music drawn from the music of the opening. Between the strains of the chorale, the orchestra comes to the fore and asserts its dotted rhythms and soaring scales that function like a ritornello. And so the movement proceeds, with strain after strain of the chorale and interpolated orchestral passages. But one surprise awaits us. For the ninth phrase of the chorale,

Bach abandons the chorale temporarily and introduces the celebratory "Alleluja" in an exultant fugal passage before permitting the chorale melody to enter:

First Movement

Al le - lu - ja,___ al - le-lu - ja,

By the end of this stately movement, we are prepared for the long-awaited event, the arrival of the Savior.

Second Movement: Recitative (Tenor and Continuo); Third Movement: Aria (Soprano, Bass, Violino Piccolo, and Continuo) Two movements intervene before that arrival, or, rather, they comment on it. The second movement is a short recitative for tenor and continuo (a **secco,** or "dry," **recitative**), in which the soloist compares the Savior to a young deer leaping from the hills above. In the splendid third movement, a duet for soprano and bass, the Savior answers questions asked by the Soul, who awaits in nervous expectation. The two voices are accompanied by a violino piccolo, which begins the movement with lilting rhythms but soon breaks into an effusion of notes that move restlessly higher, reaching several high notes before gradually descending to the lower range. Here is part of this complex violin solo, an extraordinary example of the baroque convoluted melodic style:

Cantata No. 140, Third Movement

Adagio
Violino piccolo

By its text, the third movement falls into a three-part form (*ABA*). In the *A* section, the Soul asks, "When do you come, my Savior?" In the *B* section, the Savior prepares the wedding banquet. Then the text of the *A* section is reused. Throughout the movement the music is driven by the opening figure of the violin, which, ritornellolike, recurs between passages for the singers and concludes the movement. There is thus a unity of mood that pervades the music, despite the demarcation of the text into three sections.

Fourth Movement: Chorale (Tenors in Unison, Strings, and Continuo) The fourth, central movement marks the arrival of the Savior:

Zion hört die Wächter singen,	Zion hears the watchmen singing,
Das Herz tut ihr vor Freuden springen,	Her heart springs for joy,
Sie wachet und steht eilend auf.	She awakens and arises quickly.
Ihr Freund kommt vom Himmel prächtig,	Her friend resplendent comes from Heaven,
Von Gnaden stark, von Wahrheit mächtig,	Strong in grace, powerful in truth,
Ihr Licht wird hell, ihr Stern geht auf.	Her light shines clearly, her star ascends.
Nun komm, du werte Kron,	Now come, you worthy crown,
Herr Jesu, Gottes Sohn,	Lord Jesus, God's own Son,
Hosianna!	Hosanna!
Wir folgen all	We all follow
Zum Freudensaal	To the joyous hall
Und halten mit das Abendmahl.	And partake of the Lord's Supper.

In this movement, Bach returns to the chorale melody; here, the second verse of its text is sung by the tenors of the chorus in unison. But first, we hear a new, noble melody in the strings; then, the melody appears in counterpoint against the chorale. Bach joins this hauntingly beautiful melody to the chorale in the most effortless way. There is nothing studied about this effect; here is nonimitative counterpoint at its finest:

Cantata No. 140, Fourth Movement

Text: Zion hears the watchmen singing.

Evidently, the composer was especially fond of this movement, for he later arranged it as an organ chorale prelude.

Fifth Movement: Recitative (Bass Solo and Strings); Sixth Movement: Aria (Soprano, Bass, Oboe, and Continuo) The fifth and sixth movements, neither of which is based on the chorale, concern the wedding of the Savior and the Soul. Unlike the earlier "dry" recitative of the second movement, the fifth movement is an **accompanied** (*accompagnato*) **recitative,** meaning that the continuo is reinforced with additional instruments. In this, the dramatic high point, the Savior is accompanied by both the continuo and the strings. Bach lavished great care on this recitative. When the Savior pledges to relieve the Soul's "troubled eye," the music suddenly swerves to a strained series of dissonant harmonies, revealing through the example of word painting the richness of Bach's tonal language.

The aria of the sixth movement, a duet between the Savior and the Soul, features a solo part for oboe. Throughout the aria, the vocalists frequently sing together, as if to suggest the union of Jesus and the Soul. The overall form for the movement is *ABA*. The walking bass of the *A* section is especially animated, as in the beginning of the duet, when the soloists sing of their abiding love:

Cantata No. 140, Sixth Movement

Text: My friend is mine, and I am yours.

In the *B* section, the text refers to heavenly ecstasy. There then follows a literal repeat of the *A* section. Instead of writing out this repeat, Bach uses the abbreviation **Da capo** ("From the head"), which instructs the musicians to return to the beginning. We shall later encounter other examples of this type of aria, the **da capo aria** (see pp. 139, 140).

Seventh Movement: Chorale (Chorus and Orchestra) The final movement of the cantata is a simple homophonic setting of the last verse of the chorale, with the orchestra reinforcing the four parts of the chorus. The sustained pitches of the chorale lend majesty and stability to this final celebration of faith.

By any measurement, Bach's cantatas, to which he devoted the greater part of his career, are among the supreme creations in Western music. No other genre elicited from him such extraordinary invention or brilliant technique on such a sustained level for such a period of time. Still, he did write other sacred music that surpasses the individual cantatas in scale. The *St. John Passion* (1724) and *St. Matthew Passion* (1727) are imposing sacred works that draw on Scripture and devotional poetry to relate and treat the Passion of Christ, his final days and crucifixion. With their enriched polyphonic choruses, dramatic recitatives, and reflective arias, these masterpieces match the scale of Handel's great oratorios, which we shall take up in Chapter 5. Unlike those oratorios, however, Bach's **Passions** utilize chorales, a feature that ties them to the chorale cantatas.

An even more monumental work is Bach's great Mass in B minor, the result of years of arduous work. Bach began composing Mass sections—in Latin, according to the Catholic liturgy—in the 1720s and continued his work during the 1730s; part of the composition was offered to the elector of Saxony, a Catholic region in Germany, in 1733. Only toward the end of Bach's life was he able to assemble all the various movements into one sprawling complex, the Mass in B minor. Although Bach finished a complete setting of the Ordinary of the Mass, its overwhelming size rendered it unsuitable for performance during a service. Bach seems to have intended it as a demonstration of what could be done in setting the Mass, just as he explored the limits of counterpoint in *The Musical Offering* and *The Art of Fugue*. Like his cantatas and Passions, the Mass in B minor is the fervent expression of a devout man who always sought to extol the worship of God through music and in whose hands the music of the baroque reached new levels of magnificence.

Suggested Listening

J. S. Bach
  The Art of Fugue
★*Brandenburg Concerto* No. 5
★Cantata No. 140, *Wachet auf, ruft uns die Stimme*
  Goldberg Variations
  Mass in B minor
  The Musical Offering
  Das Orgelbüchlein
  Passacaglia in C minor (BWV 582)
★Prelude and Fugue in E major (*Well-Tempered Clavier,* Book II)
  St. Matthew Passion
★Toccata and Fugue in D minor (BWV 565)

Note: Works marked with an asterisk are the principal works discussed in the chapter.

5

GEORGE FRIDERIC HANDEL

George Frideric Handel (1685–1759), Bach's great contemporary, was the second master of the late baroque. He was a man of the world who studied in Italy and worked in Germany before settling in England, where he established himself as an internationally acclaimed composer and made his fortune. Handel excelled in rendering human dramas into music. He was known at first for his serious operas in Italian, which he introduced to England in 1711. Later, he boldly changed course to develop the English **oratorio,** which featured dramatic versions of biblical stories set to music. In this new genre, Handel amalgamated elements of earlier Italian oratorios, German and English church music, and his own Italian operas. Handel's English oratorios were the mainstay of his posthumous recognition. Throughout the nineteenth century and into the twentieth, burgeoning Handelian societies regularly performed such oratorios as *Saul* (1739), *Israel in Egypt* (1739), *Messiah* (1742), *Judas Maccabaeus* (1747), *Solomon* (1749), and *Jephtha* (1752).

A keyboard virtuoso, Handel regaled English audiences with his improvisations. As a performer, he was rivaled only by Bach, though the two never met. (Indeed, Handel seems not to have known Bach's music at all.) In addition to well-crafted keyboard suites, Handel wrote several organ concertos for performance between the acts of his oratorios. There is also some splendid occasional music. The *Water Music* (probably 1717) was performed during a royal outing on the Thames River; the *Fireworks Music* (1749), written for a large, festive orchestra, celebrated with special pomp the Treaty of Aix-la-Chapelle, concluded between England and various European monarchies.

Bach spoke to the devout through his cantatas and chorale settings and to music connoisseurs through his cerebral fugues and canons; Handel addressed his audiences

George Frideric Handel.

with bold, compelling gestures and lyrical melodic lines. Handel's music has an immediate, theatrical appeal; Bach's music is to be pondered, like the moves of a master chess
player. Handel's music makes its impact directly; Bach's music engages the listener with
its dense part writing and its ornate design. Like Bach, Handel worked quickly, turning
out a major work in a matter of days. And like Bach, he was a consummate contrapuntist. Though he used counterpoint more for dramatic effect than for the sake of
complexity, Handel was a master of the discipline and criticized those who, he thought,
were deficient in it. (Once, after listening to an opera lacking in contrapuntal elaboration, he is said to have remarked that his cook knew more about counterpoint than did
the opera's composer.)

Handel was born in Halle, a small Saxon town. His father, a barber-surgeon, sent him to the university to prepare for a career in law. Not finding law to his liking, Handel went off to Hamburg, where he played in the orchestra of the municipal opera and, according to one account, became a proficient composer of "correct" fugues. It was in Hamburg that he composed and mounted his first two operas, the music of which is lost. In 1706 he traveled to Italy, which for centuries had drawn artists, writers, and composers. While in Rome, he composed sacred music and well over one hundred secular cantatas; in Florence, Naples, and Venice, he met the leading composers of Italian opera and instrumental music, including Alessandro and Domenico Scarlatti, Arcangelo Corelli, and Antonio Vivaldi.

In 1710 Handel was appointed Kapellmeister to the court of Hanover by an elector who later became George I of England. By the terms of his appointment, Handel received permission to sojourn in London, where he won ready favor at the royal court. In 1711 his opera *Rinaldo,* the first Italian opera composed for performance in England, received its premiere. The work scored a great success, though it attracted, too, its share of criticism. In *The Spectator,* the critic Joseph Addison, partial to the English theater,

ITALIAN OPERA IN LONDON, 1711

*A*s I was walking in the streets about a Fortnight ago, I saw an ordinary Fellow carrying a Cage full of little Birds upon his Shoulder; and, as I was wondering with my self what Use he would put them to, he was met very luckily by an Acquaintance, who had the same Curiosity. Upon his asking him what he had upon his Shoulder, he told him, that he had been buying Sparrows for the Opera. Sparrows for the Opera, says his Friend, licking his Lips, what[,] are they to be roasted? No, no, says the other, they are to enter towards the end of the first Act, and to fly about the Stage.

This strange Dialogue awakened my Curiosity so far that I immediately bought the Opera [i.e., the libretto]. . . . But to return to the Sparrows; there have been so many Flights of them let loose in this Opera, that it is feared the House will never get rid of them; and that in other Plays, they may make their Entrance in very wrong and improper Scenes, so as to be seen flying in a Lady's Bed-Chamber, or perching upon a King's Throne; besides the Inconvenience which the Head of the Audience may sometimes suffer from them. I am credibly informed that there was once a Design of casting into an Opera, the Story of Whittington and his Cat, and that in order to do it, there had been got together a great Quantity of Mice; but Mr. Rich, the Proprietor of the Play-House, very prudently considered that it would be impossible for the Cat to kill them all, and that consequently the Princess of his Stage might be as much infested with Mice, as the Prince of the Island was before the Cat's arrival upon it; for which Reason, he would not permit it to be Acted in his House. And indeed I cannot blame him; for, as he said very well upon that Occasion, I do not hear that many of the Performers in our Opera pretend to equal the famous Pied Piper, who made all the Mice of a great Town in Germany follow his Musick, and by that means cleared the Place of those little Noxious Animals.

Joseph Addison, The Spectator,
March 6, 1711

William Hogarth, *The Oratorio,* 1733. A caricature of an oratorio chorus.

ridiculed the special stage effects of the opera, including, in one scene, the release of a flock of live sparrows (see p. 135).

Handel stayed on in his adopted country for almost half a century, through the reigns of Anne, George I, and George II. Often, he was called on to compose music for important state functions; some of his coronation anthems, in fact, are still in use. For nearly three decades, however, he concentrated on composing Italian operas, the preferred entertainment of both the English royalty and the English aristocracy. In 1720 he was named music director of the newly established Royal Academy of Music, with a mandate to foster the development of Italian opera in England. The Academy was funded by royal patronage and by wealthy investors, who viewed it as a profit-making business enterprise. (Securities of the Academy were traded on the London stock exchange.) Handel spent much of his time on administrative matters, coddling his Italian singers and traveling to the Continent from time to time to recruit the fashionable—and temperamental—virtuosos demanded by the public.

Struggling with a host of problems, both financial and artistic, Handel managed to keep this transplanted form of entertainment alive well into the 1730s. By then, however, English audiences had begun to tire of Italian opera, and in 1737 the Academy was forced to close its doors for a second and final time. In retrospect, that failure seems almost inevitable. The English had never been altogether comfortable listening to operas sung in a foreign language. Moreover, they were uneasy with certain conventions of Italian opera, such as having sopranos or altos—among them *castrati,* castrated male singers—sing heroic male roles. The operas themselves had grown more and more stereotyped. Typically, the virtuoso singers would deliver an "exit" aria and then make an abrupt exit, bidding for applause to the detriment of dramatic continuity. With the cooling of public interest, the financial difficulties of the Academy grew more severe. Coupled with all those problems was the animosity of London critics, who viewed Italian opera as a foreign threat to the established English theater.

In 1732, while still preoccupied with writing operas, Handel produced *Esther,* the prototype of his distinguished series of oratorios with English texts. Based on an English libretto after Racine, *Esther* told the familiar Old Testament story of the queen who saved her people from massacre. The Bishop of London ruled that the work could not be produced as an opera, because that would be a profanation of a sacred subject. Therefore, Handel had it performed "after the Manner of the coronation service," without costumes, scenery, staged action, or other theatrical trappings. With its English text and its uplifting biblical story, *Esther* scored a considerable success—a response that later encouraged Handel to abandon Italian opera in favor of the English oratorio. He went on to compose nearly twenty oratorios, all presented in concert performance and many enthusiastically received by the middle-class audiences of London.

As a foreigner, Handel was a frequent butt of ridicule. His detractors caricatured his speech (he could swear, we are told, in five languages), his portly figure, and his voracious eating habits. Being a man of firm will and shrewd business sense, however, Handel prevailed, in the end, against all ridicule. Oxford University offered him an honorary doctorate in 1733 (though, curiously, he declined the distinction), and when he died, in 1759, he was buried in Westminster Abbey, the final resting place of England's distinguished poets and musicians. Posterity has viewed him as the outstanding anglicized—if not English—composer of all time.

HANDEL AND ITALIAN OPERA

By the time Handel turned to Italian opera, the genre had evolved into an art form with rigid conventions. The main attraction of Italian operas was their long series of highly ornate, stylized arias in which the principal singers commented on the events of the unfolding drama. The da capo aria was the predominant type of aria. It consisted of two contrasting sections, *A* and *B,* followed by a repeat of the *A* section, resulting in the structure *ABA.* The repetition, though it impeded the dramatic flow, gave the soloist an opportunity to indulge in a virtuoso display of improvised embellishment.

(In Handel's day, soloists were free to decorate the music with ornaments of their own devising and, indeed, often compelled composers to rewrite arias to suit their taste.) Between the arias were the recitatives, speechlike passages with simple continuo accompaniments, which laid out the dramatic action of the opera. To heighten the effect, Handel sometimes provided orchestral accompaniment for a recitative, as did Bach in his cantatas and Passions (for one example, see p. 130). In addition to writing any number of memorable arias and fluent recitatives, Handel employed ensembles, such as duets, and large-scale choruses; he was, in fact, one of the first composers to integrate fully those devices into Italian operas. Finally, to introduce his operas, Handel customarily used orchestral overtures, often recalling the seventeenth-century French overture (see p. 81), with arresting dotted rhythms and stately chords, and animated fugal passages.

GIULIO CESARE IN EGITTO (JULIUS CAESAR IN EGYPT, 1724)

Handel's operatic masterpiece is *Julius Caesar in Egypt,* a fictionalized drama about Julius Caesar, Cleopatra (the queen of Egypt), and Ptolemy (the king of Egypt and Cleopatra's brother). In this version, Cleopatra asks Caesar to help her wrest the Egyptian throne from her brother. At first, she appears as a seductress, seeking to entice Caesar with alluring music. Eventually, she falls in love with him, and after considerable adversity, the two triumph over Ptolemy.

Handel begins his opera with a majestic overture, an example of the French overture modeled on the earlier practice of Lully (see p. 81). The overture is in two sections. The first section, which opens with a flourish, is in dotted-note style with ornamental trills, and suggests Caesar's regal character:

Julius Caesar, *Overture*

The first section is repeated. The second section, in faster tempo, is in fugal style. Its subject is a buoyant figure with persistent note repetitions and lively skips:

The momentum of the fugue is ultimately interrupted by the return of dotted-note figures that recall the opening and that bring the overture to a sumptuous conclusion.

Handel captures the many sides of Caesar's character in a variety of remarkable arias. The Roman emperor is in turn triumphant, bellicose, reflective, and amorous. He is also a shrewd judge of human nature, as we learn in an aria he sings in Act I after encountering the scheming Ptolemy, "Va tacito e nascosto." Here is the text of this da capo aria:

A	*Va tacito e nascosto,* *quand'avido è di preda,* *l'astuto cacciator.*	**A**	He goes silently and concealed, when avidly stalking his prey, the wily hunter.
B	*E chi è a mal far disposto,* *non brama che si veda* *l'inganno del suo cor.*	**B**	And he who is disposed to do evil is not eager for one to see the deceit in his heart.

In the first three lines of the aria, the *A* section, the text pictures a hunter stealthily stalking his prey. In lines four through six, the *B* section, the man intent on doing evil—Ptolemy—is likened to the hunter.

To match this text with musical imagery, Handel hit upon the idea of a prominent solo for a horn, the traditional instrument of the hunter. We hear the instrument right at the outset, in an orchestral passage that, like a ritornello, later returns to conclude the *A* section. The horn begins by leaping up to a pitch that is repeated several times before it descends by step. Then the horn applies the same idea at a higher pitch level:

Julius Caesar, *Act I, "Va tacito e nascosto"*

The tempo marking, *Andante,* suggests a walking tempo, which is supported by the steady pace of the bass line (not shown). Handel specifies the dynamic marking *piano* to suggest the stealth of the hunter. When Caesar's part enters, it takes up the horn theme and pauses periodically to permit the horn to reenter:

In the *B* section of the aria, Handel withdraws the horn from the ensemble, thinning out the texture. Just as the text speaks of "the deceit in his heart," so the music winds through a maze of harmonies, ultimately reaching a dark minor key considerably removed from the major key of the opening. Then, as convention dictated, the *A* section is repeated, and Caesar exits.

Only the music for Cleopatra matches the high quality and nobility of Caesar's arias. First a seductress, then Caesar's lover, and finally a noble queen, Cleopatra appears in a great diversity of musical settings. We look briefly at the enchanting da capo aria she sings to Caesar in Act II, "V'adoro, pupille" ("You I adore, O eyes"), which reveals Cleopatra in her first role, as seductress:

A
V'adoro, pupille,
saette d'Amore,
le vostre faville
son grate nel sen.

A
You I adore, O eyes,
darts of love,
your sparks
are welcome in my heart.

B
Pietose vi brama
il mesto mio core,
ch'ogn'ora vi chiama
l'amato suo ben.

B
My dejected heart
longs for your pity,
and calls you every moment,
its own dear love.

To conjure up the exotic locale of this love scene, Handel introduces a special ensemble, which includes oboe, viol, harp, bassoons, and theorbo,* that is separate from the regular orchestra. Cleopatra entices Caesar with slow, stately music in $\frac{3}{4}$ time. Dancelike, the music suggests a sarabande (see p. 90), with its gentle pull toward the second beat:

Julius Caesar, *Act II, "V'adoro, pupille"*

This aria, too, follows the da capo plan, but with one important exception (see the study diagram). After the contrasting *B* section (in a minor key and scored for Cleopatra and just the special ensemble), Handel has the enamored Caesar comment briefly in a recitative on Cleopatra's loving strains, and in this way postpones the requisite return of the *A* section. Not even the gods in heaven, Caesar declares, are capable of a melody that can compare to such beautiful singing (*bel canto*). With this masterful interruption, Handel departs from convention to give Caesar—and the audience—a moment to savor the warm lyricism of this exquisite aria.

---

* A member of the lute family, popular during the seventeenth century, with a lengthened neck and a second set of unstopped bass strings that vibrate sympathetically.

Handel: *Julius Caesar*, Act II, Da Capo Aria, "V'adoro, pupille" (Cleopatra)

A	B	Recitative	Da Capo
Cleopatra	Cleopatra	Caesar's reaction	Repeat of *A*
Sarabande character			
String orchestra and special ensemble	Special ensemble (orchestra drops out)	Continuo	
Major key	Minor key		

HANDEL AND ENGLISH ORATORIO

In devising oratorios with English texts, Handel solved one problem posed to English audiences by Italian opera: the problem, as Addison put it, of having English people sitting "together like an Audience of Foreigners in their own Country" listening to an opera sung in "a Tongue which they did not understand." Most of Handel's oratorios deal with biblical subjects, further removing them from his Italian operas, populated by characters drawn largely from ancient history. The subjects for the oratorios range from new treatments of familiar Old Testament stories to the direct quotation of Scripture in *Messiah* and *Israel in Egypt*. The middle-class audiences that delighted in the sentimental and morally instructive novels of Samuel Richardson (1689–1761) were sure to find edification in accounts of such worthy figures as Saul, Solomon, Jephtha, and Judas Maccabaeus.

In his oratorios, Handel abandoned the operatic conventions of theatrical staging, dramatic acting, and "exit" arias. Moreover, on occasion he departed from the set plan of the da capo aria and experimented with a variety of new designs. Above all, he greatly expanded the use of the chorus. The oratorios are filled with great choral movements, particularly *Israel in Egypt* and *Messiah*. Sometimes, the chorus serves as a deliberative body that takes the place of individual roles. Thus, in *Israel in Egypt,* grand double choruses relate the tribulations of the Hebrew nation in exile. On other occasions, the chorus is directly engaged in the plot. In *Belshazzar,* three distinctive types of choral music characterize the Babylonians, the Jews, and the Persians, the principal figures of that drama.

MESSIAH (1742)

Handel's most popular oratorio is *Messiah,* composed in little more than three weeks and first performed in Dublin in 1742 as a benefit for Irish charities. When it was performed in London the following year, some critics denounced as blasphemous

Handel's use of Scripture in a nonliturgical public entertainment. The oratorio gradually won popularity during Handel's lifetime, however; today, it is recognized as one of the great choral works of all time.

Messiah consists of three parts, which recount the incarnation, crucifixion, and resurrection of Christ. The oratorio begins, like *Julius Caesar,* with a French overture, and it has an abundance of choruses (some twenty out of fifty-three numbers) and several distinguished recitatives and arias. Among the best known of the arias are "Every valley shall be exalted," "I know that my Redeemer liveth," and "Why do the nations so furiously rage?" Though these arias are sung by soloists, *Messiah* has no parts per se for individual characters and no conventional plot or dramatic action. Rather, the music comments on events as they take place and underscores the general theme of *Messiah:* the redemption of mankind through the life and work of Christ. For a closer view of Handel's method, we look at three choruses from *Messiah.*

In Part I, the chorus "For unto us a Child is born," with text from Isaiah 9:6, announces the birth of Christ:

> For unto us a Child is born, unto us a Son is given:
> And the government shall be upon His shoulder;
> And His name shall be called Wonderful, Counsellor, The mighty God,
>   The everlasting Father, The Prince of Peace!

Handel assigns three distinctive musical ideas—we shall call them *a, b,* and *c*—to the three lines of text, and builds up his chorus with four sequential treatments of those ideas. These treatments are framed by an orchestral introduction and conclusion based on *a.* The study diagram lays out the plan of the entire movement.

The lively idea for the first line of text (*a*) is presented against a vigorous bass line by the sopranos and tenors and later by the altos and basses. After an orchestral passage

---

Handel: *Messiah,* Chorus, "For unto us a Child is born"

Orchestral Introduction (based on *a*)	*a*	*b*	*c*	*a*	*b*	*c*	*a*	*b*	*c*	*a*	*b*	*c*	Orchestral Postlude (based on *a*)
	Choral polyphony in pairs of voices (soprano-tenor, alto-bass)	(tenor-soprano, alto-bass)	Full chorus	Choral polyphony in pairs of voices	Full chorus	Choral polyphony in pairs of voices	Full chorus	Full chorus					

based on *a,* the sopranos introduce *a* with a crisply declaimed motive that proclaims, "For unto us a Child is born." The second half of the line, "unto us a Son is given," is repeated and divided into four compact segments that steadily rise until the tenors enter with *a:*

Messiah, *Part I, Chorus, "For unto us a Child is born"*

The second idea (*b*) climbs in steps to a climax on "His" before receding on "shoulder." Here, too, Handel divides the chorus into pairs, with tenors and sopranos, and then altos and basses, entering. Note Handel's use of majestic dotted rhythms and the shaping of the music to suggest "shoulder":

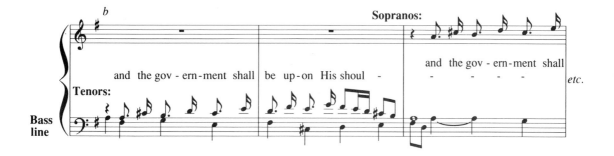

In contrast, the third idea (*c*) is scored for the full chorus; it bursts forth as several short, powerful chordal acclamations, again in dotted-rhythm style:

Quite a different mood is captured in Part II in the chorus "And with His stripes we are healed" (Isaiah 53:5). This is a severe fugue in a somber minor key. Its subject commences with a series of wide leaps, of which the last, on "His stripes," is particularly expressive and dissonant. Then, for "we are healed," Handel continues with a smooth, stepwise ascending line:

Messiah, *Part II, Chorus, "And with His stripes"*

Many composers before and after Handel wrote fugues based on this subject, though few fugues match the intensity of this choral version. Handel's method is simple: He fills the fugue with thirteen entrances of the subject, one after the other, so that the music is saturated with the subject. Then, in a stroke of genius, he abandons the deliberate fugal style to have the chorus break into fresh, contrasting music for the text "All we like sheep have gone astray" (Isaiah 53:6). Here a musical figure that strays over a wide range and a restless rhythmic energy contrast sharply with the tense solemnity of the fugue:

Messiah, *Part II, Chorus, "All we like sheep"*

The great "Hallelujah" chorus, with which Part II concludes, is easily the most celebrated movement of *Messiah*. The text, drawn from Revelation 19:6, 11:15, and 19:16, announces the reign of the Lord and of the resurrected Christ:

> Hallelujah! For the Lord God Omnipotent reigneth.
> The kingdom of this world is become the Kingdom of our Lord
>   and of His Christ; and He shall reign for ever and ever.
> King of Kings, and Lord of Lords.

This stirring choral finale is built on five basic musical ideas. A brief orchestral flourish announces the first idea (*a*), the short, compact acclamation on "Hallelujah!" taken up by the chorus, immediately repeated, and then compressed:

Messiah, *Part II, "Hallelujah" Chorus*

Handel reworks *a* on a higher pitch and then, to depict the omnipotent God, introduces a stark, powerful figure sung in unison by the chorus (*b*). The new figure rises to the "Lord God" and then moves by wide leaps to suggest His omnipotence:

Now the "Hallelujah" acclamations break in again, as Handel alternates *a* and *b* and combines them contrapuntally. The third musical idea (*c*) reflects the contrast between the "kingdom of this world" and the "Kingdom of our Lord and of His Christ." Here Handel chooses a homophonic, chordal texture to support the dramatic juxtaposition of low and high registers:

Next, Handel sets "And He shall reign for ever and ever" in fugal style, on this potent, disjunct subject that alternates between ascending and descending leaps (*d*):

And He shall reign for ev - er and ev - er

Finally, "King of Kings, and Lord of Lords" is intoned by the sopranos as a pedal point (see p. 109) with sustained pitches (*e*):

King of Kings,_____ and Lord of Lords._____

Repeatedly the soprano pedal point is heard, rising successively to higher and higher pitch levels, as the music beneath surges forward with joyous "Hallelujah" acclamations. The closing section makes use of *a, d,* and *e* in various combinations as this masterpiece comes to a triumphant "Amen" (subdominant–tonic) cadence on "Hallelujah."

TOWARD THE CLASSICAL PERIOD: THE ECLIPSE OF THE BAROQUE

One or two decades before 1742, when Handel composed *Messiah,* the late baroque style, in all its ostentation and eloquence, was beginning to give way to a more relaxed style, the purpose of which was to please and delight. A distinction came to be made between a full-blown "strict" or "high" style—involved and learned—and a lighter, "free" style. The "strict" style was most appropriate for church music; the "free" style, suitable for less serious instrumental and other secular music, gave composers greater latitude to experiment and invent. As the eighteenth century advanced, the "free" style became popular in opera and instrumental music, and, indeed, finally influenced church music as well.

Two terms, *rococo* and *galant,* are often applied to this light, transitional style that arose in music roughly between 1720 and 1750 or 1760. *Rococo* is best applied to the arts in France. The term was originally used to describe a decorative style that emerged in French architecture as early as the seventeenth century before taking hold in the eighteenth century. Its curvilinear shapes were thought to resemble light "shellwork" (*rocaille*). In painting, the rococo style is apparent in the amorous, frivolous scenes of Watteau, Fragonard, and Boucher. In music, it showed up in the **opéra-ballet,** a light form of opera that featured dances and scenes from everyday life. The opéra-ballet

Watteau, *L'Amour paisible,* ca. 1716. Known for his paintings of *galant* country fêtes, Watteau frequently incorporated music instruments in his paintings. In this detail from a relaxed gathering in the country, a guitarist entertains an amorous couple.

offered an alternative to the serious *tragédies lyriques* of Lully and others that had occupied the stage with tragic figures drawn from mythology.

Galant is another term used to describe the light style of the time, in France and elsewhere. Watteau painted a series of scenes described as *fêtes galantes;* Jean Philippe Rameau composed an opéra-ballet titled *Les Indes galantes (The Gallant Indians,* 1736), with amorous scenes set in Turkey, Peru, Persia, and America. In Germany, light instrumental dances were designated as *Galanterien.*

Composers of *galant* music rejected the contrapuntal complexities of the baroque in favor of a supple melodic style with a simplified, supporting bass line. Their *galant* music was tuneful, with short, clearly articulated and often repeated phrases, and tended to have simple harmonies. They favored the elementary forms of composition, such as straightforward dance forms with two main sections, each repeated.

By the 1730s, the *galant* style was making inroads on the late baroque style in music throughout Europe. In Italy, a new type of opera, the **opera buffa,** or comic opera, began to challenge the hegemony of **opera seria,** or serious opera. At first, comic opera had appeared as an unassuming diversion (**intermezzo**) between the acts of an opera seria. Now it gained stature as an independent type of opera. Typically, it called for just a few characters, who sang a succession of arias and recitatives written in a melodious style punctuated by short, crisp phrases.

One of the most popular and significant comic operas was *La serva padrona* (*The Maid as Mistress*) by the Italian composer Giovanni Battista Pergolesi (1710–1736), who also wrote church music in the high sacred style. This opera, about a house servant who outwits and marries her master, was first performed in Naples in 1733. It was staged in Paris in the 1750s, where it touched off a lively debate over the relative merits of French and Italian opera. Jean-Jacques Rousseau composed a French intermezzo, *Le Devin du village* (*The Village Seer,* 1752), in imitation of Pergolesi's work. The popularity of Italian comic opera increased steadily during the eighteenth century, reaching its perfection, as we shall see, in Mozart's masterpiece *The Marriage of Figaro* (1786), in which a servant outwits a count.

With the approach of the midcentury, composers of instrumental music also departed from the baroque style, though much of their work seems rather undistinguished. One exception is Domenico Scarlatti (1685–1757). The son of the illustrious opera composer Alessandro Scarlatti, Domenico began by writing operas in Italy but later took up positions at the royal courts in Portugal and Spain. There, working in relative obscurity, he wrote over five hundred keyboard sonatas, many of them in pairs. Each sonata is in one movement, and all are elaborations of the binary form basic to the baroque dance suite. They show a wealth of invention, ranging from delicate nuances to colorful imitations of guitars and mandolins. Scarlatti developed a particularly brilliant brand of keyboard virtuosity, specializing in treacherous hand crossings, wide leaps, and brash, unpredictable figurations. Marked by strong contrasts, Scarlatti's sonatas made less and less use of the continuous, homogeneous textures of baroque music.

Bach and Handel were both aware of the changes that were taking place in musical style. Bach titled several of his light dance movements *galant*, and he even borrowed from—or parodied—the new style of comic opera in some entertaining secular cantatas, including the delightful *Coffee Cantata* (ca. 1735). In England, the "ballad opera" *The Beggar's Opera* (1728) by John Gay (music by John Christopher Pepusch, 1667–1752) satirized the social order with roles for villains, pickpockets, and harlots—and spoofed the conventions of Italian opera, the basis of Handel's livelihood, as well. Its popularity contributed to Handel's decision to turn from Italian opera to English oratorio.

Throughout this period, sometimes referred to as the preclassical period, composers aspired more and more toward music of simplicity, charm, and clarity. The music of the time, along with the other arts, began to show the influence of a powerful new direction in Western thought, which we know as the Enlightenment.

Suggested Listening

J. S. Bach: Cantata No. 211 (*Coffee*)
Handel: *Jephtha*
★ _____: *Julius Caesar in Egypt*
★ _____: *Messiah*
 _____: *Saul*
 _____: *Water Music*
Pergolesi: *La serva padrona*

Note: Works marked with an asterisk are the principal works discussed in the chapter.

PART IV THE CLASSICAL PERIOD

EUROPEAN HISTORY AND CULTURE	AMERICAN HISTORY AND CULTURE	EUROPEAN MUSIC
1740–1780: Reign of Maria Theresa in Austria (coregent with Joseph II from 1765) **1740–1786:** Reign of Frederick the Great in Prussia **1748:** Discovery of ruins at Pompeii		**1732:** Birth of Haydn
1750–1772: Denis Diderot, *Encyclopédie* **1755:** J. J. Winckelmann, *Thoughts on the Imitation of Greek Works* **1755–1773:** Samuel Johnson, *Dictionary of the English Language* **1756:** Beginning of Seven Years' War **1759:** Voltaire, *Candide*		**1756:** Birth of Mozart **ca. 1759:** Haydn's first symphony
1760–1820: Reign of George III in England **1762:** Rousseau, *The Social Contract* **1762–1796:** Reign of Catherine the Great in Russia	**1765:** Stamp Act Congress	**1761:** Haydn employed by Esterházys
	1770: "Boston Massacre" **1773:** Boston Tea Party	**1770:** Birth of Beethoven **1772:** Haydn, Symphony No. 45 (*Farewell*)
1774–1792: Reign of Louis XVI in France **1776:** Adam Smith, *The Wealth of Nations*	**1776:** *Declaration of Independence*	
1780–1790: Reign of Joseph II in Austria **1781:** Kant, *Critique of Pure Reason* **1784:** Beaumarchais, *The Marriage of Figaro* **1789:** Beginning of French Revolution	**1781:** Siege of Yorktown **1783:** Treaty of Paris **1787:** *Federalist Papers;* Constitution ratified **1789:** Inauguration of George Washington as first president	**1781:** Mozart arrives in Vienna **1785–1786:** Haydn, *Paris* Symphonies **1786:** Mozart, *The Marriage of Figaro* and Piano Concerto, K. 488
1790: Burke, *Reflections on the Revolution in France* **1792:** Wollstonecraft, *Vindication of the Rights of Women* **1792–1804:** First French Republic **1793:** Louis XVI executed **1793–1794:** Reign of Terror in France **1795–1799:** Directory in France; rise of Napoleon **1799–1804:** Consulate in France	**1791–1792:** Thomas Paine, *Rights of Man* **1794–1796:** Paine, *Age of Reason*	**1791:** Mozart, *Magic Flute* and *Requiem;* death of Mozart **1791–1792, 1794–1795:** Haydn in England, *London* Symphonies **1792:** Beethoven arrives in Vienna **1797:** Haydn, String Quartets, Op. 76 **1798:** Haydn, *The Creation*
1804: Napoleon proclaimed emperor		**1801:** Beethoven, *Moonlight* Sonata **1803:** Beethoven, Third Symphony (*Eroica*) **1808:** Beethoven, Fifth Symphony, Sixth Symphony (*Pastoral*) **1809:** Death of Haydn
1812: Napoleon invades Russia **1814–1815:** Congress of Vienna **1815:** Battle of Waterloo		**1825:** Beethoven, String Quartet, Op. 132 **1827:** Death of Beethoven

BACKGROUND FOR THE CLASSICAL PERIOD

"*What* is Enlightenment?" the philosopher Immanuel Kant asked in 1784. For him, the enlightened person was a confident youth coming of age, emerging from immaturity with a new self-reliance and an insatiable curiosity about the world around him. Much of the eighteenth century was indeed an Age of Enlightenment, an Age of Reason, a time when many thoughtful men and women rejected what they regarded as religious superstitions, preferring instead to set their faith in reason and knowledge.

Kant preached the new secular faith with a motto borrowed from Horace: *Sapere aude,* "Dare to know." The philosopher John Locke had already declared that knowledge existed only in the objective world and that the mind was a blank page ready to be filled with the impressions of experience. David Hume dared to doubt even causality—the principle of cause and effect—on which, it had been thought for centuries, the very universe depended. Scholars throughout Europe strove to codify knowledge and to determine its limits: The Swedish scientist Carolus Linnaeus devised a bold new botanical classification, Samuel Johnson produced a dictionary of the English language that ran to two thousand pages, and in France, Denis Diderot labored for years over the massive *Encyclopédie,* a vast storehouse of modern thought.

Could this vigorous spirit of inquiry renew political institutions and the quality of life as well? Many rulers thought so, including the "enlightened" monarchs Frederick the Great of Prussia (reigned 1740–1786), Joseph II of Austria (reigned 1780–1790), Gustave III of Sweden (reigned 1771–1792), and Catherine the Great of Russia (reigned 1762–1796). Americans set down the rights of ordinary citizens—not monarchs—in the *Declaration of Independence* (1776), a carefully reasoned document that drew on the political thought of John Locke. A few years later, Crèvecoeur, a French immigrant to the new republic, described the new American man in glowing terms: "*He* is an American, who leaving behind him all his ancient prejudices and manners, receives new ones from the new mode of life he has embraced, the new government he obeys, and the new rank he holds." The Marquis de Condorcet, even while imprisoned in the Bastille, predicted that mankind would eventually achieve perfection.

In their search for that perfection, many eighteenth-century thinkers and writers turned with renewed fervor to classical antiquity—a symbol of an earlier golden age of mankind. The models of ancient Greece and Rome proved irresistible to eighteenth-century Europe. About the middle of the century, French taste inclined *à la grecque.* The German art historian Johann Winckelmann found Greek statuary to possess a "noble simplicity and silent grandeur," attributes, he hinted, that contemporary artists would do well to emulate. The recovery of ancient artifacts and artworks at Herculaneum and Pompeii kindled new interest in the art of the Romans as well, and the Italian antiquarian Giovanni Battista Piranesi countered Winckelmann's hellenistic leanings by pointing to the ancient Roman roadways and aqueducts as monuments of engineering.

Architects and painters eagerly took up Graeco-Roman themes. Architects modeled numerous buildings on ancient temples, with their balanced proportions, symmetrical columns, clean lines, and simple shapes. The state capitol in Richmond, Virginia, finished in 1792, is a noteworthy American example.

Virginia State Capitol. Designed by Thomas Jefferson in imitation of a Roman temple in Nîmes, the Capitol building in Richmond was built between 1785 and 1792. For Jefferson and many of his contemporaries, the classical temple represented the glory of the Roman Republic and seemed a suitable symbol of the young American Republic.

In this classical revival (often termed **neoclassicism** in art history), painters turned to the grand themes of ancient history. They went beyond mere imitations of Roman and Greek art, however. Like the philosophers of the eighteenth century, they were more interested in the moral quality of life in ancient Greece and Rome than they were in the trappings of antiquity. Thus, in the painting *Lictors Bringing Back to Brutus the Bodies of His Sons,* the French painter Jacques-Louis David (1748–1825) sought to exemplify the civic virtue of the Roman consul Lucius Junius Brutus, who condemned his own sons to death for plotting against the Republic.

The influence of the ancients continued strong well into the eighteenth century. The neoclassic poet Alexander Pope (1688–1744), for example, translated Homer into English and composed pastorals in the manner of Virgil and odes and satires in the manner of Horace and other Roman poets. Pope had ready advice for the would-be critic: "*You* then whose Judgment the right Course wou'd steer, / Know well each ANCIENT'S proper *Character,* / his *Fable, Subject, Scope* in ev'ry Page, / *Religion, Country, Genius* of his *Age:* / Without all these at once before your Eyes, / *Cavil* you may, but never *Criticize.*"

It is more difficult to document the specific effects of the classical revival of the eighteenth century on music. We commonly refer to the mature music of Haydn and Mozart as "classical" and to the latter decades of the eighteenth century as the "Classical

Jacques-Louis David, *Lictors Bringing Back to Brutus the Bodies of His Sons,* exhibited in 1789. For the subject of this neoclassical painting, David chose an incident from the early days of the Roman Republic recounted by the Roman historian Livy. Lucius Junius Brutus, one of the first consuls of the Republic (usually dated from 509 B.C.), having discovered that his sons had taken part in a conspiracy, condemned them to death. Brutus appears before the statue of *Roma,* symbol of the Republic, as the lictors carry in the bodies of his sons. David reflects Brutus's stern moral conviction in the massive Doric columns, austere and unornamented.

Period." Unlike the architects, however, who could imitate ancient temples in their designs, or the poets, who could imitate the epic poems of antiquity, composers had no comparable models. Indeed, they knew very little about ancient Greek and Roman music, nor do we know much about it today. Consequently, some historians argue that the idea of classicism has little to do with eighteenth-century music and should not be used in referring to it.

Still, the term *classical* is useful when we are considering the music of the latter part of the eighteenth century, so long as we are aware of its limitations. The music of Haydn, Mozart, and their contemporaries, though in no way imitative of antique models, does evidence the characteristics of classical art—poise, balance, mastery of form, and delight in beauty. We can interpret this new emphasis on balance and clarity as a reaction

THE CLASSICAL PERIOD   155

against the highly ornate style of the baroque and quite in keeping with the intellectual tenor of the Enlightenment.

There is another reason why *classical* is an appropriate term to describe the music of the latter part of the eighteenth century. In the nineteenth century, composers began to view the music of Haydn and Mozart (and eventually Beethoven) as timeless, exemplary works of art that could serve as models, just as the artworks of antiquity had for the eighteenth century. The music of these Viennese masters came to represent a classical canon of masterpieces against which composers measured their own progress, and from which they ultimately struggled to assert their independence.

6

MUSIC IN THE CLASSICAL PERIOD

*H*aydn and Mozart were the luminaries of the new classicism in music, but many other eighteenth-century composers contributed to the evolution of its style. The lines between historical periods are never sharply drawn, and the forces of change were already at work well before Haydn and Mozart began their careers. By mid-century, many composers were turning more and more away from the "gratuitous" complexity of the high baroque to music that, if less artful, was more immediately appealing. Instead of overwhelming listeners with ornately fashioned lines and passages fortified with counterpoint, they wrote agreeable, pleasant music that made less-strenuous demands on the audience.

The trend toward accessibility was strengthened by the rise of a new musical public. Most composers still depended on the patronage of the royal courts, but they also responded to the tastes of the musical public. Public concerts were established in the leading cities, and music publishers began to cater to the new market of musical amateurs that was emerging among the members of the prosperous middle class.

The transition from the high baroque to what became the classical style took place, roughly, between 1730 and 1775. During the last decades of the century, Haydn and Mozart brilliantly articulated the classical style, and in the early nineteenth century, Beethoven tested its limits with unprecedented vigor. Because the work of these three composers was so fundamental to the musical life of Vienna, this period is often referred to as the age of *Viennese Classicism*. Before we turn to their music, we must first explore the elements of the classical style they perfected.

MELODY IN CLASSICAL MUSIC

Baroque composers had preferred florid melodies that ran on measure after measure with little or no pause. The opening of Bach's *Brandenburg Concerto* No. 5, of the third movement of Bach's cantata *Wachet auf,* and of Vivaldi's Concerto grosso, Op. 3, No. 8, are three examples we have studied that bear out this observation (see pp. 119, 128, and 99). Classical composers, by contrast, favored melodies in short, balanced phrases. Consider, for example, the opening theme from a piano sonata by Mozart, composed in 1788:

Mozart: Sonata in C major (K.★ 545), First Movement

★ The K stands for Köchel, the nineteenth-century scholar who cataloged Mozart's compositions.

The structure of this melody is straightforward: Two rests, one in bar 2 and one in bar 4, divide the four-measure whole cleanly into two halves. Mozart emphasizes the symmetry by making the rhythmic values of bars 1 and 3 identical, and those of 2 and 4 nearly so. (Compare this melody with the Bach allemande melody on p. 73, with its generous series of undifferentiated note values.)

By balancing the parts of their melodies, classical composers achieved a certain poise and clarity of structure; and by varying the lengths of the parts, they could construct melodies with different degrees of complexity. For example, they might divide a melody of sixteen measures into halves, and then repeat each half. Here is the first half of such a melody, from Haydn's celebrated *Surprise* Symphony (No. 94) of 1791 for orchestra:

Haydn: Symphony No. 94 (Surprise), Second Movement

"Repeat" of melody

At first, this melody might sound tediously symmetrical, although, as we shall see, Haydn had a reason for making it sound that way. The first eight measures fall into pairs according to the basic rhythmic pattern |♫♫♩ | ♫ ♩ ♩ |, which begins anew in bars 3, 5, and 7. To reinforce this division, Haydn introduces the term *ten.,* or **tenuto,** at the end of bars 2, 4, and 6. *Tenuto* means "held," in contrast to the **staccato** markings (which mean "detached") elsewhere in the theme (shown by the dots below the note heads). Finally, to emphasize the two-measure divisions even further, Haydn reverses the direction of the melody. Measures 1 and 2 tend to ascend; measures 3 and 4 descend; measures 5 and 6 tend to ascend; and measures 7 and 8 descend. This simple melody has an even simpler bass accompaniment, consisting, for the most part, of one note per measure.

In bar 9, Haydn begins to repeat the melody. The second statement is played *pianissimo* (very softly), and the strings of the orchestra are instructed to pluck out their parts (in a technique known as **pizzicato**). Nothing disrupts Haydn's restraint until the sudden, orchestral crunch at the end—Haydn's surprise.★ Here, the orchestra interjects a *fortissimo* (very loud) chord, with the string players instructed to bow (**arco**) rather than pluck.

This staid melody is an extreme example of the classical style; we might say that Haydn overstates the melodic symmetry in order to make a musical joke. If we simply count out the measures and their rhythmic divisions, we get this rather regular scheme:

$$16$$
$$8 \quad + \quad 8$$
$$2+2+2+2 \; + \; 2+2+2+2$$

But if we take into account the dynamics markings—which unavoidably affect how we hear the music—we get something else:

$$16$$
$$8 \quad + \quad 7\frac{1}{2} \quad + \quad \frac{1}{2}$$
$$p \qquad pp \qquad \textit{ff}$$

★Haydn did not call his symphony the "Surprise"; that nickname came later.

MUSIC IN THE CLASSICAL PERIOD 159

Thus, Haydn's dynamics momentarily upset the studied symmetry of the melody.

Many classical melodies consist of symmetrical subdivisions that add up to larger symmetrical groupings, almost as though the composers were counting out the measures according to a rigorously planned, periodic phrase structure. That is not exactly what they were doing, however. After all, Haydn inserted his *fortissimo* chord because he wanted to *disrupt* the pattern. Rather, classical composers organized their melodies into recognizable sections to give them a clear audible structure, much as a skillful writer uses conjunctions and clauses to reveal the structure of a lengthy, complex sentence.

DYNAMICS IN CLASSICAL MUSIC

Another way in which classical composers punctuated or coordinated the sections of a theme or a movement was by altering the dynamics. For example, they might begin a twelve-bar melody *forte* for four measures, then continue *piano* for the next four, and finally return to the *forte* level for the last four. In a way, this use of contrasting dynamics was a throwback to the terraced dynamics of the baroque, in which composers sustained levels of sound in blocklike fashion. But classical composers shifted the dynamics level more frequently, and they worked with a broader range of gradations than had their baroque predecessors.

About the middle of the eighteenth century, two special techniques for treating dynamics came into favor: the **crescendo**★ (a gradual decrease in dynamics level) and the **decrescendo** (a gradual decrease in dynamics level; sometimes referred to as **diminuendo**). In modern scores, these effects are often represented by wedge-shaped notational signs:

$$\diagdown\!\diagup \qquad \diagup\!\diagdown$$

Composers of orchestral music found the crescendo especially attractive. In particular, the orchestra of the Palatine court in Mannheim (in southern Germany) became noted for its skillful handling of coordinated swells in dynamics. Composers writing in the so-called Mannheim style often opened their compositions with sensational, attention-grabbing crescendos, a practice that was soon widely imitated.

The appeal of these techniques was strengthened by the popularity of a new keyboard instrument known as the *fortepiano* (literally, "loud-soft"), the forerunner of the modern piano, which began to replace the harpsichord during the 1770s (see p. 227). The harpsichord, because its strings were plucked evenly, produced sounds at fixed levels of dynamics. But the fortepiano could produce fine shades of loud and soft sound by means of a hammerlike mechanism that struck and rebounded from the strings. A

★ From the Latin *crescere,* to "increase" (as in the "crescent moon").

firm pressure on the keys produced a loud sound; a more delicate touch, a softer sound. Amateurs and connoisseurs alike could create dramatic crescendos and diminuendos on the fortepiano.

The harpsichord did not become outdated for some time, however. Haydn still conducted his late symphonies of the 1790s from the harpsichord, and, for a while in the nineteenth century, it continued to be used in Italian operas. Nevertheless, classical composers of keyboard music, eager to exploit the sonorous richness of the fortepiano, were drawn more and more to the new instrument. Some began to explore a wide range of dynamics by entering such markings as *pianissimo (pp)* and *fortissimo (ff)* into their scores. The boldest of all was Beethoven. Here is an example from his famous *Pathétique* Sonata, probably composed near the end of the eighteenth century:

Beethoven: Piano Sonata in C minor, Op. 13 (Pathétique), *First Movement*

Beethoven achieves a powerful effect by traversing, through a crescendo, a broad spectrum of dynamics, from *pianissimo* to *fortissimo*. To intensify the effect, he calls for a sudden accent, known as a **sforzando (sf)** in the middle of bar 4. All these notations support the tempo marking, "Very fast and with fire."

RHYTHM IN CLASSICAL MUSIC

Classical composers varied their treatment of rhythm as they did their application of dynamics levels. For example, they might establish one or two types of rhythms for several measures and then shift to a contrasting pattern. A representative example is the opening of Mozart's Piano Sonata in A minor (1778):

Mozart: Piano Sonata in A minor, K. 310, First Movement

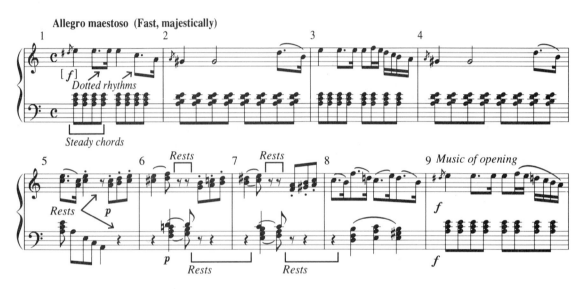

This passage begins with two basic rhythmic ideas: a majestic (*maestoso*) melody with dotted rhythms in the treble part (♩♪♫) and a steady series of eighth-note chords in the bass part (♫♫). This juxtaposition continues through bar 4. Then, in bars 5–7, Mozart abruptly breaks the melody with rests. Finally, in bar 9, he reverts to the dotted melody and chords of the opening bars. Note how he marks off the rhythmic changes by means of changes in dynamics: *piano* (m. 5) and *forte* (m. 9). Such rhythmic diversity contrasts sharply with the rhythmic uniformity of the late baroque.

TEXTURE AND HARMONY IN CLASSICAL MUSIC

By and large, the texture of classical music is more homophonic than the texture of baroque music. Innumerable compositions of Haydn and Mozart, for example, have a clearly projected melody set against a harmonic underpinning of simple chords, creating a transparent musical texture. To be sure, classical composers did not avoid contrapuntal textures altogether; yet, they tended to reserve the strict forms of counterpoint, such as fugue or canon, for special, even exceptional, effects. And they generally avoided the extravagant contrapuntal elaboration cultivated during the late baroque.

Moreover, they typically changed their harmonies less frequently than did baroque composers. Sometimes, classical composers went out of their way to use just a few types of chords, as if attempting to reinforce the harmonic clarity and stability of their music. Consider, for example, a passage from the second movement of Haydn's Symphony No. 101 (1794), which presents a graceful melody in the treble (upper staff) against an accompaniment of chords (lower staff):

Haydn: Symphony No. 101 (Clock), *Second Movement*

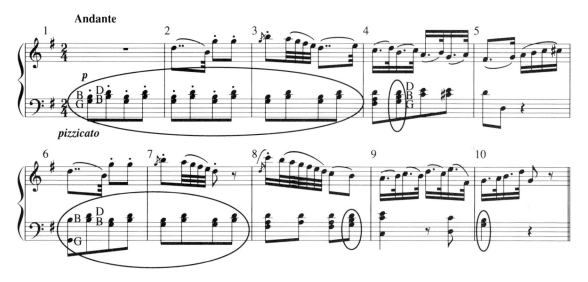

All the circled notes in the lower staff belong to the same harmony (in this case, the harmony is based on the G major triad, with pitches G, B, and D). There are changes in the harmony only in bars 4, 5, 8, and 9. (Because of this harmonic sturdiness, and the steady "tick-tock" of the bass, the symphony came to be known as *The Clock*.)

In their selection of keys, classical composers also tended toward a simplification of means. As a general rule, they found major keys more attractive than minor keys. Less than 10 percent of Haydn's hundred-odd symphonies are in minor keys, and only two of Mozart's two dozen or so piano concertos. Baroque composers had associated minor keys with strong emotions; classical composers favored the brighter major keys, perhaps with an ear to the popular demand for music pleasant to play and enjoyable to hear.

GENRES AND FORMS IN CLASSICAL MUSIC

Three new instrumental genres—the symphony, the string quartet, and the classical sonata—epitomized the various features of the classical style we have been describing. The **symphony** was a grand instrumental work that dramatically displayed the sonorities and colors of the modern eighteenth-century orchestra. The **string quartet** emerged as the exemplary type of **chamber music,** that is, instrumental music written for small groups of performers. Intended for intimate settings, string quartets were written for two violins, one viola, and one cello. Finally, the classical **sonata,** which evolved from baroque predecessors, was a work that typically featured one or two instruments and usually included a piano. Piano sonatas, the most common type, were written for piano solo; ensemble sonatas were often written for piano and another instrument.

Nearly all the instrumental genres of this period—from the symphony to the keyboard sonata—consisted of independent movements of contrasting tempo and mood. One common sequence consisted of three movements: a fast movement, a slow movement, and a very fast finale. By adding a stylized dance movement known as a minuet and trio, either before or (more commonly) after the slow movement, composers extended the sequence to four movements: for example, fast–slow–minuet and trio–very fast. These three- and four-movement sequences became the standard paradigms of classical instrumental music.

Classical composers built the movements of their sonatas, string quartets, and symphonies from several structural blueprints, or forms. The most significant classical form came to be known as **sonata form** (or **sonata-allegro form**). Before we go on, we must clarify the difference between *sonata* and *sonata form,* since the terms easily cause confusion. *Sonata* refers to an entire multimovement instrumental composition; thus, we speak of Beethoven's *Pathétique* Sonata for piano in three movements. *Sonata form* refers only to a specific form used in one, several, or sometimes all of the movements of a single composition, be it a sonata, a string quartet, a symphony, or some other instrumental type.

Most frequently, sonata form appears in the first movement or in the finale of a sonata, a chamber piece, or a symphony, although a simplified version of sonata form

Classical Instrumental Music: Typical Four-Movement Plan

Movement	*Typical Tempo*	*Form(s) Used*
First movement	Fast	Sonata form
Second movement	Slow or Very slow	Simplified sonata form, theme and variations, or rondo
Third movement	Moderate	Ternary dance form (Minuet and Trio)
Fourth movement	Very fast	Sonata form, rondo, or hybrid of the two

may appear in the slow movement. In addition to sonata form, composers relied on other forms in their instrumental compositions. Among the most common are **theme-and-variations** form, typically in the slow movement; **ternary dance** form, typically in the minuet and trio; and **rondo** form, typically in the finale. The diagram summarizes the common applications of these forms in classical music.

SONATA FORM

Sonata form became the most prevalent instrumental form in classical music—indeed, one of the most prevalent in music since the eighteenth century. For over two hundred years, the term has inspired numerous attempts at definition. The form itself has been put to different uses over the years, for composers have reserved the right to interpret it in various ways. In the eighteenth century, composers used sonata form to establish a tension between a tonic and a second key and then to resolve that tension in favor of the tonic key. Tonal tension balanced by tonal resolution might be taken as the fundamental concept behind sonata form as construed by the classical masters.

At the middle of the eighteenth century, sonata form was a fairly uncomplicated form. It consisted of two main sections, each of which was repeated. The first section presented material in two keys. If the movement was in a major key, the two keys were the tonic major and the dominant major; if the movement was in a minor key, the two keys were the tonic minor and, usually, the key on the third pitch of the scale, the mediant. To take one brief example, if the composition was in C major, the first section included material in the key of C major (the tonic) and in the key of G major (the dominant); if the composition was in A minor, the first section included material in the key of A minor (the tonic) and in the key of C major (the mediant).

Binary Sonata Form

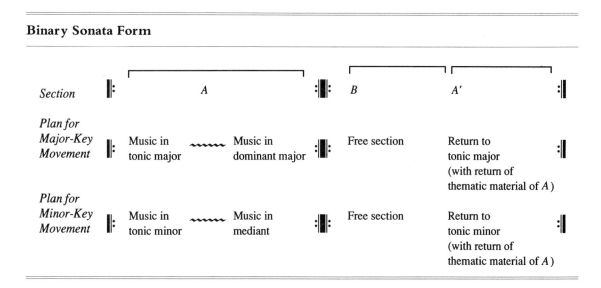

Ternary Sonata Form

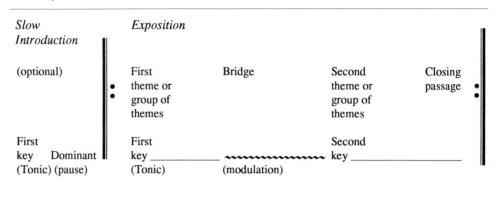

Slow Introduction

(optional)	First theme or group of themes	Bridge	Second theme or group of themes	Closing passage	

First key Dominant
(Tonic) (pause)

First key _____ ⟿ Second key _____
(Tonic)   (modulation)

Given this key plan, the composer might choose to limit the thematic material for the first section, perhaps presenting and re-presenting just one thematic idea. Or the composer might present several thematic ideas arranged in groups of themes. In either case, the thematic material of this first section (which we will label *A*) was organized into two keys to provide strong tonal contrast.

The second section was approximately the same length as the first. Its main purpose was to return to and reaffirm the tonic key, thereby resolving the tonal contrast. Sometimes, the tonic key was restated near the beginning of the second section. More often, however, the restatement came after a free, tonally unstable passage of several measures (*B*) that might wander through keys other than the tonic. The return of the tonic key usually coincided with the reappearance of thematic material from the first part of *A*. The remainder of the movement often continued to reuse material from *A*, though that material now required some modification to keep the music in the tonic key. To reflect such modifications, we label the section starting with the return of the tonic key as *A'*. The accompanying diagram (p. 165) summarizes the basic design of early sonata form, or **binary sonata form:** ‖: *A* :‖: *B A'* :‖.

From this simple binary scheme, sonata form gradually took on a remarkable sophistication. Composers still adhered to the basic design, but they began to expand the dimensions of the form and to delineate its contents more clearly and dramatically. Not only did they move to a new key in the second part of the *A* section; they sometimes also introduced a strikingly new theme (or group of themes) with the new key. Often, this secondary thematic material was gentler in character than the opening, vigorous material, heightening the contrast between the two. A **bridge,** to provide the modulation between the two keys, connected the two parts of the first section. Finally, a **closing passage,** which often consisted of a few incisive measures of chords clinching the second key, rounded out the *A* section.

The *A* section thus came to comprise four more or less distinct parts: a theme or a group of themes in the tonic key; a bridge modulating to the second key, a theme or a group of themes in the second key, and a closing passage in the second key. This much

Ternary Sonata Form, *Continued*

Development		*Recapitulation*				*Coda*
*					*	
Material from exposition developed	Retransition (preparation for return of tonic)	First theme or group of themes	Transition (based on Bridge)	Second theme or group of themes	Closing passage	(optional)
Modulations through various keys	~~~~~~~~	First key _____ (Tonic)				~~~ First key (Tonic)

* Repeat sometimes omitted.

of sonata form is called the **exposition,** because it presents or "exposes" the basic thematic materials of the movement and establishes its tonal polarity of two keys.

The *B* section of sonata form underwent an even greater transformation. Composers began to postpone the return to the tonic key (*A'*), thereby giving greater emphasis to the music of *B* that led up to that return. They used the *B* section to explore a loose succession of keys other than the two keys already introduced in the exposition. In addition, they used the *B* section to fragment, extend, revise, or develop in some other way the themes from the exposition. The *B* section, which came to be called the **development,** was far less structured than the exposition. As it meandered from key to key, it added to the tonal tension already established in the exposition; it also delayed the return of the tonic key, prepared by a passage known as a **retransition.**

The return of that key marked the dramatic highpoint of the movement—the **recapitulation,** or **reprise.** Serving as a balance to the exposition, the recapitulation reestablished the supremacy of the tonic key and resolved the tonal conflict of the exposition and the tonal ambiguity of the development in favor of the tonic key. The recapitulation also reintroduced the thematic materials of the exposition, either exactly or somewhat reordered.

The older binary sonata form thus evolved into a three-part structure consisting of an exposition, a development, and a recapitulation. Although the traditional repeats of the older binary form survived for a time, the second section (which now contained two substantial portions, the development and the recapitulation) ultimately grew to such proportions that its repeat was no longer feasible.

Finally, during the last quarter of the eighteenth century, composers expanded this three-part structure (later known as **ternary sonata form**) by adding two optional sections: a stately **slow introduction** before the exposition, and a concluding section called the **coda** (from the Italian word for "tail") at the end of the movement (see the diagram). The purpose of the slow introduction was to prepare the listener for a full-length, sonata-form movement. At its simplest, it consisted of just a few chords, or a few scraps of thematic material in no particularly structured fashion, before an arrival

Beethoven: Sonata in F minor, Op. 2, No. 1, First Movement

Exposition *(A)*

First theme *(a)*	pause	Bridge based on *a*	Second theme *(b)*	Closing passage *(c)*
First key _____ (tonic minor)		Modulation to 〰〰〰〰〰	Second key _____ (mediant)	

and pause on the dominant harmony. A slow introduction made its effect by arousing the listener's expectations, subsequently to be fulfilled or defeated in the course of the movement proper. At the other end of the sonata form, the coda gave the composer an opportunity to sum up the movement. At its simplest, a coda consisted of a few, definitive chords. More elaborate codas could include dramatic excursions before the final, unmistakable assertion of the tonic harmony. These two additions, the slow introduction and the coda, further reinforced the tonal tension and resolution, the thematic development and restatement, and the formal symmetry that are the hallmarks of classical instrumental music.

BEETHOVEN: SONATA IN F MINOR, OP. 2, NO. 1, FIRST MOVEMENT

A characteristic example of classical sonata form is the first movement of Beethoven's early Piano Sonata, Op. 2, No. 1, completed by 1795 and dedicated to Haydn. The study guide identifies its principal thematic elements and formal features.

This movement clearly shows the grafting of ternary sonata form onto the older binary sonata form. The two main sections of the movement are repeated. The exposition (*A*) contains forty-eight bars, the development (*B*) fifty-two bars, and the recapitulation (*A'*) fifty-two bars. So, the three parts are more or less equal:

A	*B*	*A'*
Exposition	Development	Recapitulation
48 bars	52 bars	52 bars

Exposition Beethoven launches the movement with a theme that moves by ascending staccato leaps before it executes a compact turnlike figure (*a*). The bass part enters in bar 2 with some simple chords to support this theme. But the momentum is soon checked by an unexpected pause. Next, Beethoven writes a bridge passage, drawn from

Beethoven: Sonata in F minor, Op. 2, No. 1, First Movement, *Continued*

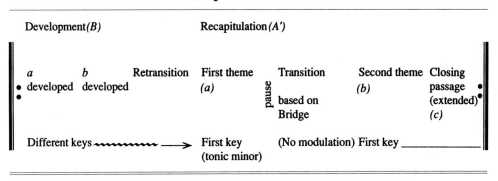

Development *(B)*			Recapitulation *(A')*			
a	*b*	Retransition	First theme	Transition	Second theme	Closing
developed	developed		*(a)*		*(b)*	passage
				based on		(extended)
				Bridge		*(c)*
Different keys ⟿ ⟶			First key (tonic minor)	(No modulation) First key _____		

Beethoven: Sonata in F minor, Op. 2, No. 1, First Movement

FIRST THEME (A)

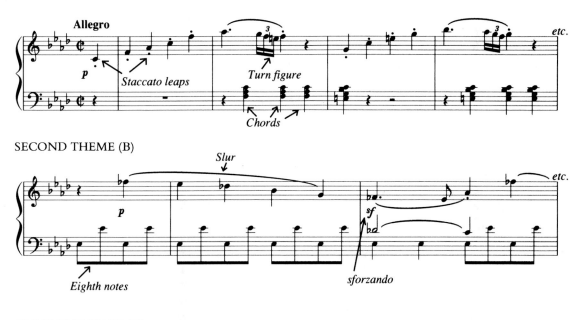

SECOND THEME (B)

CLOSING PASSAGE (C)

the first theme, that prepares, via a modulation, for the entry of the second theme (*b*) in the second key. To contrast with the detached, ascending skips of the first theme, he has the second theme describe a descending contour, performed in a smooth style known as **legato** (indicated by the curve, or **slur,** above the notes), in which the pianist takes care to play the pitches as if they were connected. At the bottom of the descent, Beethoven places an unexpected—and unsettling—accent (*sf*). As the second theme unfolds, the bass advances with restless eighth notes (♪♪♪♪) impelling the music forward and adding rhythmic momentum to the appearance of the new key.

The closing passage (*c*) of the exposition is marked *con espressione,* "with expression." Here rhythmic activity subsides, as we hear an expressive melodic gesture in the upper part that reaches a cadence strongly in the second key. (Note again Beethoven's use of the *sforzando* to accentuate the passage.) The reappearance of chords in the bass reinforces the second key and prepares the way for the repeat of the exposition.

Development In the development, Beethoven reworks the thematic material of the exposition. He begins by presenting the first theme (*a*) in the second key. Soon he abandons it to take up the second theme (*b*); this is now developed extensively through a succession of keys and at one point is introduced in the bass part. The final portion of the development initiates the return to the tonic key. Here again the rhythmic energy of the music abates, and we hear the turn figure from the first theme—at first *pianissimo* but then louder and louder as we approach the recapitulation.

Recapitulation Modeled almost measure for measure on the exposition, the recapitulation announces the return of the tonic key and retraces the events of the exposition in the same order. There are some crucial changes in the recapitulation, however. Since the tonic key is now affirmed as the ultimate tonal goal of the movement, there is no need for a modulation; thus, the transition, the counterpart to the bridge section, does not modulate, and the second theme and closing material stay in the tonic key. At the very end of the movement, Beethoven presents some *fortissimo* chords to reaffirm the principal key once again. Straightforward in design, this compact movement illustrates effectively the workings of classical sonata form.

We now turn to the other forms often used by classical composers in their instrumental music: theme-and-variations form, ternary dance form, and rondo form. Like sonata form, these forms commonly appear in the movements of sonatas, string quartets, symphonies, and other instrumental compositions.

THEME-AND-VARIATIONS FORM

Much of the appeal of classical music comes from its tuneful elegance. In a type of composition known as theme and variations, composers turned that elegance to great advantage. They selected especially memorable themes, either of their own invention or borrowed, for treatment in a series of variations. In a typical classical arrangement, the theme appears first, with a simple harmonic accompaniment; then, the composer subjects the theme to a series of variations:

Theme / Variation 1 / Variation 2 / Variation 3 . . .

Mozart: Sonata in A major for Piano (K. 331), Theme-and-Variations Movement

Theme	Variation 1	2	3	4	5	6	
‖: ▦ :‖	‖: ▦ :‖	‖: ▦ :‖	‖: ▦ :‖	‖: ▦ :‖	‖: ▦ :‖	‖: ▦ :‖	Coda
Time signature	Sixteenth notes	Triplets	Minor key	Hand crossings	Adagio (slow)	Allegro (fast)	
$\frac{6}{8}$	(♪♫)	(♪♫♫)				$\frac{4}{4}$	
	Internal variation						
p	*p f*	*p f*	*p f*	*p f*	*p f*	*p f f*	

Often, the composition ends with a culminating final variation or, more simply, with a repetition of the original theme, giving the composition a rounded symmetry.

Themes appropriated for classical variations generally exhibited clear-cut phrase structures. A typical theme was in two balanced parts, with each repeated. Each part, in turn, divided into shorter phrases. Finally, the accompaniment supporting the theme was distinguished by clearly articulated cadences and by an uncomplicated harmonic plan. The theme that Haydn used in the second movement of his *Surprise* Symphony, a theme-and-variations movement, is a good example (see p. 158).

In the variations that followed the theme, the composer might alter different features, such as its rhythm, meter, tempo, key, accompaniment, or some of its melodic details. Still, composers were usually careful to respect the integrity of the theme; its basic contours, phrase structure, and harmonic plan were generally left intact.

MOZART: PIANO SONATA IN A MAJOR, K. 331, FIRST MOVEMENT

Here is a portion of an original theme on which Mozart wrote six variations. Eight measures in length, the portion divides into two similar four-measure phrases; Mozart underscores the symmetry of the theme by having the second phrase (mm. 5–8) begin like the first (mm. 1–4):

Mozart: Piano Sonata in A major, K. 331, First Movement

This gracious, simple theme, with its lilting long–short pulse in $\frac{6}{8}$ time (♩ ♪ ♩ ♪), inspired from Mozart a remarkable breadth of variation techniques (see the study diagram). One special technique actually involved devising a variation within a particular variation. In Variation 1, for example, Mozart begins by transforming the treble melody into a series of sixteenth notes (♫) interrupted by rests. But later in the same variation, this gentle, *piano* beginning gives way to a *forte* passage in which a more straightforward version of the theme is set against an insistent sixteenth-note accompaniment in the bass:

Mozart: Piano Sonata in A major, K. 331, First Movement

VARIATION 1

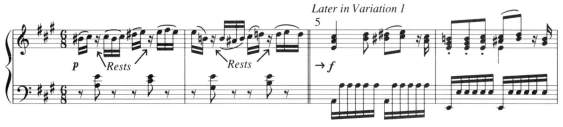

In other variations, Mozart employs faster triplets (♫♫) in the accompaniment (Variation 2), turns to the minor tonic key (Variation 3), and experiments with a passage that requires the pianist to cross left hand over right hand (Variation 4):

VARIATION 4

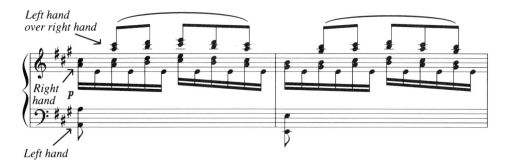

Variation 5 is a tender Adagio ("slow"), and, finally, Variation 6 is a brisk Allegro ("lively") in $\frac{4}{4}$ time. In this movement, Mozart thus varies the embellishment of the theme, its accompaniment, its key, its tempo, and its meter. But through all these imaginative modifications, he is careful to preserve enough of its basic outline and supporting harmonies so that the theme is never far removed from our musical awareness.

Minuet and Trio

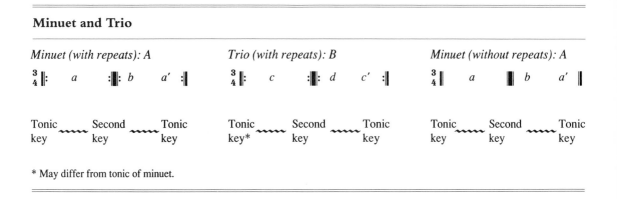

Minuet (with repeats): A	Trio (with repeats): B	Minuet (without repeats): A

* May differ from tonic of minuet.

TERNARY DANCE FORM

The preferred dance movement of the classical composers was the **minuet** (also known as **minuet and trio**). By the middle of the seventeenth century, the minuet was a fashionable dance practiced at the European royal courts. Stately and aristocratic, minuets were written in a moderate tempo with triple ($\frac{3}{4}$) meter. In the eighteenth century, composers continued to write minuets for dancing but also began to appropriate its form for instrumental music. By midcentury, stylized minuets were appearing in symphonies, string quartets, sonatas, and other instrumental music. There were two major sections in the classical minuet: the minuet proper (*A*) and the trio (*B*). Through the repetition of the minuet proper, the classical version came to assume an overall ternary, *ABA* shape.

The minuet proper (*A*) consisted of two sections, each of which was repeated. In time, classical composers expanded the second section to include a transitional passage (*b*) and a modified return (*a'*) to the music of the first section (*a*). In so doing, they transformed what had been a miniature binary form into a small-scale ternary form similar to sonata form (see the study diagram).

The trio (*B*) was essentially a second minuet. Its music usually contrasted with that of the minuet proper (*A*), and sometimes its key differed from that of the minuet proper. After the trio, the original minuet was repeated, this time, however, *without* its internal repeats. Quite often, composers employed the abbreviation *Da capo* to designate the second performance of the original minuet.

Haydn and Mozart wrote hundreds of minuets, expending great care on them (we shall have a closer look at one by Haydn in Chapter 7; see p. 190). Early in the nineteenth century, however, the popularity of the minuet began to wane.

RONDO FORM

The rondo, most frequently encountered in the finales of instrumental works, was a sectional movement organized around a recurring theme known as the **refrain** (*A*). The refrain provides the foundation of the movement: Typically in the tonic key, it stands as an independent section, often, in fact, as a small-scale binary form with repeats (‖: *a* :‖: *b a'* :‖). Other, contrasting sections, known as **episodes,** mark departures from the refrain and introduce new keys and new thematic material.

Composers devised various schemes for their rondos. Sometimes they simply alternated the refrain with a single episode (*ABABA*), and sometimes they devised more complex plans (for example, *ABACA, ABCBA,* or *ABACABA*). In the most elaborate version, they combined elements of the rondo form and the sonata form to produce a hybrid known as **sonata-rondo form.**

BEETHOVEN: PIANO SONATA IN C MINOR, OP. 13 (PATHÉTIQUE), THIRD MOVEMENT

The last movement of Beethoven's *Pathétique* Sonata, in C minor, is a rondo with an *ABACABA* plan—that is, the refrain (*A*) alternates with two episodes (*B* and *C*). Here are the principal themes for the *A, B,* and *C* sections:

Beethoven: Piano Sonata in C minor, Op. 13 (Pathétique)

A SECTION

B SECTION

C SECTION

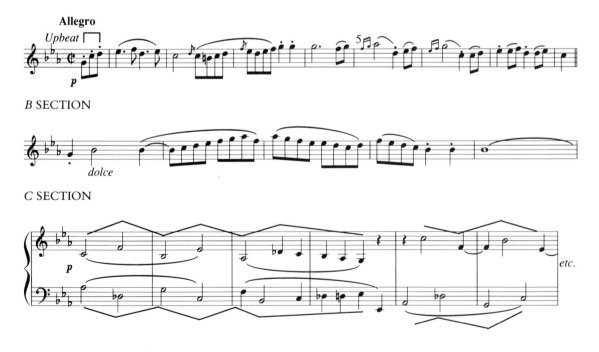

The *A* section is based on an arching theme that falls into two balanced phrases. The first, propelled by an upbeat, pauses on a high note in the fourth measure. The second phrase pushes the theme one pitch higher before gradually falling downward. In its four appearances throughout the movement, this basic theme remains in the tonic minor key. The *B* and *C* sections are contrasting episodes in major keys. *B* has a lyrical, flowing theme marked *dolce* ("sweetly"). *C* is set even further apart from the refrain by the use of longer rhythmic values and contrapuntal treatment that includes setting the theme against its rough mirror inversion. In all these sections, Beethoven emphasizes dramatically the passages leading toward and away from the refrain, the essential idea behind the rondo, perhaps the most accessible of the classical forms.

Suggested Listening

*Beethoven: Piano Sonata in C minor, Op. 13 (*Pathétique*)
*_____: Piano Sonata in F minor, Op. 2, No. 1
*Joseph Haydn: Symphony No. 94, in G major (*Surprise*)
_____: Symphony No. 101, in D major (*Clock*)
*Mozart: Piano Sonata in A major (K. 331)
_____: Piano Sonata in A minor (K. 310)
_____: Piano Sonata in C major (K. 545)

Sonata Form
Beethoven: Symphony No. 1, in C major, Op. 21, first movement
Haydn: Piano Sonata in E-flat major (Hob. XVI:52), first movement
Mozart: Symphony No. 40, in G minor (K. 550), first movement

Theme and Variations
Beethoven: Piano Sonata in G major, Op. 14, No. 2, second movement
Haydn: Symphony No. 94, in G major (*Surprise*), second movement
Mozart: String Quartet in D minor (K. 421), fourth movement

Minuet and Trio
Beethoven: Piano Sonata in F minor, Op. 2, No. 1, third movement
Haydn: Symphony No. 88, in G major, third movement
Mozart: Piano Sonata in A major (K. 331), second movement

Rondo
Beethoven: Piano Sonata in C major, Op. 53 (*Waldstein*), third movement
Haydn: String Quartet in E-flat major, Op. 33, No. 2 (*Joke*), fourth movement
Mozart: Piano Sonata in A major (K. 331, *Rondo alla turca*), third movement

---

Note: Works marked with an asterisk are the principal works discussed in the chapter.

7

JOSEPH HAYDN

*O*f all the eighteenth-century classical composers, the Austrian Joseph Haydn (1732–1809) enjoyed the widest acclaim in his own time. His vast catalog of works includes more than one hundred symphonies, and he probably wrote several others that have been lost. There are nearly seventy string quartets, a genre he was the first to master. There are numerous works for keyboard, among them some sixty-odd keyboard sonatas, and hundreds of chamber works for various scorings. His vocal music includes many operas (enjoying a revival in recent years), some oratorios (two of them, *The Creation* and *The Seasons,* still often performed), and several large-scale Masses.

So celebrated was Haydn's music that other musicians imitated it and unscrupulous publishers pirated it, taking quick profit by pawning off the work of lesser composers as the genuine article. The jumble of spurious music attributed to Haydn has created vexing problems for the modern scholar, especially because Haydn's music was so widely performed in many countries. He visited England twice, his symphonies soon reached the United States, his oratorios were performed in Russia, and he received commissions from France, Spain, and Italy. All the while, his compositions were being regularly performed in Vienna, London, and Paris.

Along with international fame, Haydn enjoyed longevity, and during his long career, he witnessed significant changes in musical style. As a boy, he was familiar with the music of the Austrian baroque, which, by the time he came of age, in the 1750s and 1760s, had given way to the lighter *galant* style. Over the next three decades, he did much to shape the classical style we described in Chapter 6. By the time Haydn died, in 1809, Beethoven had completed seven of his nine monumental symphonies, further extending the scope of the classical style. Because Haydn's music sweeps across

Joseph Haydn.

this spectrum of musical styles, an understanding of his music is essential to an understanding of the classical period itself.

Haydn was born in the southeastern part of Austria, near Hungary. In 1732 Austria, the German states, and many other territories constituted the Holy Roman Empire, still ruled by Habsburg monarchs, who traced their royal ancestry back to the tenth century.

As a child, Haydn sang in the choir of St. Stephen's Cathedral in Vienna. There he received instruction in singing and in playing the harpsichord and the violin. Dismissed from the choir when his voice changed, he earned a meager living for several years by giving music lessons. In composition, he was largely self-taught. He eagerly studied the latest keyboard music of C. P. E. Bach, the eldest son of J. S. Bach. He pored over the standard music treatise on music theory, the *Gradus ad Parnassum (Steps to Parnassus)*★ by Johann Joseph Fux (1660–1741), who had served as the imperial composer in Vienna. Published in Latin in 1725 and then widely translated, this treatise was organized as a dialogue between student and master. It offered systematic instruction and numerous exercises—all prepared and corrected under the master's watchful eye. Haydn's study of this primer prompted him to investigate traditional counterpoint in all its rigor and complexity.

★ Parnassus: a mountain in Greece that was the mythological abode of the nine Muses of the arts and a favorite haunt of Apollo, the god of the sun, poetry, and music.

In 1761 Haydn became the assistant music director at the court of Prince Paul Anton Esterházy, the head of a wealthy Hungarian family. Ennobled during the seventeenth century, the Esterházys owed their allegiance to the Austrian crown. We learn much about Haydn's responsibilities—and those of eighteenth-century court composers in general—from a document that set forth the terms of his appointment. The prince expected Haydn to comport himself in an upright manner and to encourage his musicians to follow his example. Haydn was to appear with his musicians on command, all wearing wigs and white stockings and linen. He was to compose music as ordered by the prince, in the quantity and type the prince desired, and for the prince's exclusive use. Haydn's duties did not end there. He was to serve as librarian for the music of the court orchestra and as caretaker of the musical instruments, and he was required to instruct female vocalists. In return, he received a salary and meals at the officers' table.

Haydn's patron, Paul Anton Esterházy, was succeeded in 1762 by his brother Nikolaus, known as "the Magnificent." In what is now Hungary, the new prince built a splendid palace called Eszterháza. Used at first during the summers, Eszterháza boasted an ornately furnished opera house for performances of Italian opera and German comedies.

Haydn served Prince Nikolaus for nearly thirty years (he became music director in 1766). During that long employment, he worked steadily on his symphonies, string quartets, and operas. He also produced much music for the baryton, a peculiar eighteenth-century string instrument, related to the viola da gamba family, that had an extra, freely resonating set of strings on the posterior side of its wide fingerboard. Haydn created a repertoire of hundreds of pieces featuring the baryton, which the prince played himself.

During these years, Haydn's reputation spread throughout Europe. Maria Theresa remarked in 1773 that in order to enjoy good opera she had to journey to Eszterháza. In the mid-1780s, Haydn received a commission to write six symphonies for a concert series in Paris (known as the *Paris* Symphonies, Nos. 82–87). In 1790 Johann Peter Salomon, an enterprising impresario and violinist, visited Haydn in Vienna and persuaded him to come to England to compose music for a public concert series. Haydn accepted and made two highly successful trips to England, where he was acclaimed in the press and was awarded an honorary degree by Oxford University. The fruits of the English period are the twelve grand *London* Symphonies (Nos. 93–104), the culmination of Haydn's symphonic style. Those symphonies were to provide models for Beethoven's early symphonies in the nineteenth century.

Haydn spent his last years in Vienna. Impressed by a gala commemorative performance of Handel's choral music he had heard in Westminster Abbey, Haydn himself turned to choral music after his return from England. He composed the masterful oratorios *The Creation* and *The Seasons,* which were performed first in Vienna and soon throughout Europe, and a magnificent series of Masses for soloists, chorus, and orchestra. Haydn died not long after the fall of Vienna to Napoleon's advancing armies. Fittingly, the Requiem of Haydn's great contemporary and friend, Mozart, was performed at his memorial service.

Haydn's long career embraced several stylistic periods. We focus on three, broadly defined as the early period, in which Haydn imitated the musical fashions of the time; the period of maturation, beginning during the late 1760s and lasting about a decade, in which he struck out on a bold new path in his instrumental music; and the long

Title page of one of Haydn's *London* Symphonies arranged as an "Overture" for piano solo with optional accompaniment of violin and cello. The signature of the impresario Salomon appears at the bottom of the page.

period of mastery, beginning roughly in the 1780s, in which he perfected the elements of the classical style.

HAYDN'S EARLY AND MIDDLE PERIODS

Haydn was comparatively slow to develop as a composer. His straitened circumstances during the early years in Vienna gave him little opportunity to advance his career. Although our knowledge about this early period is incomplete, we do know that he tried his hand at several types of music, ranging from church music to music for light comedies performed in Vienna, and including keyboard music of relatively simple levels of difficulty. Little of this early output has survived; what has is not particularly distinguished. Haydn appears to have worked competently in the idiom of the light *galant* style; the music was charming, but it gave little hint of what was to come.

The music Haydn wrote during his first few years at the Esterházy court gave considerably stronger evidence of his promise as a composer. Beginning in the 1760s, he became more experimental in his instrumental music, especially in his symphonies. He wrote symphonies in three and four movements, symphonies with different orders of contrasting movements, symphonies that borrow elements from such older genres as the trio sonata and the concerto, symphonies with scholarly displays of counterpoint—in short, he experimented with one approach after another as he sought to develop his own individual style.

The music of the late 1760s marked a turning point in Haydn's development. Now he was writing symphonies, string quartets, and other works with a strongly experimental bent: Sudden changes in texture, bizarre leaps in the melodic lines, abrupt pauses, and rhythmic clashes fill the pages of these extraordinary compositions. Several compositions dramatically explore minor keys, unusual at that time, but Haydn's new approach is also evident in his works in major keys. Here is a short example from one of the turbulent minor-key symphonies of these years. The jarring leaps in measures 1–3 and the syncopated, off beat rhythmic patterns (see p. 523) in measures 4–5 (♪ ♩ ♪) propel the upper part forward against a detached, running bass line:

Symphony No. 49 in F minor (1768), Second Movement

The most remarkable composition of this period is the *Farewell* Symphony (No. 45) of 1772, an experimental work of an unprecedented kind. Haydn had an ulterior purpose in mind when he wrote this symphony: His musicians had been away from their families for a long time and were eager to obtain a leave to return home. Haydn diplomatically presented their desire to the prince in musical terms. He planned the last movement of the symphony so that the members of the orchestra literally bade farewell as the movement progressed. About midway through the movement, the instruments begin to drop out; by the end of the movement, only two violins remain. As the story is told, the prince understood Haydn's message and granted the musicians their wish.

Haydn worked hard to refine his symphonic style during this period of experimentation. He once quipped that the isolation of the Esterházy court forced him to become original. Still, he was not, as he is often labeled, the father of the symphony. By the time he began to write symphonies, two basic types had already become established. The Italian symphony, or *sinfonia*, was a composition most often in three movements, characteristically in the sequence fast–slow–very fast. These pieces had originally served as overtures to Italian operas, but about the 1730s they began to be performed

The Early Classical Orchestra (ca. 1760)

Woodwinds	2 Oboes
Brass	2 Horns
Strings	Violin I
(several per part)	Violin II
	Viola
	Cello and Double Bass
	(Harpsichord used as continuo instrument)
Optional Instruments	Woodwinds: 1 or 2 Flutes, Bassoon (often doubles the bass line)
	Brass: 2 Trumpets
	Percussion: 2 Timpani (generally added with trumpets)

as separate instrumental works. Meanwhile, in Austria and Germany, composers were writing a second type of symphony: a symphony in four movements that included a minuet and trio. Haydn experimented with both types and eventually adopted the four-movement symphony as his favored type.

The orchestras that performed these early symphonies, much smaller than the symphonic orchestras we know today, typically comprised oboes and horns in pairs, and a group of strings (see the table). For an especially festive piece, Haydn enlarged his orchestra by adding two trumpets and two timpani or by adding some woodwinds, such as a flute or a bassoon. At Eszterháza, Haydn directed an ensemble of only twenty to twenty-five players, considerably closer in size to the ensembles at J. S. Bach's disposal (see pp. 118–119) than to a typical twentieth-century orchestra of about one hundred players.

There was no conductor in the modern sense—standing on a podium with a baton—to lead these eighteenth-century orchestras. Usually, the leader of the first violin section gave the musicians their cues. Haydn himself preferred to work from a harpsichord, playing the bass line with his left hand and improvising chords with his right hand according to the baroque figured bass tradition, while still managing to keep the orchestra under control.

The opening of the *Farewell* Symphony, presented here in a full modern score, is a good example of Haydn's typical orchestration from this time. The string parts appear on the bottom four staves, the oboes and the horns on the top two staves. The part for first violins carries the theme, another energetic theme marked by explosive, wide leaps. The bass part carries a forceful bass line of repeated notes. The second violins and the violas fill out the middle range of the string section, and the oboes and the horns contribute *forte* chords for harmonic support. In this dramatic opening, Haydn pits the sustained chords of the oboes and the horns against the agitated movement of the strings. (Notice how he manipulates the rhythmic structure to maximize this contrast: The notes played by the oboes and the horns are often held across the bar line, while the strings move quickly and vigorously in faster notes.)

Symphony No. 45 (Farewell), *First Movement*

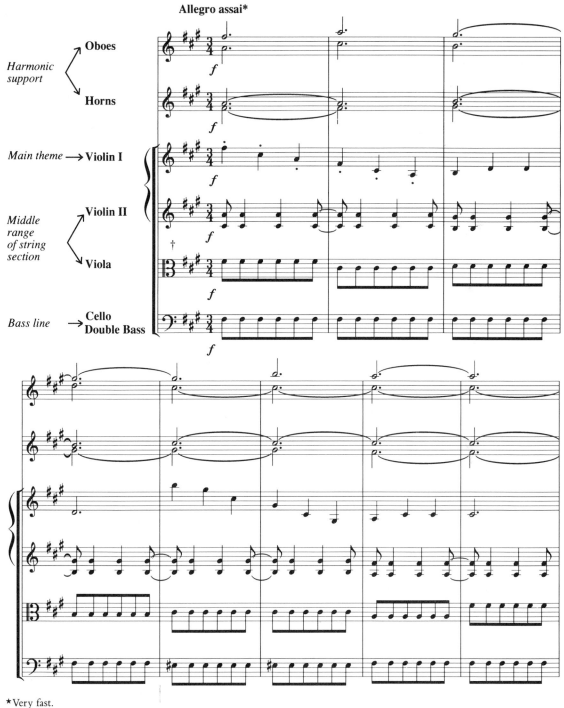

*Very fast.

†𝄡 = Viola Clef (middle line = middle C).

JOSEPH HAYDN   183

This attention to dramatic contrast characterizes Haydn's music of the 1760s and 1770s. Toward the end of this middle period, he began to consolidate and simplify his music, as if in reaction to the highly charged character of such earlier works as the *Farewell* Symphony. From this consolidation emerged the final synthesis of Haydn's mature classical style.

HAYDN'S MATURE STYLE

By the 1780s, Haydn's international fame was secure. No longer obliged to compose solely for his patron, he began to accept commissions and to submit his music to publishers in Austria and abroad. He became a celebrity among composers, a public figure who wrote music for public consumption. Nowhere is Haydn's changing status reflected more vividly than in his late symphonies, which he built on an increasingly grander scale.

The majestic quality of these symphonies is partly the result of the larger instrumental resources he could now command. In London, for example, he wrote for an orchestra of some forty musicians, nearly twice the size of his orchestra at Eszterháza. In the *London* Symphonies, he used flutes and bassoons, formerly optional instruments, as standard members of the woodwind section, along with the oboes. Some of these symphonies also have parts for two clarinets, the final addition to the woodwind group.★ Haydn buttressed the brass section by regularly including two trumpets in addition to the two horns, and in all the *London* Symphonies (and in most of the *Paris* Symphonies), he wrote parts for two timpani, which generally play with the brass section.

Finally, Haydn reorganized the lower range of the string section by separating the cellos from the double basses. The double basses continued to play the bass line, but the cellos became increasingly independent. Haydn was now writing for a five-part string ensemble instead of for the four-part ensemble common in his earlier symphonies (see the table on p. 185).

The public audiences to which Haydn now offered his symphonies had a profound influence on their style. He delighted the new concertgoers with beguiling dance rhythms, charming tunes, and all sorts of special effects. So popular were these symphonies that many were later given nicknames (none by the composer, however), such as *L'Ours* (*The Bear*, No. 82) and *La Poule* (*The Hen*, No. 83). One of the most popular was No. 100, written in 1794 and dubbed the *Military* Symphony.

SYMPHONY NO. 100 (*MILITARY*)

The time was right for a "military" symphony. England and its allies were at war with France, then gripped by revolutionary fervor. The monarchs of Europe had been shocked

---

★ The clarinet has a single-reed mouthpiece and a bell-shaped endpiece. Its range is greater than that of the oboe, and its tone more mellow (see p. 535). More than Haydn, Mozart established the clarinet as an orchestral instrument.

The High Classical Orchestra (ca. 1790)

Woodwinds	2 Flutes
	2 Oboes
	2 Clarinets
	2 Bassoons
Brass	2 Horns
	2 Trumpets
Percussion	2 Timpani
Strings	Violin I
(several per part)	Violin II
	Viola
	Cello
	Double Bass
	(Harpsichord used as continuo instrument)

by the fall of the Bastille in 1789 and by the terror that followed. The English statesman Edmund Burke, who viewed the nobility as a "graceful ornament to the civil order," regarded the French Revolution as a perversion of the "natural order of things." In 1792 the French monarchy was abolished, and a year later Louis XVI died on the guillotine. During much of this period—indeed, for many years to come—Europe was embroiled in war.

Haydn's English audience no doubt appreciated the special character of this symphony. To make doubly sure, Haydn built into it certain conventions that were common in military music of the time: the use of prominent parts for wind instruments and, more conspicuous, the use of several percussion instruments.

In the seventeenth century, Turkish armies invading Austria had brought with them bands of military musicians, called Janissaries, that used wind instruments supported by such percussion instruments as the cymbal, the bass drum, and the triangle.★ Janissary bands became quite popular among the Viennese, who proved more susceptible to Turkish music than to Turkish armies.

The Turkish vogue had reached England as well, and Haydn shrewdly alluded to it in his *Military* Symphony. To avoid abusing the Janissary sound, he limited its use to two movements, the second and the fourth. But, as we shall see, he worked in other military allusions throughout the symphony.

★ See p. 534. Cymbals: saucer-shaped metal disks struck together; bass drum: large, cylindrical drum with two sides, played with a padded mallet; triangle: a small steel rod bent into a triangular shape and struck with a metal rod. All these instruments produce sounds of indefinite pitch.

First Movement: Adagio–Allegro Instead of launching headlong into the exposition of a sonata-form first movement, Haydn begins with a stately, slow introduction (Adagio). In the opening measures, we hear an ingratiating melody, in dotted-rhythm style, played softly by the violins. The melody is in a major key:

Symphony No. 100 (Military), First Movement (Adagio)

About halfway through the introduction, Haydn turns to the parallel minor key and writes a striking crescendo from *piano* to *fortissimo*. This passage marks the entrance of the timpani. It is the first intimation of the symphony's military character:

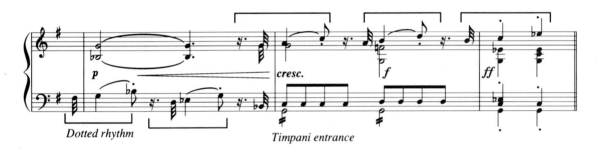

In the closing portion of the introduction, the violin melody resumes. After another crescendo, we hear a few concluding bars of repeated chords, first played *piano* but then, unexpectedly, *fortissimo*. The last chord is held by a **fermata,** or pause (⌢), as we await the Allegro, the beginning of the movement proper (see study diagram).

Haydn begins the exposition of the Allegro with a theme (*a*) related to the violin melody that began the slow introduction. For ease of comparison, we have marked with asterisks the corresponding notes between the two examples. The Allegro theme commences with an ascent followed by a descending line; this much is especially close to the melody of the slow introduction. Then Haydn extends *a* into a full-fledged, eight-measure theme:

Symphony No. 100 (Military), First Movement (Allegro)

Haydn: Symphony No. 100 (*Military*), First Movement, Adagio

Slow Introduction (Adagio)

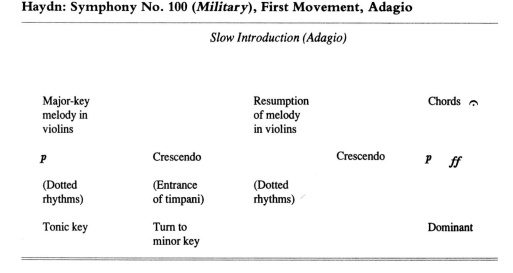

Major-key melody in violins		Resumption of melody in violins		Chords ⌒
p	Crescendo		Crescendo	*p* *ff*
(Dotted rhythms)	(Entrance of timpani)	(Dotted rhythms)		
Tonic key	Turn to minor key			Dominant

A flute, accompanied only by two oboes, plays the lively Allegro theme in a high register.* In Haydn's day, wind instruments figured prominently in military bands, and the appearance of this wind ensemble, a most striking and unusual beginning, provides another hint of the military character of the symphony. Next, Haydn repeats the theme, this time in the strings. A jolting *forte* for full orchestra extends the theme through the bridge to the second group of themes and the second key.

The second group is especially elaborate. First, the winds return to play *a* in the new key, and the strings interrupt them with an outburst in the parallel minor key. Only then does Haydn introduce his second theme (*b*), also in the new key. Ushered in by the violins and supported by the flute, this theme has an insistent tapping rhythm (♫ | ♩♩ ♫ ♩♩):

Second theme (b)

p

In the closing section of the exposition, Haydn shifts the second theme to the bass line, with a rumbling timpani roll in the background. The exposition closes with three crisp, *forte* chords. The entire exposition (but not the slow introduction) is then repeated.

The study diagram summarizes the structural highpoints of the exposition. Haydn's careful dynamic markings make it easy to identify these highpoints as we listen to the

---

* To make it easier to read the example, we have transposed the theme to a lower register. The notation *8va* above the staff indicates that the example sounds one octave above the written notes.

Haydn: Symphony No. 100 (*Military*), First Movement, Allegro

Exposition

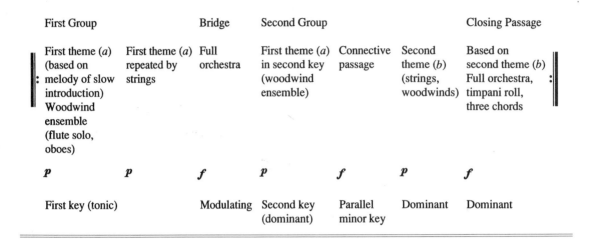

First Group		Bridge	Second Group			Closing Passage
First theme (*a*) (based on melody of slow introduction) Woodwind ensemble (flute solo, oboes)	First theme (*a*) repeated by strings	Full orchestra	First theme (*a*) in second key (woodwind ensemble)	Connective passage	Second theme (*b*) (strings, woodwinds)	Based on second theme (*b*) Full orchestra, timpani roll, three chords
p	*p*	*f*	*p*	*f*	*p*	*f*
First key (tonic)		Modulating	Second key (dominant)	Parallel minor key	Dominant	Dominant

Haydn: Symphony No. 100 (*Military*), First Movement, Allegro

Development

Two measures of rest	Second theme (*b*)	Second theme (*b*) fragmented, developed	Brief pause	Retransition: fragment of *a; b* frag-mented, developed	Return of wind ensemble
	p	*p < ff p < ff* timpani roll timpani roll		*p*	*p < f* *p*
	Remote, unprepared key	Various keys		Preparation for return of tonic key	

Haydn: Symphony No. 100 (*Military*), First Movement, Allegro

Recapitulation

First Group		Transition	Second Group (compressed)	Closing Passage (extended into)	Coda
First Theme (*a*) Woodwind ensemble	First theme (*a*) repeated by full orchestra	Full orchestra	Second theme (*b*) Strings, woodwinds	Based on second theme (*b*) Full orchestra	Chords
p	*f*	*f*	*p*	*ff*	
First key (tonic)		(No modulation) First key (tonic)	Remote, unprepared key	Re-establishment of first key (tonic)	

symphony. In particular, note how he uses *piano* dynamics for the first and second thematic group and reserves *forte* dynamics for transitional or closing material.

The development of the first movement reveals how well Haydn understood his English audience (see study diagram). He begins with a surprise: two full measures of rest followed by the second theme in a totally unexpected—and unprepared—key. He then works over the second theme, appropriating its tapping motive throughout the development. The music moves through a variety of keys, and we hear two mighty crescendos with timpani rolls and then a brief pause. Now Haydn works in bits of the first theme and begins to move the music toward the tonic key. Finally, he brings back the wind ensemble to mark the end of the development and the beginning of the recapitulation.

As the diagram shows, the recapitulation is relatively uncomplicated. When Haydn reaches the second group (*b*), however, he departs from the order of events in his exposition by curtailing the restatement of the first theme (compare the diagram of the exposition). Since the music remains in the tonic key, a restatement of the first theme would have been redundant (it has already reappeared in the tonic to open the recapitulation). Haydn simply omits it. He springs one more surprise by beginning the closing section, now extended into a coda, with an adventurous and abrupt excursion to a remote key. (This device reminds us of the beginning of the development.) He then returns to the tonic key and ends the movement in grand style with timpani rolls, rushing scales in the strings, and, for extra measure, five triumphant chords by the full orchestra.

Second Movement: Allegretto The second movement, in the form *ABA'*, is based on a hauntingly simple C major melody that became one of Haydn's most popular creations. Symmetrical in construction, the melody is in binary form (‖: a :‖: b a' :‖), with each part repeated (this much of the movement represents the A section). Here is the first part (a), which breaks down into four similar two-measure portions, for a total of eight measures:

Symphony No. 100 (Military), Second Movement

Note how the melody progressively rises by leaps, reaching its peak midway, in the fifth measure, before subsiding through a smooth, stepwise descent. This much is played by a flute and the first violins, with accompaniment by the other strings. When *a* is repeated, Haydn calls for a wind ensemble of oboes, clarinets, and bassoons. The addition of the clarinets, which appear only in the second movement, reinforces the woodwind section and suggests again the sound of a military band. Haydn orchestrates the second part of the melody (*b* and *a'*) in similar fashion, presenting it once in the flute and the strings and then repeating it with the wind band.

The contrasting minor-key middle section, *B*, is actually based on the theme of *A*. Here, Haydn brings in the full complement of Turkish percussion (triangle, cymbals, and bass drum), with horns and trumpets to add to the clangor. With its crescendos and steady beat of jangling percussion, this section creates an arresting sonorous effect.

Haydn now returns to the major-key music of the *A* section, presented first by the winds and strings, then with the Janissary complement. Just as the movement is about to finish, he introduces yet another surprise: a trumpet fanfare, like a call to arms, and a drum roll leading to a *fortissimo* crash in a distant key. This ominous passage is short-lived, however, and the movement ends triumphantly in the tonic key.

Third Movement: Minuet and Trio Having dismissed all suggestions of battle, Haydn turns in the third movement to an elegant minuet. Again, his theme is a model of classical symmetry. Here are its opening eight bars, divided by a rest into two orderly parts with rhythmic values that match exactly:

Symphony No. 100 (Military), Third Movement (Minuet)

Haydn garnishes his theme (*a*) with a gentle turn figure, always followed by clipped staccato notes,

and he supports his theme with a simple accompaniment of chords.

The second section of the minuet is more complicated. Haydn begins by breaking up the theme, giving part of it to the bass and, in one delightful passage, setting bass against treble. This sort of treatment resembles on a small scale the development sections of his sonata-form movements. In the study diagram, we have labeled the passage *b*. Following it, and rounding out the minuet proper, is a modified return of the opening theme (*a'*).

The theme of the Trio, also in binary form, is in dotted-note style. As he often does in his trios, Haydn reduces the scoring by limiting himself to winds and strings.

Symphony No. 100 (Military), *Third Movement (Trio)*

At one point, however, in a minor-key *forte* passage for full orchestra, he breaks in with yet another ominous sounding passage:

Haydn: Symphony No. 100 (*Military*), Third Movement, Minuet and Trio

Minuet			Trio			Minuet Da Capo (without repeats)
‖ *a* ‖: *b*	*a'* :‖	‖: *c* :‖‖: *d'*	*c'* :‖	‖ *a* ‖ *b* *a'* ‖
Repeat written out	Quasi develop- ment of theme	Return of theme	Dotted notes	(Turn to minor key)		
f (repeat *p*) *f*	*p*	*f* *ff*	*p*	*p* *f*	*p*	
Full orchestra			Winds, strings	Full orches- tra	Winds, strings	

But the "skirmish" is soon over, and the da capo repeat of the minuet restores the movement to its original elegance.

Finale: Presto In the finales of his late symphonies, Haydn took delight in trying out modifications of the standard forms, including ingenious combinations of the rondo and sonata form. A Haydn symphonic finale may begin simply like a rondo, with a clearly recognizable refrain suggestive, perhaps, of a popular dance. But in the course of the movement, complications inevitably arise: Sometimes, the refrain fails to return when one expects it; sometimes, Haydn extends passages into a full-fledged development, as if the movement were in sonata form after all. Nowhere is Haydn more adventurous than in the finales of his *London* Symphonies, filled with unexpected turns.

A complex version of the hybrid form known as **sonata-rondo form** occurs in the finale of the *Military* Symphony. The movement begins with a rapid, whirling theme, the *A* section, or refrain, given here in part:

Symphony No. 100 (Military), *Fourth Movement*

As the diagram shows, the first statement of the refrain is a self-sufficient section in binary form, with each part repeated. (This type of refrain is common in Haydn's rondos or rondo-derived movements.) Haydn draws out the *b* portion so that it resembles a small development section, purposefully delaying the restatement (*a'*) of the opening material. After a bridge to the second key, he moves into the *B* section. Rather than a clear-cut theme, this section has energetic leaps and crisp ornaments exchanged between bass and treble:

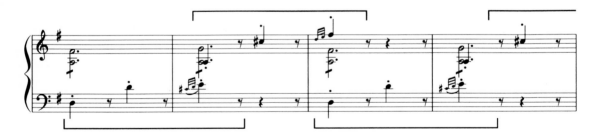

Haydn builds the movement around these two ideas. The extended *C* section functions like a development, with the *A* and *B* material subjected to a variety of reworkings, combinations, and keys. Near the beginning of this section, Haydn catches the rushing music off-guard with a surprise bombardment from the timpani. The final return of the *B* section has an even greater surprise. The Janissary percussion, which

Haydn: Symphony No. 100 (*Military*), Fourth Movement, Sonata-Rondo

A (Refrain)	Bridge	B	C (Development of material from A and B) Timpani interruption	A (Shortened)	Bridge	B	A (Shortened)
‖: a :‖: b a' :‖	Based on A					Janissary percussion	Janissary percussion
Tonic key	Modulating	Second key (Dominant)	Variety of keys	Tonic key		Tonic key	Tonic key

has been silent since the second movement, suddenly rejoins the fray and enters into every *forte* passage to the very end.

HAYDN AND THE STRING QUARTET

Along with his symphonies, Haydn is chiefly remembered for the series of string quartets that spanned his long career. He was the first undisputed master of this new genre, which supplanted the trio sonata and other types of baroque chamber music. The string quartet was written for two violins, a viola, and a cello. Haydn combined these instruments in a great variety of ways. The first violin might play the melody, accompanied by the other three instruments; or the ensemble might play as two pairs of instruments. In yet another arrangement, the four instruments might be treated as equal partners. In his mature quartets, Haydn realized the full potential of the ensemble, engaging it in a rich exchange of melodic and harmonic material, the give-and-take that was the hallmark of the classical string quartet.

Haydn's early quartets feature prominent solo writing for the first violin, with restrained accompaniment by the other instruments. Then, about the time he was writing the *Farewell* Symphony, he moved in a new direction. The six quartets that constitute Op. 20 (1772) contain several fugues that exhibit rather erudite contrapuntal techniques. Although he soon abandoned the strict fugal style, this experiment gave him experience in treating the four instruments as independent parts.

Haydn's command of the string quartet genre is fully evident in the six quartets of Opus 33, composed in 1781, which the composer declared were written in a new style. This new style amounted to a systematic elaboration of the thematic material, now broken up and reconstituted in fresh treatments by the four instruments. Through ever-original instrumental combinations, Haydn brought all four instruments into active participation in the string quartets of his mature period.

STRING QUARTET IN C MAJOR, OP. 76, NO. 3 (*EMPEROR*)

The six quartets of Opus 76, composed in 1797, mark the summit of Haydn's achievement in the string quartet. We take as our example the third quartet, known as the

Emperor. Like most string quartets, this one is in four movements. The first and fourth movements are in sonata form, the second consists of a theme and four variations, and the third is a minuet and trio. We shall examine here the first and second movements.

First Movement: Allegro In the first movement, Haydn uses thematic material sparingly. A compact theme, announced at the outset, provides the basic material for the entire movement. Four measures in length, the theme is really a short motive (♪| ♩ ♪♩♩) repeated and rhythmically modified several times:

String Quartet, Op. 76, No. 3 (Emperor), *First Movement*

Each measure is introduced by an upbeat (♪), but then diverges: Bar 2 has staccato, *piano* eighth notes; bar 3, a syncopation formed by a short note followed by a longer note (♪ ♪); and bar 4, a vigorous, *forte* conclusion. Such detailed modifications enable Haydn to build a theme out of a mere kernel of five notes.

Next, Haydn subjects the theme to a contrapuntal treatment. Still in the tonic key, he sets the motive of the first measure against an ascending scale with dotted rhythms. In three short measures, he manages to direct the motive into the viola, the second violin, and the first violin parts, and the scale figure into all four parts (in the order of second violin, first violin, viola, and cello). We give this passage in full score:

The bridge, which modulates to the dominant, is drawn from the first theme, which is also the source for the second theme of the exposition, in the dominant:

SECOND THEME

The robust closing passage of the exposition begins with a strong assertion of the dominant key, but then unexpectedly veers toward a new key, with yet another statement of the first theme, before landing firmly with a cadence on the dominant to conclude the exposition.

In the development, in two broad parts, Haydn skillfully puts his theme to further use. In the first part, he moves through several keys, reworking the opening theme in a variety of ways—for example, with the theme in the viola and the cello against the ascending scale in the violin, or with the theme in the violins accompanied by the viola.

In the climax of the development, Haydn transforms the first theme and scale figure into a robust peasant tune over a dronelike harmony:

By calling for double stops★ for the three lowest parts, Haydn thickens the texture and achieves a rustic, earthy tone. This unexpected injection of a folklike passage into an otherwise highly polished composition was an especially favorite device of Haydn.

Throughout the movement, Haydn thus makes rich use of the theme (and its germinal motive) introduced in the opening measures. The theme informs the structure of the movement by appearing in all its principal sections in some guise—as a theme and accompaniment, in counterpoint, or over a peasant drone, for example. The result is one of the most tautly constructed movements in all Haydn's string quartets.

★Executed by drawing the bow across two strings simultaneously, thus producing two pitches.

Second Movement: Theme and Variations Haydn originally composed the theme of the second movement for a patriotic hymn marking the birthday of Emperor Francis II of Austria in 1797. He then reused the theme, without text, for the slow movement of his quartet. (The theme has served, at various times, as the national anthem for both Austria and Germany; it is currently the anthem of the German Federal Republic.) This beautiful Adagio theme consists of three phrases (*a, b,* and *c*), of which two (*a* and *c*) are repeated. Phrase *a* begins with an upbeat and moves primarily in even rhythmic values before it comes to rest on a high pitch. Phrase *b* attains the same high pitch, now set off more emphatically by a fermata (⌢). Phrase *c* begins even higher, with the climax of the theme, and then describes a smooth descent:

String Quartet, Op. 76, No. 3 (Emperor), *Second Movement*

★∞, sign for an ornament known as a turn; ♩ ∞ = ♪♫♫♪.

In each of the four variations that follow, the theme is played in its entirety by one of the instruments and accompanied by the other three (see study diagram). In other words, Haydn respects the melodic integrity of the emperor's theme, so that instead of varying the pitches of the melody, he varies nonmelodic aspects of the music, such as texture, rhythm, register, or type of accompaniment. The theme itself and the fourth variation are scored for the full ensemble, with all four instruments participating in a homophonic texture. In contrast, Variation 1 is for only two instruments, and Variations 2 and 3 require, for the most part, three instruments.

Rhythmically, the first variation has a florid part in sixteenth notes (♫♫♫) for the first violin; the second and third variations flow along in eighth notes (♫♫); and the fourth variation (like the theme) moves mostly in quarter notes (♩). Toward the end, the fourth variation shifts to a high range, setting it off from the earlier variations. Haydn limits his dynamics to *piano* and *pianissimo* for the length of this exquisite movement.

Haydn: String Quartet, Op. 76, No. 3 (*Emperor*), Second Movement

Section:	Theme	Variation 1	Variation 2	Variation 3	Variation 4
Theme:	Violin 1	Violin 2	Cello	Viola	Violin 1
Basic Rhythmic Values:	♩	♫♫	♫	♫	♩
Texture:	4 parts homophonic	2 parts	3 and 4 parts	3 and 4 parts	4 parts homophonic, higher range
Dynamics:	*p*	*p*	*p*	*p*	*p* *pp*

Haydn's influence was extraordinary, both during and after his lifetime. By consolidating the accomplishments of lesser figures, he established the symphony and the string quartet as the two most important genres of classical instrumental music. Mozart and Beethoven, both of whom he knew, freely drew on his contributions, as did countless other composers. International in appeal, his music communicated through its warmth, wit, and humanity. It reached new public audiences and represented the best the classical period could offer.

Suggested Listening

Joseph Haydn
The Creation
Lord Nelson Mass
String Quartet, Op. 20, No. 5, in F minor
String Quartet, Op. 33, No. 2 (*Joke*)
★String Quartet, Op. 76, No. 3 (*Emperor*)
String Quartet, Op. 76, No. 4 (*Sunrise*)
★Symphony No. 45 (*Farewell*)
Symphony No. 49, in F minor (*Passione*)
Symphony No. 82 (*L'Ours*)
Symphony No. 83 (*La Poule*)
Symphony No. 88, in G major
Symphony No. 92 (*Oxford*)
★Symphony No. 100 (*Military*)
Symphony No. 104, in D major

Note: Works marked with an asterisk are the principal works discussed in the chapter.

8

WOLFGANG AMADEUS MOZART

*T*he career of Wolfgang Amadeus Mozart (1756–1791), the second great master of eighteenth-century classicism, contrasted sharply with that of Haydn. Mozart began to compose when he was only five years old; Haydn developed his craft considerably later in his life. Mozart, a child prodigy, was one of the great keyboard virtuosos of his time; Haydn, though a gifted performer, never won acclaim as a soloist. Mozart gained easy admission to the courts of Europe as a child; Haydn began his musical career modestly and at first lived in poverty. Mozart composed masterpieces in nearly every genre, from symphony to concerto, from sacred music to opera; Haydn's lasting contributions were mainly symphonies, string quartets, and sacred music. Finally, Mozart died in poverty at the age of 35; Haydn lived a long life and continued to reap the rewards of an international career.

Still, the two composers had much in common and admired each other's music. Mozart, younger by some twenty-four years, acknowledged his debt in a series of brilliant string quartets dedicated to the older musician. Haydn, for his part, declared to Mozart's father that Wolfgang was the greatest composer alive whom he knew "personally or by reputation." Crushed by the news of Mozart's death, Haydn paid posthumous tribute to him by arranging for the publication of his music.

W. A. Mozart.

MOZART'S LIFE AND CAREER

Mozart was born into a musical family. His father, Leopold, was educated in Salzburg, where he served as a court composer and violinist. For centuries, Salzburg had been a small church principality. It was ruled by a prince-archbishop and enjoyed strong ties to Vienna and, of course, to Rome. The archbishop supported a retinue of composers who were expected to produce a steady supply of church music. One of those composers was Michael Haydn (1737–1806), who, though overshadowed by his illustrious brother Joseph, was a competent composer in his own right. At the court, Leopold Mozart composed symphonies and other instrumental works; he also devised a successful method for teaching the violin that was published and eventually translated into several languages.

Soon realizing that his young son, Wolfgang, was a prodigy, Leopold provided him with instruction in harpsichord along with his gifted older sister, Nannerl. Before long, the boy was picking out chords for himself at the keyboard and was composing short pieces, which his father wrote down. Blessed with an uncanny musical ear, Wolfgang could identify pitches and could tell when an instrument was slightly out of tune. He improvised at the keyboard with astonishing facility and could even play blindfolded or with his hands covered. He played the violin as well as he played the harpsichord.

Leopold decided to devote himself to his children's education and to nurture their musical talents. In 1763 the family embarked on a three-year tour that took them through Germany and the Austrian Netherlands, on to Paris and London, and, on the way back, through Holland. They visited many princely courts along the way. At every stop, the children amazed their royal audiences with their talents. At the Palace of Versailles, the seven-year-old Wolfgang performed before Louis XV; in London, before George III. While they were in London, where the children were billed as "Prodigies of Nature," they met Johann Christian Bach, the youngest son of J. S. Bach and one of the first composers to write for the fortepiano. Johann Christian Bach joined in improvisation sessions with young Mozart, who learned much from the older musician. After returning to Salzburg, Wolfgang gave new evidence of his musical prowess. To win over the skeptical archbishop, he was confined to a room for an entire week to compose a sacred composition by himself, a test he easily met.

Leopold now decided to take his gifted son to Italy. There he was given several tests in musicianship and in academic counterpoint. In Rome, during Holy Week 1770, he astonished observers by writing down from memory a complex choral work he had heard only once, in the Sistine Chapel. More important for Leopold, who wanted compensation as well as praise, Wolfgang began to earn commissions to compose Italian operas during the early 1770s.

Meanwhile, the archbishop in Salzburg had died and had been succeeded by Hieronymus, Count of Colloredo, who proceeded to reorganize the court orchestra. Charles Burney, a traveling Englishman who prepared a documentary account about music in Europe, reported that the orchestra was distinguished more for its "coarseness and noise than delicacy and high-finishing." Mozart joined the entourage of musicians on his return to Salzburg in 1772, but he found Hieronymus dogmatic and authoritarian and came to resent the constraints of his position and his low social status. He composed music on command, including church music and serenades★ for visiting dignitaries. In 1777 and 1778 he traveled with his mother to Germany and France in search of a new post, but without success. His mother died while they were in Paris.

A valuable opportunity came when Mozart received a commission to write an Italian opera for the Hoftheater in Munich. The 1781 premiere of the opera, *Idomeneo,* was a success, but the archbishop soon ordered Mozart back to his service. Matters went from bad to worse, until at last the archbishop angrily dismissed the rebellious Mozart, who decided to seek his fortune in Vienna. There he lived and worked for most of the last ten years of his life. Leopold stayed on in Salzburg to serve the archbishop as assistant music master.

Mozart's move to Vienna marked a turning point in his career, and he now composed an extraordinary series of masterpieces. Estranged from the Salzburg court and from his father (he married against Leopold's wishes in 1782), Mozart struggled to

---

★ Suitelike instrumental compositions performed in the evening to honor a dignitary.

survive on a meager income from private lessons, commissions, and concerts. He arranged concerts for noblemen and managed public subscription concerts. During the Viennese years, to supply new music for his own concert appearances, he turned out several piano concertos in remarkably short order. His manuscripts reveal just how hectic his schedule was at that time: Some of the piano parts for the concertos were left blank, evidently to be finished when Mozart performed them in concert.

In 1784 Mozart joined the Masonic lodge "Beneficence" in Vienna. During the eighteenth century, Freemasonry, a secret male society dedicated to humanitarian ideals, attracted many members of the "enlightened" middle class of professionals, especially in England, France, Germany, and Austria; among its membership were many musicians, writers, and statesmen, including Haydn, the German writers Lessing, Herder, and Goethe, and, in the young American republic, George Washington and Benjamin Franklin. Mozart wrote several compositions specifically for his lodge, in which he was active for a time. Some of his other music from this period also contains Masonic allusions, including, as we shall see, his German opera *Die Zauberflöte (The Magic Flute)*.

In his last years, Mozart fell deeply into debt and was obliged to borrow from his friends, among them some fellow Masons. On his deathbed, he was still working feverishly on the Requiem Mass in D minor. Also left unfinished was a set of six string quartets for the king of Prussia. When Mozart died, he was buried in an unmarked grave.

Legends soon began to cluster around Mozart's life. According to one, Mozart had been poisoned by a less-gifted and envious court composer, Antonio Salieri (the subject of a nineteenth-century dramatic scene by the Russian playwright Aleksander Pushkin and, in our own time, of the play *Amadeus* by Peter Shaffer). According to another, a violent snowstorm raged over his burial. The early German romantics, who ascribed godlike gifts to artistic geniuses, made Mozart the object of a cult in the nineteenth century. The writer and musician Ernst Theodor Amadeus Hoffmann even took Mozart's middle name for himself (Amadeus, "beloved of God") and honored Mozart as a romantic composer.

The catalog of Mozart's works reveals the scope of his staggering achievement. Among his many operas are five that remain in the standard repertory: three Italian operas, *Le nozze di Figaro (The Marriage of Figaro,* 1786), *Don Giovanni* (1787), and *Così fan tutte (Thus Do All the Ladies,* 1790), and two German operas, *Die Entführung aus dem Serail (The Abduction from the Seraglio,* 1782), and *Die Zauberflöte (The Magic Flute,* 1791). There is also much sacred music, including the unfinished masterpiece, the Requiem in D minor. Among the many symphonies are the pensive No. 40, in G minor, and the lustrous No. 41, the *Jupiter.* Mozart wrote nearly forty concertos, the majority of them for piano and orchestra. He wrote string quintets and quartets, piano trios, violin sonatas, music for wind ensembles, music for piano, and even music for a mechanical clock. The list of compositions runs to over six hundred items, first cataloged in chronological order in the nineteenth century by the Austrian scholar Ludwig von Köchel; the "K" numbers used to identify Mozart's compositions are in honor of Köchel's name.

MOZART AND THE CLASSICAL CONCERTO

The classical concerto emerged during the eighteenth century as a synthesis of the older baroque ritornello principle (see p. 98) and elements of newer instrumental forms, especially classical sonata form. It was Mozart who perfected that synthesis. From the baroque concerto, he retained the idea of a contest between solo and orchestral forces. (Unlike the baroque concerto grosso, with its group of soloists, most of Mozart's concertos call for only one soloist. See p. 97.) Also, in his piano concertos, in which he excelled, Mozart often instructed the soloist to play the bass line during the tutti passages, after the baroque continuo practice (see p. 72). (In modern performances, that practice is rarely observed.)

The first movements of Mozart's concertos represent an amalgam of the ritornello principle and classical sonata form. Mozart commonly works with four substantial ritornelli (R) that feature the orchestra and three main solos (S) that feature the soloist with light orchestral accompaniment:

$$R_1 \quad S_1 \quad R_2 \quad S_2 \quad R_3 \quad S_3 \quad R_4$$

The orchestra occasionally interrupts the solo sections with comments of its own. In the first ritornello, preparatory in character, Mozart previews the groups of thematic material that will be treated more fully in the course of the movement. The first ritornello functions like an exposition for the orchestra, except that it tends to cling to the tonic key throughout.

The first solo functions more like a conventional exposition in sonata form. Actually, the soloist may begin with fresh material before retracing the material of the first tutti; the important point, however, is that in the first solo, Mozart observes the normal sequence of events for a sonata-form exposition, including, above all, its use of two thematic groups in two contrasting keys. The first solo typically ends strongly on the second key and is reinforced by the following second ritornello (usually less elaborate than the first ritornello).

The second solo constitutes the development proper, with florid modulations through several keys. Here, Mozart either develops themes he has presented earlier or freely introduces new material, in either case enabling the soloist to engage in an unimpeded display of virtuoso figuration.

The third ritornello coincides with the beginning of the recapitulation and the reinstatement of the tonic key; often, this orchestral passage is subtly elided with the third solo, which continues the recapitulation. The fourth ritornello is the final section of the movement. Traditionally, the orchestra here comes to a dignified pause to allow the soloist to perform alone a *cadenza,* an improvisatory passage of great virtuosity. The soloist may digress through several keys in the course of this cadenza but always returns to the tonic key. A trill inevitably signals the orchestra to reenter and conclude the movement with a few strong measures in the tonic key.

PIANO CONCERTO IN A MAJOR, K. 488

The first movement of Mozart's Piano Concerto in A major, K. 488 (1786) exemplifies the formal process we have described (see the study diagram). The movement is built

Mozart: Piano Concerto in A major, K. 488, First Movement

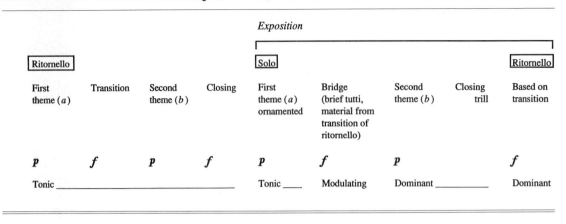

	Ritornello				Exposition				
					Solo				**Ritornello**
	First theme (*a*)	Transition	Second theme (*b*)	Closing	First theme (*a*) ornamented	Bridge (brief tutti, material from transition of ritornello)	Second theme (*b*)	Closing trill	Based on transition
	p	*f*	*p*	*f*	*p*	*f*	*p*		*f*
	Tonic _____				Tonic ____	Modulating	Dominant _____		Dominant

on two basic themes (*a* and *b*), first announced by the strings in the opening ritornello. Both themes comprise balanced eight-measure melodies. Theme *a* has two four-measure phrases that use contrasting ranges: The first begins relatively high and descends through a series of graceful leaps; the second phrase counterbalances the first by beginning relatively low and ascending to the range of the first. Theme *b* is generated by a rhythmic motive in its first measure (♩♩♩.♩ ♩♩); the motive recurs in the third measure and is modified in the fifth and sixth measures:

Piano Concerto in A major, K. 488, First Movement

FIRST THEME (*a*)

SECOND THEME (*b*)

Mozart: Piano Concerto in A major, K. 488, First Movement, *Continued*

Development			*Recapitulation*							
Solo			Ritornello (brief, elided with First theme) (a)	Solo					Ritornello	Solo cadenza	Resumption of Ritornello
Piano figuration	Brief melodic gestures in woodwinds	Ascending chromatic scale		First theme (a)	Transition	Second theme (b)	Closing	Based on transition			trill
								Pause			
p and *f*			*p*	*p*	*f*	*p*	*f*	*f*			*f*
Modulations through various keys ~~~~~		Dominant pedal point	Tonic _____					Tonic	Various keys and return to	Tonic	

In addition to these two basic themes, the ritornello includes transitional and closing material, in short, all the principal parts of an exposition—but all remaining in the tonic key. When the soloist enters, Mozart thins out the orchestra to highlight the piano. The pianist begins by taking up the first theme, now varied slightly with an overlay of ornamental figures. In our example, the basic pitches of the original theme are circled:

Sixteenth-note ornamentation

After the bridge to the dominant, the second key, we hear the tender second theme (*b*) in the piano, answered by a statement from the orchestra. In the closing section, the soloist finishes with an extended run and trill, cadencing firmly on the second key and leading to the second orchestral ritornello. The next solo serves as the development of the movement. Much of it is given over to modulating passagework for the piano, sometimes accompanied by brief melodic gestures in the woodwinds. To prepare for the recapitulation and the return of the tonic key, Mozart establishes the dominant in the bass; at its conclusion, the piano executes an ascending scale that eases us into the recapitulation.

The recapitulation, divided between a brief ritornello and a more extended solo, observes the customary sequence of events, without modulating from the tonic key. The final ritornello introduces the piano cadenza and, at its conclusion, resumes to bring the movement to a strong conclusion. Ordinarily, Mozart improvised his cadenzas during performances, without bothering to write them down. His cadenza for this movement has survived, however. Introduced by stately orchestral chords and a solemn pause, it erupts into rushing scales, sweeping figurations, and incisive trills, giving us a fair idea of Mozart's brilliant style of improvisation.

The slow movement is one of the most moving creations of Mozart. Set in a minor key, it contrasts in mood with the charming first movement. Mozart fills his Adagio with harsh dissonances, gaping melodic lines, and sublime orchestral sonorities. By using many pungent chromatic notes outside the key of the movement, he suggests a brooding melancholy. The emotional intensity of this movement provides compelling evidence, indeed, that classical music is not as cold, impersonal, or "reasonable" as the superficial view sometimes suggests. Rather, Mozart and many other classical composers evoked a broad range of emotions in communicating to their audiences.

Formally, this movement is in three sections: The outer sections (*A*) are in a minor key; the central section (*B*) is in a contrasting major key. The form of the whole is *ABA′*. The movement begins with a haunting piano melody (*a*) marked by a long–short–short rhythmic pattern (♩. ♪♪):

Piano Concerto in A major, K. 488, Second Movement

Mozart establishes the gently pulsating rhythm with long and short notes in the bass part. In measure 2, the melody is broken by a rest, and we hear a solitary bass note some three octaves below. Then the melody continues, pausing again in measure 4. A few measures later, we hear an exquisite orchestral passage, based on a theme (*b*) introduced by the clarinet and the violins and imitated in the bassoon:

Next, Mozart reworks and extends the opening theme in the piano against light orchestral accompaniment; at this point, he begins to introduce major-key harmonies in anticipation of the central section.

In the *B* section, the orchestra and the piano exchange a new theme in a major key (*c*), and the accompaniment shifts to faster triplets. The new theme is presented as a duet, first for flute and clarinet, then for the two clarinets. Against the theme, the bass line maintains the long–short pattern of the opening section:

A short transition then leads us back to the melancholy mood of the *A* section, now modified to include a closing section with an unexpected surprise: The pianist executes extreme melodic leaps while the strings gently pluck out their parts. The movement closes with hushed *pianissimo* chords.

The subdued tone of the Adagio gives way to the buoyant, lighthearted rondo of the last movement. The piano and then the orchestra begin straightaway with the principal theme, the refrain or *A* section (see p. 174), which recurs throughout the movement. Here is the opening of the *A* section; its theme is animated by energetic leaps followed by a rapid stream of notes. The bass is assigned a common classical type of chordal accompaniment in which the individual chords ($\frac{6}{3}$) are played in a "broken" arrangement,

(see also the example on p. 205):

Piano Concerto in A major, K. 488, Third Movement

Between the successive appearances of the refrain, Mozart introduces complex episodes with new themes and excursions to new keys. Each time, however, he carefully prepares for the return of the refrain; sometimes he dashes our expectations again and again by delaying its reappearance. This witty play is characteristic of Mozart's rondo finales, which bring many of his concertos to delightfully satisfying conclusions.

MOZART AND ITALIAN OPERA

Italian opera continued to dominate the opera houses of Mozart's Vienna, as it did elsewhere in Europe (its principal competition remained French opera). Earlier in the century, Italian composers had settled as far away as Dublin and St. Petersburg, turning out a seemingly endless supply of *opere serie*, or serious operas. But some connoisseurs found those operas routine and hackneyed and began to call for reform. Thus, the composer Benedetto Marcello produced a biting satire in his *Teatro alla moda (The Theater "à la Mode,"* written around 1720), which pretended to be a handbook on how to write, compose, and produce an Italian opera. Marcello advised librettists not to bother reading the ancient Latin and Greek works on which they based their plots, because the ancients would never be aware of the liberties they were now taking. Nor should they worry about observing the rules of Italian poetry; they should just force their lines into the patterns that suited the virtuoso singers for whom they were writing. Composers should avoid confusing themselves by reading the librettos they were setting to music. They should allow solo singers to tuck in a cadenza whenever they felt the urge and to alter tempos to suit their voices. Above all, composers should encourage the singers to articulate their words poorly so that the audience would pay attention to the music.

In 1730 an event took place in Vienna that helped restore serious Italian opera to its former level of dignity: The Italian Pietro Metastasio was named court poet to the emperor. Metastasio's aim was to provide edifying opera librettos of high literary quality. He wrote many of his librettos for state occasions, as thinly disguised paeans to the Austrian monarchy; typically, his librettos were serious and moralizing in tone. Virtue was always rewarded, sometimes in an unexpectedly happy ending. Composers based hundreds of operas on Metastasio's librettos. Mozart alone used them for three Italian operas: *Il sogno di Scipione (The Dream of Scipio,* 1772), *Il rè pastore (The Shepherd King,* 1775), and *La clemenza di Tito (The Clemency of Titus,* 1791).

One of the leading composers of Italian opera was Christoph Willibald Gluck (1714–1787), who studied in Italy and worked in Vienna and in Paris (where his French operas were admired by Marie Antoinette). Many of Gluck's early operas are based on librettos by Metastasio. By the 1760s and 1770s, Gluck was ready to propose a systematic reform of opera seria. Urging composers to resist the abuses of virtuoso singers, he argued for common sense and a "beautiful simplicity." Above all, for Gluck the music should serve the drama. Thus, the overture should clearly set forth in musical terms the argument of the drama, and the music for the arias should respect rather than disturb the drama's integrity. Gluck summarized these principles in a famous preface to his opera *Alceste* (1769), which was based, with some changes, on the ancient Greek tragedy by Euripides.

Mozart composed both serious opera (*opera seria*) and comic opera (*opera buffa;* plural, *opere buffe*). His best known Italian operas—*The Marriage of Figaro* and *Don Giovanni*—are viewed as opere buffe,* though they commingle serious and comic characters, occasionally dissolving the strict line between the two types. Mozart succeeded as did few other opera composers in bringing to life with unerring sensitivity the noble counts and countesses and members of the servant class who populate his operas; they are delineated not as stock figures but as credible individuals playing out human dramas.

THE MARRIAGE OF FIGARO

The Marriage of Figaro is based on the play *Le mariage de Figaro* (1784) by Pierre-Augustin Beaumarchais (1732–1799), a French dramatist who served the Bourbon monarchy as a secret agent, interceded on behalf of the American cause during the War of Independence, and almost became a victim of the French Revolution. Beaumarchais's literary fame rests on *Figaro* and an earlier play, *Le barbier de Séville (The Barber of Seville)*. These plays formed part of a trilogy about the intrigues of the comic servant Figaro.

For his opera, Mozart used an Italian version of *Le mariage de Figaro* by Lorenzo Da Ponte, an Italian poet who worked in Vienna in the 1780s (he also collaborated with the composer on *Don Giovanni* and *Così fan tutte*). Mozart built much of the opera on solo arias and recitatives—the common ingredients of Italian opera—but he also used duets, trios, and larger ensembles with telling effect. Each of the four acts of the opera, but especially the second and fourth, builds in tension to a culminating finale. In these finales, Mozart masterfully constructs complex series of ensembles that introduce the principals until the stage seems to overflow with characters. A forceful quickening of the tempo speeds the course of the finales to dramatic conclusions.

The opening scenes of Act I serve to demonstrate the masterful way in which Mozart draws his characters. In the first two scenes, we meet Figaro and Susanna, servants of the Count and Countess of Almaviva. They are to be married later that day, and the Count has offered them quarters adjoining his own. Figaro is quite content with the arrangement, but Susanna has misgivings. She fears that the Count has designs on her and may be planning to send Figaro off on a trip so that he can seduce her. The countess summons Susanna with her bell, and Figaro is left to ponder the situation. He decides to outwit the Count. (Ultimately, in the last act, the Count is outwitted when the Countess substitutes herself for Susanna during an evening rendezvous with the Count.)

This much of the action takes place in the first two scenes, apportioned as two duets and recitatives for Susanna and Figaro (Scene 1), and a recitative and a solo for Figaro (Scene 2):

Scene 1 (*Figaro and Susanna*)
    Duet
    Recitative
    Duet
    Recitative

Scene 2 (*Figaro alone*)
    Recitative
    Cavatina

---

*Mozart labeled *The Marriage of Figaro* an opera buffa; *Don Giovanni*, a *dramma giocoso* ("jocose drama").

In this scene from a modern production of Mozart's *Marriage of Figaro*, Figaro ponders how to outwit his master, Count Almaviva.

Mozart cleverly ties the two scenes together by applying the horns of the orchestra as a double musical metaphor. They serve as an emblem of nobility, but they also symbolize the count's intention to cuckold Figaro. Horn fanfares make an appearance in the first duet, and again in the second duet, where they suggest the Count's bell summoning Figaro—both as servant and as about-to-be cuckolded husband. (In the same passage, Mozart uses flutes and oboes to represent the more delicate handbell of the countess.)

In the second scene, Figaro hits on a strategy: He will pretend to play the servile lackey, but he will ensnare the Count and make him dance to the servant's tune. As he considers how to do this, Figaro sings the famous **cavatina**★ "Se vuol ballare." Here is the Italian text along with a free translation:

Se vuol ballare,	If you want to dance,
signor Contino,	my little count,
il chitarrino	on my little guitar
le suonerò.	I'll accompany you.
Se vuol venire,	If you want to enroll
nella mia scuola,	in my school,
la capriola	capers
le insegnerò.	I'll show you.
Saprò, ma piano,	Yes, I shall know, but carefully,
meglio ogni arcano,	all these plots,
dissimulando	by stealth
scoprir potrò!	I'll unveil more successfully!
L'arte schermendo,	Disguising my craft,
l'arte adoprando,	exploiting my craft,
di quà pungendo,	pinching here,
di là scherzando,	jesting there,
tutte le macchine	all his machinations
rovescierò.	I shall reverse.

This cavatina divides into three parts, in the order *ABA'* (see the study diagram). In the *A* section, Figaro invites the Count to dance. The horns, accompanied by pizzicato strings (the orchestral counterpart to Figaro's guitar), double the enticing melody to produce a remarkable orchestral effect. We give here the opening of Figaro's part:

The Marriage of Figaro, *Act I, Cavatina, "Se vuol ballare"*

Se vuol bal - la - re, si - gnor Con - ti - no, se vuol bal - la - re, si - gnor Con - ti - no,

---

★ A short setting for solo voice and orchestra, typically less complex than an aria.

Mozart: *The Marriage of Figaro*, Cavatina, "Se vuol ballare"

A	B	A′	Coda (B)
Allegretto $\frac{3}{4}$	Presto $\frac{2}{4}$	Allegretto $\frac{3}{4}$	Presto $\frac{2}{4}$
(suggests a minuet)	(suggests a popular dance)	(suggests a minuet)	
Horns, pizzicato strings	Short, repeated phrases	Horns, pizzicato strings	
p	$<$ *f*	*p*	*f*

With its moderately fast tempo (Allegretto), $\frac{3}{4}$ meter, and carefully balanced phrases (compare the rhythmic values of mm. 1–4 and 5–8), the *A* section suggests that most aristocratic of dances, the minuet (see p. 173). But in the *B* section, where Figaro sets his snare, the tempo shifts to a rapid presto and to a less-refined dance in $\frac{2}{4}$ meter. Here, Figaro sings in short, crisp phrases as he works himself up into a fury:

L'ar - te scher - men - do, l'ar - te a-do - pran - do, di quà pun - gen - do, di là scher - zan - do,

Note the rapid-fire delivery of words ending in "-do": "schermendo," "adoprando," "pungendo," and "scherzando," which accent the music and give force to Figaro's mounting rage. Then, with the return of the *A* section, considerably shortened and reworked, we are back in the world of the courtly minuet and of Figaro the servant. But a brisk coda in $\frac{2}{4}$ reminds us again of his intentions. All in all, "Se vuol ballare" is a masterpiece of characterization.

MOZART AND GERMAN OPERA

In Germany, a native operatic tradition was slow to develop. Italian opera and French academic drama ruled the German stage during much of the eighteenth century. Only gradually were voices raised for a native German drama and, in turn, for a German opera.

One type of German opera did take hold, however: the **Singspiel,** a comic opera with arias and spoken dialogue (instead of recitative). From its lowly origins around the middle of the century, the Singspiel had come to attract the attention of major composers. The opening of a national theater in Vienna by Emperor Joseph in 1778 also encouraged its popularity. It was in this theater that Mozart's delightful Turkish opera, *Die Entführung aus dem Serail (The Abduction from the Seraglio),* was premiered in 1782. Mozart's most famous German opera is *Die Zauberflöte (The Magic Flute).* It offers a range of serious and comic characters, of high moral purpose and comic relief—and it is filled with unforgettable music. Mozart died only a few months after its premiere.

THE MAGIC FLUTE

The Magic Flute concerns the moral education of Tamino, a young prince. In the first scene, he is saved from a serpent by three women dressed in black, who bid him to rescue Pamina, the abducted daughter of their mistress, the Queen of the Night. Tamino is accompanied on his mission by Papageno, a birdcatcher, to whom the women give a magic set of bells. They offer Tamino a magic flute to protect him against dangers along the way.

Tamino and Papageno reach the court of Sarastro, who is holding Pamina, only to discover that he is a benevolent and enlightened man who presides over the mysteries of Isis and Osiris. Tamino and Pamina are eventually united; then, in the closing scene, the plotting Queen of the Night is defeated, and Tamino and Pamina are welcomed into the priestly temple.

The Magic Flute is a Masonic allegory of the triumph of reason and truth over evil. Sarastro is the enlightened master priest who opposes the forces of darkness, symbolized by the Queen of the Night. Both the score and the libretto teem with subtle Masonic allusions. The poet Goethe, himself a Mason, commented that only the initiated would fully grasp Mozart's special purpose.

Goethe's caution has not deterred scholars from trying to unravel the mysteries of the score, however. The chords at the very beginning of the overture are thought to represent the applicant knocking on the door of the Masonic temple for admission. Several parts of the opera are in the key of E-flat major, which has three flats, apparently associated by Mozart with Masonic numerology. There is a good amount of formal counterpoint in the score, evidently to suggest ceremonial Masonic rituals. The overture, for example, includes a lively fugue. Similarly, in the finale to the closing act, Tamino and Pamina encounter two armored men who sing, in chorale style, an inscription on a pyramid, with the orchestra providing accompaniment in strict counterpoint. Finally, there is music for winds in several passages (including trombones, which Mozart adds to buttress his orchestral forces); wind bands were customarily used in Masonic ritual.

In his score, Mozart matches a broad spectrum of musical styles to his characters. The Queen of the Night, for example, drawn from the opera seria, sings virtuoso arias. Papageno sings irresistibly charming melodies that have the appeal of heartfelt folk tunes. Tamino and Pamina, on the other hand, are entrusted with considerably more sophisticated, elegant music. On the most serious level is Sarastro's music, noble and measured. The text of his aria in Act II, "In diesen heil'gen Hallen," reads like a manifesto of Masonry:

Stanza 1

In diesen heil'gen Hallen,
kennt man die Rache nicht,
und ist ein Mensch gefallen,
führt Liebe ihn zur Pflicht.
Dann wandelt er an Freundes Hand,
vergnügt und froh ins bess're Land.

Stanza 2

In diesen heil'gen Mauern,
wo Mensch den Menschen liebt,
kann kein Verräter lauern,
weil man dem Feind vergiebt.
Wen solche Lehren nicht erfreun,
verdienet nicht ein Mensch zu sein.

Stanza 1

Within these sacred halls,
one does not know vengeance,
and if a brother has fallen,
love returns him to his duty.
Then he turns to his friend's hand,
refreshed and joyful in the better land.

Stanza 2

Within these sacred walls,
where man loves fellow man,
no traitor can be lurking,
as we forgive our foes.
Whoever does not delight in such teaching,
deserves not to be a man.

Mozart joins the two stanzas to a simple aria, with the same music serving the two verses (*AA*). There is a reassuring simplicity about this music, with its radiant vision of a Masonic paradise; there is also a suggestion of nobility, implied by Mozart's use of dotted rhythms:

The Magic Flute, *Act II, Aria, "In diesen heil'gen Hallen"*

Sarastro sings this aria to reassure Pamina after her mother, the Queen of the Night, has arrived at the temple to foment rebellion and to incite Pamina to kill Sarastro.

In an earlier scene, the Queen's seething hatred erupts in her celebrated "rage" aria, "Der Hölle Rache" ("Vengeance of hell"), which offers melodic lines ruptured by wide leaps and a driving rhythmic energy. The strings accompany her melody, given here, with bristling repeated notes, a striking reference to the agitated style of the aria:

The Magic Flute, *Act II, Aria, "Der Hölle Rache"*

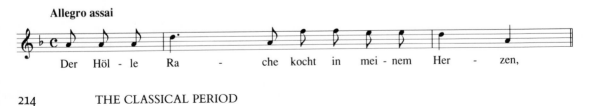

214   THE CLASSICAL PERIOD

Here is the text of the aria:

Der Hölle Rache kocht in meinem Herzen,
Tod und Verzweiflung flammet um mich her!
Fühlt nicht durch dich Sarastro Todesschmerzen,
so bist du meine Tochter nimmermehr.

Vengeance of hell is roused in my heart,
Death and despair burn all around me!
If Sarastro does not feel the pains of death at
   your hand,
Then you are no longer my daughter.

Verstossen sei auf ewig, verlassen sei auf ewig,
zertrümmert sei'n auf ewig alle Bande der Natur,
wenn nicht durch dich Sarastro wird erblassen!
Hört! Rachegötter! Hört der Mutter Schwur!

Be outcast for ever, be abandoned for ever,
all bonds of nature destroyed for ever,
If Sarastro is not destroyed by you!
Hear me, gods of vengeance! Hear a mother's
   oath!

In the aria, Mozart makes extreme demands upon the singer, and in some passages pushes the soprano to the very limits of her high range. The form of the aria, in three parts of unequal length, is equally striking: The first section quickly modulates from the tonic to the second key; the second section acts as a transition to the return of the tonic; and the third, which reestablishes the tonic, is drastically curtailed, as if to suggest that the Queen is consumed by her fury (section 1, lines 1–4; section 2, lines 5–7; section 3, line 8). This explosive music stands in striking contrast to the deliberate, reasoned tone of Sarastro's music, which ultimately prevails in the opera.

MOZART AND SACRED MUSIC

The strong ties between church and state in Austria and Italy ensured the cultivation there of sacred music and its rich tradition. It was a conservative tradition, built on centuries of polyphonic settings of the Mass and other sacred texts. In Mozart's day, learned counterpoint was still associated with sacred music. Mozart, Haydn, and countless other composers produced a great many Masses, motets, litanies, and smaller sacred works.

    The rise of the classical orchestra influenced sacred music as well as secular, and the sacred Mass grew more symphonic in character. To achieve a sense of solemnity and grandeur, composers expanded the orchestra by adding trombones,★ which were historically associated with ritual and supernatural imagery.

REQUIEM IN D MINOR, K. 626, INTROIT AND KYRIE

The supreme example of Mozart's sacred music is the Requiem in D minor, K. 626, which was commissioned in 1791 under unusual circumstances by an anonymous caller, apparently a count who intended to claim the work as his own. Mozart left the Requiem

---

★ Bass brass instruments with a cupped mouthpiece and with a bore that expands into a bell. A separate U-shaped piece called a slide can be moved to expand or shorten the length of the tubing (the column of air), thus producing the pitches of the scale. The trombone did not become a regular member of the orchestra until the nineteenth century. See p. 535.

Mozart: Requiem, K. 626 (Introit and Kyrie)

Introit (Requiem aeternam)

Adagio

Orchestral Introduction		Line 1 (*Requiem aeternam*)	2 (*Lux perpetua*)	3–4 (*Te decet*)	5–6 (*Exaudi*)	
Imitative subject in winds, string chords	trombones	Imitative polyphony in chorus	Homophonic	Soprano solo, flowing figure in strings	Chorus	Orchestral passage
					Dotted figure	
p	*f*	*f*	*f*	*p*	*f*	*p*
Tonic (minor key)			Major key			

unfinished at his death. A host of legends came to surround the work. According to one, popularized in the nineteenth century, Mozart himself viewed the composition as his own requiem. After his death, some of his acquaintances set about completing the work, and therein lies some uncertainty. We shall never know for certain exactly what Mozart left behind in the form of preliminary sketches for others to complete. Nevertheless, the authentic parts of the Requiem bear the stamp of Mozart's genius and show at its best the high sacred style of the period.

The **requiem** is the sacred Mass for the dead. The tradition of composed polyphonic requiems dates back at least as far as the fifteenth century. By convention, the more joyous texts of the Mass are omitted from requiems; also, a penitential text known as a Tract is introduced, to which is appended the text of the famous thirteenth-century sequence *Dies irae* ("Day of Judgment").

The first movement of Mozart's work, the *Introit* "Requiem aeternam dona eis, Domine" ("Grant them eternal rest, O Lord"), is combined with the Kyrie, a fugue in high contrapuntal style. The Latin text and translation follow:

Requiem aeternam dona eis, Domine,
et lux perpetua luceat eis.
Te decet hymnus, Deus, in Sion,
et tibi reddetur votum in Jerusalem.
Exaudi orationem meam,
ad te omnis caro veniet.
Kyrie eleison, Christe eleison.

Grant them eternal peace, O Lord,
and let eternal light shine upon them.
A hymn befits Thee, O Lord, in Sion,
and a vow shall be offered to Thee in
    Jerusalem.
Hear my entreaty,
all flesh shall come to Thee.
Lord have mercy, Christ have mercy.

Mozart presents the text of the Introit in distinct sections, with several different styles and textures (see the study diagram). Marked Adagio, the movement begins with a

Mozart: Requiem, K. 626 (Introit and Kyrie), *Continued*

		Kyrie eleison, Christe eleison			
		Allegro			Adagio
1–2 *(Requiem* *aeternam)* based on preceding	⌢ Pause	7 Fugue on 2 subjects presented simultaneously	Dissonant chord	⌢ Pause	Cadence
f Tonic	 Dominant	*f* Tonic			*f* Tonic

dark–colored orchestral passage that introduces a contrapuntal subject moving stepwise in the woodwinds against a background of detached chords in the strings. Four somber trombone chords signal the entrance of the chorus, which, as our example shows, takes up the first line of text and the subject in imitative fashion, with the voices entering one by one:

Requiem in D minor, K. 626 ("Introit")

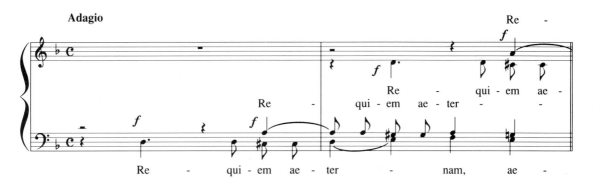

The voices are doubled by woodwinds and accompanied by the strings and an organ continuo; the effect of the whole is one of subdued gravity. For the second line of text, Mozart abandons the minor key of the opening for a brighter major key; the chorus here sings in chordal fashion, matching the reference to "eternal light" ("lux perpetua") with harmonic clarity:

et   lux   per - pe - tu - a

Again in contrast, Mozart assigns the third and fourth lines to a soprano solo, accompanied by a flowing figure in the strings. The full chorus reenters for the fifth and sixth lines, supported by a dotted figure in the orchestra that makes the supplication more emphatic. Finally, Mozart repeats, with some revisions, the music for the first two lines, pausing before the following Kyrie, set in a faster Allegro tempo.

A masterpiece of fugal writing, the Kyrie is based on two juxtaposed fugal subjects, one for the text "Kyrie eleison" and the other for the text "Christe eleison":

Requiem in D minor, K. 626 ("Kyrie")

The first subject is not Mozart's invention: It had a distinguished ancestry, including treatments by Bach, Handel (see p. 144), and other baroque masters. The second subject, which moves in faster rhythmic values, describes a florid melisma (see p. 14), with a profusion of notes for "-le" that generates great rhythmic energy. Near the end of the movement, Mozart calls a halt to this intricate polyphony with a surprise cadence that swerves to a shattering dissonant chord. After a pause, he resumes with the Adagio tempo from the opening of the work; the final chord reverberates with great force and majesty.

It remained for later generations to assess fully the magnitude of Mozart's genius. He was remembered as a great keyboard virtuoso and as a composer of prodigious talent with an astonishing artistic facility. His richly hued music made considerable demands upon listeners, yet it was filled with memorable melodies of unequaled purity and beauty. His music was truly international in scope, synthesizing as it did a variety of styles and genres. With masterpieces in nearly every genre, it assured the ascendancy of German music into the nineteenth century. No one benefited more from Mozart's music than did Beethoven, his greatest successor, whose immortal compositions would have been unthinkable without the sublime accomplishments of Mozart.

Suggested Listening

Wolfgang Amadeus Mozart
Clarinet Quintet (K. 581)
Don Giovanni
★*The Magic Flute*
★*The Marriage of Figaro*
★Piano Concerto in A major (K. 488)
Piano Concerto in C minor (K. 491)
★Requiem in D minor (K. 626)
Symphony No. 40, in G minor (K. 550)
Symphony No. 41, in C major (*Jupiter*, K. 551)

Note: Works marked with an asterisk are the principal works discussed in the chapter.

9

LUDWIG VAN BEETHOVEN

*F*ew composers have altered the course of music history as powerfully and decisively as Ludwig van Beethoven (1770–1827). The heir of the musical legacies of Mozart and Haydn, Beethoven in turn influenced nearly every major composer of the nineteenth century and beyond. In their symphonies, Schubert, Mendelssohn, Schumann, Brahms, Bruckner, and Mahler—and scores of lesser symphonists—worked in the shadow of Beethoven's mighty nine symphonies; in their chamber music, many of those same composers turned to Beethoven's exemplary series of string quartets for inspiration. Generation after generation of pianists has matched its skill against Beethoven's challenging thirty-two piano sonatas. And Beethoven's revolutionary union of music and text in the "Ode to Joy" finale of the Ninth Symphony deeply affected the course of German opera and instrumental music later in the nineteenth century.

If we discount Beethoven's early years, about which we know relatively little, his career spans three general stylistic periods: (1) up to 1802, (2) 1803–1814, and (3) 1815–1827. Those periods roughly coincide with (1) the waning days of the Enlightenment in Austria, (2) the turbulent period of Napoleon's empire, and (3) the political reaction and restoration after Napoleon's defeat. As we have seen, Mozart and Haydn brought the classical style to perfection during the 1780s and 1790s. Beethoven began his career by emulating their masterpieces; but by the time of his death, his music had exceeded the limits of classicism and was exploring the romantic aesthetic that we shall examine in Part V. From one perspective, then, Beethoven's music marked the culmination of the classical style; from another, it anticipated the outbreak of musical romanticism in the decades to come.

Two nineteenth-century views of Beethoven.

The composer's imperious personality and eccentric manner contributed greatly to his reputation as a suffering romantic artist and social recluse, and over the years many romanticized legends grew up around his tormented life (we give two nineteenth-century accounts on p. 223). However fact was transformed into fiction, Beethoven won a new artistic independence for composers who followed him. Many listeners have continued to sense in his music an intimate diary of his life's struggles.

BEETHOVEN'S EARLY PERIOD

Beethoven was born in 1770 in Bonn, the site of the court of the Electorate of Cologne, one of many German territories loyal to the Austrian monarchy. As a boy, he displayed uncommon musical gifts, and his father himself oversaw his musical education, apparently with the intention of rearing a second Mozart. From all accounts, Beethoven's childhood was miserable. His father, according to one witness, "poured out too many libations to Bacchus" (that is, drank to excess). He often beat his son to force him to practice the piano for hours on end, and he harshly criticized his son's early attempts at composition. By the early 1780s, Beethoven was serving at court as an organist and as

A NINETEENTH-CENTURY ANECDOTE ABOUT BEETHOVEN

Beethoven should by no means be offered as a model for directors of orchestras. The performers under him were obliged cautiously to avoid being led astray by their conductor, who thought only of his composition, and constantly labored to depict the exact expression required, by the most varied gesticulations. Thus, when the passage was loud he often beat time downwards, when his hand should have been up. A diminuendo he was in the habit of marking by contracting his person, making himself smaller and smaller; and when a pianissimo occurred, he seemed to slink, if the word is allowable, beneath the conductor's desk. As the sounds increased in loudness, so did he gradually rise up, as if out of an abyss; and when the full force of the united instruments broke upon the ear, raising himself on tiptoe, he looked of gigantic stature, and, with both his arms floating about in undulating motion, seemed as if he would soar to the clouds. He was all motion. . . .

From The Harmonicon *xi (1833)*

---

a violist in the orchestra. In 1783 a brief notice in a music periodical prophesied that he would follow in Mozart's footsteps.

Beethoven's early compositions were of uneven quality, though in 1790 he wrote a remarkable funeral cantata in memory of Emperor Joseph II. That monarch had instituted several reforms during his reign, and in the cantata, Beethoven recounted his good works—his struggle against fanaticism and superstition and his faith in the progress of mankind. Some fifteen years later, Beethoven chose to reuse part of that cantata in his opera *Fidelio*. That work, with its stirring dungeon scene, in which political prisoners yearn for freedom from tyranny, is one powerful reminder of Beethoven's affinity to the humanitarian ideals of the Enlightenment.

BEETHOVEN AND SOCIETY

His extreme reserve towards strangers, which is carried to such excess, . . . prevents him from displaying those excellent qualities, which, under a forbidding exterior, he is known to possess. And yet such are the contrasts that meet in his character, that occasionally his warmth of temper, extreme bluntness of remark, and singularity of manners, together with his total want of reserve in offering his opinion on others, tend to estrange him much from the prescribed forms of society. Add to all this, that deplorable calamity, the greatest ill that could befall a man of his profession, his extreme deafness, which we are assured is now [1823] so great as to amount to a total privation of hearing. Those who visit him are obliged to write down what they have to communicate. To this cause may be traced many of the peculiarities visible in his later compositions; for though, as we have before observed, the design of a composition ought to be found in the mind, without any aid from material sounds, yet its effect should be accurately heard upon some instrument, before final adoption. . . .

From The Harmonicon *i (1823)*

In 1792 Beethoven moved to Vienna, the imperial capital. He had visited Vienna briefly a few years before, and probably he had met Mozart there. Now, nearly a year after Mozart's death, he applied for tutelage in composition to Haydn, who had recently returned from his first visit to England. Beethoven's studies with Haydn were interrupted after only a year or so, however, when Haydn left for his second visit to England. There is some evidence that Beethoven was disappointed with the course of study Haydn prescribed for him; still, Beethoven never lost his regard for Haydn's music.

During his early years in Vienna, Beethoven began to appear as a virtuoso pianist in the salons of the aristocracy. His performances conjured up vivid memories of Mozart, much to the discomfort of other aspiring Viennese pianists. Beethoven also began to compose sizable works, most of them in the traditional classical forms: several piano sonatas, including three dedicated to Haydn; two piano concertos reminiscent of Mozart; an ambitious set of string quartets, with striking suggestions of Haydn and Mozart; and his first finished symphony (1800).

The Symphony No. 1 owes much to Haydn's *London* Symphonies: It is written for an orchestra of the same size, begins with a majestic slow introduction, and observes Haydn's four-movement plan with a minuet as the third movement. Here and there, however, we sense Beethoven's emerging individual style: severe and frequent contrasts in dynamics and a relentless, driving rhythmic energy. To be sure, these stylistic characteristics were not entirely lacking in Mozart's and Haydn's music, but Beethoven experimented with them in a considerably more forceful manner.

PIANO SONATA IN C-SHARP MINOR, OP. 27, NO. 2 *(MOONLIGHT)*

One of Beethoven's best-known works from the early period, the *Moonlight* Sonata (1801), in many ways adumbrated the music of the middle period. Beethoven once dismissed the work as insignificant alongside his other sonatas. In fact, this sonata is remarkable for its striking freedom from established models. In earlier sonatas, Beethoven had favored the typical classical plans of three or four movements: fast–slow–fast, or fast–slow–minuet–fast. But after the turn of the century, he grew more daring, treating each new sonata as an opportunity for experimentation. Thus, one sonata (Op. 26, 1801) has a somber funeral march for its slow movement. What is more, the march bears the extraordinary title "On the Death of a Hero," underscoring its extramusical meaning apart from its form. In another sonata, described as *quasi una fantasia,* or "like a fantasy" (Op. 27, No. 1), Beethoven builds his first movement from a juxtaposition of seemingly unrelated Andante and Allegro sections.

Beethoven described the *Moonlight* Sonata also as *quasi una fantasia*—further evidence that he was deliberately reaching beyond the limits of the classical sonata. Many of Beethoven's contemporaries (and the romantics who followed him) found the first movement of this sonata strangely evocative, with a mysterious, dreamlike quality. Its key alone—C-sharp minor—was unusual; few composers wrote sonatas in this key of four sharps. The melancholy strains of the first movement, with its unwavering triplet accompaniment and sketchlike intimations of melody, seemed to suggest a song whose text had been suppressed. One acquaintance of Beethoven's actually urged him to set a poem to this movement. Many titles were suggested for the sonata as a whole, of which *Moonlight*—coined after Beethoven's death—has endured.

The sonata has three movements, with tempo indications of Very Slow and Sustained (*Adagio sostenuto*), Relatively Fast (*Allegretto*), and Very Fast and Agitated (*Presto agitato*). The first movement, the freest in form of the three, is played at a *pianissimo* level throughout. The Allegretto, a lighthearted movement in *ABA* dance form, has *pianissimo* and *piano* levels. The third movement is in sonata form and explores a much broader dynamic range, from *pianissimo* to *fortissimo*.

Essentially, what Beethoven accomplishes in this sonata is to shift the weight of the composition from the delicate, muffled first movement to the massive finale, with its faster tempo, much more dramatic use of dynamics, and stricter formal control. To link the three movements, Beethoven instructs that there be no pause between the first two movements and, furthermore, subtly reuses traces of material from the first movement in the third. All in all, the sonata marks an adventurous reinterpretation of the traditional classical sonata.

The Adagio opens with a few introductory measures of triplets () in the middle register of the piano and a quiet bass line in octaves. Above the triplets, Beethoven presents what sound like half-formed portions of a melody, which begins by hovering around a single, repeated pitch:

*Piano Sonata, Op. 27, No. 2 (*Moonlight*), First Movement*

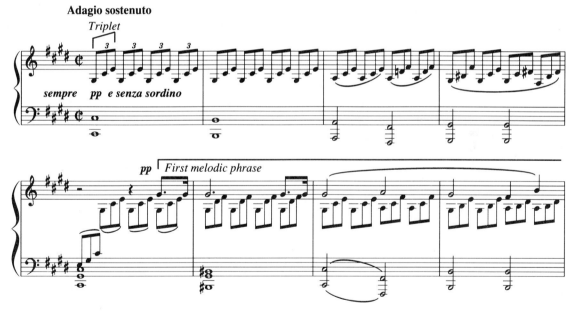

Beethoven: Piano Sonata, Op. 27, No. 2 *(Moonlight),* First Movement

Introduction	*A*	Transition	*A'*	Coda
Triplet accompaniment	4 melodic phrases in treble with triplet accompaniment	Triplets	Return of melody and accompaniment	Accompaniment, vestige of melody in bass
Tonic	Tonic, then touching on different keys	Dominant pedal	Tonic	Tonic

The melody falls into several phrases, each of which transports us harmonically away from the tonic key. With the fourth phrase, Beethoven seems to make a fresh start in a new key, but this soon gives way to a transition: Over an extended dominant pedal point, we hear the restless triplets of the accompaniment, as Beethoven prepares the return of the tonic key. The melody, somewhat recast, resumes in the tonic. A coda, again based on the triplets, rounds out the movement, with a vestige of the melody in the low register of the piano. Overall, then, the form of the movement is *ABA'*, or, more accurately, *A*–Transition–*A'*. As the study diagram shows, these sections are framed by the introduction and the coda.

Beethoven instructed that the entire movement be played with extreme delicacy and *senza sordino,* that is, "without the *sordino.*" Scholars disagree about what Beethoven meant by this instruction. Most likely, he intended that the dampers (*sordini*) of the piano be raised, allowing the strings to resonate freely and produce a gentle welling of undamped sonorities. By raising the dampers (strips of feltlike material, resting on the strings, that were typically regulated by a knee lever on the fortepiano, by a foot pedal on later pianos), the pianist could blur the various harmonies, creating evanescent harmonic mixtures. On the modern piano, the resulting volume of cacophony creates too great a distortion. But when performed with care on a fortepiano of Beethoven's time, a considerably more delicate instrument, the effect can be musically captivating.

The second movement of the *Moonlight* Sonata is a short major-key piece that functions as an interlude between the pensive Adagio and the explosive finale. Though not labeled, the movement resembles the minuet, for it has an opening section, a trio, and a repeat of the opening section. More likely, however, Beethoven conceived this movement as a **scherzo,** a lighthearted movement (the word means "joke" or "jest"). Previously employed by Haydn in some of his string quartets, the scherzo came to replace the minuet in the nineteenth century, largely owing to the efforts of Beethoven, who introduced it into his symphonies, sonatas, and other instrumental works. The basic form of the scherzo—scherzo, trio, and repeat of scherzo—derived from the ternary dance form typically encountered in the minuet (see p. 173).

THE FORTEPIANO

The fortepiano of Beethoven's time was quite different from the modern piano. It had a smaller range (generally about five octaves) and more delicate proportions. It could sustain less tension on its strings and overall was capable of producing lower volumes of sound than its modern counterpart. The concert grand piano in use today has eighty-eight keys (more than seven octaves) and a reinforced interior iron frame. Moreover, it is triple-strung; that is, it has three strings for each pitch. It incorporates several technological innovations made later in the nineteenth century, by-products of the Industrial Revolution.

On the modern piano, three foot pedals are used to create special effects. When the damper pedal, on the right, is depressed, it raises the dampers, allowing the strings to resonate freely. The pedal on the left causes a muting effect. When it is depressed, the entire set of hammers shifts slightly, so that the hammers strike only one of the three strings for each key, thereby muting the sound. This "soft" pedal is known as the *una corda* pedal, from the Italian for "one string."

The fortepiano shown here was built by the English maker John Broadwood in 1792. It has two foot pedals: One engages an *una corda* mechanism, and the other raises and lowers the dampers. Many pianos from this time used knee levers (on the underside of the case) instead of foot pedals for special effects.

The playful character of Beethoven's second movement is most evident in the Trio, where the composer accents the third beat of the measure to disrupt the meter:

Piano Sonata, Op. 27, No. 2 (Moonlight), Second Movement (Trio)

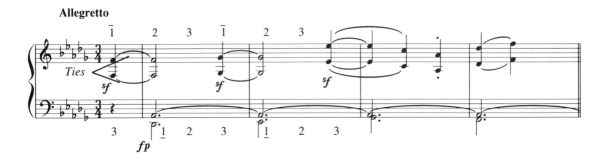

By holding (tieing) the third beat across the bar line, Beethoven creates the appearance of two opposing meters: the $\frac{3}{4}$ meter of the bass clef, and a second $\frac{3}{4}$ meter displaced by one beat in the treble clef.

The third movement, in the minor key of the first movement, is a substantial movement in sonata form. Agitated in character, it erupts with rapidly ascending material across the keyboard, abrupt leaps and pauses, and an unflagging rhythmic energy. In the opening material (*a*), Beethoven ingeniously brings back the ascending triadic figure from the opening of the first movement, now transformed from quiet triplets

into rocketing sixteenth notes

What had been the accompaniment in the Adagio now is extended to become the main material for the finale, driven by a staccato bass line and punctuated by *sforzandi* (accented) chords:

Piano Sonata, Op. 27, No. 2 (Moonlight), Third Movement

For the second theme of this movement, Beethoven introduces a yearning minor-key melody (*b*) accompanied by another triadic pattern. The new theme is distinguished by a rhythmic figure that stresses the second beat of the measure:

To close out the exposition, Beethoven varies the second theme, first with repeated staccato notes (*b'*) and then with longer note values (*b''*):

Most of the development section is dedicated to a treatment of *b* in the bass in various keys. The recapitulation seems to progress according to standard sonata form. Just as the movement is about to close, however, Beethoven launches into a fantastic coda. Rolled chords come to a halt and give way to two more statements of *b* (in the bass and the treble) and then to torrents of passagework running up and down the keyboard. Still not ready to close, Beethoven resorts to a cadenza and, in a masterly stroke, adds two bars of Adagio—two sustained piano octaves in the bass that invoke for a moment the mystery of the first movement:

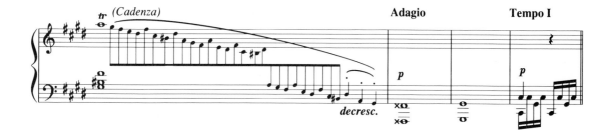

A few furious measures close out this emphatic application of sonata form.

BEETHOVEN'S MIDDLE PERIOD

Sometime early in the nineteenth century, Beethoven announced that he would seek a "new manner" in his music. Notwithstanding the innovations of such works as the *Moonlight* Sonata, he may have perceived too great a reliance on the classical masters in his early instrumental works. Now he was intent on experimenting even more freely.

There was another factor that stimulated the "new manner": Beethoven had begun to lose his hearing. The deterioration was gradual; as late as 1815, he was still able to perform publicly as a pianist, and total deafness was to come only later. The psychological consequences of the impairment, however, were overwhelming. Beethoven set down his thoughts in a poignant document written in Heiligenstadt, not far from Vienna. In this so-called Heiligenstadt Testament (1802), a remarkably frank confession, he lamented the failure of the one physical sense in which, as he put it, he should have been whole. Though close to suicide, he decided instead to live for his art. Rejuvenated, Beethoven entered the most productive period of his life.

Swiftly, he composed a bold new series of instrumental works that evidenced a powerfully "heroic" character in this middle period. Among these works are several of his most famous piano sonatas, including the *Tempest,* Op. 31, No. 2 (1802); the *Waldstein,* Op. 53 (1804); and the *Appassionata,* Op. 57 (1805); and the set of three *Razumovsky* String Quartets, Op. 59 (1806). Arguably, his most impressive achievements, however, were in the symphony.

Between 1803 and 1808, Beethoven concentrated his symphonic innovations in three monumental works: the *Eroica* Symphony (No. 3), the Fifth Symphony, and the *Pastoral* Symphony (No. 6). In these epoch-making works, Beethoven departed dramatically from tradition to produce symphonies on an unprecedented, grand scale. Most obvious of all, he began writing movements considerably longer than had been the practice. Further, he began to fortify the orchestra by adding woodwind and brass instruments. Finally, and most challenging of all to contemporary audiences, Beethoven seemed to design these symphonies to impart some sort of program or message beyond the music.

This bold new approach is first proclaimed in the Third Symphony, the *Eroica* ("Heroic") Symphony. Beethoven originally intended to dedicate this work to Napoleon Bonaparte and even planned to name it after him. To Beethoven and other liberal thinkers of the time, Napoleon had first stood as a champion of the oppressed. (In a similar way, roughly a decade before, some had found reason to praise the French Revolution: The English poet Wordsworth, for one, had predicted a golden age for France, "whence better days / To all mankind.") In 1804, however, after defeating two coalitions of European powers, Napoleon proclaimed himself Emperor of France; and at some point, Beethoven withdrew the dedication.

Conflict and contrast inform nearly every page of the score of the *Eroica,* heightening its heroic character. The lengthy first movement, in a highly charged style, teems with tense dissonances and clashing rhythmic patterns. The second movement is a lugubrious funeral march; the third, in contrast, is a joyful and explosive scherzo. In the complex fourth movement, Beethoven allies sonata form with a series of variations to achieve a crowning conclusion to the symphony; the basic theme on which this movement is based is drawn from Beethoven's ballet *The Creatures of Prometheus,* which celebrates the heroic deeds of the mythological figure who brought fire and civilization to mankind.

The mighty Fifth Symphony—perhaps Beethoven's best-known composition—is similar in mood to the *Eroica.* It seems to depict a musical struggle that is eventually resolved in the victorious finale. The symphony begins with the famous four-note motive, an attack of three short notes followed by a pause:

Symphony No. 5, in C minor, Op. 67, First Movement

Not only does Beethoven incorporate the motive into the second theme of the first movement,

but he also saturates the movement with its presence in some shape in nearly every measure. Indeed, the entire symphony is indebted to the basic motive, with its dialectical process of motion and rest. Sudden cessations of motion occur throughout the symphony. In the recapitulation of the first movement, the orchestra unexpectedly pauses to give way to a brief oboe cadenza. In the second movement, a pause occurs almost in the exact midpoint. In the third movement, only a few bars are heard before that movement pauses. And in the finale, the use of a pause is made even more dramatic: The triumphant course of the music is checked by the reappearance of material from the third movement, creating the effect of a large-scale interruption.

We have little reliable evidence about what meaning, if any, Beethoven intended the Fifth Symphony to convey. According to one interpretation, the opening motive was meant to represent Fate knocking at the door. Some critics went further. In particular, the writer, critic, and composer E. T. A. Hoffmann thought that Beethoven had won for the symphony a new stature. He applied to it such romantic words as "frightening," "mysterious," and "sinister," and proclaimed Beethoven the master of a new romantic power in instrumental music.

SYMPHONY NO. 6, IN F MAJOR, OP. 68 (*PASTORAL*)

For the Sixth Symphony, the *Pastoral,* finished in 1808, Beethoven himself provided specific descriptive titles for the movements, marking an important break from the symphonies of most classical composers. Beethoven's musical vision of the countryside suggests a romantic contemplation of nature and communion with God. Marking another break with tradition, Beethoven expanded the symphony to include five movements instead of the customary four. In addition, the third, fourth, and fifth movements are played without break and constitute an imposing stretch of continuous music. Here are Beethoven's headings for all five movements:

1. Awakening of cheerful feelings upon the arrival in the countryside

2. Scene by the brook

3. Merry gathering of peasants

4. Thunder; Storm

5. Shepherd's song; Happy and thankful feelings after the storm

Throughout the symphony, Beethoven provides musical symbols to reflect the program. There are imitations of birdcalls, flowing music to represent the brook, and dissonant music to represent the thunderstorm. As for the inhabitants of this setting, Beethoven imitates the music of the peasants with drone effects to suggest bagpipes and introduces characteristic themes to suggest the calls of shepherds.

He employs all these special effects, however, not just to imitate certain sounds and activities but also to reflect the emotions of a sensitive observer in the countryside. He made that distinction clear in a note found with his sketches for the symphony. His attempt to convey emotional release in his music proved greatly appealing to later romantic composers who were devoted admirers of the *Pastoral* Symphony.

First Movement: Awakening of Cheerful Feelings upon the Arrival in the Countryside (Allegro ma non troppo; Fast but not too fast) The arrival in the countryside is announced by a short theme (*a*) supported by a drone bass that quickly comes to a pause:

Symphony No. 6, in F major, Op. 68 (Pastoral)*, First Movement*

THE CLASSICAL PERIOD

The second measure of the theme provides a rhythmic motive that figures prominently throughout the movement (♫♫ ♫). A few bars further along, for example, this motive appears ten times in succession, again over a static bass. The passage moves in a gradual swell from *piano* to *forte,* followed by a diminuendo to *pianissimo:*

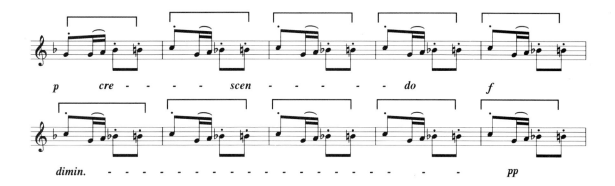

The opening measures are then taken up by the full orchestra at a *forte* level, with birdcalls in the flutes and, yet again, with the drone bass. The drone imitates the sound of bagpipes and provides a sense of tonal stability—and lack of conflict—quite in contrast to the dissonant tone of other symphonies by Beethoven, such as the *Eroica.* Moreover, the repetitions of the rhythmic motive in the second example suggest an idyllic world wholly at peace, and the gradual crescendo and diminuendo suggest the awakening of feelings in response to the peaceful scene.

The first movement is cast in sonata form. After the first thematic group, a short transition leads to the second group (*b*) in the new key. This new material consists of a smooth, flowing descending figure that foreshadows the second movement ("Scene by the Brook"). Beethoven repeats the figure several times, first in the strings (first violins, second violins, cello, double bass) and then in the woodwinds (clarinets, flutes). Here is how it first appears in the first violins:

The passage moves into a gradual crescendo, the second dynamics swell of this movement. The woodwinds, accompanied once again by a drone bass, now close the exposition with a robust motive of four pitches:

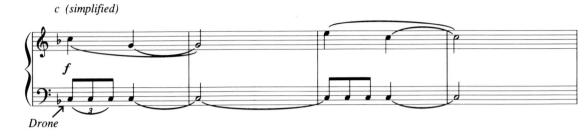

c (simplified)

Drone

As we shall see, this simple closing idea (*c*) reappears in another guise in the finale of the symphony as the Shepherd's Song of Thanksgiving. The exposition ends with a gradual diminuendo from *forte* to *piano* to *pianissimo,* with nearly thirty statements of the motive, ♫♫, drawn from *a* (♫♫ ♫).

The development is based almost entirely on that same motive. In large stretches of this section, Beethoven sustains individual major harmonies for several measures through a slowly unfolding crescendo before abruptly shifting to a fresh harmony, also prolonged for several measures. The slow rate of harmonic change in these passages once again gives the music a conspicuously static quality. Shortly before the recapitulation, the orchestra builds to a full *fortissimo,* one of the few climaxes in this movement. Then Beethoven thins out the orchestration, reestablishes the drone bass, and introduces the recapitulation. Much of this section corresponds to the exposition, though now the music remains in the tonic key. Beethoven adds a coda with one more *fortissimo* climax; the movement concludes with several *forte* chords for full orchestra followed by two *piano* chords to prepare us for the second movement.

Second Movement: Scene by the Brook (Andante molto moto; Slowly with much movement) The time signature of this movement is $\frac{12}{8}$. In choosing this compound meter, Beethoven was following a tradition of earlier composers who had used the meter for settings of pastoral texts or subjects. Typically, a measure of $\frac{12}{8}$ divides into four groups of three eighth notes each:

♫♫ ♫♫ ♫♫ ♫♫.

Beethoven uses this division, but also a subdivision that breaks the eighths into sixteenths, doubling the number of notes per measure:

♫♫♫ ♫♫♫ ♫♫♫ ♫♫♫.

These two arrangements, with their gently undulating flow, are carried through much of the movement by the lower strings, creating the effect of a murmuring brook. Above this rhythmic current is heard a slowly unfolding melody; its progress is checked periodically by the flow of the lower voices. Here are two examples from the opening measures, one with the melody accompanied by eighth notes, the other by sixteenths:

Symphony No. 6, in F major, Op. 68 (Pastoral), Second Movement

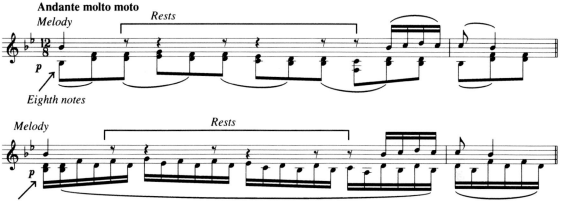

The rests that interrupt the melody permit the listener to focus attention momentarily on the tranquil motion of the accompaniment, which lends a certain rustic charm to the movement.

Beethoven uses sonata form for the second movement, though he is careful to avoid sharp thematic contrasts or any suggestion of tension. Most of the movement is played at a *piano* level, rarely reaching *forte*. In the closing bars, the composer indulges in a moment of literal imitation: He brings in three birdcalls actually identified in the score as the nightingale (flute), the quail (oboe), and the cuckoo (clarinet). For a brief moment, this natural imagery takes precedence over the steady motion of the brook; then, this exquisite movement comes to a close.

Third Movement: Merry Gathering of Peasants (Allegro; Fast) For the third movement, Beethoven writes a scherzo; a courtly minuet simply would not do to depict the peasants' lively celebration. What is more, Beethoven expands the proportions of his scherzo considerably by adding new material and by repetition. Instead of the usual scheme—*A* | *B* (Trio) | Repeat of *A*—the structural plan is *A* | *BC* | *A* | *BC* | *A* | Coda (based on *A*), in which *A* is the scherzo proper, and *B* and *C* replace the trio. The *A* section begins simply enough, with an unharmonized theme in the strings. Played detached (staccato) and at a *pianissimo* dynamics level, the descending theme has crisp ornaments that fall on the downbeats of the fifth, sixth, and seventh measures:

Symphony No. 6, in F major, Op. 68 (Pastoral), *Third Movement*

A SECTION

When Beethoven does introduce harmonies to support the thematic line, he simply restricts himself to one harmony for several measures, recalling the static passages of the first movement. The music builds steadily to a *fortissimo* climax, with the horns becoming more prominent as the gathering of peasants grows livelier. Then, abruptly, the full orchestra is interrupted by the B section, which begins with a fresh, playful theme in the high, exposed range of the oboes, accompanied only by violins and (more sparingly) by a bassoon:

B SECTION

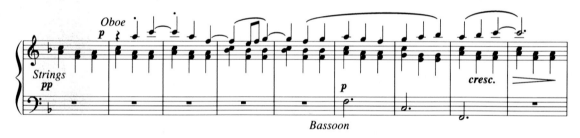

Against the regular accompaniment of the strings, the oboes enter in the middle of a measure, missing by one beat. Beethoven apparently seems to mean that the peasant musicians, though enthusiastic in their music making, are perhaps not too skillful. He carries the suggestion further by having the bassoon enter first with three notes, and later (not shown in the example) with four, as if the player were unsure of the part.

The melody of the B section is taken up in turn by the clarinet and the horn. Traditionally, this section, which corresponds to the Trio, would be followed by the return of the A section. Instead, Beethoven runs the B section into a faster C section, a rowdy Allegro dance in $\frac{2}{4}$ time:

The rhythm of this exuberant country dance derives from the first movement (compare the example on p. 232), where it appears in quite a different context. In the third and fourth measures, however, Beethoven adds one other rhythmic figure, consisting of a short note followed by a longer one (♪♩.), which produces a snaplike quality. This figure is commonly associated with folk music.

   The *C* section is halted by a shrill note from the trumpet, which has not been heard in the earlier movements. Beethoven then proceeds to repeat *A, B,* and *C* and, finally, adds an abridged statement of *A,* which culminates in a furious presto coda.

Fourth Movement: Thunder; Storm (Allegro; Fast) Without warning, the presto breaks off, and we hear instead the rumblings of an approaching storm. Beethoven turns to the minor mode for this movement, setting it off from the major keys of the other movements. Short, repeated motives in the low strings, timpani rolls, outbursts from the brass instruments—all depict the onslaught of the storm as the peasants scatter for cover. Trombones enter at the climax of the storm, and the shrill piccolo★ adds to the drama. Gradually, the violence subsides, and the woodwinds play a hymnlike melody. Without pausing, Beethoven moves directly to the finale.

Fifth Movement: Shepherd's Song; Happy and Thankful Feelings after the Storm (Allegretto; Moderately Fast) The finale is based on an authentic Alpine melody used by herdsmen to gather their flocks. In the extraordinary opening, the triadic melody is played first by a clarinet and then answered by a horn:

Symphony No. 6, in F major, Op. 68 (Pastoral), *Fifth Movement*

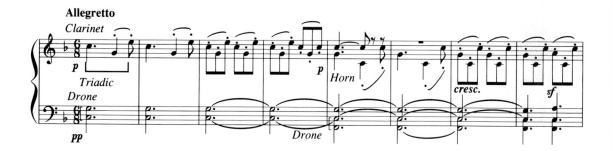

───────────

★ A small flute that sounds one octave higher than the normal flute.

Beethoven: Symphony No. 6, in F major, Op. 68 (*Pastoral*), Fifth Movement

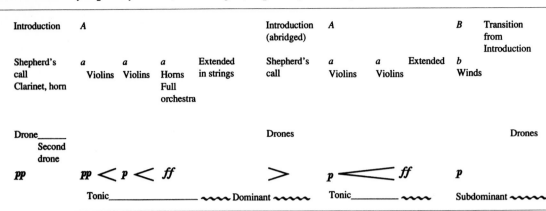

Introduction	A				Introduction (abridged)	A			B	Transition from Introduction
Shepherd's call Clarinet, horn	*a* Violins	*a* Violins	*a* Horns Full orchestra	Extended in strings	Shepherd's call	*a* Violins	*a* Violins	Extended	*b* Winds	
Drone____ Second drone					Drones					Drones
pp	*pp* < *p* < *ff*				>	*p* < *ff*			*p*	
	Tonic_____ ∿∿ Dominant ∿∿				Tonic_____ ∿∿				Subdominant ∿∿	

The clarinet is supported by a drone bass in the lower strings, and as the horn enters, Beethoven adds a second, conflicting drone. The result is a strange, mildly dissonant mixture of harmonies. This gives way to the gentle primary theme of the movement (*a*), which is drawn from the shepherd's call. Its triadic contours recall the closing theme of the first movement, as a comparison with the example on p. 234 makes clear:

*Symphony No. 6, in F major, Op. 68 (*Pastoral*), Finale*

Triadic
pp

cresc.

As the study diagram reveals, most of the movement is based on statements of *a* in the tonic key. Beethoven extends the third statement, which comes as the climax of a tremendous crescendo, through a modulation to the dominant (the key on the fifth step of the tonic scale). Then, we hear the music of the introduction, and Beethoven returns to two more statements of *a* in the tonic. There follows a fresh theme (*b*), introduced by the woodwinds in the subdominant key (the key on the fourth step of the tonic scale) and characterized by a lilting, long–short rhythmic pattern (♩♪):

p dolce
sf
sf

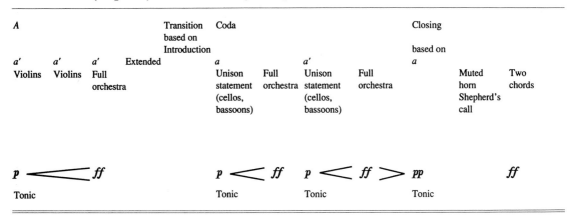

A				Transition based on Introduction	Coda				Closing based on		
a'	*a'*	*a'*	Extended		*a*		*a'*		*a*		
Violins	Violins	Full orchestra			Unison statement (cellos, bassoons)	Full orchestra	Unison statement (cellos, bassoons)	Full orchestra		Muted horn Shepherd's call	Two chords
p ———— *ff*					*p* < *ff*		*p* < *ff* > *pp*				*ff*
Tonic					Tonic		Tonic		Tonic		

Once again, Beethoven brings back the material of the introduction with its drone bass, and we have three additional statements of the shepherd's theme in the tonic, this time in a varied version we shall call *a'*. It features a flowing, smooth motion:

In the summarizing coda, Beethoven presents unison statements of *a* and *a'* that build to two mighty climaxes for full orchestra. The closing bars recall the shepherd's call *pianissimo*. Played by a muted horn, this reference affords a last glimpse of Beethoven's fleeting pastoral vision. Two *fortissimo* chords conclude this magnificent symphony.

More monumental music and more heroic music followed in Beethoven's middle period. In 1809, as Napoleon's armies marched on Vienna, Beethoven wrote his fifth and final piano concerto, which soon became known as the *Emperor* Concerto because of its martial tone. About the same time, he wrote an overture and some incidental music for Goethe's tragedy *Egmont,* which recounts the events leading to the Spanish subjugation of the Netherlands in the sixteenth century. The overture, a passionate work in F minor, concludes with the brilliant *Siegessymphonie* ("Victory Symphony") in F major, Egmont's triumphant vision of liberation as he awaits his execution.

BEETHOVEN'S LATE PERIOD

By 1814 Napoleon had fallen before a coalition of England, Prussia, Austria, and Russia, and the victorious allies convened in Vienna to restore political order.* Beethoven was in Vienna during this Congress of Vienna, and he composed patriotic cantatas and other pieces to celebrate the victory. Though well received, they were inferior to the music of the heroic period and were promptly forgotten. Now almost completely deaf, Beethoven withdrew more and more from public life. He communicated with visitors by passing written notes back and forth. Increasingly, the music of this period grew abstract and difficult for Beethoven's contemporaries to understand.

The first few years of the later period were surprisingly unproductive. Then, in 1823 and 1824, Beethoven finished two major works that had occupied him for years. The *Missa Solemnis* was a majestic setting of the Mass on a large scale. The revolutionary Ninth Symphony was a fundamentally new conception of the symphony that would profoundly influence symphonic composition well into the twentieth century. Set against the first three movements for orchestra is the gargantuan finale, which was inspired by a poem by Friedrich von Schiller (1759–1805), "An die Freude" ("To Joy"), an ode to universal brotherhood. Nearly one thousand measures long and requiring more time to perform than some entire symphonies of Haydn or Mozart, Beethoven's finale introduces for the first time vocal soloists and a chorus into the traditionally instrumental domain of the symphony. Beethoven's innovation was later emulated in symphonies by Berlioz, Mendelssohn, Liszt, and Mahler. Despite its imposing complexity, the finale of the Ninth Symphony essentially unfolds as a series of variations on the following prosaic theme, disarmingly simple in its smooth, stepwise motion, but universally recognized:

Symphony No. 9, in D minor, Op. 125, Finale

p dolce

No less innovative than the finale of the Ninth Symphony was Beethoven's other instrumental music of the late period. His last few piano sonatas, for example, were audacious in their structural freedom and in the technical demands they made on performers. Written between 1816 and 1822, these sonatas were rich in performance directions for the pianist. Instead of entering a simple tempo marking, such as Adagio or Allegro, Beethoven chose more provocative instructions, such as "With energy and with feeling and expression throughout," "Slowly and full of yearning," or "Song of lament," as if he intended to charge the music with some extramusical purpose.

---

*In 1815, Napoleon briefly returned to power before his decisive defeat at the Battle of Waterloo. He spent his last years in exile on the southern Atlantic island of St. Helena, where he died in 1821.

In his very last years, Beethoven wrote a series of six string quartets (1823–1826). By that time, he was utterly dependent on his inner ear; in a sense, he was composing for himself rather than for others. The quartets reveal the primary characteristics of Beethoven's late style: a use of complex contrapuntal textures, melodies of great lyrical beauty, and dramatic and startling contrasts. These forward-looking works proved difficult for Beethoven's contemporaries to plumb; they were, however, warmly embraced by the romantic composers who followed him. As one example, we look briefly at the slow movement of the String Quartet Op. 132.

STRING QUARTET IN A MINOR, OP. 132, THIRD MOVEMENT, *HEILIGER DANKGESANG (SACRED SONG OF THANKSGIVING)*

As he had with the symphony, Beethoven expanded the string quartet well beyond the classical models of Haydn and Mozart. One of his late quartets, for example, has seven movements; the Opus 132 quartet (1825) has five, arranged in a symmetrical plan. The first and fifth are Allegro movements in a minor key; the second and fourth are a scherzo and a march in a major key. At the heart of the quartet stands the ineffable slow movement titled "Heiliger Dankgesang," or "Sacred Song of Thanksgiving."

While working on this quartet, Beethoven was recovering from a serious illness, an event recorded in the deeply felt, central slow movement. The full title of the movement is "Sacred Song of Thanksgiving, from a Convalescent to the Deity in the Lydian Mode." Along with this remarkably frank title, we find such revealing directives within the movement as "Feeling New Strength" and "With the Most Inward Expression."

Much of this extraordinary movement is written in the Lydian mode, one of the old church modes, specifically the one built on the pitch F (see p. 9):

Lydian Mode

For Beethoven to write modal rather than tonal music in 1825 was nothing less than extraordinary; the church modes, associated with the sacred music of the Middle Ages and the Renaissance, were rarely used at that time. For listeners accustomed to tonal music, the archaic style of this Lydian music gave the quartet a mystical, supernatural quality.

There are five sections in the movement according to the plan *ABABA* (see the study diagram). The three *A* sections are in the Lydian mode; the two *B* sections are in a major key. In the first *A* section, Beethoven presents a solemn Lydian melody in the first violin, while the other instruments accompany in block-chordal fashion, suggesting the texture of a chorale. The Lydian melody divides into five separate phrases in

Beethoven: String Quartet, Op. 132, Third Movement ("Heiliger Dankgesang")

A	B	A	B	A
Molto Adagio Lydian mode (on F)	*Andante* Major key (D)	*Molto Adagio* Lydian mode (on F)	*Andante* Major key (D)	*Molto Adagio* Lydian mode (on F)
Alternating passages in imitative counterpoint and chorale-like melody	"Feeling New Strength"	Chorale phrases with imitative counterpoint	"Feeling New Strength"	First phrase of chorale melody with imitative counterpoint

sustained notes, with each phrase introduced by a short passage in imitative counterpoint for all four instruments. We give here the opening measures of the movement through the first phrase of the chorale:

String Quartet in A minor, Op. 132, Third Movement

A SECTION

*★"Under the voice" (that is, subdued).

Between the three *A* sections, all based on the Lydian chorale, are two contrasting *B* sections. For these, Beethoven reverts to tonal music: The *B* sections are firmly anchored in a major key (D major) and employ "modern" harmonic progressions. In addition, he chooses a slightly faster tempo for the *B* sections, Andante. Marked "Feeling New Strength," this music refers to the composer's convalescence. Its energetic leaps, vivacious trills and ornamental lines, and rhythmic animation are all in contrast to the meditative mood and solemn Adagio tempo of the *A* sections:

B SECTION

In the course of the "Song of Thanksgiving," the music thus alternates between the *A* and the *B* sections. Whereas the two *B* sections are essentially the same, the music for the *A* sections becomes increasingly more complex and learned. In the second *A* section, for example, Beethoven presents the chorale in long notes in the first violin while the other three instruments weave a tapestry of imitative counterpoint. In the last *A* section, Beethoven focuses on the first phrase of the chorale melody, which is allowed to stand out in the rich texture of four-part counterpoint. At the end, *pianissimo* chords in the high registers of the strings produce an ethereal, unworldly sound, as if Beethoven were taking leave of mortal concerns.

As his great contemporary Goethe was for literature, so was Beethoven the crucial link between eighteenth-century classicism and nineteenth-century romanticism. He began by thoroughly assimilating and mastering the classical idioms of Haydn and Mozart; yet, he soon transcended those idioms. For the composers who followed him, Beethoven's music took on a new, highly romanticized meaning; and his life, a certain mythical stature. Thus, he was viewed as a titan among mortals, a genius who felt compassion for mankind yet who created in inexorable solitude. In Beethoven's scores, the romantics found unleashed a new expressive power and an assertion of his unbending commitment to art. Understandably, they could not resist claiming Beethoven as one of their own.

Suggested Listening

Ludwig van Beethoven
Egmont Overture, Op. 84
Fidelio, Op. 72
Piano Concerto No. 5, Op. 73 (*Emperor*)

F I N G A L,

A N

ANCIENT EPIC POEM,

In S I X B O O K S:

Together with several other POEMS, composed by

OSSIAN the Son of FINGAL.

Translated from the GALIC LANGUAGE,

By JAMES MACPHERSON.

Fortia facta patrum.   VIRGIL.

L O N D O N:

Printed for T. BECKET and P. A. DE HONDT, in the Strand.

M DCC LXII.

Fingal/An/Ancient Epic Poem/in Six Books, London, 1762.

Title page from one of the first editions of the Ossianic poems. Note the presence of the harp in the vignette. Macpherson had Ossian accompany recitations of his poems with this instrument, in the tradition of the bards.

Revolution, which, erupting in 1789, not only rent the fabric of French society but also unleashed revolutionary new views about art and the role of the modern artist.

In England, too, the arts were undergoing profound change. Thomas Percy's collection, *Reliques of Ancient English Poetry* (1765), revived interest in popular ballads and influenced later generations of romantic poets, especially Wordsworth and Coleridge. Perhaps the most important stimulant for change came from one of the great literary forgeries of all time. In the 1760s, readers in England and on the Continent "discovered" the poems of Ossian, a mythic Celtic bard who, it was alleged, lived in the third century B.C. These poems were, in fact, the concoctions of James Macpherson, an enterprising Scotsman who had pieced together bits of epic poetry from Virgil, Homer, Milton, and others, transferring the locales to Ireland and Scotland. Loosely narrative, the rough poetic prose speaks of the noble, uncorrupted emotions of the ancient Celts, describes the rugged wilderness of their haunts, and recounts the interventions in their affairs by supernatural figures. No amount of reason—not even the enlightened scepticism of Samuel Johnson, who doubted the poems' authenticity from the start—was able to check the Ossianic craze that followed the appearance of Macpherson's "translations." Goethe had young Werther declare that Ossian had replaced Homer in his heart, and German critics found the barbaric Ossianic heroes superior to Homer's cultured Greeks. Napoleon carried a copy of Ossian with him during his military campaigns, and in Scotland, Sir Walter Scott proudly imitated the Ossianic poems in his own poetry.

What all these antecedents had in common was a reaction against eighteenth-century enlightened thought, with its objective treatment of beauty and its emphasis on artistic formulas. A new sense was abroad—that modern, "romantic" art should transcend those limitations. The romantics overturned the centuries-old aesthetic in the arts, according to which a work of art had been an imitation of an external object or idea, and artists had been best served by emulating proven, exemplary models. The newly emerging romantic aesthetic countered by asserting that the work of art had its own creative energy and, furthermore, that the work of art did not imitate the world but rather expressed the artist's own, highly original experience of the world. For the romantics, artists relied not on models but on their own feelings and emotions and on their own, innate genius; what counted was not the objective form of the art but its subjective content. This decisive shift—from art as imitation to art as expression—presented bold new perspectives for the romantics to explore.

The range of response to these revolutionary ideas was extraordinary. In England, William Wordsworth declared in his preface to the *Lyrical Ballads* (1798) that the purpose of poetry was to express the spontaneous outpouring of natural feelings. With his collaborator, Samuel Taylor Coleridge, Wordsworth offered ballads in colloquial language, rejecting the formal diction and heroic couplets of earlier practice. In the *Biographia Literaria* (1817), an early example of romantic criticism, Coleridge rhapsodized that the imagination was "the living Power and prime Agent of all human Perception."

In Germany the romantic writers Novalis (Friedrich von Hardenberg), W. H. Wackenroder, and Ludwig Tieck explored metaphysical realms in their novels, stories, and poetry. In France, Victor Hugo, defining romanticism as "liberalism in nature," wrote plays that violated the principles of neoclassic drama. The Spanish painter Francisco Goya, recoiling from the horrors of Napoleon's campaigns in the Iberian peninsula, depicted war with ugly, surreal images. In America, where romanticism was to take root later in the nineteenth century, Nathaniel Hawthorne and Edgar Allan Poe found inspiration in the macabre and the grotesque. In all their diversity, these examples testify to the impulse of the romantics to explore new avenues of expression.

Music was accorded a position of particular prominence—indeed, of preeminence—in the romantic aesthetic. In the early years of the eighteenth century, music had been regarded, like the other arts, as an imitative art; in particular, music was thought to mimic the accents and inflections of human speech and the range of human passions. Exactly how music did that, however, had never been reasoned out. Later in the eighteenth century, some aestheticians began to question whether music was in fact an imitative art and finally concluded that it was not. Instead, they decided that music by itself had the power to arouse and express emotions, rather than just imitate them in some vague fashion.

Just when this romantic quality of music began to express itself is difficult to determine. Some historians find "preromantic" signs in the music of Carl Philipp Emanuel Bach (1714–1788), the eldest son of J. S. Bach. A versatile musician, composer, and theorist at the Berlin court of Frederick the Great and later at Hamburg, Emanuel Bach wrote highly idiosyncratic keyboard music. His fantasies, sonatas, and rondos from the 1760s, 1770s, and 1780s featured a mannered, eccentric style best described by the German word *empfindsam,* which roughly translates as "extrasensitive" or "sentimental." Emanuel Bach's music was characterized by bold harmonic licenses and bizarre unprepared turns of phrase and modulations. To many of his contemporaries, Bach seemed intent on winning for instrumental music a new expressiveness, and in that regard, his work perhaps prefigures the efforts of the romantics.

Other historians claim as a harbinger of the new movement a remarkable cluster of instrumental works from the 1760s and 1770s, including several dramatic symphonies by Haydn (such as the *Farewell* Symphony; see p. 181). Evincing striking signs of stylistic discontinuity, those works stand conspicuously apart from the conventional music of the time; some have even suggested a link between them and the Sturm und Drang movement in German literature. To be sure, Haydn subjected his symphonies to extensive experimentation during that time, but whether that experimentation represented a Sturm-und-Drang-like romantic crisis or, indeed, anticipated nineteenth-century romanticism remains open to debate.

By the end of the eighteenth century, however, new voices were beginning to assert the supremacy of music in the hierarchy of the arts. The other arts, it was thought, should aspire to the romantic condition of music. Not tied to reality, music was taken to be the mysterious language of a spiritual realm that strove toward the infinite and the unworldly. Romantic composers endeavored to create their own, individual modes of expression. In part, the new individualism was a response to profound changes in societal attitudes toward composers and other artists. New economic conditions were freeing composers from their dependence on the patronage system, which had tended to regulate the type and the quantity of music they had produced. In the nineteenth century, composers enjoyed a different, and in some respects improved, social status. No longer the servants of the courts of Europe, they were sustained by an ever-broadening middle-class base that supported the rapid proliferation of public concerts and the establishment of the orchestra as a cultural institution. In short, composers were becoming more and more free to compete in the marketplace. Of course, the same economic forces that created that freedom also posed serious challenges. Few composers could survive on the income generated by the sale of their compositions alone; rather, they were forced to find additional ways to support themselves. Some gave music lessons, others embarked on strenuous concert tours, and still others turned to music journalism. In the concert halls and opera houses of England and Europe, they struggled to find new audiences to support their art; there, the most extravagant romantic composers exploited their new freedom with verve and daring.

10

MUSIC IN THE ROMANTIC PERIOD

Composers of this period by no means formed a united group or school. They pursued in their music such highly personal avenues of expression that we might denote individualism as the watchword of their romanticism. Still, nearly all romantic composers were indebted in some way to the compositional styles of the great Viennese classicists. The works of Haydn, Mozart, and Beethoven constituted acknowledged masterpieces that continued to influence music throughout the nineteenth century. The romantics' response to that canon was characteristically varied. Some relied heavily on classical forms and strove to continue the grand tradition of classical instrumental music. Others were less reliant on the past. We can, perhaps, obtain the most accurate view of music in the nineteenth century by speaking of a classical-romantic continuum—that is, by recognizing that classicism and romanticism were equally at work in much music of the nineteenth century, like two intertwining strands, with now one conspicuous and now the other. With that understanding, we can now examine how nineteenth-century composers extended and transformed classical methods—how, in short, they "romanticized" the legacy of Haydn, Mozart, and Beethoven to create a new kind of music.

MELODY IN ROMANTIC MUSIC

Romantic composers sought to write music that was spontaneous and unconstrained. Not always content to construct melodies upon evenly balanced phrases, they were capable of producing dynamic, irregular melodies marked by imbalance and unpredictability—not by the comparative "tidiness" of classical melodies. Some romantic melodies are compellingly expressive, with capricious lines that boldly transcend the boundaries of classical melodic writing. Consider, for example, this soaring melody from Frédéric Chopin's Prélude in D minor, for piano solo:

Chopin: Prélude in D minor, Op. 28, No. 24

Beginning with a descending triadic figure, Chopin creates an agitated melody, intense and passionate. The first part consists of a four-measure phrase that crests on the downbeat of bar 3. The second phrase begins with a similar triadic descent, but stretches to a higher range in bar 7. Now Chopin extends the second phrase, allowing it to grow more intense and impelling it forward with trills in bars 8 and 10. Then, to finish the phrase, Chopin adds a dramatic gesture, a rushing scale that traverses some three octaves to climax and break off abruptly in the highest reach of the piano.

Such exuberant, rhapsodic display typifies the dynamic character of romantic melodies. Here, an initial, four-measure phrase is followed by a longer phrase of nine measures, producing a decided imbalance. The indecorous, sweeping scale at the end gives further emphasis to the imbalance of the nine-measure phrase. The freshness and daring of Chopin's melody admirably suit the character he specified for the prélude, *Allegro appassionato* ("Fast, with passion"). Although not all matched the élan of Chopin's prélude, many romantic composers took pains to avoid the routine and the conventional in their melodies as they sought to capture the fanciful, the eccentric, and the incongruous.

DYNAMICS AND EXPRESSION MARKS IN ROMANTIC MUSIC

Romantic composers employed a liberal range of dynamics and expression marks, as if to underscore the expressive purpose and power of their music. In that regard, they went well beyond the limits of earlier practice. As we have seen, classical composers had generally applied dynamics to cleanly articulated divisions of phrases and sections as a reinforcement of the musical substructure. Beethoven had experimented further by introducing unexpected accents and by exploring dramatic ranges of dynamics. Later nineteenth-century composers went even further, as in this example from the *Symphonie fantastique (Fantastic Symphony)* by Hector Berlioz:

Berlioz: Symphonie fantastique, *First Movement*

In the course of just two measures, Berlioz calls for four dynamic levels, along with a diminuendo and a crescendo. The first two bars create an electrifying orchestral effect: a diminuendo, or lessening of the volume of sound, from *mezzo forte*★ to *pianissimo* that immediately reverses itself to swell to *fortissimo*. In bar 2 Berlioz provides an even more extreme contrast: The *fortissimo* is juxtaposed with *ppp* (triple *piano,* a shade below *pianissimo*). The sense of disorder and instability created by these severe shifts in dynamics corresponds well to the subject of the symphony—the sufferings of a morbidly sensitive young artist who has taken an overdose of opium (see p. 307).

In addition to bold, even extreme, treatments of dynamic levels, romantic composers filled their scores with expression markings of all sorts, as if determined to stamp their music with their individuality. They added descriptive words and phrases to tempo markings to specify the particular character or mood they wanted their music to express. For example, in an exquisite piano sketch titled "By the Lake of Wallenstadt," Franz Liszt designated the tempo as *Andante placido* ("Moderately, placidly") and even provided a motto from Byron's *Childe Harold*: "Thy contrasted lake, / With the wild world I dwell in, is a thing, / Which warns me, with its stillness, to forsake / Earth's troubled waters for a purer spring." In another piano piece depicting a tempest, Liszt entered such markings as *Presto furioso* ("Very fast, furiously"), *stringendo* ("pressing"), *sempre strepitoso* ("always tumultuously"), and—left wide open to interpretation—*cadenza ad libitum* ("cadenza, with liberty"). Behind all these expression marks was the irrepressible desire to extend the music into what was ultimately undefinable—the subjective realm of the emotions.

★ A dynamic marking, abbreviated *mf,* meaning "half loud."

TEMPO AND RHYTHM IN ROMANTIC MUSIC

In their approach to rhythm, romantic composers also took new liberties. They freely specified gradual changes in tempo, including the **ritard** (also **ritardando,** a reduction in speed) and **accelerando** (an increase in speed). Occasionally, they challenged the authority of the bar line to create the effect of a spontaneous, unpredictable rhythmic flow. An exquisite example is this excerpt from a piano composition by Robert Schumann:

Schumann: Kreisleriana, *Op. 16, No. 4*

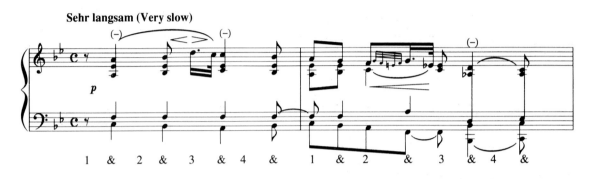

The meter of the music, c (or $\frac{4}{4}$), is obscured by Schumann's stratagem of beginning with a short rest. There is no effective downbeat, and the longer (and stressed) rhythmic values fall off the beat, contributing to the sense of rhythmic freedom.

Many nineteenth-century composers employed a rhythmic license commonly known as **rubato** (from the Italian for "robbed"). There is considerable confusion about just how this technique was used. Usually, composers did not notate rubato in their scores; rather, performers resorted to it at their own discretion. Rubato was a flexible approach to rhythm in which performers stretched or contracted the rhythmic values of a melody in order to produce an unpredictable, elastic quality, but without completely disrupting the basic meter. This "give-and-take" approach to rhythm again reflects the romantics' preference for rhythmic spontaneity and freedom, qualities that gave their music a sense of heightened expression.

HARMONY AND TONALITY IN ROMANTIC MUSIC

During the nineteenth century, the tonal system that had been developed and perfected during the baroque and classical periods was considerably expanded and transformed. We have seen that tonality was based on the concept of a tonic key and tonic triad supported by a group of triads (see pp. 68–72), of which the most important was the dominant triad on the fifth pitch of the scale. Classical composers viewed tonality primarily as an orderly, rational system of musical planning, though they were not averse to introducing tonal surprises in their music—the sudden appearance of a remote key, for example (see p. 189). Romantic composers, on the other hand, used tonality as yet another agent of expression. In their compositions, they frequently explored a broad range of keys and introduced bold excursions to keys well removed from the tonic. They began to move away from the standard dominant-to-tonic pull of the classical period in favor of other possibilities, such as modulations to keys based on pitches a third above or below the tonic (a trend already evident in Beethoven's middle-period music):

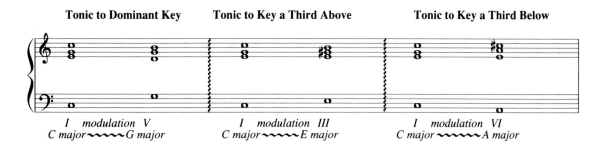

Furthermore, they ignored more and more the distinction between the major and minor modes by commingling major and minor keys. A composition in the key of C major, for example, might contain harmonies freely drawn from the key of C minor. All of these developments gradually weakened and eventually subverted the familiar tonal plans of the classical period.

Romantic composers extended the tonal system further by experimenting extensively with new formations of harmonies, especially with pitches drawn from the complete range of the chromatic scale (see p. 514). Since the chromatic scale divides the octave equally into twelve half steps, none of its individual pitches claims priority as a tonal center. The colorful harmonies of the following excerpt, from a well-known étude by Chopin, are based entirely on fragments of or complete chromatic scales:

Chopin: Étude, Op. 10, No. 3

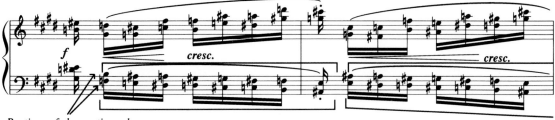

Portions of chromatic scales

(continued)

MUSIC IN THE ROMANTIC PERIOD

Complete chromatic scales

So pervasive is the chromaticism that this passage seems to lack any clear-cut key center.

As the nineteenth century progressed, composers became even bolder and freer in their tonal experimentation. With the music of Richard Wagner, tonality, already extended considerably beyond classical usage of the eighteenth century, reached a critical stage. Wagner's great music drama *Tristan und Isolde* (1865), often regarded as the culmination of German musical romanticism, is written in a musical language immersed in chromaticism; it is the crucial nineteenth-century work in the evolution of tonality. Here, long stretches of chromatically charged music more or less render irrelevant conventional perceptions of key centers.

In the *Vorspiel,* or Prelude, to Act I of *Tristan und Isolde,* Wagner displays the elements of his new musical language. Here are the celebrated opening measures:

Wagner: Tristan und Isolde, *Vorspiel to Act I*

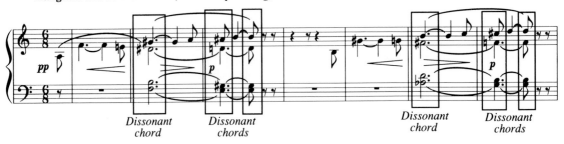

CHROMATIC FRAGMENTS

This music is constructed on sliding chromatic fragments (summarized beneath the example), with no conventional harmonic progressions and with no clear statement of a specific key. In addition, the music upends our traditional understanding of dissonance and consonance. The first chord (bar 2), a highly dissonant chord, progresses not to a consonant chord of resolution but to another dissonant chord (bar 3). There are, in fact, no consonant chords in the passage, no familiar, stable triads. By charging the music with such a level of dissonance, Wagner creates a sense of rising tension and of restless yearning.

Wagner's innovative approach to harmonic and tonal planning fundamentally affected the course of nineteenth-century music, as later composers zealously pursued the implications of the revolutionary harmonic language of *Tristan und Isolde*. Indeed, by the end of the century, some were writing music that more or less lacked recognizable tonal centers and that prepared the way for the more radical experiments of the twentieth century.

FORMS AND GENRES IN ROMANTIC MUSIC

Nineteenth-century compositions ranged in length from works of enormous size, many times the length of their classical counterparts, to short, fragmentlike pieces that lasted barely a minute or two. Both extremes reflected the romantic aesthetic: The vast romantic symphonies and music dramas seemed to approach the romantic ideal of the boundless by violating traditional limits, while, at the other extreme, the miniature pieces seemed inconclusive, unfinished, and, in their own way, romantically open-ended.

Throughout the nineteenth century, the traditional musical genres of the classical period endured. Romantic composers still created numerous examples of the sonata, string quartet, concerto, symphony, and opera, for example, and they continued to use classical forms—including sonata form, theme-and-variation, and rondo. But they now filled those objective forms with highly original, subjective contents. Romanticism was, after all, a celebration of content over form. In nineteenth-century music, this celebration is especially evident in its program music—instrumental music with extramusical references and sometimes elaborate programs—in which the romantics excelled.

The range of their imagination was astonishing. Franz Liszt wrote collections of piano pieces titled *Années de Pèlerinage (Years of Travel),* inspired partly by his experiences in Switzerland and Italy, partly by literary subjects. Among the variegated offerings of his collections are "William Tell's Chapel," "Nostalgia," "The Bells of Geneva," and "The Marriage" (after a painting of Raphael). There are three pieces based on Petrarch sonnets originally set by Liszt as songs, and a *Fantasia quasi sonata* ("Fantasy, like a sonata") inspired by a poem of the French romantic Victor Hugo.

Felix Mendelssohn-Bartholdy produced numerous *Songs without Words,* refined and evocative piano miniatures that resembled songs but lacked texts and vocal parts. Robert Schumann composed *Fantasy Pieces, Night Pieces, Scenes of Childhood,* and other collections of programmatic piano music. On occasion, he chose titles for his pieces only *after* he had composed them, letting the music itself suggest an extramusical meaning. Among Schumann's inspirations are "Soaring," "Whims," "The Entreating Child," "Of Distant

Lands," "The Prophetic Bird," and—most romantic of all—"Why?" Other nineteenth-century composers wrote orchestral music inspired by novels, poems, plays, historical subjects, paintings, myths, and exotic locales: Berlioz's *Waverley* Overture, on the novel by Sir Walter Scott; Mendelssohn's *Calm Sea and Prosperous Voyage* Overture, on a poem by Goethe; Liszt's *Faust* Symphony, on Goethe's great epic poem; and Edvard Grieg's *Peer Gynt* Suites, on the play by Henrik Ibsen.

For the romantic composers, program music was not at all irreconcilable with the traditional types of instrumental music. Thus, Liszt wrote an extravagant piano concerto with the remarkable title *Totentanz (Dance of Death),* and Mendelssohn composed a *Scottish* Symphony, with appropriate allusions to the Scottish landscape and history (though without an explicit program). Romantic composers did not always rely on the traditional classical genres for their program music, however. On occasion, their inspiration found full expression in newly fashioned genres, most notably **character pieces,** generally short piano compositions with some programmatic reference, and one-movement **concert overtures** for orchestra (we shall examine these types in Chapter 12).

TONE COLOR IN ROMANTIC MUSIC

Tone color—the timbre or quality of sound—fascinated the romantics, who exploited it in their music and raised the sensual aspects of sound to a new level of significance. The opening of Schumann's *Phantasie* (1836), one of the great works of romantic piano music, drives home the point; we have here a glorification of the idiomatic sound properties of the piano:

Schumann: Phantasie, *Op. 17*

*To be played throughout in a fantastic and passionate manner.

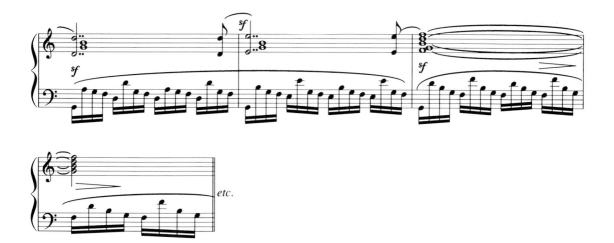

With the damper pedal depressed (indicated in the example by the abbreviation *Ped.*), Schumann introduces a melody against a background of undampened sonorities. The melody, rough and sketchlike, simply describes a descent in stark octaves; also, much of the passage is drawn from a single underlying harmony, without change. In short, Schumann here luxuriates in the sheer splendor of sound; not melody and harmony but the timbral qualities of the welling piano sonorities create the striking effect. Put more simply, tone color, more than harmonic or melodic considerations, inspired this passage.

Nowhere was the new interest in tone color more evident than in nineteenth-century orchestral music. Technological advances, brought on by the Industrial Revolution, led to modifications and improvements of instruments. The orchestra continued to expand throughout the century: New instruments were employed for special timbral effects, and the brass section was strengthened considerably. All of that encouraged the romantics in their quest for new combinations of instrumental colors. We shall have more to say about that quest in Chapter 12.

Suggested Listening

Berlioz: *Symphonie fantastique,* first movement
Chopin: Étude, Op. 10, No. 3
_____: Prélude, Op. 28, No. 24
Schumann: *Kreisleriana,* Op. 16
_____: *Phantasie,* Op. 17
Wagner: *Tristan und Isolde,* Vorspiel to Act I

Melody
Berlioz: *Symphonie fantastique,* first movement (see also pp. 307–309)
Brahms: Cello Sonata in F major, Op. 99, first movement
Chopin: Étude in C-sharp minor, Op. 25, No. 7

Dynamics and Expression Marks
Chopin: Nocturne in C-sharp minor, Op. 27, No. 1
Liszt: "William Tell's Chapel," from *Années de Pèlerinage,* Book I

Tempo and Rhythm
Chopin: Nocturne in E-flat major, Op. 9, No. 2
Schumann: Symphony No. 3 (*Rhenish,* Op. 97), first movement

Harmony and Tonality
Chopin: *Fantasie,* Op. 49
Liszt: *Faust* Symphony, first movement
_____: Petrarch Sonnet No. 104, from *Années de Pèlerinage,* Book II

Tone Color
Berlioz: *Roméo et Juliette,* "Queen Mab" Scherzo
Mendelssohn: *Hebrides (Fingal's Cave)* Overture, Op. 26

11

ROMANTIC ART SONG

"*E*very composer is a poet, only of a higher stature." Setting words to music acted as a catalyst for the imagination of the romantic composers. They were elevated to the status of "tone-poets" by Robert Schumann, who boldly asserted his faith in the primacy of music over poetry. For the romantics, music was indeed a language far richer and more suggestive than the language of words. Felix Mendelssohn, when asked to explain the meaning of some of his piano music, replied that words alone would not suffice. The nineteenth-century philosopher Arthur Schopenhauer thought that texts served only to unleash—not control—the imagination of composers. Their music, in short, was a powerful, autonomous language of emotions.

To be sure, romantic composers did set texts to music; indeed, their century saw the great flowering of the art song. Especially popular in German-speaking countries, the art song was known there as the **Lied** (pronounced *leet;* pl., **Lieder**). Lieder were typically written for a solo singer and instrumental accompaniment; the successive improvements in the design of the piano during the first few decades of the nineteenth century made it the favored instrument for accompaniment. Encouraging the remark-able burst of nineteenth-century song writing was the rise of German lyric poetry, which by 1800 had achieved extraordinary subtlety and sophistication in the hands of such poets as Johann Wolfgang von Goethe (1749–1832) and Friedrich von Schiller (1759–1805). Their short subjective poems were highly emotional, personal utterances ideally suited to the needs of the romantic composers, who valued above all else the subjective experience in their music. Romantic composers strove to wed music and poetry in their Lieder so that the music seemed to interpret in any number of remarkable ways the nuances of the poetry and the poetry seemed to inspire a range of melodic, harmonic, and musical textures. Music and poetry were fused into a new genre, the romantic art song.

Romantic songwriters drew their texts from a variety of sources. Among the German poets, they drew on Goethe and Schiller and also found inspiration in the poetry of younger German poets, especially Wilhelm Müller (1794–1827), Heinrich Heine (1797–1856), and Joseph Eichendorff (1788–1857). Folk poetry, too, both German and non-German, provided a rich source of texts; indeed, folk poetry, timeless and universal, was taken as the wellspring of romantic poetry itself. Finally, some composers turned to English poetry for their texts. They drew on the celebrated Ossianic "poems," the long narrative poems of Sir Walter Scott (including *The Lady of the Lake*), the lyric poetry of Byron, and the folklike poems of Robert Burns. They also derived texts from the plays of Shakespeare, highly regarded in Germany since the eighteenth century.

Among the most prolific nineteenth-century composers of romantic art songs were Franz Peter Schubert (1797–1828), Robert Schumann (1810–1856), Johannes Brahms (1833–1897), and Hugo Wolf (1860–1903). In this chapter, we shall look at the two outstanding romantic songwriters of the first half of the century, Schubert and Schumann.

SCHUBERT'S LIFE AND LIEDER

Born in Vienna, Schubert lived there unpretentiously for almost all of his short life. By the year of his death, his Lieder and elegant piano pieces were more and more in demand in Austrian circles, though full recognition of his genius and the enormous scope of his achievement came only posthumously. Schubert received his first musical instruction from his father, a schoolmaster of modest means, who taught him to play the violin. When he was eleven years old, the boy was sent to the Imperial and Royal City College, a boarding school for commoners. There, he furthered his education and rapidly developed his musical abilities, astonishing Antonio Salieri, the aging court composer of Italian operas. Young Schubert served as a choirboy in the imperial court chapel and played in the student orchestra, which he occasionally conducted. He pored over the scores of Mozart, Haydn, and, later on, Beethoven. Throughout his student years, he continued to compose, relying on the generosity of an older student for music paper, which he himself was too poor to buy.

After his voice broke, Schubert was obliged to leave the college. His father had always intended him to be a schoolteacher, and Schubert dutifully prepared for that career. For a few years, he taught in his father's school and sometimes gave music lessons to help support himself. Though teaching became increasingly burdensome, Schubert found time to turn out an extraordinary amount of music. In 1814 he wrote his first masterpiece, the song *Gretchen am Spinnrade (Gretchen at the Spinning Wheel)*, D. 118,★ a setting of a famous poem from Goethe's *Faust*. In 1815 he composed a setting for

---

★ The D stands for Otto Erich Deutsch, the twentieth-century scholar who cataloged Schubert's music.

Franz Peter Schubert.

Goethe's popular ballade, *Erlkönig (The Erl King)*, D. 328. In that same year, he produced some 140 songs, 30 of them inspired by Goethe's poetry; the next year he wrote another 100 songs.

Eventually, Schubert resigned his teaching position to devote himself to composition. In the ten years of life left to him, his health steadily declined, and he was beset by various misfortunes. He had few patrons, and he failed to win a regular position in Vienna. When he sent a bundle of his songs to Goethe, the aging poet coolly returned them unopened. Schubert did, however, have the support and encouragement of a small group of friends, many of them artists and middle-class professionals, who met in the evenings to hear his latest work. Through his later years, Schubert revered the music of Beethoven, whom he may have met just a week before Beethoven's death in 1827. He served as a torchbearer at Beethoven's funeral. In 1828 he himself died; he was buried, according to his wish, near Beethoven's grave.

Although Schubert is most often associated with the German art song—he composed over six hundred songs altogether—he was a remarkably versatile and prolific composer. He tried his hand at opera, though he failed to mount a successful production. He also wrote sacred music and choral works and left a quantity of instrumental music, including numerous dance pieces and miniatures for piano written for the so-called *Schubertiaden,* evening gatherings of his friends. Some of Schubert's best work is found in his piano sonatas and string quartets, worthy successor to the masterpieces of Beethoven.

Finally, Schubert wrote an impressive series of symphonies. Admittedly, they are uneven in quality, and the early ones owe a great deal to the symphonies of Mozart and Haydn. The most famous, the *Unfinished* (No. 8, 1822), is actually one of several symphonic fragments Schubert left; it did not appear in print until 1867. The Ninth Symphony, the *Great* (1825–1826), is a masterpiece, though its premiere, which took place more than ten years after Schubert's death, required the joint efforts of Schumann and Mendelssohn. Most of Schubert's music, in fact, was "discovered" only later in the nineteenth century. Only one hundred compositions or so appeared in print during his lifetime. It remained for composers of following generations—Schumann, Mendelssohn, Liszt, and Brahms, for example—to help establish Schubert's fame and his rightful place in music history.

SCHUBERT'S LIEDER; *WINTERREISE*

Schubert was not the first to compose Lieder, though his uncommon talents raised song writing to a new standard of excellence. Before him, C. P. E. Bach, Mozart, and others had written German songs, and in 1816 Beethoven created an exquisite *Liederkreis,* or song cycle (literally, a "circle of songs")—*An die ferne Geliebte (To the Distant Beloved).* Already before the beginning of the century, several minor composers had set Goethe's poems to music, especially the ballades. Goethe himself preferred simple melodic lines and unassuming piano accompaniments, little more than a background for musical recitations of his poems, designed to enhance the metrical patterns of the verses but not to interfere with the poetry.

In Schubert's mature Lieder, the music is far more than a simple accompaniment. Schubert's melodies are ideally suited to the singing voice and give a spontaneous musical expression to the poetry. The piano accompaniments, anything but unassuming, attain a high degree of complexity. Schubert typically begins with a few measures for the piano alone, often of great subtlety and beauty, in which he introduces a short theme or figure, or some colorful harmonic progressions to set the mood for the poem. After the vocal line begins, Schubert characteristically uses a wealth of pianistic figures and techniques in the accompaniment to suggest subtle interpretations of the text.

Schubert's sheer production of songs was a staggering accomplishment. On one day alone in October 1815, for example, he composed nine songs. Sometimes, the texts of his songs cluster around one poet, as if Schubert happened on a volume of poetry that sparked his inspiration. For other stretches of his song writing, he turned quickly from one poet to another, as if dissatisfied in his search for suitable verses. Thus, on another day in 1815, we find him composing eight songs on texts by seven poets.

Many of Schubert's individual songs have long been popular favorites, such as *The Trout* (D. 550), *Hark, Hark the Lark* (D. 889), *Ave Maria* (D. 839), *Death and the Maiden* (D. 531), *To Music* (D. 547), and numerous others. Schubert is especially remembered for his great song cycles, *Die schöne Müllerin (The Lovely Miller's Daughter,* 1823), which contains twenty songs, and *Winterreise (Winter's Journey,* 1828), which contains twenty-four songs. Both cycles are based on the poetry of Wilhelm Müller. Little known today (he died, like Schubert, at an early age), Müller wrote several collections of romantic poetry, which began to appear in the 1820s.

Müller's *Die schöne Müllerin* originated as a dramatic playlet about a miller's daughter, Rose, who is wooed by a young gardener, a hunter, a squire, and a young miller (a play on the name Müller). After the young miller is rejected, he drowns himself and is joined in death by the miller's daughter. Müller then reworked the playlet into a cycle of twenty-three poems, of which Schubert selected twenty to be set as songs. In this version, the action was simplified considerably. The miller has only one rival, the hunter, who makes his appearance only in the fourteenth song. The cycle ends with the miller drowning himself; he is consoled by a lullaby "sung" by the stream. In *Winterreise,* regarded by many as Schubert's greatest masterpiece, Müller's poetry again deals with rejected love. But instead of following a narrative thread, as in *Die schöne Müllerin,* the cycle reveals the emotional inner world of the rejected lover as he wanders aimlessly across a stark, winter landscape. A howling storm, tears turning to ice on the wanderer's face, a frozen pond, a menacing crow that circles overhead, snarling dogs—all give unity to the mood of alienation in the cycle. The wanderer seeks solace in the thought of death and, at the end of the cycle, throws in his lot with a strange old man who plays a hurdy-gurdy in the snow, even though there are no passersby to hear his music or reward him.

Most of Schubert's Lieder fall into three basic types: the **through-composed song,** the **strophic song,** and a hybrid of the two, known as the **modified** (or varied) **strophic song.** (Occasionally, we encounter songs that do not readily fit into one of those categories.) The through-composed song consists of new music for each stanza of the poem; Schubert generally employs this type for narrative poems or poems with shifting moods that naturally require fresh music. The strophic song, in contrast, reuses the same music from stanza to stanza; Schubert often employs this type for nonnarrative poems or poems evincing a unity of mood. The modified strophic song falls between the first two types: Its music for the first stanza is essentially repeated in subsequent stanzas but undergoes some variations, such as a change in key, a change in the accompaniment, or a slight revision of the vocal line. To give some idea of the wealth of techniques employed by Schubert in setting songs, we shall look at three songs from *Winterreise:* "Der stürmische Morgen" ("The Stormy Morning," No. 18), "Der Leiermann" ("The Hurdy-Gurdy Man," No. 24), and "Der Lindenbaum" ("The Linden Tree," No. 5).

"THE STORMY MORNING" (THROUGH-COMPOSED)

This short, powerful song depicts a storm on a wintry morning. At the climax of the poem, the wanderer, observing the raging heavens, comes to identify the storm with the passions of his own heart:

Stanza 1

Wie hat der Sturm zerrissen
des Himmels graues Kleid!
Die Wolkenfetzen flattern
umher in mattem Streit.

How the storm has rent
the grey mantle of heaven!
The tatters of clouds flutter
around in lifeless struggle.

Stanza 2

Und rothe Feuerflammen	And red flames of fire
zieh'n zwischen ihnen hin,	draw up between them;
das nenn' ich einen Morgen	I call that a morning
so recht nach meinem Sinn!	made expressly for me!

Stanza 3

Mein Herz sieht an dem Himmel	My heart sees in the heavens
gemalt sein eignes Bild,	its own image painted;
es ist nichts als der Winter,	it is nothing other than winter,
der Winter kalt und wild!	winter cold and wild!

Schubert begins his through-composed song with a short piano introduction that presents a forceful idea doubled an octave below, with several accents (indicated by the small, wedge-shaped signs, >) marking its jagged contours:

Schubert: Winterreise, *"Der stürmische Morgen"*

There is little in this turbulent opening to establish a firm harmonic foundation. Schubert suggests here the disorder of the heavens, compared in the poem to a torn, fluttering garment. When the voice does enter (m. 4), it merely doubles the piano figure, again without harmonic support. A short piano interlude, with driving, whipping triplets, prepares us for the second and third stanzas, which are sung straight through without interruption.

For "red flames of fire" (stanza 2), Schubert abruptly shifts keys and writes *fortissimo* chords in the piano, the first solidly harmonic passage in the song. But in the third stanza, he briefly reverts to the technique of the first stanza, in which the vocal line doubles the piano. The climax of the song—"It is nothing other than winter"—is given twice, accompanied by pounding chords in the piano. Then, with a short piano postlude, Schubert summarily ends the song.

"THE HURDY-GURDY MAN" (STROPHIC SONG WITH MODIFICATIONS)

This, perhaps the most moving song of *Winterreise,* concludes the cycle. As the wanderer nears the end of his journey, he meets an old man who plays a hurdy-gurdy.* Barefoot, the feeble musician stands in the snow, his only audience some ravenous dogs. With frozen fingers, he cranks out a few strains of music while the wanderer comments on his pathetic plight. Then, in the closing stanza, the wanderer responds to the musician's predicament and seeks his companionship:

Stanza 1

Drüben hinterm Dorfe	Over beyond the village
steht ein Leiermann,	there stands an organ grinder,
und mit starren Fingern	and with rigid fingers
dreht er, was er kann.	he cranks out what he can.

Stanza 2

Baarfuss auf dem Eise	Barefoot, on the ice,
wankt er hin und her,	he staggers to and fro,
und sein kleiner Teller	and his little cup
bleibt ihm immer leer.	remains forever empty.

Stanza 3

Keiner mag ihn hören,	No one may hear him,
keiner sieht ihn an,	no one looks at him,
und die Hunde knurren	and the dogs snarl
um den alten Mann.	around the old man.

---

* A boxlike string instrument with a crank that turns a rosined wheel setting internal strings in motion. Some strings create a steady drone; others are stopped by a set of keys, making it possible to produce melodies.

Stanza 4

Und er lässt es gehen	And it's all the same to him
alles wie es will,	whatever may happen.
dreht, und seine Leier	He cranks, and his hurdy-gurdy
steht ihm nimmer still.	is never quiet.

Stanza 5

Wunderlicher Alter,	Marvelous old man,
soll ich mit dir gehn?	should I follow you?
Willst du meinen Liedern	Will you take my songs
deine Leier drehn?	and play to them?

      Schubert's setting of this poem captures a mood of utter resignation and emptiness. It is essentially a strophic setting that appropriately matches the static quality of Müller's poem. There are, however, two noteworthy modifications to the strophic design. Instead of reusing the same music for each stanza, Schubert composes music for the first *two* stanzas, and then repeats this much without alteration for the third and fourth stanzas (see the study diagram). In addition, the music for the fifth stanza, though based on earlier material, differs in some striking ways; it reflects a critical change in the poem and for that reason is set off from the body of the song.

      The drone of the old musician's hurdy-gurdy is suggested by a drone in the piano accompaniment, which persists throughout the song, a static, frozen plane of sound. For much of the song, the vocal part of the wanderer alternates with fragments of melody in the piano that imitate the winding melody of the hurdy-gurdy. At first, Schubert portrays the wanderer as a detached observer pausing from time to time to listen to the melancholy music before commenting on it:

Schubert: Winterreise, *"Der Leiermann"*

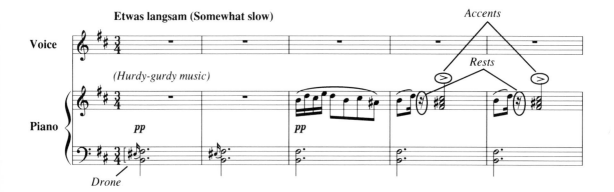

(Wanderer)

Drü-ben hin-term Dor-fe steht ein Lei-er-mann,
Kei-ner mag ihn hö-ren, kei-ner sieht ihn an,

Dissonant chords

But for the last stanza, in which the wanderer addresses the old man directly, Schubert joins the vocal line to the melody of the hurdy-gurdy, as if to suggest that here, in the depth of winter, the traveler has found the companionship he so desperately seeks:

*Wanderer and
Hurdy-gurdy
together*

Wun - der-lich - er Al - ter, soll ich mit dir gehn?

Schubert: *Winterreise,* "The Hurdy-Gurdy Man" (Strophic)

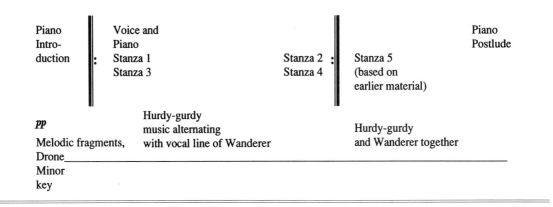

Piano Intro-duction	Voice and Piano Stanza 1 Stanza 3	Stanza 2 Stanza 4	Stanza 5 (based on earlier material)	Piano Postlude
pp Melodic fragments, Drone Minor key	Hurdy-gurdy music alternating with vocal line of Wanderer		Hurdy-gurdy and Wanderer together	

Schubert: _Winterreise_, "The Linden Tree" (Modified Strophic)

Piano Introduction	Stanzas 1	2	Piano Interlude	Stanzas 3 (based on music for stanza 1)	4 (based on music for stanza 2)
Triplets 	Melody and chordal accompaniment		Triplets 	Triplets 	Triplets 
_pp_	_p_		_pp_		
Major	Major	Major	Minor	Minor	Major

In the deliberate piano introduction (see the first example) and postlude that frame the song, Schubert not only imitates the music of the hurdy-gurdy but also captures the bleakness of the scene. The numbness of the old musician's hands is compellingly expressed in unexpected rests, in accented pitches, and in dissonant chords as the old man struggles to grind out a few more bars of music.

"THE LINDEN TREE" (MODIFIED STROPHIC)

One of Schubert's most finely crafted songs, "The Linden Tree" has achieved the status of a German folk song. In its essential outlines, it is a strophic song, but in this case the music differs enough from stanza to stanza that we shall regard it as a modified strophic song.

In Müller's poem, the traveler fondly recalls a tree he knew in his youth, how he lay dreaming in its shade and how he carved words of love into its bark. Recently, the traveler has passed by the tree late at night without stopping to heed its seductive call, "Here you will find your peace." Now the tree calls out to him, a symbol of lost happiness:

Stanza 1

Am Brunnen vor dem Thore
da steht ein Lindenbaum;
ich träumt' in seinem Schatten
so manchen süssen Traum.

Near the well by the town gate
there stands a linden tree;
I dreamt in its shade
so many sweet dreams.

Stanza 2

Ich schnitt in seine Rinde
so manches liebe Wort;
es zog in Freud' und Leide
zu ihm mich immer fort.

I cut into its bark
so many words of love;
in joy and sorrow it drew me
to it again and again.

5 (freely based on stanza 1)	Piano Interlude	Stanza 6 (based on music for stanza 1)	6 (based on music for stanza 2)	Piano Postlude
Triplets	Triplets	Triplets	Triplets	Triplets
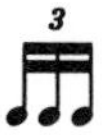 ♫ (3)	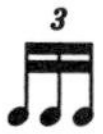 ♫ (3)	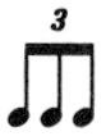 ♫ (3)	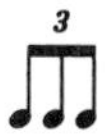 ♫ (3)	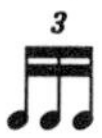 ♫ (3)
f	< >	*pp*		
Minor		Major	Major	Major

Stanza 3

Ich musst' auch heute wandern
vorbei in tiefer Nacht,
da hab' ich noch im Dunkel
die Augen zugemacht.

Today I had to pass by it
in the depth of night,
but even in the darkness
I closed my eyes.

Stanza 4

Und seine Zweige rauschten,
als riefen sie mir zu:
komm her zu mir, Geselle,
hier find'st du deine Ruh!

And its branches murmured,
as if they beckoned me:
come here to me, lad,
here you will find peace!

Stanza 5

Die kalten Winde bliesen
mir grad' in's Angesicht,
der Hut flog mir vom Kopfe,
ich wendete mich nicht.

The cold winds blew
into my face,
my hat flew off my head,
but I did not turn back.

Stanza 6

Nun bin ich manche Stunde
entfernt von jenem Ort,
und immer hör ich's rauschen:
du fändest Ruhe dort!

Now I am many hours
removed from that place,
and still I hear its rustling:
there you could have found peace!

The wanderer's recurring memory of the linden tree, the central image of the poem, might well have suggested a strophic setting to Schubert. But the poem traces the wanderer's shifting attitudes toward the tree—first he recalls it, then senses its allure once again as he passes it in a storm, and finally reminisces about it—and this feature likely prompted Schubert to modify the strophic setting. His solution is a most sophisticated treatment of the art song. Our study diagram summarizes its distinctive features.

ROMANTIC ART SONG

He begins with an extended piano introduction. Sliding triplets impel the song gently forward and create the effect of rustling leaves:

Schubert: Winterreise, *"Der Lindenbaum"*

The first two stanzas, in a major key, are set to one of Schubert's most memorable melodies, which begins with a simple triadic descent (mm. 8–10). The piano reinforces this melodic line and accompanies it with a straightforward series of chords.

After the second stanza, Schubert turns to the minor mode and inserts a piano interlude, again based on the introductory triplets. Stanzas 3, 4, and 5—in the minor, major, and minor, respectively—constitute the central portion of the song. The turn to the minor key corresponds to the wanderer's experiences as he passes the tree during the storm; the sweeter major-key music suggests the tree itself and its seductive power. Another piano interlude—this one with more intense rising and falling triplets to suggest the gusting wind—follows the fifth stanza. The sixth stanza is sung to the music of the opening stanza and then repeated to the music of the second stanza. A postlude for piano ends the song with the murmuring triplets of the introduction.

The alternation between major and minor creates a sense of temporal progression as the poet first recalls the tree from his youth, then passes it by, and finally admits that he still hears its nostalgic call. In addition, Schubert's music juxtaposes the wanderer's yearning for the linden tree of his youth (major-key music) and the cold reality of his winter odyssey (minor-key music). The modified strophic setting of the song fits all of this admirably.

ROBERT SCHUMANN

The second great master of the Lied, Robert Schumann, lived most of his life in the German cities of Leipzig, Dresden, and Düsseldorf. An impressionable youth devoted to music, Schumann had a particular fondness for Schubert's music. When he learned of Schubert's death in 1828, he broke into tears. Years later, he examined Schubert's unpublished manuscripts, and his efforts did much to rescue them for posterity. Schumann himself became a masterful composer of songs and song cycles and created numerous examples the equal of Schubert's.

Schumann's father, a publisher and bookseller, encouraged his son to read widely in German literature, and the young Schumann experimented with writing on his own. He tried his hand at writing poetry and short stories, finding inspiration in the fantastic tales of E. T. A. Hoffmann and Jean Paul (Richter). After his father's death, he was sent to Leipzig to study law but chose instead to study piano with Friedrich Wieck, a noted pedagogue and concert pianist. In preparation for a career as a concert pianist, Schumann put in long hours of practice and composed a quantity of difficult piano music. An injury or malady of his right hand evidently put an end to his plans to be a concert pianist.

Wieck's most illustrious student was his own daughter, Clara, a child prodigy who soon emerged as a composer (see p. 296) and distinguished concert pianist. Schumann, nine years older than Clara, fell in love with her and asked for her hand. For reasons that are still not clear, Wieck opposed the marriage and tried to discredit Schumann. Eventually, the matter was settled in a court of law, which ruled in the couple's favor. Robert and Clara were married in 1840.

That year marked a turning point in Schumann's career. He turned his creative energies from piano music to songs, and in 1840 he composed well over one hundred Lieder, many of them settings of romantic love poetry. In the years that followed, he

Clara and Robert Schumann.

took up in somewhat systematic fashion chamber and orchestral music and, eventually, choral music and even opera, though with mixed results.

In 1849 a revolution broke out in Dresden, and Schumann and Clara fled the city. Over the next few years, Schumann suffered nervous breakdowns and mental depression. He tried to drown himself in the Rhine River, but some fishermen rescued him, and he was committed to an asylum. Forbidden to see Clara until just before his death, he was occasionally visited by a younger musician who had been a guest in the Schumann home—Johannes Brahms. After Schumann's death in 1856, Brahms remained Clara Schumann's devoted friend for some forty years.

Schumann combined his literary and musical talents by finding time for music journalism as well as composition. He was instrumental in founding a music journal, the *Neue Zeitschrift für Musik (New Journal for Music)*, on which he worked for several years in Leipzig as editor. In the pieces he wrote for that distinguished publication, which examined a cross section of the musical life of Germany, he strove to produce music criticism of the highest kind. He warned against the commercialization of art, which he labeled as philistinism, and endeavored to guard serious art music from the encroachment of gaudy showmanship. In several of his most telling essays, the Philistines of art are confronted by a sturdy league of composers whose ranks include such figures as Mendelssohn, Chopin, and Brahms. Schumann's ambitious literary efforts were matched by the romantic spontaneity and color of his music, which marked the zenith of German romanticism in the first half of the nineteenth century.

Schumann's major compositions include several song cycles, a substantial amount of piano music, chamber works, four symphonies, orchestral overtures, and music for Byron's *Manfred* and Goethe's *Faust*. We now turn to *Dichterliebe*, his most famous song cycle. (For a discussion of Schumann's piano cycle *Carnaval*, see pp. 293–296.)

SCHUMANN'S *DICHTERLIEBE*, OP. 48

The inspiration for Schumann's *Dichterliebe (Poet's Love)* was the highly successful volume of poems titled *Buch der Lieder (Book of Songs*, 1827), which established the career of Heinrich Heine. A celebrated German poet and writer, Heine settled in 1831 in Paris, where he pondered with an ever-critical eye the contemporary values of German and French culture. His early romantic poems inspired thousands of nineteenth-century songs. The collection *Book of Songs* conveniently brought together hundreds of the early poems, many of them dealing with unrequited love and most of them compressed into two, three, or four quatrains. Heine's poems were famous for their wit, their cutting irony, and their forceful imagery. None of that was lost on Schumann, who devised an abundance of imaginative ways to set the poems to music.

Schumann selected the texts for *Dichterliebe* from a section of *The Book of Songs* titled *Lyrical Intermezzo*. In a prologue to this section (not set by Schumann), Heine introduces the poet, an old knight who is pining for his lost love. The poems begin with the awakening of the poet's love in springtime and then trace his eventual rejection and disillusionment. In the last poem—and the last song of *Dichterliebe*—the poet buries his grief and pain in an enormous coffin.

Schumann stressed the intimate relationship between text and music and made his piano accompaniments integral to the songs. Moreover, he unified the cycle by artfully linking many of the songs harmonically and melodically, giving the cycle continuity and shape, and a sophisticated key plan. Occasionally, he introduced subtle references from one song to another, again to unify the cycle poetically and musically. As had Schubert, Schumann worked with the strophic, modified strophic, and through-composed varieties of Lied construction. We shall examine briefly two songs from *Dichterliebe:* "Im wunderschönen Monat Mai" ("In the lovely month of May," No. 1, a strophic setting) and "Hör' ich das Liedchen klingen" ("When I hear the little song," No. 10, a through-composed setting).

Heine's short poem "In the lovely month of May" tells of the awakening of love and unfulfilled desire:

Stanza 1

Im wunderschönen Monat Mai,	In the lovely month of May,
als alle Knospen sprangen,	as all the buds were bursting,
da ist in meinem Herzen	there bloomed in my heart
die Liebe aufgegangen.	the beginnings of love.

Stanza 2

Im wunderschönen Monat Mai,	In the lovely month of May,
als alle Vögel sangen,	as all the birds were singing,
da hab' ich ihr gestanden	then did I confess to her
mein Sehnen und Verlangen.	my desire and my longing.

Heine uses two images, budding flowers and singing birds, to suggest the awakening of love. The only hint he gives that something may be amiss comes in the last two lines, where the poet speaks of his longing. To capture this sense of unfulfilled yearning, Schumann created music charged with poignant dissonances. In the very beginning of the song, for example, Schumann accumulates dissonant, rolled chords in the piano; no stable, consonant harmony appears in this extraordinary opening until the voice enters, and then only at the conclusion of its first vocal phrase, on the word "Mai" ("May"):

Schumann: Dichterliebe, Op. 48, No. 1, *"Im wunderschönen Monat Mai"*

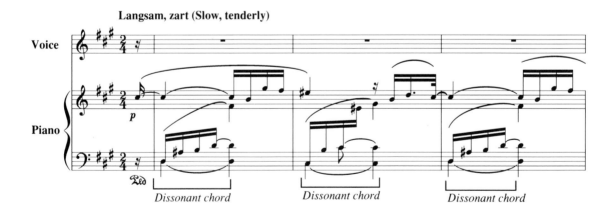

THE ROMANTIC PERIOD

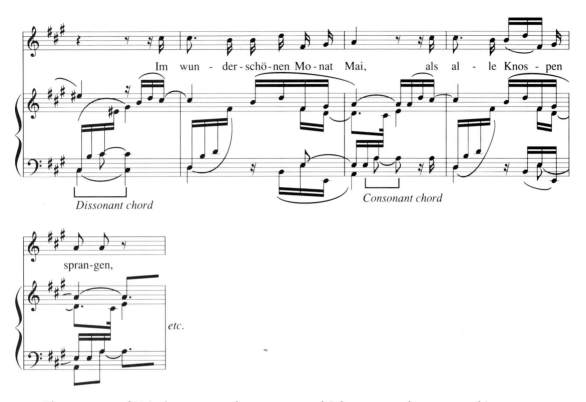

The structure of Heine's poem may have encouraged Schumann to choose a strophic setting for this short song, with the same music for each stanza. In the poem, the two stanzas share several features: The two begin with the same line of text, they have the same rhyme scheme, and they use an image from nature. Schumann frames the two stanzas with a piano introduction and postlude and separates them with an interlude for piano. In the interlude and the postlude, Schumann brings back the yearning music of the introduction. Indeed, this song ends with a symbol of the poet's longing—a held dissonant chord.

That longing finds some relief in the second song, which begins by resolving the dissonant chord to a consonant chord, but the ultimate poetic and musical resolution comes only at the end of the entire cycle.

As the cycle proceeds, the poet's love is rejected, and he is left with his grief. The through-composed tenth song is one of the most deeply felt in the entire cycle. Here, unfulfilled love gives way to unbearable misery:

Stanza 1

Hör' ich das Liedchen klingen,	When I hear the little song,
das einst die Liebste sang,	that my loved one used to sing,
so will mir die Brust zerspringen	then my breast is torn
von wildem Schmerzendrang.	by uncontrolled pangs of pain.

Stanza 2

Es treibt mich ein dunkles Sehnen	A deep longing drives me
hinauf zur Waldeshöh',	up to the high forest;
dort löst sich auf in Thränen	there in tears
mein übergrosses Weh.	my colossal woes are released.

Schumann begins with a strumming figure in the piano that outlines a melody, the "little song" of the text. When the voice enters, it takes up the melody already intimated by the piano:

Schumann: Dichterliebe, Op. 48, No. 10, *"When I hear the little song"*

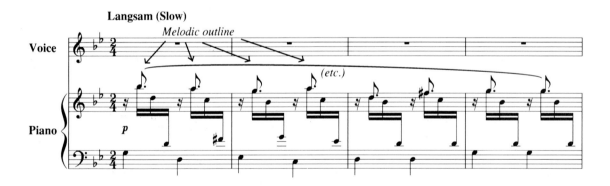

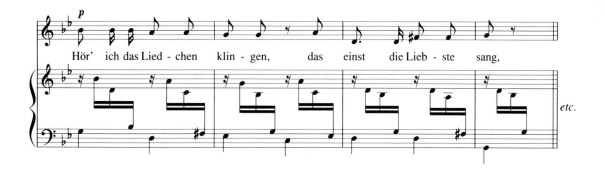

Hör' ich das Lied - chen klin - gen, das einst die Lieb - ste sang,

etc.

The voice sustains the melody, spinning out its mournful strains straight through both stanzas of poetry. Then an extraordinary effect: As the voice concludes, the piano part continues by itself and develops into a postlude nearly as long as the vocal part. Marked by severe dissonances and chromatic lines, this final section is thus deliberately made disproportionate. In turning to the piano, Schumann allows his music to continue where the poem left off, with the unburdening of the poet's woes; the romantic poetry of the piano's sonorities replaces the musical allusions of Heine's poetry.

Suggested Listening

Schubert: *Erlkönig (The Erl King)*, D. 328
_____: *Die Forelle (The Trout)*, D. 550
_____: *Gretchen am Spinnrade (Gretchen at the Spinning Wheel)*, D. 118
_____: *Der Tod und das Mädchen (Death and the Maiden)*, D. 531
*_____: *Winterreise*, D. 911
*Schumann, Robert: *Dichterliebe*, Op. 48
_____: *Liederkreis* (Eichendorff), Op. 39

Note: Works marked with an asterisk are the principal works discussed in the chapter.

12

ROMANTIC INSTRUMENTAL MUSIC

*T*he nineteenth century was an age of virtuosity. Europe was traversed by performers who captivated their audiences with pyrotechnical wizardry of inexhaustible varieties. The cult of the virtuoso accorded well with the romantic emphasis on individual expression and creativity. Many of the romantic composers were themselves virtuosos who fashioned spectacular compositions for their own performances. There were virtuosos of every kind. Some played the violin upside-down or with only one string; others drew dazzling sonorities from the piano and devised passages so intricate that the pianist seemed to have three hands. Grand soirées became the fashion, with several virtuosos competing with one another or joining together in a glittery, gala finale.

Especially in demand were the piano virtuosos. Most of the leading composers of the day were pianists, and many of them enjoyed distinguished reputations as concert artists—Frédéric Chopin, Felix Mendelssohn-Bartholdy, Franz Liszt, and Johannes Brahms, for example. Beethoven himself had launched his career in Vienna as a pianist and continued to perform in public until deafness overtook him, and Robert Schumann aspired to become a piano virtuoso; his wife, Clara, enjoyed a distinguished international career as a concert pianist.

The piano as we know it today emerged during the nineteenth century, a product of the Industrial Revolution. With its reinforced iron frame, which continued to develop in the first half of the century, it could tolerate a considerably greater tension on its strings than its eighteenth-century predecessor, the fortepiano. A new action, introduced in 1821, facilitated the rapid repetition of individual keys. The range of the modern piano increased as well, and foot pedals became a standard feature. It was—

and remains—an especially versatile instrument. Performers could manage melodic material with one hand and weave complex accompaniments with the other. The damper pedal, which raised the dampers, thereby allowing all the strings to resonate freely, permitted the pianist to introduce fresh material with both hands while prolonging blurred layers of sound. The *una corda* pedal, or soft pedal, enabled the pianist to achieve fine shades of sound, while at the other extreme the instrument could produce an intense range of dynamics as well. Finally, since the piano could sustain melodies and generate harmonic blocks of sound, whole symphonies or other orchestral music could be transcribed, or reduced, for performance on the piano. Indeed, many composers created complex orchestral scores while working at the keyboard, quickly fabricating a rough approximation of the intended effect. In the age before the phonograph, the piano became an important medium for the dissemination of new music.

FRÉDÉRIC CHOPIN

As sensational as the triumphs of the piano virtuosos were, much of their music is now forgotten. One exception is the work of Frédéric Chopin (1810–1849), who devoted himself to composing piano music of exquisite refinement and brilliance. Born in Poland, Chopin studied at the Warsaw Conservatory and concertized briefly in Austria and Germany before settling in Paris in 1831. Not long before, the romantic movement had made a vigorous impact on the arts in France, polarizing Parisian literary circles into opposing romantic and neoclassical camps. Chopin spent most of his career in Paris; finally, in 1848, to escape social upheaval there, he left Paris to concertize briefly in England and Scotland. By that time, Chopin was suffering from tuberculosis; he died less than a year after returning to Paris in 1849.

During his tenure of some eighteen years in Paris, Chopin essentially retired from the arduous career of a concert pianist. Frail in health, he preferred to compose and to teach piano to members of wealthy Parisian families, including the Rothschilds. He soon established his place in an impressive group of musicians, artists, and writers. Franz Liszt was perhaps the most flamboyant and certainly the most successful of the virtuosos (we shall examine one of his piano concertos later in this chapter). The unconventional composer Hector Berlioz shocked musical Paris in 1830 with the premiere of a "fantastic" symphony (see pp. 307–313). The painter Eugène Delacroix filled his canvases with sensual, vibrant colors; the young romantic writer Alfred de Musset was greeted as the French counterpart of the English poet Lord Byron; and the novelists Balzac and Flaubert were beginning to write starkly realistic French novels.

Finally, there was the Baroness Aurore Dudevant, who wrote a stream of novels under the pen name of George Sand. Chopin first met her in Paris in 1836, and for some eleven years she remained his lover, friend, counselor, and artistic comrade-in-arms. A determined individualist, Sand gathered around her a group of artists, occasionally wore male attire, and took up cigar smoking. The two divided their time between Paris, where Chopin taught piano to the French aristocracy, and Nohant, Sand's summer estate in southern France, where Chopin composed much of his best piano music.

Frédéric Chopin.

Chopin composed almost exclusively for solo piano; all of his music includes the piano. Much of his finest work is found in relatively short, intimate types of piano pieces. These include several examples of such stylized dances as the **waltz** (in French, **valse**), and two dances of Polish origin, the **polonaise** and the **mazurka.** There are also nearly thirty **études,** short, highly polished exercises for the piano designed to explore the technical resources of the instrument. One of the most famous is the "Black-Key" Étude in G-flat major, Op. 10, No. 5, which appeared in 1833.

ÉTUDE IN G-FLAT MAJOR, OP. 10, NO. 5 ("BLACK-KEY")

Many celebrated pianists had composed études before Chopin assembled his masterful first set of twelve in the 1830s. Generally humdrum, practical exercises, études had been designed to improve finger dexterity and to assist with certain technical problems (for example, running scales, arpeggiations, and octaves) or certain styles of playing (for example, the sustained legato and the detached staccato). A typical étude featured one or two patterns that the pianist was to master through repetition. Working with this pedagogic mold, Chopin created études that challenged even the most skillful pianists. His études, though, are more than mere exercises; they are superbly crafted studies in composition as well.

Chopin's "Black-Key" Étude is in the key of G-flat major, a key with no fewer than six flats, including the five black keys on the piano keyboard:

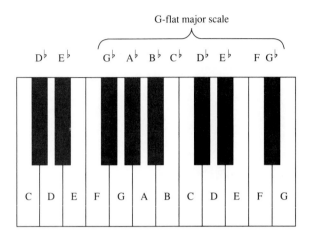

G-flat major scale

Chopin ingeniously designed this vivacious étude so that the right hand plays *only* on the black keys, a treacherous enough assignment when one considers the anatomy of the hand. Throughout the étude, the right hand endeavors to avoid any number of pitfalls as it twists and turns through rapidly changing patterns of black keys. The left hand, in contrast, provides steady, incisive chords as an accompaniment:

Chopin: Étude in G-flat major, Op. 10, No. 5 ("Black-Key")

To conclude, Chopin writes cascading octaves and *fortissimo* chords. Less than one hundred bars in length, this scintillating étude offers a brief flash of the brilliant virtuosity that animates much of Chopin's music.

NOCTURNE IN B-FLAT MINOR, OP. 9, NO. 1

Chopin reserved some of his most lyrical music for the **nocturne** ("night piece"), a moderately slow piece with a singing treble melody and a steady harmonic figuration in the bass part. His first published nocturne (Op. 9, No. 1) appeared in 1832; it shows his melodic writing at already its most elegant. Here, Chopin sets a haunting minor-key melody (*a*) against a flowing arpeggiated accompaniment. The melody begins with a delicate six-note upbeat and descends to four repeated pitches before dropping still further:

Chopin: Nocturne in B-flat minor, Op. 9, No. 1

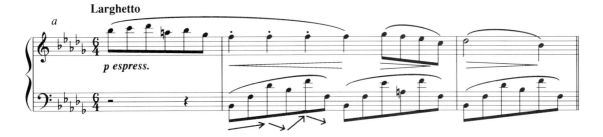

The melody recurs several times in the nocturne, and with each recurrence, Chopin enriches it with fresh embellishments of great expressive beauty and rhythmic sophistication. Our next example cites the opening bars of the melody in two subsequent, embellished versions. Thus, the six-note upbeat of the melody is transformed into a supple turnlike figure of eleven notes, and the first full measure breaks into a stream of twenty-two notes or leaps into the highest register of the piano before falling in a smooth descent. In performance, these excerpts display a hallmark of Chopin's style: the use of rubato, or subtle give-and-take between melody and accompaniment, in which the melody is stretched in rhythmic freedom while the accompaniment maintains a steady rhythmic pattern:

EMBELLISHED VERSION OF *a*

Like many of Chopin's shorter piano pieces, this nocturne describes an *ABA* structure. The *A* section is in a minor key; the extended, contrasting *B* section is in a major key. The melody of the *B* section (*b*) appears in bare octaves, with occasional accents and with a quite subtle change in the contour of the accompaniment:

In this central section, Chopin indulges in pure melodic display, with several statements of *b*. The last statement of *b*, marked *ppp,* is played with the damper pedal depressed, suggesting a dreamlike reminiscence of the melody. Chopin abridges the return of the *A* section and ends the nocturne calmly in a major key, in a gesture of understatement. The singing style of the nocturne and its pliable, melodic contours represent romantic melody at its most poetic and entrancing.

PRÉLUDE IN A MINOR, OP. 28, NO. 2

Chopin composed several works in larger forms, including three piano sonatas and two full-length concertos for piano and orchestra. Two of the sonatas rank among the most successful sonatas of the nineteenth century, though sonata form seemed more to hinder than inspire Chopin's imagination; and writing for orchestra apparently did not come easily to him. He was considerably more successful in other substantial types of piano music, some of which he himself developed. There are four **impromptus,** refreshing improvisatory compositions not bound by any particular formal design; four scherzi, *ABA* movements drawn by Chopin with ambitious dimensions; and four **ballades,** free, sectional compositions possibly inspired by Polish ballade poetry. Occasionally,

Chopin explored elements of fantasy in his larger compositions, as in the *Polonaise-fantaisie,* Op. 61, and the *Fantaisie,* Op. 49.

Chopin's Opus 28, which appeared in 1839, comprised a pathbreaking collection of twenty-four préludes, one in each major and minor key. To be sure, there had been earlier sets of piano pieces that served some preludial function, and in *The Well-Tempered Clavier,* J. S. Bach had produced two monumental cycles of preludes and fugues in all the keys. Bach had paired each prelude with a fugue in the same key, giving the preludes a clear preparatory purpose. Although the idea behind Chopin's opus owed something to Bach's example, his préludes are free, romantic creations: They are préludes to nothing at all, except whatever the listener's imagination provides. Taken individually, the préludes appear as short musical fragments; taken all together, they form one of the most enriched, rewarding collections of nineteenth-century piano music.

Many of the préludes fall into one of three types. A few, technically quite demanding, resemble études. Others, projecting singing melodies against a harmonic wash of accompaniment, resemble nocturnes. The most original and striking suggest rough improvisatory sketches, as if Chopin had hastily jotted them down before they escaped him. Perhaps the most audacious of this last group is the second prélude, in A minor. Only twenty-three measures in length, it contains some of Chopin's most dissonant and daring music. We give it here in its entirety.

Chopin: Prélude in A minor, Op. 28, No. 2

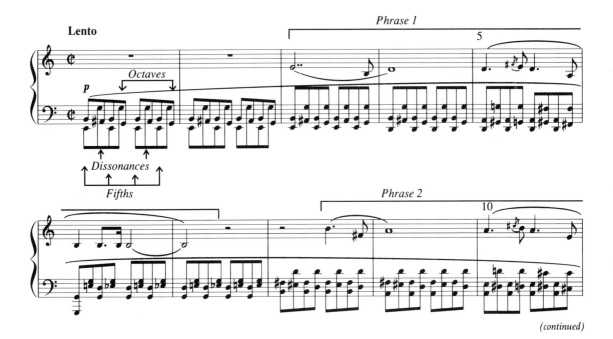

(continued)

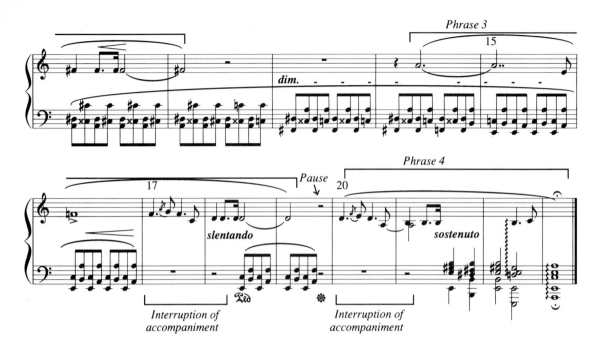

First, Chopin establishes a highly unusual accompaniment marked by open fifths on the beat and by terse dissonances and bare octaves off the beat. Because the entire prélude is performed at a soft dynamic level, the ear is able to accommodate the dissonances, though they occasionally create some unsettling clashes, and they must have struck Chopin's contemporaries as rather bizarre. Chopin sustains this peculiar accompaniment, with two interruptions, in bars 17 and 18, and 19 and following. The single long slur over the accompaniment (bars 1–16) indicates a smooth, legato style of performance and emphasizes the overall continuity of the prélude, broken only by the unexpected interruptions toward the end.

The melody of the upper part is equally perplexing. In contrast to the elaborate detailing of the *a* melody in the Nocturne in B-flat minor, the melody of this prélude offers only a sketchy outline. It suggests no particular major or minor key, since Chopin has taken great pains to conceal the tonality of the piece (in striking contrast to the procedure of classical composers, who characteristically initiate a composition by clarifying its tonality). Its four phrases (mm. 3–7, 8–12, 14–19, and 20–23) unfold against the slowly shifting dissonances of the accompaniment. In measure 19, the melody pauses, as does the accompaniment, leaving the listener with a half measure of rest. The last phrase, stripped of the accompaniment, begins with the melody alone. In the closing bars, a few cadential chords give harmonic direction to the wayward course of the prélude and secure the key of A minor, now heard unambiguously for the first time, as its tonic. As in his other préludes, Chopin here gives his inspiration free reign. This imaginative vignette exudes a certain spontaneous quality that reaches to the core of the romantic subjective experience.

Another strikingly original creator of romantic piano music was Robert Schumann, who began his career by devoting himself to compositions for the instrument, in which he developed new approaches to musical form. The best of his piano music consists of collections of contrasting character pieces that, assembled together, form formidable cycles unified by some extramusical idea or title—for example, *Papillons (Butterflies)*, *Davidsbündlertänze (Dances of the League of David)*, *Fantasiestücke (Fantasy Pieces)*, *Kreisleriana*, and *Carnaval*.

CARNAVAL, OP. 9

Carnaval, a collection of twenty-one pieces, appeared in 1837. This remarkable composition is a musical depiction of a masked ball, with its colorful personages, madcap revelries, and festive dance rhythms, that is the culmination of carnival season before Lent (a companion piano cycle by Schumann is titled *Faschingsschwank aus Wien*, or *Carnival Jests from Vienna*). Most of the pieces are pianistic renditions of dances such as the waltz. The entire work is framed by a majestic *Préambule*, or preamble, and a stirring conclusion, the "March of the League of David against the Philistines." Here the Davidites, for Schumann those upright defenders of the best in modern music, are deployed against the banal Philistines, the corrupters of good taste and standards in art.

In the course of the cycle, Schumann introduces us to the fantastic characters who inhabit the world of his carnival. Some of those depicted are Schumann's contemporaries and acquaintances. Thus, Chopin, whose music Schumann championed, is represented by a beautifully singing, nocturnelike movement. Nicolò Paganini, the great Italian violin virtuoso (1782–1840), makes his appearance with an energetic piece in which Schumann designs keyboard figurations to approximate the technical resources of the violin. One movement ("Chiarina") is about Clara Wieck, Schumann's future wife, and another ("Estrella") is about Ernestine von Fricken, to whom the composer had been engaged. There are also fictitious characters from the traditional pantomime. Among these comic masks are Pierrot, Pantalon, and Columbine. Finally, two characters, Eusebius and Florestan, stand out as literary inventions of the composer. They appear in a good deal of Schumann's piano music and in his music criticism. Eusebius represents the brooding, dreaming introvert; Florestan is his exuberant, extroverted counterpart. These two complementary personalities are really masks to Schumann's own character and thus suggest his presence at the carnival.

Carnaval achieves its musical cohesion through a network of motives based on three enigmatic "Sphinxes," which appear by themselves in the middle of the score. Not meant to be played, they provide a clue to the underlying organization of the cycle. The Sphinxes are based on a musical code Schumann used to represent his own name and the city of Asch, where Ernestine von Fricken lived. He discovered that both the city and his name could be represented by musical notes that use the same pitches. Our example shows how. (German musical nomenclature differs in some cases from the English: The letter *s* can be combined with E or A to form *Es* or *As*, that is, E-flat or A-flat in English terms; also, *h* is the same as B. No pitches are derived for the letters *u*, *m*, and *n* in Schumann's name.)

Sphinxes in Robert Schumann's Carnaval

		English notation:	German notation:	Derivations:

No. 1 — English notation: Eb C B A; German notation: (E)s C H A; Derivations: S c h uma nn

No. 2 — English notation: Ab C B; German notation: As C H; Derivations: A s c h

No. 3 — English notation: A Eb C B; German notation: A (E)s C H; Derivations: A s c h

Nearly every movement of *Carnaval* derives in some way from these Sphinxes. Two short examples, the fifth and sixth pieces, illustrate Schumann's ingenious method. Titled "Eusebius" and "Florestan," the two halves of Schumann's personality, they are constructed on the same Sphinx (the third one), but with remarkably different results. The music for Eusebius, the introvert, is deliberately vague and seemingly without direction. Note how Schumann distorts the $\frac{2}{4}$ meter by using irregular septuplets, groupings of seven notes that inject an unpredictable asymmetry. Moreover, he goes to great pains to conceal the Sphinx within the music, subtly working it into the turning, irregular melody. (Lest it be overlooked entirely, though, in many editions the four notes of the sphinx are marked with crosses.)

Robert Schumann: Carnaval, *Op. 9, No. 5 ("Eusebius")*

On the other hand, the music for Florestan, the extrovert, is exuberant and passionate. Accordingly, the sphinx is conspicuously stated, right at the outset, as the first four notes of the movement.

Robert Schumann: Carnaval, *Op. 9, No. 6 ("Florestan")*

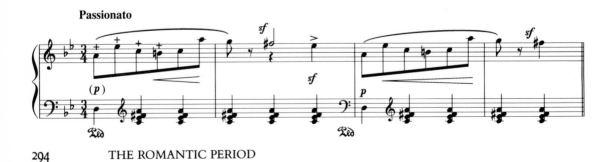

Schumann, *Carnaval*, Op. 9, No. 6 ("Florestan")

Passionate	Adagio	Passionate	(Adagio)	Passionate	Accelerando - - - - - - - - - - - -	
Statements of *a* (based on Sphinx)	*(Papillon?)* Incomplete quotation	*a*	*(Papillon?)* quotation	*a* extended and reharmonized	Return of opening statement *a*	Broken off
Melody against chords						
Minor	Major	Minor	Major	Major	Minor	

From these four notes, Schumann derives the essential thematic gesture—eight notes in all, which we shall label *a*—on which "Florestan" is based. The fertile range of his imagination is evident in the remarkable originality of the movement's form (see the study diagram). Schumann begins with strong statements of *a*, an explosive, disjunct idea that ascends to strong accents (*sf*) off the beat, propelling the music toward a minor key without, however, reaching a definitive cadence in that key. Then, the passionate course is twice checked by a contrasting idea in Adagio tempo, which Schumann teasingly labels *Papillon?*, or "Butterfly?" In deliberate, ascending, stepwise octaves, this new idea is, in fact, a quotation from Schumann's earlier piano composition *Papillons*, Op. 2, a whimsical romantic interjection that utterly deflates Florestan's passionate outburst:

The remainder of the movement uses restatements of *a*, now reharmonized to turn the music to a major key. But the minor-hued opening returns, with an increasingly faster tempo until it abruptly breaks off to give way to the next character piece, the delicious "Coquette."

The exact programmatic meaning of "Florestan" is as elusive as the capricious *papillon* that it cites, though undoubtedly the piece held some personal significance for

Schumann. Be that as it may, there is intriguing evidence scattered throughout his other music that he habitually employed a secret musical code. Suggestions for a theme in some of his compositions symbolizing his beloved Clara have been put forward; further, we know that Schumann made a habit of alluding to other composers' music—including the music of Clara—not to mention his practice of self-quotation, which probably stems from some autobiographical urge. Although we cannot always decipher his cryptic purpose, Schumann obligingly reveals some of his compositional intentions in the musical games of *Carnaval*, and he obligingly unmasks himself in his most romantic literary-musical creations, Eusebius and Florestan.

CLARA SCHUMANN

One of the most celebrated piano virtuosos of the nineteenth century was Schumann's wife, Clara (1819–1896). At the age of 5, she began to study piano with her father, Friedrich Wieck; at age 9, she made her debut in Leipzig and soon was recognized widely as a child prodigy. Her earliest compositions consisted chiefly of stylish piano pieces designed for her own concerts. A more serious tone emerged in her later efforts, which included songs (some published under Robert's name), chamber music, and a piano concerto. After her marriage to Robert in 1840, Clara greatly reduced her activities as a concert pianist and found less and less time to compose; between 1841 and 1854, eight children were born to the Schumanns. Still, Clara occasionally undertook a concert tour, and she taught, with her husband, at the newly established Leipzig Conservatory. In 1854 Robert's deteriorating mental condition led to his commitment to an asylum, and Clara was obliged to raise their family herself. A great source of support for Clara during that difficult time was her friendship with Johannes Brahms, who first visited the Schumanns in 1853 and, after Robert's death in 1856, remained a devoted admirer of Clara's. She continued to concertize extensively and became a noted interpreter of her husband's music, though she composed little after his death.

VARIATIONS ON A THEME OF ROBERT SCHUMANN, OP. 20

Clara Schumann's Variations on a Theme of Robert Schumann, Op. 20, were composed in 1853 as a birthday present for her husband. For her theme, Clara borrowed a short minor-key piano piece Schumann had composed in 1841 (Johannes Brahms also penned a variation set for piano based on this theme). Its mournful melody begins with two stepwise descents. In the contrasting middle section, the melody climbs to a higher, more expressive range; then, in the closing measures, we hear the descending lines of the opening again:

Robert Schumann: Theme

After presenting Robert's theme intact, Clara proceeds to subject it to seven variations. In the first two, she applies progressively faster rhythmic values to develop a sense of accelerating momentum. In the third, she presents the theme in the major mode, with broadly spaced, richly hued chords for accompaniment:

Clara Schumann: Variations on a Theme of Robert Schumann, Op. 20

VARIATION 3

In the fourth variation, the theme appears accented in the middle register of the piano, accompanied by chords beneath and by rapid, running passagework above:

VARIATION 4

(continued)

The strident fifth variation, marked *forte*, places the theme in the upper voice, with an accompaniment of thundering octaves below. The more subdued sixth variation treats the theme as a canon (p. 525). The concluding, seventh variation presents the theme with a rolled, arpeggiated accompaniment that sweeps up and down the keyboard. Toward the end, Clara manages to work in an allusion to one of her own piano pieces, thus leaving her signature on this musical celebration of Robert's birthday.

THE ORCHESTRA IN THE NINETEENTH CENTURY

During the nineteenth century, the orchestra evolved from the relatively small size of the classical period (see p. 185), with its fairly standard, basic woodwind, brass, and string groups, into a much larger, more versatile ensemble, with the size and the makeup we know today. Romantic composers discovered in orchestral music an expanded spectrum of new instrumental combinations and colors as they sought to achieve the extraordinary and the romantic in their music. The art of **orchestration**—that is, the art of writing for combinations of orchestral instruments—was viewed more and more as a fundamental discipline in the composer's art. An increasing number of treatises on orchestration now appeared. The most far-reaching was the *Grand traité d'instrumentation et d'orchestration modernes (Grand Treatise on Modern Instrumentation and Orchestration)*, written by the French composer Hector Berlioz and published in 1843. In Berlioz's romantic vision, the ideal orchestra was to have 467 instrumentalists and a 360-member chorus, for a total of 827 musicians! It was to have 120 violins, several times the number typically available to Haydn. And it was to have several new instruments and combinations of familiar instruments, such as 30 pianos accompanied by bells and other percussion. Berlioz's vision, never realized by the composer, reflected a bold view of the orchestra as a composite instrument capable of a multitude of new effects simply inconceivable to earlier composers.

The nineteenth-century orchestral conductor earned recognition as a new type of musician. Formerly, the concertmaster (typically, a violinist) had led the orchestra, or, in Haydn's time, a musician who played a harpsichord, an instrument that eventually fell out of favor. Now, the increasing complexity of nineteenth-century orchestral scores demanded a different arrangement. Conductors, leading their fellow musicians with batons, rehearsed the orchestra, interpreted the full scores of works to be performed, coordinated the various parts during performances, and injected their personalities into the orchestra and its music. In short, conductors stood before the orchestra as virtuoso musicians.

Many of the leading composers of the nineteenth century were noted conductors as well. Mendelssohn, one of the first conductors to use a baton, managed a superb orchestra in Leipzig; Schumann conducted in Düsseldorf, Brahms in Vienna, and Liszt in Weimar. Both Berlioz and Wagner wrote on the art of conducting and frequently conducted to ensure that their music was properly performed.

The symphony, which Haydn and Mozart had brought to a high level of achievement and which Beethoven had transformed and enlarged, continued to attract nineteenth-century composers. Schubert, Schumann, Mendelssohn, Berlioz, Liszt, and Brahms all struggled to measure up to the extraordinary level that Beethoven had set in symphonic composition. Many of these composers and others also favored the concert overture, a shorter, one-movement work inspired by some literary, dramatic, or other programmatic idea. Finally, all but Schubert wrote concertos for solo instrument and orchestra. We turn now to the life and work of three romantic composers who contributed in distinctive ways to the orchestral repertoire of the nineteenth century: Mendelssohn, Berlioz, and Liszt.

FELIX MENDELSSOHN-BARTHOLDY

Mendelssohn (1809–1847) came from a distinguished family. His grandfather, Moses Mendelssohn, was an eminent eighteenth-century Jewish philosopher who championed religious toleration; his father was a successful banker in Berlin; and his older sister, Fanny, was a child prodigy, like Mendelssohn himself, who mastered the piano and composed fluently (some of her early songs appeared under her brother's name; toward the end of her life, her music appeared under her married name, Fanny Hensel). In 1816 the children were baptized in the Protestant faith, and the family added Bartholdy to its surname.

Young Mendelssohn received an excellent education. He studied with private tutors, shared the company of noted musicians and literary figures, and attended the University of Berlin, where he heard lectures by the philosopher Hegel and the geographer Humboldt. He began to study music and to compose at an early age. He was especially devoted to the music of J. S. Bach, and while still a young man, in 1829, he conducted a performance of Bach's *St. Matthew Passion,* some one hundred years after its premiere.

Mendelssohn spent most of his early years in Berlin. In 1825 and 1826 he wrote his first two masterpieces, a *tour-de-force* Octet for string instruments and the Overture to *A Midsummer Night's Dream* for orchestra. In 1829 he set out for England and spent the summer on a walking tour of Scotland. He visited Sir Walter Scott, whose romantic poetry and novels were popular in Germany, and made a rather tedious voyage to Fingal's Cave in the Hebrides Islands. The wild, rugged terrain of Scotland inspired two of Mendelssohn's most popular and romantic works, the *Hebrides* Overture (also known as the *Fingal's Cave* Overture) and the *Scottish* Symphony.

Following his return to Berlin, Mendelssohn embarked on a second tour, which took him to Austria, Italy, Switzerland, and France. He served briefly as a music director

Felix Mendelssohn-Bartholdy.

in Düsseldorf and then, in 1835, went on to Leipzig to conduct the famed Gewandhaus Orchestra. Here, in the city of J. S. Bach, he directed an ambitious series of public subscription concerts performed by some of the leading musicians of the time. He chose for his concerts the works of both contemporary composers and composers of the past—especially Bach and Handel. And he continued to produce critically acclaimed compositions of his own, including the oratorio *St. Paul* (1836) and the Piano Trio in D minor, Op. 49 (1840).

Mendelssohn was widely respected for his insistence on high musical standards. In 1843, the king of Prussia, Frederick William IV, summoned him to Berlin to establish a music institute. That project foundered, however, and Mendelssohn returned to Leipzig, where he taught at the new Leipzig Conservatory, established largely owing to his efforts. A cultured man, Mendelssohn wrote poetry and was an accomplished painter. Among his acquaintances were the poets Goethe and Ludwig Tieck, the fairy-tale writer Hans Christian Andersen, the painter Delacroix, and the composers Berlioz, Chopin, Robert and Clara Schumann, Liszt, Rossini, and Cherubini.

Mendelssohn's interest in earlier music led him to imitate the works of Bach and Handel in his own compositions. From his study of Bach, he mastered the strict forms of counterpoint. From Handel's music, he learned to write for choral ensembles. Prompted

The Birmingham Music Festival of 1846, where Mendelssohn's oratorio *Elijah* was premiered.

in part by his enthusiasm for Handel's oratorios, he created the imposing oratorio *Elijah* (1846), based largely on the Old Testament account in I Kings, for a music festival in England.

Because of his reliance on the music of earlier periods, Mendelssohn is generally viewed as a traditional, conservative composer. Actually, much of his music is, in its own way, highly imaginative and romantic. His *Lieder ohne Worte (Songs without Words)* are inspired, if sentimental, romantic miniatures for piano. Two of his symphonies, the *Scottish* (No. 3) and the posthumous *Italian* (No. 4), contain allusions to the folk music and national characters of Scotland and Italy. The Violin Concerto in E minor, Op. 64 (1845), filled with passionate, soulful melodies and delicate filigree work for the violin, remains one of the great concertos for the instrument. Mendelssohn is perhaps at his most romantic in his one-movement orchestral concert overtures, of which the most famous is the Overture to *A Midsummer Night's Dream*.

Mendelssohn: Overture to *A Midsummer Night's Dream*, Op. 21

Four sustained chords	Exposition First Group	Bridge	Second Group		Closing
	Elves' music	Regal music Court of Athens	Lovers' music	Tradesmen's music	Hunters' calls
a	*b*	*c* (and *b*)	*d*	*e*	*f*
p	**pp**	**ff**	**p**	**ff**	**f**
Tonic major	Tonic minor	Modulating	Dominant major		

OVERTURE TO *A MIDSUMMER NIGHT'S DREAM*, OP. 21

Not a few romantic composers turned to Shakespeare's plays for inspiration. They were attracted by the bard's disregard of the dramatic unities, his mingling of tragic and comic characters, and especially his treatment of supernatural agents, as in *The Tempest* and *A Midsummer Night's Dream*. In 1826, when Mendelssohn was only seventeen years old, he composed his overture to *A Midsummer Night's Dream* after reading the play in a German translation. Though he revealed his general purpose in the title, Mendelssohn provided no specific program for the overture; instead, he left it to the listener to imagine the action and to relate his music to the play.

Shakespeare's comedy unfolds against the backdrop of the wedding festivities of Theseus, Duke of Athens, and Hippolyta, Queen of the Amazons. Hermia, in love with Lysander but betrothed to Demetrius, has fled with Lysander to a forest near Athens. The lovers are pursued by Demetrius, who, in turn, is pursued by Helena, whose love he has scorned. The woods are also visited by a group of tradesmen who are preparing an entertainment for the wedding celebration. Finally, the hunting party of Theseus and Hippolyta appears.

The forest is inhabited by the estranged lovers Oberon and Titania, King and Queen of the elves. Oberon has sent his attendant Puck to subdue Titania with a magic love potion. In the resulting confusion, the pairs of mortal lovers are mistakenly crossed when they are administered the potion, and Titania falls in love with Bottom the Weaver, one of the tradesmen who is made to wear the head of an ass. Eventually, affairs are righted, and the mortals return to Athens to join the revels at court. For the epilogue, Puck is left to muse that the events of the day are "no more yielding than a dream."

Mendelssohn: Overture to *A Midsummer Night's Dream*, Op. 21, *Continued*

Development		Recapitulation					Coda (Epilogue)		
Largely based on *b*		*a*	*b*	*d*	*e* (extended)	*f*	*b*	*c*	*a*
mainly *pp* throughout	ritard, ⌒ pause	*p*	*pp*	*p*	*ff*		*f*	*pp*	ritard, *pp* pauses
Several keys 〰〰〰		Tonic major	Tonic minor	Tonic major_____					

Mendelssohn cast his overture in a modified sonata form, into which he incorporated various musical ideas, including themes, shorter motives, and other materials that refer to the play. We shall identify six ideas. The work opens with four mysterious, sustained chords (*a*). Delicately scored for winds (to which horns are added in the fourth chord), this motive returns to mark the beginning of the recapitulation and to conclude the work. Perhaps representing the magical power of the elves, it prompts the remarkable musical transformations that occur throughout the work.

In the exposition, Mendelssohn introduces five other ideas: *b*, scurrying music for the elves (staccato, *pianissimo* material for the strings, in a minor key); *c*, regal music in dotted-note style for the court of Theseus (*fortissimo,* for full orchestra, in a major key); *d,* smooth, lyrical music for the mortal lovers (*piano,* in a major key); *e,* uncouth music for the boorish tradesmen (complete with an imitation of Bottom's braying); and *f,* hunting calls for Theseus' party. The study guide shows the principal appearances of these motives and their progress throughout the score. The development, largely based on the elves' music (*b*), suggests through its wide-ranging modulations the errant wanderings of the mortals in the enchanted forest. A ritard at the end of the development corresponds to a passage in the play where the exhausted lovers fall asleep. Then the magical four chords from the beginning (*a*) enter to mark the beginning of the recapitulation. Its order of events more or less coincides with that of the exposition, except that Mendelssohn now reserves the return of *c*, the music associated with the court of Athens, for the coda. When it appears, its former, bright regal sound is transformed into a softly scored, lyrical melody. In the play, Theseus' court is, in the end, infiltrated by the elves, who have the final say. In a similar way, Mendelssohn's overture ends with the four evocative chords of *a*, a last reference to the supernatural domain of the elves.

Mendelssohn: A Midsummer Night's Dream *Overture, Op. 21*

MOTIVES

Several years after writing the overture, Mendelssohn was asked to provide fuller music for a production of the play. For that occasion in 1843, he composed several new pieces, including a delicate Scherzo to describe the peregrinations of Titania's fairy, who wanders "swifter than the moon's sphere"; a luminescent Nocturne for the lovers in the forest; and a celebrated "Wedding March" for the nuptials of Theseus and Hippolyta. Mendelssohn not only preserved the overture intact but also ingeniously worked some of its motives into the **incidental music,** thereby providing telling clues about their programmatic meaning and succumbing once again to the romantic allure of his youthful imagination of 1826.

HECTOR BERLIOZ

The French composer Hector Berlioz (1803–1869) was born in southeastern France, near Grenoble. As a youth, he received musical instruction from his father, a medical doctor, and developed a lifelong interest in literature. In 1821 he was sent to Paris to study medicine. Quickly tiring of his studies, he decided to become a composer despite his parents' disapproval. In Paris, he regularly attended performances of contemporary French operas and the operas of Gluck. At the Conservatoire (a national music school founded during the French Revolution), he pored over Gluck's scores and painstakingly copied them out for further study.

In 1826 Berlioz gained admission to the Conservatoire, where he received academic training, by no means to his liking. He deplored the traditional curriculum, with its emphasis on counterpoint and sacred vocal music, and what he viewed as the pedantry of the director, Luigi Cherubini, an Italian composer noted for his operas and sacred music. In 1831, after he competed successfully for the prestigious Prix de Rome, he was sent to Italy, where he was required to submit compositions in an academically approved style, a duty against which he rebelled. Berlioz yearned to write music in a freer, more innovative style instead of mimicking music written in an officially approved style.

Berlioz's development as a composer was arguably influenced more by his literary interests than by his studies at the Conservatoire. As a boy he worshiped Virgil. Later, he devoured the works of Sir Walter Scott, James Fenimore Cooper, Lord Byron, and others—all in translation, for at first he knew little English. Goethe's epic poem *Faust,* which he read in prose translation, made a deep impression on him, and he later composed a great setting for orchestra, chorus, and soloists based on it, *La damnation de Faust (The Damnation of Faust,* 1846), which he referred to as a "dramatic legend."

It was the plays of Shakespeare, however, that influenced Berlioz most profoundly. In 1827 a troupe of English actors arrived in Paris to perform several of Shakespeare's plays. At the time, a literary debate was raging between the romantic writers, led by Victor Hugo, and the academic defenders of the traditional French drama. As Berlioz watched the performances, his sympathies were with the romantic writers, who viewed Shakespeare's plays as an alternative to traditional French drama. There was another attraction for Berlioz: the Irish actress Harriet Smithson, who played Ophelia in *Hamlet* and Juliet in *Romeo and Juliet.* Berlioz resolved to marry her, though first he immortalized her in his revolutionary *Symphonie fantastique,* an autobiographical composition of an unprecedented kind. After a tempestuous courtship, the two were married, though within a few years, several factors, including Berlioz's idealized vision of Harriet, contributed to the failure of their marriage.

---

* Music written for use in a dramatic production. Mendelssohn's other incidental music includes individual numbers for Racine's *Athalia* and Sophocles' *Antigone.*

Scornful of all that was conventional or fashionable in French music, Berlioz was a tireless advocate of reform. To support himself, he became a journalist and published many forceful, witty pieces of music criticism in which he lampooned the shallowness of French culture and politics. In his *Memoirs,* an endearing and eloquent account of his life, he did not hesitate to direct his critical scrutiny toward himself.

As a composer, Berlioz found inspiration in literary ideas and sources; all his important works have either a text or a musical program of some kind. Among his symphonies, *Harold in Italy* is based on Byron's *Childe Harold's Pilgrimage* and on Berlioz's own experiences in Italy, and *Roméo et Juliette* is a large-scale "dramatic symphony," with vocal soloists and choral forces, after Shakespeare. Several orchestral overtures draw on Scott, Shakespeare, and Byron. Finally, two operas, *Les Troyens (The Trojans)* and *Béatrice et Bénédict,* are based on librettos Berlioz fashioned himself after Virgil and Shakespeare, respectively.

As orchestrator and conductor, Berlioz understood the potential of the modern orchestra as did few of his contemporaries. He now worked with an orchestra considerably expanded beyond the dimensions of the classical orchestra. The chart on page 307, for example, lists the requirements of his *Symphonie fantastique.* The traditional paired woodwinds are reinforced by the addition of two bassoons (for a total of four); also, Berlioz occasionally calls for the piccolo and the English horn (see p. 309). The complement of brass is considerably expanded: Four horns rather than two are now customary; in addition, Berlioz calls for two cornets (see p. 309), two trumpets, three trombones, and two ophicleides.* The string section is in five basic parts, as in Beethoven's symphonies; however, Berlioz frequently employs further subdivisions of the strings into many additional parts. Finally, the percussion emerges as an instrumental ensemble in its own right: Along with timpani, we have a bass drum, a snare drum,† cymbals, bells, and two harps.

Berlioz's orchestral scores teem with new instrumental colors and remarkable special effects made possible by the expansion of the orchestra. He was a master at exploring the timbres of new or little-used woodwind, brass, and percussion instruments. He also coaxed new effects from familiar instruments: for example, by having woodwind instruments execute a **glissando,** or slide; by having an oboe play with its bell in a leather sack, to produce a dull, muffled sound; or by having several timpani tuned to different pitches play dull, thudding chords. Sometimes, his innovative orchestration led to grand results. In a colossal setting of the Requiem, for example, Berlioz supplemented the orchestra with four brass bands spatially separated to produce a kind of quadraphonic sound. He could also extract delicate nuances from the ensemble, however, and was constantly experimenting with subtle effects, such as writing especially sparse orchestral textures or requiring the violins to tap the strings of their instruments with the wood of their bows to create a hollow, eerie effect.

---

* A nineteenth-century bass brass instrument resembling a keyed bugle that was eventually replaced by the tuba. In Mendelssohn's overture to *A Midsummer Night's Dream,* an ophicleide graphically depicts the boorish character Bottom the Weaver.

† A small, two-sided drum with snares (typically gut or wire strings) stretched across the lower side. See p. 534.

The Orchestra of Berlioz's *Symphonie fantastique* (1830)

Woodwinds	Brass	Percussion	Strings*
2 Flutes (second doubles on piccolo)	4 Horns	Timpani	First Violins
2 Oboes (second doubles on English horn)	2 Cornets	Bass Drum	Second Violins
2 Clarinets	2 Trumpets	Snare Drum	Violas
4 Bassoons	3 Trombones	Cymbals	Cellos
	2 Ophicleides	Bells	Double Bass
		2 Harps	

*Strings are in five parts (further subdivisions employed)

SYMPHONIE FANTASTIQUE

The flamboyant work that launched Berlioz's career was the *Symphonie fantastique (Fantastic Symphony,* 1830), which earned him both critical recognition and vitriolic attack. The young composer declared that the inspiration behind this musical drama, as he called it, was his infatuation with Harriet Smithson and the emotional torment it had caused him. To explain the unusual course of his tradition-shattering symphony, he drafted a detailed, movement-by-movement program, originally intended to be distributed to the audience. From the program, which Berlioz revised in 1855, twenty-five years after completing the symphony, we learn that the work concerns an episode in which an artist takes an overdose of opium after an attack of lovesick despair. The music represents the effects of the drug—the artist's fantasies, hallucinations, and nightmares. In one bold stroke, Berlioz thus extended the realm of instrumental music to express the most intense personal feelings and to explore the subconscious depths of the mind.

The literary source of this unprecedented autobiographical symphony may have been Thomas De Quincey's *Confessions of an English Opium-Eater,* published in 1822 and translated into French (and available to Berlioz) a few years later. In that essay, De Quincey examined the "pleasures" and "pains" of opium in a remarkably frank manner and mentioned the role of music in his hallucinations (see p. 308).

The primary musical influence on Berlioz's *Symphonie fantastique* was probably Beethoven's *Pastoral* Symphony, which we studied in Chapter 9. Like that symphony, Berlioz's work is in five movements instead of the customary four. The third movement, a slow movement, depicts a pastoral scene and even includes an allusion to Beethoven's *Pastoral.* Berlioz, however, goes considerably further than Beethoven in stretching the programmatic limitations of the symphony: Where Beethoven's music suggests feelings aroused by a peaceful pastoral setting, Berlioz's slow movement remains centered on the creative imagination of the romantic artist, with the natural setting as a backdrop.

The dream commenced with a music which now I often heard in dreams—music of preparation and of awakening suspense. . . . The morning was come of a mighty day—a day of crisis and of final hope for human nature, then suffering some mysterious eclipse, and labouring in some dread extremity. Somewhere, I knew not where—somehow, I knew not how—by some beings, I knew not whom—a battle, a strife, an agony, was conducting,—was evolving like a great drama, or piece of music; with which my sympathy was the more insupportable from my confusion as to its place, its cause, its nature, and its possible issue. . . . Some greater interest was at stake; some mightier cause than ever yet the sword had pleaded, or trumpet had proclaimed. Then came sudden alarms; hurryings to and fro; trepidations of innumerable fugitives, I knew not whether from the good cause or the bad; darkness and lights: tempest and human faces: and at last, with the sense that all was lost, female forms, and the features that were worth all the world to me, and but a moment allowed,—and clasped hands, and heart-breaking partings, and then—everlasting farewells!

From Thomas De Quincey, Confessions of an English Opium-Eater, *1822*

First Movement: *Rêveries, Passions (Reveries, Passions)* The first movement expresses the malaise the artist experienced before meeting his beloved and the adulation she inspired at their first meeting. The long, slow, mournful introduction gives way to a passionate Allegro movement that announces her arrival, his "volcanic" love for her, his fits of jealousy, and his suffering. The Allegro is in sonata form, albeit a sonata form interpreted with considerable latitude by Berlioz; among its unusual features are the reversal of the first and second themes in the recapitulation and the further development of the first theme in the recapitulation. Some justification for these procedures may be found in Berlioz's program; the specially prominent role of the first theme, for example, has to do with its significance as the **idée fixe,** or "fixed idea," a melody that recurs transformed in every movement of the symphony to represent the artist's beloved. Here is the melody in full:

Berlioz: Symphonie fantastique, Idée fixe, *First Movement*

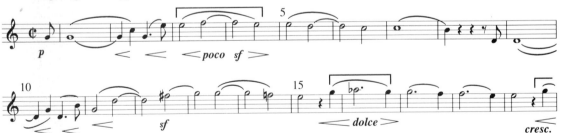

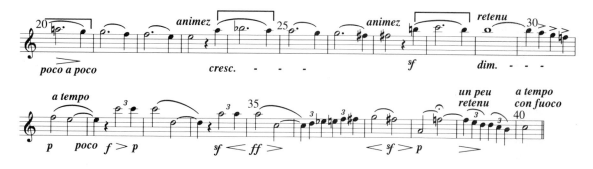

This arching melody breaks into three extended phrases: The first (mm. 1–15) reaches two crests in measures 3 and 13; the second (mm. 16–32) takes a half-step figure, bracketed in the example, and pushes it successively higher to a climax in measure 28; and the third (mm. 32–40) descends to bring the melody to a cadence. Berlioz's profuse tempo markings include *animez* ("excite"), *retenu* ("held back"), and *a tempo con fuoco* ("in tempo with energy"). There are numerous expression markings as well: in the first four bars alone, three crescendos, a *poco sf* (presumably an accent not quite as heavy as a normal *sforzando*), and a diminuendo. In his notation, Berlioz took pains to achieve the precise effect he had in mind.

Second Movement: *Un bal (A Ball)* The artist now encounters his beloved at a ball. Berlioz writes, accordingly, a waltz in triple time; the Allegro, which takes the place of a scherzo, is heard as the second of the five movements. Toward the middle of the movement, the *idée fixe* momentarily interrupts the graceful course of the waltz, before it resumes and breaks into an animated coda for its conclusion. The orchestra includes parts for harps (Berlioz specified at least four) and, at one point, a lovely solo for the cornet.★ The orchestration is clear and resilient and at times creates a shimmering effect.

Third Movement: *Scène aux champs (Pastoral Scene)* The artist now moves to the countryside, where on a summer evening he listens to two shepherds piping a slow, protracted tune. The duet is performed by an oboe and an English horn† offstage. The music calms the artist and leads him to consider how he will woo his beloved. Birdcalls reminiscent of the slow movement of Beethoven's *Pastoral* Symphony reinforce the mood. Then the *idée fixe* reappears in yet another transformation, and the artist wonders whether he has been deceived. The melody ceases and quiet returns. After threatening rolls on timpani suggest distant thunder, the shepherds' tune is heard again, and the pastoral scene ends peacefully.

★ A valved brass instrument similar in appearance to the trumpet but with a less brilliant tone. The cornet has a conical bore as opposed to the cylindrical bore of the trumpet.

† A double-reed instrument that resembles the oboe but is tuned a fifth below. The English horn plays the first six notes of the movement and is then answered by the oboe.

Berlioz: *Symphonie Fantastique,* **Finale**

Slow *Introduction*		*Allegro* *Idée fixe*			*Dies irae*	
Muted strings	Thematic fragments in winds and bass	Distorted by clarinet (twice)		Bells (Hint of fugal subject of Round Dance)	Each phrase stated three times, by ophicleide and bassoon, then in diminution by brass and woodwinds	(Hint of fugal subject)
pp Tonally vague		*ppp* *ff* Major	*f* *ff* Transposed major		*f* Minor	

Fourth Movement: *Marche au supplice (March to the Scaffold)* The fourth and fifth movements depict the nightmares the artist experiences in his opium dream. In the fourth movement, the artist dreams that he has murdered his beloved and is to be executed for his crime. The music suggests the grim procession to the scaffold, with muffled brass, dull chords for the contrabass, and an insistent marchlike rhythm in the timpani. A contrasting section features the bright, metallic sound of the full woodwind and brass, again accompanied by the thump of percussion. Near the end, a clarinet sounds the opening phrase of the *idée fixe,* rudely interrupted by a *fortissimo* chord to suggest the fall of the guillotine, a grisly symbol of decapitation. The garish scene concludes with pizzicato notes in the strings to suggest the drop of the severed head and with several bars of triumphant tonic chords.

Fifth Movement: *Songe d'une nuit du sabbat (Dream of a Sabbath Night)* The symphony culminates in a massive finale more than five hundred measures in length. In a macabre hallucination, the artist imagines himself at his own funeral, escorted by gruesome monsters and sorcerers. The beloved appears, transformed into a witchlike harlot. Solemn bells give way to a medieval plainchant, the sequence *Dies irae* from the Requiem Mass (see p. 16). Then, the witches join in a round dance. For the final section of the movement, Berlioz combines the *Dies irae* and the round dance (see study diagram).

The finale offers the most outlandish music of the symphony. Its loose, at times "chaotic," structure is dictated not by any conventional form but rather by the shape of the program. An eerie slow introduction sets the mood. Berlioz divides the strings into nine parts: Eight of the parts, which are muted, execute crisp rhythmic gestures; the ninth part, for the low strings, offers a percussionlike rumbling sound. Imprecise melodic

Berlioz: *Symphonie Fantastique,* Finale, *Continued*

Witches' Round Dance		Dies irae and Round Dance combined in two different keys		Animated
Free fugue				
	(Hint of *Dies irae*)		strings *col legno*	
f *ff*	*p*	*ff*	*mf*	*ff*
		Minor and major		
Major				Major

fragments and dissonant harmonic textures fill the introduction, without clearly stating a theme: These are the "strange noises" of the program, which seem to be answered by other sinister utterances. As the phantasmagoric introduction dissolves, we hear the *idée fixe* from afar. It is grotesquely distorted by a clarinet, a macabre parody of the original melody. We hear the noble melody transformed into a lively dance tune, with snaplike embellishments and trills added. Thus, Berlioz, suffering from unrequited love, takes his "revenge" on his beloved Harriet:

Berlioz: Symphonie fantastique, *Finale*

The beloved, now a sorceress, is riotously greeted by her compatriots as she takes her place at the artist's funeral.

In the second section of the finale, Berlioz introduced a device that doubtless offended the conscience of many: The sacred chant *Dies irae* (see p. 16) now makes its appearance in this symphony about an opium dream. It is accompanied by solemn bells, a symbol for the Church and its ritual. Berlioz divides the chant into three large portions; each is stated three times, in successively smaller note values. We give the first portion, played by the ophicleide and the bassoon, and its two compressions, or *diminutions,* heard in the brass and the woodwinds:

DIES IRAE

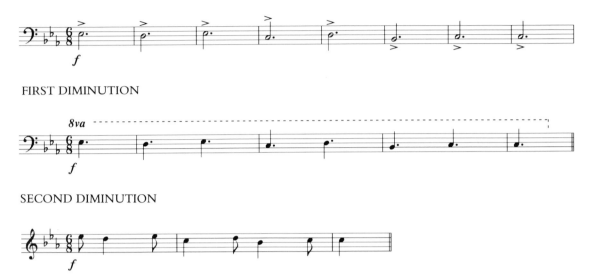

FIRST DIMINUTION

SECOND DIMINUTION

For the third section, the round dance of the witches, Berlioz turns to a mockery of counterpoint, a roistering fugue in which he disregards nearly all the conventions. Each entrance of the fugal subject is prepared by grating, syncopated chords. The wild course of the fugue suggests the witches scurrying about the body of the artist. Here is the basic subject of the fugue, executed with forceful accents and detached staccato articulations:

FUGAL SUBJECT

Berlioz concludes the symphony by combining the dance and the *Dies irae,* written in different keys. At one point, the violins and the violas tap their strings with the wood of the bows for a special, unsettling effect (*col legno*). The striking juxtaposition of the dance and the *Dies irae* is yet another example of Berlioz's extraordinary experiments that many of his contemporaries found incomprehensible.

The first performance of the *Symphonie fantastique* brought a swift critical response. Robert Schumann hailed Berlioz as a master of the modern orchestra, though he admitted that at first glance the symphony looked like music turned upside down! At the other extreme, one reactionary French critic labeled the symphony a saturnalia of cacophony, devoid of all art. From the start, the *Symphonie fantastique* embroiled Berlioz in the age-old controversy of innovation versus tradition, a controversy that continued to rage throughout the nineteenth century and, of course, well beyond. Through all that, the significance of the symphony endured: Its detailed, if fanciful, program associated with specific musical themes, its free approach to musical form and thematic transformation, its bold exploitation of the orchestra—in short, its fundamental expansion of the scope of the modern symphony—all are contributions that heavily influenced progressively minded nineteenth-century composers who followed Berlioz.

FRANZ LISZT

Born in Hungary, the pianist Franz Liszt (1811–1886) studied and concertized in Vienna, where, according to legend, he was embraced by Beethoven. Recognized as a prodigy, young Liszt scored triumphant successes in Paris and London before settling in Paris. There he experienced the upheaval of the July Revolution in 1830. Seeking spiritual comfort in this time of political instability, he turned to Catholicism and for a while attended meetings of a Utopian socialist sect. He also figured prominently in the artistic circle around George Sand (see p. 286), where he frequently encountered Chopin.

The most decisive event for Liszt during this period was a concert given in 1831 by the Italian violinist Nicolò Paganini, whose unparalleled virtuosity was taking Paris by storm. Paganini had utterly transformed violin playing by pushing its technical resources to new limits. Indeed, some observers wondered if his incredible feats might be inspired by the devil, a notion ostensibly supported by the violinist's gaunt, macabre appearance. Overwhelmed by Paganini's playing, Liszt made up his mind to accomplish on the piano what Paganini had accomplished on the violin and undertook in earnest a vast expansion of keyboard technique. The result was a set of études of "transcendental" difficulty—indeed, of such difficulty that Liszt later revised them to make them more accessible to pianists. Several of Liszt's concert études are fitted with vivid titles, for example, "Eroica" ("Heroic"); "Harmonies du soir" ("Evening Harmonies"); "Wilde Jagd," which describes a nocturnal hunt; and "Mazeppa," concerned with the legend of a Cossack leader who was strapped by his enemies to a wild horse.

Between 1838 and 1848, Liszt concertized extensively, journeying from the Iberian Peninsula to Russia, and from Ireland as far south as Turkey. Everywhere, audiences acclaimed his extraordinary skill and showmanship. His repertory included hundreds of free fantasias and transcriptions (or paraphrases) for piano solo based on works by other composers, especially famous arias and scenes from operas. Liszt also composed an enormous quantity of original piano compositions, including groups of pieces inspired by his travels in Switzerland and Italy (*Années de Pèlerinage,* or *Years of Pilgrimage)* and

Liszt: Piano Concerto No. 1, in E-flat major

First Movement (Allegro)

a		*a*		*a*		*b*	*Gradually Pressing*	*Animated*	
Orchestra	Piano cadenza	Orch.	Cadenza	Orch.	Cadenza	Piano, Clarinet, 2 Violins	Transition	*a* Orch., Piano	Cadenza
ff		*mf*		*mf*		*mf*, *p*		*ff*	

a set of Hungarian rhapsodies filled with colorful and infectious melodies and rhythms, some drawn from the music of the gypsies.

In 1848 Liszt settled in Weimar as the court conductor and, for the next several years, devoted himself to writing music of a more serious and experimental nature. (We shall discuss his innovative orchestral works, most of which date from the 1850s, in Chapter 14). While in Weimar, he championed the music of Berlioz, Richard Wagner (who married Liszt's daughter Cosima in 1870), and other "progressive" composers. During his later years, Liszt divided his time between Rome, where he took the minor orders of the priesthood, Weimar, and Budapest, where he was received as a Hungarian hero (ironically, Liszt never mastered the Magyar dialect, preferring French and German instead). Aspiring young pianists came from afar to seek instruction from the Abbé Liszt, including several American pupils who helped disseminate and perpetuate his manner of pianism.

Liszt's personal life was as sensational as his music. During the 1830s he entered into an affair with the Countess Marie d'Agoult, by whom he fathered three children. For a few years, the two lived together in Italy and Switzerland, occasionally returning to Paris, including one 1837 visit when Liszt engaged in a pianistic duel with another leading virtuoso, from which he emerged triumphant. During this period Liszt published an essay on the future course of sacred music and other pieces of music journalism; much of this prose, in fact, may have been the work of the Countess, who later wrote a novel about Liszt. By the mid-1840s, the two had separated. Then, in 1847, Liszt met Carolyn Sayn-Wittgenstein, a Russian princess and prolific author who wrote a multivolume critique of the Church. The two established their household together in Weimar, though the Princess was still married. For several years, she attempted in vain to secure a divorce and in 1861 appealed to the Pope. Her request was denied, however, and she was never able to marry Liszt.

PIANO CONCERTO NO. 1, IN E-FLAT MAJOR

Liszt was unquestionably the greatest piano virtuoso of the nineteenth century. Not surprisingly, his first attempts at orchestral music were works for piano and orchestra,

a		a		a	*Second Movement (Adagio)*					
					Introduction		*Recitative (Agitated)*			
a		a		a	c	c	d		e	c
Orch.	Cadenza	Orch.	Cadenza	Orch., Piano	Orch.	Piano solo	Piano, Orch.	Cadenza	Flute, Clarinet, Oboe, Piano	Clarinet, Piano $\longrightarrow$
mf		*mf*		*p* > *ppp*	*p*	*p*	*f*		*p*	

(continued)

including two concertos.★ We shall examine the first, in E-flat major, as an example of a romantic concerto. Envisioned as early as 1830, this work was not completed until 1849; its first performance took place in Weimar with Liszt at the piano and Berlioz conducting. It is in four connected movements, all free in form (see the study diagram). A network of themes, transformed in novel ways as the concerto proceeds, serves to tie the work together into a cohesive whole. Here are the eight most important:

Liszt: Piano Concerto No. 1, in E-flat major, Themes

FIRST MOVEMENT

SECOND MOVEMENT

(continued)

★The manuscript of a third, unfinished piano concerto has recently been discovered.

Liszt: Piano Concerto No. 1, in E-flat major, *Continued*

Third Movement (Scherzo)

Introduction	Variation	Interlude	Variation	Interlude	Cadenza		Recall of		
f	*f*	*f*	*f*	*f*	Recall of	*a*	*e*	*a*	⟶
Orch. (triangle)	Piano	Orch.	Piano	Orch.	*a*		Oboe		
p	*p*		*p*	*p*		*ff*	*f*	*ff* , *fff*	

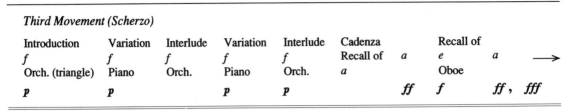

THIRD MOVEMENT

FOURTH MOVEMENT

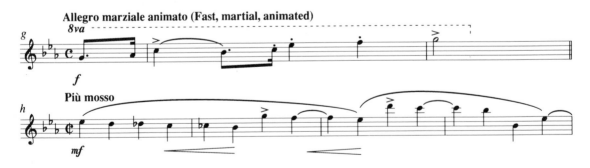

Liszt: Piano Concerto No. 1, in E-flat major, *Continued*

Finale (March)						*A bit faster - - - -*	*Very fast*
(cymbals)							
g (Recall of	Recall of	Recall of	Recall of	Recall of		Closing theme	Recall of
c transformed)	*d*	*e*	*c*	*f*		*h*	*a*
Orch.	Piano	Piano		(triangle)			
f	*ff*		*mf*		*p*		*ff* , *fff*

In the first movement, Liszt introduces two contrasting themes (*a* and *b*). They are not treated according to the eighteenth-century classical mold; the amalgamation of the ritornello principle and sonata form we observed in Mozart's concertos (see p. 203) here undergoes a process of severe compression. Thus, the opening "ritornello," which announces *a* with sturdy dotted rhythms and *fortissimo* orchestral reinforcement, is almost immediately interrupted by a dazzling piano cadenza.* Moveover, theme *b,* characterized by a long–short rhythmic pattern (♩♪), is barely introduced before it is interrupted, and it does not reappear later in the movement. Instead, the movement shifts back and forth between decisive orchestral statements of *a* and a variety of sparkling piano cadenzas carefully manufactured by Liszt to display to the full his stunning virtuoso style.

The second movement, an Adagio, introduces three new themes. Theme *c,* played by the piano with a murmuring arpeggiated accompaniment, describes an arching curve and might almost be from a nocturne by Chopin. The more impulsive theme *d* introduces a dramatic recitativelike passage with agitated tremolos (rapidly repeated pitches) in the strings. Theme *e,* played first in the high register of a solo flute and then by a clarinet and an oboe, is marked *dolce espressivo* ("sweetly and expressively").

The third movement is a scherzo (see p. 226)—more in its jesting, playful manner than in its form. To add color, Liszt uses a triangle to accompany its opening theme (*f*), a playful, staccato idea impelled by descending triplets. After presenting the theme in the orchestra, Liszt subjects it to two fanciful piano variations. In the latter part of the scherzo, themes *a, e,* and *a* again are recalled. The movement runs directly into the fourth movement, the finale.

This concluding movement, an animated march complete with cymbal crashes, serves to tie together the various strands of the concerto. The rousing march theme (*g*) is actually a transformation of theme *c* from the slow movement. Similarly, as the movement progresses, other material from the first three movements returns in some transformed guise. Toward the end, Liszt introduces a fresh closing theme, *h,* in a brisker tempo. Upon closer inspection, the descending chromatic profile of *h* is revealed to be derived from the original theme *a.* Appropriately, the concerto climaxes with the reemergence of the opening bars of *a,* now performed in a *presto* (very fast) tempo in

---

*A technique that Beethoven had earlier employed in his Piano Concerto No. 5 (*Emperor*) of 1809.

fortissimo piano octaves with full orchestral support. All in all, Liszt joins virtuosity with the expressive color of the orchestra and a free, organic approach to thematic transformation and form to produce a highly original and refreshing romantic synthesis.

JOHANNES BRAHMS

The romanticism of Johannes Brahms (1833–1897), a younger musician who worked in the second half of the nineteenth century, took a different course from that of Berlioz and Liszt. Less flamboyant in style, Brahms's music recalls the fastidious craft of Mendelssohn and the warm lyricism of Schubert and Robert Schumann. Born in the northern port city of Hamburg, Brahms was introduced to music at an early age by his father, a poor street musician who played double bass. Early on, Brahms began to study piano and soon received instruction in theory and composition as well. In 1853 he joined the Hungarian violinist Eduard Reményi on a concert tour. Through that experience, Brahms became familiar with the rhythmic zest and melodic verve of Hungarian gypsy music, qualities that were to influence his own music. The same year, Brahms met Schumann for the first time. In his music journal, Schumann welcomed the budding composer as a "young eagle" who would carry on the great tradition of Haydn, Mozart, and Beethoven. Sadly, their developing friendship was cut short by Schumann's death in 1856. Appreciative of Schumann's efforts, Brahms endeavored in his early works to emulate the music of his friend and mentor.

During those early years, Brahms gained valuable experience as a concertizing pianist and conductor. He wrote a considerable amount of piano music and several Lieder before turning to the larger genres. Frustrated in his efforts to obtain a secure appointment in Hamburg, he moved in 1862 to Vienna, the city of Mozart, Haydn, Beethoven, and Schubert. There he continued to perform as conductor and pianist until his growing fame enabled him to retire from concert life to concentrate on composition.

Brahms was an avid student of music history. He collected musical autographs and rare editions, studied problematic passages from music dating back to the Renaissance, and contributed to scholarly editions. He pored over the great works of the classical masters and earlier nineteenth-century composers such as Schubert and Schumann, and paid homage to them by modeling his own early compositions on their masterpieces. Though steeped in the grand symphonic tradition, he cautiously put off completing his first symphony until 1876, when he was forty-three years old.

Much of Brahms's music falls outside the chronological scope of this chapter; we will discuss one of his magnificent orchestral works in Chapter 14. Because his early compositions are in the style of Schumann and other romantics, however, we turn to one of them here.

PIANO QUINTET IN F MINOR, OP. 34

As a young composer, Brahms devoted considerable energies to chamber music—this at a time when most composers of the first rank were turning away from chamber

Johannes Brahms.

music. He destroyed his first attempts, but nevertheless, during the 1850s and 1860s, produced a distinguished series of works ranging in size from the duet to the sextet. In his chamber music, Brahms continued the rich classical tradition established by the string quartets and other chamber works of Haydn, Mozart, and Beethoven, and continued by Schubert, Mendelssohn, and Schumann, all of whom made important contributions to the romantic chamber music repertory. Rather than break from that tradition, Brahms sought to cultivate and extend it even further. In this he succeeded; no other nineteenth-century composer after Beethoven completed so substantial a body of chamber music of such high quality.

The Piano Quintet in F minor (1865) went through several versions before Brahms was satisfied with it. He first attempted the composition as a string quintet and then as a sonata for two pianos. In its final version as a quintet, it is scored for string quartet (first and second violin, viola, and cello) and piano. Brahms's artistry is evident in his deft manipulation of thematic material, much of which springs from a network of interrelated motives. Just as masterful is Brahms's full use of the various instrumental combinations afforded by a piano quintet, including pitting the quartet of strings against the piano, breaking the ensemble up into smaller groupings, and treating all five instruments equally. The quintet observes the traditional four-movement plan. The first and fourth movements are moderately fast, the second is a slow movement, and the third is a fast scherzo.

First Movement: Allegro non troppo In its form, the first movement is the most straightforward of the four movements. Marked *Allegro non troppo* ("Allegro but not too much"), it has a more or less regular sonata form. The tense first subject (*a*), in F minor, is played at the outset by the piano, first violin, and cello in octave doublings:

Brahms: Piano Quintet in F minor, Op. 34, First Movement

It begins modestly enough and gathers some momentum before coming to an early pause. Then, it explodes into a *forte* passage taken up by the entire ensemble. The second subject (*b*), introduced by a plummeting, descending leap, appears initially in the piano, with a triplet accompaniment in its bass register. Brahms selects a totally unexpected key for the second subject, C-sharp minor—it is another minor key, but it has several sharps in its signature and is far removed from the flat key of F minor that serves as the tonic. At the end of the exposition, in a hushed closing section (*c*), he converts the minor key of the second theme to a flat major key, D-flat major, reducing the harmonic tension that has accumulated. In deference to the traditional sonata form, Brahms calls for the repetition of the exposition.

In the first part of the development, the first subject (*a*) is led through a maze of keys. Much of this section is lightly scored, with a *piano* or *pianissimo* dynamic level. A crescendo announces the beginning of the second part of the development, in which Brahms explores the second subject (*b*). This, too, is heard in several keys, and in one ingenious passage Brahms counterposes it against its mirror inversion, as shown in the example:

DEVELOPMENT

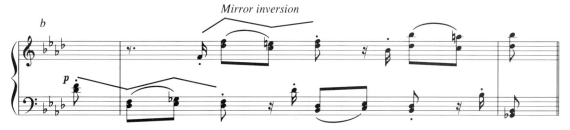

Mirror inversion

Brahms prepares for the recapitulation by establishing the dominant key, a traditional technique frequently encountered in the sonata-form movements of classical composers. Unexpectedly, when the recapitulation enters, it begins not with the opening bars but with the explosive fifth bar of the movement.

The rest of the recapitulation follows predictably enough. A tonal adjustment is made for the second group so that the tonic key is properly reaffirmed. Finally, Brahms adds an extended coda, in two sections: *Poco sostenuto* ("A bit sustained"), a quiet brooding section that includes an exquisite passage for strings alone, and *Tempo I*, a return to the first tempo, in which the music builds to a powerful climax on *a*.

Second Movement: Andante, un poco Adagio The lovely slow movement is in three broad sections with the plan *ABA*. Although each section is in a major key, Brahms uses a flat key (A-flat) for the *A* sections and a sharp key (E) for the *B* section, recalling in a way the mixture of flat and sharp keys in the first movement. The heart of the Andante is the *A* section, based on a gentle melody drawn out to some thirty bars in the piano part. Brahms places the melody in the middle range of the piano; it is paralleled a third below, suggesting a duetlike texture, and accompanied by light strings (including pizzicato cello), allowing the warm glow of the piano to prevail. We cite here the opening measures of the piano melody:

Brahms: Piano Quintet in F minor, Op. 34, Second Movement

A SECTION

Andante, un poco Adagio

p espress. sotto voce

Brahms: Piano Quintet in F minor, Op. 34, Third Movement

Scherzo A								Trio B		Scherzo A (Da Capo)
a	*b¹*	*b²*	*a*	*b¹* (extended)	*b²*	*a*	*b¹*	*c*	*c* (extended) *c*	
pp	pp	*ff*	*f*, pp	*ff*, *p*	*ff*	*f*	*ff*	Piano	Strings	Strings
6 8	2 4	6 8		2 4	6 8		2 4			
	Strings alone	Full ensemble		Contrapuntal treatment						
Minor	Major tonic (clearly defined)	Minor	∿∿∿∿∿	Major Second key	Minor	Major ending tonic	Major tonic			

Brahms: Piano Quintet in F minor, Op. 34, Third Movement

Third Movement: Scherzo The basic shape of the third movement is clear: It is an *ABA* scherzo with a scherzo proper (*A*), a trio (*B*), and a repeat of the scherzo proper (*A*). But beyond this external form, Brahms breaks from tradition (see study diagram). Instead of using repeat marks within the sections, he writes out each section in its entirety and incorporates in the process several modifications and expansions of the conventional form.

The essence of a scherzo is its lighthearted play with the listener's expectations, and this scherzo proves to be no exception. Brahms plays on our understanding of thematicism, rhythm, and meter. The scherzo begins not with a clear-cut theme but with an ambiguous triadic figure that rises in the strings (*a*). This figure is harmonically vague: There is no strong statement of the tonic key here. What is more, it is metrically off the beat. It provides a good example of syncopation, or rhythmic displacement, a technique of which Brahms was quite fond: Each weak beat is tied to the following strong beat, thereby negating the sense of a strong, regular downbeat. The meter, too, is not quite right: Brahms chooses $\frac{6}{8}$ for the opening, instead of $\frac{3}{4}$, the time-honored meter for the scherzo (and, earlier, for the minuet).

The opening gives way to a *pianissimo* passage for the strings alone, with light, staccato repeated pitches (b^1). Here, Brahms changes the meter to $\frac{2}{4}$ and comes closer to defining a theme. In a final bold stroke, he clears away the ambiguity of the minor-key opening by proclaiming a marchlike theme in the major key, played *fortissimo* by the entire ensemble (b^2), that is derived from b^1. The remainder of the scherzo proper is based on additional statements of *a*, b^1, and b^2. In the contrasting Trio, in C major, Brahms abandons his playful mood and writes a beautiful, noble melody that rises from the piano without rhythmic distortion (*c*). But with the return of the scherzo proper, we are again confronted by the earlier music of *a*, b^1, and b^2 that tries our expectations.

Fourth Movement: Poco sostenuto; Allegro non troppo In its form the most complex movement of the quintet, the finale is also the most ambitious. Nearly five hundred measures in length, it does not quite fit either of the usual forms for the finale—the sonata or the rondo form. Rather, it uses elements of both (see study diagram).

Brahms begins with a lengthy slow introduction, marked *Poco sostenuto* ("Somewhat sustained"). One of his most romantically inspired passages, this introduction suggests a kind of fantasy, with freely shifting textures and harmonies. First, we hear the five instruments in imitative counterpoint; then, a slowly descending melodic curve in the violin and cello (an allusion to Schumann's *Phantasie*, Op. 17, for piano) is set against sturdy chords in the piano. The freedom of this introductory section foreshadows what is to come. The movement proper (*Allegro non troppo*; "Fast, but not too fast") begins with a minor-key cello theme in $\frac{2}{4}$, marked by staccato notes and ornaments on the downbeat that lend it a rhythmic pungency (*a*).

Brahms: Piano Quintet in F minor, Op. 34, Finale

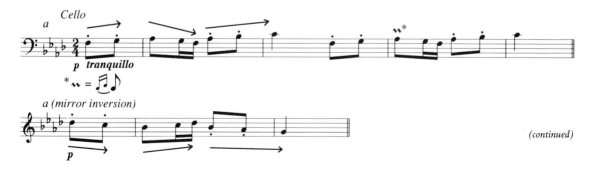

(continued)

Brahms: Piano Quintet in F minor, Op. 34 (Finale)

Poco sostenuto Slow Introduction		Allegro non troppo (Tempo I)						Little more animated (Tempo II)	
Imitative counterpoint	Melody (violin, cello) against piano chords	$\frac{2}{4}$	A a Cello	a Violin (mirror inversion)	a Piano	a drone	Bridge Based on a	B b against drone and ascending scale	Transition b developed
~~ Dominant			*p* Tonic minor			*f* Tonic ~~~~~ major		*p* Dominant ~~~~~ minor	*f* ~~~~~

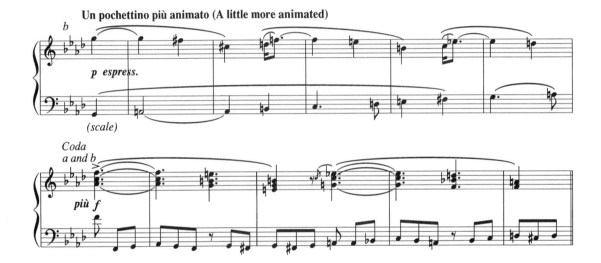

The theme is now given in mirror inversion by the violin before being stated by the piano; then, it appears in the tonic major against a drone in the bass register. An elaborate bridge leads to the second section (*B*), based on an exotically flavored tune which Brahms sets off with a slightly faster tempo. The chromatic color and rhythmic snaps (♪.) of this expressive theme give it a folklike quality, suggesting in particular Hungarian gypsy music. Against it, Brahms provides a simple scale in the cello and a drone as accompaniment. In the following extended passage, theme *b* and its accompaniment are repeated several times and led through different keys, almost as if they were part of a development section in a sonata-form movement; at the end of this passage, the first tempo is reestablished with a new version of *a*.

Next the *A* and *B* sections return, with modifications, giving the movement more the shape of a rondo. The final portion, some 150 measures in length, is a dynamic

Brahms: Piano Quintet in F minor, Op. 34 (Finale), *Continued*

Tempo I			Tempo II		Tempo I	Coda Presto, non troppo			
	A	Transition	*B*	Transition	Based				
a	modified		*b* against drone and ascending scale		on *a*	$\frac{6}{8}$ *a*		*b*	*a* and *b* combined
p	*p*	*f*	*p*	*f*	*pp*	*p*	*ff*	*ff*	*f* *p* *f*
Dominant minor	Tonic minor	〰〰	Tonic minor	〰〰	Tonic minor	Sharp minor key	Tonic minor		

large-scale coda in Presto tempo. Brahms begins with the first subject, not in the tonic key but in C-sharp minor, the contrasting minor key used earlier in the exposition of the first movement; also, the subject appears in a spirited $\frac{6}{8}$ meter. Then, to correct the deviation in key, he swerves to the tonic key and reintroduces the second subject. The final masterful stroke is the combination of the two in the closing measures, forming a weighty and dramatic conclusion to this superb quintet.

For all its original solutions to problems of form, Brahms's piano quintet is in the mainstream of the illustrious tradition of German chamber music. As we shall discover again, Brahms remained content to explore the traditional genres of instrumental music at a time when the style and the language of nineteenth-century music were rapidly evolving in new directions. For that reason, he is sometimes viewed as a musical conservative. His nostalgia for the romanticism of Schumann and his affinity for the earlier masterpieces of classicism serve to strengthen that view.

Suggested Listening

Berlioz: *Roméo et Juliette*
★_____: *Symphonie fantastique*
★Brahms: Piano Quintet in F minor, Op. 34
_____: Piano Trio in B major, Op. 8
Chopin: Ballade in G minor, Op. 23
★_____: Étude, Op. 10, No. 5 ("Black-Key")
★_____: Nocturne, Op. 9, No. 1
_____: Polonaise in A-flat major, Op. 53
★_____: Prélude, Op. 28, No. 2
Liszt: *Années de Pèlerinage,* Books I and II
★_____: Piano Concerto No. 1, in E-flat major

Note: Works marked with an asterisk are the principal works discussed in the chapter.

In a dignified, majestic recitative accompanied by the orchestra, she begins by arguing that Rome will fall one day of its own weakness. Then, in the first part of the famous cavatina that follows, "Casta diva" ("Chaste Goddess"), she calls on the Moon, another deity worshiped by the Druids, to protect the peace:

Casta Diva, che inargenti	Chaste goddess, who covers in silver
queste sacre antiche piante,	this ancient, sacred forest,
a noi volgi il bel sembiante	turn thy pleasing countenance upon us,
senza nube e senza vel.	without cloud and veil.

Into this solo Bellini poured his finest melodic expression. The scene is set by an Andante orchestral introduction that establishes in the strings a gentle accompaniment of broken chords

These move from minor to major keys. Then, in the flute we hear an extended lyrical melody (*a*) that could almost have been composed by Chopin. The soft colors of the flute are appropriate for the subdued lighting of this nocturnal scene; Norma is bathed in moonlight while the Druids prostrate themselves:

Bellini: Norma, *Act I, Cavatina, "Casta diva"*

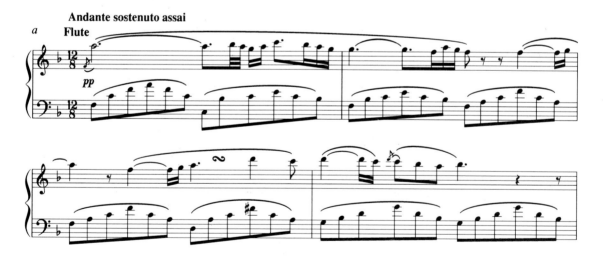

The flute melody falls into several gently turned phrases that reach higher and higher. But the melody breaks off before it can conclude and is left open, a romantic gesture. Bellini then allows Norma to make her entrance by starting afresh with the melody. At first, she retraces the contours of the flute melody; then, she extends the melody to a climax on a high note before she allows it to subside. The chorus of Druids now responds in quiet homophony as Norma sings florid runs above the chorus. For the second verse of the Andante, Bellini reuses the music of *a*, thereby producing a strophic design for the Andante, in accordance with the convention of the time. But there is one change: The chorus offers an accompanying commentary to Norma's second strophe. All of this leads up to a brief cadenza by Norma and a few cadential measures that bring the Andante to a tranquil close. Next, Norma delivers a transitional recitative (again with orchestral accompaniment); after this, she proceeds to sing an Allegro cabaletta in which she declares her passion for Pollione in an aside—this in dramatic juxtaposition to outbursts from the chorus of Druids, who demand that the Roman be punished. The entire scene then concludes with a stirring orchestral march as the Druids depart.

GIUSEPPE VERDI

The undisputed master of nineteenth-century Italian opera was Giuseppe Verdi (1813–1901). As a young man, he was turned down when he sought admission to the conservatory in Milan; indeed, Verdi was slow to develop as a composer. His early operas gave little hint of what was to come, and for a time he thought of giving up composing altogether. But in 1842, at La Scala in Milan, he scored a major triumph with *Nabucco,* based on the Old Testament account of Nebuchadnezzar and the Babylonian captivity; within a few years, performances of *Nabucco* were mounted throughout Europe and in America and South America. In a stream of operas that followed during the next ten years, Verdi turned to Schiller, Hugo, Byron, and Shakespeare, among others, for the subjects of his librettos. He later described those difficult years as his time "in the galley." They were followed by a period of artistic maturity, reached with a group of operas composed during the 1850s. Three of them are staples of the opera repertory: *Rigoletto,* based on a play by Victor Hugo (1851); *Il trovatore (The Troubadour),* based on a Spanish play (1853); and *La traviata (The Misguided Woman),* based on a play by Alexandre Dumas, the son (1853).

A good part of Verdi's long career—more than a half century elapsed between his first opera in 1839 and his last in 1893—coincided with the *Risorgimento (Resurgence),* the great movement for the unification of Italy. An Italian patriot, Verdi rejoiced when the Austrians were driven out of Italy and replaced by a monarchy under Victor Emmanuel in 1860. In fact, the composer's name was taken as an acrostic for "*V*ittorio Emmanuele, *R*è *D'*Italia" ("Vittorio Emmanuel, King of Italy"), and he was named an honorary deputy in the new Italian parliament.

Several of Verdi's operas deal with political oppression and contain allusions that Italian audiences were sure to understand. In *Nabucco,* for example, the captive Hebrews sing a hymnlike chorus that many took to be a rallying cry for Italian nationalism. (It eventually emerged as an Italian folk song.) In *Macbeth* (1847), the Scottish noblemen lament the oppression of their fatherland; and in *La battaglia di Legnano (The Battle of Legnano,* 1848), Verdi produced a rousing, patriotic work during the year of revolution.

Giuseppe Verdi.

As the unification of Italy became more and more a reality, Verdi grew less productive, but he was increasingly innovative in his approach to operatic design and relied less and less on the well-entrenched conventions of Italian opera. A tireless advocate for the rights of the composer, he did more than any other Italian to establish the notion of opera as an inviolable work of art. He was now a composer of international standing, whose operas were being performed in London, Paris, and, of course, Italy. Most noteworthy of all the operas in that regard was *Aida,* premiered in 1871 for a gala performance in Cairo following the opening of the Suez Canal in 1869.

For several years after completing *Aida,* Verdi more or less withdrew from public life. In 1874, moved by the death of the Italian romantic writer Alessandro Manzoni, he composed a Requiem Mass, but he wrote no new operas until his very last years. Then, in 1887, he returned to the stage with *Otello. Falstaff,* his final opera, was finished in his eightieth year, in 1893. These two masterpieces—one a tragedy, the other a comedy—were based on Shakespeare's *Othello,* and on *The Merry Wives of Windsor* and

Henry IV, Part II. Here Verdi continued to experiment; instead of dividing the music neatly into so many distinct arias, recitatives, and ensembles, he adopted a more flexible approach that produced long stretches of continuous music; the supple vocal lines of these scores often suggest syntheses of aria and recitative styles. Verdi also exploited the orchestra more and more as a powerful expressive agent and explored an ever broadening spectrum of harmonies and key relationships.

IL TROVATORE (THE TROUBADOUR, 1853)

The librettos of Verdi's operas typically feature dramatic human conflicts with sharply drawn characters at the center of the drama. One striking example is *Il trovatore,* which unfolds as a series of shock effects. Set in fifteenth-century Spain, it offers a rather complicated and at times entangled plot that involves four principals. Manrico, a mysterious troubadour, is thought to be the son of the gypsy woman Azucena, whom the Count di Luna, a nobleman of Aragon, seeks to capture. Manrico is in love with Leonora, a lady-in-waiting to the Princess of Aragon. But the Count, too, is courting Leonora and thus is set in strong opposition to Manrico.

Much of the action of *Il trovatore* springs from events that have taken place before the curtain goes up. We learn in Act I, for example, that Azucena's mother, a gypsy sorceress, had been burned at the stake by the former Count di Luna. In revenge, Azucena had murdered someone she thought to be one of the Count's sons, though she later learned he was her own son. Manrico is, in fact, the brother of the Count di Luna, though this fact is withheld—not always successfully—until the dramatic conclusion of the opera, when the Count has Manrico executed, only to learn from Azucena his true identity.

Il trovatore derives a strong romantic appeal from the gypsies, social outcasts whose bohemian ways clash with the aristocratic manner of the Spanish court. Act II, titled "The Gypsy," offers some of the most colorful music of the score, especially in its opening scene, which contains the famous "Anvil Chorus." As the curtain rises, we see a gypsy encampment at the foot of a mountain. Day is dawning, and the gypsies begin to stir. The orchestral introduction opens with an unharmonized figure provided with trills and accents off the beat and executed with crisp staccato articulations (*a*):

Verdi: Il trovatore, *Act II, "Anvil Chorus"*

Verdi: *Il trovatore,* Act IV (Beginning)

Introduction Adagio	Recitative			Aria (Leonora) Adagio			
Low woodwinds	Ruiz and Leonora alone	Ruiz departs Wood- winds	Leonora Strings	*a* Strings	Flute above	Cadenza	Cadence
pp				 *pp*			
Minor key				Minor key	Major key		Major key

A second motive (*b*) features a repeated pitch decorated with chromatic ornaments and impelled by an accompaniment of detached chords. The metallic ringing of the triangle adds to the exotic effect of the music:

The gypsies greet the new day and, taking up their hammers, sing the celebrated "Anvil Chorus" (*c*), with hammer blows alternating between the basses and the tenors:

c

Chi   del   gi - ta - no   i   gior - ni   ab - bel - la?

f

Text: Who makes beautiful the days of the gypsy?

Verdi repeats the music for *a, b,* and *c,* this time with the chorus of gypsies participating throughout but again culminating in the clangorous anvil chorus. Verdi's means are deliberately simple, but the use of the chorus and the application of distinctive musical means to characterize the gypsies makes a strikingly memorable effect.

In Act IV, "The Execution," the drama culminates in catastrophe. Count di Luna has captured both Manrico and Azucena; they are in prison awaiting execution (see study diagram). As the act begins, Leonora, hoping to rescue Manrico or at least bid him farewell, appears outside the prison tower, accompanied by Ruiz, a soldier in

Verdi: *Il trovatore*, Act IV (Beginning), *Continued*

Miserere Andante	Leonora's response	Manrico	*Miserere*	Leonora and Monks	Manrico, Leonora, and
b	*c*	*d*	*b*	*b* and *c*	Monks
offstage	Marchlike				*b*, *c*, and *d*
Chorus of	rhythm	Harp			
Monks					
Chordal					
texture,					
death knell					
New		Major	Minor		Major *ff*
minor		key	key		key
key					

Manrico's service. It is night, and Verdi uses low, somber woodwinds in a dark minor key to set the scene. In the introductory recitative, Ruiz and Leonora first sing unaccompanied:

Ruiz

Siam giunti.	Here we are.
Ecco la torre, ove di Stato	Behold the tower, where the prisoners
gemono i prigionieri.	of the State languish.
Ah, l'infelice ivi fu tratto!	There the unfortunate was brought!

Leonora

Vanne.	Go now.
Lasciami, nè timor di me te prenda—	Leave me, and do not worry about me—
Salvarlo io potrò, forse.	perhaps I can yet save him.

(Exit Ruiz.)

Then, Ruiz withdraws, the woodwinds return, and the strings are introduced, as Leonora's recitative grows more expressive and desperate:

| *Timor di me?—Sicura,* | Fear for me? My defense |
| *presta è la mia difesa!* | is sure and quick! |

(She examines a jeweled ring on her right hand. It contains a vial of poison.)

In quest'oscura notte ravvolta,	Veiled in this obscure night
presso a te son io, e tu nol sai!	I am close to you, without your knowing it!
Gemente aura, che intorno spiri,	Oh, wailing breeze that blows around me,
Deh, pietosa gli arreca i miei sospiri.	mercifully bring my sighs to him.

Finally, she turns to her Adagio aria, "D'amor sull'ali rosee," beginning with a minor-key melody, accompanied by triplets in the strings, that rises from her low register (a):

D'amor sull'ali rosee	On the rosy wings of love
vanne, sospir dolente,	go forth, sad sigh,
del prigioniero misero	and soothe the troubled mind
conforta l'egra mente.	of the prisoner in misery.
Com'aura di speranza	Like a breath of hope,
aleggia in quella stanza,	hover in that cell,
lo desta alle memorie,	and bring back to him all memories,
ai sogni dell'amor!	all dreams of love!
Ma, deh, non dirgli improvvido	But, pray, do not carelessly reveal to him
le pene del mio cor!	the pains in my heart!

Verdi: Il trovatore, *Act IV*

Recalling happier days with her beloved troubadour ("Com'aura di speranza"), she moves to a brighter major key and a higher register, with a flute occasionally paralleling her part above. Verdi draws the aria to a climax with an elaborate cadenza and adds a few cadential measures in the major key. Then, the death-bell tolls, and an *a cappella* chorus of monks intones a solemn "Miserere" for the condemned. They sing in a new minor key, in lugubrious chordal style with dotted rhythms, and in a slightly faster Andante tempo (b):

Miserere d'un'alma già vicina	Have pity on a soul already close to that
alla partenza che non ha ritorno!	parting moment that has no return!
Miserere di lei, bontà divina,	Have pity on that soul, O Divine Grace,
preda non sia dell'infernal soggiorno!	and save him from the infernal perdition!

Leonora shudders in terror to the chanting of the monks, as the orchestra commences a grim chordal accompaniment suggesting a funeral march (*c*):

Quel suon, quelle preci	That sound, those solemn
solenni, funeste,	prayers, like an ill omen
empiron quest'aere	filled the air
di cupo terror!	with dreaded terror!
Contende l'ambascia,	The anguish
che tutta m'investe,	that fills me entirely
al labbro il respiro,	takes the breath from my lips
i palpiti al cor!	and the pulse from my heart!

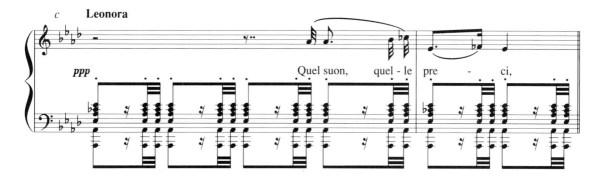

Then, contrast: Manrico sings his farewell to Leonora and to life from his cell in the tower, with a harp in the orchestra imitating the sound of his lute. His music (*d*) is in the same major key employed earlier by Leonora:

Ah! che la morte ognora	Ah! How death delays
è tarda nel venir	in coming to him
a chi desia morir!	who wishes to die!
Addio, . . . Leonora, addio!	Farewell, Leonora, Farewell!

Now Verdi repeats part of the earlier sequence of music, but this time joins the various forces together—first the monks (*b*), then Leonora and the monks together (*b* and *c*), and, finally, Manrico, Leonora, and the monks (*b, c,* and *d*). The tension builds to a final *fortissimo* cadence; a brief transition leads to the second part of Leonora's aria, an agitated allegro in which she swears her eternal love for Manrico. Once again, Verdi's method is straightforward enough; indeed, the basic structure of the scene—a recitative followed by a double aria with slow and fast sections—parallels the outline of the older "scena e cavatina." But Verdi is able to breathe new dramatic life into this staple of nineteenth-century Italian opera: Relatively simple musical means are juxtaposed and built up through combination to create a scene of great dramatic urgency and compelling interest. And the emphasis throughout remains on the sheer beauty of the human voice and its expressive capabilities as a melodic agent, the salient features of Italian opera.

FRENCH ROMANTIC OPERA

In France, the revolutionary fervor of the 1790s had carried over into the arts, especially into opera, which took on a noteworthy ceremonial character that was often unabashedly patriotic. Particularly in vogue were operas that had at their dramatic center the liberation of prisoners from tyrants of some sort, a subject not at all lost on those who had experienced and survived the recent revolutionary upheaval. Luigi Cherubini (1760–1842), an Italian composer who produced his most successful operas in Paris before the turn of the century, wrote several operas of this kind, which came to be known as "rescue operas." These operas were derived from an eighteenth-century type of French opera known as *opéra comique,* which had spoken dialogue in place of recitatives, arias of various types, choruses, and pageantry. (Despite its name, the opéra comique was not limited to comic subjects.) The trend toward political statements in opera continued during the reign of Napoleon, when opera composers glorified the emperor with lavishly ceremonial scenes.

After Napoleon, the direction of French opera changed course. More and more, composers catered attentively to the tastes of the prosperous middle-class clientele that supported the opera. The trend is especially evident during the 1820s and the reign of the "Citizen King," Louis Philippe (1830–1848), when French opera culminated in what became known as **grand opera.** This was opera on a large scale, with grand historical themes, massive choruses, spectacular ballets, and impressive stage effects. One opera, D.-F.-E. Auber's *La Muette de Portici,* premiering in Paris in 1828, climaxed with a depiction of Mount Vesuvius erupting on stage. (A performance of that opera in Brussels two years later is said to have sparked the revolution that led to Belgium's independence from Holland.)

Not just French composers but foreign composers as well tried their hand at grand opera (Rossini's *Guillaume Tell* of 1829 is perhaps the most celebrated example) or were influenced by it (Wagner, *Rienzi,* 1842; Verdi, *The Sicilian Vespers,* 1855, and *Don Carlos,* 1867). The leading practitioner of grand opera was Giacomo Meyerbeer (1791–1864), a German by birth who settled in Paris. Meyerbeer possessed a shrewd theatrical sense and a remarkable acumen for orchestration, abilities that he put to good use in his enormously successful grand operas. Typically in five long acts, they incorporate ballets as entertaining diversions (one featured a group of roller skaters intended to represent ice skaters). For most of his operas, Meyerbeer chose historical subjects, drawn not from antiquity but from more recent European history. *Les Huguenots* (*The Huguenots,* 1836) and *Le Prophète* (*The Prophet,* 1849), for example, have librettos based on sixteenth-century religious wars: *Les Huguenots* concerns the Saint Bartholomew's Massacre and the persecution of the French Protestants (1572), while *Le Prophète* concerns the rise to power of the Anabaptist John of Leyden (1534–1535).

Grand opera was the preferred entertainment of the Parisian bourgeoisie; it was successful more as a commercial enterprise than as an art form of lasting significance. In fact, in the nineteenth century, France did not produce native composers of grand opera—or of any kind of opera, for that matter—who seriously rivaled the stature of Verdi or Wagner. Nevertheless, grand opera produced a number of innovations in stagecraft and orchestral effects that exerted an influence on the development of Verdi's operas in Italy and Wagner's music dramas in Germany.

GERMAN ROMANTIC OPERA

Unlike Italy and France, Germany had no well-established native operatic tradition. Mozart, who created two German masterpieces in *The Abduction from the Seraglio* (1782) and *The Magic Flute* (1791), favored Italian opera, which was still preferred in Vienna. Beethoven, who aspired toward fame as an opera composer, managed to complete only one, *Fidelio,* and the creation of that one German opera cost him enormous effort. After lackluster performances of two early versions titled *Leonore* (1805 and 1806), he set the opera aside before revising and renaming it *Fidelio* in 1814. He wrote at least four overtures to the opera before he was satisfied. Though it has a German text, *Fidelio* derives from the French rescue opera; indeed, its libretto is a German translation of a French source.

The belated emergence of German opera in the eighteenth century proved in some ways beneficial: Unlike their Italian and French counterparts, German composers were not as bound to long-standing conventions and were somewhat freer to experiment. Romantic opera emerged during the opening decades of the nineteenth century in the further development of the *Singspiel,* a type of German opera with spoken dialogue that had already been brought to an exquisite degree of perfection by Mozart in *The Magic Flute.* The first composer after Mozart to achieve genuine success in German opera was Carl Maria von Weber (1786–1826), a contemporary of Beethoven's. Weber's masterpiece was *Der Freischütz,* which premiered in Berlin in 1821 (its title roughly translates as *The Magic Bullet*). The libretto treats a variation of the age-old tale, used by Goethe in *Faust,* in which a mortal makes a compact with the devil. Weber's protagonist is Max, a young, impressionable hunter, who accepts seven magic bullets from the devil in the belief that they will enable him to win a marksmanship contest and the hand of Agathe, daughter of the head forester.

Der Freischütz has all the ingredients of a romantic opera. Its supernatural elements are dominated by the satanic figure of Samiel, who lurks behind rocks and shrubbery and always speaks rather than sings. The libretto is rich in romantic symbolism: darkness, associated with the occult; light, associated with spiritual redemption; and a constant background of natural scenery. The action takes place in a forest, by day the haunt of the foresters, by night the abode of evil powers. Finally, there are unusual stage effects, culminating in the celebrated "Wolf-Glen" scene, in which Max, in the dark of night, enters a haunted glen to observe the casting of seven magic bullets. As each bullet is cast, a new apparition appears, including birds with flapping wings (accomplished by a mechanical device at the premiere), a wild boar, a gathering storm, an "invisible" carriage with burning wheels, a chorus of deceased hunters who have lost their souls to the devil, the full fury of the storm, and finally the terrifying emergence of Samiel himself.

Weber's score is especially noteworthy for its expressive use of the orchestra. Individual figures are allied with particular orchestral colors and motives that recur throughout the opera: Thus, Max, the hunter, twice makes his entrance to the report of hunting horns, which are associated generally with the hunt throughout the opera; Samiel is suggested by an especially ominous orchestral chord, scored with low, dark woodwinds, agitated strings and timpani strokes; and a hermit, Samiel's redeeming counterpart, makes a final entrance at the end of the opera to brass fortified by trombones, which carry traditional connotations for the Church and the divine. *Der Freischütz* is a work of great dramatic and musical coherence; in 1821 it was a milestone of German romantic opera that pointed the way toward the work of Weber's successor, Richard Wagner.

RICHARD WAGNER

No major composer of the nineteenth century commanded greater fame and greater notoriety than Richard Wagner (1813–1883), who created a revolutionary new type of opera that came to be known as **music drama.** Conceived on an unprecedented scale, his complex works typically run to several hours and employ enormous orchestral and theatrical resources. Wagner himself usually crafted his librettos and specified in exhaustive detail the special stage requirements of his dramas. He wrote numerous, pointed essays to defend the new aesthetic of his music, which Wagner's admirers and detractors referred to as *Zukunftsmusik (Music of the Future)*. A great innovator in his bold use of chromatic harmony (see p. 260), Wagner moved closer than ever before to abandoning the traditional tonal system.

Wagner's life was as controversial as his music. He was often in debt and continually hounded by creditors, whom he took special precautions to evade. He accepted money from friends, even though he lacked the means to repay them. He had affairs with the wives of his friends and supporters. The political authorities in Germany regarded him as a subversive and suspected him of associating with anarchists. His musical career began modestly enough, with several minor theatrical posts in Germany. Early on, Wagner decided to direct his principal efforts toward writing dramatic compositions for the stage. To that end—and also to escape his creditors—he left Germany and arrived in Paris in 1839. Seeking to emulate the sensational grand opera then popular in France, he wrote *Rienzi, or the Last Consul of Rome* (1842), a sprawling five-act opera that no one in Paris, unfortunately, was willing to produce. Instead, Wagner returned to Germany to oversee the opera's premiere. In Dresden, where he became the opera director, it scored a significant success.

Caricature of Wagner conducting his "Music of the Future."

His next opera was *Der fliegende Holländer* (*The Flying Dutchman,* 1843). Wagner himself constructed the libretto for this work from a story by Heinrich Heine. The opera concerns a mysterious Dutchman who is condemned to sail the seas in a phantom ship until he has been redeemed through the love of a faithful woman. Redemption through love is also explored in Wagner's next drama, *Tannhäuser* (1845). Here, Wagner drew on a variety of German legends and on works by Heine and E. T. A. Hoffmann. Tannhäuser, a Minnesinger (see p. 18), has abandoned the thirteenth-century court of the Landgrave Hermann to indulge in the carnal delights of the Venusberg, the abode of Venus. When he sings a song in praise of carnal love at Hermann's court, he is ordered to do penance by making a pilgrimage to Rome. Eventually, he is redeemed by the death of his beloved Elizabeth, the niece of Hermann, whose love for him is pure. In *Lohengrin* (1850), like *Tannhäuser* a "romantic opera," redemption is offered to a mortal (though tragically rejected) through divine intervention. At the tenth-century court of Henry the Fowler, Elsa, falsely accused of murdering her brother, the young Godfrey, Duke of Brabant, is championed by Lohengrin, who conceals his identity as a knight of the Holy Grail. Lohengrin marries Elsa on condition that she never demand to know his identity. She breaks her promise, however, and Lohengrin must leave the earthly world to rejoin his companions. At the end, Godfrey, who had been transformed into a swan by the sorceress Ortrud, is miraculously restored to life; but Elsa falls lifeless in his arms. (In 1882 Wagner returned to the theme of divine grace in his last work, the "sacred festival stage play" *Parsifal*, which also concerns spiritual redemption and, more conspicuously, the knights of the Holy Grail, the cup served by Jesus at the Last Supper.)

Lohengrin was premiered in Weimar, with Liszt as conductor. Wagner was not on hand for the performance, however, having fled Germany after it was suspected that he had taken part in the revolutionary Dresden uprising of 1849. He spent the next several years in exile in Switzerland, writing essays about music and drama (but also about music and politics, including one scurrilous anti-Semitic article and other attacks on Mendelssohn and Meyerbeer), and laying careful plans for his great cycle of four music dramas, *Der Ring des Nibelungen* (*The Ring of the Nibelung*), which took him more than a quarter of a century to bring to fruition (1848–1876).

In his essays, Wagner turned his critical gaze to the historical development of opera and set down his remarkable vision for the music of the future. For Wagner, opera was originally a serious art form that had been conceived as drama set to music. But it had deviated from its high mission and, by his time, had been corrupted by the vanity of virtuoso singers and empty stage spectacles. In his new music dramas, Wagner sought to reverse those harmful developments so that the dramatic integrity of opera could be restored. He would create works—music dramas, as he called them—that would be unified in every respect toward a dramatic end: Music, libretto, stage design, and other ingredients would all contribute to what became known as a **Gesamtkunstwerk,** a "total art work." This vision would ultimately be realized in the vast complex of the *Ring* dramas.

While he was shaping these theories, Wagner interrupted work on *The Ring* to compose two other major works. *Tristan und Isolde* (1865), which contains some of his most complex and experimental music, is based on a medieval romance from the Arthurian legends. It is a drama about illicit love, prompted in part by Wagner's passion for Mathilde Wesendonck, the wife of one of his patrons. Isolde, an Irish princess chosen to be the wife of King Mark of Cornwall, mistakenly drinks a love potion with Tristan, the king's nephew. The resulting love affair takes on a transcendental meaning as Tristan and Isolde seek to escape through their love from the world of appearances, a flight from reality heavily influenced by Wagner's own reading of the transcendental philosophy of Schopenhauer. *Tristan und Isolde* marks a milestone not only in the history of opera but also in the evolution of nineteenth-century musical style: Its freely ranging and tonally ambiguous chromatic lines (announced at the outset of the famous *Vorspiel*, see p. 260), thick orchestral textures and rich colors, complex networks of motives, and long stretches of continuous music are among its most salient features. Everything is calculated in this powerfully expressive score to emphasize the continuity of the drama. *Die Meistersinger von Nürnberg* (*The Mastersingers of Nuremberg*, 1868) is Wagner's only comic opera. It deals with a sixteenth-century singers' guild and sets musical genius, exemplified by the famous Prize Song of the young knight Walther von Stolzing, against the uncharitable criticism of those forever contemptuous of and resistant to the innovative in art—and, by extension, of Wagner's reform of opera.

In Wagner's dramas, libretto and music come together in an unbroken, continuous melodic flow, with none of the traditional divisions that were still common in Italian and French operas. Instead of articulating the course of the action into set, independent numbers, Wagner organized it around organic "poetic-musical periods" of various lengths, each with its own, complex structure. Wagner's lush, thick writing for the orchestra is a constant element to be reckoned with; no mere accompaniment to the singers, it often achieves a sophistication matched only in the symphonies of Beethoven and later German composers. What is more, the vocal lines are inextricably woven into the rich fabric of orchestral sound. There is little in them that resembles the florid melodies of Italian opera, typically set apart from a background of orchestral accompaniment. In Wagner's work, all musical elements act together to fulfill the overriding demands of the drama.

One of Wagner's major contributions was to enlarge the orchestra. He increased the number of strings and specified the exact number of instruments each score required. Instead of the traditional pairs of woodwinds (established in the eighteenth century and still employed by most of Wagner's contemporaries), he wrote for triple and even quadruple woodwinds. He enlarged the brass section even more dramatically, calling for as many as eight horns in *The Ring,* four of which were specially designed horns known as "Wagner tubas." Wagner was one of the first orchestral composers to use to full advantage tubas—brass instruments with wide conical bores and cupped mouthpieces that strengthened the lower range of the brass ensemble. Finally, he introduced

The Orchestra of Wagner's *Das Rheingold* (1854)

Woodwinds	Brass	Percussion	Strings
3 Flutes (third flute doubles as second piccolo)	8 French horns	4 Timpani	16 First Violins
1 Piccolo	4 "Wagner" Tubas (Tenor and Bass, alternating with 4 of the horns)	Triangle	16 Second Violins
	1 Contrabass Tuba	Cymbals	12 Violas
3 Oboes 1 English Horn (doubles as fourth oboe)	3 Trumpets	Bass Drum	12 Cellos
3 Clarinets	1 Bass Trumpet	Gong	8 Double Basses
1 Bass Clarinet	3 Trombones	16 Anvils of various sizes on stage	
3 Bassoons	1 Contrabass Trombone	6 Harps (seventh on stage)	

elaborate parts for harps (six are generally called for in the *Ring* cycle) and experimented with a battery of percussion instruments. The chart on page 343 gives the instrumentation of *Das Rheingold;* a comparison with the charts on page 185 (the classical orchestra) and page 307 (Berlioz's orchestra in the *Symphonie fantastique*) underscores the extent of Wagner's contribution.

No less an achievement was Wagner's new approach to the libretto and text setting. By writing his own librettos, Wagner did away with the traditional division of labor between librettist and composer and created texts ideally suited for his pliable, elastic melodic lines. Wagner came to prefer a flexible, free type of verse, with varying numbers of stresses per line, that featured rhythmic repetitions of similar syllables or vowels rather than rhymes at the end of the lines. The result was poetry that resembled a kind of poetic prose. Here is one example, fashioned by Wagner in his essay *Opera and Drama,* that demonstrates the potential of the technique: "Die Liebe bringt Lust und Leid / Doch in ihr Weh auch webt sie Wonnen" ("Love brings joy and sorrow, / But into its misery it also weaves wonderment"). In the first line, rhythmic stresses fall on "Lie(be)," "Lust," and "Leid"; in the second, on "Weh," "webt," and "Won(nen)."

To lend coherence to his gargantuan scores, Wagner used an elaborate system of short musical figures, known as motives, that were allied to some character or element in the drama. Other nineteenth-century composers had employed similar techniques: For example, there are specific, identifiable motives in Weber's opera *Der Freischütz* and in Mendelssohn's Overture to *A Midsummer Night's Dream;* and in the *Symphonie fantastique,* Berlioz systematically applied a programmatic melody, the *idée fixe,* in all five movements. The German term **Leitmotiv** (roughly, "leading motive") is generally applied to Wagner's motives, though Wagner himself did not use the term. Rather, it fell to devoted disciples to pore over his scores and identify appearances of motives, to which they appended names: the "Curse" motive, the "Sword" motive, the "Rheingold" motive, for example. What was new in Wagner's method was that such motives thoroughly permeated the music of his dramas, appearing in proliferating series of transformations in the vocal lines and in the orchestra. Sometimes, two or three were heard together, in a kind of motivic counterpoint that enriched the flow of the music. But Wagner had another purpose in mind for the motives: They could be used as a psychological tool, conditioning the audience to expect a particular dramatic situation or entrance. Above all, Wagner's systems of motives gave unity to his scores, enabling him to tie together in ingenious ways the various musical and dramatic threads.

WAGNER'S *DER RING DES NIBELUNGEN*

Wagner remained in exile from Germany for more than ten years until at last, in 1860, he was granted a partial amnesty. Then, in 1864, the young king of Bavaria, Ludwig II, offered to pay his debts and help him complete the *Ring.* What is more, he enabled Wagner to build a theater in Bayreuth, not far from Munich. Wagner designed the theater specifically to meet the requirements of the *Ring;* this Festspielhaus, or Festival Theater, became a kind of Wagnerian shrine in which the cycle was annually realized. Performed over the course of four evenings, the *Ring* consists of the prologue, *Das*

Rheingold (The Rhinegold), and three weighty dramas, *Die Walküre (The Valkyrie), Siegfried,* and *Die Götterdämmerung (The Twilight of the Gods).* After laboring for years over the libretto, drawn from old Norse and Teutonic mythology, Wagner spent twenty more years realizing the composition of these mighty scores, in many ways the culmination of nineteenth-century romanticism.

Ever since its first performance in 1876, this great cycle has attracted its champions and its detractors. Its scope and sheer size was never equalled, and its musical style set a new standard against which generations of young composers measured themselves. George Bernard Shaw, in *The Perfect Wagnerite* (1898), interpreted it as an allegory that prophesied the downfall of the modern, plutocratic, capitalist order.★ The philosopher Friedrich Nietzsche, for some time a confidant of Wagner, may have formulated his concept of the superman in part from his knowledge of the work (though after the premiere of the *Ring* in 1876 he broke decisively from Wagner). In the twentieth century, Hitler found in Wagner's superhuman heroes symbolic qualities he sought to encourage in a master race.

In turning to mythology instead of to history or legend, Wagner sought to create a dramatic cycle with timeless relevance. Underlying *The Ring* is a cosmology that consists of several levels. First, there is the neutral, primordial world of nature represented by the Rhine River. Above, there are the gods ruled by Wotan, who inhabits Valhalla, a massive fortress built for their defense. In the bowels of the earth lives the dwarfish race of the Nibelungs, ruthlessly exploited by their master, Alberich. Finally, there is the world of the mortals, through whom the drama is inexorably acted out.

The prologue, *Das Rheingold,* is in four continuous scenes. Containing some three hours of music in all, it is the shortest of the four works in the cycle. In the first scene, we are introduced to the Rhinemaidens, guardians of the gold. To broadly sustained, static harmonies, the curtain rises to reveal the maidens sporting at the bottom of the Rhine. Suddenly, the Nibelung Alberich appears, intending to win for himself one of the Rhinemaidens. For their part, they resist his efforts and mock his advances. In turn, Alberich forswears love, a prerequisite for possession of the treasure, and then, to the amazement and horror of the Rhinemaidens, steals the gold. The second scene transfers us to the mountain peaks overlooking the Rhine, where the gods have gathered: Wotan, their ruler; Fricka, his wife; Donner, god of thunder; Froh, god of sun and rain; Freia, goddess of youth; and Loge, a demigod of fire. Two giants, Fasolt and Fafner, have recently finished building the fortress Valhalla and now arrive to demand their agreed-upon payment: the goddess Freia. But hearing of Alberich's theft of the gold and its power—whoever possesses it may win control of the world—they provide Wotan with an option: They will accept the gold in payment. Now they depart, securing Freia as a hostage.

To rescue Freia from the giants, Wotan and Loge descend in the third scene to Nibelheim, the realm of the Nibelungs, and by trickery capture Alberich, who has already fashioned from the gold a ring with magic powers and a helmet that renders whoever wears it invisible. They then ascend to rejoin the gods. In the concluding,

---

★Shaw's later cycle of five plays, *Back to Methuselah* (1922), is one twentieth-century literary cycle indebted to the *Ring.*

fourth scene, the giants claim the hoard of gold as payment and release Freia. But Alberich has placed a curse on the gold, and when the giants fight over the treasure, Fasolt is slain. Disregarding this ominous incident, and rejoicing over the return of Freia, the gods enter Valhalla.

As the *Ring* continues, Wotan, Alberich, and others vie for control of the ring. As the upholder of laws and treaties, on which his rule is founded, Wotan is prevented from regaining the gold through illicit means. He cannot intervene directly and thus is forced to act indirectly through intermediaries. First, in *Die Walküre*, Brünnhilde, one of the Valkyries (women warriors, sired by Wotan, who gather slain mortal heroes for the defense of Valhalla), tries to rescue the hero, Siegmund, locked in combat with Hunding. (Earlier, Wotan had expressed the hope that Siegmund, one of his mortal sons, would be able to recapture the ring.) But Siegmund has entered into an illicit alliance with Sieglinde, his long-separated sister and Hunding's wife; Wotan, in order to satisfy Fricka, who defends the institution of marriage, reluctantly agrees that Siegmund must sacrifice his life. Because Brünnhilde, in seeking to protect Siegmund, has disobeyed Wotan, she, too, must be punished. In the exquisite concluding scene of *Die Walküre,* atop a mountain, Wotan deprives her of her divinity, kisses her to sleep, and encircles her with a ring of protective fire.

In the next drama, *Siegfried,* the course of events turns to the hero who is the issue of Siegmund's and Sieglinde's incestuous love. After forging the sword Nothung from the fragments of Siegmund's shattered weapon, the fearless Siegfried slays Fafner, who has transformed himself into a dragon in order to guard the gold and the precious ring. Siegfried recovers the ring, though he is closely watched by the scheming Mime, his foster father and the brother of Alberich, and is pursued by Alberich himself. At the end of the drama, Siegfried climbs the mountain on which Brünnhilde is asleep, shatters Wotan's spear when the god opposes him, crosses the circle of fire, and awakens the Valkyrie. The two sing of eternal love. In *Die Götterdämmerung,* the final drama, Siegfried is killed by Hagen, the son of Alberich, and the ring is finally reclaimed by Brünnhilde, who erects a funeral pyre for her slain hero. Calling upon the Rhinemaidens to take the ring from her ashes, she mounts her horse and then proceeds into the flames to her immolation. As the banks of the Rhine overflow, drowning the villainous Hagen, the Rhinemaidens finally regain the ring. As this epic cycle comes to a close, we see Valhalla in the distance, consumed in the fire.

DAS RHEINGOLD, SCENE 4, "THE GODS' ENTRY INTO VALHALLA"

Das Rheingold (finished in 1854) employs an elaborate tapestry of some thirty motives. Preeminent among them, and given priority at the very opening of the work, is the Nature motive, associated with the Rhine River, that suggests a state of pristine innocence. Welling up from the depths of the orchestra, the motive is constructed on an ascending form of a triad, the most fundamental harmonic entity, with some of its gaps filled in:

Wagner: Das Rheingold, *Scene 4*

NATURE MOTIVE

triad

As the curtain goes up, the motive is heard repeatedly, sustained in the same key for several pages of the score in a rich overlay of sonorities. From this basic motive, Wagner derives several others in an organic process of motivic transformation. The closing portion of the fourth and concluding scene of *Das Rheingold* will serve to illustrate Wagner's method and the way in which his motives undergird the essential dramatic action.

In this scene, Wotan delivers the hoard of gold to the giants as ransom for Freia. But he attempts to keep the ring for himself, well aware of its power. At this point, Erda, the Earth goddess, rises from the ground to admonish him, in somewhat veiled language, that disastrous consequences will ensue if he fails to give up the ring. Low woodwinds and brass play Erda's motive, which unfolds as a minor-key version of the nature motive:

ERDA MOTIVE

Disturbed by Erda's warning, Wotan adds the ring to the treasure heap, thereby fulfilling the conditions of his agreement with the giants and winning the release of Freia. The orchestra anticipates this gesture with the so-called Treaty motive, a firm, resolute figure that descends in scalelike fashion:

TREATY MOTIVE

f Sehr bestimmt (Very determined)

As the giants squabble over the treasure, the orchestra sounds their cumbersome bass motive along with the compact motive in triplets of the Nibelungs, whose toil for Alberich has enabled him to amass great wealth:

GIANTS' AND NIBELUNGS' MOTIVES

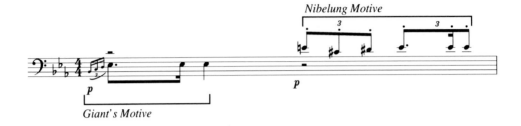

With a heavy blow, Fafner murders Fasolt and greedily snatches the ring, which has its own motive: a descending chain of thirds that then ascends by step:

RING MOTIVE

Alberich has placed a curse on the ring, and his motive is now heard in close proximity to the Ring motive. Wagner emphasizes that proximity by deriving the fateful Curse motive directly from the Ring motive; it is, in fact, based on the mirror inversion of the Ring motive, a series of *ascending* thirds:

CURSE MOTIVE

Finally, to strengthen the association even further, Wotan sings the Ring motive while referring to the force of the curse:

Text: Now fearful, I experience the power of the curse.

Now Donner, god of thunder, intervenes, summoning a storm to clear the turbulent heavens. His motive is drawn from a triad, with its pitches in broken order. It thus relates to the original nature motive:

THUNDER MOTIVE

Donner sings this motive against swirling harmonies of the strings; he is answered by heavy brass. As the skies brighten, a rainbow appears, forming a bridge to Valhalla. Six harps are added to the orchestra, which now sustains a shimmering harmony as the Rainbow motive rises in the low strings. It, too, is triadically derived, and appropriately resembles closely the Nature motive, as it slowly rises and falls, forming an arch:

RAINBOW MOTIVE

And now, Valhalla itself is given a motive, which, solemn and measured, is heard in chordal style in the brass, descending by thirds:

VALHALLA MOTIVE

Somewhat reassured, Wotan and the other gods begin their procession into Valhalla. At this point, Wagner introduces the motive of the sword, which is to figure prominently in the next drama, *Die Walküre.* The sword, to be entrusted to mortal hands, will presumably save the gods. A trumpet sounds the Sword motive with penetrating brilliance; it is a rising triadic figure, the final motive in a series that includes the Erda, Rainbow, and, of course, all-encompassing Nature motives:

SWORD MOTIVE

But there are some unsettling signs, both musical and dramatic. First of all, the Valhalla motive, a descending chain of thirds, traces its heritage to the Ring and Curse motives. And, in the closing pages of the score, Loge has misgivings about the fate of the gods; they are rushing to their destruction, he intimates. (Of course, it is his element, fire, that will eventually consume all at the end of *Die Götterdämmerung,* three dramas and some fifteen hours of music away.) Loge is assigned a motive of chromatic slides, suggesting licking flames:

LOGE'S MOTIVE

Most unsettling of all, the lament of the Rhinemaidens over their lost treasure drifts up to the gods:

RHINEMAIDENS' SONG

Text: Rheingold, Rheingold, pure gold!

Nevertheless, their plea is ignored as the gods cross the rainbow to take up residence in the magnificent new abode. *Das Rheingold* ends with the orchestra broadly restating the Valhalla, Sword, and Rainbow motives. For the moment, the gods are secure.

TEXT OF DAS RHEINGOLD, *SCENE 4 (CONCLUSION)*, *"THE GODS' ENTRY INTO VALHALLA"*

Wotan

Geheimnisshehr	Worthy of mystery
hallt mir dein Wort:	your words ring in my ears;
weile, dass mehr ich wisse!	stay, that I may learn more!

Erda

Ich warnte dich;	I have warned you;
du weisst genug:	you know enough:
sinn' in Sorg' und Furcht!	consider all in care and fear!

(Wotan attempts to detain the disappearing Erda, who sinks into the ground.)

Wotan

Soll ich sorgen und fürchten,	If I must reflect and fear,
dich muss ich fassen,	I must grasp you,
alles erfahren!	to learn all!

(Wotan is restrained by Froh and Fricka.)

Fricka

Was willst du, Wüthender?	What would you, rageful one?

"The Gods' Entrance into Valhalla" from Wagner's *Das Rheingold*. (New York Metropolitan Opera)

Froh

Halt' ein, Wotan!	Hold back, Wotan!
Scheue die Edle,	Respect the noble one,
achte ihr Wort!	Heed her words!

Donner (turning decisively to the giants)

Hört, ihr Riesen!	Listen, you giants!
Zurück, und harret;	Return and wait;
das Gold wird euch gegeben.	The gold will be yours.

Freia

Darf ich es hoffen?	Dare I hope?
Dünkt euch Holda	Do you find Holda
wirklich der Lösung wert?	worthy of the ransom?

(All turn anxiously toward Wotan, who, after reflecting, grasps his sword and turns, as if to signal a bold decision.)

Wotan

Zu mir, Freia!	To me, Freia!
Du bist befreit:	You are freed:
wieder gekauft	purchased one more,
kehr' uns die Jugend zurück!	return our youth to us!
Ihr Riesen, nehmt euren Ring!	You Giants, take your ring!

(Wotan throws the ring on the pile. The Giants return Freia. Fafner begins to fill an enormous sack with the gold.)

Fasolt

Halt, du Gieriger!	Halt, you greedy one!
Gönne mir auch 'was!	Grant me something as well!
Redliche Teilung	A fair share
taugt uns beiden.	is good for us both.

Fafner

Mehr an der Maid als am Gold	You valued the maid more
lag dir verliebten Geck;	than the gold, you infatuated fool.
mit Müh' zum Tausch	With difficulty I convinced you
vermocht' ich dich Toren. . . .	of the exchange. . . .

Fasolt

Zurück! Du Frecher!	Back! you impudent rascal!
mein ist der Ring;	Mine is the Ring;
mir blieb er für Freias Blick!	For me it replaces Freia's glance!

(Fasolt grasps the ring.)

Fafner

Fort mit der Faust!	Away with your fist!
der Ring ist mein!	The ring is mine!

(As they struggle, Fasolt seizes the Ring from Fafner.)

Fasolt

Ich halt' ihn, mir gehört er!	I have it, it belongs to me!

Fafner

Halt' ihn fest, dass er nicht fall'!	Hold it secure, lest it fall!

(Fafner strikes Fasolt with one blow to the ground. Then, he grabs the Ring from the dying Fasolt.)

Nun blinzle nach Freias Blick!	Now blink at Freia's eyes!
An den Reif rührst du nicht mehr!	The Ring you will not touch again!

(As the Gods watch in terror, Fafner places the Ring in his sack and packs the remaining treasure.)

Wotan

Furchtbar nun	Now fearful
erfind' ich des Fluches Kraft!	I experience the power of the curse!

Loge

Was gleicht, Wotan,	What can compare, Wotan,
wohl deinem Glücke?	with your luck?
Viel erwarb dir	Possession of the Ring
des Ringes Gewinn;	won for you much;
dass er nun dir genommen,	now that it is taken from you,
nützt dir noch mehr;	it serves you still more;
deine Feinde, sieh!	see how your enemies
fällen sich selbst	destroy each other
um das Gold, das du vergabst. . . .	for the gold you gave away. . . .

Fricka *(coaxingly bending toward Wotan)*

Wo weilst du, Wotan?	Why do you linger, Wotan?
Winkt dir nicht hold	Does the noble fortress
die hehre Burg,	not propitiously summon you
die des Gebieters	and now hospitably
gastlich bergend nun harrt?	await its master?

Wotan

Mit bösem Zoll	With evil toll
zahlt' ich den Bau!	I paid for the edifice!

Donner *(pointing into the distance veiled in mist)*

Schwüles Gedünst	A heavy mist
schwebt in der Luft;	hovers in the air;
lästig ist mir	its gloomy weight
der trübe Druck!	presses hard on me!
Das bleiche Gewölk	In a thunderstorm
samml' ich zu blitzendem Wetter,	I shall gather the pale clouds
das fegt den Himmel mir hell!	to sweep the heavens clear!

(Donner mounts a high rock and swings his hammer; the mist is drawn to him.)

Heda! Heda! Hedo!	Heda! Heda! Hedo!
Zu mir, du Gedüft!	To me, you mist!
Ihr Dünste, zu mir!	To me, you vapors!
Donner, der Herr	Donner, your master,
ruft euch zu Heer! . . .	beckons his host! . . .

(Donner vanishes within a thundercloud; the sound of his hammer striking a rock is heard; lightning emerges from the cloud, followed by thunder.)

Donner

Bruder, hierher!	Brother, come forth!
Weise der Brücke den Weg!	Lead the way across the bridge!

(The cloud dissipates to reveal Donner and Froh, and, before them, a rainbow which stretches across a valley to the fortress, now glowing brightly.) . . .

Wotan

Abendlich strahlt	In the evening shines
der Sonne Auge;	the eye of the sun;
in prächtiger Glut	in a magnificent glow
prangt glänzend die Burg. . . .	is displayed the fortress. . . .
Folge mir, Frau:	Follow me, wife:
in Walhall wohne mit mir! . . .	live with me in Valhalla! . . .

(The Gods begin to cross the rainbow.)

Loge

Ihrem Ende eilen sie zu,	They hasten to their end,
die so stark im Bestehen sich wähnen.	they who imagine themselves so enduring.
Fast schäm' ich mich	I am nearly ashamed
mit ihnen zu schaffen;	to be involved with them;
zur leckenden Lohe	I have a strong urge
mich wieder zu wandeln,	to change myself
spür' ich lockende Lust:	into licking flames
sie aufzuzehren. . . .	and consume them all. . . .

(As he prepares to follow the Gods, the song of the Rhinemaidens rises up from the depths of the valley below.)

Rhinemaidens

Rheingold! Rheingold!	Rheingold! Rheingold!
Reines Gold!	Pure gold!
Wie lauter und hell	How true and bright
leuchtetest hold du uns!	you did graciously shine on us!

Wotan

Welch' Klagen dringt zu mir her?	What lamenting do I hear?

Rhinemaidens

Um dich, du klares,	For you, O bright one,
wir nun klagen! . . .	we now lament! . . .

Wotan

Verwünschte Nicker! . . .	Cursed water-sprites! . . .

Loge

Ihr da im Wasser!	You there in the water!
was weint ihr herauf? . . .	Why do you cry up to us? . . .

Rheinmaidens

Rheingold! Rheingold!	Rheingold! Rheingold!
Reines Gold!	Pure gold!
O leuchtete noch	Oh if only your pure finery
in der Tiefe dein laut'rer Tand!	still sparkled in the deep!
Traulich und treu	Familiar and true
ist's nur in der Tiefe:	is the gold only in the deep;
falsch und feig	False and rotten
ist was dort oben sich freut!	is that which rejoices above!

(As the Gods cross the rainbow to the fortress, the curtain falls.)

End *of* Das Rheingold

Wagner's influence on music, drama, and European culture was incalculable. Wagnerian societies sprang up in Germany, France, England, and elsewhere, and journals devoted to Wagnerism were published. In the second half of the nineteenth century, Wagner's music and theories galvanized thinking about music, drama, and the arts. Innumerable admirers—musicians, composers, poets, dramatists among them, but many others who viewed themselves as the cultural elite—made pilgrimages to Bayreuth to hear his dramas.

Countless composers labored to imitate Wagner's lush, chromatic style and his technique of motivic transformation; every major nineteenth-century composer after Wagner came to terms with his music and work in some way. Among those who fell under Wagner's influence were Anton Bruckner, Richard Strauss and Gustav Mahler, the Belgian César Franck and many younger French composers, the Englishman Sir Edward Elgar, and the Finnish composer Jean Sibelius, to list only a few. Others struggled to break free from Wagner's influence: for example, Nietzsche, on philosophical grounds, and the young French composer Debussy, whose opera *Pelléas et Mélisande* (1902) is in many ways a radical reworking of the aesthetic behind *Tristan und Isolde*. Regardless of the reaction to Wagner, his work was of seminal significance to the course of music. His attempt to synthesize various arts in the Gesamtkunstwerk, his seamless, organic musical macrostructures, and his exploitation of a new, boldly expanded orchestra brought German musical romanticism to its extraordinary culmination.

Suggested Listening

Beethoven: *Fidelio*
*Bellini: *Norma*

Note: Works marked with an asterisk are the principal works discussed in the chapter.

Rossini: *Il barbiere di Siviglia*
Verdi: *Aida*
_____: *Otello*
_____: *Rigoletto*
★_____: *Il trovatore*
★Wagner: *Das Rheingold*
_____: *Die Walküre*
_____: *Tristan und Isolde*
Weber: *Der Freischütz*

14

LATE NINETEENTH-CENTURY MUSIC

Romantic attitudes and beliefs held sway during much of the early nineteenth century, but increasingly during its second half, two fundamental forces challenged romanticism and, indeed, reshaped the character of European society and culture. Nationalism not only remained a political force throughout the century but also encouraged the development of new national styles in the arts that more and more challenged the familiar romantic hegemony of the principal European artistic centers. The Industrial Revolution, which had set in motion not just accelerating advances in science and technology but also sweeping redefinitions of the social order, now threatened to undermine altogether the romantic faith in the subjective by replacing it with empirical truth. (Something of that attitude is suggested by Dickens's hardened schoolmaster Thomas Gradgrind, who dryly expostulates in the novel *Hard Times* of 1854, "Facts alone are wanted in life.") In the second half of the century, new movements in literature and painting marked serious challenges to the romantic aesthetic, more and more viewed as invalidated in an increasingly modernized, mechanized world.

How all those changes affected music is rather difficult to detail. For the most part, composers retained the stylistic attributes of romantic music even as the romantic aesthetic was beginning to fade. Because their music often ran counter to the new currents of intellectual thought of the period, some scholars have labeled the music of the second half of the century neoromanticism or postromanticism. During that time, music was informed with a certain nostalgia for the romantic past, and it became more and more isolated from the other arts.

EUROPEAN HISTORY AND CULTURE	AMERICAN HISTORY AND CULTURE	EUROPEAN MUSIC
		1822–1890: César Franck
		1824–1884: Smetana
		1824–1896: Bruckner
		1839–1881: Musorgsky
		1840–1893: Tchaikovsky
		1841–1904: Dvořák
	1845: Manifest Destiny	**1843–1907:** Edvard Grieg
	1853: "Opening" of Japan by Commodore Perry	**1853:** Liszt, Piano Sonata in B minor
1854: Dickens, *Hard Times*		
	1855: Whitman, *Leaves of Grass*	
	1857: Dred Scott Decision	**1857:** Liszt, *Faust* Symphony
1859: Darwin, *The Origin of Species;* J. S. Mill, *On Liberty*		**1858–1924:** Puccini
		1860–1903: Wolf
		1860–1911: Mahler
1861: Kingdom of Italy proclaimed; Emancipation of the serfs in Russia	**1861–1865:** Presidency of Abraham Lincoln; Civil War	
1862–1890: Bismarck prime minister and chancellor in Prussia and Germany	**1863:** Emancipation Proclamation	**1862–1918:** Debussy
		1864–1949: Richard Strauss
1866: Transatlantic cable; Dostoevsky, *Crime and Punishment*		
1867: Marx, *Das Kapital;* Dual Monarchy of Austria-Hungary	**1867:** Alaska Purchase	
1869: Tolstoy, *War and Peace*		
1870–1871: Franco-Prussian War		**1870:** Tchaikovsky, *Romeo and Juliet*
1871: German Empire		**1871:** Verdi, *Aida*
		1873: Brahms, *Variations on a Theme of Haydn*
		1874: Musorgsky, *Boris Godunov*
		1875: Grieg, *Peer Gynt* Suite No. 1; Bizet, *Carmen*
	1876: Telephone	**1876:** Brahms, Symphony No. 1
		1882: Wagner, *Parsifal*
1883–1885: Nietzsche, *Also sprach Zarathustra*		
	1884: Mark Twain, *The Adventures of Huckleberry Finn*	
		1887: Verdi, *Otello*
1888: Nietzsche, *Nietzsche contra Wagner*		
		1889: Richard Strauss: *Tod und Verklärung*
		1893: Dvořák, Symphony No. 9 *(From the New World)*
1895: Marconi wireless	**1895:** Crane, *The Red Badge of Courage*	
		1896: Mahler, *Lieder eines fahrenden Gesellen;* Puccini, *La bohème*
1898: Dreyfus Affair in France	**1898–1899:** Spanish-American War	
		1901: Mahler, Symphony No. 4

NATIONALISM IN NINETEENTH-CENTURY MUSIC

For the diverse populations of Europe, nationalism was a declaration of what they took to be their unique political, social, and cultural identities; it was an assertion that allegiance to a nation or a region took precedence over other allegiances, such as to a religion or a class. During the nineteenth century, a series of unification and liberation movements swept across the Continent and beyond, encouraging the definition of new national styles. By the 1870s, Germany and Italy were finally unified as countries. Earlier in the century, Spanish rule was overthrown in Mexico and South America (1820s), Turkish rule in Greece (1830), and Dutch rule in Belgium (1831), and Russian rule was resisted in Poland (1831). In the Austrian Empire, an amalgam of Czech, Hungarian, Polish, Serb, and Croat nationalist sentiments quickened. In the United States, the doctrine of Manifest Destiny (1845) was devised to justify the nation's westward expansion.

An inevitable by-product of nationalism was the notion that the artistic achievements of a nation or a region—its literature, poetry, painting, and music—should reflect its special national character. One result of that was the spurring of new interest in native folklore, dance, and poetry, and in the development of new national literary styles—for example, in Russian, Poland, and Scandinavia. Composers drew on the melodies of popular folk songs and characteristic rhythms of national dances, and they enriched traditional Western tonality by exploring the colorful harmonies and nonconventional scales of folk music. Many nationalist composers found inspiration in the great literary sagas of folk poetry. Musical nationalism made its most striking impact in regions apart from (or struggling to be independent of) the traditional European musical establishments centered in Germany and Austria, France, and Italy. Especially in the second half of the nineteenth century, nationalism figured more and more prominently in the development of musical style. By 1900 several new national musical styles had been established or were emerging. We shall consider three composers who, each in his own way, contributed to that trend.

EDVARD GRIEG: *PEER GYNT* SUITE NO. 1, OP. 46 (1875)

The Norwegian Edvard Grieg (1843–1907) is remembered today chiefly as the composer of one of the most popular piano concertos ever written (1868). But that concerto was actually influenced by a piano concerto by Robert Schumann and is not truly representative of Grieg's best efforts, which were devoted to fashioning a national Norwegian musical style. Trained at the Leipzig Conservatory in Germany, where he received a traditional European instruction, Grieg began to experiment with Norwegian musical idioms in the 1860s after returning to his homeland. His association with Henrik Ibsen (1828–1906) led the great dramatist to invite him to write incidental music to *Peer Gynt.* In later years, Grieg traveled on the Continent, attending the premieres of Wagner's music dramas at Bayreuth. He became an ardent Norwegian nationalist* and incor-

---

* In 1814 Norway had been annexed by Sweden; that event encouraged the rise of the Norwegian nationalist movement.

porated into his compositions the colorful scales and inflections of the folk music of his homeland. He died only two years after Norway won its independence from Sweden.

Peer Gynt (1875), which Ibsen called a "dramatic poem," consists of a loosely organized series of scenes centered on Peer Gynt, sometimes described as one of the first antiromantic heroes. Peer is a lazy young man, somewhat dissolute, and given to brawling. He makes off with the daughter of a neighboring farmer on her wedding day and then abandons her in the mountains. There he encounters the trolls, mischievous dwarf-like creatures who try to win him to their ranks, and a mysterious voice from the wilderness that impedes his path. For a while, Peer lives in the mountains with Solveig, a peasant woman who remains loyal to him despite his fickle ways. After visiting his dying mother, Peer sets out to make his fortune. He sets himself up as a slave dealer in America and as a messianic prophet in Africa. On his return to Norway, he meets the Button Moulder, who decides to melt Peer down in his ladle. Peer is saved by the love of Solveig.

For this unorthodox, phantasmagoric play, Grieg wrote several short orchestral movements intended as incidental music. Later, he arranged some of the movements into two orchestral suites for concert performance. Of these, the first is the better known. It has four movements: The first and fourth are for full orchestra, and the second and third are for string orchestra. The first movement, "Morning Mood," suggests a pastoral scene. It begins with a hushed, flowing melody in dialogue between flute and oboe:

Grieg: Peer Gynt *Suite No. 1, "Morning Mood"*

Accompanied by understated chords in the strings, the melody is based on a five-tone scale common in folk music, the so-called **pentatonic scale,** similar to the first five pitches of a major scale except for its larger gap between the third and fourth pitches:

Pentatonic Scale

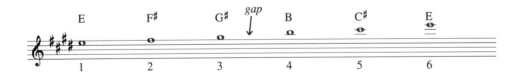

THE ROMANTIC PERIOD

In an expansive passage, the melody is repeated by the strings with a gradual crescendo, as if to suggest the dawning of a new day. Toward the end of the movement, horns and flutes (suggesting birdcalls) recall a similar tranquil mood in the slow movement of Beethoven's *Pastoral* Symphony (see p. 235). The movement ends quietly, with serene *pianissimo* chords drawn from pentatonic relationships, imbuing the music with an exotic quality.

The second movement, "The Death of Aase" (Peer Gynt's mother), is scored for muted strings and constructed on a simple four-measure rising phrase. Repetitions of this phrase, along with a few modifications, generate the entire movement. First, the strings execute a crescendo to *fortissimo,* without, however, withdrawing their mutes—a striking tone quality. Then, Grieg reverses the direction of the melody to introduce a mournful, chromatic descent. Here is the entire melodic line, with its four-measure phrases marked off:

Grieg: Peer Gynt *Suite No. 1, "The Death of Aase"*

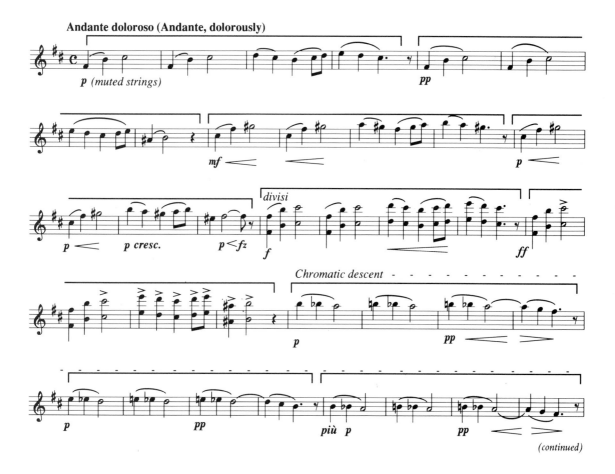

(continued)

morendo
(dying)

The third movement is a dance for Anitra, an Arab woman Peer meets in the African desert. The movement is in a simple form with two sections, each repeated. (Curiously, Grieg specifies the tempo of the Polish mazurka for this dance.)

In the last movement, "In the Hall of the Mountain King," Grieg vividly captures the infernal realm of the trolls with a lumbering motive in the bassoons and with low, pizzicato (plucked) strings:

Grieg: Peer Gynt *Suite No. 1, "In the Hall of the Mountain King"*

Alla marcia e molto marcato (In march time and very marked)

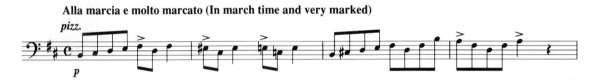

Touches of percussion and muted horn enhance the effect. Designed as a march, the frolicking movement deteriorates into a madcap free-for-all as the world of the trolls breaks down. Grieg achieves this effect with a steady repetition of the opening music and a dramatic accelerando.

ANTONÍN DVOŘÁK: SYMPHONY NO. 9 (*FROM THE NEW WORLD,* 1893)

Antonín Dvořák (pronounced d-VOR-zhock) was born in 1841 in Bohemia (later to become part of Czechoslovakia). Though part of the Austrian Empire, Bohemia was powerfully affected by a nationalist movement; in 1862, a theater was established in Prague for the performance of Czech plays and operas. During Dvořák's youth, the leading Czech composer was Bedřich Smetana (pronounced SMET-ta-na, 1824–1884), whose orchestral works and operas based on subjects drawn from Czech history and folklore were especially popular.

In 1874 the Austrian government awarded Dvořák a stipend in recognition of his talents as a composer. Johannes Brahms served on the panel of judges that decided on the award, and he became Dvořák's friend. Later, Brahms arranged for the publication of Dvořák's compositions—including the *Moravian Duets* and *Slavonic Dances,* works distinguished by their nationalist melodies, harmonies, and rhythms. In those and other works, Dvořák often used popular Slavic dances, inducing the *dumka,* a slow, melancholic dance; the *furiant,* a fast dance marked by strong changes in meter (between $\frac{2}{4}$

and ⅜); and the *polka,* a dance in moderate tempo with a characteristic rhythmic motive:
♫♪ ♫♫ | ♫ ♩. Nevertheless, Dvořák was equally capable of writing music in the traditional Germanic mold, as his substantial amount of chamber music and series of symphonies attests.

As Dvořák achieved international fame, he was invited to conduct his symphonies in England, and in 1892 he arrived in New York, where he served as director of a conservatory of music. During this "American" period (1892–1895), Dvořák sought to explore native American musical materials: He studied black spirituals and the music of American Indians and incorporated the fruits of his research in several compositions, among them some chamber works and a masterpiece, his ninth and final symphony, subtitled *From the New World* (1893). In four sizable movements, this work follows the general sequence of most nineteenth-century symphonies. Dvořák gives his symphony a special "American" character, however, by its pentatonic melodies, lively rhythms, unusual harmonies, and colorful orchestrations.

The first movement begins with a slow introduction, in which we hear fragments of themes that appear in their entirety later in the movement. The following fast movement proper, in sonata form, features three simple thematic ideas: The first (*a*) begins with a rising motive outlining a minor-key triad and has a characteristic rhythmic figure (long–short–short–long: ♩. ♪ ♪ ♩.); the second (*b*) is in a contrasting minor key and also has a compact rhythmic figure (♫ ♫♫); and the third (*c*) is a pentatonic melody in a major key that begins by recalling the long–short–short–long rhythm of *a*:

Dvořák: Symphony No. 9 (From the New World), *First Movement*

PRINCIPAL THEMES

The second and third movements were apparently inspired by Dvořák's reading of *The Song of Hiawatha,* a lengthy poem by Henry Wadsworth Longfellow based on North American Indian legends. The subtly scored second movement (*Largo*), which contains some of Dvořák's loveliest music, begins with a series of solemn brass chords (*a*), pitched in a low register and played quite softly (*ppp*):

Dvořák: Symphony No. 9 (From the New World), *Second Movement*

These chords, which include some involved, chromatic harmonic progressions, give way to the first theme (*b*), a pentatonic melody played by the English horn to the accompaniment of muted strings (the pentatonic scale on which the melody is based is included in our example):

This melody became popular later as the spiritual "Goin' Home"; Dvořák's imitation of folk music thus came to be taken as an authentic example.

Now the opening chords return, this time scored in the woodwinds, and the strings take up the melody, with muted horns playing its final strains. Turning to a slightly faster tempo, Dvořák introduces the central *B* section with a new melody in a minor key (*c*). It begins with a descending triplet:

The clarinets present a second idea (*d*), a five-measure theme that gently ascends and descends by stepwise motion:

Dvořák: Symphony No. 9 (*From the New World*), Second Movement

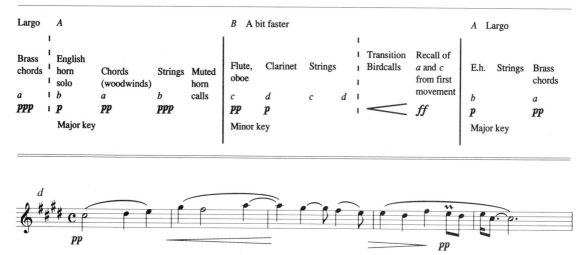

Largo	A				B	A bit faster					Transition	Recall of		A	Largo	
Brass chords	English horn solo	Chords (woodwinds)	Strings	Muted horn calls	Flute, oboe	Clarinet	Strings				Birdcalls	*a* and *c* from first movement		E.h.	Strings	Brass chords
a	*b*	*a*	*b*		*c*	*d*	*c*	*d*						*b*		*a*
ppp	*p*	*pp*	*ppp*		*pp*	*p*				*<*		*ff*		*p*		*pp*
	Major key				Minor key									Major key		

Toward the end of this section, Dvořák uses imitations of birdcalls and static drone effects to paint a pastoral scene. Beginning simply—again in a vein reminiscent of Beethoven's *Pastoral* Symphony—this passage broadens through a crescendo. Now Dvořák recalls two themes (*a* and *c*) from the first movement. The familiar English-horn melody of the opening *A* section returns, and near the end of the movement, the majestic brass chords sound again. The study diagram summarizes the overall three-part *ABA* form of the movement.

The third movement is a broadly designed scherzo in an expanded form: ‖: A :‖ ‖ BA ‖:C :‖: A :‖ BA Coda. The *A* section is introduced by the full orchestra, with triangle and timpani creating a special effect. For the principal theme, Dvořák employs a playful, descending staccato subject bantered in imitation among the woodwinds over a drone accompaniment in the strings. The drone is a static dissonant chord that remains unresolved, giving the passage a rustic, folklike flavor:

Dvořák: Symphony No. 9 (From the New World), *Third Movement*

A SECTION

Dvořák has the full orchestra repeat the theme, with biting accents in the brass, and then turns to a more sustained pentatonic melody for the *B* section:

B SECTION

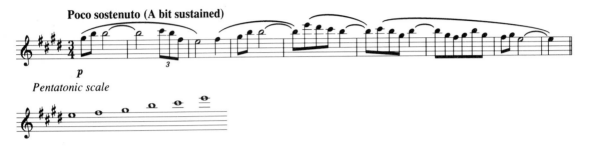

Played first by the woodwinds, this melody is repeated by the cellos. The *A* section returns, and, after a transition (with a brief allusion to theme *a* from the first movement), the *C* section begins with a new folklike melody animated by the rhythm ♩. ♪ ♩:

C SECTION

Dvořák next repeats the *A, B,* and *A* sections and concludes with a coda, making further allusions to theme *a* from the first movement.

Dvořák's technique of recalling themes is carried even further in the finale, a sonata-form movement, in which themes from the first three movements appear toward the end. Such recycling of themes became a common technique in late nineteenth-century music, as composers sought to unify their multimovement compositions by using the finale to summarize the entire composition.

In coming to the United States, Dvořák was concerned with exploring in his music the potential elements of a national American musical style. Of course, much of the flavor of the *New World* Symphony is as much Czech as it is American: The special techniques Dvořák uses in the symphony are not dissimilar to those applied in his avowedly "Czech" works. In 1893 America was a land of immigrants, a melting pot of various nationalities, and a truly American musical idiom emerged only with the work of native composers in the twentieth century (see Chapter 18). Still, it was Dvořák, a composer of international rank, who asked the pertinent question: "Every nation has its music. There is Italian, German, French, Bohemian, Russian; why not American music?"

MODEST MUSORGSKY: PROLOGUE TO *BORIS GODUNOV* (1874)

For centuries, Russia had remained more or less isolated culturally from Europe. Western influences were introduced by Tsar Peter the Great (1689–1725), who at the beginning of his reign visited Europe incognito to observe for himself Western government and culture. In the eighteenth century, foreign musicians were invited to work in Peter's magnificent capital, St. Petersburg (now Leningrad), a practice that was furthered by Catherine II (1762–1796). During Catherine's rein, Italian opera was in demand and French was the preferred language of the court.

The history of Russian music in the nineteenth century unfolded against the sweeping social changes that culminated in the emancipation of the serfs (1861) and in the emergence of Russian as a literary language. Alexander Pushkin (1799–1837), often credited with founding a distinctively Russian literature, wrote several poems on which Russian operas were later based, including *Ruslan and Ludmilla,* drawn from Russian folklore, and *Boris Godunov,* a historical tragedy. In later years, Pushkin concentrated on prose, as did a distinguished series of Russian novelists including Gogol, Dostoevsky, Turgenev, and Tolstoy, who wrote monumental, realistic novels about the Russian homeland.

By the second half of the century, many Russian composers were turning to indigenous musical sources rather than imitating Western models. In particular, a group of five composers, known as the "Mighty Handful," set out to create a national Russian style. Four of them were amateurs: César Cui (1835–1918), a military engineer; Alexander Borodin (1833–1887), a chemist; Modest Musorgsky (1839–1881), an army cadet who later became a government bureaucrat; and Nikolai Rimsky-Korsakov (1844–1908), a naval officer. Only one, Mily Alexeyevich Balakirev (1837–1910), was a professional musician. Partly because they lacked a traditional European musical training, they cultivated new, distinctively Russian manners in their compositions. The most innovative and uncompromising experimenter of this group was Modest Musorgsky.

Musorgsky had to overcome considerable adversity to pursue his interest in music. He became an officer in the army but eventually resigned his commission and took a minor position as a civil servant. Subject to bouts of alcoholism and depression, he somehow managed to produce several songs in a strikingly fresh style, and one opera, the masterpiece *Boris Godunov* (1874); he left an unfinished opera, *Khovanshchina.* He also wrote an extended piano work, *Pictures at an Exhibition* (1874), which was intended as a tribute to the painter and architect Victor Hartmann. (This composition is most familiar in the brilliant orchestral version created by the French composer Maurice Ravel in 1922.) At Musorgsky's death, only a few Russian artists and critics were aware of his genius.

Musorgsky based his great opera *Boris Godunov* on material drawn from Pushkin's drama and from various historical sources. The libretto, to which the composer himself contributed, is a chronicle of Boris's reign in several loosely knit scenes. Much of the drama unfolds in a declamatory, speechlike style that remains faithful to the natural inflections of the Russian text and that moves the action forward at a powerful, relentless pace. Great choruses suggest the shifting moods of the Russian populace, and the orchestra provides hauntingly beautiful folksonglike melodies and bright touches of color. Against this background, Musorgsky traces Boris's descent into madness and death. *Boris* is a powerful work of psychological realism, comparable in a way to the great novel *Crime and Punishment* (1866), which Dostoevsky finished not long before Musorgsky began his work on the opera.

The historical Boris Godunov acceded to the throne in 1598, after the tempestuous reign of Ivan "the Terrible" (1547–1584). Of the two heirs to Ivan's crown, one soon died and the other was demented. When the surviving heir died of mysterious causes, Boris was elevated to the crown through the intercession of the boyars, members of the Russian nobility.

In Pushkin's version (which Musorgsky followed), Boris has had Ivan's demented son murdered in order to clear his way to the throne. The opera traces the psychological deterioration of a ruler racked by guilt over his crime. Boris's downfall is hastened by an uprising staged by a youthful imposter, who claims to be Dmitri, Ivan's murdered son. Boris eventually goes mad and dies.

Different versions of Musorgsky's opera survive, including two (1869 and 1874) that he himself finished and one by Rimsky-Korsakov, who after Musorgsky's death rearranged the sequence of some scenes, severely cut other scenes, and thoroughly reorchestrated the entire score, all in an attempt to remedy the composer's perceived inexperience in dramatic composition and orchestration. We shall consider Musorgsky's second version of the Prologue, which treats the events leading to Boris's coronation.

The opera begins with a quietly winding melody, taken up by several instruments. It is a minor-key melody, though it has the irrepressible flavor of a Russian folk song:

Musorgsky: Boris Godunov, *Prologue*

SCENE 1

As the curtain rises, we see small groups of Russian peasants outside a monastery near Moscow. Boyars enter the monastery to persuade Boris to assume the throne. An official orders the peasants to pray for their success, threatening to punish them if they disobey. Twice they sing their supplication, a particularly angular melody, pitching it one step higher the second time. An official appears at the doorway of the monastery to announce that Boris still refuses to become tsar. Then a group of blind pilgrims approaches and disappears into the monastery.

In Scene 2, one of the most celebrated moments of the opera, Boris has agreed to become tsar. The scene is set at the Kremlin, in a square between the Cathedrals of the Assumption, where the tsars are crowned, and the Archangels, where the tsars are buried. The music of this Coronation Scene begins with the sound of bells, represented in the orchestra by two dissonant chords that alternate:

SCENE 2

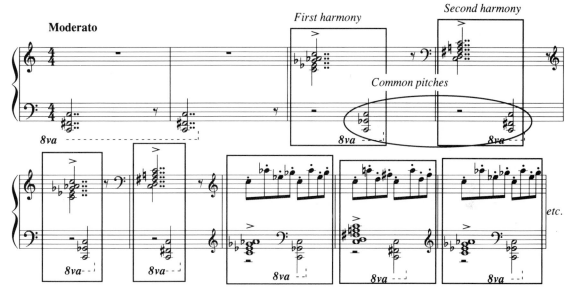

Against this harmonic pendulum, Musorgsky places faster figuration in the winds and upper strings, gradually increasing the rhythmic animation and speeding up the alternation between the two chords. The music pauses briefly and then resumes, with the order of the chords reversed. A boyar announces the entrance of the new tsar, and the throngs of peasants in the courtyard hail Boris and then break out in a joyous paean to him, based on a Russian folk song:

SCENE 2

Uzh kak na ne - be solnt - sy kras - no - mu sla - va, sla - va!
(Text: As unto the brilliant sun in the sky)

The Coronation Scene from the Prologue to Musorgsky's *Boris Godunov*.
(New York Metropolitan Opera)

Boris sings first in a recitativelike aside; guilt-ridden, he acknowledges the evil presentiments that oppress his heart. The celebration continues, and the crowd repeats its exuberant chorus.

Throughout this gripping work, Musorgsky experiments in boldly imaginative ways. He uses tonality in nontraditional applications and characteristically explores the exotic sounds of modes indigenous to Russian folk music. There are other innovative features that contribute to the drama's force: Musorgsky's harmonic vocabulary, which encompasses chords constructed upon fourths or seconds instead of conventional triads built upon thirds, and his use of incessant rhythmic patterns to create a sense of dramatic momentum. Not a few twentieth-century composers found inspiration in Musorgsky's music, which anticipated in several remarkable ways the radically modernist approaches to composition in the new century.

BRAHMS'S ORCHESTRAL MUSIC

One composer who continued to explore the established European musical traditions during the second half of the nineteenth century was Johannes Brahms. His adherence to classical forms and use of learned counterpoint were in the tradition of German instrumental music reaching back to the eighteenth century and before. Though Wagner declared the symphony to be an obsolete genre, Brahms wrote four symphonies of great power and freshness, even if their creation cost him enormous effort. Again, in a traditional vein, he composed chamber music throughout his life (see pp. 318–325), continued to write romantic Lieder, and, as one of the great pianists of the century, produced many impeccably crafted works for the piano.

Inevitably, perhaps, Brahms's music was viewed by some as a counterbalance to Wagner's "music of the future." Attracted as a young man to Robert Schumann's lyrical romanticism, Brahms's helped write a manifesto directed against Wagner and his admirers. For those who demanded "progress" in music, Brahms himself was taken as a target of ridicule. For those who stubbornly clung to older values, he stood as a champion of musical conservatism. According to another view, probably more accurate, Brahms's position in nineteenth-century music was two-sided: On the one hand, he worked to preserve the distinguished traditions of German musical romanticism; at the same time, he strove to renew those traditions by incorporating new developments in tonal and harmonic language and new approaches in thematic treatment. Indeed, his accomplishments in those areas led the composer Arnold Schoenberg, who would father radically modern musical techniques early in the twentieth century, to label Brahms a "progressive."

Appropriately, Brahms pursued his career in Vienna—the city of Haydn, Mozart, Beethoven, and Schubert. There, during the 1860s, he won renown as a pianist and as a conductor; and there, in later years, his major compositions were premiered. Among them were several orchestral works: the *Variations on a Theme of Haydn* (1873), two overtures (*Academic Festival* Overture and *Tragic* Overture, both 1880), four symphonies (1876, 1877, 1883, and 1885), and several concertos (two for piano, 1858 and 1881, one for violin, 1878, and one for violin and cello, 1887). His most ambitious composition was the *German Requiem* (1868), a large work for soloists, chorus, and orchestra, written for public performance rather than for a traditional religious service, although the text was drawn from the Lutheran Bible.

Brahms freely acknowledged that he was striving to make his symphonies worthy successors to Beethoven's nine symphonies, and his debt to Beethoven is evident. In his First Symphony, he uses a theme reminiscent of the famous melody from the "Ode to Joy" finale of Beethoven's Ninth Symphony; and in his Second Symphony, he makes occasional allusions to the style of Beethoven's *Pastoral* Symphony. Brahms's dependence on earlier music extended beyond Beethoven, however. In his Fourth Symphony, for example, he constructed an elaborate movement on a passacaglia subject (see p. 114), thereby reviving a baroque form. In the *Variations on a Theme of Haydn,* to which we now turn, he drew on a variety of eighteenth-century techniques.

VARIATIONS ON A THEME OF HAYDN, OP. 56A

This masterpiece (1873) is based on a theme that was known as the Chorale of St. Anthony, though exactly what its original religious significance was is not clear. It came down to Brahms in a version for winds attributed to Joseph Haydn. Scholarship has questioned that attribution, however, and its exact origins are unknown. Brahms himself believed that Haydn had written it down to be used in a wind divertimento, or suite. In any event, Brahms took over the theme and joined it to eight freshly composed variations and a finale, making the finale itself a series of short variations on a recurring bass pattern, another reminder of Brahms's interest in the music of earlier periods, in this case, the ostinato techniques of baroque composers (pp. 85, 114). To suggest the spirit of eighteenth-century orchestration, he used a relatively small orchestra. Mindful of "Haydn's" wind version of the theme, he reinforced the woodwind section by adding a piccolo and a contrabassoon★; he also called for four horns instead of the two customary in eighteenth-century scores. Finally, in the closing bars, he introduced a triangle to add luster to the ensemble.

The duple-meter ($\frac{2}{4}$) theme of the *Haydn Variations* consists of two parts, each repeated, and further divided into shorter phrases (marked off in our example) articulated by changes in the dynamics. A simple dotted rhythmic figure (♪.♫) appears at the outset and later permeates the theme:

Brahms: Variations on a Theme of Haydn, *Op. 56a*

THEME

★A bassoon with a basic range one octave below that of the conventional bassoon; also known as a double bassoon.

Brahms scores the theme for winds with a light pizzicato accompaniment in the low strings.

In the variations that follow, Brahms explores a range of variation techniques. The first three variations, which form a group, have increasingly faster tempos. In the first, which features the strings, he juxtaposes triplets (♫) in the bass against eighth notes (♫) in the treble, creating a gentle rhythmic tension of "threes" against "twos." By reversing (or "inverting") the bass and treble parts to "twos" against "threes," he achieves a contrapuntal tension that is clearly audible as the parts exchange their material (see the listening diagram, pp. 376–377).

Variation 2, in a minor key, features a solo for the clarinets and bassoons, with accompaniment by the strings. In Variation 3, a smoothed-out version of the melody is played by the oboes and bassoons and, at the repeats, by the strings with a flowing accompaniment in the flutes and bassoons.

Variation 4 stands apart from the others: Marked *Andante con moto,* it is in the parallel minor key and is the first variation in a triple meter, as opposed to the duple meter of the theme. Brahms uses this variation to engage in another learned type of counterpoint: With each repetition of the theme, he exchanges the parts of the theme and the accompanying line:

VARIATION 4

After this slow variation, Brahms turns in the fifth variation to a lighthearted scherzo in 6/8 time, with rapidly executed staccato work in the winds. Playful, irregular accents continually throw off the beat, adding to the humorous effect. In the sixth variation, which reestablishes the original duple meter of the theme, Brahms features a solo for the horns as the music builds to its first real climax. The seventh variation, by contrast, alludes to the **siciliano,** a graceful baroque dance of Sicilian origins that composers associated with pastoral settings. It is characterized by a long–short–short rhythmic pattern (♩.♫♩):

Brahms: *Variations on a Theme of Haydn, Op. 56a*

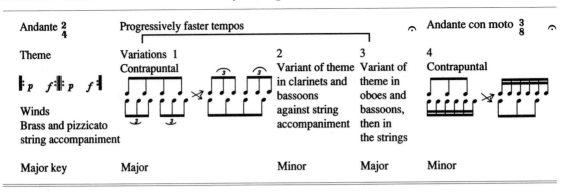

Andante $\frac{2}{4}$	Progressively faster tempos			Andante con moto $\frac{3}{8}$
Theme	Variations 1	2	3	4
	Contrapuntal	Variant of theme	Variant of	Contrapuntal
		in clarinets and	theme in	
Winds		bassoons	oboes and	
Brass and pizzicato		against string	bassoons,	
string accompaniment		accompaniment	then in	
			the strings	
Major key	Major	Minor	Major	Minor

VARIATION 7

The eighth variation, on the other hand, in the minor key, is another scherzo. Once again, Brahms resorts to learned counterpoint: The opening motive of the eighth variation, given in the strings, is answered by its mirror inversion in the winds. Later in the variation, Brahms combines the two:

VARIATION 8

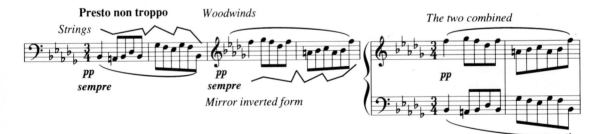

The work culminates in a finale built upon a recurring ostinato bass pattern, which comprises an ascending leap filled in by descending stepwise motion. The pattern is, in fact, derived from the fifth, sixth, seventh, and eighth pitches of the theme (see the example on p. 374). Here, Brahms once again pays reverence to the music of an earlier historical period. In this case, baroque counterpoint informs the concluding pages of this score.

Brahms: *Variations on a Theme of Haydn*, Op. 56a, *Continued*

Vivace $\frac{6}{8}$	Vivace $\frac{2}{4}$	Siciliano $\frac{6}{8}$	Presto non troppo $\frac{3}{4}$	Finale ¢	
5	6	7	8	17 variations	Return of
Staccato	Prominent		String (muted)	on a bass	theme
woodwinds,	horns		motive answered	ostinato	(triangle)
cross accents			by inverted form	derived from	
scherzolike			in winds, then	theme	
			combined		
	p *f* *ff*	*p*	*pp*	*p* and *f*	*ff*
Major	Major	Major	Minor	Major	

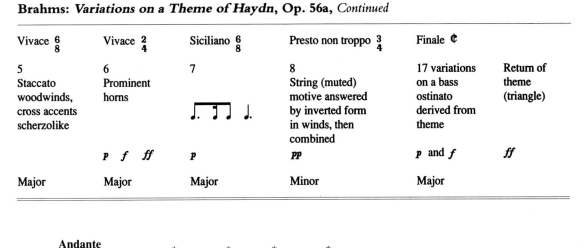

Throughout the seventeen variations of the finale, Brahms weaves florid counterpoint around the ostinato subject, which itself appears in different registers with varying instrumental combinations. Finally, the theme of the opening returns, accompanied by the shimmering sound of the triangle. Sweeping scales bring this work, with its celebration of the musical past, to a jubilant close.

PYOTR IL'YICH TCHAIKOVSKY

The music of Pyotr Il'yich Tchaikovsky (1840–1893), more than most music of his Russian colleagues, bears an affinity to nineteenth-century European music. To be sure, Tchaikovsky was not unaffected by the nationalist sentiments reflected in the efforts of the "mighty handful" to create a Russian style of music. In fact, he wrote several distinctly Russian operas himself, of which the most famous is *Eugene Onegin* (1879), with a libretto drawn from Pushkin. Moreover, his use of Russian folk songs and non-Western scales and harmonies was characteristic of the music of his contemporaries. Nevertheless, Tchaikovsky remained outside the circle of the "mighty handful"; and in certain ways, his music places him historically much closer to Brahms than it does to Musorgsky or Rimsky-Korsakov.

Tchaikovsky showed an early aptitude for music, yet he attended the School of Jurisprudence in St. Petersburg and worked as a clerk in the Ministry of Justice. In 1863 he resigned his post and enrolled in the newly formed Conservatory, which was headed by the pianist, conductor, and composer Anton Rubinstein. There, Tchaikovsky received a thorough grounding in Western harmony, counterpoint, and form. Later, Tchaikovsky himself taught at the Moscow Conservatory.

Tchaikovsky's life was not a happy one. His mother's death in 1854 was a severe emotional blow, and he struggled throughout his life to come to terms with his homosexuality. He was married for a short time to one of his admirers, but the marriage failed. For many years, he carried on a distant friendship with Madame von Meck, who admired his music and acted as his patroness. Though they corresponded regularly, they never arranged to meet. Then, in 1890, without a suitable explanation, Madame von Meck withdrew her support and broke off the correspondence.

In the last few years of his life, Cambridge University honored him with a doctorate, and his music was performed in Europe, where it won the admiration of Brahms. In 1891, during a tour in the United States, Tchaikovsky fell into a deep depression and longed to return to his homeland. The melancholy of the music he composed during his last years is most evident in the powerful slow movement of his sixth and last symphony, the *Pathétique*. He died at the age of 53, under mysterious circumstances. According to one report, Tchaikovsky consumed unboiled water and fell victim to cholera in St. Petersburg. According to another account, he committed suicide after a homosexual liaison had been exposed.

Tchaikovsky composed six symphonies, of which the Fourth (1878), Fifth (1888), and Sixth (1893) are still in the standard symphonic repertory. Some of his symphonies contain programmatic elements: For example, the Fourth has to do with Fate, and the Sixth is an intensely personal statement about life and death. Among his other works are a violin concerto (1878) and the First Piano Concerto. The latter quickly earned its place in the repertory after its premiere in Boston (1875), despite its certain liberties in form (for example, the celebrated opening theme is not recapitulated, a "weakness" first noticed by Anton Rubinstein). Tchaikovsky also wrote music for three ballets: *Swan Lake* (1876), *The Sleeping Beauty* (1889), and the ever-popular *Nutcracker* (1892).

Among Tchaikovsky's more experimental—and romantic—orchestral music are works based on Shakespeare's *Romeo and Juliet, The Tempest,* and *Hamlet,* which he described as orchestral fantasies. In another vein, the *1812 Overture* celebrates the defeat of Napoleon during the Russian campaign of 1812. Finally, he wrote two unnumbered symphonies, inspired by Byron's poem *Manfred* and by an episode in Dante's *Divine Comedy.* We shall consider here Tchaikovsky's *Romeo and Juliet* (1870), one of his most popular orchestral works.

ROMEO AND JULIET FANTASY-OVERTURE

In creating a programmatic overture about *Romeo and Juliet,* Tchaikovsky faced a particular compositional problem: how to reconcile the requirements of a sonata-form movement with the dramatic action of Shakespeare's play. Rather than follow the play directly, he based his score on three essential elements of the drama: the "ancient grudge" of the warring Capulets and Montagues, the "star-crossed lovers" Romeo and Juliet, and Friar Lawrence, who mediates between the warring factions and grants the lovers a brief asylum before their tragic end.

Curiously, Tchaikovsky chose to begin with Friar Lawrence, although in Shakespeare's play, this character appears mainly in the last act. In a slow introduction, the Friar's hymnlike melody (*a*) is intoned by low, dark woodwinds in a stately progression of even-valued notes:

Tchaikovsky: Romeo and Juliet

FRIAR LAWRENCE

This solemn beginning is followed by a dissonant passage for strings and horn, the first suggestion of conflict. Tchaikovsky now adds woodwinds and strings, and arpeggiations in the harp. Then he repeats this much of the composition one pitch lower. The music gradually builds in intensity until it erupts into the passionate Allegro, the beginning of the exposition. This passage, suggesting the feud (*b*), contains sudden interruptions and whipping scales:

FEUD

The music seethes with conflict; it features strong dissonances, clashing rhythmic figures, tense juxtapositions of orchestral groups (especially winds versus strings), and cymbal crashes. Cast in imitation between the high woodwinds and the low strings, theme *b* traces the bitter course of the feud. The struggle breaks off abruptly, and Tchaikovsky now introduces in the English horn and violas the celebrated lovers' theme (*c*):

LOVERS' THEME

This smooth, placid music is devoid of conflict and is in a major key far removed from the minor key of the feud. A subdued, more lyrical passage for muted strings (*c'*) sustains the mood of tranquility:

After a restatement of *c* with fuller scoring, the exposition ends quietly with a series of gently descending chords for the harp and light orchestral accompaniment.

Tchaikovsky appropriates the development section, with its working-out of thematic material, for the resumption of the feud. In this section, he pits the theme of Friar Lawrence against the feud music, carrying the uneasy juxtaposition through a variety of keys. The conflict grows in intensity, and at its climax a *fortissimo* statement of the Friar's theme in the trumpets prepares the recapitulation. The shortened first theme (*b*) is followed by the lovers' theme (*c*), made more ardent through its extension and by excursions into different major keys. But the passage is shattered by the resumption of the feud motive—notwithstanding appearances of the Friar's motive in the brass. A timpani roll announces the tragedy of the lovers' deaths, and a somber coda depicts the funeral procession. The lovers' theme is now gently revised and transformed, repeated several times in the high strings with conciliatory harp chords. Four *fortissimo* measures of chords conclude the work with a final allusion to the "ancient grudge."

PROGRAM MUSIC OF THE LATER NINETEENTH CENTURY

LISZT IN WEIMAR

Much of Tchaikovsky's orchestral music was inspired by extramusical ideas of some sort, a feature that ties it to earlier programmatic experiments of European romantics. After Berlioz's pioneering *Symphonie fantastique* of 1830 and Mendelssohn's refined concert overtures of the 1820s and 1830s, important contributions to programmatic orchestral music were made by Franz Liszt, who in 1848 settled at Weimar as music director. There, he gave up his illustrious career as a piano virtuoso (see pp. 313–314), championed the music of Wagner and Berlioz, and devoted himself to composing a new, experimental kind of instrumental music. One of Liszt's most impressive and demanding works from this time was the Piano Sonata in B minor (1853), dedicated to Robert

Schumann. Liszt designed an especially elaborate formal plan for this monumental composition: Its movements are linked by transitions, and the whole is unified by the reappearance of themes from the first movement later in the sonata in various transformed guises. Though Liszt did not provide a specific program for the B minor Sonata (an earlier "Fantasy-Sonata" for piano by Liszt was inspired by a poem of Victor Hugo's), there is little doubt that he had a program in mind, probably one concerned with spiritual redemption. In the grandiloquent second theme of the first movement, for example, there appears, mottolike, the beginning of *Crux fidelis* ("O faithful Cross"), an old sacred Latin hymn that Liszt used extensively in his sacred choral music. During the Weimar period Liszt now systematically refined his approach to program music by turning to orchestral music, a remarkable departure from the virtuoso, soloist-oriented music of his earlier career.

The results were a bold series of orchestral works, typically in one continuous movement, that Liszt termed **symphonic poems** (*Symphonische Dichtungen*). He drew on a wide variety of subjects, including Shakespeare's *Hamlet,* poems by Byron, Schiller, and Hugo, and the Orpheus legend. On a more ambitious scale were his *Dante* Symphony (1857, dedicated to Richard Wagner), and his *Faust* Symphony (conceived during the 1840s but not completed until 1857, and dedicated to Hector Berlioz). The *Faust* symphony is structured in three broad orchestral movements, character studies of the protagonists in Goethe's epic: Faust, Gretchen, and Mephistopheles. A chorus at the conclusion of the symphony gives the closing lines of the drama, assigned by Goethe to a "mystical chorus," which extol the womanly virtues of Gretchen, Faust's redeemer. Like the symphonic poems, the *Faust Symphony* is loosely based on the sonata principle of thematic presentation, development, and recapitulation—loosely based because the programmatic elements occasionally take precedence over the requirements of sonata form. To give unity to the entire work, Liszt exploited a technique of thematic transformation essentially analogous to Wagner's use of leitmotives; in Liszt's technique, themes embedded with extramusical meaning are brought back in various new guises and shapes. (One specialized application of thematic transformation in the *Faust* Symphony traces its origins to Berlioz: In the last movement, devoted to Mephistopheles, Liszt presents grotesque parodies of the noble themes associated with Faust in the first movement. The procedure recalls Berlioz's parody of the *idée fixe* in the culminating *Dream of a Sabbath Night* from the *Symphonie fantastique;* see p. 311.) Liszt's forward-looking orchestral music was taken as a parallel to Richard Wagner's music dramas and was considered to have divulged new possibilities for future composers of program music to explore.

RICHARD STRAUSS

One such composer was Richard Strauss (1864–1949). His father was a celebrated horn virtuoso who played in the court orchestra of Munich, where he took part in performances of Wagner's music dramas (though he loathed doing so). He urged his son to study the traditional classics, and as a result, Strauss's early music was in a decidedly conservative idiom reminiscent of the music of Beethoven, Mendelssohn, and Robert Schumann. In 1874 Strauss heard the music of Wagner for the first time, but the turning point in his compositional development did not occur until 1885, when he came to terms with the music of Wagner and Liszt. The result fundamentally changed the course of his own music. From Liszt, Strauss adopted as a compositional ideal the concept of the "poetic idea." In the instrumental music of Brahms, traditional sonata form had become an "empty shell," an artificial form devoid of poetic content. In Strauss's increasingly ambitious orchestral scores, poetic, extramusical elements would influence and guide the composer's musical decisions about thematic construction and formal designs.

When one of Strauss's orchestral works drew the attention of Hans von Bülow, a famous conductor in Meiningen, champion of Wagner, and former son-in-law of Liszt, young Strauss was taken on as an assistant conductor. During the 1880s and 1890s, he accepted conducting posts in Munich, Weimar, Munich again, and Berlin; later, he conducted opera at the Vienna State Opera. He was in fact as much celebrated as a conductor as he was as a composer, a distinction he shared with his contemporary Gustav Mahler.

As a conductor, Strauss became familiar with the large orchestras required by Wagner's works, and he came to prefer similar orchestras for his own music. Attracted to Liszt's symphonic poems, Strauss began to compose program music for orchestra. He started cautiously with a symphonic fantasy, *Aus Italien* (*From Italy,* 1886), but then ventured more boldly with a series of works he termed **tone poems** (*Tondichtungen*). Among them were *Macbeth,* after Shakespeare (1888); *Don Juan* (1889), based on a retelling of the Don Giovanni legend by the poet Nicolaus Lenau; *Tod und Verklärung* (*Death and Transfiguration,* 1889), to which we shall return; *Till Eulenspiegels lustige Streiche* (*The Merry Pranks of Till Eulenspiegel,* 1895), based on German folklore; the grandiose *Also sprach Zarathustra* (*Thus Spake Zarathustra,* 1896), based on Nietzsche's powerful work about the modern superman; *Don Quixote* (1897), after Cervantes; and *Ein Heldenleben* (*A Hero's Life,* 1898), a largely autobiographical work with one section teeming with quotations from Strauss's earlier tone poems. In these compositions, the guiding principle remained the poetic idea, which Strauss strove to ally with such traditional musical forms as the sonata, the rondo, and the variation.

Autobiographical threads run through much of Strauss's music. *Aus Italien* recounts his experiences in Italy; *Ein Heldenleben* deals with the aspirations of an artist; the *Symphonia domestica* (*Domestic Symphony,* 1903) depicts his domestic life; and the *Alpensinfonie* (*Alpine Symphony,* 1915) considers the artist's relation to broader, philosophical issues.

This outpouring of orchestral music brought Strauss both fame and notoriety. The tone poems, with their outlandish, extravagant effects, titillated some listeners and shocked others. Especially conspicuous in Strauss's scores were the severe demands they made on the technical resources of the orchestras of the day and Strauss's call for increasingly larger orchestras: The *Alpine Symphony,* for example, requires some 150 players.

Toward the end of the century, Strauss turned to opera. His tone poems already reflected the highly chromatic harmonic language of Liszt and Wagner; now he decided to carry Wagner's experiments with the music drama a step further. His first efforts—too closely modeled on Wagner's method—were failures. His next two operas, however, were masterpieces. *Salome* (1905, based on Oscar Wilde's lurid play) and *Elektra* (1909, with a libretto by Hugo von Hofmannsthal after Sophocles) outraged the moral sensitivities of early twentieth-century Vienna and won Strauss the reputation of an uncompromising modernist. *Salome,* in which the daughter of Herod dances with the severed head of John the Baptist, is a study in moral depravity; *Elektra,* in which the daughter of Agamemnon avenges his wrongful murder, is a study in retribution. The music with which Strauss treated these gruesome subjects was at once alluring and unsettling in its intensity.

Strauss now retreated from the iconoclastic, modern style of *Salome* and *Elektra.* The operas *Der Rosenkavalier* (*The Cavalier of the Rose,* 1911) and *Ariadne auf Naxos* (1916) recall the world of classical eighteenth-century opera, as if in decided reaction to the lush, romantic style of the nineteenth century. No longer at the vanguard of modernism in music, Strauss lapsed into a more conservative tonal idiom in his later operas. Meanwhile, his career was affected by world events. During the Nazis' rise to power and the Second World War, he remained in Germany, where he was used by Hitler's regime to promote its propaganda. Among his last works are the deeply moving *Four Last Songs* (1948) and the *Metamorphosen* for string orchestra (1945), the composer's pensive, nostalgic farewells.

TOD UND VERKLÄRUNG (DEATH AND TRANSFIGURATION)

Strauss himself wrote a fairly precise statement outlining the program behind *Death and Transfiguration.* His intention in this score was to represent a dying artist who, in his final hours, reviews his life from infancy through boyhood to maturity. The artist is obsessed by the artistic Ideal to which he has dedicated his life. His soul is transfigured at death, and he finds the Ideal in eternity.

As the study diagram shows in a brief summary, Strauss freely adapted sonata form to match this ambitious program. The work begins with an extended, slow introduction in a minor key. A quietly pulsating figure in the strings and irregular timpani strokes suggest the weak heartbeat of the dying artist. Gradually, two motives emerge. The first (*a*) descends from the high woodwinds:

Strauss: Tod und Verklärung

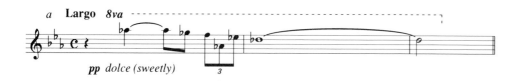

Strauss: *Tod und Verklärung (Death and Transfiguration)*

Slow Introduction	Exposition Allegro	Development		Slow Introduction (shortened)	Recapitulation Allegro	Coda Moderato
The dying artist	The artist awakens (agitated)	The artist reviews his life	Appearance of the ideal 3 statements	The dying artist	(shortened) Last agony and death of the artist	Transfiguration of the artist
Based on *a* and *b*	*c*	Based on *b* and *a*	*d*			Based on *d* Expansive Tamtam

The second, a rounded melodic curve (*b*), is introduced by the oboe and is then taken up by a solo violin, with harp accompaniment:

pp *Sehr zart (very tenderly)*

The uneasy calm gives way to an agitated Allegro, the exposition proper of the movement, as the artist awakens to agonizing pain. For this passage, Strauss couples a dissonant harmonic language with a disquieting motive in the low strings (*c*). By using syncopations, Strauss delays the emergence of a firm downbeat:

Syncopation   *Syncopation*

Instead of declaring a single theme in the exposition, Strauss propels the music forward with a complicated network of clashing motives. Well into the exposition, he seems about to introduce a second key and thematic group. But then he cuts the section short and moves into the development section, a review of the artist's life. Motive *b* suggests infancy and childhood; a more manly version of motive *a,* presented in the brass, suggests youth and manhood. Now the intensity of the music rises, suggesting the artist's passionate striving toward the Ideal. Toward the end of the development, the rising theme associated with the Ideal (*d*) emerges fully:

d **Sehr breit (Very broadly)**

ff

Strauss presents three statements of *d,* each in a higher key. Then, the slow introduction returns, followed by an abbreviated recapitulation, to suggest again the reality of the artist on his deathbed. Strident accents in the brass punctuate the artist's final agony.

The broadly conceived final section, which represents the transfiguration, is a large-scale coda dedicated to the theme of the Ideal. The conclusion begins softly, with stately suggestions of *d* in the brass accompanied by strokes of the tamtam.★ Gradually, Strauss adds woodwinds and strings and introduces faster rhythmic values. The theme of the Ideal, *d,* is given several times and is extended into the upper register of the violins. In the closing bars, we hear a breathtaking diminuendo, as this exquisite romantic vision of the artist attaining the Ideal recedes and fades. At the end, all is tranquil and resolved.

VIENNA AT THE CLOSE OF THE NINETEENTH CENTURY

While Strauss was developing the Lisztian symphonic poem further in his tone poems, other composers were vigorously pursuing new directions in other genres. Hugo Wolf (1860–1903), an ardent admirer of Wagner, devoted his difficult and irregular career to music criticism and the production of songs. In Vienna, he wrote scathing reviews of Brahms's works and, in his highly idiosyncratic Lieder, pushed the art song to a new limit of expressiveness. He arranged his best songs into sizable collections, each devoted to the verses of individual poets such as Mörike, Eichendorff, and Goethe.

These collections are not song cycles in the tradition of Schubert and Robert Schumann, but great dramatic anthologies encompassing a range of contrasting moods. Wolf's songs often have elaborate piano parts that exceed the demands of piano parts in Schumann's Lieder. The music is highly dissonant and often skirts the bounds of tonality. Some of the songs begin in one key and end in another; for others, it is difficult to assign any key at all. Wolf exploited the art song as a tool for plumbing the subjective, inner meanings of romantic poetry; he viewed his songs, in fact, as poems with musical interpretations. Extending Schumann's approach to song composition, Wolf empha-sized the subtle relationships between sound and words and uncovered disturbing visions of the darkest side of musical expression.

Other composers found the symphony to be a genre not yet exhausted. Beside Brahms's four symphonies, firmly anchored in the distinguished German symphonic tradition, the Austrian Anton Bruckner (1824–1896) laboriously completed a series of nine.† He began his career as an organist and schoolteacher. A dedicated pupil himself,

---

★ A large gong of indefinite pitch suspended in a frame.

† In a curious act of creative negation, Bruckner labeled an early symphony, not counted in the series, "die Nullte" ("nullified"); it is known today as No. 0.

Bruckner studied harmony and counterpoint through the mail with the noted music theorist Simon Sechter; Bruckner himself later taught at the Vienna Conservatory.

Devoutly religious, Bruckner produced a substantial amount of sacred music, including masses, a requiem, and shorter, motetlike compositions. In that, he was influenced by the nineteenth-century revival of interest in early sacred music, evidenced by scholarly studies of Gregorian chant and performances of the music of Palestrina and other composers of the Renaissance. Bruckner's main achievement, however, was his nine monumental symphonies. He gave none of them explicit titles, though the Fourth (1874–1880) was dubbed the *Romantic* Symphony. Still, they were embraced by the proponents of Wagner's "music of the future." (Bruckner did, in fact, dedicate one symphony to Wagner and made the "obligatory" pilgrimage to Bayreuth to meet the master.) At the same time, Bruckner won the animosity of conservative critics who loyally championed Brahms.

In scale and size, Bruckner's symphonies recall the monumentality of Beethoven's Ninth Symphony, the *Choral,* though unlike Beethoven, Bruckner never introduced texts into the domain of his instrumental music. The warm glow of Bruckner's extended themes brings to mind the lyricism of Schubert; what is more, Bruckner's expanded treatment of sonata form—often with three thematic groups instead of the traditional two—finds some precedent in Schubert's mighty Ninth Symphony, the "Great." The lush chromatic language of Bruckner's scores is often viewed as evidence of Wagner's unavoidably powerful influence. That may be, but Bruckner nevertheless kept a respectful distance from Wagner's music dramas, preferring instead to discover his identity in the symphony, a genre that Wagner had deemed obsolete. Sadly, Bruckner's creative efforts suffered an unusual fate: well-meaning friends and colleagues urged upon him drastic revisions, cuts, and other "improvements" in his symphonies, and the composer, lacking full confidence in his work, often obliged. Scholars are still trying to decipher Bruckner's original intentions in his manuscripts.

GUSTAV MAHLER

Bruckner's symphonies exhibit one feature typical of late nineteenth-century music: a trend toward extended—for some, excessive—length. Gustav Mahler (1860–1911) wholeheartedly reinforced that trend in his symphonies, which in many ways brought the German symphonic tradition to its culmination. Mahler studied at the Vienna Conservatory (where he heard Bruckner lecture) and at the University of Vienna, where, with other students, he discussed the music of Wagner and the philosophy of Schopenhauer and Nietzsche. He was first known as a conductor and moved from post to post in Kassel, Prague, Leipzig, Budapest, and Hamburg before settling down to direct the Vienna opera from 1897 to 1907. There, he conducted during the winter seasons and composed during his summer holidays.

Mahler's music reflects in sometimes frank detail the tribulations, both imaginary and real, of his tormented life. In 1897, partly to circumvent discrimination against him because he was a Jew, he converted to Catholicism. In 1907 his elder daughter died,

Gustav Mahler.

and a doctor diagnosed his heart condition. The victim of anti-Semitic intrigue, he left Vienna to join the Metropolitan Opera in New York in 1908 and the New York Philharmonic in 1909. He returned to Vienna, where he died in 1911.

Mahler wrote song cycles as well as symphonies, and much of his music is best understood, perhaps, as a synthesis of the two: His symphonies are filled with warmly lyrical passages that seem to demand texts, and his song cycles show a rigorously symphonic treatment of thematicism. A third element that impinged on Mahler's music was the program music of Liszt and Strauss; though he himself did not compose tone poems per se, he based his monumental symphonies on broadly philosophical programmatic concepts. The Second, in five lengthy movements, ends with a "Resurrection." The Fourth suggests the progression from earthly to heavenly existence and ends with a strophic song that details the "virtues of heavenly life." In the finale of the Sixth, sometimes called the *Tragic,* the hammerblows of fate correspond to tragedies in Mahler's own life.

In addition to his nine completed symphonies, Mahler left an unfinished tenth symphony written in a provocative, forward-looking musical language. He composed numerous songs, many of them on texts drawn from the classic anthology of German romantic folk poetry, *Des Knaben Wunderhorn* (*The Youth's Magic Horn,* 1805), which is referred to in some of his symphonies as well. Mahler's three major song cycles are the *Lieder eines fahrenden Gesellen* (*Songs of a Wayfarer,* 1896), *Kindertotenlieder* (*Songs on the Death of Children,* 1904), and *Das Lied von der Erde* (*The Song of the Earth,* 1909). *Das*

Lied von der Erde, which is based on Chinese poetry of the third century B.C., explores non-Western scales and harmonies.

Mahler's symphonies fall into several groups. The First Symphony, for orchestra alone, cites material from some of his songs. The Second, Third, and Fourth augment the orchestra with vocal soloists or choral forces, or both, that present texts from a variety of sources, including *Des Knaben Wunderhorn,* Nietzsche's *Also sprach Zarathustra,* and Mahler himself. The Fifth, Sixth, and Seventh symphonies are again for orchestra alone, but for an orchestra that grew larger and larger. (The gargantuan finale of the Sixth Symphony, for example, calls for an orchestra with quintuple woodwinds and an elaborate battery of percussion instruments.) The most substantial of all is the Eighth Symphony, sometimes called the *Symphony of a Thousand,* which requires enormous orchestral, solo, and choral forces. In this work, Mahler drew upon the medieval hymn *Veni creator spiritus* and texts selected from Goethe's *Faust.*

LIEDER EINES FAHRENDEN GESELLEN (SONGS OF A WAYFARER)

Mahler's *Songs of a Wayfarer* were likely originally written with piano accompaniment. At some time, he orchestrated them, and it is in this version that they are performed today. The texts for the song cycle were apparently prepared by Mahler himself. He drew heavily on German folk poetry and earlier song cycles for inspiration—in particular, on Schubert's *Winterreise,* a song cycle that also concerns a wanderer. But Mahler's approach differed significantly from Schubert's. For one thing, the orchestra afforded Mahler a wide range of colors and instrumental combinations obviously not available in Schubert's piano accompaniment. Moreover, at the end of the century, Mahler's tonal language reached new expressive limits. In particular, each song of the cycle began in one key and ended in another, suggesting the restlessness of the wayfarer and the composer's flexible approach to tonal organization.

Mahler: *Lieder eines fahrenden Gesellen,* No. 2 (Modified Strophic)

Moderate Tempo					Ritard	Slow,	Still slower
Strophe 1		Strophe 2		Strophe 3 (extended)		Strophe 4 (shortened)	Final strophe (incomplete)
Flute, voice *a*	Brief orchestral interlude	*a* in Voice and flute	Orchestral interlude	*a* in voice and violins	Orchestral	Based on opening of *a*	Solo violin, horn, harp
p <>	<*f*>	*p* <*f*> Cello in canonic imitation	*f* >	*pp*		*p*	*ppp*
Tonic major key		Tonic	Departure from tonic ~~~	New major key		New major key	

Mahler's first song reveals the event that prompts the wandering of the wayfarer (in all likelihood, Mahler himself). Rejected by his lover for another, he thinks of her on her wedding day and muses about his sorrow and the passing of spring. In the second song, the wayfarer wanders through dewy fields of flowers on a bright spring morning. The sun fills the world with light, contrasting with the sadness of the wayfarer seeking to regain his lost happiness. The third song is violent in mood. The wayfarer compares his grief to a dagger stabbing his breast. He longs to be laid upon his bier, freed from agony. Marked "stürmisch, wild" ("stormy, wild"), this is the most passionate, turbulent music of the cycle. The fourth song represents the wanderer's leave-taking from his beloved. Solemn, dirgelike music suggests a funeral procession. Then, in the exquisite conclusion, Mahler invokes the image of a linden tree—surely a reference to Schubert's "Der Lindenbaum"—in whose shade the wanderer finds solace (see p. 274).

Perhaps the most celebrated of the songs is the second (see study diagram), which is based on this gentle folksonglike melody (*a*) that rises scalelike and then subsides:

Mahler: Lieder eines fahrenden Gesellen, *No. 2*

a   **In gemächlicher Bewegung (At a comfortable pace)**

Ging heut' Mor - gen ü - ber's Feld,   Tau noch auf den Grä - sern hing

Here are its first strophe and translation:

Ging heut' Morgen über's Feld,	Went this morning through the fields,
Tau noch auf den Gräsern hing	Dew still clinging to the grass,
sprach zu mir der lust'ge Fink:	There spoke to me the merry finch:
Ei, du! Gelt?	Hey, you, fine day?
Guten Morgen!	Good morning, then!
Ei, Gelt? Du!	Hey, fine day, you!
Wird's nicht eine schöne Welt?	Hasn't it turned into a lovely world?
Schöne Welt? Zink! Zink!	Lovely world? Sing! Sing!
Schön und flink	Lovely, sing!
Wie mir doch die Welt gefällt!	But how the world pleases me!

Mahler set the poem as a strophic song with four strophes but modified the music of the second, third, and fourth strophes in various ways. The second strophe, for example, presents the theme in canon, with the cellos imitating the theme in the vocal part. The second strophe is followed by a lush orchestral interlude, which departs from the tonic key of the opening. Strophes 3 (extended) and 4 (shortened) are each cast in a new key as the wayfarer moves further afield. The final strophe, set in a slow tempo, remains incomplete, suggesting the wanderer's uncertainty: "Now does my happiness return?" he asks, only to answer his own question negatively. He will continue to yearn for that blissful state. The song ends with the brief emergence of a solo horn and solo violin and then a triple *piano* chord and arpeggio for the harp.

Mahler reused some of the material from the second and fourth songs of this cycle in his First Symphony. Indeed, many of his symphonies allude either to his songs (with or without texts) or to literary ideas of some sort. An irrepressible tone-poet, Mahler achieved at the end of the century the artistic synthesis toward which the romantics had striven.

EUROPE AT THE CLOSE OF THE CENTURY

Throughout Europe, the end of the nineteenth century signaled the critical final stage in music of the romantic tradition, if not its eclipse. By midcentury, some French composers had already begun to turn away from operas on romantic subjects to a lighter form of entertainment, the **operetta,** with its popular melodies, satirical tone, and broad appeal. Later in the century, Bizet's *Carmen* (1875) offered an antidote to romanticism: a realistic treatment of Spanish gypsy life. The philosopher Nietzsche, in fact, tiring of Wagner's seemingly ponderous scores, remarked approvingly after attending a performance of *Carmen,* an opera in four acts with spoken dialogue, "It is necessary to Mediterraneanize music."

After the humiliating Franco-Prussian War of 1870, many French composers took up traditional instrumental forms, such as the symphony, in their search for a new French music. César Franck (1822–1890), born in Belgium but active in France, Camille Saint-Saëns (1835–1921), and several younger composers sought to raise French music to a new level of achievement. In Italy, as ever, opera remained the predominant genre, but now composers began to abandon the older conventions—the predictable set numbers and the subordination of the orchestra to the soloists—in favor of continuous stretches of music and a more ambitious use of the orchestra. In the closing decades of the century a strikingly realistic style known as **verismo** came into favor in opera. *Cavalleria rusticana* by Pietro Mascagni (1863–1945) and *Pagliacci* by Ruggero Leoncavallo (1857–1919), still popular in the repertory today, are outstanding examples of the new style. Giacomo Puccini (1858–1924) moved even more boldly toward realistic settings and stark, dramatic situations in his operas *La bohème* (1896), *Tosca* (1900), and *Madame Butterfly* (1904).

Finally, the end of the century brought tonality, which had served composers for centuries, to the brink of its demise, a development we shall examine in more detail in Part VI. Composers sensed, too, that the aesthetic of expression—the lifeblood of romanticism—had been exhausted. Eager to break decisively from the grip of romanticism, they began to turn away from the legacy of the nineteenth century to seek new philosophies of music for a new, modern age.

Suggested Listening

Brahms: Symphony No. 1
★_____: *Variations on a Theme of Haydn,* Op. 56a
Bruckner: Symphony No. 4
★Dvořák: Symphony No. 9 *(From the New World)*
★Grieg: *Peer Gynt* Suite No. 1, Op. 46
Liszt: *Faust* Symphony
_____: Piano Sonata in B minor
★Mahler: *Lieder eines fahrenden Gesellen (Songs of a Wayfarer)*
_____: Symphony No. 4
★Musorgsky: *Boris Godunov,* Prologue
_____: *Pictures at an Exhibition*
Smetana: *Má Vlast (My Fatherland)*
Strauss: *Till Eulenspiegels lustige Streiche (The Merry Pranks of Till Eulenspiegel)*
★_____: *Tod und Verklärung (Death and Transfiguration)*
★Tchaikovsky: *Romeo and Juliet*

Note: Works marked with an asterisk are the principal works discussed in the chapter.

PART VI THE TWENTIETH CENTURY

EUROPEAN HISTORY AND CULTURE	AMERICAN HISTORY AND CULTURE	EUROPEAN AND AMERICAN MUSIC
		1874–1951: Schoenberg
		1881–1945: Bartók
		1882–1971: Stravinsky
1872: Monet, *Impression: Setting Sun (Fog),* exhibited 1879		**1894:** Debussy, *Prelude to the Afternoon of a Faun*
	1878: Edison patents the phonograph	
1888: Seurat, *Une Parade de Cirque*	**1888:** Eastman hand camera	
1889: Eiffel Tower completed		
1898: Radium discovered		
1899: Freud, *The Interpretation of Dreams*		**1899:** Joplin, *Maple Leaf Rag*
1901: Marconi's wireless transmission across Atlantic Ocean	**1901–1909:** Presidency of Theodore Roosevelt	**1902:** Debussy, *Pelléas et Mélisande*
1905: Einstein's Special Theory of Relativity	**1903:** First flight of Wright brothers	
1907: Picasso, *Les Demoiselles d'Avignon*		
1908: "Cubism" coined		**1908:** Bartók, *Fourteen Bagatelles*
1909: First Futurist Manifesto		**1909:** Schoenberg, *Book of the Hanging Gardens;* Mahler, *Das Lied von der Erde*
1912: Duchamp, *Nude Descending a Staircase*	**1913–1921:** Presidency of Woodrow Wilson	**1910:** Stravinsky, *The Firebird;* Vaughan Williams, *Fantasia on a Theme by Thomas Tallis*
1914–1918: First World War		**1911:** Stravinsky, *Petrushka*
1916: "Dada" coined		**1912:** Schoenberg, *Pierrot lunaire*
1917: Bolshevik Revolution in Russia		**1913:** Stravinsky, *The Rite of Spring*
		1914: W. C. Handy, *St. Louis Blues*
		1915: Ives, *Concord* Sonata
	1919: Prohibition Amendment	**1917:** Prokofiev, *Classical Symphony*
1921: Picasso, *Three Musicians*	**1920:** Women's suffrage	
1922: Joyce, *Ulysses;* T. S. Eliot, *The Waste Land*		**1923:** Berg, *Wozzeck;* Varèse, *Hyperprism*
1924, 1929: Surrealist manifestos		**1924:** Gershwin, *Rhapsody in Blue*
1925: First commercial recordings	**1925:** Fitzgerald, *The Great Gatsby*	
1926: Demonstration of television in England; sound motion pictures	**1927:** Flight of Lindbergh across Atlantic; *Show Boat*	**1927:** Louis Armstrong, "Struttin' with Some Barbecue"
1926–1953: Regime of Stalin in Russia	**1929:** Faulkner, *The Sound and the Fury;* Stock Market Crash	**1928:** Webern, *Sinfonie,* Op. 21
		1930: Stravinsky, *Symphony of Psalms*
1928: Discovery of penicillin	**1933–1945:** Presidency of Franklin Delano Roosevelt	**1931:** Varèse, *Ionisation*
		1935: Gershwin, *Porgy and Bess*

BACKGROUND FOR THE TWENTIETH CENTURY

As the twentieth century draws to a close, no one has yet proposed a term to describe adequately its music, art, and literature. For some time, the term *modernism* was used to describe new directions in the arts. That term conveyed the sense of a sharp break from the nineteenth century—not just in the arts, but also in science, technology, and,

EUROPEAN HISTORY AND CULTURE	AMERICAN HISTORY AND CULTURE	EUROPEAN AND AMERICAN MUSIC
1929: Great Depression begins		
1932: Huxley, *Brave New World*		
1933: Hitler Chancellor of Germany		**1936:** Bartók, *Music for Strings, Percussion and Celesta*
1936: Chaplin, *Modern Times*	**1939:** Steinbeck, *The Grapes of Wrath;* Mitchell, *Gone with the Wind*	**1937:** Shostakovich, Fifth Symphony
1936–1939: Spanish Civil War		
1939–1945: Second World War	**1940:** Hemingway, *For Whom the Bell Tolls*	**1944:** Copland, *Appalachian Spring*
1945: Atom bombs dropped on Hiroshima and Nagasaki; United Nations; beginning of the "Cold War"	**1941:** Welles, *Citizen Kane;* Pearl Harbor	**1947:** Charlie Parker, "Embraceable You"; Babbitt, Three Compositions for Piano
1948: First applications of the transistor; State of Israel; apartheid established in South Africa		**1948:** Hindemith, *Das Marienleben* (second version)
1949: Orwell, *1984;* People's Republic of China		
1950–1953: Korean War	**1950:** McCarthy Committee on Un-American Activities	
		1952: Boulez, *Structures I;* Cage, *4'33"*
		1953: Stravinsky, Septet
1954: Beckett, *Waiting for Godot*	**1954:** *Brown* v. *Board of Education*	**1954:** Britten, *The Turn of the Screw;* Stravinsky, *In memoriam Dylan Thomas*
1955: Salk vaccine for polio		**1956:** Stockhausen, *Gesang der Jünglinge*
1957: First Sputnik launched by Soviet Union		**1957:** Boulez, *Le marteau sans maître*
1960s: Accelerating development of computers	**1960:** Hitchcock, *Psycho*	**1960:** Penderecki, *Threnody to the Victims of Hiroshima*
1961: Berlin Wall	**1962:** Cuban missile crisis	
	1963: President Kennedy assassinated	
	1964: Civil Rights Act	**1964:** Riley, *In C;* first commercial synthesizers
1966: Chinese Cultural Revolution	**1965:** Escalation of American involvement in Vietnam	**1967:** Beatles, *Sergeant Pepper's Lonely Hearts Club Band*
	1968: Martin Luther King assassinated	
1969: Fellini, *Satyricon*	**1969:** First man on the moon	**1969:** Berio, *Sinfonia*
	1973: Watergate scandal; Vietnam peace accord	**1972:** Rochberg, Third String Quartet
		1983: Zwilich, Symphony No. 1
1986: Accident at Chernobyl nuclear reactor, Soviet Union		
1989: Opening of Berlin Wall		

indeed, the very quality of life. In music, modernism reflected a reaction against the romantic tradition. As we saw in Part V, romanticism had been by no means a coherent "movement"; the term itself was interpreted with widely different meanings, and romanticism had had an impact on different countries at different times. Still, certain persistent views had given continuity to the work of the romantics, especially the view that art involved a highly personal, subjective experience and that the artwork was shaped by the emotional attitudes of the artist. So the term gained currency over time.

Eiffel Tower, symbol of the modern age.

Claude Monet, *Impression, Setting Sun (Fog)*, 1872, exhibited 1879. Notice Monet's use of broad brushstrokes and his subordination of line to atmosphere and mood. The term *impressionism* was coined to suggest the tenuous nature of such paintings.

The term *modernism*, on the other hand, fails to accommodate satisfactorily the wildly varying trends in "modern" art or to reflect its frenzied pace of change. Rather, a host of divergent movements have made up the patchwork of twentieth-century art. We may review here some of the "isms" often applied to these movements.

The closing decades of the nineteenth century had prepared the way for bold departures in the visual arts, especially in painting. *Impressionism* was one movement that gained recognition in the 1870s and 1880s. The impressionists, including the Frenchmen Claude Monet, Auguste Renoir, and Edgar Degas, studied the ever-changing effect of light on objects and sought to capture a sense of evanescent reality by means of rapid, often broad brushstrokes. They deliberately subordinated line and structure to color and the play of light. Their subjects often featured natural, open-air settings—for example, landscapes, rivers, haystacks, lily ponds, or the setting sun, as in Monet's celebrated *Impression: Setting Sun (Fog)*, exhibited in 1879.

Georges Seurat, *Une Parade de Cirque* (1888). The scene is the area outside a French circus where the ringmaster and a clown perform a sideshow to attract an audience. They are accompanied by a trombonist and, in the background, by four other depersonalized musicians (the one on the extreme left is cut off). The figures watching the spectacle represent a cross section of Parisian society. Note the solitary fifth figure, whose outline resembles that of the musicians in the background.

In the *postimpressionism* of the 1880s and 1890s, a second group of painters carried impressionism further. The most experimental, Georges Seurat, made a careful study of color theory and used a highly regular brushwork in his canvases. Viewed close up, his paintings appear to be a sea of precise points or dots of color. Viewed from a distance, the points merge into recognizable shapes and figures. There is an order and logic about Seurat's paintings. Devoid of romantic allusions, they depict carefully balanced groups of figures, immobile and expressionless, fixed in time. Moreover, as if to celebrate modern life, Seurat and other postimpressionists painted scenes of contemporary life in Paris, which itself was undergoing rejuvenation and modernization. Seurat's *Une Parade de Cirque* (1888) offers a view of a sideshow for a circus, complete with the ringmaster, a clown, a trombonist (and other musicians), and a cross section of Parisian society drawn to the event.

Impressionism and postimpressionism signaled that painters had come to view their art in fundamentally new ways. Then, with the turn of the century, the visual arts

Pablo Picasso, *Three Musicians* (1921). A masterpiece of cubism, Picasso's canvas presents three musicians from a variety of perspectives, creating a vibrant visual rhythm. The figures are based on stock characters of the *commedia dell'arte*. (Pablo Picasso, "Three Musicians," 1921 (summer). Oil on canvas, 6'7" by 7'3¾". Collection. The Museum of Modern Art, New York.)

underwent an authentic revolution. The Spanish painter Pablo Picasso (1881–1973), in association with the French artist Georges Braque, devised a radically new approach, later dubbed *cubism*. Though the cubists painted real objects from the visible world, they undermined the centuries-old illusion of perspective, by which a flat canvas was intended to suggest a three-dimensional space. Instead, they broke up objects and figures into cubelike, multidimensional facets, all carefully arranged on the canvas. In a related

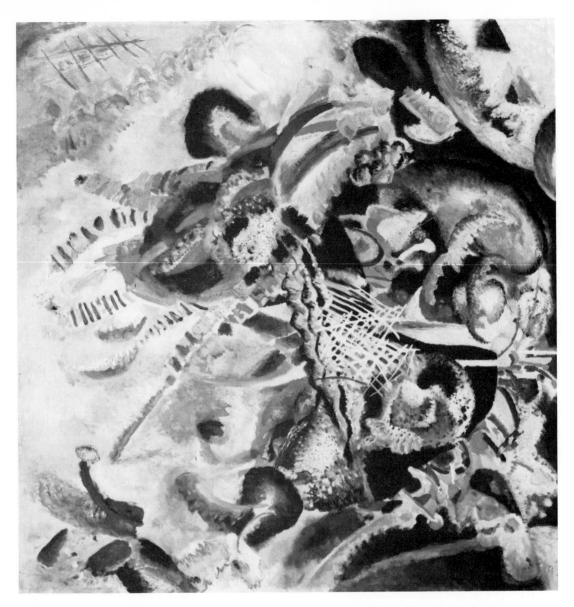

Wassily Kandinsky, *Great Fugue* (1914). A counterpoint of abstract curvilinear forms and colors fills this expressionist canvas of 1914, which Kandinsky likened to a fugue.

development, they began to assemble various objects, such as scraps of newspaper and pieces of wood, into artworks known as *collages*. The effect of all these experiments was to redefine and open up the boundaries of painting in a determined break from the traditions of Western art.

The movement called *futurism,* which took shape in the years before the outbreak of World War I, was an exploration of the dynamic quality of modern life. The futurists were a group of Italian artists and writers who chose subjects that highlighted the excitement and violent energy of modern machines and figures in motion. Like the impressionists, postimpressionists, and cubists, however, the futurists still treated real subjects and objects in their art.

Other movements led the arts away from realistic representation. In the closing decades of the nineteenth century, a new direction arose in *symbolism,* which manifested itself in the French poetry of Charles Baudelaire, Paul Verlaine, Arthur Rimbaud, and Stéphane Mallarmé. The symbolists emphasized the suggestive power of words and preferred in their poetry intimate, subjective dream states to objective narrative. They were especially drawn to music and found inspiration in the motivic networks of Wagner's music dramas. In the visual arts, striking experiments were undertaken in Paris by Henri Matisse, who headed a group of artists labeled in 1905 the *fauves* (a derogatory term meaning "wild beasts"). Matisse worked with flat planes of vibrant—to many, shocking—color to achieve unsettling distortions.

In Germany, the *expressionists* eliminated all suggestion of real objects in their paintings. Bold swatches of contrasting color and colliding fantasies of irregular lines and curvilinear shapes characterize the art of the leading expressionist, Wassily Kandinsky (1866–1944), a Russian active in Munich, who titled some of his works after musical terms and concepts. The expressionists asserted their subjective independence from an objective world—Kandinsky spoke of following an "inner voice" in his work; in a sense, their art was an art of subjective moods and impressions taken to an extreme, an art seen through the distorted lens of the artist's psychic world.

The exuberant spirit of experiment and liberation that had informed the art of the early twentieth century was crushed by the horrors of the First World War. In the postwar years, a disillusioned generation of artists and writers sought release in an art of negation, in an absolute break with the failed past. *Dadaism* (from "dada," coined in 1916 as a nonsense word for "hobbyhorse") was one of many arts of protest. Its aim was to free art once and for all from the constraints of nineteenth-century values, those same values that had led the world to destruction. A chief practitioner of this kind of artistic nihilism was Marcel Duchamp, who painted the Mona Lisa with a mustache and who constructed "readymades" out of randomly encountered objects such as snow shovels or bicycle wheels. With deliberately radical, anti-intellectual inclinations, the dadaists introduced all sorts of objects, concepts, and ideas into the art of the postwar years. Related to dadism, and no less radical, was *surrealism,* a movement first announced in 1917 and proclaimed by manifesto in 1924. Surrealism was an art of "psychic automatism"; the surrealists sought to unleash the free play of the mind, its dreams and fleeting thoughts, and to reveal the truths of the unconscious through free association. Surrealism came of age during the 1930s and 1940s but lost some of its force after the devastation of the Second World War.

In numerous ways, the arts of the twentieth century (including music, as we shall see) reflected or reacted against the social, political, and historical forces that shaped the modern world. Of course, those forces had already made an impact by the end of the nineteenth century. The map of the world had been transformed as the great powers (including England, France, Italy, the United States, and, under the iron leadership of Bismarck, the newly proclaimed German Empire) embarked on imperialist ventures in the Pacific and in Africa. The behavior of the great powers seemed to confirm the revolutionary theories of evolution of Charles Darwin (1809–1882), which gained currency as the century closed. Darwin's notion, that human beings shared with the lower orders of life the struggle for existence, was used to justify worldwide indulgence in national self-aggrandizement.

To many, the theory of evolution amounted to an assault on traditional religion. The theories of Sigmund Freud (1856–1939) brought an equally profound upheaval in views about the nature of human beings. Darwin's theories, as interpreted by many, de-idealized, deromanticized, and displaced human beings from their favored position in conventional theology. Freud's theories made them subject to the irrational forces of the subconscious. His interpretations of dreams and the role of sexuality in human behavior revealed for objective study a chaotic world that nineteenth-century thinkers had not imagined or had not dared to confront.

All this ferment propelled the arts onto strange new paths leading to unpredictable destinations. Within only a few decades, painters had abandoned the traditional use of perspective and realistic subjects, poets/writers had begun to plumb the unconscious, and many composers, as we shall see, had abandoned the time-honored system of tonality. A catastrophic world war (1914–1918), all too soon followed by a second (1939–1945), had forever altered the old political and social orders. In the following decades, new waves of an increasingly adventuresome avant-garde would arise, made up of shifting alliances of writers, artists, composers, and philosophers. Abstract expressionism, existentialism, op-art, pop-art, "happenings," "performance art," "computer art," "postmodernism"—succeeding generations would explore new paths of artistic experimentation and would continue to make bold artistic statements that frequently defied meaning.

And yet the arts have survived as an indispensable gauge of the human condition—though at a price. As the arts grew bolder in their demands, more abstract in their nature, and more elusive in their meaning, a chasm widened between artists and their audiences. That alienation became especially meaningful for music and for the revolution in sound it has engendered.

15

MUSIC IN THE TWENTIETH CENTURY

*F*or centuries, composers had based their music on tonal relationships built around the triad, universally recognized as the fundamental consonant sonority. The music of Purcell and Corelli, of Bach and Handel, of Haydn, Mozart, and Beethoven, of Schumann and Brahms, and of Wagner and Verdi all obeyed the laws of the system of tonality. The series of major and minor scales, of keys and key relationships, and of triadic harmonies were integral to that system. During the course of the nineteenth century, however, composers extended the tonal system considerably and, in doing so, subjected it to increasing stress. Wagner and Liszt, in particular, made significant contributions to new applications of tonality: In stretches of Wagner's music dramas, one is hard pressed to assign a particular key; and, in his later years, Liszt produced enigmatic, at times bizarre, compositions in which he deliberately avoided tonal principles of organization. By the end of the century, tonality was on the verge of collapse.

THE REJECTION OF TRADITIONAL TONALITY

In Chapter 14 we examined how some nineteenth-century composers began to experiment with scales outside the major and minor scales of the tonal system, such as the five-tone pentatonic scale (p. 362) and other scales of folk music. Another special scale, known as the **whole-tone scale,** began to be used more and more frequently toward the end of the century. The whole-tone scale divides the octave into six whole tones (or whole steps) instead of into the traditional mixture of seven whole and half steps. It is a symmetrical scale in which no one pitch stands out as a tonic note; rather, the ear accepts all the notes of the scale as equally important:

Whole-tone Scale

The unfamiliar, exotic sound of the whole-tone scale appealed greatly to composers seeking to enrich their music and to avoid what was perceived more and more as the routine sound of music based on major/minor scales. During the nineteenth century, the whole-tone scale was exploited with considerable daring by Liszt, and then used by later nineteenth-century Russian composers and, finally, by a younger generation of French composers who lived on into the new century. The following excerpt, from a piano prelude of 1909 by the French composer Claude Debussy, is based entirely on pitches drawn from the whole-tone scale illustrated above; the use of the scale produces a shimmering, luminescent quality:

Debussy: Voiles (Veils)

The Italian composer Ferruccio Busoni (1866–1924) went even further in proposing the development of new scales. In his provocative treatise of 1907, *Sketch of a New Esthetic of Music,* he proposed all manner of new scales, including the following, calculated to avoid the familiar patterns of the traditional major and minor scales:

Busoni: "Artificial" Scales★

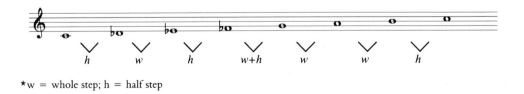

★w = whole step; h = half step

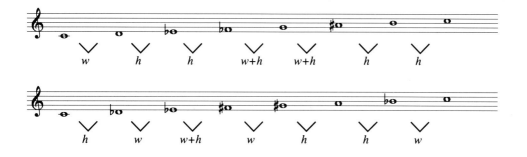

Busoni worked out 113 different scales, all of which divided the octave in irregular ways. He even encouraged composers to explore scales based on microtonal intervals smaller than the half step (for example, "third steps" instead of half steps). With these suggestions, Busoni was well ahead of his time, even though he did not actually compose with such scales. Indeed, Western composers did not explore microtonal scales thoroughly until after the Second World War.

A rash of new harmonies filled the music of the new century, in a striking departure from the traditional triad. One technique involved superimposing triadic harmonies drawn from different keys, a technique known as **polytonality,** with often striking results. A famous polytonal passage occurs in Igor Stravinsky's ballet *Petrushka* (1911); in the following excerpt, performed by a piano, the treble part outlines harmonies from the key of C major; the harmonies of the lower part are from a distant, clashing sharp key (F-sharp major):

Stravinsky: Petrushka

C major harmonies

F# major harmonies

By combining these two triadic levels, Stravinsky creates a swirling mass of dissonant sound to portray Petrushka, a wooden puppet who, having come to life, curses his grotesque features. By themselves, the C major and the F-sharp major harmonies sound familiar enough; when they are combined, however, they create a distinctly unsettling, modern effect.

In another technique, known as **pandiatonicism,** composers extended individual triads by adding pitches drawn from their underlying scales. For example, in the following harmony, a C major triad is extended by other pitches from the C major scale to form a pandiatonic harmony that is dissonant by traditional standards:

Pandiatonic Harmony

Passages with pandiatonic harmonies appeared frequently in the works of twentieth-century composers. Here, for example, is another excerpt from Stravinsky's *Petrushka,* a boisterous Russian Dance that features blocks of pandiatonic harmonies:

Stravinsky: Petrushka

As novel as these harmonic experiments were, they all retained the triad as the underlying harmonic unit. But some composers decisively turned away from the triad to test harmonies based on radically new principles of organization. For example, the enigmatic Russian composer Alexander Skryabin (1872–1915), who associated pitches with colors, preferred harmonies of superimposed fourths, so-called **quartal harmonies,** rather than triads built up of thirds. For Skryabin, the following sonority, highly dissonant by conventional measurement, was imbued with mystical associations:

Skryabin: "Mystical" Chord

The new freedom in harmonic organization reached a decisively dissonant extreme in the music of Arnold Schoenberg, who about 1908 began to write music without key signatures—indeed, without any vestiges of tonal triads. To signify his emancipation from traditional pitch relationships and harmonies, Schoenberg labeled his iconoclastic music *pantonal*. It was Schoenberg who came forward to proclaim that the tonal system had become obsolete and that all conventional notions of consonance and dissonance had lost their meaning.

How Schoenberg arrived at those conclusions is a complicated chapter in the evolution of musical style roughly spanning the period from 1890 to 1910 (see also pp. 424–426). We can only summarize it here: Schoenberg's early, tonal music, in which he retained key signatures, became increasingly chromatic through the liberal introduction of altered pitches lying outside the scale of the key. He kept that music barely within the bounds of tonality by introducing occasional, recognizable cadences firmly rooted in triadic harmonies. The move to pantonality came when he omitted those triadic cadences, yielding music—to many, seemingly chaotic music—with no basis in tonality.

Most listeners greeted Schoenberg's pantonal compositions with incomprehension, bewilderment, frustration, and uncompromising rejection. Music without tonal references was something like a gravity-free field, and perplexed listeners struggled to grasp strands of disordered pitches that at best sounded vaguely familiar. In place of Schoenberg's preferred "pantonal," the pejorative term **atonal** ("without tonality") came to be applied to this music.

Through the First World War and beyond, Schoenberg continued to work in the free atonal idiom, creating challenging compositions of unprecedented harmonic complexity and difficulty. Then, in the 1920s, he devised a new approach to composition that allowed him a rigorous control over his atonal music. Known variously as **twelve-tone music, serial music,** or **dodecaphonic music,** this fundamentally new approach to composition marked Schoenberg's second great contribution to twentieth-century music.

In much of his earlier atonal music, Schoenberg had sought to avoid immediate or proximate repetitions of individual pitches. He sensed that such repetitions would emphasize certain pitches and possibly create the impression of a tonal center. Instead, he desired to maximize the newfound equality of all twelve pitches of the chromatic scale. To achieve that goal in a systematic way, he marshaled the twelve pitches into what became known as a **tone row** or **series.** This is an atonal arrangement of the twelve chromatic pitches, all of which have to be used up before any one is repeated. Simple mathematics shows that Schoenberg had at his disposal an enormous number of possible tone rows. But he rigorously selected only those rows that gave few, if any, hints of tonal associations. Thus, his rows employ a seemingly free mixture of intervals that may be drawn from seconds, thirds, fourths, fifths, sixths, and sevenths; concentrations of thirds and fifths, which would suggest triads, are avoided. We take the liberty here to compose a **twelve-tone row** as an example (the twelve pitches are marked off according to their order in the chromatic scale):

Twelve-Tone Row

P–0 (PRIME)

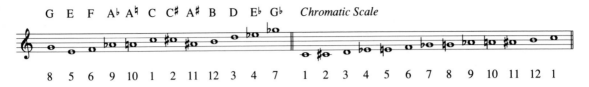

G E F A♭ A♮ C C♯ A♯ B D E♭ G♭   *Chromatic Scale*

8 5 6 9 10 1 2 11 12 3 4 7   1 2 3 4 5 6 7 8 9 10 11 12 1

In Schoenberg's system, such a tone row, known as the original prime row (or P–0), could be transposed up or down by any number of half steps, though after eleven transpositions, the basic row would return an octave above or below. Here, for example, is our row transposed up seven half steps (which we label P–7):

P-7 (ROW TRANSPOSED UP 7 HALF STEPS)

D B C E♭ E♮ G G♯ E♯ F♯ A B♭ D♭

The twelve forms of the row (that is, the original row and its eleven transpositions) constitute the twelve "prime" (P) forms. By performing the prime forms backwards, Schoenberg produced twelve **retrograde** (R) forms of the row. The next example presents our original row backwards, yielding the retrograde of the original row (labeled R–0):

R-0 (RETROGRADE OF ORIGINAL ROW)

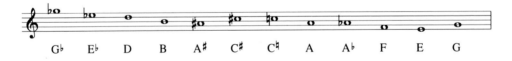

G♭ E♭ D B A♯ C♯ C♮ A A♭ F E G

Then, by inverting the contours of the original prime form of the row, Schoenberg could produce the **inversion** (I) of the row, thus (compare the contours of I-0 with those of P-0):

I-0 (INVERSION OF ORIGINAL ROW)

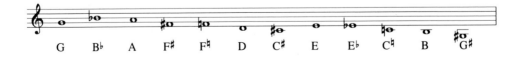

G B♭ A F♯ F♮ D C♯ E E♭ C♮ B G♯

Finally, by executing the inverted form in reverse, Schoenberg obtained the **retrograde inversion** (RI):

RI-0 (RETROGRADE INVERSION OF ORIGINAL ROW)

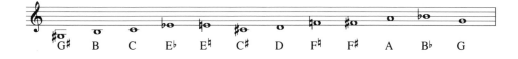

G♯ B C E♭ E♮ C♯ D F♮ F♯ A B♭ G

Each of the four basic forms—prime, retrograde, inverted, and retrograde-inverted—were transposed to yield twelve row forms, for a total of forty-eight rows. Those rows provided the raw material for Schoenberg's serial music. To create his twelve-tone compositions, Schoenberg first determined the shape of the row and generated a row table that listed all the transformations and transpositions of the row. After completing this "precompositional" planning, he then selected the particular rows to be used in the composition and developed thematic and harmonic material compatible with the row forms.

In the new twelve-tone music, the tone row thus served as the generating and unifying element. Melodies and harmonies were shaped to conform to the requirements of the row. One might assume that such music was nothing more than a mechanical process, in which individual pitches moved according to their position in predetermined, fixed tone rows, forcing the composer to sacrifice a large measure of spontaneity and the element of choice. But such a view is an oversimplification, because some aspects of the row forms were indeed left open to the composer's choice. For example, the registers of the twelve pitches (that is, their various octave levels) in a given tone row were not fixed. The following example presents the same prime form we introduced earlier, with its pitches in different registers:

P-0 WITH ALTERED REGISTERS

G E F A♭ A♮ C C♯ A♯ B D E♭ G♭

Nor were the nonpitch aspects of the row—its rhythms, dynamics, and articulation markings—predetermined. All this latitude Schoenberg and his followers used to great advantage. On rare occasions, he even permitted himself minor deviations from the row.

Of all the new alternatives to tonality that have emerged in the twentieth century, the twelve-tone system has perhaps proved to be the most enduring. Schoenberg introduced the system to his students Alban Berg and Anton Webern, who explored its potential further during the 1930s and 1940s (see pp. 428–434). In Europe and the United States, many composers adopted the technique after the Second World War and developed it in new directions. Today, Schoenberg's early twelve-tone works are often looked upon as classic examples of what became accepted as a standard compositional technique. Once considered revolutionary and at the vanguard of the radical extreme, the twelve-tone system more and more was embraced by the musical establishment.

NEW EXPERIMENTS WITH NONPITCH ELEMENTS

Polytonality, pandiatonicism, free atonality, and twelve-tone technique—all exemplify the development by twentieth-century composers of new alternatives to late nineteenth-century tonality. All represented solutions to the problem of structuring pitch in the new music. But the urge to experiment extended to nonpitch aspects of music as well. Such aspects as rhythm, dynamics, and timbre came to be viewed as independent musical determinants no longer subordinate to pitch. The emancipation of these elements is comparable to the emancipation of pitch that Schoenberg brought about with his atonal revolution.

In the early decades of the twentieth century, certain composers eagerly seized on nonpitch components as new resources for modern music. In their approach to meter and rhythm, for example, they tended to avoid regular, recurring patterns in favor of asymmetrical subdivisions. One technique involved a constant redefinition of the bar line. In the following passage from Igor Stravinsky's *Renard* (1922), the meter continuously alternates between $\frac{2}{4}$ and $\frac{3}{4}$, disrupting the regular downbeat and invigorating the music with a dynamic, rhythmic energy. (As we shall see in Chapter 16, Stravinsky was capable of far greater rhythmic complexity than this relatively simple example.)

Stravinsky: Renard

Bassoon

sempre ff e marcatissimo (always ff and most marked)

In another technique, known as **polyrhythm,** composers built up layers of competing rhythms and meters, creating a kind of complex rhythmic counterpoint—and at the same time making heavy demands on the musicians who performed their scores and on the audiences who struggled to appreciate them. All these techniques reflected an effort to break the tyranny of the traditional, regular bar line.

Some composers scrutinized the quality of sound itself—its timbre and color. In 1911 Arnold Schoenberg coined the term **Klangfarbenmelodie** (a composite German noun meaning "sound-color-melody") in an attempt to elevate the timbral properties of sound to the level of a compositional principle. In his most developed example of this concept, Schoenberg experimented with repeating single pitches or chords several times while subtly changing their instrumental scorings to suggest a kind of kaleidoscope of sound. The shifting colors of the music became the determining compositional factor, usurping the traditional role of pitch.

In many ways, the pioneers of modern music were irreverent nonconformists who avoided the trappings of tradition—and whatever was familiar in music. The eccentric French composer Eric Satie (1866–1925), protesting the tedium of academic musical forms, composed pieces with such tongue-in-cheek titles as *Trois morceaux en forme de poire* ("Three pieces in the form of a pear"). Stravinsky opened his ballet *Le Sacre du printemps (The Rite of Spring)* with an unheard-of high bassoon note and filled his radical score with unprecedented demands on the orchestra and the dancers. Schoenberg chose for his extraordinary atonal music lurid, expressionist subjects as shocking as the new sounds themselves.

The decisive break from nineteenth-century music took place in the early years of the twentieth century. After the First World War, as if in reaction to the prewar radicalism, the leading composers redefined their relation to earlier traditions. Some, seeking to incorporate the musical values of earlier periods in their modern music, embraced a direction known as neoclassicism. Others continued to cultivate national styles and were influenced by developments in popular music, especially by the rise of American jazz. Then, the end of the Second World War, followed by accelerating gains in technology, triggered a new round of experimentation that proved to be more radical than that before the First World War. In brief, experimentation and renewal have been the watchwords for the development of music in our century, which we shall now examine more closely.

Suggested Listening

Debussy: *Voiles,* from *Préludes,* Book I (whole-tone formations)
Schoenberg: *Farben (Colors),* from Five Orchestral Pieces, Op. 16 (*Klangfarbenmelodie*)
_____: Piano Suite, Op. 25 (twelve-tone style)
_____: Three Piano Pieces, Op. 11 (free atonal style)
Stravinsky: *Petrushka* (polytonal and pandiatonic harmonies)
For additional listening, see pp. 434, 453–454, 476, 509.

16

THE MUSICAL REVOLUTION

*P*aris and Vienna were the centers for the revolution in music that greeted the twentieth century. In Paris, Claude Debussy, rejecting the complex tonal thickets of nineteenth-century German music, developed a fundamentally new approach based on nuance and suggestion. In Paris, too, Igor Stravinsky won notoriety for several singular scores animated by powerful treatments of rhythm and meter. In Vienna, Arnold Schoenberg introduced his radical atonal music, which was taken up and further refined by Alban Berg and Anton Webern. The results of all these experiments varied strikingly; yet, composers in Paris and Vienna shared a common desire: to discard the familiar in sound and to explore unfamiliar, innovative means in their work. Not just in music but in the other arts as well, Paris and Vienna seethed with revolutionary ideas and attitudes; there, the seeds of modernism were sown.

CLAUDE DEBUSSY

Initially, there was little in the background of Claude Debussy (1862–1918) to suggest the decidedly modernist bent his music would take. He trained at the Paris Conservatoire, still an academic bastion, and eventually competed successfully for the Prix de Rome, which he viewed as a "national sport." His obligatory two-year tenure in Rome did little to inspire him; like his predecessor Berlioz, Debussy became impatient with the conventional routine he found there. As did many of his contemporaries, Debussy made the popular pilgrimage to Bayreuth to hear Wagner's music dramas, but he came

Claude Debussy.

to find them overtaxing and inflated; for him, Wagner's "Religion of Art" had become a "Religion of Luxury." Much of Debussy's own music sounds like a calculated reaction to the Germanic qualities of Wagner's music—a rejection of its dense, contrapuntal structure, its thick orchestration, its unrelieved seriousness, and its romantic aesthetic. Debussy preferred a music of simpler means and of carefully coordinated understatement.

As a young man, Debussy visited Russia, where he was employed as a pianist by Madame von Meck, Tchaikovsky's eccentric patroness (see p. 378). While there, he studied the scores of Russian composers, especially Musorgsky's. The highly individualistic music of that composer, with its folklike modal melodies and rhythms, made a deep impression on Debussy. No less significant for him was the opportunity in 1889 to hear an ensemble of Indonesian musicians at the International Exposition in Paris. These performers employed non-Western scales in their music, including five-note pentatonic scales (see p. 362). The fresh sounds of this non-Western music and its idiosyncratic rhythmic patterns revealed further possibilities for Debussy to explore. Yet another influence on him was the music of Liszt, especially Liszt's later, experimental music, in which Debussy found imaginative applications of whole-tone scales and harmonies. Intrigued by all these possibilities, Debussy strove to fashion a new kind of modern music. Summing up his sense of artistic liberation, he declared that he had lost all faith in the C major scale, with its trappings of traditional tonality.

Along with his contemporary Maurice Ravel (1875–1937), Debussy is often labeled an impressionist. But the comparison does not totally withstand a critical review. Debussy did not associate directly with impressionist painters such as Monet, Renoir, or Degas. Though he often used graphic titles for his compositions—for example, *Voiles* (which means either "veils" or "sails") and *Reflets dans l'eau (Reflections in the Water)*—Debussy's inspiration seems to have been more poetic than pictorial. Still, the shimmering textures of his compositions, dappled with soft, shifting harmonies, suggest at least superficially the play of variegated color in impressionist paintings.

Debussy once declared that for him the ideal music drama would consist of a loose series of dreamlike scenes. His belief in the power of music as a suggestive, symbolic art reveals his special affinity to the French symbolist poets; indeed, there is much to argue for labeling Debussy a symbolist rather than an impressionist. Debussy not only knew the work of the symbolists intimately but also enjoyed fruitful associations with some members of the group, including Stéphane Mallarmé (1842–1898). Mallarmé's symbolist poem "Prélude à l'après-midi d'un faune" ("Prelude to the Afternoon of a Faun") inspired Debussy to compose an orchestral work that, despite its date of 1894, is accepted as one of the seminal works of twentieth-century modernism.

PRELUDE TO THE AFTERNOON OF A FAUN (1894)

During a first hearing, Debussy's Prelude may strike the listener as a rather unassuming composition. It lasts only about ten minutes, it rarely attains a *fortissimo* dynamic level, and it uses an orchestra decidedly small in comparison with the Wagnerian standard of the day. There are prominent parts for woodwinds and strings (the latter generally play with their mutes applied), but the brass section is reduced to just four horns. Debussy adds the unobtrusive colors of two harps and, near the end of the work, introduces a few notes for "antique" cymbals, small finger cymbals that produce a delicate tinkling. He blends all these instrumental colors to evoke the pastoral, blissful world of Mallarmé's faun.

In the poem, the faun, a deity in Roman mythology that appears as half man and half goat, dreamily recalls his erotic adventures with some woodland nymphs. But Mallarmé never makes clear whether those adventures have actually happened or whether the faun merely imagines them. The poem moves back and forth between the present and the faun's recollection of the past. (In the poem, this is underscored by alternating roman and italic types.) The poem is suggestive rather than literal. Debussy translates that suggestiveness into subtle musical allusions and gentle distortions of melodies and harmonies—transporting us to the faun's amoral, sylvan world.

The work begins with a gesture of understated but striking originality: a solo for flute (*a*), the modern symbol of the panpipes familiar to us in Greek mythology (see study diagram). Suggesting a free improvisation, this remarkable solo is tonally amorphous and begins with nothing more than a descending chromatic fragment that retraces its steps:

Debussy: Prelude to the Afternoon of a Faun

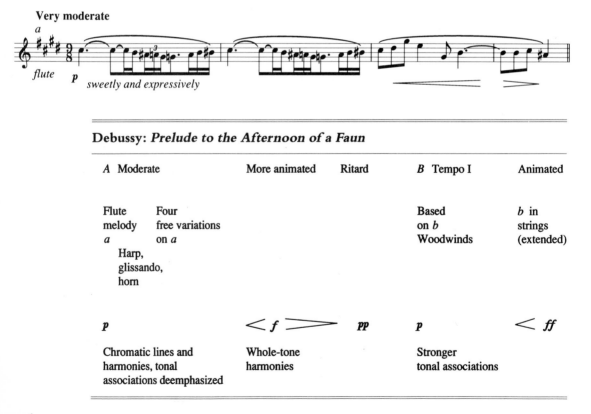

Debussy: *Prelude to the Afternoon of a Faun*

A Moderate		More animated	Ritard	B Tempo I	Animated
Flute melody *a*	Four free variations on *a*			Based on *b* Woodwinds	*b* in strings (extended)
Harp, glissando, horn					
p		*< f >*	*pp*	*p*	*< ff*
Chromatic lines and harmonies, tonal associations deemphasized		Whole-tone harmonies		Stronger tonal associations	

The flute is answered by a woodwind chord, by a harp glissando suggesting, perhaps, a cool summer breeze, and by a melodic fragment from the horn. From those materials, Debussy builds up the first section of the Prelude (*A*), which can best be described as a series of variations on the opening material. The variations are freely conceived; Debussy is careful to avoid direct repetition of thematic or harmonic material, for that would lull his audience into an easy familiarity with the music and negate the poem's play between the imagined and the real. Instead, the music seems to suggest the faun's idyllic existence in a timeless mythic-poetic world. With each recurring variation, Debussy changes the faun's theme in some way, by altering its melodic shape or by revising the supporting harmonies or orchestrations.

The *A* section contains four variations on the opening flute solo, suggesting four shifting perspectives in the faun's memory of the past. Throughout the section, the harmonies are intensely chromatic, effectively blurring our sense of a tonal center, though individual triads do emerge occasionally in Debussy's rich vocabulary of harmonies. In addition, Debussy incorporates whole-tone scales (p. 404), which underscore the effect of suspended tonality. A gentle swell and an increase in tempo prepare us for the central portion of the composition (*B*), which is based on a haunting tonal melody (*b*). First played by the woodwinds and then repeated and extended by the strings, the melody describes two descending phrases separated by an especially wide, expressive leap:

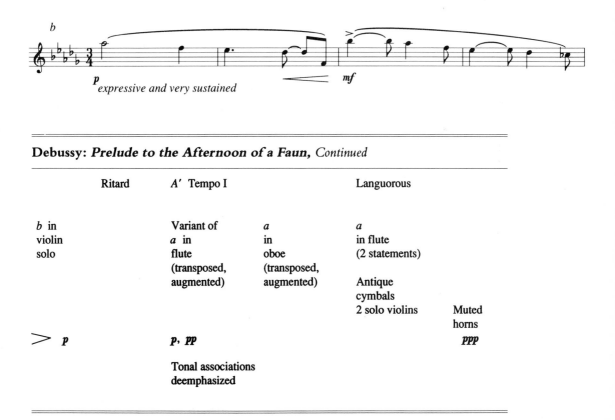

Debussy: *Prelude to the Afternoon of a Faun,* *Continued*

	Ritard	A′ Tempo I		Languorous	
b in violin solo		Variant of *a* in flute (transposed, augmented)	*a* in oboe (transposed, augmented)	*a* in flute (2 statements) Antique cymbals 2 solo violins	Muted horns
	> *p*	*p*, *pp*			*ppp*
		Tonal associations deemphasized			

Could this contrasting section, much of which can be analyzed in conventional tonal terms, represent the faun's recall of his experience? Perhaps, though in due course Debussy returns to the opening flute melody (*A'*), again heard in four varied statements. The first two are in lengthened note values, accompanied by harp arpeggiations and gentle chords in the strings. The third and fourth are in a more langorous tempo, accompanied by the antique cymbals and two solo violins. Finally, in the closing bars, muted horns sound a distant echo of the faun's melody, in a last, fleeting reminder of his world.

Most of Debussy's relatively short, though profoundly influential, career unfolded in Paris. There he wrote several major orchestral works with evocative titles; among them are the three Nocturnes (1899), *Nuages (Clouds), Fêtes (Festivals),* and *Sirènes (Sirens);* the "symphonic sketch" *La Mer (The Sea,* 1905); and the ballet *Jeux (Games,* 1913). He also composed a great deal of piano music, in which he adapted the technical resources of the instrument to his new musical language. Moreover, Debussy tried his hand at opera, including some unsuccessful attempts based on the tales of Edgar Allan Poe, a favorite of the symbolist poets. For all Debussy's reaction to Wagner's music dramas, his one complete opera, *Pelléas et Mélisande* (1902), has some curious ties to *Tristan und Isolde:* Like Wagner's drama, *Pelléas* is a story of illicit love; what is more, it uses Wagner's method of continuous music and referential motives (see p. 344). But there the resemblance ends. Debussy's drastically understated score is enveloped by soft orchestral tissues of sound; it employs a musical language of veiled intimation rather than direct statement. (In a similar way, the stage action takes place behind a gauze screen, through which our perceptions of the drama are filtered.) Finally, there are hardly any *forte* passages in the entire score, in decided contrast to Wagner's full-blown scores.

It was Debussy who led the French revolt against the domination of music by German composers. Not all his countrymen supported his efforts, however. The French composer Camille Saint-Saëns, for example, found his music pretty but unrefined, and asserted that the *Prelude to the Afternoon of a Faun* was no more a piece of music than a painter's palette was a finished painting. Indeed, there is an unfinished, spontaneous quality about Debussy's scores, as if he systematically broke music down into its components and quickly reconstituted them in novel patterns to create his compositions. In rejecting traditional notions about the unified work of music, notions heavily influenced by nineteenth-century German music and thought, Debussy emerged as a composer of the modern age. And the unassuming melodic nuances of his faun prepared the way for even more far-reaching and revolutionary experiments in sound.

IGOR STRAVINSKY

Russian by birth, Igor Stravinsky (1882–1971) enjoyed a long, distinguished life that extended across nearly three fourths of the twentieth century. After abandoning a career in law, he turned for instruction in composition to Rimsky-Korsakov, who, following Musorgsky's death in 1881, had become the most celebrated and versatile Russian composer by the beginning of the twentieth century. In 1910 Stravinsky arrived in Paris, where he began to develop his own revolutionary approach to composition. His first

Pablo Picasso, *Portrait of Igor Stravinsky,* May 24, 1920.

major efforts were the scores for two ballets: *The Firebird* (1910) and *Petrushka* (1911). These works were commissioned by Sergey Dyagilev (1872–1929), the enterprising impresario of the Ballets Russes, a Russian company based in Paris. Dyagilev, himself an innovator, experimented with replacing the set dance numbers of traditional ballet with extended passages of pantomime, thereby giving the composers whose works he commissioned great latitude with which to experiment. Dyagilev sought out the most gifted dancers, composers, and choreographers available for his ambitious productions. For his part, Stravinsky continued to compose scores for the Ballets Russes—including *The Rite of Spring* (1913), *Pulcinella* (1920), *The Wedding* (1923), and *Oedipus Rex* (1927);

other twentieth-century composers who wrote for the company included Debussy, Ravel, and Richard Strauss.

Stravinsky's *Firebird,* based on a Russian fairy tale, tells of the adventures of Tsarevich Ivan, who encounters a benevolent fairy endowed with magical powers (the Firebird) and the evil magician Kastchei. The lush orchestration of the score and its opulent tonal language suggest the music of Rimsky-Korsakov, whose popular orchestral suite, *Scheherazade* (1888), was revived by Dyagilev in a ballet production of 1910. Stravinsky turned to other Russian folk tales as his source for *Petrushka,* a ballet about a hapless puppet who comes to life and mingles with a group of colorful characters at a Russian fair during Shrovetide, the period immediately preceding Ash Wednesday. In many ways, the score of *Petrushka* is more adventuresome than that of *The Firebird.* Stravinsky uses snatches of Russian folk tunes and short melodic motives that are repeated in various configurations to produce a hypnotic effect. He is bolder, too, in his treatment of harmony, as his experiments in polytonality attest (see p. 405). In long passages of so-called pandiatonic harmony, he freely mixes notes of the C major scale without regard for their conventional consonant or dissonant values.

Stravinsky's major masterpiece of those years, however, and the work that sharply divided public opinion, was the third score he wrote for Dyagilev, *Le Sacre du printemps* (*The Rite of Spring,* 1913). Its composition entailed about two years of arduous work; the composer referred to its creation as an "act of faith." The premiere of the ballet threw the audience into an uproar and provoked a brawl between its supporters and its detractors. The main action of the ballet, in which a sacrificial virgin dances herself to death, was deemed scandalous by many members of the audience. They, and other audiences as well (see below), also found Stravinsky's score scandalous. Driven by unrelenting barbaric rhythms, it called for an enormous orchestra (including quintuple woodwinds, considerably augmented brass, and boisterous percussion sections) and was filled with primitive-sounding melodic utterances and clamorous harmonies. Uncompromisingly modern in its style and message, *The Rite of Spring* asserted a defiant rejection of traditional tonality and of the romantic aesthetic of expression that had permeated music of the nineteenth century.

The music of *Le Sacre du Printemps* baffles verbal description. To say that much of it is hideous as sound is a mild description. There is certainly an impelling rhythm traceable. Practically it has no relation to music at all as most of us understand the word.

London, *The Musical Times,* August 1913

Le Sacre du Printemps has as its essential purpose to be the most dissonant and discordant piece of music ever written. Never has the cult of the wrong note been practiced with such industry, zeal, and fury. From the first measure to the last, whatever note one expects never arrives, but rather the note to its side, which should not arrive. Regardless of what one is led to expect from a preceding chord, one hears another chord. These chords and notes are chosen expressly to give the impression of acute and nearly atrocious falseness.

Paris, *Le Temps,* June 1913

THE RITE OF SPRING (1913)

To have appreciated *The Rite of Spring,* Stravinsky's audience in 1913 would have been required to abandon almost all standard preconceptions about melody, harmony, form, and musical unity—something that audience, and indeed most trained musicians of the time, were unprepared to do. Unlike Debussy, who coolly explored new musical resources through understated nuance, Stravinsky assaulted his listeners head-on, violating their expectations and subjecting them to daring effects deemed at the time to be beyond the bounds of musical propriety. *The Rite of Spring* suggests a forceful realignment of the rudiments of music, reshaped into a startlingly new order. Like Debussy's *Prelude to the Afternoon of a Faun,* Stravinsky's score reflects a mythical, timeless world. We are introduced to that world, however, not by innuendo but by a forceful musical confrontation. Instead of the smooth sensuality of Debussy's faun, we experience the raw energy of a pagan Russian tribe.

The first part of the ballet, titled "The Adoration of the Earth," consists of an orchestral introduction and seven scenes connected without pause:

Introduction

Augurs of Spring: Dance of the Adolescents

The Game of Abduction

Spring Rounds

Games of the Rival Tribes

Procession of the Sage

Adoration of the Earth

Dance of the Earth

We look here at two celebrated passages, the "Introduction" and the "Augurs of Spring" (see study diagram, pp. 422–23).

Stravinsky opens the Introduction with an ungainly solo for bassoon, ranging into the instrument's uppermost register. This solo sounds more like a raucous croaking than a refined theme; it is, in fact, built upon a short motive of eight notes, which are immediately repeated with different rhythmic values (*a*):

Stravinsky: The Rite of Spring, "Introduction"

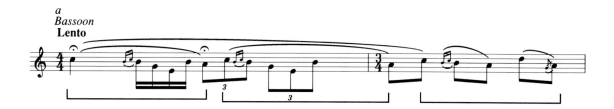

Stravinsky: *The Rite of Spring,* "Introduction" and "Augurs of Spring"

Introduction

Based on *a* (Bassoon solo)	Free Counterpoint in woodwinds, increasing in complexity, with variants of *a*	⌢	Return of *a* (Bassoon)	Transition *b'* in strings

p, mf

Notice how the two pauses (⌢) in the first measure violate the sense of a regular meter and how the revised rhythmic values of the motive violate the sense of a regular beat. This free treatment of meter and rhythm is one of the distinctive traits of Stravinsky's style.

The bassoon is joined first by a horn and then by clarinets, with each instrumental part asserting its own independent line in a kind of rough-hewn, primitive counterpoint. Stravinsky juxtaposes the bassoon motive with swelling and diminishing masses of woodwinds—suggesting the awakening of spring (as Stravinsky described it, the "sublime uprising of Nature renewing herself"). Eventually, he amasses a dense woodwind choir of polyphony, with an irregular order of lines, meter, and rhythm. Suddenly, the music halts and the opening bassoon solo returns. Now a short motive plucked by the strings,

brings a transition to the first scene, the "Augurs of Spring: Dance of the Adolescents."

If the Introduction is a free study in counterpoint, the Augurs of Spring is a free study in a rhythmic ostinato: a single dissonant chord (*b*), repeated with numerous, varying rhythmic groupings, that drives the dance forward with the pulsing lifeblood of spring. Here, we are forced to concentrate on pure rhythm as the essential principle of musical organization:

Stravinsky: *The Rite of Spring,* "Introduction" and "Augurs of Spring,"
Continued

Augurs of Spring: Dance of the Adolescents

Irregular chords *(b)* alternating with *b′* *f* (English horn)	*c* (Bassoons) against chords	⌒	*d* (Horn) against *b′*	*e* (Trumpets) against *b′*	*d* (Flute) against *b′* Several repetitions, *f* with buildup of full orchestra
	f		*mp*	*mp*	

Stravinsky: The Rite of Spring, "Augurs of Spring"

The dissonant chord is vigorously repeated by the strings. After two regular measures, strident exclamations from the horns (shown by accents in the example) mark off the pulses into asymmetrical rhythmic groupings. The chord itself contains two traditional, though unrelated, triadic harmonies; taken together, they form a sonority unrelenting in its dissonant quality. There is no easily apparent rhythmic pattern to the chords; animating the music is the energy of the basic pulse—the chord—and not the predictable pattern of a traditional meter.

Occasionally, Stravinsky redistributes part of the chord in a broken arrangement (*b'*), previously heard in the strings in the transition to the scene,

heard now in the throaty register of an English horn. In addition, against the dissonant ostinato, Stravinsky sets short, crisp fragments of melodies. We may discern three fragments (*c, d,* and *e*), which are presented by the bassoons, the horns, and the trumpets:

Against the throbbing, dissonant backdrop of the chords, these fragments stand out as tonal reference points. They appear like incipient folk songs just starting to take shape in a world of primitive sounds and harmonies. Additional instruments join in as the dance gains momentum. There is no definite break to mark the conclusion of the dance; instead, the music eventually spills over into the next dance, the "Game of Abduction," which surges forward in an animated Presto tempo, also driven by a relentless rhythmic power.

ARNOLD SCHOENBERG

Of all the modernist composers working during the early twentieth century, Arnold Schoenberg (1874–1951) ultimately found critical recognition the most elusive. Nevertheless, though his music has failed to win the popular acceptance eventually accorded the works of Debussy and Stravinsky, his deep influence on twentieth-century music is unarguable. Schoenberg lived and worked primarily in Vienna and Berlin until 1933, when he emigrated to the United States to escape persecution by the Nazis. His early, tonal compositions were in the late romantic vein of Wagner's chromatic musical language. They found an early culmination in one quite successful work, *Gurrelieder* (*Songs of Guerre;* 1903, revised 1911), a tonal work on a grandiose scale for orchestra, soloists, chorus, and narrator based on Danish symbolist poetry. (The orchestra required for this work was so large that Schoenberg had special music paper prepared to accommodate the score.) In the increasingly adventurous compositions that followed, such as the Chamber Symphony, Op. 9 (1906), Schoenberg experimented with quartal har-

Arnold Schoenberg, *Self Portrait* (1911).

monies (chords built on the interval of the fourth) and applications of whole-tone scales and harmonies.

In 1908, in a decisive break with tonality, Schoenberg abandoned all use of conventional tonal harmony. The critical work in which he took this fateful step was the Second String Quartet, Op. 10, a work that still displayed key signatures and recognizable, if attenuated, tonal features during the course of its first three movements. In the finale, Schoenberg added a soprano solo to sing a setting of the expressionist poem "Entrückung" ("Enrapture") by Stefan George. Here she announces prophetically, "Ich fühle Luft von anderen Planeten" ("I feel a fragrance from other planets"); here, Schoenberg finally liberated himself totally from the use of tonality.

In his revolutionary new music, Schoenberg came to avoid the immediate or adjacent repetition of pitches, preferring to work with all twelve chromatic pitches on an equal basis. His own term for this practice, pantonality, implied that the twelve pitches were to be treated equally. Schoenberg was convinced that pantonality (or atonality, as it became known) was the logical successor to the outworn system of tonality. He regarded his work as the inevitable result of historical development, and he took great pains to relate it to the work of such earlier composers as Wagner and Brahms. Although on a first hearing Schoenberg's music seems worlds apart from the music of the late nineteenth century, the links are there, even if obscured in the thick textures of atonal melodies and harmonies. For example, Schoenberg developed his themes in much the same way as Wagner or Brahms did; the difference is that Schoenberg's themes lack triadic reference points. Moreover, Schoenberg continued to cultivate the traditional forms favored by Brahms—sonata form, the rondo, the scherzo, for example—as well as the hallowed forms of high counterpoint—fugue, passacaglia, and canon. Despite his revolutionary abandonment of tonality, Schoenberg was unwilling to disassociate himself completely from the great tradition of German music.

PIERROT LUNAIRE (1912)

Schoenberg's embrace of atonality corresponded roughly to the movement in German art known as expressionism, centered mainly in Berlin, Vienna, and Munich. An associate and friend of the Russian expressionist painter Wassily Kandinsky, Schoenberg himself painted lurid expressionist canvases and was preoccupied with discovering relations between sound and color. Just as the expressionist painters distorted and ultimately abandoned realistic images, so Schoenberg distorted and ultimately rejected tonality. With its emphasis on expression, even if of an increasingly nonrealistic kind, expressionism was descended from German romanticism; similarly, Schoenberg's provocative and highly emotional atonal works were linked to the romantic aesthetic of musical expression. But the subjects of Schoenberg's expressive urges were new: the psychological world of hidden, tormented feelings, the dark underside of the artist's subconscious, for example. Thus, *Erwartung* (*Expectation,* 1909), a monodrama for soloist and orchestra, is about the hallucinations of a betrayed lover; and the expressionist song cycle *Das Buch der hängenden Gärten* (*The Book of the Hanging Gardens,* 1909) is rich in sexual innuendos and Freudian associations.

One of the most impressive—and difficult—works from Schoenberg's atonal period is *Pierrot lunaire (The Moonstruck Pierrot),* based on a volume of symbolist poetry by the Belgian Albert Giraud. Composed and performed in 1912 (after some forty rehearsals), the work is scored for a soprano and a small chamber ensemble of five players, some of whom double on other instruments, for a total of eight: piano, flute, piccolo, clarinet, bass clarinet, violin, viola, and cello. Each song is scored for a different ensemble that includes soprano and instruments. The soprano does not sing in the conventional sense but, rather, uses a technique Schoenberg called **Sprechstimme** ("speaking voice"), somewhere between speaking and singing. (In the soprano part, the notes are designated with small x's, thus: ♩.) Sprechstimme became a powerful technique in Schoenberg's battery of expressionist devices. By its nature it involves distortion: It has accurately notated rhythmic values, but it is meant to be executed with uneven inflections in pitch. Thus, it is neither singing nor speaking; the Sprechstimme part may be profitably compared to the role of a singing actress or, conversely, an acting singer.

The cycle has a pathetic subject: the stock pantomime character Pierrot, in this version a moonstruck clown who is revealed as a rejected, terror-stricken creature when his comic mask is taken away. The chamber ensemble weaves an intricate web of atonal sound around the recitation of the poetry, which contains a series of shocking images. The twenty-one poems are loosely arranged in three groups of seven each, and Schoenberg has set them to terse miniature movements that generally last only a few minutes. Each poem consists of three stanzas of four, four, and five lines, with recalls, in the second and third stanzas, of lines from the first stanza.

The poem of the fifth song, "Valse de Chopin," compares a melancholy waltz of the Polish composer to the bloodstained lips of an invalid. Of course, Chopin's waltz is not identified, and there is no waltz melody clearly recognizable as such in Schoenberg's music. Rather, the song is a freely composed atonal setting that suggests a grossly distorted version of a waltz. Here are the text and translation:

Wie ein blasser Tropfen Bluts	Like a faint drop of blood
Färbt die Lippen einer Kranken,	coloring the lips of an invalid,
Also ruht auf diesen Tönen	There rests in these tones
Ein vernichtungssücht'ger Reiz.	A charm in search of negation.
Wilder Lust Akkorde stören	Chords of wild lust disturb
Der Verzweiflung eisgen Traum.	The icy dream of despair.
Wie ein blasser Tropfen Bluts	Like a faint drop of blood
Färbt die Lippen einer Kranken.	coloring the lips of an invalid.
Heiss und jauchzend, süss und schmachtend,	Hot and rejoicing, sweet and pining,
Melancholisch düstrer Walzer,	melancholy, dark waltz,
Kommst mir nimmer aus den Sinnen!	You never leave my senses!
Haftest mir an den Gedanken,	You seize my thoughts
Wie ein blasser Tropfen Bluts!	Like a faint drop of blood.

This macabre movement is scored for flute, clarinet, and piano. For the third stanza, Schoenberg replaces the clarinet with the bass clarinet, whose lower range effectively distorts the original timbre of the ensemble. The music, in the triple time $(\frac{3}{4})$ of a waltz, begins with what sounds like a piano accompaniment to a clarinet line, possibly the beginning of a waltz melody. In the poem, the waltz is interrupted by "chords of wild lust"; in the music, the melody and accompaniment give way to irregular piano chords. The stanzas are separated by instrumental interludes, and a postlude in which the piano accompaniment dies away suggests the end of the somber waltz.

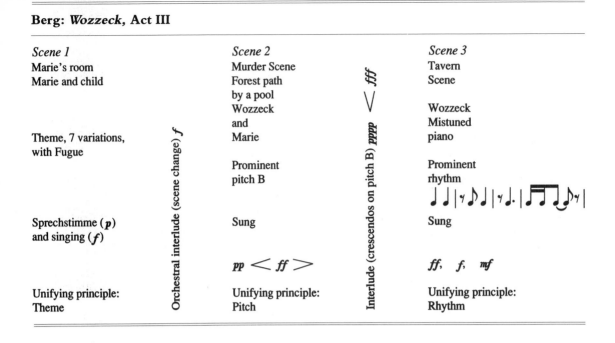

Scene 1	*Scene 2*		*Scene 3*
Marie's room	Murder Scene		Tavern
Marie and child	Forest path		Scene
	by a pool		
	Wozzeck		Wozzeck
	and		Mistuned
Theme, 7 variations,	Marie		piano
with Fugue			
	Prominent		Prominent
	pitch B		rhythm
Sprechstimme (*p*)	Sung		Sung
and singing (*f*)			
	pp < *ff* >		*ff, f, mf*
Unifying principle:	Unifying principle:		Unifying principle:
Theme	Pitch		Rhythm

(Orchestral interlude (scene change) *f*)

(Interlude (crescendos on pitch B) *pppp* < *fff*)

ALBAN BERG

Alban Berg (1885–1935), considerably less prolific than Schoenberg, composed slowly and carefully. Along with Anton Webern, he studied composition with Schoenberg in Vienna; there, under Schoenberg's watchful eye he developed his own approach to atonality and eventually adopted the twelve-tone system. Berg's principal works include two masterpieces, the operas *Wozzeck* (1923) and *Lulu* (Berg left *Lulu* unfinished; its first "complete" performance, with the third act reconstructed from the composer's sketches and drafts, was not given until 1979). He also produced works for chamber ensembles, a violin concerto, orchestral pieces, and songs. Although Berg's music is on the whole atonal, it does not exhibit Schoenberg's severe, uncompromisingly dissonant style. Rather, it is replete with flowing melodies and voluptuous harmonies, and even carries some fleeting touches of tonality. There is a romantic warmth about Berg's music that makes it, perhaps, more accessible than the music of either Schoenberg or Webern.

WOZZECK, ACT III

The expressionist opera *Wozzeck* is based on a fragmentary drama by the nineteenth-century playwright Georg Büchner (1813–1837); Berg himself arranged the libretto. The protagonist is a common soldier brutalized by a military doctor who practices a sadistic kind of therapy. Taunted by his commanding officer and roughed up by a drum major, he is finally driven insane by the imagined or real faithlessness of his mistress,

Berg: *Wozzeck,* Act III, *Continued*

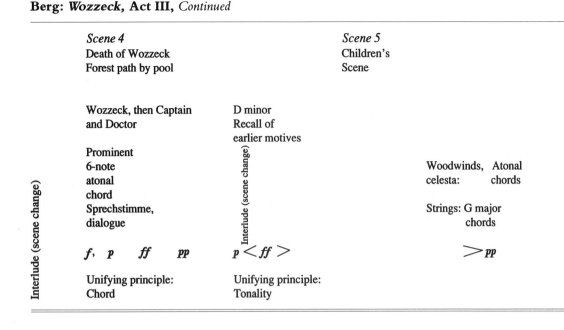

Scene 4		Scene 5
Death of Wozzeck		Children's
Forest path by pool		Scene

Wozzeck, then Captain and Doctor — D minor, Recall of earlier motives

Prominent 6-note atonal chord

Sprechstimme, dialogue

Interlude (scene change)

Interlude (scene change)

Woodwinds, celesta: Atonal chords

Strings: G major chords

$f, \; p \quad ff \quad pp$

$p < ff >$

$> pp$

Unifying principle: Chord

Unifying principle: Tonality

Marie. In the last act, Wozzeck stabs Marie and drowns himself. A modern everyman, Wozzeck is the victim of a dehumanized world. Berg conceived the idea of the opera during the First World War (he served in the Austrian army), and the music reflects the despair of postwar Germany and Austria.

The design of *Wozzeck* is highly complex. Each act consists of five scenes connected by orchestral interludes. Each scene, in turn, is loosely based on a traditional form or genre (for example, suite, sonata, rondo, fugue, passacaglia) or on some unifying musical technique. In addition, throughout the opera, a network of atonal motives, reminiscent of Wagner's leitmotives, gives the music a tight thematic unity. The rich variety of styles includes full-fledged tonal music with key signatures as well as atonal music and the use of a twelve-tone row. Finally, the vocal passages range from spoken dialogue and conventional singing to Sprechstimme.

Berg organizes the five scenes of the third act around different musical elements and textures, a technique calculated to highlight the unfolding events of the drama (see study diagram). Scene 1, for example, consists of a theme and seven variations that culminate in a fugue on two subjects. Marie, alone with her child, delivers passages from the Bible in Sprechstimme and then, in singing voice, begs God for mercy; she has been unfaithful to Wozzeck. The successive distortions of the theme through the variations parallel her mounting feelings of guilt, and Berg's use of counterpoint gives the somber scene a religious cast.

In Scene 2, Marie encounters Wozzeck, who has arrived to confront her with her infidelity. He remarks on the red color of the moon, which rises like an expressionist symbol. Then, in a frenzy, he stabs her to death. This scene is organized around the pitch B, which gradually comes to the forefront of the atonal music with the approach of Wozzeck's murderous act. In the interlude, during the scene change, the orchestra plays two tremendous crescendos based on that pitch alone, driving home the reality of Wozzeck's insanity.

In Scene 3, Wozzeck appears in a tavern. Concentration on a single pitch gives way to concentration on a rhythmic pattern. On the stage, a mistuned piano (again, a kind of expessionist distortion) plays a polka with this erratic rhythm that serves to unify the scene: ²₄♩♩ | ⸗ ♪♪ | ⸗ ♩. | ♫♫ ♪ ⸗ |.★ A barmaid notices blood on Wozzeck's hand, and the other characters join in to torment Wozzeck, who rushes out in a drunken stupor.

In Scene 4, Wozzeck returns to the murder scene searching for his knife. Finding it, he casts it into a pool and then wades into the water to wash the blood from his hand. In his delirium, he imagines that the water is blood. At last he drowns. His commanding officer and doctor pass by but decide to ignore sounds coming from the pool and leave the scene. (They communicate in spoken dialogue.) Berg sustains the eerie mood with this six-note atonal chord, repeated over and over in various transpositions and scorings:

Berg: Wozzeck, *Act III, Scene 4*

SIX-NOTE CHORD

The final scene is prefaced by an extended interlude in D minor. Here, tonality operates as the unifying element. Berg drew on an unfinished symphony for this interlude, and the music, in a lush, glowing minor key, could almost have been written by Mahler. Berg brings together the leading motives of the opera in an especially passionate passage. As the curtain goes up, we see Wozzeck's and Marie's child playing with some children. They are interrupted by another group of children, who announce that the boy's mother is dead. As they run off to see the corpse, the child continues to play on his wooden horse; oblivious to the tragedy, he sings, "Hop, hop." The music closes with soothing G major chords in the strings against oscillating chromatic harmonies in the flutes and the celesta.† The tragedy seems to have come full circle, perhaps to be repeated some day by the child; indeed, the closing chord also appears at the conclusion of Acts I and II, reinforcing the sense of dramatic circularity. Berg gives us, at last, no final resolution—only a comment about the modern human condition.

★ The normal rhythmic pattern of the polka is ²₄ ♫♫ ♫♫ | ♫ ♩.

† A small, boxlike keyboard instrument. When the keys are depressed, hammers strike a series of metal plates to produce a transparent, shimmering sound. Invented in 1886, the celesta was used by Tchaikovsky in the "Dance of the Sugar-Plum Fairy" from the ballet *Nutcracker* (1892).

ANTON WEBERN

Anton Webern (1883–1945), Schoenberg's other principal disciple, attended the University of Vienna, where he studied musicology and wrote a thesis about the music of Heinrich Isaac, a sixteenth-century Flemish composer. He worked in and near Vienna for most of his life. Despite all the thorny modernisms of his music—which many listeners find impenetrable—Webern was a serious student of the history of music. Like Schoenberg, he took great pains to justify in historical terms the revolutionary character of his music.

While still at the university, Webern began to study privately with Schoenberg. His early music includes a few essays in a tonal idiom. In fact, his first opus was a Brahmsian passacaglia in D minor for orchestra. But in 1908, under Schoenberg's influence, he abandoned tonality and began a series of stark atonal settings of expressionist texts. During this atonal period, Webern crafted compositions out of a minimum of notes, a few fragile seconds of sound that seem imposed on silence. This severe compression was rarely matched by Schoenberg or Berg, who generally worked on a much larger scale. In his approach to composition, Webern labored intensively over individual pitches, carefully coordinating their individual rhythmic values, dynamics, articulations, and registers, and thereby placing pitch and nonpitch elements on an equal basis.

Webern's aesthetic of music has been described as "unity through variation," or "constant variation." It was an aesthetic that demanded a new kind of hearing. In his compositions, he typically kept some element of the music constant while deliberately varying other elements. For example, he might repeat a rhythmic pattern with a different set of pitches, or he might repeat an atonal chord with different dynamic markings. Ironically, in searching for a metaphor to describe this unprecedented approach, Webern turned back to the nineteenth century, to Goethe's concept of the primeval plant—an organic, unified whole made up of disparate parts.

Many listeners find Webern's music abstruse and overly intellectual. Indeed, on first hearing, it sounds like a succession of isolated points of sound in no particular order; only after repeated hearings do the patterns begin to emerge. Without question, Webern's music is intellectually demanding and intricate, but perhaps no more so than the music of J. S. Bach. And, for all its intellectual rigor, it is infused with feeling. Webern's scores are filled with detailed expression markings and performance instructions, all directed to an expressive end. Not one note is superfluous.

When Schoenberg announced, in 1923, the development of his twelve-tone method of composition, Webern and Berg adopted the new system. At first, Schoenberg applied the technique cautiously. His early twelve-tone works (and those of Webern and Berg) typically use only one form of a tone row, perhaps with a few of its transpositions, as if the composer were just tentatively testing the system. Then, having gained confidence, Schoenberg went on, in the 1920s, 1930s, and 1940s, to apply twelve-tone composition to more ambitious instrumental works in the traditional genres and forms: for example, chamber music (String Quartet No. 3, 1927); theme and variations (Variations for Orchestra, 1928); and, from his American period when he settled in Los Angeles, concerto (Violin Concerto, 1936, and Piano Concerto, 1942).

Berg and Webern stamped their twelve-tone works with their own musical personalities. Berg was rather flexible in his use of row technique. For example, in his masterful twelve-tone Violin Concerto, finished in 1935 at the end of his life, he made overt references to tonality in the basic tone row, by building up much of the row from alternating minor and major triads.★ Webern, on the other hand, followed Schoenberg's practice more faithfully. Among his strict twelve-tone compositions are a string trio, a symphony, a chamber concerto, a string quartet, two sets of variations (for orchestra and for piano), and two cantatas. But unlike Schoenberg, Webern continued to work on a small scale; he continued to devise his tone rows with the same exacting care and inscrutable logic that he applied to the other elements of his music.

SINFONIE, Op. 21 (1928)

In comparison with the symphonies of Brahms or Mahler, Webern's sole work in the genre seems almost like an antisymphony. It consists of just two movements, and lasts, according to Webern's own timing, only about ten minutes. The first movement is in sonata form—not the full-fledged ternary form typically encountered in nineteenth-century music, but a simplified, binary form that derives from the eighteenth century: ‖:A:‖‖:B A':‖. The movement has no conventional theme; rather, all is derived from the tone row, which is repeatedly transposed and altered with respect to rhythm, orchestration, and register.

The orchestration, as well, is in marked contrast to nineteenth-century standards. Webern calls for a small orchestra of two clarinets, two horns, one harp, and strings in four (not five) parts: first violins, second violins, violas, and cellos. To these modest forces he rations out concise groups of notes, points of sound that collide with one another like molecules. Their interactions are not random, however; all derive from a series of rows to contribute to the unity of the work.

The tone row on which the symphony is based typifies that unity. It is a palindrome—that is, a tone row in which the intervals, or distances between the pitches, are the same forwards and backwards. Put another way, its second half presents a version of the first half in reverse order:

Webern: Sinfonie, *Op. 21, Tone Row (P-0)*

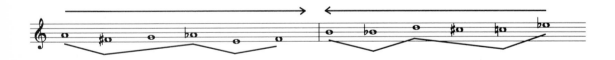

★ The last movement of the concerto employs a setting by J. S. Bach of the chorale "Es ist genug" ("It is enough").

Webern delighted in devising tone rows with special symmetrical properties; indeed, he almost seems to have taken as much trouble working out his tone row as he did in crafting the details of the whole symphony. The palindromic symmetry of the row is reflected in many ways throughout the course of the composition. At the exact midpoint of the first movement, for example, Webern writes a pause to remind us that the movement is half completed. And for the beginning of the *B* section, a short, sparse transition, he writes a passage that describes an exact musical palindrome, an extension of the palindromic properties of the basic row.

As if that were not enough, Webern imposes further order by unfolding the movement in canonic imitation, or, more precisely, as a double canon. Each canon includes two forms of the twelve-tone row, so that at its most complex the music presents four twelve-tone rows simultaneously:

Webern: Sinfonie, *Op. 21, First Movement*

The second row imitates the first, and the fourth row imitates the third, with the same succession of rhythms, registers, dynamics, and instruments. Here we see the logic behind Webern's pairings of instruments: The first violin can imitate the second violin (canon 2, mm. 6 and 8), the viola can imitate the cello (canon 2, mm. 3 and 5), the bass clarinet can imitate the clarinet (canon 1, mm. 6 and 8), and the first horn can imitate the second horn (canon 1, mm. 1 and 3). Spun out like four fine threads throughout the movement, the four series of rows describe a delicate, though strict, counterpoint. Every pitch follows the rigorous logic of the tone rows; yet, we can enjoy the music on a less cerebral level, as a crystalline, multifaceted structure of minute sounds that combine to create a remarkably taut and, in its way, flawless work of art.

In the second movement, a theme with seven variations, Webern continues to work with his fastidious symmetries. The theme, played in the clarinet with sparse accompaniment from the harp and horns, is another palindrome, and so is each variation. Variation 1 is for the string ensemble; Variation 2 erupts with a *forte* horn solo; Variation 3 contraposes two-note and three-note groupings throughout the orchestra; Variation 4, the midpoint of the movement, is restrained in tone; Variation 5 is driven by a restless rhythmic ostinato; Variation 6 is for wind instruments; and Variation 7, apportioned among the full ensemble, draws the work to a close with a series of carefully calculated ritards.

In his later years, Webern moved toward an even more abstract style and a more determined simplification of means. His life ended tragically in 1945: He was shot to death in the Austrian town of Mittersill during a curfew, after the armistice that ended the Second World War went into effect. Only in the 1950s was his significance fully realized, when a generation of younger composers began to emulate Webern's discipline and exquisite control. They were joined by the aging Stravinsky, who diligently studied Webern's twelve-tone works and found them to be elegantly cut diamonds.

Suggested Listening

Berg: Violin Concerto
★_____ : *Wozzeck*
Debussy: *La Mer*
_____ : *Pelléas et Mélisande*
★_____ : *Prelude to the Afternoon of a Faun*
_____ : *Préludes for piano*
Schoenberg: *Das Buch der hängenden Gärten*, Op. 15
_____ : Piano Concerto, Op. 42
★_____ : *Pierrot lunaire*
_____ : Three Pieces for Piano, Op. 11
Stravinsky: *The Firebird*
_____ : *Petrushka*
★_____ : *The Rite of Spring*
Webern: Concerto, Op. 24
_____ : Five Pieces for String Quartet, Op. 5
★_____ : *Sinfonie*, Op. 21

Note: Works marked with an asterisk are the principal works discussed in the chapter.

17

NEOCLASSICISM

To the audiences of 1913, Stravinsky's *The Rite of Spring,* with its brutish rhythms, jagged lines, and overwhelming power, must have seemed a willful assault on the foundations of the music itself. Schoenberg's atonal scores, too, must have seemed a pernicious foray into the unsettling and uncharted realm of modernism. Pioneers as they were, the early modernists were determined to break with the musical language of the late romantic style. Increasingly after the First World War, however, many of them began to think about tempering their iconoclastic bent and looking again at the traditions of the past, especially those of the eighteenth century (and earlier). The term used to describe this line of development in twentieth-century music is **neoclassicism.** Having declared their independence by deriving fundamentally new principles of musical organization, composers now found fresh inspiration in the forms, genres, and styles of an earlier, preromantic past.

This looking back to the past was not an act of slavish imitation but a highly selective process. Maurice Ravel wrote a minuet to suggest the style of Haydn (1909), and a piano suite, titled *Le tombeau de Couperin* (1917)★ to suggest the style of the French baroque harpsichordists. His countryman Darius Milhaud (1892–1974) composed a series of eighteen string quartets and numerous other works in such baroque and classical genres as the suite and the sonata. Richard Strauss, abandoning the discordant tone of his operas *Salome* and *Elektra,* revived the eighteenth-century German Singspiel (see

★ *Tombeau:* in the seventeenth century, a French poem or instrumental composition that commemorated the death of a nobleman or distinguished person.

p. 213) in his comic opera *Ariadne auf Naxos* (1916) and, furthermore, invoked the style and spirit of Mozart's *Marriage of Figaro* in the delightfully elegant music of *Der Rosenkavalier* (1911). The Brazilian Heitor Villa-Lobos sought to demonstrate similarities between the music of J. S. Bach and Brazilian folk music in a series of compositions for various scorings titled *Bachianas brasileiras* (1930–1945).

The scope of neoclassicism was broad. Composers revived the strict forms of counterpoint, including fugue and canon. (The first movement of Webern's *Sinfonie*, p. 433, evidences the renewed interest in counterpoint and, in a sense, could be viewed as neoclassical.) They rediscovered such genres as the baroque suite, concerto, and oratorio, and such standard classical forms as the sonata form, minuet, and rondo; in titling their music, they preferred to feature those genres and forms in lieu of vague, romantic programmatic titles. Employing an economy of means, they wrote for reduced orchestras and intimate chamber ensembles, shunning the sprawling scores of the late nineteenth century. (Stravinsky suggested that nineteenth-century orchestral composers had "overfed" audiences with music that was too rich.) The neoclassicists did not, however, return to traditional triadic tonality; their harmonies remained modern. To suggest the range of neoclassicism, we shall examine four works by composers with widely divergent styles.

SERGEY PROKOFIEV

After Stravinsky, the most significant Russian composer of the century was Sergey Prokofiev (1891–1953). He attended the St. Petersburg Conservatory before establishing himself as a concert pianist in Russia. In 1914 he met Sergey Dyagilev, for whom he wrote several ballet scores. One of them was a determinedly modernist work, *Le pas d'acier* (*The Step of Steel*, 1926), a glorification of the machine age. For some time, Prokofiev had the opportunity to live and work in the West; unlike Stravinsky, however, who eventually settled in the United States, Prokofiev decided to return to Russia for good in 1936. There, during the Stalinist era, he was subjected to criticism for what the state authorities perceived as "modernisms" in his music.

Prokofiev's style was a mixture of percussive rhythmic effects and lyrical melodies with characteristically wide leaps. A versatile composer, he wrote operas, ballets, seven symphonies, several concertos, chamber works, a wealth of piano music, film scores for the great Russian filmmaker Sergey Eisenstein, and a charming children's tale for narrator and orchestra, *Peter and the Wolf* (1936). Because Prokofiev chose to work in traditional Western instrumental forms, Stalinist critics branded him a formalist and admonished him to write patriotic music extolling the motherland and glorifying the aims of the socialist revolution. Among his works that won official approval were the ballet *Romeo and Juliet* (1936) and the Fifth Symphony, finished during the Second World War in 1944. The authorities refused, however, to approve a full-scale production of his opera *War and Peace* (1943), based on Tolstoy's novel; the opera had its first fully staged production in 1957, after the composer's death.

Picasso, *The Dance*. An economy of means is evidence of neoclassical tendencies in this work of 1925.

Although Prokofiev never allied himself with any particular style of composition, strong neoclassical tendencies are evident in his music, especially in some of his symphonies and chamber works. In fact, he called his First Symphony the *Classical*. In this exuberant student work of 1917, he meant to suggest how Haydn might have composed had he lived in the twentieth century. The result is a delightful example of how a twentieth-century composer sought to translate the classical style of the eighteenth century into modern terms.

SYMPHONY NO. 1, IN D MAJOR (*CLASSICAL*)

Prokofiev scored this symphony for a classical orchestra, with double woodwinds, two horns, two trumpets, timpani, and strings. (His one nonclassical indulgence was to use three timpani instead of two.) The symphony is in four movements and has key signatures. The first and fourth movements are in sonata form; the second (a slow movement) is in *ABA* form; and the third, curiously, replaces the classical minuet with a baroque dance, the **gavotte.**

Prokofiev begins with a rousing triadic figure, a stock figure used by Haydn and many other classical symphonists (*a*). The scurrying theme that follows is played by the strings:

Prokofiev: Symphony No. 1, in D major (Classical), *First Movement*

A flute then introduces the bridge subject (*b*), which prepares us for the dominant key:

The contrasting second theme (*c*) follows in the dominant key, in accordance with classical practice:

It appears in the high register of the violin, with a simple staccato accompaniment in the bassoon. In a distinctly modern departure from Haydn's mature style, however, are the gaping leaps in the melody and the "incorrect" harmonies implied by the accompaniment, a kind of humorous parody of the high classical style. Prokofiev carries this naive melody through three statements. For the closing section of the exposition, he takes up the opening material and ends with sweeping descending scales and a strong cadence on the dominant. Again departing from Haydn's practice, he does not repeat the exposition.

A bar of rest prepares us for the development. First, Prokofiev states *a* in the minor tonic and then leads *b* through a range of modulations. The second theme (*c*), which now undergoes development, is energetically exchanged between the violins and the bass. Finally, the music approaches what promises to be the recapitulation. Prokofiev does indeed bring back the opening material, but in the wrong key. This deliberate "error" is a device known as the "false reprise"; Haydn himself had used it to befuddle unsuspecting connoisseurs in his *London* Symphonies of the 1790s. After returning the music to the proper tonic, Prokofiev continues the recapitulation according to the traditional plan.

The slow movement, a Larghetto, is relatively simple in structure. Four measures of string chords introduce this singing melody in the high range of the first violins:

Prokofiev: Symphony No. 1, in D major (Classical), Second Movement

Repeated by the flute, the melody gives way to the central section of the movement, which is animated by a faster detached bass figure:

Gradually, the passage rises to a climax. The opening theme now returns, accompanied by the bass figure. The movement closes as it began, with chords in the strings. This final touch rounds out the Larghetto and gives it a sense of classical poise.

Why Prokofiev chose to use a gavotte instead of a minuet for the third movement is unclear. Unlike the stately minuet favored by Haydn and Mozart, the gavotte was a baroque dance in duple time with pastoral associations. Prokofiev's gavotte is a delightful movement, built on four-measure phrases, with the overall *ABA* plan of the Minuet and Trio. A deliberately light scoring supports a simple theme and chordal accompaniment. The theme itself begins with an upbeat followed by several energetic leaps:

Prokofiev: Symphony No. 1, in D major (Classical), Third Movement

The central *B* section features a simple melody performed over a drone bass, an allusion to the country origins of the gavotte. With the return of the opening section, Prokofiev reverses the instruments that carry the theme and the accompaniment. He gradually thins out the scoring and ends the movement with two pizzicato string chords.

The fourth movement is an orchestral *tour de force* that rushes along at breakneck speed. Its opening theme uses another arrangement of material based on the tonic triad, recalling Prokofiev's technique employed at the beginning of the first movement:

Prokofiev: Symphony No. 1, in D major (Classical), Fourth Movement

Prokofiev brings this ingratiating symphony to a close with rapid ascending major scales, a vivid reminder of his debt to the classical symphonists.

STRAVINSKY AND NEOCLASSICISM

From the end of the First World War to about 1950, Igor Stravinsky explored a variety of neoclassical procedures in an especially brilliant series of compositions that substituted intimate chamber ensembles and reduced orchestras for the gargantuan orchestra he had used in *The Rite of Spring*. This economy of resources is particularly evident in the "dramatic spectacle" *Histoire du soldat* (*The Soldier's Tale*, 1918), the *Symphonies of Wind Instruments* (for twenty-three winds; composed in 1920 in memory of Debussy), and the Octet for wind instruments (1923). After the war, Stravinsky worked primarily in France and in 1934 became a French citizen. But a series of commissions from the

United States led to American concert tours, and in 1939, on the eve of the Second World War, Stravinsky emigrated to the United States. He eventually settled in Los Angeles and became an American citizen.

According to Stravinsky's instructions, *The Soldier's Tale* is to be "read, played, and danced" by a narrator, a small group of instruments, and other actors and a dancer. The libretto tells of a hapless soldier who gives his fiddle to the Devil in exchange for a magical book, only to discover eventually that he has been outwitted. In the original production of 1918, the soldier appeared in the contemporary uniform of a Swiss army private, intended, appropriately, to symbolize a luckless victim of the First World War. The various movements of the score include a waltz; a ragtime, inspired by Stravinsky's discovery of American jazz; a tango; chorales; and marches, all clothed in distinctly modern, neoclassical styles.

The Octet for wind instruments illustrates Stravinsky's use of such classical forms as sonata form, theme and variations, and rondo. In a kind of manifesto, Stravinsky declared the work to be a "musical object" free of any "emotive qualities," by which he meant the subjective elements of the late romantic style. The absence of strings in the instrumentation is another indication of Stravinsky's new objectivity: He found the pure, clean sound of the winds ideally suited to his purpose. Moreover, the dynamic markings are limited to *piano* and *forte;* Stravinsky deliberately avoided a greater range of levels, as well as intervening dynamic gradations. In short, he intended the Octet to be an abstract work of art, stripped of all expressive nuance, and to be valued for its formal perfection.

Other neoclassical works borrow quite directly from eighteenth-century models. In the ballet *Pulcinella* (1920), for example, Stravinsky adapted material from the music of the eighteenth-century composer Giovanni Battista Pergolesi (see p. 148). The *Dumbarton Oaks* Concerto (1938) for chamber orchestra was inspired by his study of Bach's *Brandenburg Concertos.* The Symphony in C (1940) seems indebted to the symphonies of Haydn, whom Stravinsky revered as a "celestial power." Finally, in *The Rake's Progress* (1951), an opera with a libretto by W. H. Auden, Stravinsky returned to the operatic conventions of Mozart's time.

In still other neoclassical works, Stravinsky found inspiration in classical mythology and antiquity. Among those works are the ballets *Apollon musagète* (*Apollo, Leader of the Muses,* 1928) and *Orpheus* (1948), the melodrama *Perséphone* (1934) for speaker, soloists, and orchestra, and *Oedipus Rex* (1927). For *Oedipus Rex,* an opera-oratorio in Latin (with a libretto by Jean Cocteau), Stravinsky directed that the soloists appear on pedestals, to suggest the timelessness of Greek statues.

SYMPHONY OF PSALMS (1930)

Stravinsky's *Symphony of Psalms,* written for the fiftieth anniversary of the Boston Symphony, is not a symphony in the traditional sense. Rather, it consists of settings of three psalms for chorus and orchestra. The orchestra is made up of woodwind and brass sections, percussion (including harp and two pianos), and a curtailed string section of cellos and double basses. Absent are the lush sonorities of the violins and violas; instead, Stravinsky places in relief the clear sonorities of the woodwind and the brass. The texts of the psalms are declaimed in straightforward, chantlike melodic lines against orchestral material that features compact repeated figures, firmly anchored tonal references, and finely crafted counterpoint—all of which suggest that Stravinsky intended his work as an impersonal offering to God.

The first movement, with verses from Psalm 38, begins with an orchestral prologue in which single chords (E minor) alternate with a flowing, winding motive in the oboes and bassoons:

Stravinsky: Symphony of Psalms *(I)*

The first line of text, "Exaudi orationem meam, Domine," is an entreaty to the Lord to hear the supplicant's prayer. It is sung by the altos with a figure that simply alternates between the pitches E and F:

Text: "Hear my entreaty, O Lord."

The altos are answered by a *forte* from the full chorus. Then, after a short orchestral interlude, the chantlike figure resumes, with steady ostinato accompaniment in the winds and bass strings. Rituallike, the music proceeds with entries of one choral part answered by the full chorus. A *fortissimo* cadence on a G major harmony brings the movement to an end. Throughout the movement, the pitches E and G serve as tonal reference points to anchor the music. The stark choral entreaties are simple and direct.

The second movement is a testament of faith. It is based on verses selected from Psalm 39:

Expectans expectavi Dominum et intendit mihi.

I waited patiently for the Lord; and he inclined unto me, and heard my cry.

Et exaudivit preces meas: et eduxit me de lacu miseriae, et de luto faecis.

He brought me up also out of an horrible pit, out of the miry clay,

Et statuit super petram pedes meos: et direxit gressus meos.

and set my feet upon a rock, and established my goings.

Et immisit in os meum canticum novum, carmen	And he hath put a new song in my mouth,
Deo nostro.	even praise unto our God:
Videbunt multi, videbunt et timebunt: et sperabunt	many shall see it, and fear, and shall trust in
in Domino.	the Lord.

Designed as a double fugue, with two fugal subjects (see study diagram, p. 444), this is the most complex of the three movements. In the instrumental opening, we hear the first fugal subject announced by the oboe and flute. It is based on a four-note motive, which is repeated in various rhythmic configurations and then extended in a disjunct, intensely chromatic line:

Stravinsky: Symphony of Psalms *(II)*

FIRST FUGAL SUBJECT

Now the chorus enters with the second fugal subject, while portions of the first subject are preserved in the orchestra. The new subject begins with a descending skip followed by stepwise motion, but then leaps up on the word "Dominum" ("Lord"):

SECOND FUGAL SUBJECT

Eventually, Stravinsky presents the second subject in a choral stretto (see p. 109); then, he has the orchestra return to the first fugal subject, and it, too, is presented in stretto. In the closing measures of the movement, he combines the two subjects.

The final movement is a setting of Psalm 150 in its entirety; it is the most substantial of the three movements. Much of it alternates between a slow, stately tempo for "Alleluia" and a fast Allegro for the recital of praises to the Lord. The slow sections feature a short motive in the chorus repeated over a tonally stable pattern in the bass. The majesty of this music reflects the majesty of the text: The Lord is to be praised "in the firmament of His power." The Allegro recounts the ways in which that praise is to be offered. It begins with an extended orchestral interlude, which, according to Stravinsky's comment, represents the prophet Elijah, who ascended to heaven in a flaming

Stravinsky: *Symphony of Psalms,* Second Movement

Double Fugue

Subject I	Subject II	Subject II in stretto (Chorus)	Subject I in stretto (Orchestra)	1-bar rest	Subject I (Orchestra) and part of Subject II (Chorus)
ob	Chorus	S			
fl	Soprano	A			
fl	Alto	T			
ob	Tenor	B			
	Bass				
	References to Subject I in orchestra				
mf	*mf*	*p*	*p*	*ff*	*p*

chariot. The choral parts of this section are remarkably restrained, as in this passage based on a single, crisply declaimed note:

Stravinsky: Symphony of Psalms *(III)*

Lau - da - te DO - MI - NUM   in   vir - tu - ti - bus   E - jus,

Text: "Praise the Lord in His virtues."

The final section of the movement is a broad coda, in a tempo even more restrained than that of the Alleluia. Against a four-note bass pattern, stated some thirty times, the chorus sings its final praise in another static, chantlike figure:

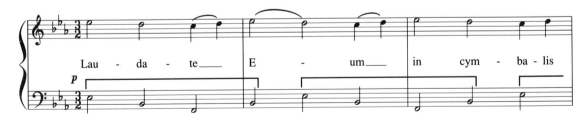

Lau - da - te___ E - um___ in cym - ba - lis

Text: "Praise Him with cymbals."

In the concluding measures, Stravinsky recalls the music for "Alleluia." The work ends with two C major chords, spaced thinly over several octaves and lacking the G (the fifth of the triad), sounding pure and resonant.

Béla Bartók.

BÉLA BARTÓK

The Hungarian composer Béla Bartók (1881–1945) allied a neoclassical approach with a deep love for the folk music of his country. Trained as a concert pianist, he was deeply influenced by the music of Liszt. As a young man, Bartók composed a rhapsodic fantasy for piano and orchestra and a symphonic poem about the nineteenth-century Hungarian nationalist Kossuth. Eventually, Bartók realized that Liszt's showy Hungarian Rhapsodies had little to do with authentic Hungarian folk music; so, he set out to research, transcribe, and analyze that music for himself. He traveled extensively through Hungary, and to Turkey and North Africa as well, and recorded thousands of melodies on an Edison phonograph. In their modal structure, microtonal (smaller than a half step) intervals, and asymmetrical rhythms, he found inspiration for much of his own music (for one example, see p. 456).

For many years, Bartók taught piano at the Budapest Royal Academy of Music, where he continued to compose and carry on his studies of folk music. Alarmed by the rise of the fascists in Germany and Italy, he sent his music to England to be published; finally, in 1940 he emigrated to the United States. In poor health, he struggled to earn his livelihood through concertizing and a research appointment at Columbia University, and began work on a collection of Yugoslav folk music. When he died, he left several planned compositions unrealized.

Bartók's principal contribution was in instrumental music. He wrote three concertos for piano and one each for violin and viola. Of the piano concertos, the first (1926) features dissonant clusters of chromatic pitches in irregular rhythmic groupings. The second (1931) contains an elaborate display of contrapuntal techniques. The third (1945), sketched in Asheville, North Carolina, is a contemplative work written in the last year of Bartók's life. One other concerto deserves separate consideration: The Concerto for Orchestra (1943) extends the idea of virtuoso display to the entire orchestra and has become a classic of the modern orchestral repertoire.

Bartók's instrumental music includes many compositions for piano solo, among them the *Allegro barbaro* (1911), filled with percussive rhythms that look ahead to the *Rite of Spring;* a Sonata for piano (1926); arrangements of many folk songs; and *Mikrokosmos,* a six-volume collection of short pieces of increasing difficulty. His six string quartets (1908–1939) are the epitome of quartet writing in the twentieth century; no less successful are the Sonata for Two Pianos and Two Percussionists (1937) and the *Music for String Instruments, Percussion and Celesta* (1936), discussed below.

Bartók embraced neither the atonal idiom of Schoenberg nor traditional tonality. Rather, his music celebrated the inflections of folk music and incorporated distinctly new approaches to the problem of tonal organization. In works based on triadic harmonies, Bartók typically replaced the tonics and dominants of traditional tonality with tonal plans of his own devising. In works not based on triadic harmonies, he characteristically suggested tonal centers by repeating individual pitches or clusters of pitches continually. Despite his innovative approaches to harmony and tonality, however, Bartók often relied on traditional forms for his compositions, as did other neoclassic composers.

MUSIC FOR STRING INSTRUMENTS, PERCUSSION AND CELESTA

Bartók conceived this four-movement neoclassic work for a modest chamber orchestra, one nevertheless that enabled him to explore an impressive range of new instrumental combinations and techniques. The orchestra consists of two five-part string groups complemented by drums, cymbals, timpani, celesta, harp, piano, and xylophone.* In his own seating arrangement for this singular ensemble, Bartók suggests positioning the strings on the two sides, with the double basses at the back and the percussion in between the two string groups.

---

*A percussion instrument with a series of wooden bars, struck by wooden mallets, that is supported on a stand and arranged in the order of a keyboard.

Despite the unusual scoring—there are no woodwinds or brass instruments—Bartók extracted a wealth of special instrumental effects from his ensemble. The strings, for example, play with mutes and without them, produce high-pitched **harmonics** (see p. 529) by lightly touching and bowing the strings, and in one passage strike the strings with the wood of their bows (*col legno*). Finally, they occasionally use pizzicato, including what is known as the Bartók pizzicato, an especially striking effect in which the players snap the strings sharply against the fingerboard of the instrument.

Bartók uses the percussion instruments sparingly in the first movement, selecting only two or three, which are introduced one at a time; only in later movements do they appear in various combinations. One special effect is the glissando, or slide, heard at various times in the piano, harp, and timpani (where it yields a kind of hollow, chromatic sound). From time to time, the delicate colors of the celesta provide a soft metallic backdrop to the orchestra.

Of the four movements, the first is a fugue, the second is in sonata form, the third is in a symmetrical rondo form, and the fourth is another rondo. The first movement is built on a fugal subject, presented by muted strings, that divides into clusters of chromatic pitches. As the example shows, the subject unfolds in four segments that expand and contract in range:

Bartók: Music for String Instruments, Percussion and Celesta, *First Movement*

From this subject, Bartók constructs a learned fugue, perhaps in homage to J. S. Bach, the master of fugues. Recall that in German nomenclature, Bach's name spells the four-note chromatic subject B♭-A-C-B♮ (p. 106); Bach himself and other composers used this subject in fugues. Bartók's allusion is more subtle: His fugue begins with five pitches, not four; but among them are the pitches of Bach's name, though they occur in a scrambled order.

In the opening section of the fugue, Bartók introduces twelve entries of the fugal subject, one for each pitch of the chromatic scale. The string polyphony steadily thickens until a timpani roll announces the climax of the section. At this point, the mutes are removed. Then Bartók reverses the procedure: Employing the mirror-inverted form of the subject, he gradually thins out the dense counterpoint and reapplies the mutes. In the final step, he combines the subject and its inversion against a chromatic flurry in the celesta. At the very end of the movement, we hear the strings alone.

The energetic second movement is in sonata form. The two string groups exchange the lively first theme back and forth:

Bartók: Music for String Instruments, Percussion and Celesta, *Second Movement*

The tonal center of this theme is C, despite the chromatic notes that engulf it. Bartók establishes that pitch by placing it on strong beats, as marked in the musical example. Corresponding to the traditional plan for the exposition of sonata form, Bartók's second theme is cast in the dominant, or G, and indeed the pitch G assumes a prominent role:

In Bartók's heavily chromatic music, the term *tonic* or *dominant* does not mean a *triadic* tonic or a *triadic* dominant; rather, the music has an emphasis at times on the two individual pitches C and G, and that emphasis gives them prominence as pitch or "tonal" centers. Even so, Bartók does follow traditional practice by closing the exposition with

Bartók: *Music for String Instruments, Percussion and Celesta,* **Third Movement**

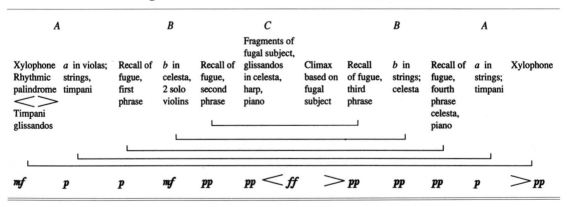

four G major chords—a stirring allusion to the classical tonality of the eighteenth century.

The third movement is a rondo with the symmetrical five-part plan *ABCBA*. Between the sections, Bartók recalls the four segments of the fugue subject from the first movement (see the study diagram). He prefaces the *A* section with a repeated, solitary high pitch in the xylophone and chromatic glissandos in the timpani. The xylophone figure describes a symmetrical pattern, with the same rhythmic values forwards and backwards; this rhythmic symmetry reflects the larger-scale formal symmetry in the overall plan of the rondo. The principal motive of the *A* section (*a*) is a mournful figure in the strings. Probably inspired by Hungarian folk music, it features a snaplike rhythmic pattern (♪♩.):

Bartók: Music for String Instruments, Percussion and Celesta, *Third Movement*

In section *B,* the celesta and two solo violins take up a new theme to the accompaniment of crisp piano chords, and string glissandos and clusters of trills. Again the new theme (*b*) displays intense chromaticism:

Section *C* features fragments of the fugal subject in the strings, performed *pianissimo* and with each pitch repeated rapidly, and rapid glissandos in the piano, harp, and celesta. The section works up to a climax for the full ensemble based on the fugal subject. Bartók brings back the *B* and *A* sections, with the material restated, compressed, and transposed to different pitch levels. The movement ends as it began, with the xylophone solo.

The finale is a complex rondo based essentially on four sections (*A, B, C,* and *D*). It begins with pizzicato chords in the strings, strummed like an ensemble of guitars.

The theme of the *A* section enters, a roistering folk dance with irregular, syncopated rhythmic groupings off the beat:

Bartók: Music for String Instruments, Percussion and Celesta, *Fourth Movement*

A SECTION

The theme of the *B* section, given by the piano in detached notes, is more straightforward and begins with a single pitch repeated insistently:

B SECTION

In section *C,* the strings introduce another folksonglike melody, in detached staccato articulations:

C SECTION

Now the *B* section returns, this time noisier and more frenzied. The *D* section recalls the fugal subject of the first movement and borrows material from the second and third movements. The final section brings back the *A* section, first calmly, with even triplets smoothing out the syncopated rhythms of the dance. Then the music surges forward and is checked again just before an allegro flourish that ends the work.

One of the most versatile twentieth-century composers was Paul Hindemith (1895–1963), whose career was established in Germany between the two world wars. He studied the violin as a youth, played the viola in a string quartet, and was proficient on several other instruments as well. He broke from the sway of romanticism early in his career and experimented with a variety of styles. For a series of one-act operas on lurid sexual themes, he chose an aggressively expressionist idiom and a style close to Schoenberg's atonality. He also incorporated elements of jazz into his music, sometimes in parody. Hindemith was one of the first "serious" composers to write for film and radio. One of his works for radio performance was a cantata in celebration of Lindbergh's flight across the Atlantic in 1927.

Hindemith's mature style developed during the 1920s, when Germany was struggling to recover from the disastrous consequences of the First World War. The sense of disillusionment was reflected in the evolving style of Hindemith, who now abandoned the experimental idioms of his early music for a leaner, simpler style rooted in counterpoint and the traditional forms and genres of the eighteenth century, and founded upon firm principles of tonal organization.

Hindemith believed that music should have a moral, educational purpose. In an effort to narrow the gulf between modern composers and their audiences, he wrote what became known as *Gebrauchsmusik*—"workaday music," or "music for use." He wrote music that called for audience participation, along with several compositions for children. And he accepted a commission to work up a plan for music education in Turkey, which was trying to modernize itself along Western lines.

The Nazis rejected Hindemith's music as decadent and inappropriate for the new Aryan state. Hindemith left for Switzerland and then emigrated to the United States in 1940. For several years, he taught at Yale University, where he founded a *collegium musicum* that specialized in the performance of medieval and Renaissance music. He also revised his theoretical works on composition, which he had begun to publish while he was still in Germany. Hindemith never abandoned tonality altogether, and he continued to defend it as a system validated by natural acoustical properties. In his mature music, we find both traditional triads and nontriadic chords, which Hindemith carefully arranged in a theoretical system according to their level of dissonance.

Hindemith wrote music in almost every genre, including a series of sonatas for each of the standard instruments with piano accompaniment. His major piano work is *Ludus tonalis* (literally, *Tonal Game;* 1942), a kind of counterpart to Bach's *Well-Tempered Clavier,* with fugues and interludes in the twelve keys of Hindemith's theoretical system.

Among his operas are *Die Harmonie der Welt* (1957), which concerns the German astronomer Johann Kepler (1571–1630). A second, more widely known opera, *Mathis der Maler* (1938), concerns the sixteenth-century German painter Matthias Grünewald, who joins the Peasants' Rebellion but then, disillusioned by its excesses, withdraws to seek solace in his art. Despite its sixteenth-century historical basis, *Mathis der Maler* may be taken as a comment on the plight of the artist in the twentieth century. Hindemith himself wrote the libretto for the opera and studied Grünewald's famous Isenheim altarpiece, which depicts events in the lives of Christ and Saint Anthony. Later, Hindemith fashioned a symphony in three movements based on the music of his opera.

DAS MARIENLEBEN (SECOND VERSION, 1948)

Das Marienleben (The Life of Mary) is a song cycle with texts drawn from the cycle of poems of the same name by the Austrian poet Rainer Maria Rilke (1875–1926). Based on biblical and apocryphal accounts, Rilke's poetry recounts events in the life of the Virgin. Hindemith composed the cycle in 1923. Later, he completely reworked it, softening its dissonant language, expunging its expressionist tendencies, and bringing it into line with his mature theories about tonality. The second version, completed in 1948, is the version that is usually performed today. For it, Hindemith prepared a long preface in which he elucidated his use of tonality in the cycle, its elaborate system of keys, and their symbolic meanings. Thus, the key of E stands for the human qualities of Christ; A, for his divinity; and B, for Mary. What is more, these three principal keys appear in consecutive order in the traditional circle of fifths (see p. 72), and thus are closely linked to one another.

Beyond reasserting traditional tonal relationships, reaffirmed by the frequent appearance of triads, Hindemith also revived traditional forms. He was especially fond of indulging in learned counterpoint. Thus, the second song, "Die Darstellung Mariä im Tempel" ("The Depiction of Mary in the Temple"), is a passacaglia (see p. 114) with a recurring bass pattern, above which the soloist and the pianist weave a complex counterpoint. Our example shows the bass pattern, which moves by leaps as it describes a gradual descent:

Hindemith: Das Marienleben, *"Die Darstellung Mariä im Tempel"*

PASSACAGLIA SUBJECT

The passacaglia is meant to symbolize the massive columns and sturdy architecture of the temple visited by the child Mary. Hindemith suggests its solidity in reinforced musical terms, as nearly twenty statements of the bass subject are unfolded against a gripping crescendo and diminuendo.

The ninth song, "Vor der Hochzeit zu Kana" ("Before the Wedding at Cana"),* opens with a lengthy piano solo that breaks into a full-length fugue based on this powerful subject:

---

* After John 2.

452   THE TWENTIETH CENTURY

Hindemith: Das Marienleben, *"Vor der Hochzeit zu Kana"*

FUGAL SUBJECT

Along the way, this subject is metamorphosed into two forms, suggesting the conversion of the water into wine. First, its staccato articulations are replaced by a legato slur; then, its triple meter is abandoned in favor of a more measured, extended $\frac{4}{2}$ meter:

Hindemith's use of learned counterpoint and his reaffirmation of tonal procedures represented no mere reliance on the music of the past. Rather, his procedure was to use the rich resources of the past to give coherence and structure to his own, uniquely twentieth-century musical language. This procedure informed the music of the other neoclassic composers as well.

Suggested Listening

Bartók: Concerto for Orchestra
★_____ : *Music for String Instruments, Percussion and Celesta*
_____ : *Piano Concerto No. 3*
_____ : *String Quartet No. 5*
Hindemith: *Ludus Tonalis*
★_____ : *Das Marienleben*
_____ : *Mathis der Maler* Symphony
★Prokofiev: Symphony No. 1, in D major *(Classical)*

Note: Works marked with an asterisk are the principal works discussed in the chapter.

Ravel: *Bolero*

_____ : *Le tombeau de Couperin*

Stravinsky: Octet

_____ : *Oedipus Rex*

_____ : Symphony in C

★_____ : *Symphony of Psalms*

18

NATIONAL STYLES
AND AMERICAN MUSIC

*T*he fashioning of distinctively national musical styles continued to motivate twentieth-century composers, especially composers working outside the major European musical centers that already enjoyed long national traditions—Germany and Austria, France, and Italy. In turning to the indigenous culture of their homelands, these composers found fresh sources of inspiration in the modal melodies and characteristic cross rhythms of folk music. In Chapter 14, we looked at the careers of three nineteenth-century composers who had drawn on national idioms: Edvard Grieg in Norway, Antonín Dvořák in Czechoslovakia and America, and Modest Musorgsky in Russia. Of those, it was Musorgsky who exercised the strongest influence on twentieth-century composers, especially on Debussy and other French composers, but also on the young Stravinsky. As the twentieth century progressed, the enthusiasm for national styles strengthened. And, as we shall see, American music, a melting pot of musical styles, came into its own during the new century.

In Scandinavia, Grieg was followed by Jean Sibelius (1865–1957), a Finn whose first language was Swedish. Much of Sibelius's music reflected the rising tide of Finnish nationalism that manifested itself in growing opposition to the rule of the Russian tsar and to Russian culture. Sibelius's *Finlandia* for orchestra (1899), for example, was such an overtly patriotic work that its performance was banned in Finland. Partly in response to Richard Strauss's orchestral works of the 1880s and 1890s, and to Wagner's *Ring* cycle, Sibelius wrote a series of programmatic tone poems based on the saga *Kalevala,* the Finnish counterpart of the *Nibelungenlied,* and seven symphonies, generally dark and brooding in tone, but firmly anchored in tonality. Then, about 1925, he withdrew from public life as Finland's most distinguished composer and entered a retirement of some thirty years.

In Czechoslovakia, Dvořák was followed by Leoš Janáček (1854–1928), who was born in Moravia, the eastern district of what later became Czechoslovakia. Janáček incorporated elements of Moravian folk music into a colorful style faithful to the accents of the Slavic dialect. Among his major works are the popular *Sinfonietta* (1926), which he dedicated to the military forces of his country, and his masterpiece, the opera *Jenůfa* (1904), cast in a realistic style, with melodies that approximated the irregular patterns of everyday speech.

Several composers in Latin countries also responded to the appeal of nationalism. The Spaniard Manuel de Falla (1876–1946) wrote a number of popular works on Spanish subjects before his creativity was impaired by the horrors of the Spanish Civil War (1936–1939): for example, *Nights in the Gardens of Spain* for piano and orchestra (1915) and *The Three-Cornered Hat* (1919), a ballet premiered by Dyagilev's Russian troupe with stage designs by Picasso. The prolific Brazilian Heitor Villa-Lobos (1887–1959) devoted himself to music education in his homeland during the 1930s and 1940s and incorporated popular Brazilian melodies and dances in extended series of works. The Argentinian Alberto Ginastera (1916–1983) treated Argentine themes and rhythms in a variety of genres before exploring twelve-tone idioms in his Second String Quartet (1958) and other works. And the Mexican Carlos Chávez (1899–1978) emerged in the 1920s after the Mexican revolution to produce colorful scores filled with materials drawn from Mexican culture, including ballets on Aztec subjects.

BARTÓK: *FOURTEEN BAGATELLES,* OP. 6, NOS. 4 AND 5

The music of Béla Bartók exudes a melodic freshness and harmonic color that derive from Hungarian folk music. Bartók's *Fourteen Bagatelles,* Op. 6 (1908), were among his first collections of piano music to appear in print. Mostly freely composed, the individual movements are short pieces that range in length from less than a minute to about three minutes. Numbers 4 and 5 stand out as settings of two folk songs, the first Hungarian, the second Slovakian. The Hungarian folk song consists of two phrases, both of which are repeated, yielding the scheme *aabb*. Though preserving the integrity of the tune, Bartók accompanies it with a free mixture of modal chords and dissonant, chromatic harmonies.

Bartók gives the second folk song (Bagatelle No. 5) a more extended treatment. After some light introductory chords in the treble, we first hear the melody in the bass. Compact in range, the melody fills out a seven-measure phrase with lively rhythms and staccato articulations and concludes with a firm accent:

Bartók: Fourteen Bagatelles, *Op. 6, No. 5*

The melody is based on a modal scale built on the pitch G, somewhat like our modern minor scale:

Mode Based on G

The chords that accompany the melody are drawn from a pentatonic scale (p. 362) based on G:

Pentatonic Scale on G

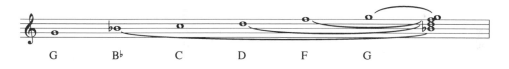

After the first statement, the chords descend to the bass register. Now we hear the melody in the treble (still drawn from the modal scale on G), with a fresh chordal accompaniment. After completing the second statement, Bartók once again directs the chords to the treble register, and the third and final statement of the melody reappears in the bass. Apart from a few modifications, the melody remains intact and recognizable; but the chordal harmonies change once again, lending charm and harmonic variety to this delightful setting.

Beginning in 1906, Bartók spent his summers collecting native folk songs in the rural areas of Hungary. The results of his researches powerfully affected the course his own music would take. Joining him in his travels was his compatriot, Zoltán Kodály (1882–1967), whose masterpiece, the Singspiel *Háry János* (1926), was inspired by Hungarian folk music. Kodály's art, Bartók once declared, expressed the very spirit of their country.

NATIONAL STYLES AND AMERICAN MUSIC

ENGLISH MUSIC

Not since the time of Henry Purcell in the seventeenth century had England produced a native composer of the first rank. In the eighteenth century, Handel established himself in London, and in the nineteenth, Mendelssohn made several trips to England, where his tasteful and impeccably crafted music was especially popular during the long reign of Queen Victoria.

With Sir Edward Elgar (1857–1934), the English once again had a major composer of their own. Among Elgar's most successful scores were his *Enigma Variations* for orchestra (1899)—a curious work, riddled with mysteries and written as a tribute to his friends—and the "symphonic study" *Falstaff* (1913), a humorous orchestral work based on Shakespeare's celebrated comic figure. Elgar's music was deeply indebted to the German romantic tradition: His Cello Concerto (1919) and two weighty symphonies (1908, 1911) suggest at times the sophistication of Wagner's chromatic harmony and the lyricism of Brahms's melodic style. His oratorios, including *The Dream of Gerontius* (1900), recall at times the style of Mendelssohn's oratorios, long favored at English music festivals. But for all Elgar's accomplishments, a modern English style in music emerged only at the turn of the century.

The leader of that musical renaissance was Ralph Vaughan Williams (1872–1958). Educated at the Royal College of Music and Cambridge University, Vaughan Williams sought further training in Berlin, where he was influenced by the late German romantic style, and in Paris, where he studied with Maurice Ravel, his junior by three years. But he found his real inspiration in English folk music and hymns and in the music of the Tudor, Elizabethan, and Jacobean periods.

Vaughan Williams wrote an impressive series of nine symphonies, some with programmatic titles (including the *Pastoral,* 1921; and *Antartica,* 1952), several other orchestral and chamber works, film music, and a wealth of choral music. For his vocal music, he drew on texts ranging from Chaucer and Shakespeare to Thomas Hardy, A. E. Housman, and Walt Whitman.

Vaughan Williams was an avid student of English folk songs, many of which were assembled by his countryman Cecil Sharp (1859–1924), who authenticated nearly five thousand English folk songs and dance melodies. A hymnologist himself, Vaughan Williams prepared a new edition of English hymns, to which he contributed some of his own melodies.

His music has the sound and the appeal of folk music, even when he does not cite actual folk melodies. In defending his affinity for traditional English melodies, Vaughan Williams decried the romantic aesthetic of originality. There was no need, he argued, for all musical ideas to be original. What mattered was to make an authentic musical statement, even if that meant reusing or borrowing from existing material. In his hymn editions and in his own music, he did much to preserve native English music, much as Bartók did for native Hungarian music.

Vaughan Williams was less adventurous than Bartók, however, in his approach to tonality, and he never succumbed to Schoenberg's atonal or twelve-tone methods of composition. For him, the traditional tonal triad remained the fundamental harmonic sonority, even though he often flavored his use of major and minor keys with modal melodies and harmonies. Moreover, Vaughan Williams was a keen practitioner of traditional counterpoint, an interest he derived from the vocal English polyphony of the sixteenth and seventeenth centuries. Not a small part of his own musical identity was derived from the glorious English music of an earlier time.

VAUGHAN WILLIAMS: *FANTASIA ON A THEME BY THOMAS TALLIS* (1910)

Thomas Tallis (ca. 1505–1585) was one of the masters of sacred music in Tudor England. He worked in a variety of styles, ranging from simple settings of psalms to an impressive forty-part motet for eight five-part choirs, which he treated antiphonally and in various combinations. As a member of the Chapel Royal, Tallis served both Henry VIII and Elizabeth I. When Henry VIII established the Anglican church, Tallis devoted his energies to composing music for the new liturgy. For the *Fantasia on a Theme by Thomas Tallis* (1910), Vaughan Williams chose a modal melody from one of Tallis's psalm settings.

The *Fantasia* is scored for a string orchestra organized in three groups. Sometimes the groups play together, sometimes they alternate, and sometimes they play separately. The strings of the first group (Orchestra I) are divided into six parts, generally with several players per part. The strings of the second group (Orchestra II) are divided into five parts, with only one or two players per part. The third group is a string quartet, with four soloists. This unusual organization makes possible a broad range of expression, from the subtle nuances of solo lines to a full-bodied, majestic sound of the entire ensemble.

The Tallis melody, presented here in the version used by Vaughan Williams, describes a long arch, gently rising and falling to end on its opening pitch. Occasionally, the basic $\frac{3}{4}$ meter shifts to a lilting $\frac{6}{8}$, disrupting the regular beat and giving the melody a certain spontaneity:

Vaughan Williams: Fantasia on a Theme by Thomas Tallis

The *Fantasia* opens with the entire ensemble playing *pianissimo* chords (see study diagram). Against a sustained high pitch in the violins, the lower strings pluck out the opening motive of the melody. Then we hear a series of triads that move in strict parallel motion, imparting an exotic, modal sound. When the melody appears, it is given first by the cellos (*piano*) and is repeated by the violins (*forte*). A transition follows, in which

Vaughan Williams: *Fantasia on a Theme by Thomas Tallis*

Largo			
Introduction	Tallis Theme	Tallis Theme	Transition
Full ensemble	(Cellos)	(Violins)	
			Orchestra I
			vs.
			Orchestra II
			(muted)
Chords, pizzicato			
Foreshadowing			
of theme			
			Loud-soft
pp	*p*	*f*	echo effects

the two orchestras engage in an antiphonal exchange. Orchestra I uses a broad dynamic range; Orchestra II plays with mutes applied, producing an eerie, distant echo.

The central portion of the work shifts to a slightly faster tempo. It is announced by a graceful viola solo drawn from the Tallis theme but now freely elaborated:

Poco più animato (A little more animated)

Viola

Against the backdrop of the two orchestras, the viola is answered by a solo violin, and then the solo string quartet engages in a display of free counterpoint. The three groups come together as the music reaches a climax in this free, quasi-development section. A tempo change to *Molto Adagio* prepares for the return of the opening: A solo violin accompanied by a solo viola plays the Tallis theme, with softly trembling chords from the two orchestras in the background. In the closing measures, the solo violin climbs to its high register, and the orchestra concludes with a swell and diminuendo to *pppp* on a major chord.

AMERICAN MUSIC

So far, we have not had ample occasion to discuss American music, and a review of its development before the twentieth century is appropriate here. The English settlers who colonized New England and the mid-Atlantic and southern coastal regions during the seventeenth and eighteenth centuries brought with them music from the homeland, mostly sacred music for worship. Their firm religious beliefs soon took root in the New World. The singing of psalms was featured in their congregational services, and,

More animated		Molto adagio	
Free Fantasia			Theme
on Theme			Solo violin
Viola solo, then	Gradual		(solo viola)
violin solo, then	addition of forces	Chords,	accompanied
string quartet		pizzicato	by Orchestra
	Orchestra I, II,		I and II
Quasi development	and string		
	quartet		
p	$<ff>p$		*p* *ff* $>$ *pppp*

not surprisingly, the first few music publications to appear in America contained music for worship. (The first published book in America, known as the Bay Psalm Book, appeared in 1640, with the title *The Whole Booke of Psalmes Faithfully Translated into English Metre;* the ninth edition of 1698 appeared with thirteen appended tunes.)

There were few well-trained musicians or composers among the early colonists. During the eighteenth century, in an effort to improve the quality of congregational singing, reform-minded ministers set up makeshift singing schools to disseminate the rudiments of music. To facilitate the ability of their congregations to read music, they devised new teaching methods and occasionally experimented with new styles of notation. One of them, known as *shape-note notation,* employed notes of various shapes ($\triangle$, $\bigcirc$, $\square$, and $\diamond$) as a means of teaching hymns. By the beginning of the nineteenth century, shape-note singing had spread throughout the rural areas of America and eventually was taken over in Southern hymnody.

Compared with European taste, native American music was rough-hewn and straightforward. One of the first American composers to achieve some measure of success was the Bostonian William Billings (1746–1800), who composed unaccompanied choral music such as psalm settings and anthems; during the Revolutionary War, he produced patriotic pieces for the American cause. He also wrote a few so-called *fuging tunes* ("fuging" was possibly pronounced "fudging"). These were hymns in block-chordal style that concluded with sections of simple imitative counterpoint. In a remarkable exaggeration, Billings was dubbed "the rival of Handel." There were, of course, no musical centers in the colonies that could match London or Paris, few established musical institutions, orchestras, or schools. By European standards, native American music was indeed unsophisticated, uncomplex, and untutored. But it was also nonconformist and ruggedly individualist, two qualities that endured and, indeed, that ultimately determined the character of American music.

A remarkably sophisticated musical culture developed in the Moravian church, a sect that traced its origins to the mid-fifteenth century. The Moravians, followers of the Czech martyr Jan Hus, had been displaced by the Thirty Years' War during the seventeenth century. During the eighteenth century, they began to settle in the colonies, forming communities such as Bethlehem in Pennsylvania, and Salem (now Winston-Salem) in North Carolina. These deeply devout immigrants produced and consumed a vast amount of church music and insisted on rigorous standards of performance in their services. They introduced meticulously built instruments into their church music, and in their *collegia musica,* they performed and preserved European music as well as their own.

By the nineteenth century, popular music of every description was flourishing throughout the country, including hymns, fuging tunes, anthems, dances, marches ("Washington's March" and "Yankee Doodle Dandy" were special favorites), ballad operas, and, finally, an ever-increasing amount of unnotated music brought from Africa by the slaves. At revivalist meetings, hymnody, shape-note singing (a classic anthology, *The Sacred Harp,* appeared in 1844), and **spirituals**—American folk songs with religious texts—were the standard fare. Minstrel shows, a popular entertainment that blended theater, music, and vaudeville—at first given by whites in blackface—became established in the 1840s and widespread in the decades that followed. Minstrel shows featured small bands of instruments, including the five-string banjo, tambourine, "bones,"* violin, and the accordion. One American composer who wrote for the minstrel shows, which were often referred to as "Ethiopian operas," was Stephen Foster (1826–1864). Foster made a career as a songwriter, composing both the music and the lyrics for some 150 songs. Among his minstrel songs are *Oh! Susanna* (1848), *Camptown Races* (1850), and *My Old Kentucky Home* (1853). During the Civil War, he composed some patriotic songs for the North. Foster is especially remembered for his cultivated household songs *Jeanie with the Light Brown Hair* (1854) and *Beautiful Dreamer* (1864), love songs with a special blend of sentiment and nostalgia that characterized his art.

Band music also became popular in the nineteenth century. During the Civil War, military bands were a common sight. About the middle of the century, improvements in brass instruments (especially, the addition of valves, which enabled brass instruments to execute chromatic pitches with greater ease than before) encouraged the writing of band music. The most distinguished American bandmaster was John Philip Sousa (1854–1932), who directed the Marine Corps Band from 1880 to 1892. Then, striking out on his own, he formed the Sousa Band, which he took on national and international tours. Sousa composed well over one hundred marches, along with several lighthearted operas. *The Stars and Stripes Forever* (1897) has remained his most famous composition, surviving all manner of arrangements and versions.

During the nineteenth century, the United States remained susceptible to trends in European arts and letters. Romanticism influenced the panoramic paintings of landscapists, the frontier novels of James Fenimore Cooper, the supernatural stories of Nathaniel Hawthorne, the macabre tales of Edgar Allan Poe, and the work of the transcendentalists Emerson and Thoreau. Although no romantic composer of the first rank emerged, at least one American musician followed in the footsteps of the great romantic virtuosos. The New Orleans pianist Louis Moreau Gottschalk (1829–1869) assimilated the spicy flavors of Creole and black music into his extravagant piano compositions. He performed his music in France, where it won the admiration of Berlioz

---

* Bone castanets.

and Chopin, and he was acclaimed in Spain. He toured the Caribbean and South America, where he staged grand musical galas of monumental proportions. He gave his fanciful works eye-catching titles: *Le Banjo, esquisse américaine* (*The Banjo, an American Sketch,* 1855), in which he applied the banjo's plucking technique to the piano; *The Union* (1862), a flamboyant piece of battle music dedicated to General McClellan and first performed on George Washington's birthday; *The Last Hope: Religious Meditation* (1854), a (cloyingly) sentimental salon piece.

Other Americans traveled abroad to study European art music firsthand. They particularly favored German music. Alexander Wheelock Thayer's biography of Beethoven, a model of scholarship, began to appear in installments during the 1860s and 1870s. A stream of American musicians enrolled at the Leipzig Conservatory or traveled to Weimar to study with Franz Liszt.

By the closing decades of the century, a group of American composers in New England were writing respectable symphonies and string quartets, operas, cantatas, and programmatic symphonic poems. The leading members of this group were John Knowles Paine (1839–1906), George Chadwick (1854–1931), Horatio Parker (1863–1919), and Edward MacDowell (1860–1908). Much of their music is redolent of the music of Brahms, Wagner, and Liszt and at times exhibits a certain academic rigor. In fact, these four composers held posts at Harvard, the New England Conservatory, Yale, and Columbia, respectively. The most successful of them was Edward MacDowell, who used American Indian melodies in his music and yet was comfortable writing traditional piano sonatas and concertos, and symphonic poems in the grand, Lisztian manner. Other distinguished Americans included Arthur Foote (1853–1937), who produced chamber and instrumental works, and Amy Beach (1867–1944), a prodigy whose *Gaelic* Symphony (1896) was the first symphony composed by an American woman.

As the century drew to a close, Dvořák's challenge—to found a distinctive American style of music—remained unanswered. By its very nature, American music was a heterogeneous art that drew on a variety of sources. While MacDowell and his New England colleagues produced abundant compositions in emulation of established European styles and genres, others were collecting melodies of the American Indians and other native folk songs or cultivating various popular, vernacular styles. Diversity—art and popular music, imported and native music—remains to this day the hallmark of American music.

The music of one American working early in the new century was remarkably eclectic. Charles Tomlinson Griffes (1884–1920) studied in Germany (his teacher, Engelbert Humperdinck, wrote the children's opera *Hänsel und Gretel,* premiered in 1893) and was drawn to the work of Debussy and Stravinsky. Griffes produced delicate music on oriental themes, music in a style that has been likened to impressionism (his most famous work is the piano composition *The White Peacock* of 1915), and music in a harsh, dissonant vein (as in his Piano Sonata of 1918). Many of his compositions remained unfinished when he died at an early age.

CHARLES IVES

Among the most innovative twentieth-century American composers has been Charles Ives (1874–1954), a stubborn individualist who in his art and life set a bold imagination against the constraints of convention. For most of his life, Ives worked in isolation; his music was played and understood by only a few. Only after his death was his genius fully recognized, and historians are still trying to assess his achievement. Ives's father, a Union bandmaster during the Civil War, had a quirk for experimenting with odd combinations of instruments and microtonal intervals. Raised in Danbury, Connecticut, young Ives received his first musical instruction from his father, who encouraged his nonconformist tendencies.

In 1894 Ives entered Yale and during his four years there played the organ at a local church. He did not distinguish himself academically. From Horatio Parker he received rigorous though traditional instruction in composition: Parker asked him to compose fugues and settings of German lyric poetry. Ives obliged, but he composed some of those fugues in four different keys, in a determined display of polytonality. He interposed quotations from hymns and familiar tunes in his music—with no warning to the listener. The titles of some of his compositions reflect his idiosyncratic approach to music making. He labeled his First String Quartet "From the Salvation Army"; another chamber work he titled "An Old Song Deranged."

Ives decided early on not to pursue a career in music. That was probably a wise decision, for few took his eccentric compositions seriously. He went into the insurance business and eventually was quite successful. On evenings and weekends, however, he continued to compose. Toward the end of the First World War, he suffered a heart attack; by 1920, he had more or less given up composition and, ten years later, retired from business. After his retirement, his music began to be performed more and more often. His Third Symphony was awarded a Pulitzer Prize in 1947, but he declined the honor.

Although Ives subscribed to no particular style of composition, his music is decidedly modern. He evidently knew little of Schoenberg's music, yet he devised his own powerful atonal language, used speechlike recitation that resembles Sprechstimme, and employed complete sets of twelve pitches similar to tone rows. He evidently knew little of Bartók's music, yet he often used chromatic clusters of pitches (to be played by the pianist's forearm, or even by a heavy wooden board depressed on the keys). Ives's music is a mixture of clashing rhythms, unorthodox harmonies and contrapuntal lines, and familiar tunes; in its complex interplay of elements, it suggests the collage techniques of later American artists. Somehow, all the elements come together into a unified work of art.

Ives devised an aesthetic of music that was as radical as his compositions. Above all, he wanted to extend the scope of music beyond the limits of familiar, correct sounds. He filled his scores with all manner of "wrong" notes, subtle and obvious allusions to other music, and cryptic marginal notations. He sought a spontaneous universal music that would transcend the ordinary, the routine. He demanded that music be strong, vigorous, and multifaceted; he rejected "arm-chair" music—music emasculated by "pretty little sounds" or "niceties."

Among Ives's available works are four thoroughly unconventional symphonies (the Third is titled *The Camp Meeting;* a Fifth Symphony, titled the *Universal,* may perhaps be reconstructed some day from the composer's drafts), band pieces, string quartets, piano sonatas, and some two hundred songs. Two chamber pieces of 1906, *The Unanswered Question* (strings, solo woodwinds, and a trumpet) and *Central Park in the Dark* (strings, solo winds and brass, and percussion with two pianos), Ives described as "contemplations."

One of Ives's greatest works is his second piano sonata, subtitled *Concord, Mass., 1840–60.* Though composed between 1911 and 1915, its premiere came only in 1939. The title refers to the center of New England transcendentalism in the nineteenth century. Concord, Massachusetts, was the meeting ground of Emerson, Hawthorne, the Alcotts, and Thoreau, and the four movements of the sonata present their musical portraits. The first movement, "Emerson," is the weightiest of the four and the closest to conventional sonata form. "Hawthorne" is Ives's version of a scherzo. Described by him as a series of "fantastical adventures," it was clearly inspired by Hawthorne's supernatural tales. The third movement, "The Alcotts," is a slow movement of great beauty, with quotations of hymn tunes, the opening of the "Wedding March" from Wagner's *Lohengrin,* and the famous four-note motive from Beethoven's Fifth Symphony, so well known that it assumes a "universal" significance in the music (and appears in other movements of the sonata as well). For the last movement, "Thoreau," Ives provided a programmatic description of Thoreau in meditation at Walden Pond; at the end, the piano is joined by a flute, Thoreau's favorite instrument.

GENERAL WILLIAM BOOTH ENTERS INTO HEAVEN

In 1914 Ives composed a song setting of Vachel Lindsay's poem *General William Booth Enters into Heaven,* a remarkable meeting of composer and poet. Lindsay's poem is about the first director of the Salvation Army and his fanaticism in trying to save the unfortunate members of society. The poem itself contains many parenthetical cues for musical instruments: bass drums to accompany the procession of Booth's tattered army, banjos played by "big-voiced lassies," and trumpets for militant fanfares. The line "Are you washed in the blood of the Lamb?" recurs throughout the poem, serving as a free refrain.

The imagery and the rhythms of Lindsay's poetry drew from Ives's rich imagination a work that transcends the limits of traditional song. It is music to be intimately experienced and pondered. Ives includes optional notes for a chorus and shouts of "Hallelujah!" to give the effect of a revivalist meeting. He gives the piano strumming banjolike textures, rousing fanfares, and especially dull thumping chords to suggest the bass drum, as at the beginning of the song:

For the refrain, Ives quotes the melody of the hymn "Cleansing Fountain," which appears throughout the song at various transpositions. As General Booth rouses his troops, the music reaches a frenzied climax. Then, in a dignified Adagio, Ives sets the lines "Jesus came from the courthouse door, / Stretched his hands above the passing poor. / Booth saw not, but led his queer ones, / Round and round, round and round and round. . . ." Here the music itself moves round and round, with a mesmerizing, calming effect, suggesting the blessing of Jesus. As the procession passes on, the piano sounds its percussive chords once again, and we hear a complete statement of "Cleansing Fountain." This singular march ends with the distant sound of the drum.

Ives was the pioneer of modern American music. His art is a synthetic art that pulls together various strands of popular and serious music into a colorful, vibrant fabric. It is a transcendent art that conveys meaning through its cumulative power. Finally, it is an intensely personal art that echoes Emerson's advice: "Trust thyself; every heart vibrates to that iron string."

AARON COPLAND

Born in 1900, Aaron Copland won recognition as a leading American composer during the 1920s and 1930s. He first studied music in New York City and then, in 1921, traveled to Paris, where he worked with Nadia Boulanger. (Many other American composers were students of Boulanger, including Virgil Thomson, who collaborated with another American living in France, Gertrude Stein, on the opera *Four Saints in Three Acts,* premiered in 1934.) In his early compositions Copland incorporated elements of jazz and other American musical idioms. The clashing rhythms and polytonal sonorities of his music from the 1920s reflect the influence of Stravinsky's music, which he greatly admired.

With the advent of the Great Depression in 1929, experimentalism in the arts underwent a general retrenchment as the United States retreated into isolationism. Reflecting the mood of the times, Copland turned to American subjects and produced scores with a broad popular appeal. He is perhaps best known for three ballet scores, *Billy the Kid* (1938), *Rodeo* (1942), and *Appalachian Spring* (1944), and, in a musical response to Franklin Roosevelt's Good Neighbor Policy, the orchestral work *El salón México* (1937), which employs Mexican musical materials. During the 1930s and 1940s, Copland wrote music for radio and film and, in keeping with the patriotic mood of the 1940s, composed the *Lincoln Portrait,* for orchestra and speaker (1942), and the *Fanfare for the Common Man,* for brass and percussion (1942). In a series of later works, most notably Piano Quartet (1950), *Piano Fantasy* (1957), and two orchestral works, *Connotations* (1962) and *Inscape* (1967), Copland tested elements of twelve-tone technique. But he never departed far from his earlier mission: to write American music in a style accessible to a wide audience.

APPALACHIAN SPRING

The ballet *Appalachian Spring* was commissioned for a performance at the Library of Congress by Martha Graham's dance company. Set in rural Pennsylvania in the early nineteenth century, it is a celebration of spring, a nostalgic reminder of simple American values as seen through the eyes of a newlywed couple.

The original score employed only thirteen instruments, including woodwinds (without oboe), strings, and piano. Copland later arranged it as a concert suite for full orchestra, and this version is the one that is usually performed. The suite consists of eight sections. In the first, an introduction in a slow tempo, Copland blends simple triads to create tranquil polytonal textures as the principals of the ballet—the bride, the groom, a neighbor, and a revivalist minister and his congregation—are introduced. The second section is an Allegro with wide leaps and forceful accents reminiscent of Stravinsky:

Copland: Appalachian Spring, *Allegro*

The third section, in a moderate tempo, is a duo danced by the couple. In the fourth section, a revivalist and his following dance to music that suggests a square dance, with prominent interruptions by the violins. The fifth section is a fast dance for the bride, who reflects on motherhood. The sixth section returns to the restrained music of the opening. The seventh section, which depicts scenes in the couple's daily life, is based on the well-known Shaker melody "Simple Gifts," first heard in the clarinet:

Copland: Appalachian Spring, *"Simple Gifts"*

p simply expressive

Copland uses the melody with little thematic alteration but subjects it to five variations before ending the section with a broad statement for full orchestra. The last section depicts the couple in their new house. Hushed and reverent, the music recalls the opening strains of this classic American work.

THE RISE OF JAZZ: RAGTIME AND BLUES

In the early decades of the twentieth century, popular music, which had continued to thrive in all its diversity, was enriched by a new type of music—**jazz**—that proved to be a quintessential expression of American culture. The derivation and meaning of the term is still being investigated, but its roots were in the vibrant rhythms and melodies of Afro-American slave music. Early jazz constituted a type of improvised performance; in time, jazz came to have its own set of recognized traditions and performance practices. Though it was a distinctly American music, it served as a rich source for modern art music: Debussy, Stravinsky, Hindemith, Ravel, Copland, and many other "serious" composers freely drew on jazz idioms in their music. Today, its popularity is worldwide; jazz plays a fundamental role in the modern musical experience.

In the nineteenth century, the music brought to America by the slaves was transformed into a rhythmic, dynamic music that found expression in spirituals, in field hollers, and in complex drum patterns. Much of this music was handed down by oral tradition, but much of it was improvised. By the end of the nineteenth century, two distinct types of black music had emerged—ragtime and blues. Together, they would form the basis of the great flowering of jazz during the 1920s.

SCOTT JOPLIN, *MAPLE LEAF RAG*

Ragtime featured a regular, strong chordal bass accompanying a treble melody animated with syncopations against the beat. "Rags" had been common in the parlors of bordellos before they achieved general popularity at the beginning of the twentieth century. They were generally performed on the piano, an instrument versatile enough to imitate the sounds and rhythms of a small band of instruments. There were several successful composers of rags, but the "King of Rag" was Scott Joplin (1868–1917), a black musician who settled in Sedalia, Missouri, and then lived for a time in St. Louis and New York. Joplin was well versed in harmony and composition, as the secure structure and the melodic flair of his music show. He aspired to become a recognized composer and even thought of writing a symphony in ragtime; he did complete two ragtime operas, *A Guest of Honor* (1903) and *Treemonisha* (1911), for eleven voices and piano accompaniment. His principal fame, however, rested with his rags, all written down and published. So popular was the new style that a market was created for ragtime instruction manuals; Joplin responded to the demand with a *School of Ragtime* in 1908.

Many of Joplin's rags are in duple meter. They consist of several sections, sometimes repeated, with each usually of sixteen measures. In form, meter, and tempo, these rags resemble marches. But their main effect depends on the tension between the cross-cutting syncopations of the upper part and the thumping, steady beat of the bass.

Joplin's most famous composition is the *Maple Leaf Rag;* it was an immediate success when it appeared in 1899, and it sold copies in the hundreds of thousands. It consists of four sections of equal length, which we shall label *A, B, C,* and *D.* The overall form of the composition is *AABBACCDD.* Joplin designated the tempo as *Tempo di Marcia* ("in the tempo of a march"). The *C* section, written in a contrasting key, is marked Trio (as are the contrasting sections of many Sousa marches). The bass moves along in eighth notes, the treble in sixteenth notes. But while the bass progresses in a regular succession of beats, Joplin continually peppers the treble melody with syncopations by holding the second or fourth sixteenth of each four-note group, that is, ♪♪ or ♪♪♪♪ ♪, thereby injecting accents that fall off the regular beats of the bass:

Joplin: Maple Leaf Rag

Ragtime was highly popular in both the United States and Europe until about 1915, when it was displaced by what became known as jazz, a livelier music that depended on a free, improvisational style. A key figure in the transition from ragtime to jazz was the New Orleans pianist "Jelly Roll" Morton (1890–1941), often viewed as one of the first jazz composers of distinction. By the late 1920s, Morton's ensemble, the Red Hot Peppers, was recording carefully prepared renditions of his compositions.

W. C. HANDY, *ST. LOUIS BLUES*

The origins of the **blues** are no less obscure than those of ragtime. The blues are songs of misery and oppression. They chronicle every sort of misfortune, from infidelity to

Standard Plan for Blues Stanza

First Phrase First line of text		Second Phrase Second line of text (same as first)		Third Phrase Third line of text	
Soloist	Instrumental answer	Soloist	Instrumental answer	Soloist	Instrumental answer
Tonic		Subdominant	Tonic	Dominant	Tonic

unemployment to depression ("Lost Your Head Blues," "Yellow Dog Blues," and "Friendless Blues," for example). The blues probably were sung by slaves before their emancipation, and the so-called country blues have remained part of the unwritten tradition of black American music. "City blues" were popularized during the 1920s by singers such as "Ma" Rainey (1886–1939), the "Mother of the Blues," and Bessie Smith (1894–1937), the "Empress of the Blues," both of whom disseminated the art form during the 1920s through sound recordings. Such musicians as "Jelly Roll" Morton and the trumpeter-cornetist Louis "Satchmo" Armstrong (1900–1971) developed instrumental styles for the art form.

Typically, the blues are built on a standard harmonic plan that fills out twelve measures divided into three phrases of four measures each. The three phrases deliver a stanza of three lines of text, of which the first and second are the same. Generally, a line of text occupies the first two measures of the phrase, leaving a gap that is filled in by an improvised instrumental response. This give-and-take creates a tension in the music that builds toward the third line of text, which gives the reason for the singer's woes. Here, for instance, is the opening stanza of the classic *St. Louis Blues* (1914), written by W. C. Handy (1873–1958), the "Father of the Blues":

> I hate to see de ev'nin' sun go down,
> Hate to see de evenin' sun go down.
> Cause my baby, he done lef dis town.

Supporting the three-line blues stanza is a harmonic foundation built of sturdy tonic, subdominant, and dominant chords, shown in our diagram in their stripped-down, basic plan. The blues are generally strophic, with the same music for successive stanzas, although sometimes more complicated formal schemes are employed, as in the *St. Louis Blues*.

The characteristic sound of the blues comes from the use of **blue notes,** certain pitches of the scale that are stretched to sound slightly off-key:

Blue Notes★

★ Marked in the example with an asterisk.

These microtonal alterations are not precisely notated; rather, they are added by the performers and are understood as a distinguishing feature of the art form and its performance practice. In a famous 1925 recording of the *St. Louis Blues,* for example, Bessie Smith's blue notes are answered by Louis Armstrong's improvised cornet solos. A reed organ provides the background accompaniment.

The *St. Louis Blues* consists of three main sections: a twelve-bar blues of three lines, which is repeated; an eight-bar transitional section, also repeated; and a concluding twelve-bar "chorus" (again based on the standard blues scheme), which revolves around a blue note as the vocalist sings "Got de St. Louis Blues."

JAZZ AND POPULAR MUSIC TO THE SECOND WORLD WAR

Early jazz was a synthesis of ragtime and blues. Its first center was Storyville, the red-light district of New Orleans, where the version known as Dixieland emerged; from there it spread north to Memphis, Kansas City, and Chicago, and east to New York. In New Orleans, Dixieland was played by small groups or "combos" resembling marching bands. A typical band included a cornet, clarinet, trombone, banjo, and drum, a mobile ensemble that could play outdoors as well as indoors. Such groups played for funerals and other outdoor processions, in taverns, and in brothels. Indoors, they were often joined by a piano. The leading figures of the New Orleans jazz style were two cornetists, Joe "King" Oliver (1885–1938) and Louis Armstrong, and the pianist "Jelly Roll" Morton.

LOUIS ARMSTRONG, *STRUTTIN' WITH SOME BARBECUE*

Early jazz bands were organized into two sections. The melodic section, or "front line," projected and embellished the theme. The front line was led by a cornet, which was eventually replaced by a trumpet. Along with the cornet, the front line typically included a clarinet and a trombone. The clarinet, when it was not playing a solo, generally executed florid lines around the cornet part. The trombone played in a lower range, where it engaged in short solos, provided a kind of free counterpoint against the main melody line, and occasionally erupted in colorful glissandos. The second section was

Creole Jazz Band (1923). From left to right, the instruments include trombone, drums, "slide" trumpet (with Louis Armstrong), cornet (with King Oliver), piano, banjo, and clarinet.

the **rhythm section,** made up of a piano, a banjo, and drums. This section provided a steady beat and gave the melodic section a firm harmonic foundation. In a typical arrangement, a performance began with the entire ensemble, continued with improvised solos for the front line, and concluded with the ensemble.

Louis Armstrong's *Struttin' with Some Barbecue,* recorded in Chicago in 1927, features Armstrong on the cornet in a band that includes trombone, clarinet, piano, and banjo. A short introduction for the full band leads directly to a cornet statement of the essential melodic line. A few chords on the banjo prepare for the second statement, which is divided between a clarinet solo and a trombone solo. The clarinet is accompanied by steady chords on the piano and banjo; when the trombone enters, the chords are cut in half and placed on the offbeat. A short connective passage for cornet and trombone leads to the final statement for full band. The piece ends with a surprise: The rhythm section drops out and the front line finishes the piece on its own.

Originally designed about 1849 by the Belgian
Adolphe Sax as an instrument for orchestras and military bands, the saxophone was later used by such
composers as Meyerbeer, Richard Strauss, Ravel, and
Pro'ofiev. In the 1920s and 1930s, it became a regular
member of the new, larger jazz bands that took hold
in Chicago and elsewhere. With its mellow yet powerful tone, the saxophone figured prominently as
well in the dance bands of the Swing Era. The
instrument has a single-reed mouthpiece and a metal
body with a wide-conical bore. It is available in sizes
ranging from soprano to bass.

OTHER DEVELOPMENTS IN JAZZ AND POPULAR MUSIC

During the 1920s—the "jazz age"—and 1930s, the small Dixieland jazz combos expanded. In Chicago—which attracted such musicians as Louis Armstrong, Leon "Bix" Beiderbecke (the first white jazz musician of distinction, 1903–1931), and Earl "Fatha" Hines (1903–1983)—and elsewhere, the larger ensembles attained the size of big bands. New instruments, such as the saxophone, were added or were substituted for traditional instruments, for example guitar for banjo, trumpet for cornet. Louis Armstrong had worked with two small combos in the New Orleans tradition, the Hot Five and the Hot Seven. By the end of the Roaring Twenties, Jelly Roll Morton's band, the Red Hot Peppers, boasted eleven members; and by the mid-1930s, a typical band might include thirteen musicians: five brass (trumpets and trombones), four saxophones, and four members of the rhythm section (piano, drums, guitar, and string bass).

The new, larger bands required more careful coordination than had the smaller Dixieland groups, which had relied heavily on their improvisational skills. Compositions were now set down in arrangements known as "charts," which summarized for each member of the band the essential harmonic and rhythmic shape of the music; solo improvisations were coordinated within these plans. The most brilliant of the new arranger/composers was Edward "Duke" Ellington (1899–1974), who built even bigger bands and excelled in new effects, such as blending the contrasting timbres of the various instruments (*Black and Tan Fantasy,* 1927) and muting the brass instruments. His total output amounts to thousands of compositions, including several hundred short works, three minutes or so in length, created for 78 rpm recordings. But Ellington went well beyond this miniature time frame to create numerous other, ambitious works in which he investigated progressively more complex forms and adventurous harmonies (for example, the *Creole Rhapsody* of 1931 and *Black, Brown, and Beige,* 1933–1943, a five-part work designed to portray the history of blacks in their music; or *Ko-ko* and *Concerto for Cootie,* both of 1940).

The 1930s brought the era of **swing** in jazz—polished, arranged music played by carefully rehearsed dance bands. Several white musicians joined Ellington in the new style, of whom the most gifted was the clarinetist Benny Goodman (1909–1986), the "King of Swing." (In 1938 Benny Goodman's band appeared at Carnegie Hall in New York, an event that helped "legitimatize" the position of jazz in American music.) Superb bands led by such celebrated musicians as Glenn Miller (1904–1944), Tommy Dorsey (1905–1956), and "Count" Basie (1904–1984), to name only a few, spread swing throughout the country with concert tours, recordings, and radio broadcasts. The period produced such celebrated musicians as the saxophonist Coleman Hawkins (known as "Bean" or "Hawk," 1904–1969) and the singer Billie Holiday (1915–1959). The popularity of swing began to wane only with the onset of the Second World War, when the enthusiasm for the suave big-band sound was dampened by the realities of the worldwide conflagration.

Other forms of popular music flourished alongside the remarkable proliferation of jazz. The songwriters of Tin Pan Alley gave the public an unending stream of memorable tunes; among the most successful were George M. Cohan (1878–1942; "You're a Grand Old Flag," "Over There," "Give My Regards to Broadway"), Jerome Kern

Band of the Swing Era.

(1885–1945; "Smoke Gets in Your Eyes"), Irving Berlin (1888–1989; "Alexander's Rag-time Band"), and Cole Porter (1891–1964, "Begin the Beguine"). Several of these composers produced Broadway musicals, a uniquely American art form that inclined toward light operetta (Victor Herbert's *Babes in Toyland* of 1903) or vaudeville (George M. Cohan's musical comedy *Little Johnny Jones* of 1904). Later successful musicals included Jerome Kern's *Show Boat* (1927), Irving Berlin's *Annie Get Your Gun* (1946), Cole Porter's *Kiss Me, Kate* (1948), and Rodgers' and Hammerstein's *Oklahoma!* (1943) and *South Pacific* (1949), among many, many others.

The most gifted composer of American musicals was George Gershwin (1898–1937), a distinguished songwriter ("Swanee," "I've Got Rhythm"), who wrote a series of highly successful Broadway shows, including *Funny Face* (1927), *Girl Crazy* (1930), and *Of Thee I Sing* (1931). Gershwin consulted with Maurice Ravel in Paris about orchestration, played tennis with Arnold Schoenberg in Los Angeles, and in his spare time painted portraits. He produced three major concert works, all indebted to American jazz: *Rhapsody in Blue* for piano and orchestra (1924; originally written for Paul Whiteman's jazz band and later orchestrated); Concerto in F, a full-fledged concerto for piano and orchestra (1925); and *An American in Paris* for orchestra (1928), a charming piece that combines the street sounds of Paris, blues music for the homesick traveler, and a frolicking Charleston. Gershwin's masterpiece is the three-act "folk opera" *Porgy and Bess* (1935), set in Catfish

Row, a black tenement in Charleston, South Carolina, and intended for a company of black singers and actors. With such American classics as the songs "Summertime," "It Ain't Necessarily So," and "Bess, You Is My Woman Now," *Porgy and Bess* suggests what splendid music Gershwin might have given us had his career not been cut short by his early death in 1937.

Suggested Listening

Louis Armstrong: *Hotter Than That*
★_____ : *Struttin' with Some Barbecue*
★Bartók: *Fourteen Bagatelles,* Op. 6
Duke Ellington: *Concerto for Cootie*
_____ : *Creole Rhapsody*
Gershwin: *Porgy and Bess*
_____ : *Rhapsody in Blue*
★W. C. Handy: *St. Louis Blues*
Charles Ives: *Concord* Sonata
★_____ : *General William Booth Enters into Heaven*
_____ : *The Unanswered Question*
Joplin: *The Entertainer*
★_____ : *Maple Leaf Rag*
Kodály: *Háry János* Suite
★Vaughan Williams: *Fantasia on a Theme by Thomas Tallis*
_____ : *A Pastoral Symphony*

Note: Works marked with an asterisk are the principal works discussed in the chapter.

19

NEW DIRECTIONS
AND THE RECENT PAST

*T*he end of the Second World War brought a new era of experimentation in the arts. In the decades since, the very meaning of music—and of the other arts as well—has been tested and retested, defined and redefined. Music now means just about anything anyone wants it to mean, from compositions for concert hall performance to the random sounds of the everyday environment, including silence, the lack of sound. In the last few decades, probing questions have been raised about the nature of music, its philosophical justification, and its purpose. And yet, while this second revolution has commanded the energies of the avant-garde, older musical traditions have somehow managed to survive. Contemporary music is a bewildering juxtaposition of the old and the new, the familiar and the unknown.

Technology helped fuel this second revolution. The phonograph, the tape recorder, radio, television, and the cinema gave composers and musicians access to mass audiences and disseminated music of every sort, from art music to jazz and other forms of popular music, around the world. The electronic studio, the computer, the synthesizer, and other technological enhancements enabled composers to explore previously uncharted musical territory and to realize the sounds of their music with unprecedented precision. The new technology gave composers more and more control over their work, but it also raised complex new issues about musical creation—indeed, about the relation between composers and their sonic environment, and between composers and their audiences.

In this final chapter, we shall survey some of the leading developments in music of the postwar years. In brief, these developments have included the revival and preservation of tonality in some form; the systematic extension of serialism to nonpitch

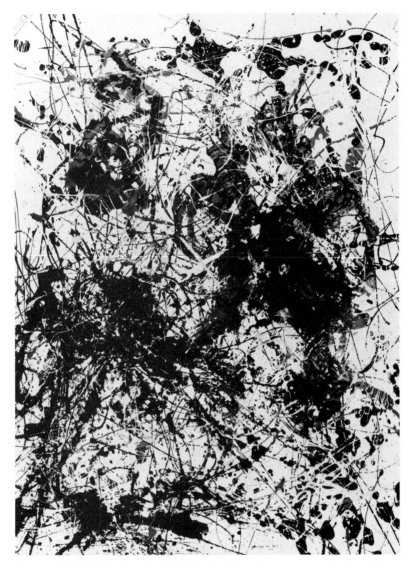

Jackson Pollock, *Number 12, 1949*. The leading abstract expressionist of the postwar era, the American Jackson Pollock became celebrated for his unorthodox painting techniques that derived in part from surrealism. By dripping, splattering, or pouring paint directly onto the canvas, Pollock produced dynamic works charged with unpredictable, random effects. (Jackson Pollock, "Number 12," 1949. Oil on paper, mounted on composition board, 31″ by 32½″. Collection, The Museum of Modern Art.)

elements, giving composers greater control over the organization of their musical material; the use of electronic media to expand drastically the boundaries of conventional musical sound; and the introduction of chance into music to achieve, paradoxically, lack of control. Along with these trends the postwar years witnessed the accelerating evolution of jazz and the dynamic development of rock and other types of popular music.

NEOTONAL MUSIC AND MUSICAL CONSERVATISM

Several composers active just before and after the war chose to write music that retained some sort of tonal principles. In the United States, Roy Harris (1898–1979) perfected a populist style in a long series of stylistically conservative symphonies, many of them inspired by American folk elements. Samuel Barber (1910–1981) won recognition for his song cycles *Dover Beach* (with string quartet accompaniment, 1933) and *Knoxville: Summer of 1915* (with orchestral accompaniment, 1948). The libretto of Barber's opera *Vanessa* (1958) was prepared by Gian Carlo Menotti (b. 1911), who composed successful operas for radio and television, among them *Amahl and the Night Visitors,* first broadcast in 1951. Other American composers began by writing neotonal music and then adopted atonal idioms. For example, Roger Sessions (1896–1985), who studied with Horatio Parker at Yale before working for several years in Europe, produced a neoclassical symphony and piano sonata and a violin concerto with an inscrutable tonal logic before he changed course to explore a twelve-tone idiom and other styles in the 1950s.

BENJAMIN BRITTEN

Tonality proved to be especially resilient in England. After Vaughan Williams, Benjamin Britten (1913–1976) emerged as the most distinguished English composer; he came of age musically during the Second World War. Possessed of enormous musical talent, Britten was a facile composer even as a child. After studying at the Royal College of Music, he wrote music for documentary films in collaboration with the poet W. H. Auden. Britten traveled to the United States in 1939, only to return to England after the outbreak of hostilities. In 1948 he founded a music festival in the East Anglian town of Aldeburgh; many of his compositions were premiered there. A prolific composer, Britten worked in many different genres. *The Young Person's Guide to the Orchestra* (1946), based on a theme of Henry Purcell, is a finely crafted primer on the modern orchestra. Britten displays the various instruments of the four basic groups (woodwinds, brass, strings, and percussion) in a cunning series of variations and ends with a fugue for the entire orchestra. Among his other works are the *Ceremony of Carols* (1942) for boys' chorus accompanied by harp, the *Serenade for Tenor, Horn, and Strings* (1943), and the moving *War Requiem* (1962), in which he juxtaposes verses by the poet Wilfrid Owen with a setting of the Requiem Mass.

Britten's best efforts, however, were in opera. He drew on a variety of sources for his librettos, though he favored English and American literature. His first successful opera, *Peter Grimes* (1945), was inspired by the eighteenth-century poetry of George

Crabbe, from Britten's native Suffolk. *Billy Budd* (1951) was based on Melville's short novel about man's inhumanity to man. *The Turn of the Screw* (1954) and *Owen Wingrave* (1971) were drawn from stories by Henry James. *A Midsummer Night's Dream* (1960) was based, though freely, on Shakespeare's comedy. Among Britten's more innovative works are three church parables, *Curlew River* (1964), *The Burning Fiery Furnace* (1966), and *The Prodigal Son* (1968). Britten drew his inspiration for these parables from Japanese plays, though he shifted the action to English settings, and employed plainchant in a kind of revival of the medieval English religious drama.

In most of his operas, Britten used a direct tonal language based on triads. But in *The Turn of the Screw*, a two-act opera for small vocal and instrumental forces, he devised a twelve-note theme and subjected it to serial manipulations, almost as if it were a twelve-tone row. The theme is constructed on a series of spiraling fourths and thirds, soft consonances that are compatible with Britten's carefully planned sequence of tonalities (all indicated by the use of traditional key signatures throughout the opera):

Britten: The Turn of the Screw

Each act consists of eight scenes with interpolated variations. The scenes of the first act are written in a rising, spiraling sequence of keys. The second act reverses that sequence as the plot unwinds. Tonality is thus coordinated with the tone row to symbolize the title of James's celebrated "ghost" story. The various turns of the plot—the first meeting between the Governess and her charges, Flora and Miles; the successive appearances of the apparitions, Mr. Quint and Miss Jessel; and their evil influence on the children—find their musical counterparts in Britten's elaborate key plan, based, in turn, on the pitch relationships of the twelve-note theme.

Throughout his career, Britten's music evinced an articulate musical logic and impressive craftsmanship. Notwithstanding his decidedly conservative outlook, Britten demonstrated convincingly the viability of English opera as an art form in the twentieth century.

DMITRY SHOSTAKOVICH

Throughout the twentieth century, tonality remained firmly entrenched in the Soviet Union as well. There, state policy discouraged composers from experimenting with new compositional techniques that were emerging in the West. That rigidity first set in a few years after the outbreak of the Bolshevik Revolution in 1917. For a brief period Russian musicians, artists, and writers actually enjoyed a good measure of freedom, and some Russian composers managed to achieve international recognition. Thus, as we have seen, Stravinsky left Russia for the West early in his career. Prokofiev, too, spent many years in the West and became familiar with the experiments of his Western counterparts; indeed, his early music reflects the steely dissonance of the modern machine age. Prokofiev's principal successor, however, spent little time in the West. Dmitry Shostakovich (1906–1975) attended the conservatory in Petrograd; his graduation exercise, the First Symphony, was especially well received both at home and abroad as the work of a promising young symphonist.

The year was 1925, shortly before Stalin seized power. Determined to transform Russia into a modern totalitarian state, Stalin ruthlessly crushed political opposition, instituted a series of five-year plans to strengthen the economy, and, through the party machinery, decreed what was acceptable in the arts. Composers were to expunge all traces of "decadent," bourgeois music from their works; they were to serve the state by conveying the themes of communism to Soviet citizens in lucid melodies expressed in uncompromising tonality. Music, in short, was to be an idealization of the Soviet state.

Shostakovich more or less abided by these directives in his early music; his first symphonies are based on unabashedly patriotic programs. He wrote his Second Symphony, titled *To October* (1927), to celebrate the tenth anniversary of the Bolshevik Revolution; he wrote his Third Symphony, titled *May Day* (1929), to commemorate the international day celebrated by all socialist workers. A more ambitious project, which marked a turning point in his career, was the opera *Lady Macbeth of the Mtsensk District* (1934), a sordid tale of nineteenth-century bourgeois life under the tsars. For two years, the opera played in Moscow to great acclaim. Then, abruptly, it was denounced in the Russian press for its modernist tendencies. The thirty-year-old composer, finding himself ostracized, withdrew both the opera and his Fourth Symphony, which he had just placed in rehearsal.

Shostakovich won rehabilitation with his Fifth Symphony (1937), which he ostensibly offered as a response to "justified criticism." The symphony was immediately acclaimed as a masterpiece, both in Russia and in the West. With the onset of the Second World War, he directed his energies to writing symphonies celebrating the homeland. He conceived his Seventh Symphony during the German siege of Leningrad in 1941, and his Eighth Symphony (1943) was a somber reflection on the cruelties of war. The Ninth (1945) was a joyous celebration of victory. But once again Shostakovich came under attack: In 1948 a party resolution censured him (and other composers) for yielding to "formalism"—that is, for subordinating the content of his music to abstract (and, presumably, contagiously Western) designs. He responded by purging his scores of the offending "mannerisms" and by writing in a simpler, more accessible style. His symphonies now extolled socialist realism, including the symphonies he wrote after the death of Stalin in 1953 and the relaxation of party pronouncements on the proper purpose of Russian music. The Eleventh Symphony (1957) deals with a 1905 uprising during the waning reign of the tsars that anticipated the events of 1917; the Twelfth (1961) is dedicated to the memory of Lenin.

In his last years, Shostakovich's music grew increasingly somber and contemplative. The Thirteenth Symphony (1962), titled *Babi Yar,* is a dark-hued symphonic cantata with texts drawn from the protest poetry of Yevgeny Yevtushenko; because of its text, it, too, met with official criticism. The Fourteenth Symphony (1969), dedicated to Benjamin Britten, is a symphonic song cycle with texts drawn from Western poetry.

Its subject is death. In a different, quasi-satiric vein, the Fifteenth Symphony (1971), for orchestra alone, presents the listener with occasional quotations from Rossini and Wagner.

After Prokofiev's death in 1953, Shostakovich stood as the preeminent Soviet composer, a position he enjoyed for two decades. Throughout his life, he adapted his music to the needs and directives of the state. We can only speculate about what course his music might have taken had he enjoyed the full artistic freedom of the West.

STRAVINSKY AND SERIALISM

After the war, many composers turned to a methodical exploration of Schoenberg's twelve-tone system and its implications for composition. Among them was Igor Stravinsky, who had worked during the 1920s, 1930s, and 1940s to master a neoclassical idiom. Now, in the postwar years, he became thoroughly familiar with the music of Anton Webern. Won over by its pristine craft, Stravinsky took the decision to adopt serialism.

At first, he applied serial techniques cautiously, in a cluster of carefully executed works. The most striking of these compositions are the *Three Songs from William Shakespeare* (1953, for voice, flute, clarinet, and viola) and a moving tribute to the poet Dylan Thomas, *In memoriam Dylan Thomas* (1954, for tenor, string quartet, and trombone quartet). The latter work consists of instrumental dirge canons that frame a setting of Dylan Thomas's poem on the death of his father, "Do not go gentle into that good night." The music is strictly serial, but the basic row comprises only five notes, which fill out the chromatic pitches between C and E, the interval of a third:

Stravinsky: In memoriam Dylan Thomas, *Tone Row*

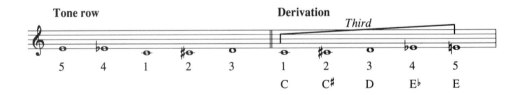

The row is thus not a conventional twelve-tone row but a succinct row of five pitches that can be inverted, performed backwards (retrograde), and transposed. Because the row spans the interval of a third, it carries certain tonal associations and can combine with triadic harmonies. In this way, Stravinsky is able to explore serial technique on a small scale without abandoning altogether tonal principles of organization.

SEPTET (1953)

Stravinsky's Septet (1953), scored for three winds (clarinet, horn, and bassoon), piano, and three strings (violin, viola, and cello), is another work from his experimental serial period; here, he occasionally achieves lean, sparse textures of sound that recall Webern's reserved style. The first movement unfolds as a sonata-form movement. Though its harmonic language is polytonal, it has a key signature that identifies A major as its central tonality. The second movement is a passacaglia that alludes to the intricacies of baroque counterpoint. The subject of the passacaglia is the following sixteen-note theme, which moves throughout its angular course by wide leaps:

Stravinsky: Septet, Second Movement

PASSACAGLIA SUBJECT

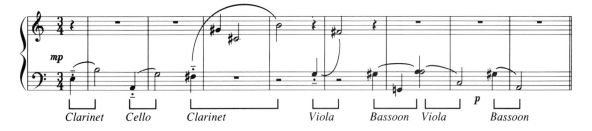

The theme is followed by eight variations; the movement concludes with a simple statement of the theme itself. Again, Stravinsky avoids committing himself to using a twelve-tone row; his sixteen-note theme has several repeated pitches, giving it a tonal stability lacking in Schoenberg's or Webern's twelve-tone scores. But from a different perspective Stravinsky's theme is closely related to Schoenberg's method: The initial statement of the theme recalls the technique of *Klangfarbenmelodie* (p. 411), first introduced by Schoenberg and applied by Berg and Webern. Stravinsky divides the theme among the registers of the winds and the strings, permitting the various colors of the ensemble to emerge like dabs of sound. We hear the clarinet (two notes), then the cello (two notes), the clarinet (four notes), the viola (two notes), the bassoon (three notes), the viola (two notes), and the bassoon (two notes). Subsequently throughout the movement, the theme appears in its entirety in the piano, where it mediates between the distinct sonorities of the wind and string groups and provides a firm center for the rich instrumental polyphony of the variations that envelops it.

In the last movement, Stravinsky again explores a neobaroque idiom: He writes a gigue and now allows his serial technique to take firmer shape. Each instrument is assigned an eight-note, scalelike row from which the pitches of its thematic material are drawn. Here is the first row, for viola, together with the derived subject, which uses pitches from that row:

Stravinsky: Septet, Gigue

ROW

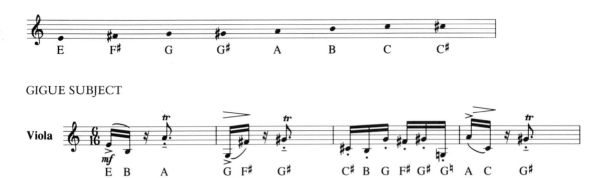

GIGUE SUBJECT

Once again, Stravinsky avoids employing a strict twelve-tone row; nevertheless, he achieves in the gigue a masterpiece of contrapuntal inventiveness within a limited serial context. In the first section (see study diagram), the subject is introduced by the three strings, which enter in turn in a mock fugal exposition. Reaching a cadence, they yield to the piano and the winds (section 2); the piano takes up the gigue subject, and the winds answer with a version of the subject in augmented note values. At the end of this section, the strings return to introduce the subject in mirror inversion and in combination with the original version (section 3). In the fourth and final section, the

---

Stravinsky: Septet (Gigue)

Section 1		*Section 2*		
Fugue				
on gigue				
subject				
Strings	Cadence	Piano and	Cadence	
Viola		winds (in		
Violin		augmented		
Cello		values)		
		Bassoon		
		Horn		
		Clarinet		
mf		*mf*		

---

piano and the winds answer with various serial manipulations of the subject; the work concludes with two polytonal chords for the full ensemble.

In later works of the 1950s and 1960s, Stravinsky did adopt fully the twelve-tone method, though for him serialism involved much more than the facile manipulation of row forms. He used serialism as an ordering process that sometimes extended beyond the notes themselves. Thus, in the *Canticum sacrum* (1955)—a work written for Venice, for soloists, chorus, and orchestra, and with texts drawn from the Vulgate—he created a musical design that reflects the architecture of St. Mark's Cathedral. In the ballet *Agon* (1957), he coordinated his use of row forms with "serialized" patterns of twelve dancers and various subgroupings.

Stravinsky's late music came closer and closer to attaining Webern's severe compression of means: Such works as the *Movements* for piano and orchestra (1959), the Variations for Orchestra (1964), and the *Requiem Canticles* (1966) last only a few minutes. In the end, Stravinsky mastered the twelve-tone system, but he never let his music be controlled by its rigor. His late music is energized by the same rhythmic vitality that marked the *Symphony of Psalms* from his neoclassical period and *The Rite of Spring* from his early period.

THE NEW ORDER: TOTAL SERIALISM

Schoenberg's twelve-tone system had been conceived as a means of serializing or organizing the twelve pitches of the chromatic scale. The logical next step was for composers to organize other aspects of music such as rhythm, dynamics, and register to achieve music that was "totally" serialized. The first composer to do so systematically was the

---

Stravinsky: Septet (Gigue), *Continued*

	Section 3		*Section 4*	
	Subject			
	in mirror			
	inversion and			
	combined with			
	original subject			
	Strings	Cadence	Piano and	Cadence
	Viola		winds (in	Full
	Violin		augmented	ensemble
	Cello		values)	(chords)
			(prime and retrograde)	
			Horn	
			Clarinet	
			Bassoon	
	(mf)		*mf*	

American Milton Babbitt (b. 1916), who taught for many years at Princeton, where he trained many young American composers. Educated himself as a mathematician, Babbitt embraced Schoenberg's twelve-tone system and began to explore twelve-tone rows that exhibited special mathematical properties. In the *Three Compositions for Piano* (1947), he made use of "rows" of rhythmic and dynamic values, in addition to a rigorous system of twelve-tone rows. Then, on a more ambitious scale, he applied similar serial techniques in the chamber work *Composition for Twelve Instruments* (1948).

In Europe, the French composer Olivier Messiaen (b. 1908) began to explore the structuring of nonpitch elements in his music of the postwar years. Trained at the Paris Conservatory, Messiaen was a church organist in Paris for many years. During the war, he spent time in a prisoner-of-war camp, and his experience there inspired him to compose the *Quatuor pour la fin du temps* (*Quartet for the End of Time,* 1940), for clarinet, piano, violin, and cello. Messiaen found inspiration for his music in a variety of sources, including antique Greek meters, Hindu rhythmic patterns, Peruvian folk song, and, above all, birdcalls. An avid ornithologist, he based several works on birdcalls he had meticulously notated on field expeditions; among those works are *Oiseaux exotiques* (*Exotic Birds,* 1956) and *Catalogue d'oiseaux* (*Catalogue of Birds,* 1958). He explored "nonretrogradable" rhythmic patterns—patterns that retain their sequence of rhythms when performed in reverse. He also worked with symmetrical scales which permit only a few transpositions before they reproduce their original form.

In 1949 Messiaen finished four rhythmic studies for piano solo. The third of these, *Mode de valeurs et d'intensités* (*Mode of durations and intensities*), was a pioneering work. It is built from four basic "modes," which define its pitches, rhythmic durations, types of attack (for example, staccato, legato, accented, unaccented), and dynamic levels. The music is assigned to three registers of the piano (high, medium, and low), which are made to coincide with rhythmic values of short, medium, and long duration. The result is a scintillating constellation of bursts of sound, now brittle, now elastic, now fleeting, now sustained.

BOULEZ: *STRUCTURES I* (1952)

In Darmstadt and in Paris, two younger composers, Pierre Boulez (b. 1925) and Karlheinz Stockhausen (b. 1928), studied Messiaen's music and followed his attempt to structure nonpitch elements. Boulez's major essay in **total serialism** was *Structures I* for two pianos, first performed in 1952. This remarkable work is a *tour de force* of precompositional planning. In homage to his teacher Messiaen, Boulez took as a starting point a twelve-tone row from the pitch mode of Messiaen's *Mode de valeurs et d'intensités*. Then, he generated a complete row table, using numbers 1 through 12 to represent the twelve pitches. Next, he fabricated three basic series of rhythmic values, dynamics, and types of articulations. The rhythmic values extended from one to twelve thirty-second notes; the dynamics included twelve levels, ranging from *pppp* to *ffff*; and the articulations comprised twelve methods of attack.

Boulez deliberately conceived these nonpitch series so that they could be represented by numbers from 1 to 12 and so that they could be ordered to correspond with the succession of pitches in any given row. Here is his original row, with the twelve numbers corresponding to its twelve pitches:

Boulez: Structures I*

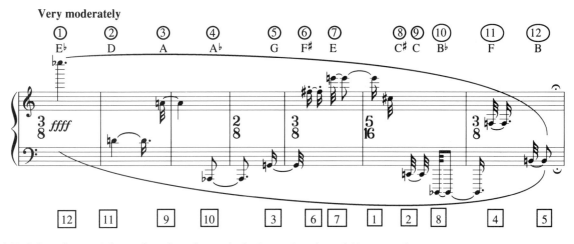

*Circled number = pitch row; boxed number = rhythmic row (in values of thirty-second notes).

To determine the rhythmic values (calculated in numbers of thirty-second notes) of this passage, Boulez turned to another row (not shown), whose pitches formed this numerical sequence: 12, 11, 9, 10, 3, 6, 7, 1, 2, 8, 4, 5. Thus, in our example the first pitch (E-flat) has a duration of *twelve* thirty-second notes, the second (D) a duration of *eleven* thirty-second notes, the third (A) a duration of *nine,* and so on. In this way, Boulez was able to predetermine with exactitude the dimensions and particulars of his composition. Much of his effort was devoted to precompositional planning; once he had designed his system of generating rows of pitches, rhythms, dynamics, and articulations, he could proceed to notate the work as a matter of course—almost as an afterthought.

Karlheinz Stockhausen was also fascinated by Messiaen's experiments in serialism; he described them as the "fantastic music of the stars." Stockhausen's first major composition to show total serialization was *Kreuzspiel* ("Cross-Play") of 1951. This was an experiment in musical pointillism, in which Stockhausen freed points of sound from the traditional connotations of theme and harmony. He organized the work as a series of intersections of different musical components—pitch, rhythm, and register, for example. (Boulez undertook a somewhat similar experiment in his *Polyphonie X* of 1951, a work he later withdrew.) *Kreuzspiel* is scored for piano, oboe, bass clarinet, and percussion. The piano controls the extreme registers of pitch, while the oboe and the bass clarinet control the middle ranges. In the first section, the piano part is gradually made to "intersect" with the oboe and the bass clarinet; by the conclusion of the section, what was originally heard in the high range of the piano has been transferred to its lowest register, and vice versa. The composition is thus a highly complex coordination of register in a serial context.

In *Kontra-Punkte* (1952), Stockhausen worked with an ensemble of ten instruments arranged in six groups: flute and bassoon, clarinet and bass clarinet, trumpet and trombone, piano, harp, and violin and cello. Through the course of the piece, the groups are reduced, so that only the piano remains at the end. Instead of controlling isolated points of sound, as in *Kreuzspiel,* Stockhausen now manipulated groups of pitches, which he subjected to no less exacting a control. The result was a fluid juxtaposition of varying groups of pitches rather than a precise counterpoint of individual notes against notes. Stockhausen's title, *Kontra-Punkte,* is an allusion to "Kontrapunkt" ("counterpoint"), but, it turns out, it also symbolizes a critical rejection of an earlier work titled *Punkte* ("Points"), which Stockhausen had written in the pointillistic idiom.

The strict control exercised by Stockhausen and Boulez in their new music marked a milestone in the use of the serial technique. As we shall see, both composers later sought to inject into their music elements of spontaneity, but during the early 1950s, they were content to regulate their approach to composition with scientific precision.

NEW RESOURCES IN SOUND

The advancing technology of the electronic age after the Second World War opened up new sonic worlds to composers. Even before the war, however, a few adventurous composers had begun to explore the possibilities of new sounds, some of them extracted from familiar instruments. The prolific American composer Henry Cowell (1897–1965), for example, drew unconventional sounds from the piano. He produced percussive "tone clusters" by striking a range of keys with his forearm, and harplike sounds by playing on the piano strings (*Aeolian Harp,* 1923; *The Banshee,* 1925). Other composers, impatient with the limitations of the Western chromatic scale, investigated microtones— tones smaller than the traditional half step. Still others sought to capture in their music the dynamism of modern life, its machines, energies, and motions. The Swiss composer Arthur Honegger (1892–1955) wrote orchestral movements depicting an accelerating and decelerating locomotive (*Pacific 231,* 1923) and a rugby match (*Rugby,* 1928).

One especially focused, though short-lived, movement that sought to harness the sounds of the machine age was *futurism.* Centered in Italy, the futurists were most active in the visual arts, though they worked to extend the composer's domain to the world of noise. In 1913 one of the principal futurists, the painter Luigi Russolo (1885–1947), published a bold manifesto titled *The Art of Noises.* This tendentious document contrasted the "silence" of antiquity with the booming, gurgling, crackling sounds of the modern age, which he attributed to the imposition of man-made machines on the natural environment. It was the duty of modern composers to identify and regulate such sounds, Russolo proclaimed, and to incorporate them into their music. Russolo identified various classes of sounds, including the sounds made by humans and animals, percussive noises made by striking objects, and various whistles, explosions, and hisses. The futurists looked forward to a time when composers would systematically convert the sounds of factories into a throbbing music of noise.

EDGARD VARÈSE: *HYPERPRISM* (1923)

A composer particularly emboldened to exploit new musical resources was the Frenchman Edgard Varèse (1883–1965). Though Varèse wrote most of his music before the Second World War, his influence became particularly meaningful after the war. Varèse arrived in the United States in 1915, having destroyed the early compositions he had written in Paris. He followed no particular trend, preferring to strike out on his own. (He once likened Schoenberg's twelve-tone system to hardening of the arteries.) An uncompromising experimenter, he brought unconventional sounds into his modernist scores and used traditional instruments in unusual ways, all in an effort to create "organized noise."

Varèse was perhaps most innovative in his approach to musical structure. Rejecting the traditional notions of thematic and harmonic development, he viewed his music as masses of sounds that collided, repelled each other, and occasionally interacted. He compared his music to crystals, which have an infinite variety of shapes but only a limited number of internal molecular structures. Each of his compositions projects its own, unique form, the result of Varèse's rigorous control of the sound masses that make it up. To describe his innovative creations, he turned to quasi-scientific titles: *Hyperprism, Ionisation,* and *Density 21.5,* for example.

Varèse wrote most of his music during the 1920s and 1930s. The requirements of his scores vary from *Amériques* for large orchestra (1921) to *Density 21.5* for solo flute (1936; written for a flute made of platinum, whose density is 21.5). Varèse also produced a group of compositions for relatively small chamber ensembles. *Ionisation* (1931), for example, is for percussion instruments alone, most of them unpitched, so that pitch is more or less eliminated as a structural component. Varèse uses a variety of familiar unpitched instruments, including drums, castanets, triangle, tambourine, and cymbals. But he also introduces a group of sirens, whose arching crescendos project parabolic curves of sound. In addition, there are a cencerro, a cowbell that is struck with a drumstick; sleigh bells; anvils; woodblocks; slapstick; and a güiro, a Cuban notched gourd that is scratched with a stick. Most unusual of all is the "lion's roar," or string drum, a tub-shaped drum with a rope drawn through its membrane to produce a dull roaring sound. Varèse has all these indefinitely pitched instruments engage in an ever-changing counterpoint of rhythms. Toward the end of the work, in a kind of coda, bells and a piano execute a few pitched, atonal clusters of sound.

In *Hyperprism* (1923), Varèse combined a percussion group with an ensemble of wind and brass. Against the rhythmic backdrop of the percussion instruments, we hear first a single pitch from a trombone that is answered by French horns and by a second trombone. This sound mass gives way to a second mass executed by the flute and clarinet. Trumpets marked *haletantes* ("panting") provide yet another sound mass. Throughout this short work, various groups of instruments intersect, sometimes coming together with the percussion and sometimes going their own way. The composition concludes with a tremendous crescendo and crash.

From 1936 to 1947, Varèse more or less withdrew from composition. He was demoralized by the neglect his music was suffering, and he felt severely limited by what he could achieve with conventional instruments. He yearned for new musical instruments and resources that would enable him to explore widely ranging vistas of pitches, harmonies, and rhythms previously not available to composers. That wish was to be answered after the war, with the development of electronic music.

ELECTRONIC RESOURCES

Even before Varèse struggled to realize his vision of a new sound world, scientists had begun to work on electronic musical devices. As early as 1920, for example, the Russian physicist Léon Thérémin had invented an instrument that used oscillators to generate audible frequencies. In 1928 the French scientist Maurice Martenot produced the *ondes martenot,* a keyboard instrument that controls a variable oscillator that, in turn, produces sound amplified and projected through a loudspeaker. Also during the 1920s, the first electric organs began to appear.

A more significant advance in manipulating electronic sounds was made in the late 1940s by Pierre Schaeffer (b. 1910) and Pierre Henry (b. 1927), who worked in a sound laboratory for Radiodiffusion Française, the French national radio. Schaeffer and Henry used phonograph discs to record sounds of everyday life, including the sounds of locomotives, musical instruments, cries, and laughter. They then dissected, reassembled, played backwards, accelerated, or otherwise manipulated those sounds to produce a type of music they described as **musique concrète,** or "concrete music." These pioneers of electronic music drew their sounds from the environment with objective detachment. Their early work culminated in the *Symphonie pour un homme seul* (*Symphony for One Man Alone,* 1950), a twenty-two minute multimovement "symphony" of noises made up of a collection of human sounds.

At first, composers of *musique concrète* were hampered by the limitations of phonograph discs. But by the early 1950s, the tape recorder had become available, and its advent greatly facilitated the editing of material. One of the first composers to exploit this new device was Varèse, who produced a major contribution in his *Déserts* (1954), a hybrid work in which sections for orchestra (without strings) alternate with three interpolations of *musique concrète. Déserts* was the first work to combine electronic sounds with an orchestra; it was the first work, in short, to bring electronically manipulated sounds into the concert hall. In choosing the title *Déserts,* Varèse meant to suggest both barren landscapes of sound and the loneliness of the modern individual.

STOCKHAUSEN: *GESANG DER JÜNGLINGE* (1956)

During the 1950s, an electronic studio in Cologne attracted composers eager to compose with electronic sounds. Among them was Karlheinz Stockhausen, who used an array of oscillators, filters, modulators, and tape recorders to generate pure electronic sounds. Thus was born **electronic music.** Instead of borrowing sounds from their environment, as in *musique concrète,* composers now used generators to produce strata of sounds that could subsequently be combined in various mixtures; or, they commenced with "white noise," a mixture of the full range of audible frequencies, and filtered out particular bands of frequencies. Having established the raw material, they modified it by adding reverberation, altering the intensity of the sound, splicing various segments, or manipulating it in some other way. The final product was then recorded on tape.

The advantage of electronic music was that composers could control the end product with absolute precision. There was no need for rehearsals. Indeed, there was no need for a score or even a performance in the conventional sense. Composers encoded their intentions on magnetic tape, and by simply playing the tape those intentions were preserved with unerring accuracy. Nothing was left to chance; every detail of the music was clinically controlled in the sound laboratory. The possibilities of electronic music seemed boundless.

At first, Stockhausen explored the new electronic resources in a series of etudelike compositions. Then, in 1956, he realized in the studio a more ambitious work, *Gesang der Jünglinge* (*Song of the Youths*). For this work, Stockhausen introduced a texted element, the canticle sung by the three boys in Nebuchadnezzar's fiery furnace, as described in the Book of Daniel (in 1956 the image of a fiery furnace was all too vivid to a Europe still recovering from the horrific cataclysm of the Second World War). To reduce the contrast between pure electronic sounds and the recorded textual elements, Stockhausen used electronic means to alter the text, which is spoken and sung by a boy soprano. Occasionally, distinct words, such as "Preiset den Herrn" ("Praise the Lord"), emerge from the shifting textures of sound, but mostly the listener hears only an occasional vowel or consonant or an unintelligible cacophony of voices. Occasionally, Stockhausen organized the purely electronic sounds to approximate parts of words. The whole composition was channeled through five sets of speakers surrounding the audience, transforming the space into an engulfing labyrinth of sound.

On a first hearing, *Gesang der Jünglinge* proves to be a disorienting experience for the listener, who inevitably struggles to comprehend its bewildering array of gurgling, cackling, and humlike sounds that are emitted unpredictably from now this speaker and now that one. But in fact the work is a carefully crafted composition that divides into several discernible sections. The first 2:45 comprise one such section representative of the composer's method of fashioning electronic sounds. First we hear a series of bubbling noises that die out, leaving a high-pitched sound that gives way in turn to what sounds like the high pitch of a boy soprano (:10). A faint, distorted chorus of voices emerges (:14), followed by bell-like sounds (:17). The voice and the chorus alternate before giving way to a long, held sonority that gradually disintegrates (:38). Now the voices resume their unintelligible cacophony (:59); finally, the command "Preiset den Herrn" ("Praise the Lord") is given, sung twice in disjunct fashion by the boy soprano (1:04). Indistinguishable portions of words emerge and disappear, all connected by varying strands of electronic sounds. "Preiset den Herrn" reappears (1:52), with swooping strata of sounds. Near the conclusion of the section, the word "Preiset" is given by itself.

After Stockhausen's pathbreaking work, other composers began to introduce texts into their electronic music, as if to demonstrate that the new music was not devoid of human emotion and meaning. For example, the Italian composer Luciano Berio (b. 1925) based his *Thema—omaggio a Joyce* (1958) on a passage from James Joyce's novel *Ulysses*. The passage is first read by a female voice and is then subjected to electronic distortion. The electronic medium is ideally suited to this musical treatment of stream of consciousness. In *Visage* (1961), Berio combined the voice of the soprano Cathy Berberian with electronic sounds. Nonsense sounds, including sobbing and moaning, are heard in a free succession before the word "parole" (Italian for "words") is formed. The effect is that of a dramatic scene in which the voice ultimately emerges as a character in its own right.

The electronic works we have mentioned were all created as tape compositions; no live performers took part in "performances" of the music. The interaction of live performers and taped elements was thoroughly explored during the 1960s. Mario Davidovsky (b. 1934) and Jacob Druckman (b. 1928) produced two series of works, titled *Synchronisms* (1962–1974) and *Animus* (1966–1969), which feature virtuoso parts for solo instruments as well as taped electronic sounds. Milton Babbitt, who first essayed electronically synthesized sound in his *Composition for Synthesizer* (1961), created works that call for a live voice and taped sounds, including *Vision and Prayer* (1961), with a text by Dylan Thomas, and *Philomel* (1964), with a poem by John Hollander based in turn on a Greek myth from Ovid's *Metamorphoses*. In *Philomel*, the mute Philomela is transformed into a bird. The metamorphosis is represented musically by a subtle interplay between a live solo soprano voice, electronic sounds, and the voice recorded and transformed on tape.

In so-called live electronic music, electronic manipulations are achieved during the actual performance. One of the pioneers in this technique was Stockhausen, who first tested it in *Mikrophonie I* (1964), for tam-tam (or large gong), played by two performers, and a group of assistants who record and modify the sound during the performance. In effect, Stockhausen completed the evolution of electronic music from the laboratory to the live concert hall by finally combining the two sources of music making in a new synthesis.

In recent decades, the equipment composers have used to produce their electronic music has become far more flexible and sophisticated than the elementary tape recorders and awkward sound synthesizers of the 1950s. The early tape recorders were cumbersome: Each bit of sound had to be constructed and recorded, and then the whole composition had to be painstakingly spliced. Modern synthesizers, the products of the computer age (the first commercial instrument appeared in 1964), now make it possible to generate and modify electronic sounds accurately and swiftly. The first synthesizers were bulky instruments, but with advances in technology, synthesizers became more compact, affordable, and manageable. In the 1960s and 1970s, computers of ever-increasing sophistication were linked with synthesizers, affording composers far more accuracy and range in exploring the realms and limits of quantifiable sound.

THE NEW FRONTIER: INDETERMINACY IN MUSIC

Although the new electronic music of the 1950s and 1960s seemed the ideal vehicle for totally controlled music, some composers reacted against that control and began to reintroduce elements of spontaneity. Thus, Boulez abandoned the total serialism of *Structures* to compose *Le marteau sans maître* (*The Hammer without a Master,* 1957), a chamber work based on surrealist poetry by René Char. This work is scored for alto solo and six instrumentalists (alto flute, xylorimba, vibraphone, various percussion instruments, guitar, and viola★). It consists of nine movements, four of which use texts, while the other five function as instrumental preludes, postludes, and commentary. The scoring varies from movement to movement, recalling the freedom of Schoenberg's earlier chamber work, *Pierrot lunaire* (see p. 426). Although Boulez uses the twelve-tone system, he takes special pains to conceal the selection of row forms and to lessen the rigor of the serial method. Contributing to the captivating, exotic sound of the work is its pervasive use of non–Western rhythmic patterns, which lend it a spontaneous, natural quality.

In later works, Boulez went even further in freeing his music from methodological constraints. His *Pli selon pli* (*Fold according to Fold,* 1962), a major work for voice and orchestra, was conceived as a musical portrait of the French symbolist poet Mallarmé; the order of some of its parts is left to the discretion of the performers. In the Third Piano Sonata (1957), of which he completed two major sections, Boulez gave the soloist latitude in deciding on the order in which the music is played. The second section, titled "Trope," includes two smaller portions ("Parenthèse" and "Commentaire") that alternate between passages based strictly on the underlying tone row and passages of a freer nature, marked off like parenthetical interpolations in the score, that deviate from strict adherence to the row. More or less paralleling Boulez's efforts, Stockhausen introduced greater freedom into his music. The score for *Klavierstück XI* (1956), for example, presents the pianist with nineteen groups of music that may be played in any order, yielding an ever-changing musical mobile. In somewhat similar fashion, *Available Forms I* (1961) by the American composer Earle Brown provides clearly notated fragments for orchestra that may be performed in any order the conductor chooses. All these experiments were responses to the radically new musical philosophy of the American John Cage (b. 1912), who pioneered the use of chance elements to redefine fundamentally the scope of music and its meaning.

JOHN CAGE

As early as the 1940s, Cage demonstrated his unorthodox bent in a series of works composed for "prepared piano." He altered the piano by attaching various objects, such as screws, bolts, and wedges, to its strings, producing a battery of unfamiliar, metallic sounds. Later on, Cage studied Eastern philosophy and Zen Buddhism. Rejecting conventional Western notions of order and musical syntax, Cage began in the early 1950s to produce works whose components were ordered by random sequences drawn from the *I Ching,* the ancient Chinese book of changes. Among those works are the *Music of Changes* for piano (1951), in which pitches, rhythmic values, and timbres were derived from the *I Ching; Imaginary Landscape No. 5* (1952), the first electronic work to use random ordering; and *Williams Mix* (1952), in which Cage subjected six hundred bits of recorded sound to the *I Ching.*

★Slightly larger than the conventional flute, the alto flute has a range a fourth lower. The xylorimba is a xylophone with an extended lower range. The vibraphone is a percussion instrument with metal bars arranged in the order of a keyboard. The bars are amplified by a series of revolving blades set inside vertical tubes below the metal bars.

In those early efforts, Cage used random procedures to generate a fixed result. In time, he sought even greater freedom by progressively eliminating evidence of the composer's decision-making process. At the first performance of his *4'33"* (1952), which many viewed as a notorious statement against music, the pianist did not play the instrument during the duration of the "composition" but merely signified the beginning and the ending of its three parts by closing and opening the keyboard lid. The silence was filled by the random noises of the surroundings, which of course were different in each "performance." Other compositions that were, in Cage's words, "indeterminate of their performance," include the *Concert for Piano and Orchestra* (1958), which calls for instrumental parts generated by chance but provides no score. The musicians are to play anything they wish from their parts, beginning and ending on signals from the conductor.

Cage thus gradually withdrew into an unpredictable sound world of chance, abdicating the semblance of control over the course of his music. During the 1950s and 1960s, with each successive offering, he seemed determined to broaden the domain of music even further. Using what he called the circus principle, Cage conceived two works in 1958, an *Aria* for soprano and *Fontana Mix* for tape, that could be performed separately or together. The *Aria* used different styles of singing (determined by the soloist) and texts randomly drawn from five languages; *Fontana Mix* appeared initially as a tape prepared using random procedures (Cage's "score" left open the possibility of other interpretations). *Theatre Piece* (1960) and *HPSCHD* (1969, for as many as seven harpsichordists, electronic tapes, and various entertainments) combined random musical and theatrical gestures. The point of such "performance art," as it came to be known, was to discover and celebrate the work of art in the actual performance itself. The result was to upend radically the conventional relation of the composer to the work of art.

Not surprisingly, traditional musical notation held no meaning for Cage's random creations. Instead, Cage turned to startling graphic designs that the performers were to interpret for themselves. Finally, along with other composers, he reduced his music to mere verbal descriptions to suggest the general limits within which random sounds were to be generated and experienced.

Music with chance elements is known as **chance music** or **aleatoric music** (from the Latin noun for dice, *alea*). By the 1960s, aleatoric music had established itself as an innovative movement in music to be reckoned with. Cage and his adherents pursued total freedom from control as doggedly as serial composers had sought total control in their music.

EXPERIMENT AND RENEWAL: JAZZ

While composers at the leading edge of the avant-garde explored the limits of serialism and aleatoric music, jazz musicians were enriching their music by devising new approaches to the art and by modifying old ones. In the United States, the blues retained its popularity after the Second World War but remained susceptible to new influences. As early as the 1920s, an adaptation of the blues for piano known as **boogie-woogie** had come into its own. Boogie-woogie borrowed its harmonic structure from traditional

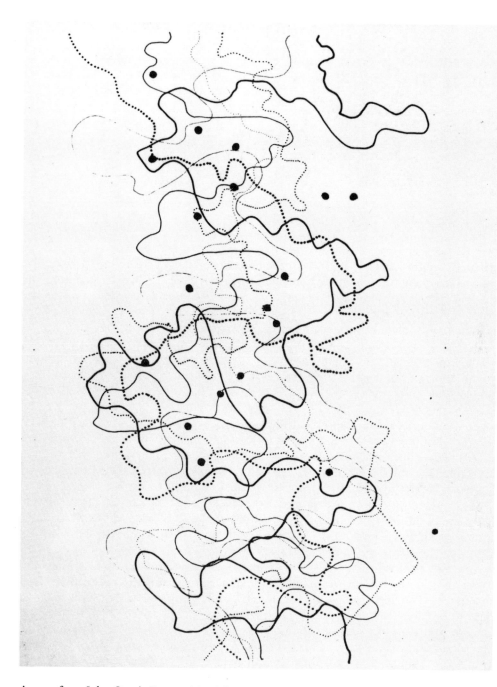

A page from John Cage's *Fontana Mix*. The score consists of ten "transparent sheets with points"; ten drawings, each with "six differentiated curved lines"; a transparent graph (not shown); and a straight line (not shown). A transparent sheet with points is placed over a drawing. Over these the transparent graph is placed, and the straight line is situated so that it connects two points. The graph is used to measure units of time (according to Cage's instructions, each unit is the equivalent of "any time unit"). The intersections of the curved lines and the straight line may indicate "actions to be made." The material may generate "tape music," but also instrumental and vocal music, and theatrical events.

blues but added a recurring bass pattern, generally some form of a "walking" pattern or a pattern in doubled notes:

Boogie-Woogie Bass Patterns

Above this bass pattern the pianist improvised energetic treble parts, with percussive dissonances and virtuoso melodic flourishes. Boogie-woogie quickly spread throughout the country, made popular by fashionable stylists who continued to perform their piano renditions of blues after the war. Musicians favored it because it gave them a solid foundation from which to launch their improvisations.

CHARLIE PARKER: "EMBRACEABLE YOU" (1947)

By the end of the Second World War, the polished style of the big bands had more or less run its course, and a younger generation of independently minded jazz musicians eager to experiment was coming to the fore. Some musicians joined together to reject the euphonious big-band sound in favor of a dynamic new style called **bebop,** also known as "rebop" or, simply, **bop.** Among the distinguished musicians who engaged in this energetic, volatile style of jazz were the saxophonist Charlie Parker (1920–1955), known as the "Bird" or "Yardbird," the pianist Thelonious Monk (1917–1982), and the trumpeter Dizzy Gillespie (b. 1917). Bop was first heard in a stunning series of late-night "jam" sessions in a Harlem nightclub. Played by small, elite groups of musicians with a reduced rhythm section (for example, a saxophone and trumpet accompanied by a piano, string bass, and drums), it featured soaring, irregular improvisational lines superimposed on the harmonic progressions of familiar tunes of earlier jazz and popular music, not infrequently performed at extremely fast tempos. The result, anything but familiar, consisted of bursts of melodic energy over an enriched harmonic structure. For example, in Charlie Parker's 1947 version of "Embraceable You," a classic Gershwin song, there is little hint of the familiar melody, even though its basic harmonic structure is preserved. After a short piano introduction, Parker launches into two statements, or interpretations, of the melody. He begins simply enough with a six-note motive:

Charlie Parker and Miles Davis.

Charlie Parker: "Embraceable You" (1947)

and continues with some ornaments that disguise but do not completely mask Gershwin's melody. But then Parker veers toward a series of complex rhythmic patterns and melodic turns that seem to take him further and further afield from the melody. Further on, a fresh improvisatory explosion of notes conceals the return of the opening; only the steady pattern of the string bass suggests the return.

Several types of jazz arose during the postwar years. "Hard bop" pushed the dynamic energy of bebop to new extremes. As if in reaction "cool jazz," practiced by such musicians as the trumpeter Miles Davis (b. 1926) and the saxophonists Gerry Mulligan (b. 1927) and Stan Getz (b. 1927), featured a transparent sound from the brass and reed instruments, with little or no vibrato.

By the early 1960s, the limits of jazz had broadened considerably. In a movement known as the Third Stream, the composer Gunther Schuller (b. 1925) mixed elements of jazz with the elements and resources of contemporary Western art music. In Free Jazz (or Free-Form Jazz), musicians began to depart substantially from the traditions that had served jazz for half a century. In the album *Kind of Blue* (1959), Miles Davis produced compositions based on jazz scales rather than on predetermined harmonic progressions. Ornette Coleman (b. 1930) and John Coltrane (1926–1967) engaged in freer, more radical improvisation, pushing jazz toward the realms of atonality and chance music.

DEVELOPMENTS IN POPULAR MUSIC

About the middle of the 1950s, a new kind of popular music emerged to rival jazz. Rock and roll, as it was known, had its origins in the music of Southern blacks of the 1950s, known as rhythm and blues. Often based on the harmonic pattern of the blues, rock and roll was performed at fast tempos and with an earthy, guttural vocal quality; performers often added nonsense syllables to create a careening, rhythmically pulsating sound. Because rock and roll was rich in thinly disguised sexual innuendos, many found it obscene and tried to have it banned. Others found it irresistible and began to imitate it, often doctoring the texts. Soon, rock and roll was absorbed into the mainstream of popular music. In 1954 Bill Haley recorded "Rock around the Clock," which sold twenty million copies. In 1956 Elvis Presley (1935–1977), the first superstar of rock and roll, took the country by storm with "Heartbreak Hotel" and "Hound Dog." "Elvis the Pelvis" captivated audiences with the gyrating motions of his stage manner. He became a film star and an idol of American youth.

Following the prosperity and calm of the 1950s, the 1960s brought social disenchantment and upheaval. In the United States, John F. Kennedy's "New Frontier," Lyndon Johnson's "Great Society," the civil rights movement, the women's liberation movement, and the protest against the Vietnam War were the great motivating forces of the decade. The popular music of the time, now known simply as **rock,** reflected the social ferment. Rock bands featured heavily amplified electronic guitars, which projected their deafening metallic sounds to mesmerized audiences. The guitars were supported by a strong beat provided by the percussion. Usually in common $\frac{4}{4}$ time, rock typically had accents on the second and fourth beats

$$\text{♩ ♩ ♩ ♩}$$
$$\text{ >   >}$$
$$1 \quad 2 \quad 3 \quad 4$$

that generated great rhythmic energy. The words were delivered in a rough, throaty manner of singing, often resembling shouting, that drove the message of the text home with unrelenting force.

Rock developed to be the music of social protest. It became a music directed as aggressively against the establishment as were the idealistic youth who protested through drug use, draft dodging, and attending rock festivals like the one at Woodstock in 1969, where half a million gathered. Rock reached its greatest popularity with the music of the Beatles, a quartet of English musicians who started out in the taverns of Liverpool, achieved their first success in England, and then launched an immensely successful career with their first United States tour in 1964. The Beatles thoroughly synthesized the styles of the blues, rhythm and blues, rock and roll, and other forms of American popular music. They were led by John Lennon and Paul McCartney, who wrote the words and music of most of their songs. George Harrison played lead guitar, and Ringo Starr played the drums. The ensemble usually consisted of three amplified guitars—the lead guitar, a bass guitar, and a rhythmic guitar—and drums; to this configuration was added or substituted keyboard instruments. All four members served as vocalists.

For a few years, the Beatles enjoyed international acclaim. "She Loves You" (1963), "Yesterday" (1965), "Eleanor Rigby" (1966), "Strawberry Fields Forever" (1967), and many other songs achieved the status of classics of popular music. Then, in 1966, the Beatles retired from public performance and produced a series of full-length albums, all carefully produced and assembled in the studio. In *Sergeant Pepper's Lonely Hearts Club Band* (1967), they brought together a variety of styles, including blues, jazz and Indian music, and a variety of instrumentations, including the Indian sitar, orchestral groups, and electronic modification. The album was held together by recurring themes of alienation and loneliness in the texts of the songs and by the music of Sergeant Pepper's band, which was heard at the beginning and the end, giving the album a cyclical unity.

Soon thereafter, the Beatles released the cartoon film *Yellow Submarine* (1968) and the experimental film *Magical Mystery Tour* (1968), which included "Fool on a Hill" and "I Am the Walrus." Their last albums were *The Beatles* (1968) and *Let It Be* (released in 1970), in a vein of parody, and *Abbey Road* (1969), to which all four musicians contributed compositions. Of all the rock groups, the Beatles were the most versatile and the most creative. Their music struck a resonant chord in the social conscience of the decade. Tragically, in 1980, ten years after the group had disbanded, John Lennon was murdered.

The protest music of rock continued well into the 1970s with the renewed fervor of "hard rock," "acid rock," and, in the early 1980s, "punk rock." An interminable number of rock groups sounded their deafening messages of nonconformity (and contributed richly to the multibillion-dollar industry of carefully packaged sound). The course of rock and other forms of popular music cannot be predicted, but they will no doubt continue to mirror the social reality of the future, as troubling or comforting as that may prove to be.

TOWARD THE FUTURE

As the postwar generation of composers of art music entered the 1960s, serialism, electronic music, and aleatoric music remained the principal directions of the avant-garde. Some individualists, though, pursued alternatives. The American composer Elliott Carter (b. 1908), for instance, began by producing two sonatas for piano (1946) and cello (1948) that displayed neotonal principles. Then, in the 1950s, 1960s, and 1970s, Carter turned to a freely expressive, atonal idiom and produced instrumental works of remarkable harmonic, rhythmic, and textural complexity, including three String Quartets (1951, 1959, and 1971), Variations for Orchestra (1955), and three concertos—a Double Concerto for harpsichord, piano, and two chamber orchestras (1961), a Piano Concerto (1965), and a Concerto for Orchestra (1969). As one means of organizing his music, Carter turned to rhythm and meter and devised intricate passages with slowly shifting tempos and metrical combinations. In another effort, Carter explored new textural resources by assigning to groups of instruments distinctive melodic and harmonic elements, which were then contraposed, like so many competing musical gestures.

The Greek composer Iannis Xenakis (b. 1922), trained as an engineer, used laws of probability, Boolean algebra, set theory, and other mathematical sources to "discover" models for his music, which he described as "stochastic." Xenakis subscribed neither to the aesthetic of chance music nor to the aesthetic of traditional serial music. He used large complexes or galaxies of sound that rendered individual pitches and rhythms imperceptible. *Metastasis* for orchestra (1954), his first composition, displays curvilinear glissandos that expand and contract, suggesting a kind of architectonic music of space that obeys its own principles of organization. In *Herma* (1964), for piano solo, Xenakis applied the principles of set theory to the keyboard, juxtaposing contrasting sets and subsets of the available pitches of the piano. Not surprisingly, the composer's search for ever-changing densities of sound led him to explore electronic means, as in *Bohor I* (1962), a twenty-minute work for four-track tape.

PENDERECKI: *THRENODY TO THE VICTIMS OF HIROSHIMA* (1960)

Other composers, too, worked with new techniques of massing sound. György Ligeti (b. 1923), who left Hungary for the free West before the unsuccessful uprising of 1957, won acclaim for two large orchestral scores, *Apparitions* (1959) and *Atmosphères* (1961), which feature subtly changing layers and volumes of sound. (*Atmosphères* was later used in the film *2001: A Space Odyssey*.) Perhaps the most shocking use of clustered sound was the *Threnody to the Victims of Hiroshima* by the Polish composer Krzysztof Penderecki (b. 1933). In this gripping composition, first performed in 1960, Penderecki drew extraordinary sounds from a string orchestra of fifty-two musicians by calling for special techniques, all carefully explained in a page of instructions attached to the score. These techniques include lowering or raising a pitch by quarter tones and clustering a group of such quarter tones to create dense textures, playing the highest note (undefined as to pitch) possible on each instrument, using other means to generate unidentifiable, high-pitched sounds, striking the wooden soundboard with the nut of the bow or with

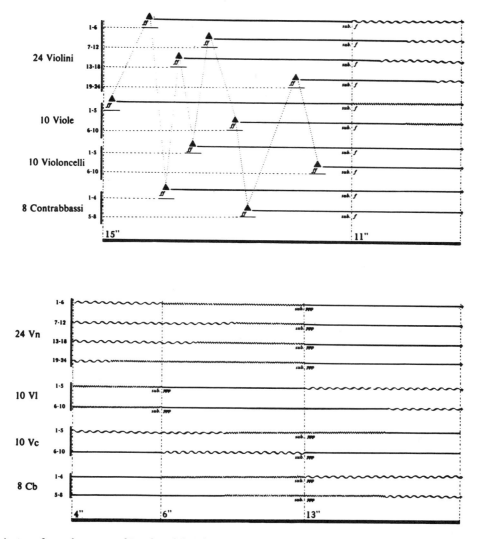

A page from the score of Penderecki's *Threnody to the Victims of Hiroshima*. The heavy line at the bottom of each system is a time line in which the various events of the composition are marked off in seconds. The solid triangular symbols instruct the musicians to play the highest available pitches on their instruments. The wavy lines instruct them to apply vibrato.

fingertips, and applying slow or fast vibrato. The result was a startling new world of sounds that seemed to shriek, howl, mourn, and beckon, a fitting tribute to the victims of the first atomic bomb.

By its very nature, Penderecki's composition demanded its own type of notation. To map out the various passages of the work, the composer marked off a continuous line that denoted the lengths in seconds of the various events. The entire composition

NEW DIRECTIONS AND THE RECENT PAST · · · 501

Penderecki: *Threnody to the Victims of Hiroshima*

Highest pitches	Slow vibrato	Rapid vibrato	Series of seven attacks in cellos, violas, violins, and double basses		Expanding and contracting chromatic clusters of sounds	
ff	*f*	*ppp*			*ppp, mf, p, ff*	
49"			60"		143"	

lasts between eight and nine minutes. Repeated hearings reveal six main sections in the *Threnody* (see study diagram). In the first, the various string groups enter with their highest available sounds, in a series of screeching noises. As their *fortissimo* attacks drop to lower levels of sound, Penderecki instructs the musicians to apply vibrato, a slow, then rapid vibrating of the finger and wrist, creating a wailing effect (49"). In the second section (about 60"), the instruments execute a series of seven attacks: striking the sound-board, plucking the highest available pitch, playing between the bridge and the tailpiece on one string,★ doing the same on all four strings, striking the soundboard, bowing the highest available pitch, and playing between the bridge and the tailpiece; this occurs in the order of cellos, violas, violins, and double basses.

In the third section (143"), Penderecki groups the strings into expanding and contracting chromatic strata that employ quarter steps to obtain dense clusters of sound; in the fourth section (79"), he builds up these masses more deliberately one pitch at a time. The fifth section (about 85") features attacks of pitches by individual instruments as well as chords, producing a pointillistic effect somewhat reminiscent of Webern's music. In the concluding section (90"), the clusters of chromatic sound return, but now are heard as solid bands of sound; the work concludes with a deafening *fff* attack and decay of a chromatic mass that fills the pitches between two octaves.

★ Bridge: in string instruments, a wooden, wedge-like piece, placed at a right angle to the strings, over which the strings are raised; tailpiece: a wooden piece, placed at the lower end of a string instrument, to secure the strings to the instrument.

Penderecki: *Threnody to the Victims of Hiroshima,* *Continued*

Expanding chromatic clusters (built up one pitch at a time)	Contracting clusters	Individual pitches in pointillistic style	Series of attacks	Band of chromatic clusters
f < *ff* *fff* > *pppp*				*pp, ff, ppp, fff* > *pppp*
79"		85"		90"

MINIMALISM

Yet another direction has been pursued since the 1960s by a group of American composers who construct their music of the simplest elements. The minimalists, as they are known, work with scraps of material—a short motive, a triad, a turn of phrase—which are repeated with a regular pulse to build up an entire composition. *In C* by Terry Riley (b. 1935) is one of the earliest results of minimalist composition (1964). Intended for any number of instruments, *In C* consists of fifty-three short motives, mostly bits of triads or scales, which are to be repeated as often as the performers wish. Each performer decides when to move on to the next motive. When they have all played all the motives, the composition is finished. Supporting the performance is a piano "pulse," which repeats the top two C's of the keyboard with metronomic regularity. Thus, each performance of *In C* is different, consisting of a patchwork of bits of melody answering each other in a (paradoxically) free, canonic association. (The commercial recording of *In C* occupies both sides of a record and lasts for about forty-five minutes.)

Other composers have explored more complex minimalist techniques. Philip Glass (b. 1937) has absorbed the intricate rhythmic patterns of Indian music into his music. In 1967 he formed an ensemble to perform his work, a series of mesmerizing instrumental compositions. Then, he turned to the theater. His major work is *Einstein on the Beach* (1976), an extravagant full-length opera in four acts set off by five shorter sections, known as "knee plays," which serve to introduce the essential bits of melodic and harmonic material on which the opera is based. An essential image of the work, an accelerating railroad train, is suitably captured in the repetitive, though shifting, patterns of the music. Throughout the opera, the character Einstein appears as a violinist, placed midway between the actors onstage and the small chamber orchestra consisting of flute, saxophones, bass clarinet, organ, and various synthesizers and keyboard instruments. Steve Reich (b. 1936), who like Philip Glass performs with his own ensemble, has

Bridget Riley, *Fission,* 1963. In this work of op-art, shifting patterns of circles that seem to accelerate toward the center create a giddying effect of fission. (Bridget Riley, "Fission," 1963. Tempera on composition board, 35″ by 34″. Collection, The Museum of Modern Art, New York. Gift of Philip Johnson.)

investigated the rhythms of African drumming and writes compositions for multiple numbers of a single instrument. In *Violin Phase* (1967), for one violin and taped violin material, three parts execute patterns of tonal material that gradually become out of phase with one another; a fourth part performs elementary rhythmic patterns that are created by the overlapping parts of the phasing procedure. In *The Desert Music* (1984), Reich uses an orchestra of eighty-nine musicians and a chorus of twenty-seven voices in a setting of selected poems by William Carlos Williams. Planned by the composer in a five-movement arch form, the work begins and ends with pulsing harmonic cycles in the orchestra that form a throbbing background of rhythmic energy. Other minimalists, notably John Adams (b. 1947), have explored traditional tonal, formal, and instrumental resources, as in Adams's *Harmonielehre* for orchestra (1985) and the opera *Nixon in China* (1987).

POSTMODERNISM, QUOTATION TECHNIQUES, AND THE REINVIGORATION OF TONALITY

For many composers, the most recent decades have been a time of reassessment. Not all have chosen to submit to the rigor of serial music or the undisciplined latitude of chance composition, or even to explore new musical resources. Some have chosen to reinvestigate the music of the past, and some indeed have found a musical identity there, through paraphrasing, quoting, or parodying earlier music. For example, the English composer Peter Maxwell Davies (b. 1934) has turned for inspiration to medieval plainchant and rhythmic techniques and to the music of John Taverner (ca. 1490–1545) and Monteverdi. The American composer George Crumb (b. 1929) has employed quotation, including the use of the *Dies irae* (see p. 16), in his *Black Angels: Thirteen Images from the Dark Land* for electronically amplified string quartet (1970), which he described as a "parable on our troubled contemporary world."

BERIO: *SINFONIA* (1969), THIRD MOVEMENT

One of the most impressive compositions to use quotation was Luciano Berio's *Sinfonia*. Finished in 1969, the *Sinfonia* is scored for large orchestra and eight solo voices. The voices recite, sing, and declaim a wide variety of quotations ranging from Claude Levi-Strauss and Samuel Beckett to student slogans of the 1960s. In the deeply moving second movement, Berio uses the words "O Martin Luther King" in tribute to the slain civil rights leader. In the celebrated third movement, Berio turns to the scherzo from Gustav Mahler's Second Symphony and borrows it, more or less intact, as a kind of scaffolding. He then assembles a series of musical quotations, including Debussy's *La Mer,* Berg's *Wozzeck,* Stravinsky's *Rite of Spring,* and Beethoven's *Pastoral* and Ninth Symphonies. The Mahler scherzo interacts with the quotations, providing a sense of structure behind their free, stream-of-consciousness associations.

ROCHBERG: STRING QUARTET NO. 3 (1972), *INTRODUCTION: FANTASIA*

Some composers, embracing a direction loosely described as postmodernism or neo-romanticism,★ went beyond quotation to return determinedly to the tonal idioms of the eighteenth and nineteenth centuries. Thus, in a series of sacred works from the 1960s and 1970s, Penderecki's atonal clusters of sound began to give way to tonal materials (*Stabat Mater*, 1962; *St. Luke Passion*, 1965; *Te Deum*, 1979; *Polish Requiem*, 1984). The American composer David Del Tredici (b. 1937), in an extended series of works composed between 1968 and 1981 on the Lewis Carroll *Alice in Wonderland* books, gradually reverted to a simple tonal style based on triads. The American George Rochberg (b. 1918) turned to tonality to protest what he viewed as the dehumanizing tendencies of modern technology and science. Rochberg began his career by mastering the twelve-tone system, but he found it too constricting and abandoned it in the 1960s. In *Contra mortem et tempus* (1965) and *Nach Bach* (1966), he began to experiment with collages of tonal quotations. In the String Quartet No. 3 (1972) and the Piano Quintet (1975), he juxtaposed atonal and tonal styles. The string quartet, in five movements, describes a symmetrical plan. The center of the work is the expressive third movement, a series of variations on a classically balanced theme in A major. On either side of this slow movement is a march. The first movement is a free fantasia, and the finale alternates between scherzos (including one, in B-flat major, cast in fugal style) and serenades. Along the way, Rochberg pays homage to several earlier masters. The two marches, for example, with their biting pizzicato notes and chromatic cells of pitches, recall the music of Béla Bartók; the warm lyricism of the tonal third movement, on the other hand, suggests the late quartets of Beethoven.

The first movement, titled *Introduction: Fantasia,* serves to demonstrate Rochberg's technique of juxtaposing contrasting styles and idioms. Highly sectional, this movement takes its shape from three essential ideas that unfold in a fantasylike flow of thematic and harmonic materials. The work begins with a bold statement: a rapidly executed atonal idea of five notes, played *fortissimo* by all four instruments in various forms. Marked *violente, furioso* ("violently," "furiously"), this first idea is heard in the high shrieking registers of the instruments. Repeated intact after a brief pause, it is then broken up into several irregularly spaced fragments that resemble an unpredictable series of bursts of energy.

Rochberg presents the second idea in a slower tempo: Against sustained chords in the second violin and viola, the first violin and cello perform an ascending figure that reaches an intensely expressive *forte* level before diminishing to *pianissimo*. Now the violent first idea returns, followed by a varied treatment of the second idea. Rochberg reduces the texture of the quartet to prepare for the unexpected third idea: a hymnlike tonal melody, played in the lower strings with an accompaniment of traditional triadic harmonies. Interrupted by an atonal passage marked *poco agitato* ("a bit agitated") and later *impetuoso* ("impetuously"), the tonal hymn melody resumes. Its lyrical melodic

---

★ Not to be confused with the term *neoromanticism* sometimes applied to later nineteenth-century music (see p. 359).

strains contrast compellingly with what follows: the resumption of the first idea, now at a *fff* level and emphasized by a restless undercurrent of atonal sonorities. The wild course of the music is checked by a brief reappearance of the second idea; then the furious outbursts resume until the very end of the movement.

ELLEN TAAFFE ZWILICH: SYMPHONY NO. 1 (1983), THIRD MOVEMENT

In recent decades, a growing number of talented women composers, including Thea Musgrave (b. 1928), Pauline Oliveros (b. 1932), Ellen Taaffe Zwilich (b. 1939), and Barbara Kolb (b. 1940), have produced a series of compositions of the first rank. In 1983 Zwilich won the Pulitzer Prize in Music for her Symphony No. 1; she is the first woman composer to receive the prestigious prize. Born in Florida, she studied at Florida State University and later at the Juilliard Conservatory in New York with Elliott Carter and Roger Sessions. Among her works are several chamber compositions, including a string trio (1982), a string quartet (1974), and a chamber symphony (1979); the song cycle *Passages* (1981), based on the poetry of A. R. Ammons; and the orchestral works *Symposium* (1973), *Prologue and Variations* (1984), and *Celebration* (1984).

Zwilich's first symphony is in three movements. All three draw their material from the opening measures of the composition, where we hear the motive of a rising third gently played by the harp and violas. This, a quintessential interval in the symphony, is subsequently extended to form a chain of intervals from which the primary thematic and harmonic elements of the symphony derive. In the first movement, rather free in form, Zwilich practices a technique of thematic transformation, whereby short thematic gestures gradually evolve to take new shapes and suggest new musical characters. Such a technique reveals her to be responsive to certain techniques of thematic elaboration and transformation employed by nineteenth-century symphonists; still, in sound and in appearance, her symphony remains unquestionably a product of the 1980s.

For the short, brisk finale, Zwilich makes use of a rondo form (*ABA'CA"*) and again ties herself to older musical traditions. The *A* section is animated by the most simple of musical figures: a single pitch, which the composer repeats persistently in various rhythmic patterns. Heard first in the timpani, the repeated pitch is set against a rising chain of thirds that are amassed into a chord; the chain of thirds recalls similar harmonies from the first movement:

Ellen Taaffe Zwilich: Symphony No. 1, Third Movement

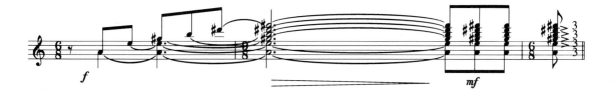

Eventually, the rushing music culminates in a rising line of thirds that sweep across the full register of the string section. A chord played by the tubular bells★ announces the conclusion of the *A* section. In the short *B* section, the bells, doubled by high harmonies in the strings, play a simple descending melodic line. Then the entrance of the repeated timpani pitch announces the return of the *A* section, now reworked and considerably abridged. Section *C* recalls the opening measures of the first movement and its restrained tempo. Against undulating thirds in the harp and strings, an oboe plays a brief melodic line. Finally, the insistent rhythmic repetitions of *A* return in yet another transformed version. Toward the end of the movement, the momentum of the music is checked by two chords in the woodwind, brass, and bells. In a brief epilogue, Zwilich gathers the orchestral forces together for a dramatic crescendo. The symphony ends with the appropriate gesture: three repeated pitches, drawn from *A,* that serve as an emphatic cadence.

Where the mercurial musical evolution of the recent past will lead remains to be heard, seen, felt, and experienced. By the end of the 1980s, composers seem to have paused for a moment to look to the past and to peer into the future. No one style definitively points the way to the future; no single method of composition seems to offer the greatest potential for young composers. Clearly, though, music will continue to amuse, please, entertain, annoy, vex, astonish, and profoundly move us. And, no doubt, as long as humankind survives, the musical art will endure in all its rich diversity.

★A series of metal tubes, suspended in a frame, that are struck by wooden mallets (see p. 534).

Suggested Listening

Babbitt: *Philomel*
The Beatles: *Abbey Road*
———— : *Sergeant Pepper's Lonely Hearts Club Band*
★Berio: *Sinfonia*
★Boulez: *Le marteau sans maître*
★———— : *Structures I*
★Britten: *The Turn of the Screw*
★Cage: *Fontana Mix*
Carter: String Quartet No. 3
Crumb: *Black Angels: Thirteen Images from the Dark Land*
Davis: *Kind of Blue*
Del Tredici: *Final Alice*
Ligeti: *Atmosphères*
★Messiaen: *Mode de valeurs et d'intensités*
★Charlie Parker: *"Embraceable You"*
———— : *KoKo*

Note: Works marked with an asterisk are the principal works discussed in the chapter.

★Penderecki: *Threnody to the Victims of Hiroshima*
  Reich: *The Desert Music*
★Riley: *In C*
★Rochberg: String Quartet No. 3
  Shostakovich: Fifth Symphony
★Stockhausen: *Gesang der Jünglinge*
  Stravinsky: *Agon*
★———— : *In memoriam Dylan Thomas*
★———— : Septet
★Varèse: *Hyperprism*
★———— : *Ionisation*
★Zwilich: Symphony No. 1

APPENDIX: The Elements of Western Music

In this section, we shall review briefly the characteristics of Western music—chiefly pitch, rhythm, musical texture, and tone quality—that distinguish it from the music of other cultures. And we shall examine the traditional notation of Western music—that is, the conventions of setting music down on paper for the guidance of performers and listeners. What we say here will not enable the student to follow all the intricacies of a complex musical score, but it will give the student some familiarity with the musical conventions encountered throughout this book.

PITCH AND MUSIC NOTATION

Central to Western music is the concept of **pitch,** which refers to the relative height or depth of a distinct sound. When we experience music, we often take pitches for granted. Consciously or unconsciously, we are aware that certain pitches are considerably higher or lower than others, that some pitches group closely together in range, whereas other pitches seem widely separated from one another. When we sing the opening of "The Star-Spangled Banner," for example, we are aware that the pitch sung to the word "say" is considerably lower than the pitch sung to the word "see":

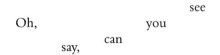

When we participate in a choir, we are aware that the female vocal parts (**sopranos** and **altos**) sing pitches that exceed the range of their male counterparts (**tenors** and **basses**). When we hum a tune to ourselves, we are aware of its general contours: whether the tune tends to ascend or descend, whether it centers on a few pitches in a narrow range, or whether it actively leaps about. With some training and considerable experience, musicians are able to develop a highly refined sense of pitch; indeed, some gifted individuals are able to identify distinct pitches with uncanny accuracy by relying solely on their sense of hearing. Of course, not many are blessed with this talent, known as perfect pitch or absolute pitch. But music is, after all, a succession of distinct sounds, and we rely in part upon our ability to distinguish how high or how low those sounds are in order to make sense of the music and, ultimately, to derive pleasure from our listening experiences.

In the West, a special type of **notation** is employed to chart and thereby identify pitches. In its earliest forms, Western music notation appeared during the Middle Ages. Almost from the beginning, it used signs to represent pitches. At first, those signs appeared successively by themselves, as a rough approximation of the various pitch heights; eventually, the signs came to be placed on lines and in the spaces between lines as a kind of time graph. By about the sixteenth century, most of the features of modern notation, including the familiar **staff** of five lines, had become standardized:

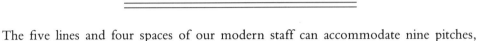

The five lines and four spaces of our modern staff can accommodate nine pitches, represented by signs known as **notes.** The lower pitches occupy the lower lines and spaces; the higher pitches occupy the higher lines and spaces. Extensions of this staff, called **ledger lines,** can accommodate still lower and higher pitches below and above the staff. The notes are read from left to right:

Seven letters are used to identify the various pitches: In ascending order, they are A, B, C, D, E, F, and G. After the pitch G, the cycle begins anew. A complete series of pitches—for example, A, B, C, D, E, F, G, and A—spans a distance known as an **octave,** that is, A to A, or B to B. Within any octave may be placed a consecutive series of *eight* pitches that begin and end with the same letter name. Octaves are often used to measure roughly the ranges of the various musical instruments. For example, the modern piano has a range of a little more than seven octaves. To determine precisely which pitches of an instrument's range fill which lines and spaces of a staff, a sign known as a **clef** (a "key," as in a "key to a puzzle") appears at the beginning of the staff. Different clefs are employed for different instruments, but two occur most frequently: The **treble clef** (𝄞) identifies the higher pitches, and the **bass clef** (𝄢) identifies the lower pitches. In the following example, a representation of part of the piano keyboard shows which pitches the two clefs locate. By convention, the treble clef, which curves around the second line of the staff, establishes that second line for the pitch G above "middle C" on the piano (middle C lies on the first ledger line below the treble staff):

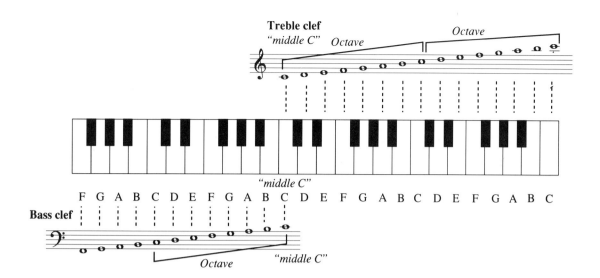

The bass clef establishes the fourth line from the bottom of the staff as the pitch F *below* middle C. In the example, middle C lies on the first ledger line *above* the bass staff.

In addition to the seven basic pitches represented by the letters A through G, Western music employs other pitches (and their octave duplications), represented by signs known as **accidentals.** The most common are five pitches that appear on the piano keyboard as black keys. They are located between the white keys (except for the white keys E and F, and B and C, which have no black keys between them; see the preceding example). Depending on the context, different names are used for these black keys. For example, consider the black key between middle C and D. In relation to C, the pitch produced by this key sounds a bit higher; so, it is labeled with a **sharp** sign (♯) as C♯. In relation to D, however, the same pitch sounds a bit lower; so, it is sometimes labeled with a **flat** sign (♭) as D♭. (Similarly, the black key between D and E is sometimes labeled D♯ and sometimes E♭; the black key between F and G is either F♯ or G♭; the black key between G and A is either G♯ or A♭; and the black key between A and B is either A♯ or B♭.) In short, sharps are used to raise pitches, and flats are used to lower pitches. A third accidental, the **natural** sign (♮), serves to cancel a preceding flat or sharp. In notation, all accidentals are placed before the pitches they modify:

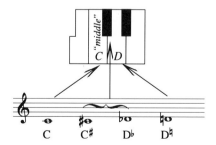

Often, a group of sharps or flats prevails throughout an entire musical composition. As a convenience, the composer lists the appropriate accidentals at the beginning of the staves immediately after the clefs. This listing of accidentals constitutes what is known as a **key signature:**

Key Signatures

In the modern Western tuning system, the octave is divided into twelve pitches separated by distances known as **half steps** or **semitones** (on the piano, the succession of seven white keys and five intervening black keys). This was not always the case, however. Medieval music relied primarily on the seven basic pitches from A through G (represented today by the white notes of the modern piano). Gradually, accidentals were introduced for the five alternative pitches, giving rise to the twelve pitches we know today. The complete series of twelve pitches is termed a **chromatic scale,** which spans an octave and includes all the available half steps in between. The thirteenth pitch of the chromatic scale duplicates the first pitch one octave higher:

Chromatic Scale

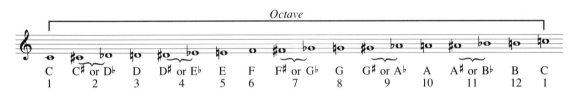

These twelve pitches, together with their duplicating octaves above and below, constitute the basic pitches on which Western music is based.

Down through the centuries, Western composers have arranged pitches in various sequences, one after the other, to form memorable progressions known as **melodies.** We shall begin with a well-known melody, "The Star-Spangled Banner," and present first only the text of its opening, arranged to approximate the contours of the melody:

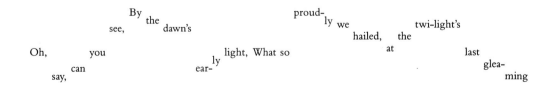

Next, we present the text along with the melody in musical notation:

"The Star-Spangled Banner"

MELODY

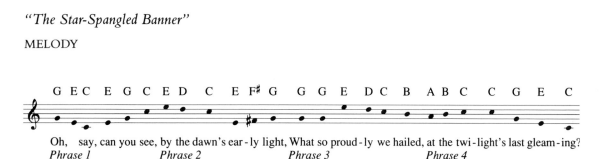

Oh, say, can you see, by the dawn's ear-ly light, What so proud-ly we hailed, at the twi-light's last gleam-ing?
Phrase 1   *Phrase 2*   *Phrase 3*   *Phrase 4*

Melodies typically consist of several more or less distinct sections known as **phrases.** Sometimes, phrases are strikingly similar: An initial phrase may be literally repeated or slightly modified to form a second phrase. In other instances, phrases are dissimilar and are marked by contrast, as in our example from "The Star-Spangled Banner." Here, the first four musical phrases, each with its own contour of descending and ascending pitches, correspond to portions of the text marked off by points of punctuation. Occasionally, a phrase ends with a pause, known as a **cadence,** which gives a sense of articulation or of conclusion. Here, for example, the music pauses at the end of the phrase "at the twilight's last gleaming?" Each phrase, in turn, is made up of a succession of movements from pitch to pitch. The distance between two consecutive pitches is known as an **interval.** Some intervals are relatively small; in fact, some entail only smooth motion by step between neighboring pitches, as in "by the dawn's," which moves through three adjacent pitches. Other intervals are larger and entail "broken" motion by skip between nonadjacent pitches, as in "Oh, say, can you see," which clearly moves by skips. The sizes of the intervals are determined by the number of steps between consecutive pitches. Thus, two adjacent pitches (that is, pitches that occupy a line and the space immediately above or below) form the interval of a second. By gradually increasing the distance between the two pitches, we may generate intervals of a third, fourth, fifth, sixth, seventh, and finally, octave (*not* an eighth). When two instruments play exactly the same pitch, sounding as though there were only one pitch, the interval is known as a **unison** (*not* a first). Here is a summary of the basic interval types:

Basic Interval Types

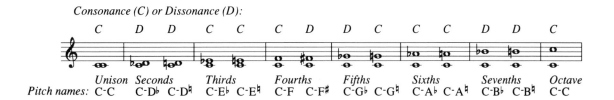

Consonance (C) or Dissonance (D):

C   D   D   C   C   C   D   D   C   C   C   D   D   C

Pitch names: Unison Seconds Thirds Fourths Fifths Sixths Sevenths Octave
C-C   C-D♭ C-D♮   C-E♭ C-E♮   C-F C-F♯   C-G♭ C-G♮   C-A♭ C-A♮   C-B♭ C-B♮   C-C

THE ELEMENTS OF WESTERN MUSIC   515

To Western ears, seconds have an unstable, harsh quality and are placed in a category of intervals known as **dissonances.** Of the larger intervals, thirds and sixths typically have a mild, pleasant quality and are classed among the **consonances.** Some common fourths and fifths (for example, C–F, C–G) have a hollow, stable quality and are considered consonant. Sevenths, like seconds, have a dissonant, unstable quality and are regarded as dissonances. The last interval type, the consonant octave, forms a special category, because its pitches (for example, C–C) duplicate each other and seem to blend together. (When male and female voices sing the same melody, they naturally duplicate, or double, one another at various octave levels.)

Melodies usually contain a mixture of **conjunct** (by step) and **disjunct** (by leap) **motion,** as in "The Star-Spangled Banner." But some melodies move largely by stepwise motion. For example, the well-known anthem "My Country, 'Tis of Thee" employs almost exclusively smooth motion by step:

"My Country, 'Tis of Thee"

Western composers, regardless of which intervals they select, have typically organized their melodies around recurring, prominent pitches, thereby achieving a degree of stability and order. They have tended to develop a melody from and around a basic pitch, which is often, in fact, the final pitch of the melody. By isolating the basic pitch of a given melody, we can generate a **scale** of consecutive pitches from that pitch on which the melody is based. A scale is simply a succession of ascending pitches that fill out the interval of an octave—the familiar series Do-Re-Mi-Fa-Sol-La-Ti-Do. The most important scales in Western music, in common use since about the sixteenth century, are the **major scale** and the **minor scale.** Major and minor scales have eight pitches (with seven steps among them), in contrast to the chromatic scale, discussed earlier, which has thirteen pitches (with twelve steps among them).

Here is a major scale based on C—that is, a C major scale:

C major Scale

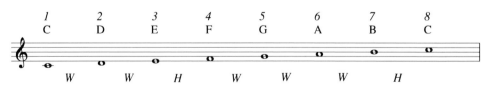

W = whole step; H = half step

As our example shows, this scale consists of eight pitches, with seven steps among them. There are two types of steps. Half steps, the smallest interval commonly used in Western music, occur between the third and fourth pitches and between the seventh and eighth pitches. The slightly larger **whole step** (or **whole tone**), which contains two half steps, occurs elsewhere in the scale. Our version of "The Star-Spangled Banner" consists almost exclusively of pitches from this scale; moreover, the focal (and concluding) pitch of the melody is C, with which the C major scale begins and ends.

The *minor* scale based on C—that is, a C minor scale—also consists of half steps and whole steps, but they occur in a different order, as the next example reveals:

C minor Scale

The primary distinguishing feature of the minor scale is its third pitch, which is always one half step lower than the corresponding third pitch of the major scale. This change affects the basic character of the scale; for many, it sounds dark and somewhat melancholy in comparison to the major scale, which may sound bright and cheerful. However we describe the difference, it is readily apparent if we consider well-known melodies based on minor scales, such as the carol "We Three Kings of Orient Are," or "When Johnny Comes Marching Home Again." In "We Three Kings," the lower third step occurs on the word "kings"; in "When Johnny Comes Marching Home Again," the lower third occurs on the word "home":

"When Johnny Comes Marching Home Again"

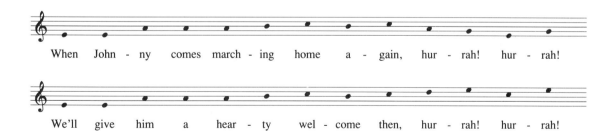

All these scales share certain characteristics, however: They are successions of ascending pitches arranged in stepwise order and framed by the octave. Over the centuries, these scales have provided the raw materials of Western melodies and a means with which to organize them.

RHYTHM AND MUSIC NOTATION

Music exists in time. In fact, one might define music as a series of sounds ordered in some temporal sequence. We are reminded daily of temporal relationships, which we understand in a general sense as **rhythm:** thus, the fluctuating rhythm of the waves, the accelerating rhythm of a locomotive, the brisk rhythm of a tennis game, the steady rhythm of a ticking clock, the pulsating rhythm of our heartbeats, or the dynamic, irregular rhythm of our speech. In music, rhythm has to do with the relative durations of pitches, or, in the broadest meaning, the sense of temporal movement between successive sounds. For example, when we sing the beginning of "The Star-Spangled Banner," we are aware that the pitch sung to the word "see" has a longer duration than the pitches sung to the words "say," "can," and "you":

Oh,   say,   can   you   see

When we tap our feet in listening to music, take note of the intricate patterns of a drummer in a jazz band, or follow the up-and-down gestures of a conductor's baton at an orchestral concert, we are reminded of the fundamental role that rhythm plays in music.

In Western musical notation, we use several types of notes to indicate the duration of pitches, or rhythmic values. The longest value normally encountered is represented

Table 1   Rhythmic Values (Binary Division)

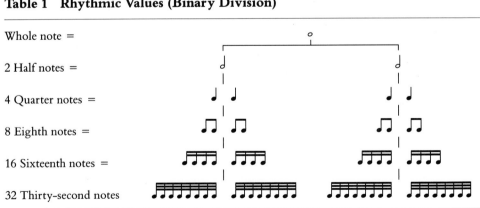

Whole note =	
2 Half notes =	
4 Quarter notes =	
8 Eighth notes =	
16 Sixteenth notes =	
32 Thirty-second notes	

by the oval-shaped **whole note** (o). A whole note is the equivalent of two **half notes,** which are represented by an oval with a stem attached (♩ ♩). A half note, in turn, is equivalent to two **quarter notes,** which are represented by a solid note head with a stem (♩ ♩). A quarter note is the equivalent of two **eighth notes,** which have a flag attached to the stem (♪♪ or ♫); an eighth note is the equivalent of two **sixteenth notes,** with two flags (♬ or ♬); and so on. (By adding more flags, we can represent even shorter rhythmic values, such as thirty-second notes and sixty-fourth notes.) Table 1 summarizes the basic types of rhythmic values encountered in notation.

Notice that these values are divided in a binary fashion—that is, a whole note is the equivalent of *two* half notes; a half note is the equivalent of *two* quarter notes. We can, however, achieve a ternary division by placing a **dot** directly after the note head. In **dotted notes,** the dot effectively adds half the value of the original note. Thus, a dotted whole note (o.) is the equivalent of *three* half notes (♩ ♩ ♩); a dotted half note (♩.) is the equivalent of *three* quarter notes (♩ ♩ ♩); and so on. Table 2 summarizes the use of the dot.

Rhythmic values can be altered in other ways as well. For example, a curved line known as a **tie** joins two notes to produce a rhythmic value equal to the sum of their individual values:

$$o = ♩\underset{\smile}{♩} = ♩♩\underset{\smile}{♩♩} = ♩.\underset{\smile}{♩}$$

Triplets are groups of three notes marked with the numeral 3. In a triplet, three notes have the same duration as two notes of the same value. Thus,

has the same value as

Table 2 Rhythmic Values (Ternary Division)

Dotted whole note =	o.	Dotted eighth note =	♪.
3 Half notes	♩ ♩ ♩	3 Sixteenth notes	♪ ♪ ♪
Dotted half note =	♩.	Dotted sixteenth note =	♬.
3 Quarter notes	♩ ♩ ♩	3 Thirty-second notes	♬ ♬ ♬
Dotted quarter note =	♩.		
3 Eighth notes	♪ ♪ ♪		

Table 3   Rests (Binary Division)

Whole rest =	
2 Half rests =	
4 Quarter rests =	
8 Eighth rests =	
16 Sixteenth rests =	
32 Thirty-second rests	

Similarly, quintuplets are groups of five notes that take the place of four

and septuplets are groups of seven notes that take the place of six

.

Finally, composers often employ bits of silence that have definite rhythmic values. These are known as **rests.** They have their own set of notational symbols (see Table 3). As with note values, the normal division of rests is binary. For example, a quarter rest is the equivalent of *two* eighth rests; an eighth rest is the equivalent of *two* sixteenth rests; and so on. By adding dots, we achieve a ternary division of rests. Thus, a dotted eighth rest is equivalent to *three* sixteenth rests (see Table 4).

These basic rhythmic values are the building blocks of Western rhythm, just as pitches drawn from scales are the building blocks of Western melodies. By themselves, however, rhythmic values do not tell performers all they need to know, for there is no absolute standard for measuring rhythmic values during a performance. Consequently, composers typically provide directives to indicate the **tempo**—that is, the speed or basic rhythmic pace—of a composition. Once performers know the tempo, they can determine the actual duration of the various rhythmic values—for example, how long a whole note or how short a sixteenth note will actually sound in a particular performance. Sometimes, the composer's directive is nothing more than a vague word or two: **Allegro** (Fast), or **Adagio** (Slow), for example. (Table 5 gives a few of the most common tempo directives.) Sometimes, composers provide more precise indications of tempo by including numbers for settings on a **metronome,** a clocklike mechanism with a sliding scale that emits ticking sounds at varying rates of speed. By rehearsing a composition with a particular metronome setting in mind, performers can obtain a fairly accurate idea of the composer's intentions about tempo.

Table 4 Rests (Ternary Division)

Dotted whole rest =	▬•	3 Eighth rests	ɤ ɤ ɤ
3 Half rests	▬ ▬ ▬	Dotted eighth rest =	ɤ•
Dotted half rest =	▬•	3 Sixteenth rests	ɹ ɹ ɹ
3 Quarter rests	ƨ ƨ ƨ	Dotted sixteenth rest =	ɹ•
Dotted quarter rest =	ƨ•	3 Thirty-second rests	ɹɹɹ

Whatever the composer's directives, the performers must set the basic pulse, or **beat,** of the composition. When we listen to music, we are usually conscious of an underlying series of beats. (A common analogy compares beats to the footsteps of a marching band.) For example, in a waltz, the beats occur in groups of three: "One-two-three, one-two-three," and so on. Similarly, in "The Star-Spangled Banner," the beats fall in groups of three. We can demonstrate this first by placing the beats beneath the text. The example shows how some words are held for exactly one beat, as in "say," "can," and "you." On the other hand, the words "see" and "light" are held for two beats each; and the words "by" and "the" are held for less than one beat each:

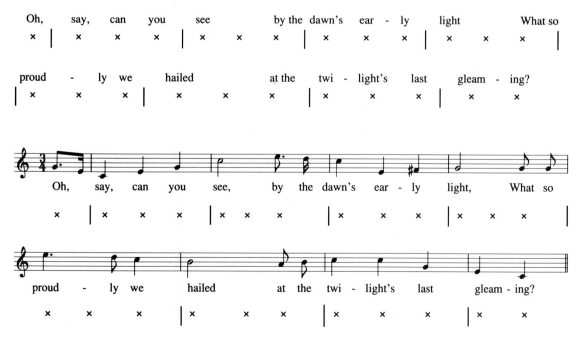

Table 5 Tempo Indications

Presto:	Very fast	Andante:	Moderately slow
Vivace:	Lively	Largo:	Slow
Allegro:	Fast	Adagio:	Slow
Allegretto:	Moderately fast	Lento:	Slow
Moderato:	Moderately	Grave:	Slow, gravely

Most Western music is **metrical;** that is, its various rhythms are organized into equal segments of time, known as **measures** or **bars,** which contain regular patterns of beats known as **meters.** Naturally felt **accents** mark off the beginning of each pattern. Here is a succession of nine undifferentiated beats, with no indication of meter:

x   x   x   x   x   x   x   x   x

By stressing the first beat and then every third beat, we create three equivalent groups of three beats each, and a sense of meter is established:

x   x   x   x   x   x   x   x   x
1   2   3   1   2   3   1   2   3

By convention, vertical lines known as **measure lines** or **bar lines** are used to suggest such metrical divisions:

| x   x   x | x   x   x | x   x   x |

The natural accent falls on the first beat, or **downbeat,** of each measure, while the other beats within each measure remain relatively unaccented. The last of these "weak" beats in each measure is known as an **upbeat.** The upbeat prepares for the next measure, which begins with a stressed downbeat:

| x   x   x | x   x   x | x   x   x |
downbeat   upbeat   downbeat   upbeat   downbeat   upbeat

Stressed beats thus serve to divide musical time into recurring patterns. Sometimes, however, a composer may choose to violate the basic meter by placing stresses off the downbeat. In the following example, the stress falls on the second beat of each measure instead of on the first beat. This technique is known as **syncopation** (in which the ac*cent* is placed on the wrong syl*la*ble):

Syncopated pattern:	1	**2**	3	1	**2**	3	1	**2**	3
Beats:	|x	x	x	|x	x	x	|x	x	x
Normal pattern with downbeats:	**1**	2	3	**1**	2	3	**1**	2	3

There are three basic types of meters in Western music: **duple meter,** with two beats to a measure; **triple meter,** with three beats to a measure; and a few types of **compound meter,** which subdivides its beats into smaller groupings of three. Examples of duple meter include most marches (for example, John Philip Sousa's *The Stars and Stripes Forever*); their basic pattern of beats is ONE-two, ONE-two, and so on. In a common variant of duple meter (sometimes known as *quadruple meter*), there are four beats per measure, in which the third beat receives a slight stress, in addition to the stronger stress of the downbeat:

| ONE two *three* four | ONE two *three* four |

Typical examples of this arrangement include "America the Beautiful" and "The Battle Hymn of the Republic." Here is a line from "America the Beautiful," with its beats marked off:

A - mer-		i-ca!		A - mer-		i-ca!	God	shed	His	grace	on		Thee	
four|ONE		two *three*	four|ONE	two *three*	four |	ONE	two	*three*	four |	ONE etc.

Examples of ternary meter include waltzes and "The Star-Spangled Banner"; their basic pattern of beats is ONE-two-three, ONE-two-three, and so on. Finally, in compound meter, the number of beats per measure (two, three, or four) divides into groups of three. Stephen Foster's popular song "Beautiful Dreamer," for example, has three beats per measure, which divide into groups of three each, for a total of nine divisions: ONE-two-three-*four*-five-six-*seven*-eight-nine:

Beau-ti-	ful	Drea-				mer,			wake	un-	to
|**x**	x	x	*x*	x	x	*x*	x	x	|**x**	x	x
1	2	3	*4*	5	6	*7*	8	9	**1**	2	3

me,						Star-	light	and	dew-	drops	are
x	x	x	*x*	x	x	|**x**	x	x	*x*	x	x
4	5	6	*7*	8	9	**1**	2	3	*4*	5	6

wai-	ting	for	thee.								
x	x	x	|**x**	x	x	*x*	x	x	*x*	x	x|
7	8	9	**1**	2	3	*4*	5	6	*7*	8	9

Another example of compound meter is "Three Blind Mice," with two beats per measure, divided into groups of three each: ONE-two-three-*four*-five-six, ONE-two-three-*four*-five-six, and so on.

In music notation, the choice of meter is indicated by a **time signature,** a vertical series of two numbers placed after the clefs (and key signature) at the beginning of the staff: for example, $\frac{2}{4}$, $\frac{3}{4}$, $\frac{6}{8}$. In the simple duple and triple meters, the upper number indicates how many beats there are in each measure; the lower number indicates the rhythmic value that is to be assigned to each beat. Thus, in $\frac{2}{4}$, the common duple meter, each measure has two beats, and each beat is equivalent to a quarter note. In $\frac{3}{4}$, the common triple meter, each measure has three beats, and each beat is equivalent to a quarter note. In compound meters, the upper number indicates how many divisions there are in each measure. In $\frac{6}{8}$, one of the compound meters, each measure has six divisions, and each division is equivalent to an eighth note (there are two beats, with each beat equivalent to three eighth notes). Other time signatures include $\frac{4}{4}$ (also indicated as **c**), $\frac{2}{2}$ (also indicated as **¢**), $\frac{3}{8}$, $\frac{9}{8}$, and $\frac{12}{8}$.

In all the basic meters we have so far discussed—duple, triple, and compound—the pattern of beats is regular and symmetrical. From time to time, however, composers have experimented with asymmetrical meters—indicated by time signatures such as $\frac{5}{4}$, in which each measure has five beats, usually divided into groups of three and two, or two and three:

|x	x	x	*x*	x	|x	x	x	*x*	x|
1	2	3	*4*	5	**1**	2	3	*4*	5

|x	x	*x*	x	x	|x	x	*x*	x	x|
1	2	*3*	4	5	**1**	2	*3*	4	5

Such experiments have been especially common in music of the twentieth century among composers seeking to escape the "tyranny" of the bar line. Nevertheless, duple, triple, and compound meters are the meters we encounter most often.

MUSICAL TEXTURE: COUNTERPOINT AND HARMONY

So far, we have been using single lines of music as examples. Actually, single-line music, or **monophony** (meaning "one voice"), was the prevalent type of music for several centuries in the West, and it is the only type of music that has come down to us in notated form from the very early periods (see Chapter 1). Around the tenth century, music was forever transformed when individually composed lines were set against each other to be performed at the same time. The shift from music with one line to music with multiple, simultaneously sounding lines transformed musical notation as well. Such multiline music is called **polyphony** (or "several voices"), and the art of fitting one line of music against another is called **counterpoint** (from the Latin *punctum contra* *punctum* for "point [that is, "note"] against point"). Often, the terms *polyphony* and *counterpoint* (and their adjectives *polyphonic* and *contrapuntal*) are used interchangeably.

The term **texture** refers to the various ways in which musical lines are combined. In the simplest example, a piece of music may consist of only one line, in which case its texture is said to be **monophonic.** Obviously, considerably more complex textures are produced when several lines are set against one another in counterpoint. In a texture known as **imitative counterpoint** (or **imitative polyphony**), after one line begins, it is imitated in turn by other lines of music known, along with the original line, as **voices** or **parts.** Sometimes, the **imitation** is quite literal, as in a type of composition known as a **canon** or, when provided with a popular text, as a **round** (for example, "Row, Row, Row Your Boat," "Three Blind Mice," and "Frère Jacques"). In the following example, the opening of the round "Row, Row, Row Your Boat" in three-part counterpoint, the identical contours of the three lines are shown above the notes for ease of comparison:

Round, "Row, Row, Row Your Boat"

STRICT IMITATIVE POLYPHONY

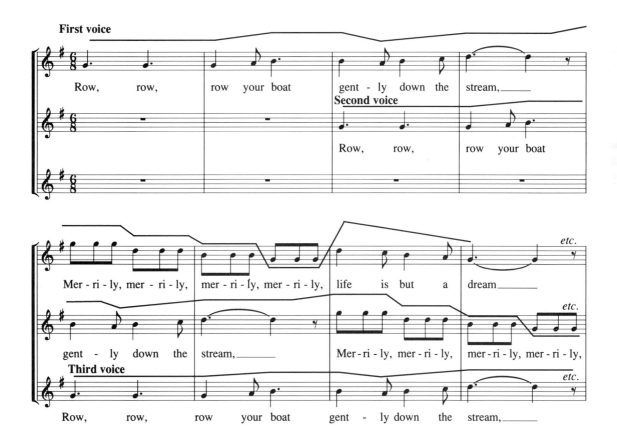

In other instances, though the imitating voice does not always follow the leading voice note for note, it follows closely enough that the similarity is apparent. The listener again comprehends the passage as imitation. In the following abstract example of free imitative counterpoint, the second voice initially imitates the first strictly but then takes its own course, sometimes paralleling the first voice and sometimes diverging from it.

Free Imitative Counterpoint

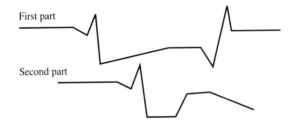

In nonimitative counterpoint, the voices are even more independent, as in the following abstract example. Here, the second voice shares no material at all with the first; yet, we hear the passage contrapuntally, as one articulate line of music set against another:

Nonimitative Counterpoint

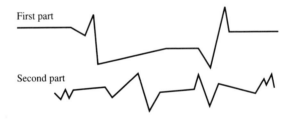

Whereas counterpoint is the art of setting lines of music against each other, **harmony** is the art of using **chords:** combinations of two or more pitches that are sounded simultaneously. The typical harmonic texture is known as **homophony** (or "similar voices"). Homophony features a melody supported or accompanied by other voices forming chords, as when a singer is accompanied by a guitar or when a church choir sings a well-known hymn:

Homophonic Texture

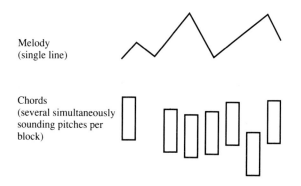

Melody
(single line)

Chords
(several simultaneously
sounding pitches per
block)

The melodic line, usually the uppermost voice, is said to be "harmonized" by the chords of the other voices. For example, we can harmonize the first two phrases of the melody of "The Star-Spangled Banner" by adding beneath it a series of chords to produce the following, familiar version:

"The Star-Spangled Banner," Harmonized

Like polyphony, homophony thus involves several parts that move against each other. There is a basic distinction, however. In polyphony, we hear the music as individual lines made up of individual pitches moving in time. In homophony, we hear the music as a succession of simultaneously sounding chords.

Since about the mid-fifteenth century, the basic type of chord used in Western harmony has been a three-note chord known as a **triad.** We may produce triads by taking a portion of a scale and extracting from it every other pitch:

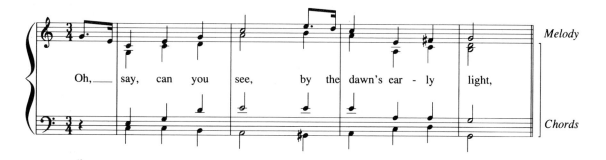

The study of harmony involves a set of rules that regulates the progression from one chord to the next. Two concepts that are of fundamental importance in harmonic progressions are consonance and dissonance. We have already described the distinction between consonant and dissonant intervals (see p. 516). In harmony, we extend the distinction to consonant and dissonant chords. Some chords, such as certain triads, are regarded as consonant; to Western ears, they sound euphonious, pleasant, and stable. Other harmonies contain intervals that give them an unstable, dissonant quality, while still other harmonies are extremely harsh and grating. Generally, in music before the twentieth century, a dissonant chord required a **resolution** to a consonant chord; that is, the dissonant chord could not stand by itself but was required to progress to a consonant chord that released the tension of the dissonance.

Throughout the history of music, the distinction between consonance and dissonance has never been absolute but has depended on context. Dissonance has been viewed as the absence of consonance; similarly, consonance has been viewed as the resolution of dissonance. In Western music, the distinction between the two has been steadily redefined over the centuries. Thus, in the music of the Middle Ages, for example, only a few, select types of chords were accepted as consonant. By the fifteenth century, notions of consonance had broadened. Of course, many other chords continued to remain dissonant. By the end of the nineteenth century, however, as composers favored more and more dissonant harmonic styles, the traditional distinction between consonance and dissonance had grown much weaker. Put another way, the tolerance level for dissonance had increased significantly. Finally, in the twentieth century, adventuresome composers rejected the distinction altogether. In their experimental modern music, consonance and dissonance ceased to have any meaning.

By the seventeenth century, composers were using a sophisticated system of musical organization known as **tonality** (adjective **tonal**), which was based on a complex hierarchy of harmonic relationships built upon triads. Most of the music with which we are familiar today uses the same system. For a further discussion of the tonal system, see pages 68–72.

TONE QUALITY AND THE CLASSIFICATION OF INSTRUMENTS

When we describe the tone quality of a pitch, we refer to special qualities independent of the pitch's specific identity and rhythmic value. One such quality concerns the relative loudness or softness of sound, referred to as **dynamics.** By convention, various Italian terms are used to designate dynamic levels. Here are the most common ones:

pianissimo	*(pp)*	very soft
piano	*(p)*	soft
mezzo piano	*(mp)*	half soft

mezzo forte	(*mf*)	half loud
forte	(*f*)	loud
fortissimo	(*ff*)	very loud

These terms are in no way absolute; indeed, practices in applying dynamics have varied considerably over the centuries. We can only speculate about performance practices in early music; not until the seventeenth century did composers begin to use dynamic markings in their music, and then cautiously to suggest shifts from loud and soft. Only in the eighteenth century did composers adopt generally the idea of moving from one dynamic level to another by gradually increasing the sound (**crescendo**) or decreasing it (**decrescendo**). In the nineteenth and twentieth centuries, composers have experimented with a broader range of dynamics, such as triple or quadruple forte (*fff* or *ffff*) and softer shades of *piano*. (For example, in an extraordinary symphonic passage, the nineteenth-century Russian composer Tchaikovsky even called for quintuple *piano: ppppp*.)

Tone color, or **timbre,** also affects the quality of sound. Though a difficult concept to explain, tone color is easy to recognize. Tone color reflects the character of sound produced by different instruments, enabling us to distinguish between the nasal sound of an oboe, the mellow sound of a violin, and the wooden sound of a xylophone.

All musical instruments produce sound by setting in motion a series of vibrations. Pianos and violins use strings as the vibrating medium; organs and flutes use columns of air; and drums use stretched membranes. The sound generated typically projects a **fundamental pitch** that is determined by the length of the vibrating column of air or by the tautness of the string or membrane. Thus, the longest pipes of an organ produce its lowest fundamental pitches; the shortest strings of a piano produce its highest fundamental pitches.

In addition to the clearly audible fundamental pitch, a vibrating medium emits considerably fainter, secondary sounds known as **partials, harmonics,** or **overtones.** Different instruments emphasize partials in different ways. Two different instruments playing the same pitch will emit, in addition to the fundamental, different configurations of "stressed" and "unstressed" partials. It is this physical property that determines the distinctive "color" of, say, a violin or a flute.

Over the centuries, composers have written music for an endless variety of musical instruments—some simple, some remarkably complex—each with its own timbre. Anthropologists have classified instruments according to five groups. **Idiophones** are instruments made of solid materials that produce sound when they are struck, rubbed, or shaken. Among them are cymbals, gongs, rattles, the glass harmonica, and the xylophone. **Membranophones** are instruments with tautly stretched membranes, such as drums (for example, timpani, bass drum, and snare drum). **Aerophones** are instruments that use a column of air, including wind and brass instruments (recorder, flute, French horn, trumpet, cornet, trombone, tuba, and sousaphone, for example) and organs. With some aerophones, the musician blows across reeds, or strips of pliable cane or metal, to produce the column of air (for example, saxophones, oboe, clarinet, bassoon). **Chordophones** are instruments with strings, including lutes, guitars, harps,

A pitch is a blend of many vibrations generated through a medium such as a taut string or a column of air. Represented below is a string fixed at two points. When the string is plucked, the entire length vibrates to produce the basic fundamental pitch that we hear. When the same string is fixed at its midpoint and is plucked, the fundamental pitch sounds one octave higher. Along with a fundamental pitch, a plucked string produces fainter pitches, blending in with the fundamental, known as partials, harmonics, or overtones. These are generated by vibrations that occupy portions of the string (that is, a half, a third, a quarter, and so on). Shown below is a representative series of overtones, all of which blend with a fundamental to create the low pitch we identify as the C two octaves below middle C.

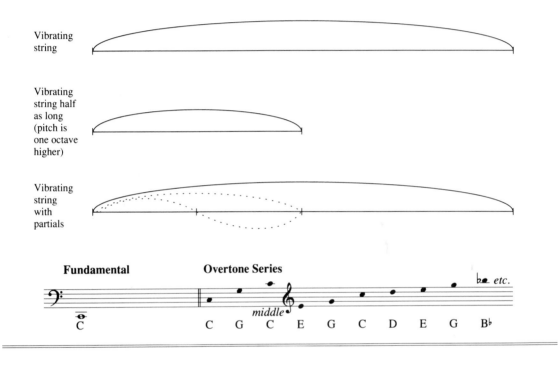

Vibrating string

Vibrating string half as long (pitch is one octave higher)

Vibrating string with partials

Fundamental

Overtone Series

C

C   G   C   E   G   C   D   E   G   B♭

middle

the members of the violin family (violin, viola, cello), the double bass, and the piano. Finally, **electrophones** are instruments that generate sound by electronic means, including the modern pipe organ and the synthesizer.

A second, more familiar system is used to classify common Western instruments, such as those typically encountered in the modern orchestra. There are four basic categories. The **woodwinds** are aerophones that are so named because they are primarily constructed of wood. The most common include the flute and the piccolo (in the twentieth century constructed of metal), the oboe and the English horn, the clarinet and the bass clarinet, and the bassoon and the contrabassoon. The **brass** are aerophones that are made of metal. The most common include the trumpet, the French horn, the trombone, and the tuba. The **percussion,** with examples of membranophones and idiophones, include both instruments that produce distinct pitches—for example, timpani, xylophone, vibraphone, and tubular bells—and instruments that produce sounds too indefinite to be identified as precise pitches—for example, cymbals, gongs, snare drum, and triangle. The fourth group, the **strings,** are chordophones that include the violin, the related viola and cello, and the double bass (also known as the string bass, contrabass, or bass). See pages 534–537 for an illustration of common instruments.

Finally, we may usefully compare instruments according to their range—that is, whether they occupy a high, middle, or low range. The study chart on pages 532–533 locates the approximate ranges of many common instruments in comparison to the wide range of the piano keyboard. At the bottom of the instrumental compass is the contrabassoon, a woodwind instrument whose low range matches the very lowest pitches of the piano. At the other extreme is the piccolo, whose piercing high range matches the high notes of the piano. Of course, each instrument has its own tone color and special properties, in addition to its specific range. For a further discussion of the characteristics of individual instruments and how some instruments became members of the modern orchestra, see pages 84, 118–119, 182–184, 306, and 343.

PRACTICAL RANGE OF THE INSTRUMENTS

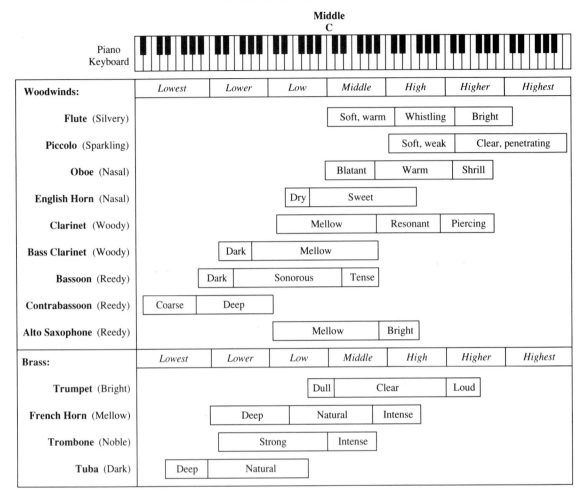

Woodwinds:	Lowest	Lower	Low	Middle	High	Higher	Highest
Flute (Silvery)				Soft, warm	Whistling	Bright	
Piccolo (Sparkling)					Soft, weak	Clear, penetrating	
Oboe (Nasal)			Blatant	Warm	Shrill		
English Horn (Nasal)		Dry	Sweet				
Clarinet (Woody)			Mellow		Resonant	Piercing	
Bass Clarinet (Woody)		Dark	Mellow				
Bassoon (Reedy)		Dark	Sonorous	Tense			
Contrabassoon (Reedy)	Coarse	Deep					
Alto Saxophone (Reedy)			Mellow		Bright		

Brass:	Lowest	Lower	Low	Middle	High	Higher	Highest
Trumpet (Bright)			Dull	Clear		Loud	
French Horn (Mellow)		Deep	Natural	Intense			
Trombone (Noble)		Strong	Intense				
Tuba (Dark)	Deep	Natural					

PRACTICAL RANGE OF THE INSTRUMENTS

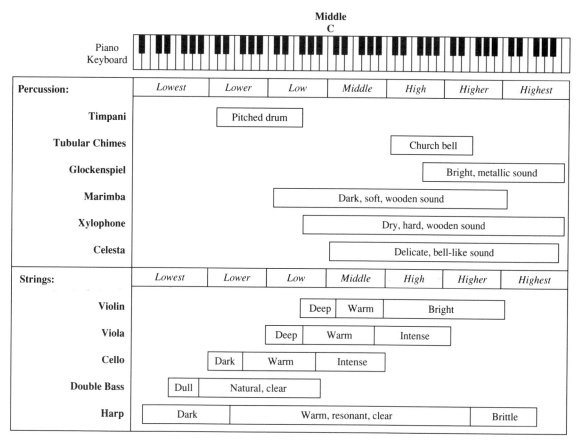

Percussion:	Lowest	Lower	Low	Middle	High	Higher	Highest
Timpani		Pitched drum					
Tubular Chimes					Church bell		
Glockenspiel						Bright, metallic sound	
Marimba			Dark, soft, wooden sound				
Xylophone				Dry, hard, wooden sound			
Celesta				Delicate, bell-like sound			

Strings:	Lowest	Lower	Low	Middle	High	Higher	Highest
Violin				Deep	Warm	Bright	
Viola			Deep	Warm	Intense		
Cello		Dark	Warm	Intense			
Double Bass	Dull	Natural, clear					
Harp	Dark	Warm, resonant, clear				Brittle	

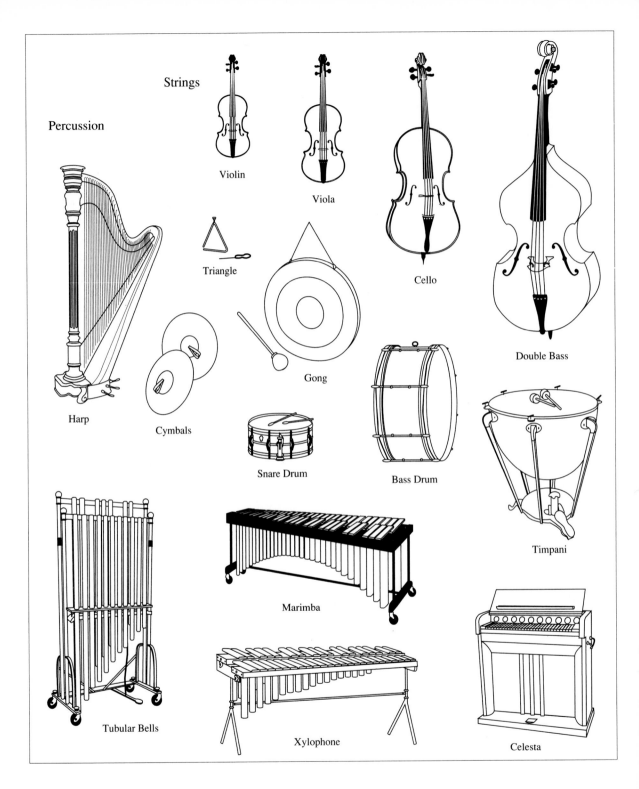

Strings

Percussion

Violin

Viola

Cello

Double Bass

Triangle

Gong

Harp

Cymbals

Snare Drum

Bass Drum

Timpani

Tubular Bells

Marimba

Xylophone

Celesta

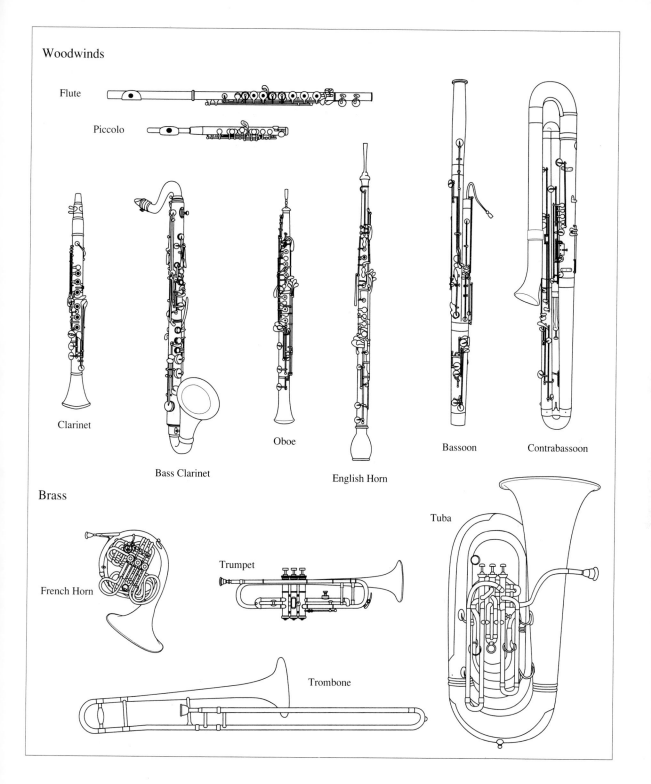

Woodwinds

Flute

Piccolo

Clarinet

Bass Clarinet

Oboe

English Horn

Bassoon

Contrabassoon

Brass

French Horn

Trumpet

Trombone

Tuba

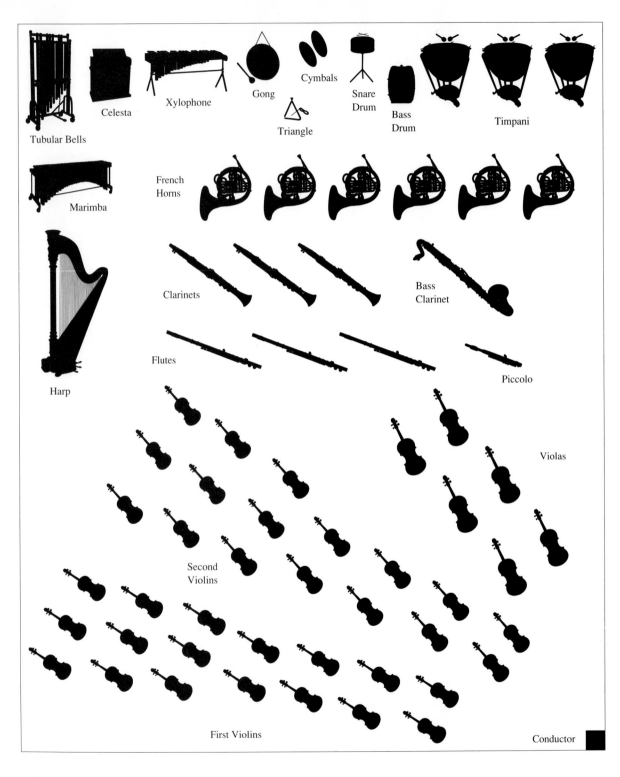

Tubular Bells

Celesta

Xylophone

Gong

Triangle

Cymbals

Snare Drum

Bass Drum

Timpani

Marimba

French Horns

Harp

Clarinets

Bass Clarinet

Flutes

Piccolo

Violas

Second Violins

First Violins

Conductor

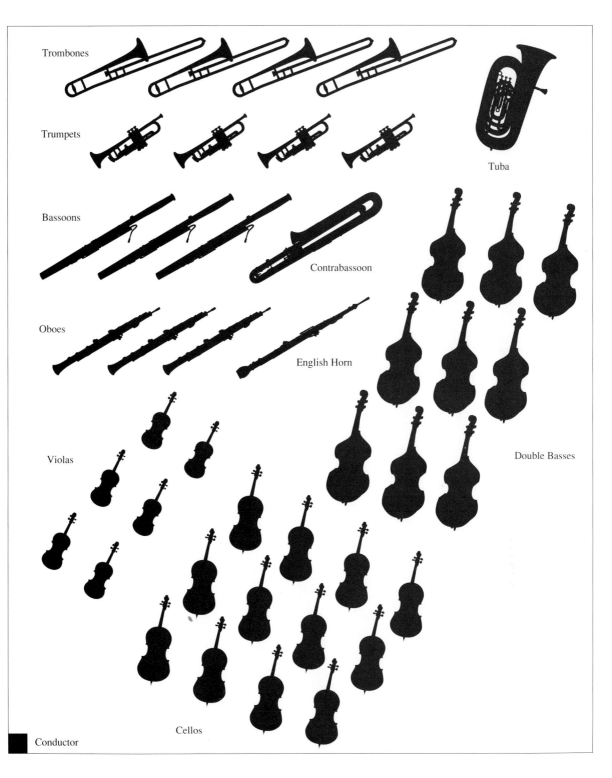

Trombones

Trumpets

Tuba

Bassoons

Contrabassoon

Oboes

English Horn

Double Basses

Violas

Conductor

Cellos

GLOSSARY

Italicized terms indicate cross-references.

A cappella: choral music without instrumental accompaniment.

Accelerando: a gradual increase in *Tempo* (abbr. *accel.*).

Accent: emphasis placed on a *Note* or *Chord,* often indicated by a wedge-shaped mark (< or >).

Accidental: a sign used to alter a *Pitch: Sharp* (♯), *Flat* (♭), *Natural* (♮).

Accompanied recitative: a *Recitative* with orchestral accompaniment. See also *Secco recitative.*

Adagio: slow; a movement in a slow *Tempo.*

Aerophone: a class of musical instruments that employ a column of air as the vibrating medium to produce their sound.

Aleatory (aleatoric music): see *Chance music.*

Allegretto: moderately fast.

Allegro: fast.

Allemande: a baroque dance in a slow *Duple meter,* typically the opening movement of a baroque *Suite.*

Alto: the low female vocal *Register* (also *Contralto*); also, a *Part* that employs that *Register.*

Andante: moderately slow, a "walking" *Tempo.*

Answer: a version of a fugal subject that typically follows a statement of the *Subject,* as if in response to it.

Anthem: an English choral work for use in church services; also, a national patriotic *Hymn.*

Antiphony (antiphonal): a style of performance with alternating *Choirs.*

Arco: a direction for players of *String instruments* to bow rather than pluck the strings. See also *Pizzicato.*

Aria: a movement in an *Opera,* an *Oratorio,* or a *Cantata* for solo voice and orchestra.

Arioso: a style of singing less melodic than an *Aria* and more melodic than a *Recitative.*

Arpeggio: a "broken" *Chord,* with its *Notes* played successively rather than simultaneously.

Art song: a composed *Song,* typically for voice and piano, as distinguished from a folk song.

Atonality (atonal): music written without a *Key* center; a musical style developed by Arnold Schoenberg about 1908.

Augmentation: the technique of increasing the rhythmic values of a *Melody,* typically by doubling them.

Augmented: a class of *Intervals* expanded by a *Half step;* a rhythmic value that has been lengthened. See *Augmentation.*

Avant-garde: the vanguard of radical, advanced movements in the arts.

Ballad: a narrative poem in several stanzas, often set to music as a *Song.*

Ballade: a type of fourteenth- and fifteenth-century secular music and poetry; in the nineteenth century, a *Programmatic* instrumental composition, typically for piano.

Bar (bar line): see *Measure; Measure line.*

Baritone: a male vocal *Register* between *Tenor* and *Bass.*

Bass: the low male vocal *Register;* also, the lowest-sounding part in a vocal or an instrumental composition (hence, bass line).

Bass clef: a *Clef* ($\mathcal{9}\colon$) used to locate the lower sounding *Pitches.*

Basso continuo: see *Continuo.*

Basso ostinato: a bass *Ostinato* pattern.

Beat: the fundamental pulse in a musical composition; the basic subdivision within the *Measure lines* of a composition.

Bebop: a style of *Jazz* developed in the 1940s and 1950s that featured incisive rhythmic patterns and small *Virtuoso Ensembles.*

Bel canto: a style of singing, common in nineteenth-century Italian *Opera,* that emphasizes the lyrical qualities of the voice.

Big bands: the *Jazz* bands of the 1930s and 1940s, typically comprising ten to twenty musicians.

Binary form: a musical form in two basic parts, often repeated, as in the following designs: ‖: *a* :‖: *a'* :‖ or ‖: *a* :‖: *b a'* :‖.

Binary sonata form: *Sonata form* that divides into two basic sections that are repeated.

Blue note: in the *Blues,* a *Pitch* that is sung or played slightly below its notated value.

Blues: a variety of Black-American popular music featuring texts of lament and a standard harmonic pattern.

Boogie-woogie: in *Jazz,* a style of piano playing, developed in the 1920s, with short repeated bass patterns.

Bop: see *Bebop.*

Brass instruments: instruments with bent, straight, or coiled sections of brass and cupped mouthpieces, including the French horn, trumpet, trombone, and tuba.

Bridge: in *Sonata form,* a modulating *Transition* that links the first and second thematic sections of the *Exposition.*

Cabaletta: a short operatic *Solo,* often preceded in nineteenth-century Italian *Opera* by a slower *Cavatina.*

Cadence: a series of notes or chords that suggests a musical pause; in *Harmony,* a series of *Harmonic progressions* that serves to define a *Key.*

Cadenza: a virtuoso display passage, often improvised, by a soloist, as in an *Aria* or a *Concerto.*

Canon (canonic): a high style of counterpoint; a composition in which the pitches of one part are strictly imitated by one or more other parts.

Cantabile: in a "singing" manner.

Cantata: a chamber composition, often in several movements, developed during the baroque period for various combinations of soloists, a chorus, and an instrumental ensemble, with a sacred or secular text.

Cantus firmus (pl., **cantus firmi**): in medieval and Renaissance music a borrowed melody, such as a *Plainchant* or tune, used as the basis of *Polyphonic* compositions.

Canzona: a Renaissance instrumental composition, sometimes based on a *Chanson.*

Cavatina: in eighteenth-century opera, a short *Aria;* in nineteenth-century Italian opera, a complex aria that generally includes a slow, lyrical section and a fast, brilliant section (known as a *Cabaletta*).

Chaconne: a slow baroque dance in triple meter, often featuring a *Basso ostinato.*

Chamber music: music intended to be performed in an intimate setting by a small ensemble (e.g., *Piano trio, String quartet*).

Chamber sonata: see *Sonata da camera.*

Chance music: post–World War II music in which elements of chance determine the shape or structure of a composition (also called *Aleatory, Aleatoric music*).

Chanson: French for "song"; a *Song* with a secular French text.

Chant: a *Monophonic* melody; see *Plainchant.*

Character piece: a short composition, often for piano solo, with *Programmatic* elements, especially common during the nineteenth century.

Choir: a vocal or an instrumental ensemble, with more than one musician per part.

Chorale: a German (Lutheran) *Hymn.*

Chorale cantata: a church *Cantata* in which one or more movements employ a *Chorale* melody.

Chorale prelude: an organ composition based on a *Chorale.*

Chord: two or more notes sounded simultaneously.

Chordophone: a class of musical instruments that use strings as the vibrating medium to produce their sound.

Chord progression: the progression from one *Chord* to a second chord.

Chorus: a vocal *Choir.*

Chromatic (chromaticism): tonal music that draws on the pitches of the *Chromatic scale* rather than on a *Diatonic Scale.*

Chromatic scale: the Western *Scale* in which the *Octave* is divided into twelve *Half steps*.

Church modes: in medieval and Renaissance music, *Diatonic* scales based on D, E, F, and G.

Church sonata: see *Sonata da chiesa*.

Circle of fifths: a circular representation of the *Keys* arranged in ascending order of *Flats* and *Sharps*.

Clef: a musical symbol placed at the beginning of the *Staff* that indicates which pitches are represented on the staff. See *Bass Clef; Treble Clef*.

Closing passage: the closing section of the *Exposition* and *Recapitulation* in *Sonata form*.

Coda: the closing section of a *Movement*.

Coloratura: a highly ornate style of singing, often employed by sopranos.

Common time: a meter with four quarter-note *Beats* per measure, indicated by $\frac{4}{4}$ or c.

Compound meter: meter with subdivisions of the main *Beats* into groups of three, as in $\frac{6}{8}$ (*1* 2 3 *4* 5 6) or $\frac{12}{8}$ (*1* 2 3 *4* 5 6 *7* 8 9 *10* 11 12).

Con brio: with energy.

Concertino: the group of solo instrumentalists in a *Concerto grosso*.

Concerto: an instrumental composition for a soloist and an orchestra.

Concerto grosso: a type of baroque *Concerto* featuring a group of soloists (*Concertino*) set off from an orchestra (*Ripieno*).

Concert overture: a one-movement work for orchestra, often with *Programmatic* elements, developed during the nineteenth century.

Conjunct motion: melodic motion by *Half step* or *Whole step*.

Consonance (consonant): an interval or a chord that sounds stable and mellifluous, as opposed to *Dissonance*. See also *Imperfect consonance; Perfect consonance*.

Continuo: a practice of musical accompaniment developed during the baroque period in which a bass line is provided with figures (hence, *Figured bass*) that indicate a series of chords to be performed or *Realized* above the bass line; the term also applies to the instrumental ensemble entrusted with this task.

Contralto: the low female vocal register (also called *Alto*).

Contrary motion: melodic motion in which two parts move in opposite directions.

Counterpoint (contrapuntal): the art of contraposing and combining musical lines; also, a musical part composed to be set "in counterpoint" against another part. See also *Polyphony*.

Countersubject: a *Contrapuntal* part set against the *Subject* of a *Fugue*.

Courante (also **corrente**): a moderately fast baroque dance in *Triple meter*, often the second dance of a baroque suite.

Crescendo: growing louder.

Da capo: "from the beginning," an instruction to the performer to return to the beginning of the composition.

Da capo aria: a type of *Aria* developed during the baroque period with the plan *ABA*; the repeat of the A section is indicated by the term "Da capo" placed at the end of the B section.

Dance suite: see *Suite*.

Decrescendo: becoming softer; *Diminuendo*.

Development: the technique of reworking or developing in some way previously stated *Themes* and *Motives*; the central portion of *Ternary sonata form*. See also *Exposition; Recapitulation*.

Diatonic: based on the pitches of a *Major* or *Minor scale*, as opposed to *Chromatic*.

Diminished: a class of *Intervals* that have been decreased by a *Half step*.

Diminuendo: becoming softer; *Decrescendo*.

Diminution: the technique of shortening the *Rhythmic* values of a melody, typically by halving them.

Disjunct motion: melodic motion by skip, as opposed to *Conjunct motion*.

Dissonance (dissonant): an *Interval* or a *Chord* that sounds unstable and harsh, as opposed to *Consonance*.

Divertimento: an eighteenth-century instrumental composition in a light style, typically consisting of several dance movements.

Divine Office: in the Roman Catholic church, the daily services apart from the *Mass*.

Dodecaphonic: see *Twelve-tone music*.

Dominant: the fifth degree of a *Major* or *Minor scale*; the *Triad* built upon that degree; the *Key* or *Tonality* based upon that degree.

Dot: see *Dotted note*.

Dotted note: a note with a dot placed after it to increase its rhythmic value by half (e.g., ♩., ♪., ♪.).

Dotted rhythm: a stately *Rhythmic* pattern with a *Dotted note* followed by a short note (e.g., ♪. ♪ ♪. ♪).

Double bar: vertical lines placed at the end of a staff to denote the end of a section of a composition or of the entire composition.

Double dots: dots placed within *Double bars* to indicate music that is to be repeated (‖: :‖).

Double stop: on a *String instrument,* stopping and bowing two strings simultaneously to produce a *Chord.*

Downbeat: the accented *Beat* at the beginning of a *Measure;* see also *Upbeat.*

Drone: a sustained tone, often in a *Bass* part, typically held for several measures.

Duple meter: a meter with two beats per measure: 1 2 | 1 2 (e.g., $\frac{2}{4}$ or $\frac{2}{2}$).

Dynamics: the levels of loudness and softness in music.

Eighth note: ♪, a note one half the value of a *Quarter note,* one quarter the value of a *Half note,* and one eighth the value of a *Whole note.*

Electronic music: music that employs electronic means to generate its sounds.

Electrophone: a class of musical instruments that use electronic means to produce their sound.

Embellishment: see *Ornament.*

Ensemble: a small group of instrumental or vocal musicians; a *Movement* in a vocal work that calls for more than two soloists.

Episode: in a *Fugue,* a passage between statements of the fugal *Subject;* in a *Rondo,* a passage between statements of the *Refrain.*

Espressivo: with expression.

Estampie: an instrumental dance form of the medieval period.

Étude: a work for a solo instrument intended as a technical exercise.

Exposition: the first main section of *Sonata form* (see also *Development* and *Recapitulation*); in a *Fugue,* the opening and subsequent passages that present the *Fugal subject* successively in all the *Voices.*

Fantasia (fantasy): a contrapuntal instrumental composition of the Renaissance; a composition in free form.

Fermata: a sign (⌢) placed above or below a note indicating that it should be held beyond its *Rhythmic* value.

Figured bass: the technique employed in the baroque *Basso continuo* in which a bass line is provided with figures to indicate the chords to be realized above the bass line. See also *Continuo.*

Finale: the movement that concludes an instrumental composition (e.g., *Symphony, Concerto*); the *Ensemble* that concludes an act of an *Opera.*

First theme (first thematic group): the first theme or group of themes in the *Exposition* of *Sonata form.*

Flat: an *Accidental* sign before a note (♭) indicating that the note should be lowered one *Half step.*

Form: the structural organization of a composition (e.g., *Sonata form, Theme-and-variations form*).

Forte (f): loud.

Fortissimo (ff): very loud.

Four-part harmony: *Harmony* in four parts, referred to as the *Soprano, Alto, Tenor,* and *Bass* parts. In four-part harmony, one part typically doubles a pitch of the basic *Triads* used.

Free imitation: in *Counterpoint,* a type of *Imitation* in which one *Part* is freely imitated by other parts.

French overture: a baroque instrumental *Movement* with a slow opening section, often featuring *Dotted rhythms,* followed by a faster section in *Fugal* style.

Fugal exposition: see *Exposition.*

Fugato: a portion of a composition in *Fugal* style.

Fugue (fugal): a composition in a high style of *Counterpoint* in which a *Subject* is introduced and elaborated in various combinations by two or more *Parts.* In highly complex fugues, more than one *Subject* may be employed (hence, double fugue, triple fugue, etc.).

Fundamental: a basic pitch that generates a series of *Harmonics.*

Galliard: a Renaissance dance in *Triple meter,* in a lively *Tempo;* frequently performed with a *Pavan.*

Gavotte: a baroque dance in *Duple meter* encountered in *Suites.*

Genre: a category or type of composition; e.g., *Concerto, Opera, Symphony.*

Gesamtkunstwerk: "Total work of art"; applied to Wagner's revolutionary music dramas.

Gigue (jig): a fast baroque dance in *Compound meter;* often the last *Movement* of a *Suite.*

Glissando: sliding through a range of *Pitches* to produce a continuum of sound.

Grand opera: a type of nineteenth-century French *Opera* characterized by spectacular stage effects and scenery, ballets, and pageantry.

Grave: slow, gravely.

Gregorian chant: *Monophonic Chant* used in the early Roman Catholic church; named after Pope Gregory I (590–604).

Ground (ground bass): see *Ostinato.*

Half note: ♩, a note half the value of a *Whole note,* twice the value of a *Quarter note,* and four times the value of an *Eighth note.*

Half step (semitone): the *Interval* between successive *Pitches* of the *Chromatic scale;* the smallest interval in conventional Western music.

Harmonic: a term in acoustics used to describe the various "partial" sounds generated by a vibrating medium in addition to the *Fundamental pitch;* the frequencies of the partial are multiples of the fundamental pitch.

Harmonic progression: a progression from one *Chord* to another.

Harmony (harmonic): the vertical combinations of *Pitches* to produce *Chords;* the study of chord relationships.

Heterophony: a performance practice in which different musicians perform different versions of the same *Melody* simultaneously; used in ancient Greek and in non-Western music.

Homophony (homophonic): a *Texture* characterized by a single *Melodic* line accompanied by blocklike *Chords,* as opposed to *Polyphony.*

Hymn: a stanzaic religious song sung by a congregation.

Idée fixe: a "fixed idea"; a term used by Berlioz in his *Symphonie fantastique* to describe the recurrent *Melody* that represents the beloved in each *Movement.*

Idiophone: a class of musical instruments that produce their sound by being struck or rubbed.

Imitation: a *Contrapuntal* technique in which one *Voice* is imitated by one or more others.

Imitative polyphony (imitative counterpoint): *Polyphony* that makes extensive use of *Imitation.*

Imperfect consonance: a class of *Consonant* intervals that includes thirds with three or four *Half steps* and sixths with eight or nine *Half steps.*

Impromptu: a *Character piece,* typically for piano, that suggests an *Improvisation.*

Improvisation: music that is improvised, without benefit of a notated *Score.*

Incidental music: music composed for a dramatic production.

Indeterminacy: see *Chance music.*

Instrumentation: see *Orchestration.*

Intermezzo: in the eighteenth century, a comic dramatic work performed between the acts of an *Opera seria;* in the nineteenth century, a section of a larger instrumental work, or a short, independent instrumental composition.

Interval: the distance between two *Pitches,* heard either simultaneously or successively.

Inversion: playing a *Melody* "upside-down," so that its *Intervals* move in opposite directions from its original order (also known as *Mirror inversion*); also, a reordering of the pitches of a chord by *Transposing* the bass note so that it is no longer the lowest-sounding note.

Jazz: twentieth-century Black-American music characterized by an improvisatory melodic style, with strong rhythmic and harmonic organization.

Key: the *Major* or *Minor mode* of a composition (e.g., G major, E minor, F major, D minor, and so on).

Key signature: the collection of *Sharps* or *Flats* at the beginning of a *Staff* to indicate the *Key* of a composition.

Klangfarbenmelodie: "Sound-color-melody," a term coined by Arnold Schoenberg in 1911 to identify *Tone color* as an element of composition.

Largo (larghetto): slow; a slow movement.

Ledger lines: small parts of imaginary lines above and below the *Staff* to accommodate extra *Pitches.*

Legato: a smooth manner of performance, as opposed to *Staccato.*

Leitmotiv: in Wagner's music dramas, a "leading" *Motive* associated with a character or a dramatic element.

Lento: slow.

Libretto: the text of an *Opera* or *Oratorio* (Italian for "little book").

Lied (pl., **lieder**): German for art song.

Liturgy: the official ritual for a church service.

Lute ayre: a type of *Song* with lute accompaniment that flourished in England during the early seventeenth century.

Madrigal: a secular vocal work cultivated during the Renaissance in Italy and then transplanted to England.

Madrigalism: see *Word painting.*

Major intervals: seconds, thirds, sixths, and sevenths with two, four, nine, and eleven *Half steps,* respectively.

Major mode: applied to music in a *Key* based on a *Major Scale* and using primarily *Major triads.*

Major scale: a *Diatonic* scale with half steps between *Scale degrees* 3 and 4 and 7 and 8 and characterized by a major third between degrees 1 and 3 (C major scale: C, D, E, F, G, A, B, C). See also *Minor scale.*

Major triad: a *Triad* consisting of a major third and a minor third; the two together constitute a *Perfect fifth* (e.g., C major triad: C-E-G).

Masque: a staged dramatic entertainment of the sixteenth and seventeenth centuries, especially popular in England.

Mass: the principal service of the Roman Catholic church; in music, the *Ordinary* of the Mass is frequently set to music.

Mazurka: a Polish dance in a moderate or lively *Triple meter.*

Measure: the basic temporal division of Western music, periodically indicated by *Measure lines;* also, *Bar.*

Measure line: a vertical line across a *Staff* to indicate the division of the music into *Measures.*

Mediant: the third *Scale degree;* the *Triad* built on the third *Scale degree.*

Melisma (melismatic): several notes sung to one syllable of text.

Melody (melodic): a succession of *Pitches* with a memorable shape.

Membranaphone: a class of musical instruments that use a stretched membrane to produce their sound.

Meno: less.

Meter (metrical): a regular arrangement of stressed and unstressed *Beats.*

Metronome: a mechanical device that emits regular *Beats* according to an adjustable scale.

Mezzo: half; hence, *mezzo forte,* "half loud."

Microtone: an *Interval* smaller than a *Half step.*

Minor intervals: seconds, thirds, sixths, and sevenths with one, three, eight, and ten *Half steps,* respectively.

Minor mode: applied to music in a *Key* based on a *Minor scale* and using primarily *Minor triads.*

Minor scale: a *Diatonic* scale with *Half steps* between *Scale degrees* 2 and 3 and (usually) 5 and 6 and characterized by a minor third between degrees 1 and 3 (e.g., A minor scale: A, B, C, D, E, F, G, A).

Minor triad: a *Triad* consisting of a minor third and a major third; the two together constitute a *Perfect fifth* (e.g., A minor triad: A-C-E).

Minuet (minuet and trio): a baroque dance in a moderate *Triple meter;* often used as a *Movement* in such classical instrumental works as the *Symphony, String quartet,* and *Sonata.*

Mirror inversion: see *Inversion.*

Mode (modal, modality): applied to music based on scales; in Western music through roughly the sixteenth century, Modal is applied to music based on one of the *Church modes;* in music since roughly the seventeenth century, Mode refers to the *Major* or *Minor mode.*

Moderato: moderately.

Modified strophic song: A *Strophic song* in which the recurring music for each strophe is somewhat modified.

Modulation (modulate): the technique of changing *Keys* within a composition.

Molto: much.

Monody (monodic): a style of music developed in Italy about 1600 in which a solo singer is accompanied, typically by a *Basso continuo.*

Monophony (monophonic): a type of music with a single melodic line, as opposed to *Polyphony.*

Motet: a sacred *Polyphonic* vocal composition, usually with a Latin text, first developed in the thirteenth century.

Motive: a short musical gesture, such as a *Melodic* fragment or *Rhythmic* pattern.

Movement: an independent portion of a larger composition, such as a *Symphony, String quartet,* or *Sonata.*

Music drama: a term used by Wagner to describe his later *Operas.*

Musique concrète: a type of music developed about 1950 in which natural sounds are recorded and manipulated electronically.

Mute (muted): an object applied to an instrument to soften its sound.

Natural: a sign (♮) used in *Notation* to cancel a previous *Sharp* or *Flat.*

Neoclassicism (neoclassical): music of roughly the 1920s, 1930s, and 1940s that makes use in some way of eighteenth-century musical techniques and procedures.

Neumatic: a type of text setting in medieval *Chant* in which a few *Notes* are sung to each syllable of text.

Neume: a notational sign used in early *Chant* manuscripts of the Middle Ages that groups *Pitches* to show which ones are to be sung to each syllable of text.

Nocturne: "night piece"; a lyrical instrumental composition of the nineteenth century, typically for piano.

Non troppo: not too much.

Notation: the system of symbols used in writing down music.

Note: the notational symbol for a *Pitch*.

Octave: the *Interval* between the first and last *Pitches* of a *Scale,* as in C–C, D–D, etc. The ratio of frequencies in an octave is exactly 2:1, with the higher pitch vibrating twice as fast as the lower.

Office: see *Divine Office.*

Opera: a staged dramatic work that employs solo singers, ensembles and choruses, an orchestra, costumes, sets, and scenery, and occasionally dance.

Opéra-ballet: a type of French baroque *Opera* popular in the waning years of the reign of Louis XIV.

Opera buffa: Italian comic *Opera* of the eighteenth and early nineteenth centuries.

Opéra-comique: a type of eighteenth-century French *Opera* that uses spoken dialogue instead of *Recitative.*

Opera seria: Italian serious *Opera* of the eighteenth century.

Operetta: a light *Opera,* usually on a comic subject.

Opus (abbr., **Op.**; pl., **opera**): Latin for "work"; opus numbers are used to catalog the works of composers.

Oratorio: a dramatic work on a religious subject similar to an *Opera* but without staged action.

Orchestra (orchestral): a large *Ensemble* of instrumental performers; a contemporary orchestra typically has about one hundred performers.

Orchestration: the technique of choosing different instrumental combinations for an *Orchestral* work or a large instrumental *Ensemble;* also, *Instrumentation.*

Ordinary: the *Chants* of the *Mass* whose texts remain the same from day to day in the liturgical calendar. See also *Proper.*

Organum: early medieval *Polyphony* in which a freely composed *Part* or *Parts* are added to a preexistent *Plainchant.*

Ornament: patterns of *Pitches,* such as a *Trill,* used to decorate a melodic line; also known as *Embellishment.*

Ostinato: a relatively short figure repeated over and over; such a figure in the *Bass* is known as a *Basso ostinato.*

Overtone: see *Harmonic.*

Overture: an instrumental (often orchestral) composition that prefaces a larger work such as an *Opera* or *Oratorio;* an independent overture is known as a *Concert overture.*

Pandiatonicism: the addition to triads of pitches drawn from their underlying *Diatonic* scales, a technique developed in the twentieth century.

Parallel motion: two musical *Parts* that move in the same direction while preserving the same distance between them.

Parallel organum: *Organum* in which the *Parts* move in *Parallel motion.*

Paraphrase technique: in Renaissance music, an elaboration of a *Plainchant* melody.

Parody technique: in Renaissance music, a composition that borrows heavily from a preexistent composition so that it is, in effect, a reworking of its model.

Part: one of the lines in a *Polyphonic* composition; also, the music played by a musician, as in "oboe part," "soprano part," etc.

Partial: see *Harmonic.*

Partita: a baroque *Suite* of dance movements, originally *Variations* of one another.

Passacaglia: a type of composition developed during the Baroque, usually instrumental, comprising a series of *Variations* based on an *Ostinato* figure.

Passion: a sacred musical work relating the events of the suffering and the crucifixion of Christ.

Pavan (also **pavanne**): a slow dance in *Duple meter* of the sixteenth and early seventeenth centuries, often paired with a *Galliard.*

Pedal point: a *Pitch,* usually in the *Bass,* that is sustained while other *Parts* move more rapidly; pedal points are frequently encountered in *Fugues.*

Pentatonic scale: a five-pitch *Scale* common in folk music and non-Western music; on the piano, a pentatonic scale may be produced by playing the black keys.

Percussion: a classification of instruments that are played by various means of striking or shaking. Some percussion instruments, such as various drums, triangle, cymbals, and castanets, produce no definite *Pitch;* others, such as the timpani, xylophone, and tubular bells, produce definite pitches.

Perfect consonance: a class of intervals including the *Unison,* fourths with five *Half steps,* fifths with seven *Half steps,* and *Octaves* with twelve *Half steps.*

Perfect fifth: an *Interval* of a fifth with seven *Half steps* (e.g., C to G).

Phrase: a self-contained portion of a *Melody.*

Pianissimo *(pp):* very softly.

Piano *(p):* softly.

Piano trio: a piece of *Chamber music* for piano, violin, and cello.

Pitch: the relative "highness" of sound in music.

Più: more.

Pizzicato: plucking the strings of a string instrument rather than bowing them. See also *Arco.*

Plainchant, plainsong: the official *Monophonic* texted music of the Roman Catholic *Liturgy.*

Poco: somewhat.

Point of imitation: in *Polyphonic* music, a *Texture* in which the various *Voices* enter in *Imitative* style with the same musical figure.

Polonaise: a Polish dance in *Triple meter.*

Polychoral: music for two or more *Choirs* that perform either in *Antiphonal* style or together.

Polyphony (polyphonic): a *Texture* in which two or more independent musical lines are contraposed, as opposed to *Homophony.*

Polyrhythm: the juxtaposition or contraposition of distinct rhythmic layers.

Polytonality (polytonal): a twentieth-century technique in which music is written in two or more *Keys* presented simultaneously.

Prelude (prélude): a short instrumental piece intended as an introduction; in the nineteenth century, a short instrumental piece, typically for piano.

Presto: very fast.

Program music (programmatic): instrumental music with some extramusical element or idea, often drawn from literature or the other arts.

Progression: see *Harmonic progression.*

Proper: the *Chants* of the *Mass* whose texts change from day to day in the liturgical calendar.

Psalmody: the singing of psalms.

Quartal harmony: harmony constructed of fourths.

Quarter note: ♩, a *Note* one fourth the value of a *Whole note,* one half the value of a *Half note,* and twice the value of an *Eighth note.*

Quartet: a work for four musicians, as in *String quartet.*

Ragtime: a type of Black-American music, popular from roughly 1890 through the 1920s, that was one of the precursors of *Jazz.* Ragtime featured a *Syncopated* treble line and a regular chordal accompaniment.

Rallentando: becoming slower.

Range: the range of *Pitches* in a composition, from the lowest to the highest *Note.*

Realization (realize): the act of producing *Chords* from a *Figured bass.*

Recapitulation (reprise): the third principal section of a *Movement* in *Sonata form* in which the events and materials of the *Exposition* are brought back in the *Tonic* key.

Recitative: a type of vocal style intended to approximate the natural inflections of speech, used especially in *Operas, Oratorios,* and *Cantatas.* See *Secco recitative.*

Refrain: a passage that periodically returns throughout a composition.

Register: a particular range of *Pitches;* vocal registers include *Soprano, Alto (Contralto), Tenor, Baritone,* and *Bass.*

Repeat sign: see *Double dots.*

Requiem: in the Roman Catholic liturgy, the *Mass* for the dead.

Resolution: a *Progression* from a *Dissonant* chord to a *Consonant* chord, releasing or "resolving" the tension of the *Dissonance.*

Responsorial: a type of performance, as in a *Plainchant,* in which a soloist is answered by a *Choir.*

Rest: silence in music; a notational sign, for example, 𝄾 , 𝄿 , ▬ , ▬ , specifying a momentary pause.

Retransition: in *Sonata form,* a passage toward the end of the *Development* that prepares for the return of the tonic key in the *Recapitulation.*

Retrograde: the presentation of a given musical line backwards.

Retrograde inversion: the presentation of a given musical line backwards and in *Mirror inversion.*

Rhapsody: a free *Fantasy,* typically for piano solo, often with a nationalistic character.

Rhythm (rhythmic): a fundamental aspect of music that concerns the organization of sounds into discernible temporal relationships; also applied to a particular rhythmic pattern.

Rhythm section: in *Jazz,* a part of the *Ensemble,* typically the piano, drums, and bass, that reinforces the basic *Meter.*

Ricercar (ricercare): in the Renaissance, an instrumental composition characterized by *Imitative polyphony;* forerunner of the *Fugue.*

Ripieno: in a *Concerto grosso,* the *Orchestra* that accompanies the *Concertino.*

Ritard: a slowing down of the *Tempo.*

Ritornello: in baroque music, a kind of musical *Refrain,* especially the opening section of a *Concerto* or an *Aria.*

Ritornello form: a form structured around a recurring *Ritornello;* especially common in baroque music.

Rock: popular music developed in the 1960s characterized by heavy electronic amplification.

Rondeau: French form of secular *Song* and poetry of the fourteenth and fifteenth centuries.

Rondo: an instrumental form cultivated from the seventeenth century on in which a *Refrain* alternates or is juxtaposed with contrasting *Episodes* (for example, *ABACA, ABACABA, ABCA*).

Root: in *Harmony,* a *Pitch* on which a *Triad* or *Chord* is constructed.

Round: a vocal *Polyphonic* work in *Canonic* style with *Strict imitation* between the *Voices.*

Row: see *Tone row.*

Rubato: "robbed" time; in performance, a technique in which the available time within *Measures* is stretched or distorted in some way.

Sarabande: a slow baroque dance in *Triple meter* encountered in *Suites,* often with an emphasis on the second *Beat* of the *Measure.*

Scale: a group of consecutive *Pitches* filling out an *Octave,* as in *Major scale, Minor scale,* or *Chromatic scale.*

Scale degree: an individual *Pitch* of a *Scale.*

Scherzo: Italian for "joke"; an instrumental movement of humorous character in rapid *Triple meter* developed in the eighteenth and nineteenth centuries; in the nineteenth century, the scherzo and trio replaced the *Minuet and Trio.*

Score: the complete musical *Notation* for a composition, usually involving several aligned parts for different performers, for use by the conductor.

Secco recitative: "dry" recitative; recitative accompanied only by a *Continuo* section, as opposed to *Accompanied recitative.*

Second theme (second thematic group): the second theme or group of themes in the *Exposition* of *Sonata form.*

Semitone: see *Half step.*

Sequence: the repetition of a melodic portion or *Harmonic progression* at higher or lower pitch levels; in medieval *Plainchant,* a texted melody added after the Alleluia in the *Mass.*

Serenade: "evening music"; a light instrumental composition cultivated in the eighteenth and nineteenth centuries.

Serial (serial music, serialism): a twentieth-century technique in which a composition is based on a *Series* or ordering of pitches, most commonly a *Twelve-tone row.*

Series: an ordering of *Pitches,* as in a *Twelve-tone row.*

Sforzando (sf): a sharp accent.

Sharp: an *Accidental* sign before a *Note* (♯) indicating that the note should be raised one *Half step.*

Siciliano (siciliana): a baroque dance in *Compound meter.*

Sinfonia: Italian for *Symphony.*

Singspiel: German *Opera* of the eighteenth and nineteenth centuries with spoken dialogue replacing *Recitative.*

Sixteenth note: ♪, a *Note* one sixteenth the value of a *Whole note,* one eighth the value of a *Half note,* one fourth the value of a *Quarter note,* and one half the value of an *Eighth note.*

Slow introduction: an introductory passage in a slow *Tempo* that precedes the *Exposition* of *Sonata form.*

Slur: a curved line over two or more *Notes* directing the performer to play them in a smooth, *Legato* fashion.

Solo: for performance by one performer.

Sonata: an instrumental composition in several *Movements,* usually three or four. In the baroque, sonatas were typically performed by one or two *Treble* melody instruments and a *Basso continuo;* since the classical period, sonatas are generally written for one or two instruments.

Sonata da camera: in the baroque period, a "chamber" *Sonata,* often consisting of various dances, as in a *Suite.*

Sonata da chiesa: in the baroque period, a "church" *Sonata,* more serious in mood than a *Sonata da camera,* and often in four *Movements* in the succession slow–fast–slow–fast.

Sonata form (sonata-allegro form): a form most often used in the first *Movements* of *Sonatas, String quartets, Symphonies,* etc., with three principal sections: *Exposition, Development,* and *Recapitulation.*

Sonata-rondo form: a form that uses elements of *Sonata form* and *Rondo,* most often found in the finales of *Sonatas, String quartets, Symphonies,* and so on.

Song: a musical setting of a poem or other text for one or more voices and accompaniment.

Song cycle: a collection of *Songs* unified by a narrative or poetic idea or by musical means.

Sonority: a term used to describe the general sound quality of a composition or musical passage; sometimes used to refer to a *Chord.*

Soprano: the highest female vocal *Register;* a high musical part.

Spiritual: a kind of religious folk song cultivated by American blacks in the nineteenth century; also, a type of religious folk song cultivated in American revivalist meetings during the eighteenth and nineteenth centuries.

Sprechstimme (Sprechgesang): a style of singing, developed by Arnold Schoenberg, halfway between speech and song; "spoken song."

Staccato: a detached manner of performance indicated by dots above or below note heads, as opposed to *Legato.*

Staff (stave): a series of five lines and four spaces used to notate music.

Stretto: in a *Fugue,* a passage in which entries of the *Subject* overlap; also, an increase in *Tempo.*

Strict imitation: *Canonic* imitation.

String instruments: instruments that produce sounds by means of vibrating strings; in the modern *Orchestra,* the string section includes the violin, viola, cello, and double bass.

String quartet: a composition for a chamber group, consisting of two violins, a viola, and a cello, developed during the eighteenth century, principally by Haydn.

Strophic song: applied to *Songs* in which the various stanzas of text are set to the same music, as opposed to *Through-composed songs.*

Subdominant: the fourth degree of a scale; the *Triad* built on that degree.

Subject: in a *Fugue,* the initial *Theme;* also, a musical idea.

Suite: an instrumental composition consisting of a series of stylized dance movements. In the standardized baroque suite, a typical plan consists of an *Allemande,* a *Courante,* a *Sarabande,* and a *Gigue.*

Swing: a type of *Jazz* practiced by *Big bands* during the 1930s and 1940s.

Syllabic: a type of text setting in which each syllable is set to one *Note;* see also *Melismatic* and *Neumatic.*

Symphonic poem: a piece of *Program music* in one *Movement* for orchestra developed in the nineteenth century by Franz Liszt.

Symphony: a work for orchestra, usually in three or four *Movements,* developed in the eighteenth century.

Syncopation: a rhythmic device in which normally unaccented *Beats* are accented (e.g., $|1\,\underset{<}{2}|1\,\underset{<}{2}|$ instead of $|\underset{<}{1}\,2|\underset{<}{1}\,2|$).

Tempo: the speed of a musical composition.

Tenor: the high male vocal *Register,* also a part that uses that register; in medieval church *Polyphony,* the tenor is the voice entrusted with the *Plainchant* or other preexistent *Melody* on which the composition is based.

Tenuto: held.

Ternary form: three-part *Form,* ABA.

Ternary sonata form: *Sonata form* that emphasizes a division into three parts, the *Exposition, Development,* and *Recapitulation.*

Terraced dynamics: shifts in *Dynamic* levels, typically between *Forte* and *Piano,* common in baroque music.

Tetrachord: a succession of four consecutive *Pitches* (e.g., C, D, E, and F; D, E, F, and G).

Texture: a general term used to describe the blending of melodic lines and harmonies in a composition.

Theme (thematic): a *Melody* or musical idea on which a composition is based.

Theme-and-variations: a composition in which a *Theme* is presented and subsequently varied, modified, or altered in some way in a series of *Variations*. Each variation is typically the same length as the theme.

Thoroughbass: see *Figured bass*.

Through-composed song: a *Song* in which each stanza of text is set to different music, as opposed to a *Strophic song*.

Tie: in *Notation*, a curved line connecting two pitches to indicate that they should be held as one continuous sound.

Timbre: see *Tone color*.

Time signature: in *Notation*, a ratio at the beginning of the staff to indicate the *Meter* of a composition (e.g., $\frac{2}{4}$, $\frac{3}{4}$, $\frac{6}{8}$).

Toccata: an instrumental composition, often for a keyboard instrument, in a free, virtuoso style.

Tonality (tonal): the principal musical system in Western music from the baroque period to the twentieth century. Tonal music conveys a feeling of gravitational pull toward a principal *Tonic* pitch, a *Tonic Triad* constructed on that pitch, and a hierarchy of triads around the *Tonic Triad;* also, a *Key* of a tonal composition.

Tone: a *Pitch* of definite height.

Tone color: the quality of sound of a musical instrument or *Part;* also, *Timbre*.

Tone poem: a *Programmatic* composition for orchestra, developed by Richard Strauss, similar to a *Symphonic poem*.

Tone row: see *Twelve-tone row*.

Tonic: in *Tonal* music, the central or "home" *Pitch* or *Triad;* the first degree of a *Diatonic Scale*.

Total serialism: a type of *Serial* music developed about 1950 in which pitch and nonpitch elements such as *Rhythm, Dynamics,* and *Register* are controlled or serialized according to a *Series* or some ordering.

Transition: a passage leading from one section of a composition to another.

Transposition (transpose): a repetition of a musical line or idea so that it begins on a different pitch; for example, C-D-E-F-G may be transposed to G-A-B-C-D or to F-G-A-B♭-C.

Treble: a high *Voice* or *Part,* as opposed to *Bass*.

Treble clef: a *Clef* (𝄞) used to locate the higher sounding pitches.

Tremolo: on string instruments, the rapid reiteration of a single *Pitch,* produced by short up-and-down bow strokes.

Triad: a *Chord* consisting of three *Pitches,* constructed by adding pitches a third and a fifth above a fundamental pitch (e.g., C-E-G, D-F-A, etc.).

Trill: an *Embellishment* in which two adjacent *Pitches* are alternated rapidly, indicated by the sign *tr* placed above a note.

Trio: a work for three instruments or voices; the middle section of a *Minuet, Scherzo,* etc.

Trio sonata: in baroque music, a *Sonata* for two *Treble* instruments and a *Basso continuo*.

Triple meter: a *Meter* with three *Beats* per measure, the first of which is accented: |1 2 3 |1 2 3|.

Triplet: a *Rhythmic* grouping of three notes (e.g., $\overset{3}{\sqcap\!\sqcap}$) with the same duration as two similar notes.

Tritone: the interval of three *Whole steps*.

Trope: in medieval *Monophony,* an addition to the *Liturgy* involving a new text or melody joined to a *Plainchant*.

Troubadour, trouvère: in the Middle Ages, aristocratic French poet-musicians who composed courtly love songs.

Tune: a simple *Melody* easy to sing.

Tutti: "all"; in a baroque *Concerto grosso,* the entire ensemble, including the *Concertino* and the *Ripieno*.

Twelve-tone music: twentieth-century music that employs *Twelve-tone rows*. See also *Serial*.

Twelve-tone row: first devised by Arnold Schoenberg, an ordering of the twelve *Chromatic* pitches to which the techniques of *Retrograde, Mirror inversion,* and *Retrograde inversion* may be applied; in addition, the four basic forms of the *Tone row* may be *Transposed;* also *Tone row, Row, Series*.

Unison: the *Interval* formed when two voices or instruments perform the same *Pitch*.

Upbeat: a weak *Beat* that precedes a *Downbeat*.

Valse: French for *Waltz*.

Variation: a varied or elaborated statement of a previously stated *Theme* or passage. In a variation, certain aspects of the *Theme* or passage remain the same while others are altered.

Verismo: applied to late nineteenth-century Italian opera, which was distinguished by its realism.

Vespers: a service of the Roman Catholic *Office* held during the early evening.

Vibrato: an expressive shaking effect caused by rapid, minute variations in a pitch during its production.

Virelai: a French form of secular *Song* and poetry of the fourteenth and fifteenth centuries.

Virtuoso: a highly skilled performer.

Vivace: lively.

Vocal: having to do with the human *Voice;* hence, music with text.

Voice: the human voice; a musical part or line in a *Polyphonic* texture.

Waltz: a nineteenth-century dance in *Triple meter;* also, *Valse.*

Whole note: o, a *Note* twice the value of a *Half note,* four times the value of a *Quarter note,* and eight times the value of an *Eighth note.*

Whole step (whole tone): the *Interval* of a second consisting of two *Half steps.*

Whole-tone scale: a *Scale* consisting solely of *Whole steps,* used especially by Liszt and by Debussy and other twentieth-century composers.

Wind instruments: instruments in which sound is produced by means of a column of air.

Woodwind (wind): a section of the modern *Orchestra* that includes the flute, oboe, clarinet, and bassoon and their families of instruments.

Word painting: a musical illustration of a word or phrase by means of a *Rhythmic, Melodic,* or *Harmonic* motive or figure.

Name and Title Index

Boldface page numbers indicate compositions discussed in detail.

Symphony No. 100 (*Military,* Haydn), **184–93**
Symphony No. 101 (*Clock,* Haydn), 163
Symphony of a Thousand, 388
Synchronisms, 492

T

Tallis, Thomas, 459
Tannhäuser, 18, 341
Tate, Nahum, 83
Tchaikovsky, Pyotr Il'yich, 378
   1812 Overture, 378
   Eugene Onegin, 377
   Hamlet, 378
   Nutcracker, 378
   Pathétique Symphony, 378
   Romeo and Juliet, **378–80**
   Sleeping Beauty, 378
   Swan Lake, 378
   Tempest, The, 378
Telemann, Georg Philipp, 105
Tempest Sonata, Op. 31, No. 2 (Beethoven), 230
Tempest, The (Tchaikovsky), 378
Terpsichore, 88
Tertullian, 3
Theater Piece, 494
Thema—omaggio a Joyce, 491
Theresa, Maria, 179
Thomson, Virgil, 466
Three Compositions for Piano (Babbit), 485
Three-Cornered Hat, The, 456
Three Musicians, 399
Three Songs from William Shakespeare, 482
Threnody to the Victims of Hiroshima, **500–2**
Tieck, Ludwig, 251
Till Eulenspiegels lustige Streiche, 382
Tinctoris, Johannes, 33
Toccata and Fugue in D minor (BWV 565), 105, **114–17**
Tod und Verklärung, 382, **383–85**
Tombeau du Couperin, Le, 435
To Music (D. 547), 268

To October (Symphony No. 2), 481
Torelli, Guiseppe, 98
Tosca, 391
Totentanz, 262
Tragic Overture, 373
Traviata, La, 331
Treemonisha, 469
Trio Sonata, Op. II, No. 6 (Corelli), **91–97**
Tristan und Isolde, 260–61, 342, 418
Triumphs of Oriana, The, 52
Trois morceaux en forme de poire, 411
Trout, The (D. 550), 268
Trovatore, Il, 18, 331, **333–38**
Troyens, Les, 306
Turn of the Screw, The, 480

U

Unanswered Question, The, 465
Unfinished Symphony (No. 8), 268
Union, The, 463
Universal Symphony, 465

V

Varèse, Edgard, 488–89
   Amériques, 489
   Density 21.5, 489
   Déserts, 490
   Hyperprism, **489**
   Ionisation, 489
Variations on a Theme of Haydn, Op. 56A, **373–77**
Variations on a Theme of Robert Schumann, Op. 20, **296–98**
Vasari, Giorgio, 33
Vaughan Williams, Ralph, 458–59
   Antartica Symphony, 458
   Fantasia on a Theme by Thomas Tallis, **459–60,** 461
   Pastoral Symphony, 458

Verdi, Giuseppe, 331–33
   Aida, 332
   Battaglia di Legnano, La, 331
   Falstaff, 332
   Macbeth, 331
   Nabucco, 331
   Otello, 332
   Rigoletto, 331
   Traviata, La, 331
   Trovatore, Il, 18, 331, **333–38**
Verlaine, Paul, 401
Viderunt omnes
   Gradual, **12–15**
   Organum, **23–25**
Villa-Lobos, Heitor, 436, 456
   Bachianas brasileiras, 436
Violin Concerto in E minor, Op. 64 (Mendelssohn), 301
Violin Phase, 503–4
Virgil, 7, 83, 306
Visage, 491
Vision and Prayer, 492
Vitry, Philippe de, 27
Vivaldi, Antonio, 66, 98–99, 117
   Concerto Grosso for Two Violins and Orchestra, Op. 3, No. 8, **99–101**
   Four Seasons, 99

W

Wachet auf (Cantata No. 140, J. S. Bach), **124–30**
Wackenroder, W. H., 251
Wagner, Richard, 299, 314, 328, 340–44, 356, 383, 387
   Fliegende Holländer, Der, 341
   Lohengrin, 341–42
   Meistersinger von Nürnberg, Die, 342–43
   Parsifal, 342
   Rienzi, or the Last Consul of Rome, 340
   Ring des Nibelungen, Der, 342, **344–46**
   Götterdämmerung, Die, 345, 346
   Rheingold, Das, 344–45, **346–56**

Wagner, Richard (*continued*)
    Siegfried, 344–45, 346
    Walküre, Die, 345, 346
    Tannhäuser, 18, 341
    Tristan und Isolde, 260–61, 342,
      418
Waldstein Sonata, Op. 53, 230
Walküre, Die, 345, 346
War and Peace, 436
War Requiem, 479
"Washington's March," 462
Water Music, 133
Watteau, Antoine, 146, 147
Waverley Overture, 262
Weber, Carl Maria von, 339
    Freischütz, Der, 339–40, 344
Webern, Anton, 410, 413,
    431–32, 434
    Sinfonie, Op. 21, **432–34,**
      436
Wedding, The, 419
Weelkes, Thomas, 52

Well-Tempered Clavier, 103, 108,
    291
"When Johnny Comes Marching
    Home Again," 517
White Peacock, The, 463
Wieck, Clara. *See* Schumann,
    Clara
Wieck, Friedrich, 277, 296
Wilbye, John, 52
"Wilde Jagd," 313
Williams Mix, 493
Winckelmann, Johann, 153
Winterreise, 268–69
    "Hurdy-Gurdy Man, The,"
      269, **271–74**
    "Linden Tree, The," 269,
      274–77
    "Stormy Morning, The,"
      269–71
Wolf, Hugo, 266, 385
Wordsworth, William, 251
Wozzeck, **428–30**

X

Xenakis, Iannis, 500
    Bohor I, 500
    Herma, 500
    Metastasis, 500

Y

"Yankee Doodle Dandy," 462
Yellow Submarine, 499
*Young Person's Guide to the
    Orchestra, The,* 479

Z

Zauberflöte, Die, 202, **213–15,**
    339
Zwilich, Ellen Taaffe, 507
    Symphony No. 1, **507–8**

Subject Index

Boldface page numbers indicate compositions discussed in detail.

Blues, 469–70
  of Handy, 470
    St. Louis Blues, **470–71**
  influence of, on rock, 498
Boogie-woogie, 494–95
Bop, 496-98
Brass instruments, 119, 530
  ancient Roman, 7
  Beethoven's use of, 230
  in classical symphonies, 184
  ranges of, 532
  in romantic orchestra, 263
  Wagner's use of, 343
Breve, 42
Bridge, 166, 502
Broadway musical, 475

C

Cabaletta, 328
Caccia, 29
Cadence, 24, 515
Cadenza, 118, 206
Canon, 107, 525
Cantata, 105
  of Bach, 124, 130–31, 148
    Cantata No. 140 *(Wachet auf),* **124–30**
  early Italian, 124
  eighteenth-century German, 124
Cantus, 28
Cantus firmus, 41
Canzona, 55–57
  of Gabrieli, 57
    Canzona septimi toni, No. 2, **57–58**
Cavatina, 211, 328
Celesta, 430
Cello, 85
Chamber music, 163
  baroque, 91
  of Bartók
    Music for String Instruments, Percussion and Celesta, **446–50**
  of Brahms, 318–19, 373
    Piano Quintet in F minor, Op. 34, **318–25**
  classical, 164, 193

of Dvořák, 365
  See also specific genres (e.g., String quartet)
Chamber sonata, 91
Chance music, 494
Chanson, 41
  of Dufay, 41
Chant, 11. *See also* Plainchant
Chants of the ordinary, 12
Chants of the proper, 12
Character piece, 262
Chitarrone, 77
Chorale, 124
Chorale cantata, 124
Chordophones, 529–30
Chords, 526
Chromatic scale, 514
Chromaticism, in romantic music, 259–61
Church modes, 8–9
  Ave maris stella, **9–10**
  Beethoven's use of, 241
  use of, in Renaissance, 37
Church music
  baroque, 81–82, 91, 124, 130
  classical, 215
  and Counter-Reformation, 49
  hymn, 9
  Jewish influence on, 7–8
  modes in, 8–9
  monophonic, 10–16
  organ in, 18, 115
  plainchant, 10–11, 15–16
  polyphonic, 21–25
  psalmody, 8
  in Renaissance, 37, 41, 49, 54
  sequence in, 15–16
  trope, 15
  See also Sacred music
Church sonata, 91
Clarinet, 184
Classical period
  Beethoven as bridge from, 243
  concerto, 203
  cultural background, 153–56
  dynamics in, 160–61
  forms in, 164–67, 170–74
  genres in, 163–64
  harmony and texture in, 162–63

keyboard music, 158–59
  musical background, 154–56, 157
  opera, 208–9, 212–13
  orchestra, 182
  rhythm in, 161–62
  sacred music, 215
  string quartet, 193
  symphony, 163–64, 181–85
  timeline for, 152
  tonality in, 258–59
Clavier, 109
Clef, 512
Closing passage, 166
Coda, 167
Comic opera. *See* Opera buffa
Compound meter, 523, 524
Concerted manner, 75
Concertino, 97
Concerto
  of Bach, 103, 117
    Brandenburg Concerto No. 5, **117–23**
  baroque, 97–98
  of Bartók, 446
  of Beethoven, 239
  of Brahms, 374
  of Carter, 500
  of Chopin, 290
  classical, 203
  of Corelli, 91
  of Handel, 133
  of Liszt
    Piano Concerto No. 1 in E-flat major, **314–18**
  of Mozart, 202, 203
    Piano Concerto in A major (K. 488), **203–8**
  in romantic period, 261
  of Vivaldi, 98–99
    Concerto Grosso in A minor, Op. 3, No. 8, **99–101**
Concerto grosso, 97–98, 99
Concert overture, 262
  of Mendelssohn
    A Midsummer Night's Dream, Op. 21, **302–5**
Conductor, in romantic period, 298–99

Conjunct motion, 516
Consonance, 516, 528
Consort song, 52
Continuo, 72
    in *Brandenburg Concerto* No. 5
        of Bach, **120–22**
    in concertos of Mozart, 203
    in early Italian opera, 76
    harpsichord as, 87
    in madrigals of Monteverdi, 75
Contrabassoon, 374
Contrapuntal. *See* Counterpoint
Contrary motion, 21
Contratenor, 28
Cornet, 309
Cornu, 7
Council of Trent, 16, 49
Counterpoint, 20, 524
    Bach's use of, 107, 109–10
    Beethoven's use of, 241
    Brahms's use of, 375–77
    in classical music, 162, 215
    Handel's use of, 134
    Hindemith's use of, 453
    imitative, 525–26
    and musical texture, 524–26
    neoclassical revival of, 436
    nonimitative, 526
    Palestrina's use of, 50
    in Renaissance music, 39
    Stravinsky's use of, 483–84
    Webern's use of, 432–34
    See also Polyphony
Counter-Reformation, 49
Courante, 90
Crescendo, 160, 529
Cubism, 399–400
Cymbals, 185
Czechoslovakian music,
    nationalism in, 455

D

Da capo, 130
Da capo aria, 130, 137
Dadaism, 401
Damper, 226
Damper pedal, 286

Dance music
    in baroque period, 88–91
    chamber sonata derived from,
        91
    in classical period, 172–73
    medieval, 18
    minuet, 172–73
    in Renaissance, 54
    in romantic period, 287
    suite, 88
Decrescendo, 160, 529
Development, 167
Diaphony, 20
Diminuendo, 160
Diminution, 109
Disjunct motion, 516
Dissonance, 516, 528
Divine Office, 11
Dodecaphonic music, 407. *See
    also* Serial music
Dominant triad, 69
Dorian mode, 5, 7, 9
Dot, 519
Dotted note, 519
Dotted rhythms, 81
Double aria, 32
Double bass, 85
Double harp, 77
Double-reed shawm, 118
Double stop, 195
Downbeat, 522
Drone, instrumental, 19
Dry recitative, 128
Dumka, 364
Duple meter, 523, 524
Duplum voice, 23
Dynamic markings. *See*
    Dynamics
Dynamics, 528–29
    in baroque music, 74–75
    in classical music, 160–61
    in romantic music, 256–57
    terraced, 74

E

Eighth note, 519
Electronic music, 490–91
    of Berio, 491

of Cage, 493–94
    interaction of live and taped
        elements in, 492
    rock, 498–99
    of Stockhausen, 490–92
    Gesang der Jünglinge, **490–91**
Electrophones, 530
English horn, 309
English music
    early opera, 81–82
    fourteenth-century, 29
    instrumental, in Renaissance, 55
    Italian opera in, 134–35
    madrigal, 52–54
    masque, 81
    oratorio, 137
    rock, 499
    twentieth-century, 458, 479
Enlightenment, The, 66, 146,
    153, 221, 223
Ensemble sonata. *See* Sonata
Episode, 108, 174
Estampie, 18
Étude, 287
    of Chopin, 287
        "Black Key" Étude, **287–88**
    of Liszt, 313
Exposition, 166
Expressionism, 401
    Schoenberg and, 426
Expression marks, in romantic
    music, 256, 257

F

Fantasia, 55
Fauvism, 401
Fermata, 117, 186
Fifteenth-century music, 37
    Dufay's influence on, 39–44
    Franco-Flemish style, 39–41,
        44–45, 47
    Josquin's influence on, 44–47
Figured bass, 73
Flat sign, 513
Flute, 118
Folk music
    Bartók's use of, 445–46,
        456–57

Motet *(continued)*
  polychoral, 57
  thirteenth-century, 26
Motive, 43–44
  in Liszt's Piano Concerto No.
    1, 315–16
  in Mendelssohn's Overture to
    A Midsummer Night's Dream,
    304
  Wagner's use of, 344
Musical, Broadway, 475
Musical notation. *See* Notation
Music drama, 340
Musique concrète, 490

N

Nationalism
  effect of, in nineteenth-century
    music, 361
  effect of, in twentieth-century
    music, 455–56
  in twentieth-century Russian
    music, 481
Natural sign, 513
Neoclassicism, 154, 435–36
  Bartók and, 445–46
  Hindemith and, 451
  Prokofiev and, 436–38
  Stravinsky and, 440–41
Neumatic text setting, 14
Neumes, 11
Nocturne, 288
  of Chopin
    Nocturne in B-flat minor,
      Op. 9, No. 1, **288–90**
Notation
  Basso continuo and, 72–73
  Cage's view of, 494, 495
  in medieval polyphony, 25
  in medieval secular music, 18
  Penderecki's use of, 501–2
  and pitch, 511–18
  in plainchant, 11
  and rhythm, 518–24
  shape-note, 461
Notes, 512
  rhythmic values of, 518–19
Notre Dame polyphony, 22–23, 26

O

Oboe, 118
Oboe da caccia, 124
Octave, 512–14
  basic ratio underlying, 8
Opera, 75
  aria in, 80, 328
  of Auber, 338
  of Beethoven, 223, 339
  of Bellini, 329–31
    Norma, **329–31**
  of Berg, 428
    Wozzeck, **428–30**
  of Berlioz, 306
  of Britten, 479
  comic, 148, 328
  of Debussy, 418
  of Donizetti, 329
  eighteenth-century *galant* style,
    146–48
  in England, 81, 135–37, 479
  in France, 81, 338–39
  German, 81, 212–13, 339–40
  of Handel, 133, 137–38
    Julius Caesar in Egypt,
    137–41
  of Hindemith, 451
  Italian. *See* Italian opera
  libretto for, 75
  of Lully, 81
  of Meyerbeer, 338–39
  of Monteverdi, 76–80
    Orfeo, **76–80**
  of Mozart, 201, 202, 208–9
    The Magic Flute, **213–15**
    The Marriage of Figaro,
    209–12
  of Musorgsky, 369–70
    Boris Godunov, **370–72**
  of Purcell, 81–82
    Dido and Aeneas, **83–86**
  recitative in, 78, 81–82
  in romantic period, 261,
    327–28
  of Rossini, 329
  serious, 148, 208–9, 328
  of Shostakovich, 481
  spread of, in eighteenth
    century, 80–83

  of Richard Strauss, 383
  of Tchaikovsky, 377
  of Verdi, 331–38
    Il trovatore, **333–38**
  of Wagner, 340–44
    Ring des Nibelungen, Der,
    342, **344–56**
  of Weber, 339–40
Opéra-ballet, 146
Opera buffa, 148, 209, 328
Opéra comique, 338
Opera seria, 148, 208, 209, 328
Operetta, 390
Ophicleide, 306
Oratorio, 133
  of Elgar, 458
  of Handel, 133, 137, 141
    Messiah, **141–46**
  of Haydn, 179
  of Mendelssohn, 301
Orchestra, 77
  baroque, 118–19
  classical, 160, 182, 185
  of Monteverdi, 77
  nineteenth-century, 262–63,
    298–99, 307
  program music for, 261, 381
  romantic, 298–99
  of Stravinsky, 420
  of Wagner, 343–44
Orchestral music
  of Bach, 117–23
    Brandenburg Concerto No. 5,
    117–23
  of Beethoven, 232–39
    Pastoral Symphony, **232–39**
  of Berio, 505
  of Berlioz, 298, 306
    Symphonie fantastique,
    307–13
  of Brahms, 373
    *Variations on a Theme of
    Haydn,* Op. 56A, **374–77**
  of Bruckner, 386
  of Copland, 467
  of Debussy, 418
    *Prelude to the Afternoon of a
    Faun,* **415–18**
  of Dvořák, 365–68
    Symphony No. 9, **364–68**

Polyphony *(continued)*
  at Notre Dame, 22–26
  origins of, 20–21
  of Perotin, 25–26
  rise of, 21–22
  sacred. *See* Sacred polyphony
  secular. *See* Secular polyphony
  See also Counterpoint
Polyrhythm, 411
Polytonality, 405
Postimpressionism, 397–98
Prelude, 88
  of Bach, 103
  of Chopin, 290–92
    Prélude, Op. 28, No. 2,
    290–92
  of Debussy
    *Prelude to the Afternoon of a
    Faun,* **415–18**
Primary triad. *See* Tonic triad
Program music, 99
  of Berlioz, 307–13
  in late nineteenth century, 380
  of Liszt, 380–81
  of Mendelssohn, 302–5
  in romantic period, 261
  of Richard Strauss, 382–83
  of Vivaldi, 99
Proper, chants of the, 12
Psalmody, 8
Psalteries, 8, 18

Q

Quartal harmonies, 406
Quarter note, 519
Quartet. *See* String quartet

R

Ragtime, 468
  of Joplin, 468–69
    Maple Leaf Rag, **469**
Range, practical, of selected
    instruments, 532–33
Recapitulation, 167
Recitative, 78
  accompanied, 130

Bach's use of, 128, 130
in early Italian opera, 80
Handel's use of, 138
Mozart's use of, 209
secco (dry), 128
Recorder, 52
Refrain, 174
Renaissance
  cultural background, 33–35
  Franco-Flemish music, 39–47
  harmony in, 38–39
  instrumental music, 54–59
  Italian composers, 48–51
  madrigals, 51–54
  modality in, 37–38
  musical background, 34, 35
  musical trends in, 37–39
  timeline for, 32
  Venetian instrumental style,
    57–59
Repeat marks, 19
Reprise, 167
Requiem, 216, 332
Requiem mass, 16
Resolution, 528
Responsorial chant, 12
Rests, 520–21
Retransition, 167
Retrograde form, 408
Retrograde inversion, 409
Rhythm, 518
  in baroque music, 73–74
  in classical music, 162
  dotted, 81
  in early Greek music, 6
  in early twentieth-century
    music, 410–11
  in thirteenth-century motet, 26
  notation for, 518–24
  in organum, 25
  in romantic music, 258
  and pitch, 518–20
Rhythmic modes, 25
Rhythm section, 472
Ricercar, 55
Ripieno, 97
Ritard, 258
Ritardando, 258
Ritornello, 79, 98
  Bach's use of, 117–18, 120

Mozart's use of, 203
Vivaldi's use of, 98
Rock, 498–99
Rococo, 146–47
Roman music, 7
  organ in, 115
Romantic period
  art song, 265–66
  Beethoven as link to, 243
  chamber music, 318–19
  cultural background, 246–52,
    359
  decline of, 391
  dynamics in, 256–57
  forms and genres, 261–62
  harmony in, 259–62
  Lieder, 265–66
  melody in, 255–56
  musical background, 252–53
  nationalism in, 359, 361
  opera, 327–29, 338–44
  orchestra, 298–99
  piano in, 285–86
  rhythm in, 258
  timelines for, 246–47, 360
  tonality in, 259–61
  tone color in, 262–63
Rondo form, 165, 174–75
Round, 525
Rubato, 258, 289
Russian music
  eighteenth-century, 369
  late nineteenth-century, 369,
    377
  nationalism in, 361, 481
  twentieth-century, 480–81

S

Sacred monophony, 10–16
Sacred music
  of Bach, 103, 105, 124
  of Bruckner, 386–87
  in colonial America, 460–61
  of Handel, 141–46
  medieval
    monophonic, 10–16
    polyphonic, 22–25
  of Monteverdi, 75

Sacred music *(continued)*
 of Mozart, 215
 of Purcell, 81–82
 in Renaissance, 37, 44
 See also Church music
Sacred polyphony, 20–21
 of Dufay, 39–44
 fourteenth-century English, 29
 of Josquin, 44–47
 of Leonin, 23–25
 of Palestrina, 49–50
 of Perotin, 25–26
Sarabande, 90
Saxophone, 473
Scales, 516
 artificial, of Busoni, 404–5
 chromatic, 514
 and church modes, 362
 five-tone pentatonic, 362
 major, 516–17
 minor, 516–17
 modern, emergence of, 68–72
 origins of, 38
 pentatonic, 362
 whole-tone, 403–4, 517
Scandinavian music, nationalism
 in, 361, 455
Scherzo, 226, 322
Secco recitative, 128
Secular monophony
 of Machaut, 19–20
 medieval, 16–19
Secular polyphony, 26–27
 ballade, 27
 of Machaut, 27–29
 motet, 26
 in sixteenth-century Italian
 music, 51–52
Semitones, 514
Sequence, 15–16
Serenade, 201
Serial music, 407
 of Boulez, 485, 492
 Stravinsky's adoption of, 482,
 484
 total serialism, 485–88
 See also Twelve-tone music;
 Twelve-tone row
Sforzando, 161

Shape-note notation, 461
Shape-note singing, 461, 462
Sharp sign, 513
Shawm, 118
Siciliano, 375
Sinfonia, 181
Singspiel, 213, 339
Sixteenth note, 519
Slow introduction, 167
Slur, 170
Snare drum, 306
Soft pedal, 286
Sonata, 57
 of Bach, 114
 in baroque period, 86
 of Beethoven
 Moonlight Sonata, **224–29**
 Sonata in F minor, Op. 2,
 No. 1, **168–70**
 in classical period, 164
 of Gabrieli, 57
 of Hindemith, 451
 of Liszt, 380–81
 in romantic period, 261
 of Domenico Scarlatti, 148
 and sonata form, 164–67
Sonata-allegro form. *See* Sonata
 form
Sonata da camera, 91
Sonata da chiesa, 91
Sonata form, 165–70
 Beethoven's use of, 168–70,
 268–70
 Berlioz's use of, 308
 binary, 166
 Brahms's use of, 320–21
 in classical music, 165–67
 Haydn's use of, 186–89
 Liszt's use of, 317
 Mendelssohn's use of, 302–3
 Mozart's use of, 203
 in romantic music, 261
 ternary, 167
Sonata-rondo form, 174
Song cycles
 of Barber, 479
 of Hindemith
 Marienleben, Das, **452–53**
 of Mahler, 387–88

of Robert Schumann, 279–83
 of Schubert, 268–77
 of Wolf, 385
Songs. *See* Lieder
Soprano, 511
Spanish music
 medieval polyphony, 22
 nationalism in, 456
 and Renaissance, 51
Spirituals, 462
 Dvořák's use of, 365
Sprechstimme, 426–27
Staccato, 159
Staff, musical, 512
Steps
 in ancient Greek music, 6, 9
 in church modes, 9
 half, 514
 tonality and, 68–71
 whole, 517
Stretto, 109
String instruments, 531
 ancient Greek, 6–7
 ancient Roman, 7
 in baroque orchestra,
 118–19
 Bartók's use of, 447
 in classical symphony, 184
 Penderecki's use of, 500–502
 range of, 533
 in string quartet, 163, 193
 violin family, 85
 Wagner's use of, 343
String quartet
 of Bartók, 446
 of Beethoven, 241
 String Quartet in A minor,
 Op. 132, **241–43**
 in classical period, 164
 of Haydn, 193, 197
 String Quartet in C major,
 Op. 76, No. 3 *(Emperor)*,
 193–97
 of Mozart, 202
 in romantic period, 261
Strophic song, 269
Sturm und Drang, 248, 252
Subdominant triad, 69
Subject, 107

Credits

EUROPEAN HISTORY AND CULTURE	MUSIC	AMERICAN HISTORY AND CULTURE
	1829: Rossini, *Guillaume Tell*	1829–1837: Presidency of Andrew Jackson
1830: July Revolution in France	1830: Berlioz, *Symphonie fantastique*	
	1831: Bellini, *Norma*	1831: McCormick's reaper
1832: Goethe, *Faust* (Part II)	1833: Chopin, Études, Op. 10	
	1833–1897: Johannes Brahms	
	1835: Schumann, *Carnaval*	
	1836: Meyerbeer, *Les Huguenots*	
1837–1901: Reign of Queen Victoria in England		
1838: Dickens, *Oliver Twist*	1839: Chopin, 24 Préludes, Op. 28	1839: Poe, "Fall of the House of Usher"
1839: Daguerreotype process of photography	1839–1881: Modest Musorgsky	
	1840: Schumann, *Dichterliebe*	
	1845: Wagner, *Tannhäuser*	1844: Morse's telegraph
1848: Marx and Engels, *The Communist Manifesto;* Revolutions in Europe	1848–1876: Wagner, *Ring of the Nibelung*	1846–1848: Mexican War
	1849: Liszt, Piano Concerto No. 1	1849: California Gold Rush
		1853: "Opening" of Japan by Commodore Perry
	1853: Verdi, *Il trovatore, La traviata*	1854: Thoreau, *Walden*
	1854: Liszt, *Faust* Symphony	1855: Whitman, *Leaves of Grass*
1859: Darwin, *Origin of Species*	1860–1911: Gustav Mahler	1861–1865: Presidency of Abraham Lincoln
1861: Emancipation of serfs in Russia	1862–1918: Claude Debussy	
1862–1890: Bismark prime minister and chancellor in Prussia Germany		1861–1865: Civil War
	1865: Wagner, *Tristan und Ísolde;* Brahms, Piano Quintet, Op. 34	1863: Emancipation Proclamation
1866: Dostoevsky, *Crime and Punishment*		
1867: Marx, *Das Kapital;* Dual Monarchy of Austria-Hungary		
1870-1871: Franco-Prussian War	1870: Tchaikovsky, *Romeo and Juliet*	
	1871: Verdi, *Aida*	
1872: Monet, *Impression: Setting Sun*	1873: Brahms, *Variations on a Theme of Haydn*	
	1874: Musorgsky, *Boris Godunov*	
	1874–1951: Arnold Schoenberg	1876: Alexander Graham Bell's telephone
	1874–1954: Charles Ives	1878: Edison patents the phonograph
	1875–1937: Maurice Ravel	
	1881–1945: Béla Bartók	
	1882: Wagner, *Parsifal*	
	1882–1971: Igor Stravinsky	
1883–1885: Nietzsche, *Also sprach Zarathustra*	1883–1945: Anton Webern	1884: Mark Twain, *The Adventures of Huckleberry Finn*
	1885–1935: Alban Berg	
	1887: Verdi, *Otello*	
1889: Eiffel Tower	1889: R. Strauss, *Tod und Verklärung*	
	1893: Dvořák, Symphony No. 9 (*From the New World*)	
	1894–1937: Bessie Smith	
	1894: Debussy, *Prelude to the Afternoon of a Faun*	
	1895–1963: Paul Hindemith	
	1896: Mahler, *Lieder eines fahrenden Gesellen;* Puccini, *La bohème*	1898–1899: Spanish-American War
	1899: Joplin, *Maple Leaf Rag*	

20134055

MT 6 T62 M9 1990   20134055

20134055

Todd, R. Larry

The musical art:

JUL   5 JF

552

Todd, R. Larry

The musical art:

DEMCO